Rankin

To my dear friend
and supporter, Rabbi
Bob and his lovely
Bunny

— Walter Mulins

Zion in the Valley

Rabbi Bernard Illowy, United Hebrew,
1854–1855. First rabbi in St. Louis.

Zion
IN THE VALLEY

The Jewish Community of St. Louis

—— *Walter Ehrlich* ——

Volume I
1807–1907

University of Missouri Press
Columbia and London

Library of Congress Cataloging-in-Publication Data
Ehrlich, Walter, 1921–
    Zion in the valley : the Jewish community of St. Louis / Walter
Ehrlich.
        p.   cm.
    Includes bibliographical references and index.
    Contents: v. 1. 1807–1907.
    ISBN 0-8262-1098-8 (alk. paper)
    1. Jews—Missouri—Saint Louis—History.   2. Saint Louis (Mo.)—
Ethnic relations.   I. Title.
F474.S29J53   1997
977.8'66004924—dc21   96-49340
                                                                  CIP

∞ ™ This paper meets the requirements of the
American National Standard for Permanence of Paper
for Printed Library Materials, Z39.48, 1984.

Designer: Mindy Shouse
Typesetter: BOOKCOMP
Printer and binder: Thomson-Shore, Inc.
Typeface: Palatino

This book was brought to publication with generous
assistance from the Arthur and Helen Baer Charitable
Foundation, the Lubin-Green Foundation, and Mildred Simon.

To Sylvia and to the memory of Jacob Rader Marcus

CONTENTS

PREFACE

Raised in St. Louis in an Orthodox Jewish family, I always had an avid interest in matters Jewish. When I returned from the service after World War II and did my graduate work, I hoped to specialize in American Jewish history. My graduate school mentors dissuaded me, however, pointing out that the American historical profession considered ethnic, religious, or local history on a "lesser" academic level than something more national in scope, a view quite different from the historiographic approach that Europeanists took. So I went into constitutional history, and my scholarly research and publications have been in that area. Then came the civil rights movement and with it the popularity of cultural pluralism—and everything changed. By then, though, I was already deeply immersed in high school and university teaching in constitutional history. But decades later, as retirement loomed, I decided that having paid my dues, so to speak, and having attained all the academic goals and honors one might wish for, I would go back to my first love. Hence my current scholarly work and this book.

Why a history of St. Louis Jewry? One good reason is that it has never been done. There are little bits and pieces here and there—several acceptable congregational histories and anniversary pamphlets; a number of journal articles about individual Jews successful in civic or business circles; a few institutional studies (for example, the Jewish Federation, the YMHA); a smattering of brief newspaper feature stories devoted to various individuals and institutions; and even a few recent articles that I have written for scholarly journals. But no comprehensive history of St. Louis Jewry has ever been written, although we do have histories of other midwestern Jewish communities (New Orleans, Indianapolis, Cincinnati, Kansas City—even Columbus, Ohio). My bibliography is somewhat deceiving in that it cites many secondary works. Most of those items compare with the recipe a good cook uses—a little of this and a little of that. I have found most of my materials in primary sources: newspapers, archival documentary collections, personal reminiscences, and congregational and institutional records.

With a population of about sixty thousand, the St. Louis Jewish community ranks as the largest in the interior of the United States, away from the East and West Coasts (Chicago and Cleveland are larger, of course, but they are located on the Great Lakes along the northeastern extremity of the country, not in the "interior"). More than just in numbers, though, St. Louis Jewry contributed in many ways to the development of both American and world Jewry. Some of its rabbis have been major figures in the metamorphosis of American Judaism. A St. Louis Jew led the fight to abolish slavery in Missouri. St. Louis Jewish businessmen have been in the forefront of department store retailing and merchandising. Several Jewish women have been leaders in philanthropic and cultural ventures whose ramifications extended far beyond just the St. Louis community. A St. Louis journalist and statesman headed the world Mizrachi organization, the religious wing of the Zionist movement. Jewish Hospital in St. Louis for many decades has ranked as one of the very finest in the country. The St. Louis Vaad Hoeir is the only such Jewish community organization in the country. These and many more achievements have emanated from the "Zion in the Valley," achievements that have affected Jews not only in St. Louis but also throughout the nation and the world. Yet this history has never been written. I hope what I have produced will prove worthwhile.

When I started this project, I anticipated a single volume comparable with histories of other Jewish communities. But as my data accumulated, I realized that either I would have to leave out a lot of very important and interesting detail, or I would have to expand my work to more than one volume. With more than a little encouragement and support from Beverly Jarrett, director and editor-in-chief of the University of Missouri Press, I chose the latter course. The organization seemed self-evident: one volume on the "German" era, one on the "Russian" era, and one on the "American" era. The first two, however, overlapped so much that it proved impossible to find a satisfactory point of separation. I therefore went to "Plan B" and chose an arbitrary breaking point: the year 1907, the one hundredth anniversary of the first Jew in St. Louis. It turned out to be a very sound historical choice. The succeeding volume of this history, then, will begin at that point and go from there.

I wish I could claim that this is the definitive history of St. Louis Jewry. It is not. Many details that I might have covered had to be left out completely simply because of space limitations, and parts of my narrative barely skim the surface. Many institutional histories remain to be written, as do biographies of important individuals and families. My sincerest wish is that this book will engender interest for continued research into St. Louis Jewish history by professionals and amateurs, leading to more books and articles and historical programs.

This work focuses on Jews in the city of St. Louis only. In my next volume "St. Louis" will include St. Louis County, for as Jews moved westward in the 1900s, they moved into the county, and there was a tangible connection between Jews who lived there and Jews who lived in the city (in fact, by the 1980s very few Jews remained in the city proper). In addition, other small Jewish enclaves developed separately nearby, in places such as East St. Louis and Belleville in Illinois, and in several outstate Missouri communities such as Cape Girardeau, Louisiana, and Hannibal, but they are not included in this study. Although located near St. Louis physically, Jews residing in these places have never been viewed as part of the "St. Louis" Jewish community; each has had its own independent albeit isolated identity. If any Jews with ties to those communities feel ignored or overlooked, I extend to them my apologies.

Some might feel offended in not finding names of friends or relatives who engaged prominently in one activity or another. Not all could be included. That is not to infer that Montefiore Bienenstock or Nicholas Scharff lacked importance. Space and editorial limitations simply forced me to make certain choices, and I confess to probably having omitted some who might indeed have left their imprint on St. Louis Jewish history. I take full responsibility for any such oversights.

The spelling of names posed a constant problem. Newspapers in particular often misspelled names; yet in most instances I have to go by their spelling. When I had other documentation, I corrected those errors. I admit, though, that probably some fell through the cracks. Another dilemma resulted from data with only an initial for the first name. The reader will appreciate that the initial "A." can stand for a multitude of possible first names. I could not chance guessing incorrectly.

In a project such as this, there are countless people to thank. Many archival centers provided invaluable assistance, and I want to thank their directors and staffs: the American Jewish Archives in Cincinnati; the Missouri Historical Society in St. Louis; the St. Louis Jewish Community Archives; the American Jewish Historical Society in Waltham, Massachusetts; the Judah L. Magnes Museum in Berkeley, California; and the Museum of the Jewish Diaspora located at Tel Aviv University in Israel. This work would not have been possible without St. Louis Jewish newspapers, many of which no longer exist but microfilm copies of which were made available through the generous cooperation of the American Jewish Periodical Center in Cincinnati, the St. Louis Public Library, the Missouri Historical Society, the Library of Congress, and the University of Missouri–St. Louis Thomas Jefferson Library. I extend to them all my sincerest gratitude.

Many St. Louis synagogues and temples graciously opened their records for me. I am indebted especially to United Hebrew, B'nai El, Shaare Emeth, Temple Israel, Shaare Zedek, and Nusach Hari B'nai Zion. I wish to thank also the many community service and philanthropic groups that made their records available, though personnel at those agencies were the first to admit to the incompleteness of those records: the St. Louis Jewish Federation, Jewish Hospital, Vaad Hoeir of St. Louis, the Jewish Center for the Aged, the Jewish Community Centers Association, and the Central Agency for Jewish Education.

I received several research grants that helped considerably in my work. For them I wish to thank Eric P. Newman and the Harry Edison Foundation of St. Louis, the Rapoport Fellowship Program of the American Jewish Archives in Cincinnati, and the Summer Faculty Research Program of the University of Missouri–St. Louis.

I am indebted also to many individuals for their counsel and assistance. Donald I. Makovsky's master's thesis on the origins of United Hebrew Congregation is a seminal work on the history of St. Louis Jewry. Burton A. Boxerman has written several scholarly articles on St. Louis Jews prominent in the city's civic and business growth; his assistance in helping research those areas and in reading parts of my manuscript has been invaluable. Samuel L. Rosen wrote a master's thesis on the early development of the St. Louis Jewish Federation. I have relied heavily on their research in some parts of this book, especially since some of the primary materials that they used no longer exist. Abraham Peck (American Jewish Archives), Glen Holt (St. Louis Public Library), David Young (St. Louis Jewish Community Archives), Diana Kline (Shaare Emeth Temple Library), and Alice Handelman (Jewish Center for the Aged) went out of their way to make available records in their institutions. Kay Kulfinski of Edwardsville, Illinois, and Muriel Ziskind of St. Louis provided me with valuable information about early ancestors in St. Louis, and Dr. Burton A. Shatz made available his excellent materials on the 1904 World's Fair. For scholarly criticism and advice, my thanks to historian colleagues Jonathan Sarna, formerly of Hebrew Union College–Jewish Institute of Religion in Cincinnati; Leonard Dinnerstein, University of Arizona; Ben Procter, Texas Christian University; Roger Daniels, University of Cincinnati; Herbert H. Paper, Hebrew Union College–Jewish Institute of Religion, Cincinnati; William B. Faherty, St. Louis University; Abraham Peck, American Jewish Archives, Cincinnati; and Gary A. Tobin, Brandeis University Institute for Community and Religion. Steven Rowan, William S. Maltby, Jack Langleben, and James Neal Primm of my home University of Missouri–

St. Louis from time to time rendered invaluable scholarly criticism and advice. In fact, I have even borrowed from Professor Primm (with his approval, of course) the title for this book; he wrote a very well-received scholarly St. Louis history, *Lion of the Valley.* May the *Lion* and the *Zion* be a good match!

I would be terribly remiss if I did not mention here Rabbi Robert P. Jacobs of St. Louis, whose interest in this work has never lagged. Several other rabbi/historians have also been of great assistance: Jeffrey B. Stiffman of Temple Shaare Emeth, Jerome W. Grollman and Howard G. Kaplansky of United Hebrew Temple, Alvan D. Rubin and Mark L. Shook of Temple Israel, Joseph R. Rosenbloom of Temple Emanuel, Aaron Borow of Nusach Hari B'nai Zion, and Kenneth Greene of Shaare Zedek. They merit special mention not only for their sound and critical advice but also for making available their congregational records. Last but certainly not least, I want to extend my deepest appreciation to the late and revered Jacob Rader Marcus of Hebrew Union College–Jewish Institute of Religion in Cincinnati for his continuous inspiration, who passed away just as I was completing this work. Just hearing Dr. Marcus refer to me as one of his "boys" has been one of the warmest honors bestowed on me. I know I could mention more people, but space constrictions prevent me from including them all. Unpublicized though you are, I sincerely thank you. You have all contributed to what is good about this book. Any negatives are completely my own responsibility.

No published work could be readable without the indispensable and laborious contributions of a good editor. John Brenner of the University of Missouri Press has performed yeoman and diligent service in editing my manuscript, and I express to him my sincerest appreciation.

Last but certainly not least, I can never put into words the deepest gratitude I have for my dear wife, Sylvia, without whose devotion and endless sacrifices this work could never have been done. She is a gem in every sense of the word; the biblical expression *aishes chai-il* had to have been coined especially for her. The same loving and affectionate sentiments are true for my children and their families. I have been indeed fortunate for their continuous and inspirational support.

W.E.

St. Louis, Missouri

Zion in the Valley

1

In the Beginning

"No Jew is ever the first Jew anywhere. There has always been at least one there before him." So wrote Jacob Rader Marcus, undisputed dean of American Jewish historians.[1] If that is the case, then, the "first Jew" in St. Louis may have been there either sub rosa or outright illegally.

Pierre Laclede and his young protégé Auguste Chouteau founded St. Louis during the winter of 1763–1764 as a frontier trading post for the New Orleans–based firm of Maxent, Laclede and Company. American Jewish bibliography identifies the "first Jew" in St. Louis as the merchant Joseph Philipson, who arrived there in 1807. But a combination of intriguing circumstances suggests that one or more of his coreligionists might have preceded him.

French hegemony over the Mississippi River valley dated back to seventeenth-century claims and conquests by a long list of bold and colorful voyageurs and coureurs de bois, probably the most well known in our history books being the stalwart Father Jacques Marquette, the intrepid Louis Joliet, and the flamboyant Rene Robert Sieur de la Salle. France held sway over this vast and sprawling "Louisiana" until 1763. Then, as a consequence of the Seven Years' War (called the French and Indian War in American history annals), France ceded everything east of the Mississippi to England and everything west of the river—which included the lonely bluff where Laclede and Chouteau were just then establishing the future St. Louis—to Spain. Louisiana remained under Spanish control until 1800, when Spain secretly ceded it back to France. Almost immediately, though, complex developments associated with the westward growth of the infant United States led to the famous Louisiana Purchase of 1803. On March 10, 1804, Captain Amos Stoddard raised the Stars and Stripes in St. Louis, symbolically designating the city for the first time as part of the

---

1. Jacob R. Marcus, *The Colonial American Jew, 1492–1776,* vol. 1, 216.

United States. Conceived under France, born and nurtured under Spain, St. Louis now was American. Three and a half years later Joseph Philipson arrived.[2]

But what of Professor Marcus's adage about the "first Jew"? Were there any Jews in St. Louis before it became part of the United States? The evidence is not substantial enough for an unequivocal "yes" or "no." The most judicious claim is a tenuous and shaky "maybe." There are too many intriguing circumstances combined with admittedly tortuous historical evidence that simply cannot be rejected peremptorily. Even if they suggest only possibilities, we must investigate them.

Prior to 1763, France's *Code Noire* determined the status of Jews in her possessions in the Caribbean and the Mississippi valley. Simply put, that law excluded all non-Catholics in general, and Jews in particular. Nevertheless, enforcement of the *Code Noire* often depended less upon the letter of the law than upon more persuasive economic matters of mercantilist and trade necessities. As a result, some officials turned their heads, some did not; some times and places proved to be less restrictive to Jews, some proved to be more restrictive. Accordingly, Jews on a number of French Caribbean islands engaged prominently from time to time in trade and commerce, and even established synagogues and developed other vestiges of Jewish community life.[3]

It is no great surprise, then, that Jews found their way onto the mainland and into French Louisiana, especially in the New Orleans area, the hub of trade and commerce along the Gulf coast. At least six Jews conducted business there in the 1750s and 1760s; perhaps the most important was Isaac Rodriguez Monsanto, scion of a prominent Spanish Sephardic Jewish family. Though the French government never granted those Jews official

---

2. Many excellent studies detail the history of the Mississippi valley and of early St. Louis. Among others, see J. Thomas Scharf, *History of Saint Louis City and County from the Earliest Periods to the Present Day, Including Biographical Sketches of Representative Men*, 2 vols.; William Hyde and Howard L. Conard, eds., *Encyclopedia of the History of St. Louis*, 4 vols.; Louis Houck, *A History of Missouri*, 3 vols., and *The Spanish Regime in Missouri*, 2 vols.; LeRoy Hafen and Carl R. Rister, *Western America*; McCune Gill, *The St. Louis Story: Library of American Lives*, 3 vols.; Eugene M. Violette, *A History of Missouri*; Selwyn K. Troen and Glen E. Holt, eds., *St. Louis*; and James Neal Primm, *Lion of the Valley*.

3. Scholarly accounts of Jewish life in the French Caribbean islands include, among others, Marcus, *Colonial American Jew*; Anita L. Lebeson, *Jewish Pioneers in America, 1492–1848*; Bertram W. Korn, *The Early Jews of New Orleans*; Bernard Postal and Lionel Koppman, eds., *American Jewish Landmarks*, especially vol. 2; I. Harold Sharfman, *Jews on the Frontier*; Ellis Rivkin, *The Shaping of Jewish History*; and Isaac S. Emmanuel, *Precious Stones of the Jews of the Netherlands Antilles*.

toleration, they were nevertheless permitted to settle. Some penetrated into the hinterland to trade, especially in the Natchez area. On at least one occasion the Monsanto organization sent an expedition to Kaskaskia, on the east side of the Mississippi River not far from St. Louis. Evidence suggests that Isaac Monsanto himself, described by another frontier trader as a "very worthy little French Jew," accompanied that group. Evidence also indicates business dealings between Monsanto and Pierre Laclede, not surprising since both were important traders in Louisiana, but nothing related to the founding or settling of St. Louis. Nothing in available records suggests that any of the Laclede-Chouteau group that founded St. Louis were Jewish. Nor is there any indication that any of the New Orleans Jewish merchants or their agents ever came to the site of the future St. Louis prior to 1763. The closest was Monsanto in Kaskaskia, and that was only a "maybe."[4]

If evidence is lacking that any Jews might have come to the site of St. Louis prior to 1763 up the Mississippi River via New Orleans, there are intriguing possibilities that some might have approached from the north or northeast by way of the Great Lakes and the Illinois Territory. A small number of Jews settled in French Canada in the 1700s, mostly along the St. Lawrence River, despite restrictive regulations. Perhaps the most successful was Aaron Hart, who lived in the small town of Three Rivers (Trois Rivieres) midway between Montreal and Quebec. Related to him by marriage was Ezekiel Solomons, reputed to be one of Canada's most picturesque pioneer merchants and the first Jewish settler in what is now the state of Michigan. Solomons established an important fur-trading center at Michilimackinac, on Mackinac Island, located strategically where Lakes Huron and Michigan come together. At least four other Jewish frontier merchants lived or did business there along with Solomons:

---

4. The Monsanto family was a longtime Sephardic Spanish family that fled the Inquisition to Holland. Isaac Rodriguez Monsanto eventually emigrated to America, later bringing over his brothers and sisters. The family became prosperous merchants, shippers, fur buyers, and bankers in New Orleans, despite the *Code Noire*. Furthermore, they practiced their Judaism openly, but some in succeeding generations abandoned their ancestral faith. In 1896 Olga Mendez Monsanto married John Francis Queeny, hard-driving chemical entrepreneur. He and his son Edgar Monsanto Queeny created the Monsanto Chemical Company, naming it after Olga Mendez Monsanto. Eric P. Newman to author, August 16, 1988, letter in possession of author; Dan J. Forrestal, *Faith, Hope and $5,000: The Story of Monsanto*, 12–13; Korn, *Early Jews of New Orleans*, 9–23, 266–71; Gill, *The St. Louis Story*, vol. 1, 297. See also Marcus, *Colonial American Jew*, vol. 1, 373–76 and vol. 3, 1446; Postal and Koppman, *Landmarks*, vol. 2, 135–36; and Joseph L. Blau and Salo W. Baron, *The Jews of the United States, 1790–1840: A Documentary History*, vol. 3, 847–54, 985.

Isaac Levy, Benjamin Lyon, Chapman Abram, and Ezekiel's cousin Levy
Solomons. There is reason to believe that on several occasions some if
not all of them went down Lake Michigan and the Illinois River as far
as Cahokia to trade for furs. Thus Jews from Canada were near St. Louis
before Laclede selected the site in 1763, but on the Illinois side and only
as itinerant and transient fur traders.[5]

There is yet another suggestion that Jews were near St. Louis prior to
1763. In 1907 the American Jewish Historical Society reprinted an article
that had appeared eight years earlier in a Chicago journal, alleging that
about three hundred Jews had settled in the Mississippi valley in the
early 1700s. Pursuant to the *Code Noire*'s mandate that all Jews were to be
removed, the article stated, those settlers were herded together at Fort des
Chartres in Illinois, their property was confiscated, and they were all then
expelled from the territory. Three Jews were said to have been burned at
the stake, one on the north bank of the Ohio River, one near Vincennes, and
a third in the Yazoo district farther down the Mississippi. This harrowing
story, which sounds as though it came right out of Inquisition Spain, is
of course intriguing, because if true it would place a fairly large number
of Jews very near the site of St. Louis well before either Laclede or the
Mackinac fur traders. But there is no verifiable evidence to support the
story. It remains, therefore, pure conjecture.[6]

So much for possibilities of Jews being in or near the site of St. Louis
prior to its founding in 1763–1764. In 1763, French Louisiana east of the
Mississippi became first English and then, in 1783, part of the new United
States, while everything west of the Mississippi, including the newly
founded village of St. Louis, became Spanish. What then, after 1763, of
Professor Marcus's adage?

Once the Ohio valley became English, religious restrictions no longer
forbade Jews from being there. Jews of course had been in the English
colonies east of the Appalachians since 1654, first in New Amsterdam
(which shortly became New York) and then, during the next one hundred years, scattered throughout the coastal settlements. Sephardic Jews
came first, from Portuguese and Spanish possessions in the Western
Hemisphere, followed by English, Dutch, and French coreligionists. By
the mid-1700s, however, Ashkenazic Jews from various Germanic states
outnumbered their American forebears.[7] Nevertheless, their combined

---

5. Marcus, *Colonial American Jew*, vol. 1, 376–88 and vol. 2, 728–30. For more on the
Jewish settlers in Canada, see Arthur Daniel Hart, ed., *The Jews in Canada*.

6. The article appeared originally in the Chicago *Inter-Ocean*, October 1, 1899. Max J.
Kohler, "Some Jewish Factors in the Settlement of the West," 33–35.

7. Sephardic Jews are predominantly of Mediterranean and Iberian descent; most
who came to America came via Holland and Latin America, especially the Caribbean

number totaled perhaps twenty-five hundred, representing a mere one-tenth of 1 percent of the English colonial population. Only a handful lived on farms or plantations; most were small middle-class urban shopkeepers, tradesmen, and artisans. During and after the French and Indian War, however, venturesome Jews joined intrepid frontier merchants and traders who penetrated into the dangerous transmontane Ohio valley. They supplied scattered and beleaguered military outposts with vitally needed supplies. England's war with France ended in 1763, but Indian difficulties continued, and mere existence was precarious for everyone moving into the hostile frontier. Yet English colonials came, individuals and families, farmers and tradesmen, slowly but inexorably populating the Ohio valley. The westward movement abated temporarily during the Revolutionary War, but after 1783, with the fertile expanse between the Appalachians and the Mississippi now part of the new United States, the flow accelerated. And in that flow were Jews—not many, because there were not many to begin with—but they were there.

Annals of the westward movement document activities of a number of Jewish merchants and traders who either themselves or through agents left their imprint on American frontier history. Jacob I. Cohen and Isaiah Isaacs, for instance, came out of Philadelphia and Richmond to trade for furs. The Gratz brothers of Philadelphia, Barnard and Michael, became prominent businessmen of the frontier, as their agents traversed the dangerous West. Joseph Simon dispatched men and merchandise from Lancaster and Pittsburgh. The account books of Isaac Levy indicate a lucrative Illinois trade in the 1770s. The Gratz brothers and David Franks established important mercantile posts in Vincennes, Cahokia, Kaskaskia, and Fort des Chartres. Jewish entrepreneurs also participated in several Ohio valley land and colonization projects, among them the George Croghan venture, the Indiana Company, the Vandalia colony, and the Illinois and Wabash Land Companies.[8]

Ample evidence exists, then, that after St. Louis was founded in 1763–1764, Jews or their agents engaged in trade and commerce right across the

---

islands. Ashkenazic Jews came predominantly from western and central (later eastern) Europe. They differ mostly in ritual and liturgy, as well as in Hebrew pronunciation. Yiddish, a German-Polish-Hebrew dialect, is widely used among Ashkenazic Jews; prevalent among Sephardic Jews is Ladino, a Spanish-Hebrew dialect. Although the American Jewish population was at first mostly Sephardic, it had become predominantly Ashkenazic by the mid-1700s.

8. The best scholarly accounts of this phase of American Jewish history include Marcus, *Colonial American Jew;* Lebeson, *Jewish Pioneers in America;* Blau and Baron, *Jews of the United States;* and Sharfman, *Jews on the Frontier.* See also Marcus, *Early American Jewry,* 2 vols., and Marcus, *American Jewry: Documents, Eighteenth Century.*

Mississippi River in Illinois. Some Jews also lived there. Isaac Monsanto was in Kaskaskia; another Jewish merchant there was Simon Nathan. One of Cahokia's most prominent citizens in the 1770s was Isaac Levy, apparently a man of many talents; he served the town as physician, shopkeeper, moneylender, Indian trader, liquor dealer, and army supplier.[9]

But did any of those Jews who lived in Illinois cross over to Spanish territory? There is no evidence involving any of those already mentioned. But as early as 1769 agents of the Gratz brothers and David Franks bartered for furs with Indians in St. Louis. This might have been in outright defiance of Spanish law; more likely, it was one of numerous instances of relaxed enforcement. What is not known, however, is who those agents were, and whether any of them were Jewish. As a matter of fact, many people crossed over from Illinois into Spanish Louisiana, to St. Louis and elsewhere, some illicitly and some with approval of Spanish officialdom. In 1789, for instance, Colonel George Morgan laid the foundation for New Madrid, considered the first "American" settlement west of the Mississippi, opposite the mouth of the Ohio River. Spanish authorities granted Morgan's settlers, many of them non-Catholic Germans from Pennsylvania, "perfect freedom in religious matters." One of several businessmen who set up shop in New Madrid was Jacob Myers, a Jewish native of Lancaster, Pennsylvania. A statistical census of the District of Cape Girardeau, dated November 1, 1803, lists "Ezekial Block, or Bloch, a German Jew," who came from Richmond, Virginia (other members of the Block family would later be among the early Jewish settlers in St. Louis). Clearly, then, some Jews came from east of the Mississippi into Spanish Louisiana and settled in what later became Missouri.[10]

But did any come specifically to St. Louis? Annals of early St. Louis indicate that Spanish authorities often permitted non-Catholics to trade and even to reside there. That certainly could explain the Gratz and Franks connection. Aside from that one instance, though, no evidence points to any Jews coming specifically to St. Louis from the east. Yet it would seem perfectly reasonable that if Jewish merchants and traders were only a few miles away in Illinois settlements, some of them from time to time

---

9. Sharfman, *Jews on the Frontier*, 294. Marcus, *Colonial American Jew*, vol. 1, 375–76, describes Levy as "a Jew by descent only," who married a French woman and was "completely Gallicized and took his oath on the New Testament."

10. Postal and Koppman, *Landmarks*, vol. 3, 169; Houck, *Spanish Regime in Missouri*, vol. 2, 393, 412. Houck lists among the settlers of New Madrid one William Cohen (also spelled "Cowen," "Culhoon," and "Cooene"), a native of Carlisle, Pennsylvania, who married Marie Block, daughter of Henry Block and Marie Hamer of Huntingdon, Pennsylvania. Houck, *History of Missouri*, vol. 2, 149, 156, 274.

would have come over for business purposes when appropriate needs or opportunities presented themselves, just as non-Jews did. Nevertheless, lacking actual evidence, that too must remain only conjecture.

One final approach must be explored to complete all "first Jew" possibilities: Spanish Louisiana via New Orleans, from 1763 until the Louisiana Purchase. (For the sake of simplicity, "Spanish Louisiana" here includes not only the 1763–1800 period but also that short 1800–1804 span when Louisiana nominally was French territory again. Actually, the French never did reassume control, and Spanish law and officialdom continued until the United States took over.) The key factor was that just as the French before 1763 had waxed hot and cold in enforcing the *Code Noire*, so too the Spanish authorities after 1763 were inconsistent with restrictive Inquisition regulations. Technically, all non-Catholics were excluded. But recognizing the need to attract settlers, Spain relaxed those restraints. There is no question that some Jews took this opportunity to settle in southern Louisiana. Some located in the New Orleans area, some in New Madrid and Cape Girardeau, but none can be placed as far north as St. Louis.[11]

What we find in St. Louis, however, is something that suggests engaging possibilities, yet is fraught with all sorts of pitfalls for the student of American Jewish history. From the very beginning in 1763, the population of St. Louis was overwhelmingly Roman Catholic, and it was still so when Amos Stoddard raised the American flag in 1804.[12] But that population also included a few who fell into one of two intriguing situations due, of all things, to their names. No discriminating person, of course, should be deceived by the "Jewish sound" of a name as proof of anything. After all, countless Jews and non-Jews bear similar names, both family and given names. Yet there is no denying what statisticians and mathematicians refer to as "statistical probability," that a person named "Gottfried

---

11. Houck, *History of Missouri*, vol. 3, 201. In 1772, reviewing the religious scene in Louisiana, Governor Don Luis de Uzanga wrote: "The King of France, the former sovereign, left the province in complete and absolute liberty. . . . So long as a settler was active, diligent, and laborious, he was inconvenienced by no exactions. Religious opinions were tolerated in order that disputes on such topics might not embarrass the development and progress of the country. . . . Such was the state of affairs [when Spain took over in 1763 and they remained] in the same state without any change *except the expulsion of some Jews and Protestants*." Houck, *Spanish Regime in Missouri*, vol. 1, 144–45 (emphasis added). See also Primm, *Lion of the Valley*, 22. Among the prominent Jews there was Antonio Mendez, a pioneer of the sugar industry in Louisiana during the late 1700s. Marcus, *Colonial American Jew*, vol. 3, 1397.

12. By 1807 there were "so few Protestant American families" in St. Louis that they still were "not able to erect a church of their own." Houck, *History of Missouri*, vol. 3, 224.

Heimberger" or "Manfred Schlosser" *probably* will be Germanic, or that someone named "Pablo Mendez" or "Fernando Vasquez" *probably* will be Hispanic—or that someone named "Benjamin Levy" or "Abraham Cohen" *probably* will be Jewish.

What does one make, then, of a Joseph Alvarez Hortiz? On the surface Hortiz was a solid and stable Spanish resident of early St. Louis. Born in Lienira, Estremadura, Spain, in 1753, the son of Francois Alvarez and Bernarda Hortiz, he came to St. Louis as a soldier in the Spanish garrison. His parents had educated him in his youth, and he became secretary to at least two Spanish governors of St. Louis. In 1780 he married Margaret Marianne Becquet of Fort des Chartres, raised a family in St. Louis, and also moonlighted as proprietor of a small general store. When Spanish authority departed in 1804, Hortiz left with the Spanish flag. Nothing distinguished Hortiz from other Spaniards in St. Louis—except his name. The horrors that the Spanish Inquisition perpetrated against Hispanic Jews are all too well recorded. How many perished probably never will be known. Many survived only by becoming Marranos, professing Catholicism publicly but secretly retaining their Judaism. Some emigrated and resumed their Jewish identity elsewhere. Many abandoned their ancestral faith by conversion or assimilation into the Christian population through intermarriage. Among Spanish Jewish families caught in the grip of the Inquisition were many named Alvarez and Hortiz. In truth, "Alvarez" and "Hortiz" and "Mendez" were not uncommon names in Spain, among both Jews and non-Jews, as perhaps "Smith" or "Fields" are in America. Nevertheless, the question that cannot be avoided is: was Joseph Alvarez Hortiz of Spanish St. Louis perhaps a descendant of Jews who had evaded the long arm of the Inquisition? The answer is simply that we do not know. There is no evidence even to suggest it, only the name. All we know about Hortiz indicates that he was no more nor less devout a Catholic than the rest of the St. Louis population—but withal a Catholic and not a Jew. If Hortiz descended from Jewish ancestry, he did not consider himself a Jew, nor did any of his contemporaries. Only his name raises a subtle uncertainty, but that is totally unreliable historic evidence.[13]

The Hispanic "Jewish-sounding" name was not the only one of its kind found on the frontier. Records of early Americans in various parts of the western wilderness include such "Jewish-sounding" names as Samuel Moses, Isaac Cohen, and Solomon Abrahams, none of whom were Jewish; the same is true of Jacob Abrahams, Benjamin Jacobs, and Joseph Levy.

---

13. "Index to St. Louis Register: Baptisms, Marriages and Burials, 1766 to 1781" (transcribed by Oscar W. Collett), Missouri Historical Society, St. Louis.

Despite their fathers' names or religions, their mothers were not Jewish, and by traditional Jewish law one's identification as a Jew by birth comes from the mother. American frontier conditions compounded difficulties of ascertaining who was or was not Jewish, or who was or was not descended from Jews. As late as the American Revolution, few marriageable Jewish women could be found in the West. Those who lived along the East Coast were very reluctant to move to the western wilderness where, in addition to myriad physical dangers, they also faced life without such requisite Jewish accoutrements as synagogues, facilities to maintain dietary laws, and especially Jewish social and cultural companionship. Lacking Jewish women, Jewish men on the frontier married others, white, black, or Indian, but invariably women outside their faith. Children of those marriages, because of traditional Jewish law, were not considered Jewish. Frontier Jews who resisted intermarriage faced almost insurmountable obstacles trying to perpetuate any Jewish religious continuity or identification, as they were virtually isolated from all aspects of Jewish social and cultural life, let alone religious life. Only the most dedicated could overcome such difficulties. It is no surprise, then, that many strayed from their faith either through intermarriage or gradual lack of observance.[14]

How, then, does one categorize an early St. Louisan named Samuel Solomon? In his book about Jews on the American frontier, I. Harold Sharfman relates a fascinating tale about "the Jew Samuel D. Solomon . . . the first of his people to settle in St. Louis." According to Sharfman, Solomon came to America from Liverpool, England, where he claimed to have earned a medical degree from the University of Aberdeen and a fellowship in the Royal Humane Society in London. Actually, Sharfman asserts, Solomon was no more than a "cure peddler who convinced the naive of the medical wonders wrought by his cordial balm of Gilead and other liquid remedies." "Doctor" Solomon practiced for a while in Philadelphia, "touting a cordial elixir" from which he was reputed to have amassed a fortune. Unmasked as a quack and with charges pending against him, Solomon fled from Philadelphia, eventually alighting in St. Louis in 1806. There the "suave" Solomon opened a shop "visited by the French madames and mademoiselles who in addition to fancy

---

14. Marcus, *Colonial American Jew*, vol. 3, 1193; Sharfman, *Jews on the Frontier*, 295; Joseph R. Rosenbloom, *A Biographical Dictionary of Early American Jews: Colonial Times to 1800*, 4, 73, 92. Identifying someone as Jewish has always been a problem, as traditionally Jewish identity has passed from generation to generation through the mother. It became a divisive issue when some proposed recognizing patrilineal as well as matrilineal descent. For purposes of this study, the author readily accepts as Jewish anyone who is so identified either by himself (or herself) or by others.

lace and racy outfits procured his youth balms." Apparently those po-
tions did not charm certain macho voyageurs in St. Louis, especially one
Joseph LeBlond. For whatever the provocation, LeBlond soundly thrashed
Solomon, precipitating one of the city's early assault and trespass court
cases. Solomon not only lost the suit but also was beaten up again by
three of LeBlond's henchmen. Solomon filed charges against them, but
either prudence or his assessment of frontier justice—or fear of further
beatings—influenced him to drop the charges. Nevertheless, according
to Sharfman, "Solomon's trade grew with the town," and "he became a
merchant of standing, a warden in the Catholic church, influential and
patronized by the leading families."[15]

Sharfman's claim that Samuel Solomon was "the first of his people to
settle in St. Louis," in 1806, is intriguing, but it does not comport with verifiable evidence. Unfortunately, challenged to document his allegations,
Sharfman was unwilling or unable to do so. True, some of what he claims
about a Samuel Solomon in Philadelphia is verifiable, as is some of what
he alleges about a Samuel Solomon in St. Louis, but there is no evidence
that they were the same Samuel Solomon.

As a matter of fact, early records actually muddle the picture, because
they indicate the possibility of several Solomons in St. Louis in those
days. Early St. Louis church records note the birth, death, and burial of
an infant "son of Mrs. Solomon" on March 8, 1795. Those documents do
not give the father's name—one can only assume that his last name was
indeed Solomon—but no evidence suggests his first name to be Samuel.
On April 8, 1807, a twelve-year-old Solomon Solomon was buried. Church
records do not name his parents. Simple arithmetic, though, indicates that
twelve-year-old Solomon Solomon was born in 1795, the same year as
the birth and death of the infant "son of Mrs. Solomon." Unless the two
were twins—and nothing indicates that—it is possible that there were two
Solomon families in St. Louis in 1795 to whom sons were born. Of course,
Solomon Solomon might have been born elsewhere in 1795 and later
moved to St. Louis. In any event, clearly one or maybe two Solomon families were in St. Louis sometime between 1795 and 1807, although available
data does not associate a *Samuel* Solomon with either. Then, on January
7, 1801, according to early church records, "Samuel Solomon" married
Genevieve Gueret. That full name appears in the records for the first time.
With it, too, arises the strange possibility of yet a third Solomon family, all
distinct from Sharfman's Samuel Solomon who allegedly came in 1806.[16]

---

15. Sharfman, *Jews on the Frontier,* 109–10.
16. "Index to St. Louis Register: Baptisms, Marriages and Burials, 1766–1781" and
"Indexes to St. Louis Cathedral and Carondelet Church Baptisms, Marriages and
Burials" (transcribed by Oscar W. Collett), Missouri Historical Society, St. Louis.

Compounding the confusion are other unrelated early references to "Samuel Solomon." A partial list of St. Louis residents in 1802 includes that name, as does another roster dated March 10, 1804, the date of the Louisiana cession. In 1808 "Samuel Solomon" filed suit against Joseph LeBlond, as indicated above, but nothing in court records further identifies him. A "Saml. D. Solomon" communicated from St. Louis several times with General William Clark in 1813 about Indian and related military affairs in the Mississippi valley during the War of 1812. As secretary of the St. Louis Board of Commissioners, "Samuel Solomon, Clerk" signed numerous documents between 1809 and 1816. In 1821 residents of Carondelet proposed "Saml Solomon" for justice of the peace. Were these Samuel Solomons and the Samuel Solomon married in 1801 all the same? Who was the father of the "son of Mrs. Solomon" born and buried in 1795, and of twelve-year-old Solomon Solomon buried in 1807? Historic and genealogic data so far fail to provide accurate and adequate answers.

One thing is certain, however; none of those Solomons can be identified as a Jew. The name alone is not enough. As a matter of fact, available data associates all of the Solomons with Catholicism. Solomon children were baptized in 1795, 1801, and 1803 in the Catholic Church. Solomons who died in 1795 and in 1807 were buried as Catholics. The "Samuel Solomon" married in 1801 was married in the Catholic Church, as were other Solomons later in the 1820s. "Samuel Solomon" was a "church warden" who between 1810 and 1813 "superintended and certified to the burial of the dead" for the Catholic Church in St. Louis when no regular priest was available. Aside from the suggestive name, the only evidence about any person named Solomon, Samuel or otherwise, is that he was not Jewish at the time he (or any of them) can be placed in St. Louis. True, he (or they) might have been born Jewish and then lost or abandoned that identification, but once again, substantiating data is lacking. Available information about the Solomons of early St. Louis identifies them only as Catholics. Thus none can qualify as an early Jew, let alone as Professor Marcus's "first Jew."[17]

---

17. See "Index to St. Louis Register: Baptisms, Marriages and Burials" and "Indexes to St. Louis Cathedral and Carondelet Church Baptisms, Marriages and Burials" as well as "Samuel Solomon" collections in American Jewish Archives (Cincinnati) and Missouri Historical Society (St. Louis). See also Houck, *History of Missouri*, vol. 2, 56; Scharf, *Saint Louis City and County*, vol. 1, 148 and vol. 2, 1642; Blau and Baron, *Jews of the United States*, vol. 3, 842–46; and Robert L. Kirkpatrick, "History of St. Louis, 1804–1816," 144. A longtime student of early Missouri history, Eric P. Newman of St. Louis has gathered some interesting data on "Samuel Solomon" and believes "that the probability is that he was of Jewish descent and probably conformed to whatever

In addition to his unverifiable claim about Samuel Solomon, Sharfman maintains also that one Edward Rose, a "Jewish mulatto," lived briefly in St. Louis in 1807. In a frontier town where "hundreds of boisterous *voyageurs* dominated the wild community," and "horse thieves were hanged at Bloody Island," Sharfman asserts, Edward Rose suddenly appeared, a "dogged, sullen, silent fellow of sinister aspects . . . an outlaw, a member of a river gang infesting the Mississippi River islands." After a very brief and stormy few months in St. Louis, in 1807 Rose joined the Ezekiel Williams fur-trapping expedition into the western wilderness and lived the rest of a turbulent life among the Indians in the middle Missouri River basin.

Valid historical evidence dramatically verifies Edward Rose as the violent and treacherous outlaw and villain portrayed by Sharfman, and places him briefly in St. Louis in 1806–1807 before he moved westward. As with Samuel Solomon, however, there is no evidence that Rose was, or that anyone considered him to be, Jewish. All that exists is a totally unsupported "may have been" reference. On the other hand, reliable evidence indicates that Rose was born in Kentucky about 1787 or 1788, "the son of a white trader and a half-breed woman, mixed Indian and Negro." Whether that "white trader" was Jewish cannot be ascertained, but it seems safe to assume that Rose's mother undoubtedly was not; therefore, by traditional Jewish law, Edward Rose also was not Jewish. Like Samuel Solomon, then, he cannot qualify as an early Jew in St. Louis, and certainly not as Professor Marcus's "first Jew."[18]

Yet another entry into the "first Jew" derby is Zachary Mussina. As will be shown in the next chapter, Mussina was the agent sent by the Philipsons of Philadelphia to St. Louis to handle their business affairs there before Joseph Philipson eventually moved west in 1807 and settled permanently on the banks of the Mississippi. In a well-researched article published in 1986, Ira Rosenwaike, a scholar of early Jewish families in the Midwest, examined whether Mussina may have been Jewish. Rosenwaike concluded the possibility of European Jewish roots, and even that some of Mussina's contemporaries may have thought him to be Jewish. However,

---

religious beliefs the area and his wife (who was not Jewish) required." Newman may be correct; unfortunately, though, it is something that is at most probable, yet lacks satisfactory historical evidence. Newman letter to author, August 16, 1988.

18. Sharfman, *Jews on the Frontier*, 111; Bernard Postal and Lionel Koppman, *A Jewish Tourist's Guide to the United States*, 655; David H. Coyner, *The Lost Trappers: A Collection of Interesting Scenes and Events in the Rocky Mountains*, 59–63; Washington Irving, *Astoria, or Anecdotes of an Enterprize Beyond the Rocky Mountains*, 92–93, 152–63, and *The Adventures of Captain Bonneville*, 118–20; Reuben Holmes, "The Five Scalps," 3–54.

even if a case can be made to identify Mussina as a Jew, his sojourns in St. Louis were brief and sporadic, and he eventually settled elsewhere. At best, Rosenwaike concurs, Mussina might be the first *possible* Jew known to be *temporarily* in St. Louis. Under no circumstances, however, can he be considered the first *permanent* Jewish resident there.[19]

What, then, of Professor Marcus's aphorism about the "first Jew" in St. Louis? Historical evidence indicates that prior to the consummation of the Louisiana Purchase in 1804, some identifiable Jews were *near* St. Louis, but none lived *in* St. Louis. As for residents within St. Louis, some at most *might* have had Jewish origins, but none can be verified as having been or thought to have been Jewish or of Jewish ancestry. Not until after the Louisiana Purchase, when St. Louis became part of the United States, did a clearly identifiable "first Jew" finally settle in St. Louis.[20]

19. Ira Rosenwaike letter to author, May 23, 1989, letter in possession of author; Ira Rosenwaike, "The Mussina Family: Early American Jews?" 397–404.

20. In addition to those already mentioned, three more persons have been suggested as candidates for the "first Jew of St. Louis," but based solely on their names. One was Joshua Bloch, a slave in pre-American St. Louis. Brothers David and Philip Fine owned property in St. Louis. Donald I. Makovsky, "Jewish Haven of Freedom," 69. Aside from their suggestive names, however, no proof exists that any were Jewish.

2

THE FIRST JEWS

In 1883 Isidor Bush, post–Civil War Missouri's most famous and influential Jew, wrote a series of newspaper articles about early St. Louis Jewry. "As early as 1816," he wrote, "three years before the first steamboat arrived at St. Louis, four years before Missouri was admitted into the Union as a state, we find our co-religionists among its few inhabitants. . . . The Bloch (or Block) family was undoubtedly the first and most numerous Jewish family that settled west of the Mississippi River."[1] This designation of the Blocks as St. Louis's first Jews remained almost universally accepted for half a century, partially, no doubt, because of Bush's personal stature and integrity, but especially because he proffered firsthand knowledge of early people and records as the source of his information. Then in 1935 Bernard A. Ehrenreich, a St. Louis businessman with tangential interests in local history, wrote a seminal article in the Rosh Hashannah issue of the *Modern View*, a St. Louis English-language Jewish newspaper, entitled "Three Brothers: A Saga of St. Louis' First Jewish Family." Ehrenreich identified the Philipson brothers, Joseph, Jacob, and Simon, as the first Jews of St. Louis, preceding the Blocks by almost a decade. Ehrenreich did not

---

1. *Jewish Tribune* (St. Louis), November 23, 1883. Isidor Bush's "Historical Sketches," written in late 1883, constitutes the only history of the Jews of St. Louis, albeit sketchy, until this present project. At the request of the *Tribune*'s coeditors Moritz Spitz and Solomon H. Sonneschein (also then rabbis of Temples B'nai El and Shaare Emeth, respectively), Bush formulated his history as a series of articles for the newspaper. He wrote three articles, which appeared in the November 23, December 7, and December 21 issues. Then misfortune struck. Fire destroyed Bush's materials, prompting the *Tribune* to alert its readers to a delay of several weeks while Bush attempted to reconstruct those "well-kept records." *Tribune,* January 4, 1884. Just at that time Spitz withdrew from the editorship of the paper, the result of a number of simmering disputes with Sonneschein, leaving the latter in sole control. Not one of Sonneschein's most ardent admirers anyway, Bush discontinued his association with the paper, and with it his historical sketches. *Jewish Voice* (St. Louis), May 21, 1909.

document his claim, his story being written as a newspaper article rather than as an annotated piece of scholarship.[2] Shortly thereafter a Columbia University doctoral candidate, Sister Marietta Jennings, also named the Philipsons as the first Jews in St. Louis. Apparently she did not know of Ehrenreich's work; nevertheless her extensive footnotes and reliable historical data reinforced his basic thesis, albeit with minor modifications.[3]

Somewhat surprisingly, St. Louis Jewry reacted indifferently, almost unconcernedly. Perhaps the community considered other matters more important. It was, after all, the era of the Great Depression and of widespread international and domestic turmoil. Ominous war clouds were gathering, soon to erupt into the bloodbath of World War II. The St. Louis Jewish press unceasingly detailed a shocking chronicle of anti-Jewish barbarities in Poland, Rumania, and Nazi Germany. At home, in addition to privations engendered by economic hard times, a virulent antisemitism festered menacingly in heavily German-populated St. Louis, as Bundists, Coughlinites, and Christian Frontists associated Jews with virtually every evil or misfortune at home and abroad. Little wonder that St. Louis Jewry paid scant attention to its early history.[4]

But others did, albeit modestly. Editors of the 1943 *Universal Jewish Encyclopedia* included a brief piece on the Philipsons, but cited only the Ehrenreich article as their source. At the same time, oddly, they let stand unchanged, in the selection entitled "St. Louis," the incorrect reference to the Block family as the first Jews in the city. Meanwhile, in St. Louis, under the able leadership of director Charles Van Ravenswaay, the Missouri Historical Society expanded its files on local ethnic groups, including Jews, and those additional collections reflected the work of both Ehrenreich and Jennings.[5]

By 1950 the atmosphere had changed considerably. The Great Depression and World War II were over. The state of Israel had blossomed into a thriving reality, infusing Jews of St. Louis, as it did Jews all over the world,

---

2. Bernard A. Ehrenreich, "Three Brothers: A Saga of St. Louis' First Jewish Family," in *Modern View* (St. Louis), September 26, 1935. Almost fifty years later Ehrenreich recalled: "I don't remember where I got my information. I just went down to the [St. Louis] Public Library and browsed around there." Bernard A. Ehrenreich, interview by author, November 20, 1984.

3. Marietta Jennings, *A Pioneer Merchant of St. Louis, 1810–1820: The Business Career of Christian Wilt*, 33–35. Some of the materials Jennings used were in the St. Louis Public Library. It seems she and Ehrenreich crossed paths there and used the same sources, but neither knew of the other's work.

4. Burton A. Boxerman, "Rise of Anti-Semitism in St. Louis, 1933–1945," 251–69.

5. Director's File, Missouri Historical Society, St. Louis; *Universal Jewish Encyclopedia*, vol. 7, 312–15.

with a new sense of pride and esteem. Forces that earlier had split the St. Louis Jewish community no longer seemed as divisive. The American Jewish Tercentenary of 1954 rekindled a broad and prideful interest in American Jewish history, especially local history. Stimulating leadership by Rabbi Ferdinand M. Isserman of Temple Israel, a moving proponent of interracial and intercultural relations, also spurred St. Louis Jewry to a renewed awareness of its own place in the chronicle of St. Louis.[6]

In the 1950s, accordingly, St. Louisans produced a number of works that dealt with the early days of their Jewish community. Some works examined individual institutions and congregations. One reiterated the defunct Block family legend, but others, especially those by Rabbi Isserman, correctly reflected the Ehrenreich-Jennings "Philipson thesis." Perhaps the most unique was a remarkably well-researched term paper written in 1954 by University City High School student Allan Lazaroff, who used materials in St. Louis probate court records and in the updated archives of the Missouri Historical Society. Thanks to his history teacher Wesley E. Kettelkamp, a copy of that paper was placed in the Missouri Historical Society and also was reprinted, in eight installments, in the *National Jewish Post*, a journal serving the St. Louis Jewish community. In 1958 Donald I. Makovsky wrote a master's thesis on the origins and early years of United Hebrew Congregation, the first Jewish congregation in St. Louis. His comprehensive background for the establishment of that institution included an extensive recounting of the early Jews of St. Louis, including the Philipsons. Just at that time, cognizant that 1957–1958 represented the 150th anniversary of the first identifiable Jew in the city, the St. Louis Rabbinical Association established the Judaism Sesquicentennial Committee to mark the anniversary with a commemorative pamphlet about the Philipsons. Rabbi Isserman chaired a committee of lay and religious leaders who secured Makovsky's services to write it. Entitled *The Philipsons: The First Jewish Settlers in St. Louis,* the pamphlet was distributed at the annual combined Reform-Conservative service on Thanksgiving Day, 1958. At long last the Jewish community accorded to the Philipsons their due recognition as the first identifiable Jews in St. Louis.[7]

_____

6. Oscar Handlin, *Adventure in Freedom: Three Hundred Years of Jewish Life in America,* 180–84, indicates that by the 1950s many ethnic fears of the thirties and forties had relaxed. See also John Higham, *Send These to Me: Immigrants in Urban America,* 96–97.

7. Charles Klotzer, "Ten Jews Met in 1836 and Created the United Hebrew Congregation," in the *National Jewish Post* (Missouri Edition), September 11, 1953; also Hyman Flaks, "Thirty Years of Vaad Hoeir," in Norman Paris, ed., *Brocho L'Mnachem: Essays Contributed in Honor of Rabbi Menachem H. Eichenstein,* 25–26. The Lazaroff paper can be found serialized in the *National Jewish Post* (Missouri Edition), December 9

Very little information exists about the early years of the Philipson brothers.[8] Simon apparently was the oldest, born in 1771; then came Joseph, born in 1773, and Jacob, the youngest, born in 1778. Simon and Jacob were born in that part of Poland which later came under Prussian rule; one might assume Joseph was born there too. Contemporaries referred to the Philipsons as "Polish Jews." That could have referred to their native land. It also could have meant merely that they adhered to *Minhag Poland*, the eastern European rituals of Ashkenazic observance. In fact, the terms "Polish Jews" and "German Jews" often were used interchangeably for many who emigrated from the eastern German states that formerly had been part of Poland and who followed *Minhag Poland*. No specific evidence corroborates why the Philipsons came to the United States, but one probably can assume the same general political, social, and economic forces that impelled so many others, Jews and non-Jews. The Philipsons came to the United States reportedly from Hamburg, Germany, and settled in Philadelphia. Existing records indicate Simon arrived on September 14, 1796. One cannot ipso facto assume the same date for the others; a safer assertion is that they came in either the late 1790s or early 1800s. They were known as highly educated and cultured gentlemen as well as accomplished musicians. Apparently Simon and Jacob were the more observant, for they became members of Philadelphia's Rodeph Shalom Congregation, the oldest Ashkenazic synagogue in the United States.[9]

---

and 23, 1955, and January 6 and 20, February 10, 17, and 24, and March 16, 1956. Donald I. Makovsky's graduate work culminated in his "Origin and Early History of the United Hebrew Congregation of St. Louis, 1841–1859," followed by his pamphlet *The Philipsons: The First Jewish Settlers in St. Louis, 1807–1858*.

8. Unless otherwise indicated, the major sources for the following narrative about the Philipsons are the Jennings book, the Ehrenreich article, and the Makovsky thesis cited previously.

9. Jennings and Makovsky incorrectly refer to Joseph as the youngest brother. When Simon died, a brief obituary in the *Daily Missouri Republican* (St. Louis), July 1, 1841, gave his age as seventy-five; that would mean he was born in 1766. But probably more reliable is Simon's more contemporary petition for citizenship in 1799. He gave his age then as twenty-eight, which would mean he was born in 1771. Simon Philipson's Petition for Citizenship, June 17, 1799, Division of Archives and Manuscripts, Pennsylvania Historical and Museum Commission, Harrisburg, copy in possession of Murray Darrish, former president of the Jewish Genealogy Society of St. Louis. The dates for Joseph's and Jacob's births come from newspaper obituaries, admittedly not infallible. Simon's petition for citizenship states that he was "a native of Poland now [1799] under the Possession of the King of Prussia." The St. Louis City Death Register, a copy of which is in the Missouri Historical Society in St. Louis, lists "Prussia" as Jacob's place of birth. References to the Philipsons in St. Louis can be found also in

It was not their religion, though, that brought the Philipsons to St. Louis;
it was their business. By 1803 Jacob and Simon were partners in a Philadelphia firm dealing with furs and lead, products that by their very nature
directed the brothers' attention and interests westward. With financial
help from Joseph Hertzog, a wealthy and prominent Philadelphia merchant, the Philipsons expanded into the Missouri fur and lead markets.
They engaged Zachary Mussina, Simon's brother-in-law, as their western
agent, and in short order he established lucrative contacts with lead
miners in southeastern Missouri and with fur interests in St. Louis. Among
others, the Philipsons dealt with John Jacob Astor and the American Fur
Company, and with Moses Austin, the lead magnate whose son Stephen
would be prominent in American involvement in Texas. Business was
good, and brother Joseph also became involved, although it is not clear
whether as a partner or independently. One of the brothers may have
visited St. Louis, but if he did he stayed only briefly before returning
to Philadelphia, and agent Mussina continued to direct the Philipson
business in the Mississippi valley.

Before long the Philipsons decided to move to St. Louis. Already doing
well in furs and lead, they envisioned unlimited opportunities in general merchandising, not only in supplying everyday needs for St. Louis
residents but also in outfitting the increasing numbers of hunting and
trading expeditions passing through the city on their way west. In 1807
the Philipsons persuaded Hertzog to finance them again, in a general
mercantile enterprise that they would establish in St. Louis. At the same
time they concluded that someone other than Mussina should represent
them. Although a good salesman and experienced in both western lead
and mercantile affairs, the industrious and ambitious Mussina wanted to
be more than just an agent for someone else. In addition, personal discord
between the refined and cultured Philipson brothers and the "quick tem-
pered" and "at times sullen" Mussina created dissension. The Philipsons
preferred a less irascible person, not only to ensure a steady flow of lead
and furs to the East but also to establish and operate a challenging and
demanding new business enterprise in the West.[10]

The responsibility fell to thirty-four-year-old Joseph Philipson. Why
the mantle fell on this particular brother is not known; it may have been
because he was not married and therefore was unencumbered with family

---

Frederic L. Billon, *Annals of St. Louis in Its Territorial Days from 1804 to 1821*, vol. 2, 229,
and in Blau and Baron, *The Jews of the United States*, vol. 1, 264.

10. Mussina's ambitions for wealth led to a partnership in Philadelphia with Hertzog
and the latter's nephew Christian Wilt. In 1810 Mussina returned to St. Louis with
Wilt, established a profitable mercantile house, and became a major competitor of the
Philipsons. Jennings, *Pioneer Merchant*, 15–16.

responsibilities. At any rate, Joseph left Philadelphia in September 1807. His first stop was Baltimore, where he purchased some ten thousand dollars' worth of goods from at least twelve different firms, mostly on long-term (twelve-month) notes, managing to pay down only $552.90 in cash. Then it was on to St. Louis. In the archives of the venerable St. Louis Mercantile Library one still can see Joseph Philipson's original account book. The first page is dated "St. Louis, December 13, 1807." On it are recorded business transactions numbered "84" to "92." They constitute a list of the Baltimore firms from whom Philipson had purchased his inventory. The eighty-three prior transactions remain unknown, as their record no longer exists. But what is left in that musty old journal unquestionably confirms that as early as December 13, 1807, Joseph Philipson already had established himself in business. The first identifiable Jew had settled in St. Louis.

Contemporary records do not give the address of Philipson's first establishment. However, a description of St. Louis at that time locates the "business district," which by 1810 already consisted of twelve stores, "on Main Street, between Spruce and Pine." Today that is on the grounds of the famous Gateway Arch complex on the St. Louis riverfront. In 1821, John Paxton's first *St. Louis Directory and Register* listed him as "Philipson, Joseph, Merchant, 6 North Main." He conducted business alone for a while, but in 1808 his brother Jacob joined him, leaving Simon in Philadelphia to look after matters there. Customers listed in the Philipson account book include some of St. Louis's most famous early personalities: Alexander McNair, later the first governor of Missouri; Auguste and Pierre Chouteau and Madame Labadie, pioneer settlers; Meriwether Lewis, explorer; Frederick Bates, secretary and several times acting governor of the Territory of Louisiana and later the second governor of Missouri. Philipson also did a lot of business with the government, outfitting exploring parties and provisioning troops. The Philipson store was a general merchandising store in every sense; products ranged from coffee ($.75 a pound) to almonds (also $.75 a pound) to Spanish cigars ($.02 each) to butter ($.20 a pound). A violin sold for $6.25; an umbrella, on the other hand, cost $8. Two volumes of a history of Virginia sold for $8; a silk shawl brought $16.

There is no clear evidence that Joseph and Jacob Philipson joined as actual partners in that store, though it seems likely that they did. Nevertheless, they did combine in other ventures, including real estate and lead. Competitors sometimes resented their unscrupulous tactics and hard bargaining; other contemporaries saw in them the traits of "educated refined gentlemen."[11]

---

11. One student of early St. Louis states that Philipson was the first American to establish a "permanent" store in St. Louis. That statement bears critical scrutiny. Kirk-

The period before and during the War of 1812 produced many difficulties for trade and commerce in the Mississippi valley. Problems with
hostile Indians seemed never-ending. Governmental restrictions on trade
with European nations, combined with retaliatory measures by England
and France, had a devastating effect on Mississippi valley business. Merchants found themselves short of goods, and businessmen of excellent
character and repute turned to smuggling and price gouging just to
survive. Some have hinted that Joseph Philipson practiced some of those
indiscretions. On the other hand, while others in St. Louis, including a
few of his close associates, suffered prosecution and conviction, Philipson
never even faced trial. Either he was indeed totally innocent, or he proved
shrewd enough to evade detection.

Joseph Philipson also stands out as one of the pioneers of the renowned
St. Louis beer industry. For a long time many considered him to have been
the first brewer not only in St. Louis but also west of the Mississippi, but
recent scholarship shows that that distinction belongs to others. In 1815
Philipson established the "St. Louis Brewery," the third such enterprise in
St. Louis. The company operated in two frame buildings, one a two-story
structure, on Main (or Third) Street, between Biddle and Carr Streets, near
the city's northern limits. The beer was brewed in a wooden pirogue (a
canoe-shaped boat hollowed out of a log) propped up on the north side
of the building.

Joseph Philipson stayed in the beer business for only a few years, but
in that brief time he left his mark as a pioneer in brewing procedure. He
introduced in the Midwest the steel roller technique for grinding malt
and hops. Heretofore millers ground those products with stones in a grist
or flour mill. In 1816 Simon Philipson, still in Philadelphia, learned of a
superior steel roller system then being experimented with in European
and eastern American breweries. Apparently the brothers maintained a
business relationship involving the brewery, for Simon purchased a set
of the new rollers and sent them to Joseph, who installed them in the
St. Louis plant.

Joseph Philipson was responsible for additional "firsts" in the St. Louis
beer industry. Other brewers produced their wares only for the St. Louis
market and sold directly from their brewery. Philipson sold from the
brewery too, by the barrel and the half barrel, but he also sold to retail

---

patrick, "History of St. Louis," 99. Shortly after he arrived in St. Louis, Jacob Philipson
opened "*his* new Store, opposite the Post Office" (emphasis added), and advertised
the sale of "dry goods and a general assortment of groceries." The advertisement did
not mention Joseph Philipson at all. *Missouri Gazette* (St. Louis), November 9, 1808.
See also Billon, *Annals of St. Louis*, vol. 2, 229.

outlets in scattered St. Louis stores where people could buy in smaller consumer-sized quantities. In the meantime, brother Jacob Philipson had moved to Ste. Genevieve and opened a general store there. Joseph shipped St. Louis Brewery products downriver and provided the Ste. Genevieve market with a constant supply of beer, ale, and a "strong palatable porter." Thus Joseph Philipson was the first in St. Louis to package beer for the small consumer and to export it to markets outside the city.

One of Joseph Philipson's pricing practices promised to be uniquely promotional and beneficial for the St. Louis community. He offered to lower his prices when grain and hops could be secured from the nearby countryside. This would be a boon for local farmers as well as for his customers. Unfortunately Philipson did not remain in the brewery business long enough for this policy to make much of an impact, and his competitors and successors did not show the same concern for the welfare of the community. Evidently Philipson was a good salesman and a novel go-getter. He reputedly offered a standing bargain to his customers: "A dollar refunded if you return the barrel." At the same time, unlike his competitors, Philipson did not sell beer on credit, because he had to pay cash, often in advance, for all his materials. Understandably this "no credit" policy, despite his other favorable practices, did not endear him to some of his customers.[12]

As early as 1812, even before he began brewing beer and ale, Philipson had considered establishing a whiskey distillery. That idea finally reached fruition in 1820, when he formed a partnership with Matthew Murphy and James Nagle to operate an expanded enterprise called the "St. Louis Brewery and Distillery," located at the same site as the existing brewery. It was the first commercial distillery in the city. In 1821 Murphy and Nagle withdrew from the firm, leaving Philipson to run it alone. By then, too, his brewery remained the only one in St. Louis, his competitors having either died or gone out of business.[13]

Being the sole brewery did not prove to be as favorable as one might expect. The arrival of the steamboat *Zebulon M. Pike* in St. Louis in 1817, a monumental turning point in the city's economic development, signaled

12. The best account of the early brewing industry in St. Louis is still James Lindhurst, "History of the Brewing Industry in St. Louis, 1804–1860."

13. As early as 1808 "Samuel Solomon" advertised twelve hundred gallons of "Good Old Whiskey" for sale, but there is no mention whether it was imported or home distilled. *Missouri Gazette* (St. Louis), November 30, 1808, cited in Kirkpatrick, "History of St. Louis," 101. A commercial distillery was established in 1817 by Christian Wilt, but it was across the river in Illinois. Jennings, *Pioneer Merchant*, 192–93. Of course, private "backyard" breweries and distilleries were common.

for Philipson a potentially disastrous competition from long-established breweries in the East. His problems were compounded in January 1821 when a fire in the malt house partially destroyed his plant, forcing a temporary shut-down. The loss sustained in that fire, combined with other financial reverses following the Panic of 1819, forced Philipson to sell out to wealthy businessman John Mullanphy. By that time Simon Philipson had joined his brothers in St. Louis, and he immediately arranged a three-year lease with Mullanphy. When the lease expired in 1824, complete control of the brewery reverted permanently to Mullanphy. Prominent though the Philipsons had been in the early history of brewing in St. Louis, they would never again associate with that industry.[14]

Joseph Philipson did not restrict his enterprising career to merchandising and brewing. He bought and sold real estate in and around St. Louis. He engaged in lead mining in southeast Missouri. He owned one of the earliest sawmills in St. Louis. He was a stockholder in the Bank of St. Louis, the first bank chartered in Missouri, and one of the largest incorporators of the next bank, the Bank of Missouri. As bank director, he shared financial responsibilities for St. Louis with such historic personages as Auguste Chouteau, J. B. C. Lucas, Thomas F. Biddle, Joseph Charless, and Thomas Hart Benton. His civic accomplishments included service on a jury unique in St. Louis history because it resulted in the first legal execution in the city. Philipson was associated with a variety of more pleasant civic activities, including endeavors to build a courthouse, an art museum, and other public buildings. Contemporaries characterized him as an individual of civic pride and concern, and acclaimed him as one of the city's "leading citizens."[15]

By 1817 western political maneuverings triggered the movement for Missouri statehood. Events soon erupted into an acrimonious national debate that pitted North against South over the convulsive issue of slavery. What Thomas Jefferson feared as "the firebell that rang in the night" finally abated in 1820 and 1821 with the Missouri Compromise and statehood for Missouri. Of course feelings ran high in St. Louis, where the prose was seething and the oratory bombastic. But Joseph Philipson did not play much of a role in those political debates. That may seem strange,

---

14. When Simon Philipson returned the brewery to Mullanphy, he attempted to retain the steel rollers that he had sent to his brother Joseph in 1816. He claimed they were part of a separate malt rolling enterprise not included in the 1821 sale of the brewery. The case was finally settled in Mullanphy's favor in the Missouri Supreme Court. *Philipson v. Mullanphy*, 1 Missouri Reports 620–26 (1821).

15. Primm, *Lion of the Valley*, 101; Richard Edwards and M. Hopewell, eds., *Edwards' Great West and Her Commercial Metropolis*, 310; Billon, *Annals of St. Louis*, vol. 2, 15.

considering his status as a "leading citizen"; apparently that recognition saluted his civic, cultural, and economic contributions rather than political achievements.

Other issues also furthered controversy in the years when Missouri awaited statehood. Discord between "hard money" and "soft money" advocates plagued the American scene, as did rampant western land speculation. Those problems inextricably brought about the Panic of 1819 and an ensuing depression that affected financial institutions for several years. Both the Bank of St. Louis and the Bank of Missouri went under. Their collapse and the hard times of the early 1820s devastated Philipson financially. He sold virtually everything to meet his obligations. But meet them he did, even at the cost of financial ruin. Thus a promising career in business and commerce came to an abrupt and ruinous end. For the rest of his life Joseph Philipson would remain disassociated from the larger St. Louis business community, except for some minor fur and land dealings.

But he did not disappear from the public scene. No longer a man of financial means, Philipson fell back on his cultural talents. Until he died at age seventy-one on June 19, 1844, he supported himself primarily as a musician and by giving music lessons. He never married, and the meager income from this urbane and refined occupation satisfied a bachelor's financial needs.[16]

Philipson's lengthy career in music disclosed to the St. Louis public an individual quite different from the Shylock-type, shrewd-dealing, and hard-bargaining businessman characterized earlier. The community now saw more of the refined and cultured Joseph Philipson, the talented musician, the linguist, the patron of literature and the arts. St. Louis did not rank in the 1820s and 1830s as a mecca of culture and intellect; it was, after all, still a lusty and burgeoning river city on the turbulent frontier. That is not to say, though, that the area was totally devoid of civilized accoutrements. Chroniclers of early St. Louis attest to private book collections, amateur and professional theatrical productions, and oratorical and musical presentations. In that sphere appeared yet another of Joseph Philipson's contributions to St. Louis history, perhaps his most important. For more than twenty years he projected the image of the finer cultural life, of music, of the fine arts, of literature. Clearly his fellow citizens respected his cultural profile; when he died, his funeral cortege included at least ten carriages conveying St. Louis's "oldest and most

---

16. Philipson's career is characterized in an obituary in the *Daily Evening Gazette* (St. Louis) on the occasion of his death.

respectable citizens." One St. Louis newspaper eulogized his cultural endowment to the community as follows: "His highly cultivated mind— his dignified manners—and his fine taste in letters and the arts would have adorned the most polished circles of society."[17]

The second identifiable Jewish settler in St. Louis arrived in 1808; he was Jacob Philipson, Joseph's brother. On November 9, 1808, the *Missouri Gazette* advertised the opening of Jacob's new general store, opposite the post office, where St. Louisans could find "A seasonable supply of Dry Goods and a General Assortment of Groceries." Merchandise included blankets, ladies' Morocco leather spangled shoes, linseed oil, coffee and tea, hymn books, imported liquors, chocolate, sugar, writing paper, German and English Bibles, salted shad and mackerel, and even a 40-gallon and a 114-gallon still. Philipson evidently believed in intensive advertising; he ran the same notice in five consecutive issues of the paper. It remains the earliest known advertisement of a Jewish-owned establishment in St. Louis.

Jacob Philipson operated several general stores in the St. Louis waterfront business district during the next two years. Then in January 1811 he moved to Ste. Genevieve, about seventy miles south on the Mississippi River. No evidence indicates why he chose that particular destination; perhaps the attraction was another Jewish family, the Block family, who had lived nearby for more than a decade. Philipson opened a general merchandising store in Ste. Genevieve, which he ran until 1814, when wartime constrictions forced him to close.

His whereabouts and activities for the next few years are a bit hazy, although unquestionably he remained in southeastern Missouri. His Ste. Genevieve establishment gave way to a joint Block-Philipson enterprise, the one to which Joseph Philipson's St. Louis Brewery later shipped beer and ale products. He also built and lived in a stone house in Ste. Genevieve, on the corner of Second and Merchant Streets. That building, known as the Philipson-Valle house (it later was bought by J. B. Valle), still remains as one of the historic sites of Ste. Genevieve. He lived for a time in the Potosi

---

17. *Daily Evening Gazette,* June 21, 1844. An indication of Philipson's cultural interests is revealed in his meager estate: a piano, a forty-five-volume encyclopedia, four dictionaries, four music books and lots of music, a Bible, a French grammar, a chemistry book, an atlas of Europe, a volume of Faust's tragedies, and a large collection of prints and paintings. The complete inventory is found in Estate of Joseph Philipson, Estate No. 1907, Probate Court Files, Probate Court of St. Louis. The probate records of Simon Philipson are in Estate No. 1666, and those of Jacob Philipson in Estate No. 5154. In addition to the records in the St. Louis Probate Court, copies are in the archives of the Missouri Historical Society (St. Louis) and the American Jewish Archives (Cincinnati).

area, where he probably handled Philipson family lead interests. Most important of all, though, he married Elizabeth Block, daughter of Simon Block, a Jewish merchant of Ste. Genevieve and Washington County. In contrast with many other Jewish pioneers, Jacob Philipson married within his faith.

Philipson returned with his bride to St. Louis, where they remained the rest of their lives. Although existing evidence cannot substantiate whether Jacob and Joseph Philipson became actual partners in their merchandising establishments, they did cooperate in extensive real estate holdings and in lead mining. Then, just as the Panic of 1819 and the ensuing depression destroyed Joseph Philipson's business edifice, so did it devastate Jacob Philipson. And just as Joseph Philipson abandoned a career as merchant and businessman and became a teacher, so too Jacob Philipson abandoned his career as a merchant and businessman and also became a teacher. But where Joseph taught music, Jacob, an accomplished linguist as well as a musician, gave private lessons in English, German, and French. Giving language lessons proved no more profitable than giving music lessons, and Jacob too lived the rest of his life in meager circumstances, especially with a family to support. Nevertheless, like Joseph, he nurtured a strong interest in literature, art, and music. Indeed, up to almost the very end, his home at 224 South Third Street served as a salon for not only language lessons but also music, art, and literary appreciation. Thus, though he came to St. Louis to undertake a career in business, Jacob Philipson's legacy to St. Louis was primarily cultural.[18]

By the time the third Philipson brother, Simon, settled in St. Louis, several other Jews already had done so. Simon had remained in Philadelphia to handle family business affairs there, but in 1821, following the financial cataclysm in which his brothers suffered so disastrously, he joined them in St. Louis. He associated briefly with John Mullanphy in the St. Louis Brewery, and then went into the poultry and egg business, along with some dabbling in real estate. Neither wealthy nor impoverished, he

---

18. Jacob Philipson's marriage produced at least seven children. Philip died before his father. Joseph married twice; neither wife was Jewish (one of his descendants by Joseph's second wife reputedly donated the land in Cape Girardeau on which the state of Missouri established what is now Southeast Missouri State University). Lavinia married Antonio Prietto, a non-Jew. Esther married Alexander Lewis, a Jew and early member of United Hebrew Congregation. Theodore never married. Anna Mierree (Marie) married a Jew named Moses. Rose Adelaide married a Jew, Adolph Mayer. The only known descendants of Jacob Philipson are those of his children Joseph, Esther, and Rosa Adelaide. Kay B. Kulfinski in interview with author, February 4, 1985. Kulfinski, a resident of Edwardsville, Illinois, is a descendant of Jacob Philipson through Philipson's son Joseph and Joseph's second wife.

occasionally saw to his brothers' financial needs. He had been a merchant and businessman in Philadelphia, but his activities in St. Louis, except for the first few years, focused elsewhere.

In the twenty years that Simon Philipson lived in St. Louis, he achieved a reputation as a charming eccentric. British author William Drummond Stewart, traveling through St. Louis in 1830, described him as a "Polish Jew, an agreeable old man, who had an old wooden house on a square plot . . . he had a large poultry yard and very much lived upon eggs, either in kind or converted into money." A familiar sight in old St. Louis, according to Stewart, was that "agreeable old man" trudging to the brewery every two or three days carrying under his arm a barrel that he replenished with beer. Philipson collected curios of all sorts, and his home overflowed with odds and ends, some valuable, some worthless junk. "His abode . . . was never swept," wrote Stewart, "save when a plume of ostrich feathers was called to clean anything for exhibition to a rare hunter of the old and curious in these parts."[19]

That disarray resulted partially from the lack of someone to look after the household. Simon had married the former Susanna Mussina, the well-educated sister of his former employee and later business rival Zachary Mussina. They had six children, all born in Philadelphia. On October 7, 1821, shortly after the family arrived in St. Louis, Mrs. Philipson passed away. This may be the earliest recorded death of a Jew in St. Louis, if indeed she was Jewish. Susanna Mussina was of Italian extraction, but it is not clear whether she was also Jewish. At any rate, she was interred in the city cemetery, there being no Jewish burial grounds in St. Louis at the time.[20]

Joseph and Jacob Philipson settled into relatively serene and tranquil lives after they changed careers from prominent and wealthy merchants to modest and unpretentious teachers; Simon Philipson, on the other hand, led a troubled and lonely life. Within a few years after his wife died, he lost three children. One son, Philip, "a promising and adventurous lad . . . possessed of true pioneering spirit," sought his fortune in the Rocky Mountains. He survived four years of danger there, but died in Lexington, Missouri, on the return trip. Another son, Louis, also challenged the western wilderness, only to lose his life by drowning. Daughter Amanda's undisciplined lifestyle added to the Philipson family

19. William Drummond Stewart, *Edward Warren* (London, 1854), 482, as cited in Makovsky, "History of United Hebrew Congregation," 121. See also Charles Van Ravenswaay, *Saint Louis: An Informal History of the City and Its People, 1764–1865*, 306–7.

20. For possible Jewish identification of Susanna Mussina Philipson see Ira Rosenwaike, "The Mussina Family," 397–404.

discomfiture. Married to "a most accomplished violinist," she strayed from accepted moral patterns and eventually gave birth to an illegitimate son. Several tempestuous years later the child ended up in New York, and Amanda in a tragic early grave.

All this family sorrow was counterbalanced somewhat by considerable musical talent, a trait that characterized many of the Philipsons. Ill-fated Louis and Amanda, for instance, were brilliant musicians. William Drummond Stewart described them as "the most extraordinary pianists I ever heard." Louis composed several works that were published by a New York music company. When a Coblenz, Germany, official visited St. Louis in 1834, the Philipson children so impressed him that his endorsement of their talent "furthered the cause of music in the City." Unfortunately, neither was able to develop their talent into a productive life or career.[21]

Through their common interest in music, the Philipsons became acquainted with two more gifted musical families in St. Louis. Johann Heinrich Weber was a linguist, scholar, composer, and former counselor at the court of Frederick William III of Prussia. When he came to St. Louis in 1834, Weber brought with him a large musical library containing scores by Bach, Haydn, Mozart, Beethoven, Handel, and others. William and Henry Robyn were also accomplished musicians. With St. Louis beginning to show signs of cultural growth in the 1830s and 1840s, these three families assumed prominence in cultivating musical appreciation, and St. Louis citizenry became acquainted with many musical masterpieces. According to a St. Louis historian and former director of the Missouri Historical Society, the Philipson, Weber, and Robyn families "established classical music in St. Louis."[22]

Important as were the Philipson brothers' legacies to St. Louis in business, linguistics, and music, all these might have been transcended by a remarkable family art collection. Simon Philipson's potpourri accumulation in his disheveled house included about 150 paintings. When he died in August 1841, the paintings went to his brother Joseph. Added to what Joseph already owned, the collection totaled about 390 paintings and 100 prints. They included *Portrait of an English Lady* by Hans Holbein, *Portrait* by Titian, *Capture and Conflagration of Troy* by Rembrandt, *The Savior on the Cross* by Peter Paul Rubens, *Hagar in the Desert* by Bartolome Esteban Murillo, and more by artists such as Botticelli, Francis Hals, Leonardo da Vinci, Raphael, and others. No one knows where or how the Philipsons acquired such art treasures. There had been more, but Simon sold some on

21. Van Ravenswaay, *Saint Louis*, 306.
22. Ibid., 306–7.

at least two occasions in August 1839 and September 1840. In November 1840 he proposed that the St. Louis Board of Delegates purchase the collection and establish a municipal art museum. The offer was turned down. Some maintained the city government lacked authority to make such a purchase. Others considered it "too expedient a luxury" to justify a municipal expenditure. The *St. Louis Daily Evening Gazette* editorialized, however, that "from the rarity and value of this collection it is certainly desirable that it should be retained in this city. It would present a good opportunity to establish a gallery which would be creditable to the city."[23]

After Simon died and the collections merged, the paintings were displayed publicly, but under private auspices. For a while Joseph Philipson exhibited them in a suite he rented from James Lucas located over the surveyor general's office on Chestnut Street. In 1843 the "Philipson Galleries" occupied rooms at the corner of Main and Olive. For reasons unknown, when Joseph Philipson died in 1844, instead of bequeathing the collection to a surviving relative (the closest was his brother Jacob), he specified that the executors of his estate, Peter Chouteau and James Sarpy, could dispose of the collection to its best advantage, either by outright sale or by exhibition to raise revenue. They stored the paintings for a while in a room over the post office at an annual rental of one hundred dollars. In 1846, deeming that an unnecessary and unreasonable expense, Sarpy obtained probate court permission to sell the paintings. Instead of selling them, though, in 1848 he turned them over to Robert E. Clary, husband of Simon Philipson's daughter Esther, as trustee. What happened next to

---

23. According to Simon Philipson's will, a tract of land in Washington County, Missouri, was left in trust for the children of his brother Jacob, and the rest of his land in trust for his own daughters Amanda and Esther. In addition to sons Philip and Louis who died in the western wilderness, two more sons, Joseph Jr. and William Hyman, died as youths in St. Louis. Amanda's dissolute lifestyle has already been alluded to. Esther married Lt. Robert Emmett Clary, a West Point graduate, whose classmate Jefferson Davis served as best man at the wedding. Despite that close friendship, Clary served with distinction on the Union side during the Civil War. One of the Clary children, Capt. Robert Emmett Clary Jr., died in action during that conflict. Another child, Marie Louise Clary, married General Charles P. Stone, noted as the chief engineer in the construction of the pedestal base for the Statue of Liberty. Thus the only known descendants of Simon Philipson are those of his daughter Esther. Of course Amanda might have had descendants, but considering her marital indiscretions they would be difficult to trace. Kay B. Kulfinski, interview by author, February 4, 1985. The inventory of Simon Philipson's estate contains a list of his paintings. See Estate of Simon Philipson, Estate No. 1666, Probate Court Files, Probate Court of St. Louis. Copies of that list are also in the archives of the Missouri Historical Society (St. Louis) and the American Jewish Archives (Cincinnati). See also *Daily Evening Gazette*, November 13, 1840, and Van Ravenswaay, *Saint Louis*, 306–7.

the art treasures is unknown; apparently they were sold or given away piece by piece and literally scattered to the four corners of the globe. Thus the earliest art collection in St. Louis, in spite of being offered to the city, simply vanished. One can only speculate what its value, both cultural and monetary, would be today had it been kept intact and preserved.[24]

Despite the noteworthy business, civic, and cultural legacies St. Louis's first Jewish family left to the city, one important legacy is conspicuously missing. Its absence actually creates a dilemma in even identifying the Philipsons as Jews. No evidence exists that the Philipsons associated in St. Louis with anything Jewish, either in their personal lives or in dealings with others. True, when Joseph and Jacob arrived in 1807 and 1808, they faced the same overwhelming problems of religious isolation that so many other single Jewish trailblazers experienced on the American frontier. Yet when Simon came in 1821, other Jews already had settled. By the 1830s enough Jews had come to St. Louis to end religious isolation. In the lifetime of all three Philipson brothers, religious services were held in St. Louis and synagogues, cemetery associations, and benevolent societies came into being. True, one does not have to be a "joiner" to demonstrate one's Judaism. At the same time, it is not unreasonable to expect some relationship, at least, considering who the Philipsons were and the small size of the Jewish community. Yet there is no evidence of any demonstration of Judaism by any of the three brothers.[25]

That is why the Philipsons present such an enigma. Virtually every contemporary description characterized them as modest men of unimpugnable character who led exemplary lives. The little that is known of

---

24. An extant legend is that many of the pieces ended up in the possession of the Chouteau, Sarpy, and Clary families in St. Louis. Kay B. Kulfinski, interview by author, February 4, 1985. St. Louis would wait until 1881 before it acquired a municipal art museum, donated to the city by Wayman Crow, a pioneer dry goods wholesaler and part-time educator. Primm, *Lion of the Valley*, 352, 523.

25. Bernard Ehrenreich wrote in his article about the Philipsons: "Simon was the most sturdily Jewish of all the brothers. He observed prayers in the morning and at all other appropriate times. He ate only that which was ceremonially pure, which unfortunately necessitated a constant diet of eggs and milk. He implanted a strong Judaism within his and his brothers' children and was known throughout the community for his religious and general knowledge. It was at Simon's home that the Philipson clan gathered to hold their religious services and observances. It was he that led them in prayer, and taught the newer generation the essence of Judaism." *Modern View*, September 26, 1935. Unfortunately, no evidence supports Ehrenreich's contentions. Yet if his observations are true, it is incomprehensible that those who possessed such an "essence of Judaism" did not associate with any Jewish organizations or synagogues when they came into existence. Accordingly, because Ehrenreich cites no corroborative evidence, we must view his account as containing considerable journalistic license.

their background indicates that they were Jewish by birth and undoubtedly grew up with at least a minimal knowledge of Judaism and Jewish
practice. Jacob and Simon even belonged to Rodeph Shalom Congregation
in Philadelphia. Jacob married a Jewish woman, and some of his children
married Jews; Simon's wife may have been Jewish. Even their non-Jewish
descendants recognized their forebears as Jews. Still, certain facts elude
explanation. Simon was the first of the brothers to die, in August 1841.
By then the United Hebrew Cemetery had been established. Yet Simon
was buried in the city cemetery. That could be explained because Simon
chose interment alongside his wife, who had been buried there in 1821,
long before a Jewish cemetery existed. Joseph died in 1844, and he too
chose burial in the city cemetery, where he already owned a plot, alongside his brother. The laudatory obituary for Joseph that appeared in the
St. Louis press compounds the Philipson conundrum. It characterized
him as "distinguished by his many virtues; and, although a member
of no religious denomination, by the constant practice of the precepts
of Christianity." Yet that "member of no religious denomination" who
constantly practiced "the precepts of Christianity" was born and raised
a Jew, even though during his years in St. Louis he was a nonpracticing
and totally secularized Jew.[26]

Jacob Philipson was the last of the brothers to die, on January 10, 1858, at
age seventy-nine. Unlike his brothers, however, Jacob chose to be buried in
a Jewish cemetery. The choice may have been dictated, though, not by any
religious considerations but rather by economic constraints. Apparently
Jacob found himself in such dire financial difficulty that he feared he could
not even afford the cost of a decent burial. He therefore requested in his
will that his Jewish son-in-law Alexander Lewis, a member of United
Hebrew Congregation, seek funds from his fellow congregants to pay for
a plot and interment in the United Hebrew Cemetery. But the wording of
Jacob's unique burial request adds fuel to the dilemma of the Philipsons'
identification with Judaism. He asked his son-in-law to solicit "money
sufficient for my funeral among *his* followers in creed, . . . [so I might be]
interred in *their* cemetery." Was Jacob affirming merely that he was not
a member of either their congregation or their cemetery association? Or
was he suggesting that any donors would be Lewis's "followers in creed"
but not his? Was this his way of saying he did not consider himself to
be Jewish—he who had married a Jewess, and who had children who
had married Jews? If so, he would not be the first nor the last to deny
being Jewish just because he was nonprofessing and nonpracticing and

---

26. *Daily Evening Gazette*, June 21, 1844.

totally assimilated. The history of religious persecution records too many victims of sword and fire who made an equal disavowal for exactly the same reasons, yet were considered Jews no less than the most professing, the most observant, and the least assimilated.[27]

The Philipson brothers thus left a record in both life and death that raises questions about their religiosity. The most guarded conclusion is that they identified with Judaism before they came to St. Louis, but that once in St. Louis, they did little or nothing by way of either overt or covert practice or observance to enhance that identity. They became totally secularized. The ancient and revered Hebrew scholar Hillel taught in *Ethics of the Fathers* (chapter 2, verse 5) what has become one of the basic tenets of Judaism: "Do not separate yourself from the community; every Jew should think of himself as part of his people, sharing their joys and troubles." No record exists of what any of the Philipson brothers thought about being Jews; but the record of what they did—or rather what they did not do—indicates that they did not pursue Hillel's fundamental precept. Even when others took the lead, they neither joined nor helped. Indeed, the Jewish community developed in St. Louis not because of anything the Philipson brothers did, but rather in spite of what they did *not* do. If they made noteworthy contributions to the larger St. Louis community—and indeed they did—their contribution to St. Louis Jewry remains only the incidental fact that they happened to be first. Isidor Bush, writing in 1883, identified himself publicly and proudly with his faith, and deplored that "in those [early] days many young Israelites were yet ashamed to avow themselves as such." Accordingly, he admonished, "such men as continued to conceal or to disavow their being Jews or of Jewish descent, I shall not honor by counting them among the Jews of St. Louis."[28] Bush undoubtedly was referring precisely to the Philipsons. It seems almost impossible that he did not know of them, considering the small size of the Jewish community and the Philipsons' many achievements, and especially since some of the Philipsons had married members of the Block family, whom Bush wrote about in considerable detail. The Philipsons were not the first, and certainly not the last, in St. Louis or anywhere else, to be Jews in name only. If they led almost completely secular lives, at least there is no evidence that they ever disavowed their Judaism. Undoubtedly others considered them to be Jews. But it is understandable

---

27. Emphasis added. For the original, see Estate of Jacob Philipson, Estate No. 5154, Probate Court Files, Probate Court of St. Louis. For more information on the Philipson and Block families, see Philipson Family Papers, Block Family File, and Rosa Mayer Grant File in the manuscript collections of the American Jewish Archives, Cincinnati.

28. *Tribune*, November 23, 1883.

that a man of Isidor Bush's integrity, and with his fierce pride in his Judaism, would find it difficult to honor the Philipsons. Little wonder, then, that Bush did not even mention them when he wrote of the early Jews of St. Louis.[29]

---

29. Bush conceded that he might have made some errors in his research since some materials and information were "already difficult to obtain," but he emphasized that he wrote "with care." *Tribune,* December 7, 1883. Still, the Jewish community was so small and the Philipsons so well known, that it is very unlikely Bush was unaware of them; he simply refused to acknowledge them as worthy of being considered Jewish.

———— 3 ————

THE BRIDGE YEARS

Members of the Block family settled in St. Louis and in other parts of Missouri shortly after the Philipsons. In contrast, though, the Blocks contributed importantly to Jewish life in St. Louis. They paved the way for the emergence of a Jewish community. Judaism always has recognized the capability of any person to practice his or her faith as an individual, even in a totally isolated situation, but Orthodox Judaism has required a *minyan,* a minimum of ten adult males, for certain rituals. (True, Reform Judaism differs, but Reform did not reach the Mississippi valley until the mid–nineteenth century.)[1] No worship services or activities such as weddings, baby namings, or burials could be conducted without a *minyan.* Simply stated, numbers counted. Since the Blocks represented a sizable portion of the Jews in early St. Louis, and since many of them practiced their Judaism, they were an important element of the "bridge years" from the first Jew to the first *minyan* in the late 1830s and the first organized Jewish institutions in the early 1840s.

Those who formed that bridge came to St. Louis beginning in 1816 or 1817. They fell into two categories: members of the Block family, and others. In both cases, in contrast with many who came to America in large organized groups, these immigrants came singly or in very small family groups. Some husbands brought wives and children; some came alone and brought their families later; some came unattached and married here. Not all came directly to St. Louis; some settled first in scattered midwestern communities and then gravitated to St. Louis. Some came to St. Louis

---

1. Reform Judaism originated in western Europe in the late eighteenth century, a part of the Enlightenment of the French Revolution. The first synagogue in the United States to associate with Reform was Beth Elohim, in 1824, in Charleston, South Carolina. The first in St. Louis was Shaare Emeth in 1869. Prior to then, Jews and Judaism in St. Louis identified overwhelmingly with traditional or Orthodox Judaism, albeit modified to reflect attempts to "Americanize" and "modernize" religious practices.

and then moved away to other midwestern locations. They followed no distinct pattern, except that a good many ended in St. Louis. Furthermore, they immigrated to America and to the Midwest over a period of several decades. In many instances those already in St. Louis attracted others from the East Coast or from Europe. As with other Jews who ventured into the frontier, some married non-Jews and assimilated. According to Isidor Bush, because of "the love, the warm, faithful attachment to their family and to their people," only one Block who intermarried actually gave up his faith. Bush undoubtedly exaggerated; more than one loosened ties with traditional Judaism, and later generations even severed ties completely. In fact, Bush even identified a number of prominent St. Louis families in the 1880s who were no longer considered Jewish, yet descended from Block ancestry: "the Carrs, Edgertons, Van Phuls, Taylors, Meisenburgs and others," he specified, "are grandchildren of the Blocks." Nevertheless, many also retained their ties with Judaism.[2]

Emanating from roots in Bohemia, portions of the large Block family came to the United States over a period of four decades, beginning during the administration of George Washington in the 1790s. Isidor Bush labeled the Blocks "the most numerous Jewish family that settled west of the Mississippi River." Another writer, estimating that at least twenty-three settled west of the Mississippi, seventeen at one time or another in St. Louis alone, called them "the chief nourisher of St. Louis Jewry." The Block family poses a gratifying yet frustrating enigma. The historian finds no shortage of Blocks to write about. That abundance, however, actually muddles exact genealogical relationships, because of ambiguous records, different Blocks with the same given names, and different spellings of those names (for example, Eleazer versus Eliezer, Bloch versus Block versus Black). Furthermore, even though the Blocks constituted a large family, there were other Blocks not related, in spite of the same surname. On the other hand, though some strayed, many Blocks remained staunchly Jewish, the product of "pious parents in Bohemia" who raised and educated them "with all the rigor of the Jewish orthodoxy of those days."[3]

Abraham Block probably paved the way for the Block family, migrating to America in 1792 when he was twelve. He grew up in Virginia, married, and raised a family, and in 1823 moved west to become one of the pioneer

---

2. *Tribune*, November 23, 1883. When the Missouri Historical Society reprinted the Bush articles, the Society's editor inexplicably omitted the names of these prominent families. A similar omission deleted reference to the well-known Taussig family. See in *Missouri Historical Society Bulletin* 8 (October 1951): 62, 66.

3. *Tribune*, November 23, 1883; Makovsky, "Early History of the United Hebrew Congregation," 137.

settlers of Washington, Arkansas. Jacob Block, either a brother or a cousin, also immigrated to Virginia in the 1790s, perhaps with Abraham Block. He opened grocery stores in several places, including Baltimore and Williamsburg, before settling permanently as a merchant in Richmond. (His son Eleazer would come to St. Louis.) Jacob's brother William (anglicized from Wolf) also immigrated in the 1790s, to Baltimore. Successful as a merchant, he went back to Bohemia to bring his wife over. She refused; when he insisted on living in America, she secured a divorce. Wolf Block thereupon returned to Baltimore, without a wife but accompanied by two cousins, both named Simon. One lived briefly in Richmond and then for many years in Cincinnati, where he associated with Joseph Jonas, the first Jew of that city, and also helped found Cincinnati's first synagogue. The other Simon Block lived briefly in Williamsburg and then went west to Cape Girardeau, Missouri. At about the same time, in the 1790s and early 1800s, other Blocks migrated into the Mississippi valley, Andre Block to New Madrid, Ezekiel Block to Cape Girardeau, and another Simon Block to Ste. Genevieve. They were in southeast Missouri even before the Louisiana Purchase, despite Spanish and French law officially barring Jews.[4]

With Block family members already in the Mississippi valley, some inevitably settled in St. Louis. According to Isidor Bush, the first was Wolf Block in 1816—apparently the same Wolf Block who had returned earlier to Baltimore *sans* wife. Except for Bush's statement, however, no extant evidence corroborates a Wolf or William Block in St. Louis at that early date.[5] The first Block in St. Louis appears to have been Wolf's nephew, Eleazer. Eleazer Block was born on March 26, 1797, in Williamsburg, Virginia, and moved when still a boy with his father to Richmond. He returned to Williamsburg to study at the College of William and Mary, where in 1814 he earned a bachelor of arts degree. Block thereby became one of a select group of Americans of the time who attained a higher education. He practiced law in Baltimore and Richmond, and in about 1817 he succumbed, along with some of his relatives, to the lure of the West. His kinsmen joined other Blocks in Cape Girardeau and Ste. Genevieve; Eleazer went instead to St. Louis. He became the city's first Jewish lawyer. Records in St. Louis associate him professionally with prominent attorneys Edward Bates and Thomas Hart Benton. The city's first printed directory, published in 1821, listed him as "Block, Eleazer,

---

4. The author is indebted to Donald I. Makovsky for his research on the Blocks and other Jews of the "bridge" years, incorporated in his graduate thesis on the origins of United Hebrew Congregation. See also Ira Rosenwaike, "Eleazer Block—His Family and Career," 142–49.

5. *Tribune,* November 23, 1883.

attorney at law, north Church, n.e. corner B." More specifically, his office was in a one-story brick building on the northeast corner of Pine and Second. Sometime in the mid-1820s, perhaps tiring of bachelor life, he returned to Richmond and married Abigail DePass, a member of one of the leading Sephardic families of Virginia and a niece of Gershom Mendez Seixas, New York's famous Revolutionary War patriot rabbi. Block continued to practice law, but gradually drifted into his father's grocery and merchandising business. In 1826, following the death of cousin Simon Block in Cape Girardeau, Eleazer Block was designated guardian of his cousin's ten minor children. Although Eleazer wanted to be close to his wards, he reluctantly decided not to return to either Cape Girardeau or St. Louis because "a town without a Jewish congregation was not an appropriate place to raise his own family." He moved instead to Cincinnati, the closest city in which a synagogue existed. It would be almost fifteen years before St. Louis attained its first Jewish congregation.[6]

Meanwhile more Blocks migrated to America and settled in scattered Missouri communities. Wolf Block's younger brother Emanuel came to St. Louis in about 1817, when lawyer Eleazer arrived. Two cousins settled in outstate Missouri, Levi Block in Troy, about fifty miles northwest of St. Louis, and Hyman Block in Perryville, about ninety miles to the south. Both later moved to St. Louis. Another Block, Jacob, lived briefly with cousins in rural Missouri before settling in St. Louis. He opened a mercantile establishment at 153 North Main, and by 1840 had become a wealthy man.[7]

Phineas Block stands out as a uniquely interesting member of the group. A distant cousin of Wolf Block, Phineas came to America in 1821. He located first in Cape Girardeau, where he married his cousin Delia, daughter of Simon Block. The young couple moved shortly thereafter to Louisiana, Missouri, on the Mississippi River about eighty-five miles north of St. Louis. There Block amassed a fortune, starting with a mill and a commission and grocery business. The widely known firm of Block and McCune, owners and managers of the Northern Mississippi Steamship

---

6. Rosenwaike, "Eleazer Block," 142–44, and Scharf, *Saint Louis City and County,* vol. 1, 151. After about a decade in Cincinnati, Block went back to the East, first to Richmond and then to New York, where in the 1840s he joined the famed Rabbi Isaac Leeser of Philadelphia in an unsuccessful attempt to establish "a seminary of classical learning, combined with religious instruction." Block eventually moved to New Orleans, where he died in 1886 at the age of eighty-eight. Rosenwaike, "Eleazer Block," 144–49.

7. Levi Block married a Catholic girl, a Miss Massey, of the Massey Iron Works, in Troy, Missouri. According to Isidor Bush, he was the only Block who abandoned his faith as a result of intermarriage. *Tribune,* November 23, 1883.

Company, developed a lucrative business on the Mississippi River. In 1838 Phineas Block became president of the Upper Mississippi Insurance Company. Then in 1840 his wife Delia died at the young age of thirty-four, and Phineas retired to St. Louis to live with family members there. His daughter Annie, who frequently had visited St. Louis and stayed with her wealthy uncle Jacob Block, became a very attractive belle of St. Louis society. Writer Charles Edward Pancoast, who "went much in Society," later wrote that "this girl seemed to have the power of drawing me to her more than any other Ladies."[8]

Besides being a successful business and family man, Phineas Block was a devout practicing Jew. Pancoast styled him a "Rabbi" who, while still living in Louisiana, Missouri, acted as "the Spiritual Advisor of all the Hebrews for many miles around." He also served as their *shochet,* or ritual slaughterer. Traditional Jewish law prescribes a precise and humane method of slaughter that the *shochet* must employ, using only one thrust of the knife, otherwise the meat is not kosher. "The Rabbi never missed killing with only one blow while I was there," Pancoast recalled.[9]

In addition to persons bearing the Block name, extended family relations (in-laws and cousins) also settled in St. Louis and constituted parts of the link to a Jewish community. Some played important roles later in establishing early St. Louis Jewish institutions. Among them were Abraham Schwartzkopf, a *shochet,* and Joseph Kohn, who immigrated with their wives, sisters Esther and Ellen Block. Abraham Weigle came over with his wife, the sister of Eliezer Block. Described as a "true, genuine Israelite," Weigle was a *mohel* (one who performs the ritual of circumcision), and for a long time the only one in the mid-Mississippi area. He sometimes traveled as far as two hundred miles, without compensation, to perform a circumcision on a Jewish child. Nathan Abeles was engaged to Rachel, the sister of Phineas and Jacob Block, while still in Europe. They did not marry there because young Abeles was too poor. Nevertheless they immigrated to America together, still unmarried, first to Louisiana, Missouri, where Abeles left his betrothed with her brothers. Unable to find a clerking job in St. Louis, Abeles peddled in the Louisville, Kentucky, area. Starting with only fourteen dollars, within a year he improved his financial status sufficiently to return to Missouri and marry his patiently waiting fiancée. Characteristic of difficulties early Jews faced, it is not clear whether Abeles and his bride were joined in a "marriage-ceremony according to Jewish

---

8. Ibid. Annie Block eventually married a non-Jew.

9. This vignette about Phineas Block and similar examples of other Blocks, both in St. Louis and other Missouri communities, contrast pointedly with the lack of Judaism demonstrated by the Philipsons.

rite, or whether it was not so performed at all." The chronicler indicates that if a ceremony was performed, it was by either Eliezer S. Block or Abraham Weigle; no rabbi or equivalent official was available in St. Louis in those days. Abeles faced no problem, however, in securing a marriage license; whereas he could not afford the exorbitant fees in Bohemia, in St. Louis the "same privilege" cost him only twenty-five cents.[10]

Jews other than the extended Block family also settled in St. Louis during the bridge years between 1807 and the late 1830s and early 1840s. Like the Blocks, they came either singly or in small groups. Some resided in St. Louis only temporarily before moving on elsewhere. Others settled permanently, but their descendants moved away. Still others became the patriarchs and matriarchs of families whose descendants still call St. Louis their home. Most were poor young Jewish artisans or small retail shopkeepers who, like others who migrated westward, primarily sought economic opportunity. Like the Blocks and other Jews who came to America, some arrived in St. Louis as ardent Jews, while others were not not so devout. Some retained their fidelity to Jewish belief and practice, others relaxed their religious bonds. Some assimilated and abandoned their Jewish identity entirely, others maintained that identity, in varying degrees of piety and commitment. The only discernible pattern concerned national origins: most, though not all, came from the European Germanic states and northwestern parts of the Austrian Empire, and were commonly referred to as "German Jews."

A notable exception was Phineas Israel Johnson, who came from England. He lived only briefly in St. Louis, but his importance lies more in his English family ties and in his offspring. Phineas was born to a pious Jewish couple whose family name was "Israel"; it was the same family whose name metamorphosed to "d'Israel" and then "Disraeli," and which produced the famous British prime minister Benjamin Disraeli, Lord Beaconsfield. Brothers Phineas and David Israel immigrated to America in 1818, and almost immediately adopted the name "Johnson." They went first to Cincinnati, where David Israel Johnson and his wife and child settled. Phineas Israel Johnson moved on to Louisville, and then in 1819 to St. Louis. He entered the auction business with Patrick Walsh. Starting as a clerk, Phineas rose to a full partner in the firm of Walsh, Johnson and Company.

Although his Cincinnati brother remained a devout Jew, Phineas abandoned his religious ties. A contributing factor may have been his marriage,

---

10. As related by Isidor Bush in the *Tribune*, November 23, 1883. Bush erred somewhat; the couple was married in Louisiana, Missouri, not in St. Louis. *Voice,* September 7, 1917.

shortly after coming to St. Louis, to non-Jewish Clarissa Clark, a native of Virginia and a niece of Abraham Clark of New Jersey, a signer of the Declaration of Independence. In 1822 the Phineas Johnsons had a daughter, Mathilda Marian, born at the Johnson home on Second Street. Shortly thereafter the family moved to Louisville.[11]

Two decades later the daughter returned to St. Louis. She grew up and was educated in Louisville, where on January 16, 1840, she married Solomon J. Levi, a rising young St. Louis lawyer and businessman. The following year the young couple moved back to St. Louis. At the time of her marriage, Mathilda Marian embraced Judaism; she also changed her middle name to Sarah, "so as to bear one of the biblical names of her ancestors." For the rest of her life she was known as Mathilda Sarah Levi and was a devout and devoted Jewess. Her husband, described as a "zealous Hebrew," was involved in forming the first Jewish cemetery and synagogue in St. Louis, and both Solomon and Mathilda were actively engaged in religious and benevolent affairs of the emerging Jewish community. Solomon Levi participated also in St. Louis business and civic matters, beginning even before his marriage. In 1839 the governor of Missouri appointed him captain in the volunteer militia. Solomon engaged actively in local Whig politics; he worked on ward vigilance committees, labored diligently though unsuccessfully for the election of Thornton Grimsley to Congress, and on at least one occasion served as delegate to a party convention. Contemporaries justifiably referred to him as "prominent" in professional and social circles.

Mathilda Sarah Levi holds a unique place in St. Louis Jewish history. Her offspring always have traced through her a dual and prideful genealogical heritage: to Benjamin Disraeli on her father's side, and to Abraham Clark on her mother's side. Her descendants may put forward another claim. Available evidence establishes her as probably the first Jewish girl, and perhaps the first Jewish child of either sex, born in St. Louis. (Jacob Philipson's first two children were sons and might have been born in St. Louis, though no evidence verifies where they were born. His third child, a daughter, was born after Mathilda Sarah Levi.) True, one might raise questions about Mathilda's exact Jewish status at birth in light of her parents' religious affiliation (or lack of it). But no doubts exist once she

---

11. Phineas Johnson's career later would take him to Texas, where a band of adventurers settled on the site of present Dallas. Johnson reportedly acquired about eight thousand acres of that land, located in what is now the downtown area of that metropolis. His descendants still dream of that claim, obviously worth a fortune. The claim, however, is virtually useless, as documents presumably proving Johnson's ownership were destroyed in a fire long ago. *Voice*, September 7, 1917.

married. Some have suggested that Mrs. Levi might even be considered
the first Jewish female born west of the Mississippi. Considering the Jewish families scattered in the early 1800s in such places as Ste. Genevieve,
Cape Girardeau, and New Madrid in Missouri, and in other communities
in Arkansas and farther to the south toward New Orleans, that claim is
not readily verified. Being the first Jewish girl born in St. Louis merits
sufficient recognition.[12]

Among the small number of Jews who came to St. Louis during the
bridge years, several shared at least one characteristic: like the Philipson
brothers, they migrated to the Midwest from Philadelphia. Some even
had been members of the same synagogue there, Rodeph Shalom. That
common association might explain their going to St. Louis rather than
elsewhere, but that is only conjecture. Included were Joseph and Mitchell
Bomeisler, either brothers or cousins, and Alexander Friedlander, all in
St. Louis for only a few years in the 1830s. Another transplanted Philadelphian and former Rodeph Shalom member was Herman Van Beil, a native
of Amsterdam, who immigrated in the mid-1830s with his wife Elizabeth
and their two children David and Fannie. Van Beil later was prominent in
establishing St. Louis's first Jewish congregation in 1841.

Two more who came to St. Louis from Philadelphia in those years merit
special mention because of their singular records of achievement. Louis
Bomeisler (his relationship to Joseph and Mitchell Bomeisler mentioned
above is unknown) was born in Munich, Bavaria, on November 15, 1780,
the son of Rebecca Heller and Nathan Loebl Bomeisler. The latter became
quartermaster general for Bavaria during the Napoleonic Wars. As a
youth Louis received a thorough and liberal education; in preparing for
Heidelberg, for instance, he traveled extensively with a tutor throughout
Europe and the Middle East, and became fluent in seven languages. He left
Heidelberg when still in his teens to become a general's aide-de-camp, and
saw duty with Bavarian forces at the historic battles of Jena and Austerlitz.
In 1814 he represented Bavaria at the Congress of Vienna, and in 1815, now
a resident of Paris, he was decorated by Louis XVIII of France with the
Order of the Lily.

Bomeisler became an American by happenstance. In 1818 he sailed to
the United States as cargo officer on a merchant vessel. While his ship
was docked in Philadelphia, he became ill; by the time he recovered, the
vessel had sailed. Dr. James Rush, the noted Philadelphia physician who
treated him during his illness, befriended Bomeisler and convinced him
to remain in the United States. Bomeisler thereupon began a new career in

---

12. Ibid.; author interview with Muriel Ziskind, St. Louis, September 6, 1996.

this country, and within a few years "Louis Bomeisler & Co., Merchants" ranked among the better-known business establishments in Philadelphia. In 1824 Bomeisler became an American citizen. Along with involvement in local civic matters, he renewed his Masonic ties (he originally had joined the Freemasons in Paris) as a member of a Philadelphia lodge. More importantly, he affiliated with Rodeph Shalom Congregation (or the "Hebrew German Society" as it also was known then), and became one of its leaders. In 1827 the members elected him *parnass* (president), one of several congregational offices he held intermittently over the next two decades. Bomeisler's interests and leadership also involved him actively with the United Hebrew Beneficial Society of Philadelphia, the Jewish Foster Home of Philadelphia, and with Jewish education at Rodeph Shalom Synagogue. Relations with fellow Jews thus played a prominent role in Bomeisler's life in Philadelphia; he would demonstrate that same affinity in St. Louis, even though his sojourn in the Midwest lasted no more than two or three years.

Exactly when and why Bomeisler came to St. Louis is shrouded in uncertainty. The earliest verifiable date is May 2, 1836. That his wife Elizabeth accompanied him suggests he came to settle permanently rather than to conduct business transiently. Nevertheless he remained in St. Louis only briefly. In 1838 Bomeisler and his wife returned to Philadelphia, probably because of financial difficulties engendered by the Panic of 1837. But during that brief stay Louis Bomeisler made an indelible imprint on the history of St. Louis Jewry through his role in bringing about the first *minyan*.[13]

Another prominent former Philadelphian was Simon Gratz Moses, the first known Jew to practice medicine in St. Louis. Moses was born in Philadelphia on October 6, 1813, the son of Rachel Gratz and Solomon Moses. His father was a well-to-do Philadelphia merchant whose ancestors had settled in Pennsylvania in the early eighteenth century. Young Simon, distantly related to the beauteous and famous Rebecca Gratz, received a liberal education in several schools before emerging from the University of Pennsylvania in 1835 as Doctor of Medicine. Several years of private practice in Bordentown, New Jersey, were followed by a stint in Europe as private physician to Joseph Bonaparte, former king of Spain and brother of the famous Napoleon, and for many years after his downfall a resident of Bordentown. Dr. Moses's association with Bonaparte brought him in contact with some of France's most prominent citizens and physicians.

---

13. S. M. Fleischman to Editor, Germantown, Pennsylvania, December 17, 1916, in *Voice*, December 29, 1916; *St. Louis Jewish Light*, March 21, 1971.

In 1840 Dr. Moses returned to Philadelphia, and the following year, at age twenty-eight, he moved to the Midwest. Except for one brief interruption, he lived and practiced medicine in St. Louis for the rest of his life. In addition to being a successful and popular general practitioner, he also identified with educational and charitable work incidental to his profession. In 1842 he helped establish the city's first organized dispensary and became its president. He assisted in creating the sewer system and took part in other sanitary programs. He was on the medical staff of Kemper College and the Missouri Medical College. A specialist in obstetrics and women's diseases, he was a founder of the St. Louis Obstetrical and Gynecological Society and served twice as its president.

Although Dr. Moses was born and raised a Jew, he apparently drifted from his ancestral faith and assimilated into a non-Jewish life. His two marriages were to gentiles, the first to Mary Porter Ashe of Wilmington, North Carolina, daughter of a planter and Revolutionary War veteran, and the second to widow Marie Atchison, née Papin, a native St. Louisan and descendant of early French settlers. Records of St. Louis's first synagogue list "S.L. Moses" as one of its early members, but there seems to be no verifiable relationship between that person and "S.G [ratz] Moses." All we know for certainty about Simon Gratz Moses is that he, like his contemporaries the Philipsons, was raised Jewish, but that once he settled in St. Louis he apparently did nothing to associate with the faith. He died in St. Louis on February 21, 1897.[14]

Of some other Jews in St. Louis during the bridge years, nothing more is known than that they either subscribed to the first Jewish cemetery association in 1840 and 1841, or that they were listed as early members of United Hebrew Congregation. Some also were recorded in city records because they secured merchants' licenses. Maurice P. Silverburg received such a license in 1837. One "N. Weinburger," who helped organize the cemetery association, may have been the "N. Weisenberger" who received a merchant's and grocer's license in 1837, or the "Weisenberg" who ran a stable in 1839. Martin Krafter was a merchant in St. Louis in 1839, as were Samuel Pecare, Abraham Myers, Charles Weinberg, Joseph Massalsky, and Simon Mandlebaum. Martin Newberger, a merchant and another of the cemetery's founders, was fined five dollars for breaking the peace in 1839, an uncommon occurrence among early Jews in St. Louis. The event was reported in the *St. Louis Daily Missouri Republican* in a singular fashion: Newberger was referred to as a "Jew." This may have been the first time

---

14. Scharf, *Saint Louis City and County,* vol. 2, 1531; Hyde and Conard, eds., *Encyclopedia of the History of St. Louis,* vol. 3, 1572–75.

that designation was used in the St. Louis press; earlier references were "Israelite" or "Hebrew" or some variation on those terms. As a matter of fact, throughout the entire nineteenth century those expressions were much more widely used in the press than the word "Jew," even in such nationally circulated Jewish publications as Isaac Leeser's *Occident* and Isaac Mayer Wise's *Israelite*, as well as in the Jewish papers published later in St. Louis.

Not all Jews who came to St. Louis remained as permanent residents. John Worm obtained a merchant's license in 1837, but apparently did not remain in the city long after that. Alexander Levi, the first permanent Jewish settler in Iowa (1833), came to St. Louis in 1837 to take out his final citizenship papers, but he returned shortly thereafter to his home in Dubuque. Jacob Emanuel came to St. Louis in 1835 from Cape Girardeau, and a few years later Joseph Newmark came from Cincinnati, but both stayed only a few years before going elsewhere. John Meyer Levy, son of a London cantor and educated in Amsterdam and Paris, came to St. Louis in 1837 at the age of seventeen. He married a St. Louis girl "of German descent," and later moved to Prairie du Chien, Wisconsin, where with partner Isaac Marks he became a successful Indian trader.

Other St. Louis residents included those with "Jewish-sounding" names, but for whom no other proof exists attesting to their being Jewish. Joseph Kaufman was a butcher who erected a frame home on Fourth and Green Streets in 1821. Jacob Fry bought and sold land on the southeast corner of Fourth and Locust in 1821. Successful fishermen in the 1830s were A. H. Cohen and Thomas Cohen; the latter even served on the city's governing council. Licensed at various times in the 1830s as merchants or grocers were Jacob Baum, Samuel Lyons, Henry Morris, Frederich Myers, William Harris, and Conrad Katz. Of course, a Jewish-sounding name alone is not acceptable evidence that these men actually were Jewish.[15]

Undoubtedly more Jews lived in St. Louis during the bridge years, though not too many more, for in 1841 they numbered no more than forty or fifty altogether. But not all can be identified, simply because of the lack of historical data.[16]

---

15. Scharf, *Saint Louis City and County*, vol. 1, 154, 156, 200; Gill, *St. Louis Story*, vol. 1, 112–13.

16. At least one early St. Louis Jew is recorded to have converted to Christianity. Undoubtedly there were many more. The newspaper obituary for one Joseph McCormick—certainly not a "Jewish-sounding" name—states that he was formerly an "Israelite in whom there was no guile," but at the time of his death he was a member of the Presbyterian Church in Washington County, Missouri. *Daily Missouri Republican*, November 6, 1840.

The Jews in St. Louis during the bridge years were only a tiny portion of the city's total population. In 1810, when Joseph and Jacob Philipson were the only Jews in the city, St. Louis residents numbered about fourteen hundred. Most of the natives were French and Catholic; most of the newcomers were American and Protestant. Beginning about 1818, however, the arrivals in St. Louis represented more and more Irish and German immigrants fleeing the post–French Revolutionary domestic problems that bedeviled central and western Europe. By 1850 more than half of the city's population of 77,860 represented those two ethnic groups, with the Germans outnumbering the Irish by more than two to one. Most of the Jews, being of German origin, were counted as part of the German population.[17]

The proliferation of this new element led to several important developments in St. Louis. One was the emergence of the so-called Irish Crowd, a group of influential Irish businessmen and politicians whose prominence in city leadership had started even in territorial days. With men such as John Mullanphy, Thomas Brady, William Christy, John O'Fallon, and Jeremiah Connor in the fore, the Erin Benevolent Society brought many Irish immigrants to St. Louis. By 1840 they numbered several hundred families; during the next decade that number multiplied considerably as refugees from the potato famines and the ill-fated "Young Ireland" rebellion streamed to American havens, including St. Louis.[18]

Germans came to St. Louis in even larger numbers. As late as 1833 only eighteen German families lived in the city, but in the next two decades that number increased dramatically, for a variety of reasons. One no doubt was Gottfried Duden's romantic characterization of opportunities in Missouri, reprinted several times and read widely throughout the German states in Europe. Coming at a time when internal problems of the 1830s and 1840s created turmoil and discontent throughout most of western Europe, Duden's exaggerated representations of parts of Missouri as virtually a Rhineland transplanted onto a Missouri pastoral paradise attracted thousands of Germans to the Midwest. Many got no farther than St. Louis for a variety of reasons, not the least of which was that their funds ran out. Probably few Jews numbered among the Duden-inspired immigrants, because so many of the latter came in church-oriented groups, some of which consisted of quite conservative Catholics and Lutherans. On the

---

17. "Jews at St. Louis," in the *Occident and American Jewish Advocate* (hereinafter referred to as *Occident*) 2 (January 1845): 510.

18. Primm, *Lion of the Valley*, 171–73.

other hand, some German Jews had become so secular in their reaction to the French Revolution that they blended easily with the more liberal German Christian immigrants. Unfortunately immigration records did not indicate religion, and only in 1850 did the census records begin to show nativity.[19]

The influx of Irish and Germans affected the city's social, economic, and political atmosphere. By the late 1830s some perceived the new arrivals as a threat to the Whigs, who dominated politics in St. Louis. Concurrently there developed, not only in St. Louis but in other cities as well, an antiforeign sentiment that spawned the birth of the Native American Party in the 1840s. In St. Louis the party started as a pressure group within the Whig organization, primarily anti-Irish, anti-German, and anti-Catholic, and it spread as "WASP" types sought to forestall what they feared as societal domination by the "dirty Irish and Dutch." Native American sentiment spread forebodingly, and influenced both local and national politics in the 1840s and 1850s.

In St. Louis, though, early Native American supporters did not openly, at least, single out Jews to vilify as underminers of "true American" values. If they meant to include Jews, they readily did so under the rubric "dirty Dutch." Besides, not many Jews had settled yet in St. Louis, and those who did reside there had not yet organized institutions that would make them visible as Jews. A visitor to St. Louis in 1841 described the Jewish presence as follows:

> I found about forty or fifty Jews, all, with four or five exceptions, men. They had no place of worship, and lived not as Jews.[20]

Three years later the same observer found that

> the number of Jews here had increased to about sixty or seventy, nearly all men. They have a room in which divine service is held every Saturday. They also have a Shochet. But alas! the state of religion is far from being as it should.[21]

Perhaps the state of religion was not what the observer hoped for. Nevertheless, the Jewish population in St. Louis had grown from a single Jew to enough Jews to consider the state of the religion, for at least services were being conducted. The atmosphere may have been permeated with

---

19. Ibid.; George H. Kellner, "The German Element on the Urban Frontier: St. Louis, 1830–1860," 85–109; Lewis W. Spitz, "The Germans in Missouri: A Preliminary Study," 1–15; Kirkpatrick, "History of St. Louis," 142–49.

20. "Jews at St. Louis," in *Occident* 2 (January 1845): 510.

21. Ibid.

antiforeign prejudice and bigotry, but the bridge from individual Jew to Jewish community had been crossed.[22]

---

22. The following are persons known or thought to be "bridge Jews" who lived in St. Louis at one time or another by 1841, when the first cemetery association and the first congregation were organized. Some are identified only by their names on a roster. The spelling of some names might be incorrect: Abeles, Nathan (Abeles & Kohn Clothing, 112 N. Main); Arlburg, L.; Bach, M.; Bamberg, I.; Baum, Jacob (tailor, 81 N. Main); Block, Abraham; Block, Eli; Block, Eleazer; Block, Eliezer S.; Block, Emanuel; Block, Ezekiel; Block, Hyman (came from Perryville, Mo.); Block, Jacob (merchant, 153 N. Main); Block, Levi (came from Troy, Mo.); Block, Moritz; Block, Phineas (from Cape Girardeau and Louisiana, Mo.); Block, Simon; Block, Wolf; Bomeisler, Joseph; Bomeisler, Louis; Bomeisler, Mitchell; Carr, E. N. (pawnbroker, 57 1/2 N. Main); Cohen, Hyman H. (merchant, 57 N. Front); Cohen, Thomas (merchant, 39 S. First); Cohen, William (clerk, rear 39 S. First); Davidson, Samuel; Emanuel, Jacob; Emmanuel, Jacob (grocer, Krafter & Emmanuel); Fasuskey, Louis (tailor, Second St. above Cherry); Flateau, Isaac (merchant, 36 N. Front); Freiesleben, Julius (yarn store, 60 S. Second); Friedlander, Alexander; Gustraff [Gustorf ?], Ephraim; Harris, Solomon; Harris, William; Jacks, Samuel (tailor, 54 N. Front); (?) Jacobs (Morris & Jacobs, merchants, 64 N. Front); Johnson, Phineas Israel; Joseph, Moses (merchant, 157 N. First); Kaiser, David (clothing store, 26 S. First); Katz, H. C. (tailor, corner Market and Third); Kaufman, Joseph (butcher, Fourth and Green); Klein, Joseph (clerk, rear Fourth between Poplar and Almond); Klein, M. (tailor, 181 1/2 N. First); Kohn, Joseph; Krafter, Louis; Kratzer, Lewis; Latz, Adolph J. (merchant, 55 N. Front); Latz, Benjamin; Latz, Louis; Latz, Simon; Levi, Alexander; Levi, Joseph (merchant, 37 N. Front); Levi, Solomon J. (merchant, 164 N. First); Levinson, David (clothing store, 6 N. First); Levy, G.; Levy, John M. (merchant, 31 N. Front; moved with family to LaCrosse, Wisconsin, in 1846); Levy, S.; Lewis, Alexander; Lewis, C. (hatter, 9 N. First); Lyons, Alexander; Lyons, Samuel; Mandelbaum, A.; Mandelbaum, Samuel; Marks, Dennis (merchant, 53 N. Front and 176 N. Fourth); Marks, Henry (clerk, 2 N. Front); Marks, Isaac; Massalsky, Joseph (lottery & exchange broker, 36 N. Front); Morris, Henry; Morris, M.; Morris, W. B.; Moses, S. L.; Moses, Simon Gratz, M.D.; Myers, A. (merchant, 172 N. Front); Myers, Abraham (merchant, 32 N. Front); Myers, Louis (barber, 32 N. Front); Newberger, Mark (merchant, 46 1/2 N. Front); Newberger, Martin (clothing store, 144 N. First); Newmark, Joseph; Pecare, Samuel; Philipson, Jacob; Philipson, Joseph; Philipson, Simon (Third between Mulberry and Lombard); Phillips, Cohen (merchant, 34 N. Front); Rose, Edward, M.D. (rear, 63 N. First); Rosenbaum, J. (shoemaker); Roth, Jacob (mattress maker, 125 S. Second); Samuel, M.; Schneider (merchant, Chestnut between Front and First); Schwartz, Wolf; Schwartzkopf, Abraham (*shochet*); Silberburg, Maurice; Silverstone, Jacob; Van Beil, David; Van Beil, Herman (clothing store, 161 N. First); Weigle, Abraham (clothing store, 109 N. First); Weinberg, A. (clothing merchant, 15 N. First); Weinberg, Casper (dry goods merchant, 2 N. Front); Weisenberger, Andrew (tailor and clothing store, Oak between Front and First).

—— 4 ——

THE BRIDGE IS CROSSED
A Community Established

Four events signaled that St. Louis Jewry finally had crossed the bridge from the single Jew to a Jewish community: the gathering of a *minyan*, the creation of a cemetery, the establishment of a synagogue, and the organization of a benevolent society.

The full details of the first *minyan* may never be known. Although at least ten men attended, none left any testimony of the event. Nor did anything appear in contemporary records, the press, or other documentary sources. Obviously no one at the time viewed the occasion as anything more than an ordinary worship service meriting no special consideration. More than four and a half decades passed before any reference to the gathering finally appeared in print.

The credit for recording the first *minyan* belongs to Isidor Bush. In the November 23, 1883, installment of his series, "Historical Sketches: The Jews in St. Louis," Bush wrote about the first *minyan*:

> A Mr. Baumeisler, who had removed to [St. Louis] from Philadelphia, where he had been Parnass [president] of a small Jewish Congregation, together with Eliezer S. Block and Abraham Weigel, the latter two having just commenced business in co-partnership at St. Louis, and young Nathan Abeles, succeeded with the aid of some peddlers, who were just stopping at St. Louis over the Holy-Days, Rosh-Hashanah (New Year) of 1836 (5596), to hold the *first* Jewish Prayer-meeting (minjan), in the Mississippi Valley. They had rented a room, at "Max's Grocery and Restaurant" corner Second and Spruce streets, which served as Temple for these days. Baumeisler had ordered a Sepher Thora from Philadelphia and Tephiloth (Prayer-books) at his own private expense. They had no Rabbi, every member of the minjan considered himself Rabbi, and those able to do so served in rotation as readers.

Bush's brief piece is the only known account of the first *minyan*. That obviously makes it an important historical record. But one must read Bush critically, because he wrote almost fifty years after the fact, and in some instances he erred. As to his account of the first *minyan*, he may have relied on some written documentation; if so, apparently none of it still exists. It seems, though, that Bush depended more on the reminiscences of three elderly surviving members, of whom he identified only one, Eliezer S. Block, age ninety-two. The accuracy of three old men recalling an obscure event fifty years earlier may evoke some doubts, especially if contemporary historical evidence suggests differences.

Although Bush's account did not specify precisely who instigated the *minyan*, it leaves little doubt that Louis Bomeisler played a prominent role by securing a Torah scroll and prayer books.[1] A man of Bomeisler's stature and reputation undoubtedly attracted others, but we know the identity only of the three mentioned in the Bush article: Eliezer S. Block, Abraham Weigle, and Nathan Abeles, all members of the extended Block family. The other six (or more) remain anonymous. We know only that some were "peddlers, who were just stopping at St. Louis over the Holy-Days."[2]

Bush's enthusiasm probably led to an overstatement when he asserted that this was the first *minyan* "in the Mississippi Valley." Undoubtedly he meant only St. Louis or west of the Mississippi. Certainly Bush knew that Jewish services had occurred earlier in New Orleans and Cincinnati, both in the Mississippi valley. On the other hand, writers occasionally have used the term "Mississippi valley" loosely when they really have meant "west of the Mississippi." If that was Bush's intent, then he was correct. As far as is presently known, the *minyan* held in St. Louis in the 1830s was indeed the very first that assembled west of the Mississippi River.

For some time, however, uncertainty has prevailed over exactly when in the 1830s the first *minyan* occurred. The most commonly accepted year has

---

1. It seems safe to assume that this Torah scroll—and they are difficult to obtain—was the first in St. Louis. There is no record of what eventually happened to it. There is every reason to suspect, though, that some Jews in St. Louis already owned prayer books, either a *siddur* (daily prayer book) or a *machzor* (High Holy Day prayer book). They are common household possessions of even moderately observant Jews. By importing a number of prayer books at one time, though, Bomeisler made sure that he had enough books, and probably that they were all the same imprint or edition or *minhag*.

2. In his study of the beginnings of United Hebrew Congregation, Donald I. Makovsky identified Jewish merchants and peddlers in St. Louis in the 1830s who also were listed in 1841 as members of the first synagogue and cemetery association. Makovsky, "Early History of the United Hebrew Congregation," 164–71. Although Makovsky does not indicate it directly, the inference is that some may have been present at the first *minyan*. He probably is correct. Nevertheless, the mere fact that one affiliated later with a Jewish organization cannot be construed ipso facto as evidence that he participated in an earlier *minyan*. In truth, only four persons attending the first *minyan* can be identified with any historical certainty: Bomeisler, Block, Weigle, and Abeles. The others remain anonymous.

been 1836, the date Bush cited based on the recollections of his three elderly informants. Indeed, United Hebrew Congregation in St. Louis, which claims direct descent from that first *minyan*, for many years included in its temple bulletin the statement: "First Jewish Congregation West of the Mississippi River—First Service Conducted in 1836," and a plaque with a similar inscription long adorned the front of its edifices. But in his study of the origins of United Hebrew Congregation, Donald I. Makovsky questioned the accuracy of Bush's senior-citizen sources, and suggested that an indefinite and broader "between 1836 and 1838" would be more valid. By examining merchants' licenses and other contemporary records of those who later affiliated with the congregation, Makovsky placed enough of them in the city to have attended a *minyan* definitely in 1838 and probably in 1837. But lacking similar evidence for 1836, he questioned that year, although he conceded that the lack of admittedly spotty data did not necessarily preclude it. Accordingly, writers since Makovsky have hedged, preferring the safer 1837 or 1838 dates.[3]

A careful scrutiny of the data indicates, however, that the 1836 date can be substantiated. The time Bush gave was Rosh Hashannah, the Jewish New Year, in 1836. Bush also identified the year on the Jewish calendar as 5596. Unfortunately those dates did not coincide. Rosh Hashannah (the first day of the Jewish month of Tishri) in the Jewish calendar year 5596 corresponded with September 24, 1835. The Rosh Hashannah that occurred in 1836 was the first day of the Jewish year 5597. Bush obviously erred in one of those dates, either the secular 1836 or the Jewish 5596; or perhaps the *Tribune* printed a typographical error.

Fortunately, though, the slip is corrected elsewhere. Bush also identified the time as coinciding with the dedication ceremony in Cincinnati of the first synagogue erected west of Philadelphia. That dedication ceremony occurred in September 1836. Following the publication of the first Bush article, a reader wrote to the editor disputing the September 1836 date for the Cincinnati dedication ceremony. Bush replied in a prologue to his second *Tribune* article. He had checked his sources very carefully, he responded, and he assured the reader that he (Bush) had not erred, and that the Cincinnati ceremony definitely had occurred "at the same

---

3. One cannot fault Makovsky for insisting upon hard data. According to Bush, the aged survivors of the first *minyan* informed him that some of its members were itinerant peddlers. But itinerant peddlers' names were not listed in early St. Louis directories or in municipal records of merchant licenses. Furthermore, merchant license owners were not listed by name anyway until the fall of 1837—only by trade, such as grocer, clothier, druggist, etc. Thus information readily available for 1837 and 1838 is not available for 1836.

time, September 1836 (when the *first Jewish* prayer meeting or *minyan* was held) in St. Louis." Bush's reexamination and reconfirmation of his data reinforces the credibility of the 1836 date. Even if the elderly survivors of the first *minyan* erred in their recollections of exact dates, Bush's incontrovertible association of the event with the Cincinnati dedication established the precise time. The date of the first *minyan* in St. Louis, then, was Rosh Hashannah, the first day of Tishri, in the Jewish year 5597, coinciding with the secular date September 12, 1836.[4]

The only information about the location of the first *minyan*, like everything else about that event, derives from the Bush article and apparently is based on the recollections of his three aged informants: "They had rented a room, at 'Max's Grocery and Restaurant' corner Second and Spruce streets." Later observers assumed that room was on the second floor over the grocery. They probably were correct; in fact, though, it may have been a back room or a basement room. Unfortunately contemporary records show no grocery or similar store at Second and Spruce, but city directories in those days were notoriously inaccurate and incomplete. Later descriptions of the Second and Spruce neighborhood indicate two- and three-story buildings proliferating; so the "upstairs room" assumption probably was correct.[5]

There is no record of how often a *minyan* convened after 1836 before a congregation finally was organized. That St. Louis Jews continued to gather at least on Sabbaths, holidays, and festivals, is certain, but one cannot ascertain how regularly. They met in different places, sometimes in private homes, sometimes in rented rooms, no one location serving as a permanent place of worship. We can only presume that the participants shared expenses. Sometimes assembling ten men proved difficult; Bush's elderly informants reminisced that at times "they had to seek their brethren far and near to get the required number." They even recalled that

---

4. Since by the Jewish calendar a "day" actually begins on the previous evening, a more accurate statement would be that Rosh Hashannah in the secular year 1836 actually began at sundown on the evening of September 11.

5. The earliest known reference to an "upstairs" room seems to be in Marshall S. Snow, *History of the Development of Missouri and Particularly of St. Louis,* vol. 1, 88. It was published in 1908. Snow probably was correct, although he did not cite the source of his information. One writer suggests that the first *minyan* met at 54 N. Front Street, at R. A. Mack's grocery store, "which may have been corrupted in Bush's account to Max's Grocery." Murray Darrish, "The First St. Louis Minyan," in *St. Louis Jewish Light,* December 30, 1987. Unfortunately his arguments lack adequate historical validation and must be viewed as nothing more than interesting speculation.

once, by mistake, or because they could not possibly find more than nine, they called in a non-Israelite with some biblical name, (an Irishman!) to make the tenth man. He joined the prayer-meeting, and ever afterwards punctually attended their divine services on all Jewish Holy-days.[6]

On another occasion a gang of thugs threw rocks into the room where a *minyan* was praying, temporarily disrupting services. Affronted by this bigotry, a Masonic group offered its hall to the Jewish worshipers, but the generous offer was declined, with the hope that it would not be needed in the future. Apparently it was not; according to Bush, the rock-throwing incident never was repeated.[7]

With enough Jews finally living in St. Louis to gather in a *minyan* periodically to pray, and with the Jewish population slowly growing, other institutions inevitably followed. Pinpointing specific events that led to their establishment is virtually impossible, considering the lack of data, but they invariably emanated from groups already meeting in a *minyan* to worship. Whenever Jews in St. Louis found themselves in distress, for instance, *minyan* members took collections among themselves to render necessary assistance. Sometimes that aid consisted of money to bide over troubled times; sometimes it was "in kind" benevolence, food or clothing or lodging. Whatever was done, though, was informal and on an ad hoc basis. But as more Jews moved into the city, even though still in small numbers, the need was felt to organize not only for worship services but also for general humanitarian purposes. Jewish history had left a legacy, even in America, that Jews had best look out for their own.[8]

An incident that perhaps precipitated community action occurred in August 1839. One Louis Krafter, a German Jew despondent over the state of his health, committed suicide. Instead of burial in St. Louis, Krafter's body was taken to Cincinnati, where he had relatives and where a Jewish cemetery existed.[9] The exact impact of the Krafter incident is not clear—that is, whether his remains were taken to Cincinnati to relatives or to a Jewish cemetery—but within a year the Jews of St. Louis took appropriate action. On May 31, 1840, a meeting occurred at the Waverly House, on Main Street near Olive, for the purpose of establishing a Jewish

---

6. *Tribune,* November 23, 1883.

7. The Masons' attitude favorably impressed members of the Jewish community, for, according to Isidor Bush: "From that time most of the intelligent Israelites of St. Louis sought and obtained admission to the lodges of Freemasonry, and were ever since among its most faithful and devoted members." *Tribune,* December 7, 1883.

8. Ibid.

9. *Daily Missouri Republican,* August 26, 1839; *Daily Evening Gazette,* August 26, 1839.

cemetery. Who called the meeting cannot be ascertained, but Abraham
Weigle presided and Abraham Myers served as secretary. At least thirty-
three people showed up and pledged a total of $207 to purchase a burial
ground.[10]

The meeting was as important a milestone in St. Louis Jewish history
as the earlier first *minyan*. Out of no more than forty or fifty Jews living in
St. Louis at the time, thirty-three showed up, a remarkably large turnout.
It showed that St. Louis Jews would and could work together for a
project purely Jewish in nature. They were now numerous enough, they
obviously desired identification and visibility as Jews, and they were
willing and able to face the necessary financial burdens. Clearly it was
the expression of a Jewish community; it augured well for other Jewish
community institutions.

The men at the meeting designated Adolph J. Latz, Nathan Abeles, and
Casper Weinberg as a committee to purchase a desirable plot of ground.
Within two months the committee had acted. On July 24, 1840, Abeles and
Weinberg paid two hundred dollars to Charles and Elizabeth Carpenter
for an L-shaped plot of land, about 200 feet by 211 feet, outside the city
limits in St. Louis County. Located in the Mill Creek valley at what was
later to be the southwest corner of Pratte Avenue and Twenty-Sixth Street
(Jefferson Avenue), the site today is in the little-used railroad marshaling
yards just to the west of the Jefferson Avenue Viaduct, and slightly north
of where that viaduct intersects with Chouteau Avenue.

It is not clear who held actual title to the land at first. Apparently, it
was Abeles and Weinberg. Nevertheless, within a very short time the
United Hebrew Congregation was organized, and one of its first acts was
to take over the cemetery. The congregation instituted measures in that
direction as early as the fall of 1841; two years later, on November 4,
1843, it assumed full ownership, and the cemetery officially became the

---

10. *Tribune*, December 7, 1883. As listed by Isidor Bush, the group included A. Weigle,
$10; G. Levy, $3; A. Myers, $10; A. Latz, $10; Nathan Abeles, $10; A. Lyons, $5;
C. Weinberg, $10; Cohen Phillips, $3; Samuel Pecard, $10; L. Jacks, $10; Joseph Kohn,
$10; I. Bamberg, $3; S. Levy, $5; A. Friedlander, $4; E. N. Carr, $10; [?] Nenberger, $5;
M. Joseph, $5; H. H. Cohen, $5; M. Morris, $5; Jacob Block, $5; Joseph Macsalsk, $5;
M. Bach, $3; D. Levison, $10; Eli Block, $3; N. Weinburger, $5; A. Mandelbaum, $3;
Jacob Silverstone, $10; A. & L. Latz, $5; Henry Marx, $5; L. Arlburg, $5; S. Harris, $5;
Moritz Block, $5; Isaac Flatan, $5. Some of the names were misspelled in the *Tribune*
article, something which constantly and irritatingly plagues researchers. "Pecard"
should have been "Pecare," "Macsalsk" should be "Massalsky," "Flatan" should be
"Flateau," and "Nenberger" should be "Newburger." The date Bush gives for this
meeting is May 31, 1840; a copy of the original subscription paper in the American
Jewish Archives in Cincinnati is dated July 24, 1840. United Hebrew File, AJA.

United Hebrew Cemetery. The first person buried there was one who earlier had subscribed to the purchase of the land. In the spring of 1841, while probably on a business trip, Samuel Pecare died in Greene County, Illinois, about forty miles north of St. Louis. His remains were brought back to the city and interred in the new cemetery.[11]

The United Hebrew Cemetery remained at the Mill Creek location until 1868, during which time several hundred burials took place. A large number were children, victims of dread childhood maladies such as childbed fever, typhoid and scarlet fevers, consumption, and cholera. A frightening number were stillborn infants. Burial services were conducted according to traditional Orthodox procedure. A small two-story building was erected on the grounds for *tahara* (ritual purification) purposes, and women of the congregation prepared the bodies for burial according to Orthodox *halachic* procedure.[12] Following the Civil War, St. Louis's population grew rapidly, and the city expanded westward. As did other cemeteries, United Hebrew faced the problem of onrushing residential and business growth. A decision was virtually forced in 1867 when the city prohibited any further use of the grounds as a burial place. Accordingly, United Hebrew acquired a new western location out in the county, on high ground north of the Olive Street Road in what later became University City. Formal dedication of the new cemetery, called Mount Olive, did not occur until 1880. At that time, after careful consideration of both *halachic* and secular civil law, the bodies in the old graveyard, as well as some of the stones, were transferred to Mount Olive. A well-attended memorial service on June 6, 1880, culminated the move. Eighty years later, in 1960, Mount Olive reverted to its original name, United Hebrew. A visitor to its site (North and South Road and Canton Avenue) will note that the original gate on North and South (first called Spring Avenue) has been replaced by a more impressive entranceway on Canton. Near where the old gate stood one will find a special monument erected in 1880 for the dedicatory ceremony. Flanked by smaller stones, this fourteen-foot American marble cenotaph is a memorial to all whose remains were moved from the old grounds to the new, as well as to those who remained behind. Though no longer legible, the following is inscribed on its base:

> This monument, erected by the United Hebrew Congregation, is dedicated to those whose remains were transferred from the burial ground on

---

11. Makovsky, "Early History of the United Hebrew Congregation," 153–60.

12. *Halacha* is traditional Jewish law, evolved over the past two thousand years, to provide for Jewish needs in the diaspora following the destruction of the ancient Temple.

Jefferson Avenue to this, Mt. Olive Cemetery, on Sunday, June 6, 1880—
5640.[13]

Events that resulted in the first congregation also emanated from the
existence of a *minyan*. Beginning with the Rosh Hashannah service in 1836,
St. Louis Jews continued to gather in a *minyan* to worship. In 1841, as the
fall season approached, they rented a room for the coming High Holy Days
of Rosh Hashannah and Yom Kippur. In St. Louis at the time was a man
who can be identified only as a "South Carolina businessman." In some
unknown manner he suggested that those interested enough in attending
a *minyan* might consider organizing formally for worship services, just as
some had done previously to meet burial needs. After the High Holy Days,
two important meetings took place. The first was attended by most of
St. Louis's forty or fifty Jews. The meeting was addressed by Herman Van
Beil, who discussed the needs and procedures of formal congregational
organization.[14]

Van Beil's role in creating the first congregation paralleled Louis Bomeisler's earlier role in instituting the first *minyan*. Both had come to
St. Louis from Philadelphia, bringing highly regarded reputations and
impressive backgrounds, especially in matters Jewish. Both saw a com-
pelling necessity for community action to solve a particularly pressing
need. Thanks to their leadership and the magnetism of their character
and persuasion, St. Louis Jews responded to their initiatives. Bomeisler's

---

13. *Tribune,* June 11, 1880. On the occasion of the dedication ceremony on June 6,
1880, a parade of omnibuses and carriages carried a large crowd out to the site. The
procession began at the Hebrew Free School, 623 Locust, and a special fare of seventy-
five cents for adults and fifty cents for children enabled about five hundred people
to enjoy the beautiful day in the country. Transportation to the cemetery proved to
be a serious problem for many years, because of not only the distance but also the
poor condition of the roads. Aaron Gershon, for many years the superintendent of
the cemetery, often complained to the United Hebrew Board of Trustees that in bad
weather even the stoutest of horses could not pull funeral carriages up the steep
slope of Spring Avenue. Mourners often had to dismount and walk through mud
and slush. To avoid such inconvenience, portions of Spring Avenue and Olive Street
Road occasionally were paved at the congregation's expense. *Tribune,* January 23,
February 20, May 28, and June 6 and 11, 1880, and December 7, 1883; *Voice,* March 2,
1888; Richard J. Compton, ed., *Pictorial Saint Louis: The Great Metropolis of the Mississippi
Valley,* 111; Jane Priwer, *The United Hebrew Congregation, 1837–1963,* 13–14.

14. That meeting occurred sometime between Saturday, September 25, which was
Yom Kippur, and Sunday, October 3, the known date of the second meeting. Since
Sunday was a very popular day for organizational gatherings, it would seem that
the first meeting occurred on Sunday, September 26, the day after Yom Kippur. That
could account for the large turnout, as most Jews undoubtedly attended Yom Kippur
services, where the prospect of creating a congregation probably was the main topic
of conversation.

legacy was the first *minyan;* Van Beil's was the first congregation. In both instances, coincidentally, once they took the first crucial steps, both soon returned to Philadelphia, leaving others to create the institutions without which there could be no St. Louis Jewish community. Unfortunately the identity of the "South Carolina businessman" who paved the way for Van Beil remains unknown.

A native of Amsterdam, Herman Van Beil came to the United States in 1817 at the age of eighteen and settled in Philadelphia.[15] Well versed in several languages, he worked occasionally as an interpreter. His primary livelihood, though, was the garment business; he started as a dealer in secondhand goods and eventually became owner of his own clothing store. An observant Jew, Van Beil took an active role in Philadelphia's Rodeph Shalom Congregation. Rodeph Shalom was an Orthodox synagogue, and accordingly its members, including Van Beil, followed traditional observances and practices. Louis Bomeisler also was active in the same synagogue, and undoubtedly the two were acquainted and may even have been close friends; in fact, in 1831 Van Beil had succeeded Bomeisler as president of the congregation. In addition to making liberal financial contributions to the synagogue, Van Beil occasionally conducted services; once, when the congregation could not engage a regular *chazzan* (cantor), Van Beil served in that capacity. Exactly why Van Beil left Philadelphia for St. Louis is not clear; at any rate, he obtained a merchant's license in St. Louis in the summer of 1837 and opened a clothing store at 171 North First Street, a business district already housing several other Jewish merchants.

Not much is known about Van Beil's activities once he settled in St. Louis. Like Bomeisler before him, apparently he too intended his move to St. Louis to be permanent, for he brought his wife Elizabeth and their children David and Fannie.[16] The Jews in the city evidently held him in high regard; he seems to have done well in business, and certainly he was regarded as knowledgeable in Jewish religious matters. Considering his synagogue activities in Philadelphia, one would presume he attended a *minyan* to worship as often as possible. Not surprisingly, then, St. Louis Jews looked to Van Beil for guidance when the matter

---

15. For brief biographical sketches of Van Beil see Edward Davis, *The History of Rodeph Shalom Congregation of Philadelphia,* 51–56; Henry S. Morais, *The Jews of Philadelphia,* 411; and Makovsky, "Early History of the United Hebrew Congregation," 169–70, 209–12.

16. David Van Beil enrolled in St. Louis University, where he earned awards in English, French, and German. Fannie Van Beil married Joseph Levi in St. Louis on October 4, 1840. *Daily Missouri Republican,* August 16, 1839, and August 22 and October 5, 1840.

of creating a congregation arose. That he had been president of such an institution in Philadelphia added, of course, to his credentials.

Accordingly, when St. Louis Jews met after the High Holy Days in 1841, Herman Van Beil led the discussion on congregational organization. By the time the meeting adjourned, several important decisions had been reached. The most important was that they would indeed organize a congregation. They apparently agreed tentatively on a name: United Hebrew Congregation. They then appointed a committee of three—Van Beil, J. Pecare, and Hyam H. Cohen—to formulate a governmental structure for the new body.[17]

The three acted very quickly. A second meeting convened on Sunday, October 3, 1841, to vote on the proposed constitution and bylaws. It met at a coffee shop, "The Oracle," at 24 Locust Street.[18] In contrast with the large attendance at the earlier meeting, only twelve men attended the second gathering, probably because it occurred so soon afterward that it could not be adequately publicized. Only one of the three committee members, Cohen, attended (Pecare later joined the new congregation, but Van Beil's name never appeared in its records). At any rate, the twelve men who attended the meeting at The Oracle unanimously approved the proposed constitution and bylaws. United Hebrew Congregation thus came into existence on October 3, 1841. It was the first congregation in St. Louis; it was also the first congregation west of the Mississippi. The twelve men who took the formal action and whose signatures, in English and Hebrew, still appear in the congregation's Minute Book, were Abraham Weigle, Alexander Lyons, Simon Latz, Samuel Jacks, Adolph Latz, Nathan Abeles, Joseph Kohn, Isaac Flateau, Henry Marks, David Levison, Hyam H. Cohen, and Ephraim Gustorf. That group then chose as the first set of officers Abraham Weigle, president; Hyam H. Cohen, treasurer; and Joseph Kohn, David Levison, and Adolph Latz, trustees. Although not formally elected, Nathan Abeles served as secretary. Weigle and Abeles, it might be noted, had attended the original 1836 *minyan*. The other known *minyan* member, Eliezer S. Block, though not one of the original twelve, became a member shortly thereafter.[19]

-----

17. Apparently the name first proposed was "German Hebrew Congregation." That name appears on the congregation's constitution and bylaws of 1841, but the word "German" is crossed out and "United" substituted for it.

18. Although "The Oracle" was known as a coffee shop, it also sold hard liquor and advertised itself as "dedicated to Divine Bacchus" and "the doctrine of Heathen Inspiration." It seems a rather singular birthplace for a religious institution. *Daily Missouri Republican*, May 27, 1841.

19. "Minute Book of the Board of Trustees of United Hebrew Congregation," United Hebrew Temple, St. Louis. A copy is in the American Jewish Archives in Cincinnati.

Because United Hebrew was the first congregation in St. Louis, its beginnings merit additional observations. Since about 1880, United Hebrew has identified officially with moderate Reform Judaism; but it started as strictly Orthodox. In fact, when Rabbi Isaac Mayer Wise, one of Reform's chief advocates, visited St. Louis in 1855, the congregation received him quite coolly. United Hebrew was known for many years as the "Polish" synagogue. Even though its members were overwhelmingly German Jews, most of them came from areas that had been part of Poland but had been annexed by Prussia in the late eighteenth century. It should come as no surprise, then, that United Hebrew's first constitution provided specifically for *Minhag Poland*: "prayers shall never be said otherwise than among the Polish Jews"; indeed, *Minhag Poland* "shall never be altered or amended under any pretence whatsoever." In ritual matters the congregation followed the traditional *Shulchan Oruch*, the Orthodox ways codified in the mid–sixteenth century by the Spanish scholar Joseph Caro. This traditionalism obviously pleased those with similar religious proclivities; but Isidor Bush, who tended toward a more liberal approach, later opined that the newer and younger Jewish immigrants "felt rather repulsed than attracted" by that Orthodoxy. Bush's evaluation of the German Jewish immigrants proved correct; they tended overwhelmingly to prefer more liberal congregations or no congregation at all.

Among other traditional practices in those early years, United Hebrew maintained a *mikvah* (a ritual bath), a *mohel*, and a *shochet*. Fees at the *mikvah*, located in the basement of the synagogue after the congregation obtained a permanent building, ranged from twenty-five cents for a man to fifty cents for a married woman and one dollar for an unmarried woman. The *mikvah* was unheated, and at times its users undoubtedly endured some rather chilling immersions. The *shochet*, who sometimes doubled as *chazzan*, tried to visit every Jewish householder twice a week to kill poultry. Those who wanted his services usually paid a small stipend, although Nathan Abeles apparently served as *shochet* without a fee.[20]

Because of the Weigle-Block-Abeles association with the first *minyan*, United Hebrew Congregation claims its date of origin as 1836, despite the clearly documented October 3, 1841, date. Considering those three men as a direct tie between the first *minyan* and the organization of the first congregation five years later is highly speculative and tenuous, and is unsubstantiated by any solid historical evidence. See Walter Ehrlich, "Origins of the Jewish Community of St. Louis," 525–26.

20. United Hebrew was described as an "Orthodox synagogue" as late as 1863. Yet for more than a decade modifications had been made that liberalized the congregation and paved the way for official acceptance of Reform by the 1880s. See, for instance, *Israelite*, June 12, 1857, December 10, 1858, and March 28, 1863; and *Occident* 21 (June

United Hebrew Congregation had no permanent home for a number of years. Like the numerous precursor *minyanim*, it met in different places, whether for services or for other congregational purposes, sometimes in private homes, sometimes in rented rooms. On some occasions the membership convened at the home of Henry M. Marx, on Locust between Third and Fourth Streets. They met sometimes at a private residence on Carondelet Street, in the section known as "Frenchtown," just to the south of the main part of the city. Population and membership increases in the 1840s created the need for something more stable. In 1848, accordingly, the congregation leased the four-year-old North Baptist Church, a brick building on Fifth Street (now Broadway) between Washington and Green (now Lucas), and converted it into a synagogue. The lease, for seven years, did not guarantee permanency, but it certainly did afford the congregation greater stability and prestige. The immediate neighborhood, overwhelmingly residential at the time, contained about half a dozen churches of various denominations, all larger than the new Jewish house of worship.

Renovating the leased building posed a singular problem. Traditional Jewish practice prescribes that the synagogue's Ark, which holds the scrolls of the Torah (Pentateuch), should be at the east end of the sanctuary, so that worshipers faced it and *mizrach* (the east)—that is, toward Jerusalem—when they prayed. The building stood on the west side of Fifth, its front end and two entranceways on the east end, with the existing sanctuary facing toward the west. To accommodate the *halachic* prescription of facing east while praying, the congregation blocked off the two east-end doorways, opened a new entry and vestibule on the south side of the building, and constructed a walkway from Fifth Street around the building to the new entranceway. Inside the remodeled structure the seating was rearranged to conform with Orthodox procedure: the Ark and the scrolls of the Torah stood against the closed-in east wall, and the congregation prayed facing toward *mizrach*. The main sanctuary accommodated about four hundred worshipers; in conformity with Orthodox practice, women sat separately in a second-floor gallery that already existed in the building.[21]

1863): 139–40. One need only peruse the Minute Books of the board of trustees through the 1880s to note the many entries that clearly direct Orthodox procedure and ritual.

21. *St. Louis Republic*, March 15, 1915; *Voice*, March 19, 1915; *Modern View*, 25th Anniversary Edition (1925) (hereinafter referred to as *Modern View 25*), 8, 22. See also Makovsky, "Early History of the United Hebrew Congregation," 244–51. One St. Louis newspaper described the consecration ceremonies as follows: "Yesterday a portion of the Society of Jews in this city consecrated, with the usual and solemn ceremonies of their church, the brick building on Fifth Street, between Washington Avenue and Green

United Hebrew Congregation remained without a formal religious leader for a number of years. Traditional Judaism looks upon a rabbi as a teacher as much as a spiritual leader, and indeed any knowledgeable Jew is qualified to conduct services or perform other ritual functions. Ample evidence exists that weddings, burials, and circumcisions were performed in St. Louis for years without the benefit of a rabbi's presence, and that was also true, of course, for religious services. The various ritual functions merely devolved upon any who were able and available. Occasionally the congregation employed a learned Jew as a paraprofessional *chazzan* or *shochet*, or even to serve as a *melamed* (tutor) to instruct the young, but none remained very long. By the early 1850s, however, as the Jewish population increased—and after a competing congregation (B'nai El) was founded—United Hebrew decided to employ a rabbi.[22]

That rabbi was Dr. Bernard Illowy, who came in 1854, the first rabbi of United Hebrew and also the first rabbi in St. Louis. Illowy came from a long line of distinguished rabbis and scholars whose collective achievements included serving as *haus-rebbe* (private chaplain) to the Austrian Court-Jew Oppenheim family, heading a *beth din* (Jewish court of law), directing a famous *yeshivah* (talmudic academy), and authoring numerous theological tracts. Born in Kolin, Bohemia, in 1814, Bernard L. Illowy received a broad and thorough education. Trained in religious matters at first by his father, Illowy completed his theologic studies in Pressburg and was ordained by Rabbi Moses Schreiber, leader of Hungarian Orthodoxy.

Street, to be used as a Synagogue, the ownership of which they have acquired. We had the pleasure of being present and witnessing the ceremonies, which were conducted by the President, or principal Rabbi, assisted by other Rabbins. The main floor of the building was occupied by the males; the ladies were in the gallery. The prayers and service were in the Hebrew language. The books of Moses on parchment, after the usual ceremonies, were duly deposited. Our ignorance of the language prevented a full understanding of all that transpired. This sect now constitutes a large and influential portion of our community, and their devotion to their church is exemplary." *Daily Missouri Republican*, September 28, 1848.

22. Henry Myers to Isaac Leeser, St. Louis, November 6, 1849, in Missouri Box, AJA; "Minutes of the Board of Trustees of United Hebrew Congregation," especially September 24, 1849, United Hebrew Congregation, St. Louis; *Israelite*, July 25, 1856; *Occident* 7 (December 1849): 77–81. Minutes of the United Hebrew board of trustees for February 28, 1845, refer to a Mr. Herschfeld coming to the congregation for three hundred dollars per annum as *chazzan* and *shochet*, but there is no further mention of him nor any evidence that he actually served the congregation in any capacity. Ample evidence substantiates Reverend Nathan Davidson's association as *chazzan* and *shochet*. Davidson also officiated at weddings and attempted to establish some form of religious education. He left, apparently, because he felt the congregation demanded too much of him.

In contrast with most European Orthodox rabbis, Illowy also was well grounded in secular studies, an education that culminated at the University of Budapest where he earned a doctorate in philosophy. For a few years he served as professor of French and German in a gymnasium for young women; during that period, too, he married Katherine Schiff, daughter of Wolf Schiff, a prominent merchant of Raudnitz, Bavaria.

The advent of the revolutionary movement of 1848 proved to be a turning point in Illowy's life, as it was for so many German Jews. He seems not to have engaged in violent antigovernment activities. On one occasion, though, he addressed revolutionary forces passing through Kolin. At another time, on his return from a visit to Paris, a customs search of his luggage turned up a handbill containing the incriminating phrase "Liberté, Egalité, Fraternité." For these supposed revolutionary activities, a local government functionary barred Illowy from holding any rabbinic post in his native Bohemia. He thereupon applied for, and was unanimously elected to, the position as chief rabbi of Hesse. Once more a reactionary minor bureaucrat intervened and refused to sanction Illowy's appointment because of alleged revolutionary political associations. In February 1853, therefore, Illowy and his family emigrated to the United States. He obtained a position initially as rabbi of Congregation Shaare Tzedek in New York, but shortly thereafter moved to Philadelphia to Rodeph Shalom, where he served as educational director. Then in 1854 he accepted the position as the first rabbi of United Hebrew Congregation in St. Louis.[23]

The St. Louis Jewish community has been served by many outstanding rabbis; its very first fell into that category. Rabbi Dr. Bernard Illowy was a strict adherent of Orthodox Judaism, respected by both laymen and fellow clergy for his religious demeanor, his rabbinic scholarship, and his congregational ministrations. Shortly after Illowy arrived in the United States, he met Rabbis Isaac Mayer Wise and David Einhorn, two of Reform Judaism's most ardent champions. Despite unmistakable and clearly defined theological differences, they became fast personal friends. That did

---

23. Rabbi Illowy's son Henry, who authored a biography of his famous rabbinic father, spelled his own name "Illoway." The brief biographical sketch of Rabbi Bernard Illowy comes mostly from Henry Illoway, *Sefer Milchamot Elohim: Being the Controversial Letters and the Casuistic Decisions of the late Rabbi Bernard Illowy, Ph.D., with a Short History of his Life and Activities,* and David Ellenson, "A Jewish Legal Decision by Rabbi Bernard Illowy of New Orleans and Its Discussion in Nineteenth Century Europe," 174–95. See also Moshe D. Sherman, "Bernard Illowy and Nineteenth Century American Orthodoxy." Although primarily United Hebrew's rabbi, Illowy also served the newly formed B'nai El Congregation. See various entries in B'nai El congregational minutes, B'nai El Congregation, St. Louis, and Minute Books of Board of Trustees of United Hebrew Congregation, St. Louis.

not deter them from engaging in lengthy and heated religious debates. Their disputations, in Hebrew, German, and English journals and newspapers, were lauded as definitive scholarship on various theologic issues.[24]

A powerful and erudite speaker, a "commanding figure with piercing gray eyes," Illowy regularly attracted capacity crowds for his sermons. On one Yom Kippur afternoon he discoursed past sunset, the traditional end of the sundown-to-sundown Day of Atonement fast; yet the congregation insisted he continue, even though his talk lasted until after nightfall. Many of his sermons and addresses were published in denominational and secular journals and newspapers throughout the United States and abroad. He was thoroughly versed in Latin, Greek, and Hebrew, and spoke fluently in German, French, English, and Italian. At United Hebrew, he alternated between English and German with his sermons, in deference to his German Jewish congregants. Illowy possessed an extraordinary command of Hebrew, and some of his published polemics in that language served as models of Hebrew composition.

Although an observant Orthodox Jew, Illowy did not publicly display his piety; in fact, he often suspected the sincerity of those who did. A brilliant preacher, he taught mostly by example. His son wrote of him:

> He was of a most agreeable disposition, and always ready to participate in the festivities of his parishioners. He [and Mrs. Illowy] visited his members socially—he made it a point to do so—and was everywhere a most welcome guest. . . . No doubt this greatly added to his influence in promoting religious life and religious observance—especially Kashruth, as many a word thus spoken in the home fell upon fruitful ground and bore good fruit.[25]

Rabbi Illowy served the St. Louis Jewish community for only one year, 1854–1855. Even though he ranked as one of the country's leading rabbinic scholars, his Judaism proved to be too conservative for the members of his congregation. For in spite of their apparent strict adherence to Orthodoxy, many United Hebrew congregants, reflective of so many German Jewish immigrants, sought almost desperately to acculturate to their new midwestern environment. If they did not openly sympathize with much of the new American Reform, at least they sought to "modernize" and "Americanize" their Orthodoxy, and thereby better accommodate their religious lives with their secular lives. In 1855 the Cleveland Rabbinical Conference began work on *Minhag America*, a new prayer book and a

---

24. Wise referred often to Illowy as *y'didi ha-chochom* (my close and very wise friend). See for example *Occident* 11 (March 1854): 614–19 and 12 (May 1854): 33–38; and *Israelite*, May 11, 1855.

25. Illoway, *Sefer Milchamot Elohim*, 22.

revised ritual approach that modified and Americanized many traditional observances. Leading American rabbis, both Orthodox and Reform, attended that conference. Illowy had been instrumental in organizing the meeting, but he ultimately refused to attend, sensing that a too-radical element had taken control. For some time Illowy had pushed for cooperation and reconciliation between Orthodox and Reform; he was a prime mover behind such a meeting in New England earlier in 1855. But the excessively liberal recommendations that emanated from Cleveland were more than he could tolerate. The breaking point came when some members of his own congregation in St. Louis insisted upon using a new prayer book published by Rabbi Max Lilienthal, then leading a Reform congregation in Albany, New York. "I even announced to them [my congregants]," Illowy wrote to Isaac Mayer Wise, "that any Israelite who uses this book in house for the purpose of prayer is entirely excluded from all religious communion by the decision of the Jewish canon law . . . because the prayer book departs completely from the statutes of the Talmud and the teachings of the Shulchan Aruch." Dissension obviously prevailed within United Hebrew. Unwilling to compromise on so basic an issue, Illowy resigned.[26]

One more "first" in the early 1840s signaled unmistakably the existence of a Jewish community. *Tzedakah* (charity, sharing, helping those in need) and *tikkun olom* (literally, "repairing the ills of the world") are basic tenets of Judaism, as they are, of course, in other faiths. Individuals often give *tzedakah* without recourse to organizational efforts. But when a group works together to institutionalize *tzedakah*, whether the group is large or small, that cooperative effort in itself represents some sort of community action. Thus the organization of a benevolent association, coming at about the same time as the first cemetery and the first congregation, clearly demonstrated the emergence of a Jewish community in St. Louis.

As was the case with the cemetery and congregation, the roots of the first benevolent society can be traced to the existence of a *minyan*. "Whenever an Israelite wanderer needed some assistance," wrote Isidor

26. Illowy to Isaac Mayer Wise, n.d., in *Occident* 12 (November 1855): 414–17. See also *Occident* 13 (January 1855): 585–86; and *Israelite,* March 2 and August 17, 1855. Illowy remained long enough to conduct the Rosh Hashannah and Yom Kippur services in 1855 at B'nai El, and then left for a congregation in Syracuse, New York. In 1861 he went to New Orleans, where he ministered until he died in 1871. Rabbi Illowy still ranks among the nation's outstanding scholarly rabbis. His works include a tract justifying postmortems on deceased Jews under certain circumstances, a volume on Jewish *minhagim* (customs), and several *halachic* decisions on circumcision and intermarriage. See for example *Occident* 12 (April 1854): 60, and 14 (June 1856): 134–36; also Ellenson, "A Jewish Legal Decision," 174–95.

Bush, "the minyan-members had made a collection among themselves." As the number of Jews in St. Louis slowly increased, though, some felt the need to change from an ad hoc procedure to something more institutionalized and organized. One particular incident probably precipitated action. A peddler named Isaacs became ill. Joseph Kohn, of the mercantile partnership of Abeles and Kohn, engaged a physician to tend to Isaacs. At the same time the *minyan* worshipers took up a collection that they turned over to the ailing peddler. Isaacs soon recovered and went on his way, but he overlooked paying the doctor who had treated him. Feeling entitled to his fee, the doctor sued Kohn, who had to pay the bill.[27]

On November 6, 1842, on the initiative of Joseph Levy, Adolph J. Latz, and A. Jacobs, twenty-seven men organized a benevolent society that they called *Chesed v'Emeth,* or "Mercy and Truth." Its purpose was to aid indigent Jews. Even though several associations already served other ethnic and religious groups in St. Louis, the new *Chesed v'Emeth* did not restrict its benevolence to coreligionists. It was a selfless and altruistic trait that characterized later Jewish benevolent associations, down to the present time. Although its membership was small (only twenty-nine members in 1845) and its funds limited, it became the prototype of other benevolent associations that followed.[28]

In December 1846 the group formally incorporated as the Hebrew Benevolent Society. Often referred to in Jewish circles as simply "H.B.S.," the association still exists. Its broader purposes, not unlike those of other benevolent societies, have been to promote a brotherly feeling among its members, to visit the sick, to facilitate medical care, to provide sickness and funeral benefits, and in general to give financial aid to those in need. One of its most important practices was to provide small loans to individuals or groups for personal or business needs; interest charges on repayment of those small loans constituted a major source of income. Many an immigrant—or even individuals settled for a long time—owed

---

27. *Tribune,* December 7, 1883. Actually, the doctor sued the firm of Kohn and Abeles.

28. A fascinating yet puzzling aspect of *Chesed v'Emeth* was the establishment of a subsidiary branch known as *Chevrai Meshivas Nefesh,* or "Society for the Revival of Life." This group was singular in that its sole purpose seems to have been to help persons *not* of the Jewish faith. Ibid. No other similar beneficial groups are known to have existed. Did it come into being to counter some antisemitic forces current at the time? Did St. Louis Jews feel compelled to treat non-Jewish indigents in any special way? Certainly other Jewish organizations helped non-Jews; but this group's uniqueness was the exclusivity of its beneficiaries. Unfortunately additional documentation is lacking to answer those questions. The *Chevrai's* functions soon were incorporated within the broader framework of the Hebrew Benevolent Society, which continued to serve both Jews and non-Jews.

his health or business revival, or just being able to keep a family together, to the four or five dollars borrowed from the Hebrew Benevolent Society.

In the tradition of Jewish history and consciousness, as the Jewish population of St. Louis increased, additional benevolent associations came into existence. Within a decade, by 1856, six already existed, three consisting of men, three of women. Some were affiliated with specific congregations; some were open to the broader public. The editor of the *St. Louis Jewish Voice* would proudly assert in 1880 that not a single Jew had ever been an inmate of the St. Louis poorhouse. In 1919 Louis Renard, president of the Jewish Home for Chronic Invalids (later called the Jewish Sanatorium) on Fee Fee Road, would state that "it is customary for the Jewish people to take care of their own dependent ones." The implementation of that sentiment is the tradition behind and the legacy of the Hebrew Benevolent Society, and is reflected more than a century and a half later in the numerous eleemosynary and charitable institutions thriving in the St. Louis Jewish community.[29]

29. *Daily Missouri Republican,* December 15, 1846; *Occident* 2 (March 1845): 516, and 7 (December 1849): 77–81; *Israelite,* July 25, 1856; *Tribune,* January 2, March 12, and May 7, 1880, December 7, 1883, and January 4, 1884; *Voice,* January 27, 1888, November 4, 1898, November 26, 1903, February 6, 1914, and February 8 and December 13, 1918; *Modern View,* December 6, 1918, December 12, 1919, and February 8, 1929.

B'nai El Temple, Sixth and Cerre, 1855–1875. First synagogue built in St. Louis.

B'nai El Temple, Eleventh and Chouteau, 1875–1906.

B'nai El Temple, Spring and Flad, 1906–1930.

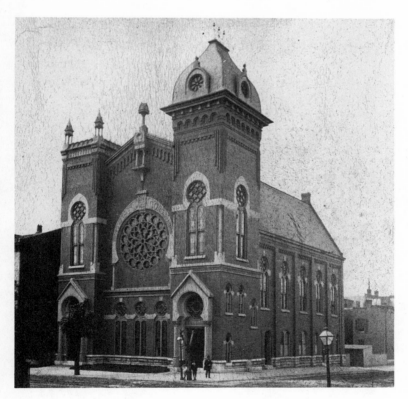

United Hebrew Temple, Twenty-First and Olive, 1881–1903. (Courtesy Missouri Historical Society, St. Louis.)

United Hebrew Temple, Kingshighway and Von Versen (Enright), 1903–1927.

Shaare Emeth Temple, Seventeenth and Pine, 1869–1897.

Shaare Emeth Temple, Lindell and Vandeventer, 1897–1932.

Temple Israel, Leffingwell and Pine, 1887–1908.

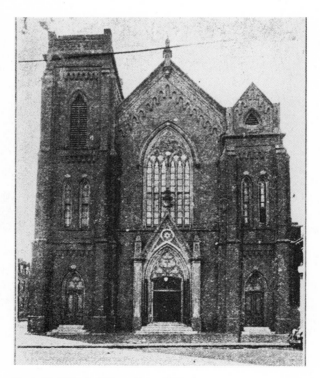

Sheerith S'fard, Fifteenth and Wash.

Rabbi Henry Kuttner,
United Hebrew, 1857; B'nai
El, 1857–1870; United
Hebrew, 1870–1875.

Rabbi Henry J. Messing,
United Hebrew, 1878–1911.

Rabbi Samuel Wolfenstein, B'nai El, 1870–1878.

Rabbi Moritz Spitz, B'nai El, 1870–1920. (Courtesy American Jewish Archives, Cincinnati.)

Rabbi Solomon H. Sonneschein, Shaare Emeth, 1869–1886; Temple Israel, 1886–1890.

Rabbi Samuel Sale, Shaare Emeth, 1887–1919.

Rabbi Leon Harrison, Temple Israel, 1891–1928.

Rabbi Adolph Rosentreter, B'nai Amoona. (Courtesy Missouri Historical Society, St. Louis.)

Mathilda Sarah Levi. First
Jewish woman born in St.
Louis. (Courtesy Mrs.
Muriel Ziskind, St. Louis.)

Solomon J. Levi.
(Courtesy Mrs. Muriel
Ziskind, St. Louis.)

Dr. Simon Gratz Moses.

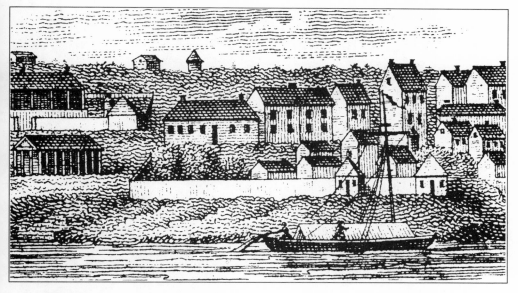

St. Louis, 1817.

The Great Fire of 1849.

Broadway, 1850.

St. Louis riverfront, 1855.

Louis Bauman.

Isidor Bush.

United Order. B'ne B'rith. Missouri Lodge
St Louis. Jan 5' 1863.

To His Excellency
Abm Lincoln
President U.S.

Sir

An Order, Expelling and Ostracising all Jews,
as a class has been issued by Maj. Genl U.S. Grant
and has been enforced at Holly Springs, Trenton,
Corinth, Paducah, Jackson and other places.—

In the name of that class of _loyal_ citizens
of these U.S. which we in part represent.

In the name of hundreds, who have been driven
from their homes, deprived of their liberty; and injured
in their property _without_ having violated any law
or regulation.

In the name of the thousands of our Brethren
and our children who have died and are now willingly
sacrificing their lives and fortunes for the Union and the
suppression of this rebellion

In the name of religious liberty, of justice and
humanity — we Enter our solemn Protest
against this Order, and ask of you — the De-
fendor & Protector of the Constitution — to
annull that Order and to protect the liberties
[of] your humblest Constituents

Morris Hoffman   Henry Kuttner
                                  President

Letter to President Lincoln protesting General Grant's Order Number 11. (Courtesy
American Jewish Historical Society, Waltham, Massachusetts.)

5

Pre–Civil War Growth
Synagogues

The 1840s and 1850s saw spectacular and traumatic developments in the history of St. Louis. Events ranged from tragic to ennobling. A rampaging flood in 1844 brought unprecedented destruction, yet paled in comparison with the twin disasters of fire and disease that struck five years later. On May 17, 1849, fire broke out on the steamboat *White Cloud* anchored on the St. Louis riverfront. Uncontrolled flames soon spread to other vessels crowded along the wharf area and to exposed freight piled on the levee. Strong breezes quickly spread the conflagration through the downtown area, turning block after block into a raging inferno. A failing water supply and a deficient fire-fighting system worsened the disaster, as twenty-three steamboats, more than four hundred buildings, and fifteen city blocks were devastated. Thousands were forced out of their jobs, and hundreds became homeless.

But the worst was yet to come: epidemic cholera. No newcomer to St. Louis (a cholera epidemic had struck in 1832), this time it was deadlier than ever. Beginning on a small scale in 1848—it may have been brought by immigrants from Germany and Holland via New Orleans—cholera had already claimed about four thousand victims by the time of the Great Fire. Sickness and mortality among the immigrants were especially rampant, wrote Dr. Simon Pollack ruefully, and "parentless children and childless parents were found everywhere." Emergency health measures, including a quarantine, finally brought the epidemic under control; still, 883 deaths were recorded in 1850, and another 845 in 1851. The numbers gradually decreased, but not until 1855 could city health officials consider the threat gone.[1]

---

1. S. Pollack, "The Autobiography and Reminiscences of S. Pollack, M.D., St. Louis, Mo.," AJA, 56–57. See also Van Ravenswaay, *Saint Louis,* 382–91; Primm, *Lion of the Valley,* 161–75; Oscar M. Ross, "The History of Saint Louis, 1848–1853," 76–84. According to one chronicler of St. Louis history, among the many businesses destroyed

Natural disasters were compounded by man-made difficulties. Smoldering racial and nationalistic prejudices erupted across the nation in the 1840s and 1850s, especially against immigrant Irish and Germans. Symptomatic of widespread xenophobia was the emergence of the Native American Party, often called "Know-Nothings" because they "knew nothing" about any racial or nationalist bigotry. In St. Louis, as elsewhere, bloodletting ethnic brawls and riots occurred. Rowdy and often drunken nativists openly taunted and physically assaulted Irish and German newcomers—Jews were included among the latter—and "uppity" black slaves, adding to an impression, created from fact and fiction about riverboat toughs and boisterous frontier and mountain men, of St. Louis as an uncommonly violent city. And as the slavery controversy grew heated, so too did the atmosphere in St. Louis.

Yet St. Louis in the 1840s and 1850s witnessed many other events of a distinctly laudatory nature. In 1842, for instance, a free dispensary came into existence. That same year saw the opening of the Benton School, followed within several years by the Clark, Mound, Jefferson, and Eliot Schools. Lafayette Park was purchased in 1844. The Mercantile Library was incorporated in 1846. City Hospital opened in 1847. In that same year the streets of St. Louis were illuminated by gas lamps. Eliot Seminary—it later became Washington University—began in 1853; St. Louis University was already about fifteen years old. It was also in 1853 that Central High School opened, on the first floor of Benton School, with a principal, four teachers, and seventy students. Businesses of all kinds came into being, especially those that serviced the many thousands moving west. In 1857 the Merchants' Exchange was organized, in 1859 a horse-drawn street railway system was born, and 1860 saw the St. Louis Public Library established at Fifth and Olive. Thus St. Louis faced many trying growth problems, but it also emerged by the Civil War as the eighth-largest city in the country and perhaps the most important urban center and transportation hub in the Midwest. This was the city to which some five thousand Jews immigrated in the decades prior to the Civil War.[2]

St. Louis's population grew phenomenally in the 1840s and 1850s, multiplying tenfold, from 16,439 in 1840 to 160,773 in 1860. Thousands

---

by the 1849 fire were those owned in whole or in part by the following Jews: Isaac Jacobs, Abraham Jacobs, Lewis M. Levy, Simon Lewis, Raborg & Shaffner, Helfenstein & Co., Charles Roderman, Weil & Bros., L. Newman, Helfenstein, Gore & Co., Levy & Bros., H. Cohen, and Simon Abeles. Scharf, *Saint Louis City and County*, vol. 1, 821 and vol. 2, 382–91.

2. Primm, *Lion of the Valley*, chaps. 5 and 6; Ross, "History of St. Louis"; Helen D. Williams, "Factors in the Growth of Saint Louis from 1840 to 1860."

of Irish settled, but Germans constituted the largest number, drawn to the Midwest for several reasons. Many still dreamed of the pastoral paradise advertised earlier by Gottfried Duden. Escapees from abortive political upheavals in central Europe flocked to the democratic environs of America, as did many apolitical refugees who fled from crop failures and devastating famines. Bad times caused by the transition from a dying feudal system to a new preindustrial society hit many central European areas. And of course there were the attractive lures of gold and glory (although for many it proved instead to be grief), as St. Louis became a springboard for military operations against Mexico, for California-bound adventurers, and for traders and travelers on the Santa Fe and Oregon Trails.[3]

Several distinct characteristics apply to those pre–Civil War German immigrants who settled in St. Louis. Most came from western and southern German and Austrian states. They came more often as family units than as individuals. They were mainly artisans and laborers rather than farmers, and they brought with them crafts and other economic skills associated more with the city than with the farm. That probably explains why many settled in St. Louis rather than going to the rural Midwest. Of course, many who wanted to go farther west simply ran out of money and had no choice but to end their travels in St. Louis. The German immigrants, at first at least, were generally liberal, even radical, in their politics, a carryover from their European backgrounds. They became overwhelmingly antislavery Republicans who supported Lincolnian Unionism. On the other hand, those who placed much credence on religion tended toward spiritual conservatism. Many, though, because of their political liberalism and negative reactions to religiously oriented autocratic experiences in Germany, viewed religion with less enthusiasm, and tended toward disaffection or even total disassociation from any organized faith.[4]

The latter proved true for many German Jews who settled in America and in St. Louis. Simply put, large numbers of Jewish immigrants to America in the nineteenth century distanced themselves from their Judaism. Many felt impelled to throw off "old fashioned" and "European" ways

---

3. Of course other midwestern cities also grew. By the time of the Civil War, St. Louis had become the eighth-largest city in the country. In the Midwest, only Cincinnati, by just a few hundred, and New Orleans, by about eighteen thousand, surpassed St. Louis in population; Chicago trailed St. Louis by nearly fifty thousand. See Troen and Holt, *St. Louis*, 53; Postal and Koppman, *Landmarks*, vol. 3, 27–35; Primm, *Lion of the Valley*, 147–238; Lebeson, *Jewish Pioneers in America*, 311; Gill, *St. Louis Story*, vol. 1, 133–40; Herman Eliafson, "The Jews of Chicago," 117; Kellner, "German Element on the Urban Frontier," 85–109; and Ross, "History of St. Louis," 1–3.

4. Kellner, "German Element on the Urban Frontier," 85–109; Spitz, "The Germans in Missouri," 1–15.

to become more readily "Americanized." To many it was important to blend into their new environs as inconspicuously as possible; that meant getting rid of racial, national, or religious characteristics that might make them stand out. Furthermore, not all Jews came to America as traditional observers of Judaism; many had started the distancing process in Europe. The evidence is very strong that many liberal western European Jews in particular deemphasized or even totally abandoned the traditional Jewish ritual life that had prevailed in the ghettos so that they could meld better into the broader non-Jewish society, first in Europe and then in America. When the French Revolution broke down ghetto walls in the late nineteenth century, it opened completely new vistas for Jews who previously had been constrained by centuries-old patterns of life and behavior. Many viewed the new Reform Judaism as a way to acculturate, to "modernize" their Judaism and to not appear, on the surface at least, too different from their Christian neighbors. Many became secular and assimilated; many gave up Judaism completely, often through intermarriage with non-Jews. Their views toward their Judaism were not unlike similar views taken by many coreligionists, both Sephardic and Ashkenazic, who had come to America during the colonial period. The plain truth was that while many Jews clung tenaciously and against almost insurmountable obstacles to their ancient faith, many others no longer wished to adhere to the religious tenets of their ancestors; or that many adhered to only as little as they felt either necessary or advisable in order to make a successful transition to a new life as "Americans." There was nothing new to this phenomenon; Jewish literature throughout the ages is replete with dismay about what was to become of the Mosaic faith because so many Jews were abandoning their religion, yet Judaism survived and even thrived. This explains to a large degree, as noted earlier, the lengthy three-decade gap from the arrival of the first Jews in St. Louis to the gathering of the first *minyan*. It also explains the considerable secularism among immigrant German Jews as well as their tendencies toward liberal Reform Judaism when they came to St. Louis.[5]

Census and population figures in those days identified nationality rather than religion, and so most St. Louis Jews were categorized simply as "Germans," since most of them came originally from Germanic Europe. Many, in fact, were Bohemians, natives of Pilsen and surrounding communities, then a part of Austria. St. Louis probably harbored the foremost Bohemian settlement in America, and as early as the mid-1850s boasted of a Bohemian benevolent society, the Bohemian Slavonic Protective Association, housed at Ninth and Soulard. That neighborhood

5. See Ehrlich, "Origins of the Jewish Community," 507–29.

was popularly known as "Bohemian Hill"; one of its most striking land-marks was the Church of St. John Nepomuk at Eleventh and Soulard, the first Czech Catholic Church in America. The neighborhood also housed many Jews.[6]

Still, the question of actual Jewish identification poses problems: who among the St. Louis "Germans" were indeed Jews, and how many were there? Certainly "Jewish-sounding" names are meaningless. Proper iden-tification necessitates checking rosters of synagogues, cemetery records, charitable association lists, and any other possible Jewish affiliation. That, of course, poses the perennial problem of identifying those secularized Jews who never affiliated with any Jewish organization or who even lapsed into nonobservance, but who still were considered, by themselves and by others, as Jewish. In any event, contemporary accounts indicate that the sixty or seventy Jews who lived in St. Louis in 1844 increased by 1853 to between six hundred and seven hundred, and by the outbreak of the Civil War to approximately five thousand, about 3 percent of the total city population. In fact, by 1860 St. Louis was identified as one of the fifteen cities in the United States "significant as Jewish centers."[7]

Why did Jews come to St. Louis in such large numbers during that period? They came for the same reasons others came. The Jewish increase was in the same proportion as that of the rest of St. Louis, about tenfold. Westward expansion, and especially the attractions of land, trade, and gold, offered innumerable prospects for easterners and European immi-grants. As a major gateway to the West, St. Louis itself was one of those magnets, especially if friends or family already lived there. Accordingly, if many Jews and non-Jews passed through St. Louis looking for oppor-tunities farther west, so too did many view St. Louis itself as the final site of their hoped-for happiness and prosperity.

Nevertheless, one observer would write later that "up to [the Civil War] no one heard of St. Louis Jewry." Its communal affairs were still in a "primitive state." Individual Jews struggled to establish themselves, and the newly created Jewish community sought to find a role for itself.[8] The

---

6. Irving Gersten, "The Freund Story," 181.

7. Louis J. Swichkow, "The Jewish Community of Milwaukee," 34. The fifteen cities were New York, Philadelphia, Cincinnati, Baltimore, Louisville, St. Louis, San Francisco, Boston, Cleveland, New Orleans, Newark, Milwaukee, Detroit, Pittsburgh, and Chicago. Those fifteen cities contained about two-thirds of all Jews in the United States in 1860. See also Ross, "History of St. Louis," 3; Eliafson, "The Jews of Chicago," 117; and David Philipson, "The Jewish Pioneers of the Ohio Valley," 49–50.

8. *Tribune*, January 7, 1884; "Reminiscences of Samuel Bowman," *Modern View* 25, 7. Of course a more complete answer to why Jews came to St. Louis involves the reasons that impelled them to leave their European homelands in the first place, regardless

most obvious manifestation of those efforts was the establishment of new Jewish institutions, especially congregations.

But before the Jewish population began to grow appreciably, and before additional Jewish institutions came into existence, war broke out in 1846 between the United States and Mexico. This is not the place to discuss either the broad causes and implications of that conflict or how it unfolded; rather, the concern here is the participation by the Jews of St. Louis. Since they numbered only about a hundred when the war began, one should not look for any large-scale Jewish involvement. In fact, the sparse evidence identifies only one St. Louis Jew in actual combat in Mexico: Benjamin J. Latz, younger brother of Adolph J. Latz, one of the founders of United Hebrew Cemetery and United Hebrew Congregation. Latz rose to be a sergeant in the Missouri Volunteers, an Army of the West unit commanded by Colonel Alexander W. Doniphan, which participated in the long overland march from Fort Leavenworth to Santa Fe that culminated in the conquest of New Mexico. American forces then continued through the wilderness and deserts of northern Mexico where, on February 28, 1847, near Chihuahua, the Missouri Volunteers defeated a large entrenched Mexican force, inflicting heavy losses. Latz fought also at Sacramento and against marauding Comanche Indians. On June 30, 1847, Colonel Doniphan and his Missouri Volunteers, Sergeant Latz among them, arrived back in St. Louis, triumphantly bearing trophies of their now-famous Mexican campaign. Shortly thereafter Latz was discharged from the service. He did not remain in St. Louis, however; apparently smitten with the Southwest, he soon went back to New Mexico and lived the rest of his life there.[9]

Whereas Latz left St. Louis after the war, Jacob Hirschorn was a Jewish Mexican War veteran who settled in St. Louis after the war. Born in Bavaria, Hirschorn came to New York in 1846 at just about the time the war with

of where they emigrated to. Many excellent modern Jewish histories give details. See especially Howard M. Sachar, *The Course of Modern Jewish History*, 165–68.

9. *Tribune*, December 21, 1883. St. Louis newspapers understandably and properly gave maximum coverage to the arrival of the local heroes from Mexico, up the Mississippi by steamboat by way of New Orleans. *Daily Missouri Republican*, June 30–July 5, 1847; *St. Louis Daily Evening News*, June 30–July 5, 1847. Following the Mexican War, Benjamin Latz returned to New Mexico and an adventurous life there and in California. In the Civil War he fought on the Union side at the Battle of Valverde in New Mexico, one of a series of critical engagements that secured the Southwest for the Union. He died in Santa Fe on June 9, 1864, where the local *New Mexican* eulogized him as "a man with an almost entire insensibility to fear and danger . . . [and] a devoted friend with a heart of the kindest and most charitable impulses." *Tribune*, December 21, 1883.

Mexico broke out. A youth of sixteen, he immigrated to this country to find work, leaving his widowed mother and only sister behind in Bavaria. Along with some new acquaintances, he enlisted in the First Regiment of New York Volunteers, which saw a great deal of action in Mexico, some quite bloody. Of the 1,200 who left New York, only about 260 returned. Hirschorn kept detailed notes of his war adventures. Years later he moved to St. Louis, where he became a prosperous merchant. In 1903, at the urging of his children and grandchildren, Hirschorn finally wrote his war memoirs in a volume entitled *The Mexican War: Reminiscences of a Volunteer.* His colorful accounts of the battles at Contresas, Churubusco, and Chapultepec provide vivid first-person and eyewitness descriptions of those and other engagements of the Mexican War. They also throw considerable light on the courage and self-reliance characteristic of so many young immigrants who served in the United States armed forces so soon after coming to this country, many of them speaking very little English and relying much more on their native European tongues to survive.[10]

Since St. Louis served as a jumping-off place for military expeditions, one might reasonably assume that some St. Louis Jewish merchants, along with non-Jewish merchants, contributed indirectly, at least, to the war effort by furnishing United States armed forces with food, horses and transport, clothing, medical supplies, ordnance, and other material necessary for military operations. It was undoubtedly lucrative for some. Equally important, though, were the many local groups that patriotically undertook all sorts of fund-raising projects to outfit and supply many Missouri Volunteer units, and, if needed, to care for their families. The scanty St. Louis Jewish community contributed "liberally" to those endeavors, especially in light of "their small number and means," wrote Isidor Bush later. Indeed, Mayor Bryan Mullanphy, treasurer of various fund-raising efforts, more than once commended the small Jewish community's "active aid and liberality."[11]

---

10. Hirschorn died in St. Louis on February 2, 1906, and was buried in Mount Sinai Cemetery. Jacob Hirschorn File, AJA; Jacob R. Marcus, *Memoirs of American Jews, 1775–1865,* vol. 2, 88–98. A great-grandson, Ralph Goldsticker, was a highly decorated bombardier-navigator in World War II. *St. Louis Jewish Light,* January 17, 1996. Though Dr. Simon Gratz Moses and Dr. Simon Pollack appear to have been the only Jewish doctors in St. Louis during the Mexican War, there is no evidence that either served with the military during that conflict. For that matter, though, there is no evidence that any non-Jewish St. Louis doctors served either, since the war proved relatively short and the army was able to get by with its regular medical personnel and did not have to engage in any broad recruiting endeavors.

11. *Tribune,* December 21, 1883, and January 7, 1884.

During the 1840s and 1850s at least five congregations were started in St. Louis in addition to United Hebrew. We know very little about the first. In January 1843 a list of "grievances" was presented to the board of trustees of United Hebrew Congregation by a group that identified itself as the "Gates of Mercy Congregation," or *Shaare Rachmonios*. There is no evidence of when or by whom the group was started. One of the leaders, though, was the highly respected Joseph Newmark, a native of Prussia and an ordained (in Europe) rabbi. Newmark apparently never practiced his learned profession formally, but came to America in 1824 at the age of twenty-five and entered the garment business, first in Somerset, Connecticut, and then in New York. In 1841 he moved to St. Louis and established a clothing store on Main Street. Newmark was not among those who organized United Hebrew in 1841 (perhaps he had not yet arrived in the city), but shortly thereafter his name was associated with Gates of Mercy Congregation and its list of grievances. Those concerns dealt with United Hebrew's policies on dues, membership requirements, and especially burial fees and procedures. Apparently the issues were soon resolved, for within a few months Newmark—and possibly the entire membership of that small congregation—joined United Hebrew. (In fact, United Hebrew soon elected him to its board of trustees and then as its president.) Once the "grievances" were settled, nothing more ever was heard of the Gates of Mercy Congregation.[12]

The next two congregations founded in the 1840s reflected not only the growth of the St. Louis Jewish population but also other reasons why American Jewish communities have experienced a proliferation of congregations: personality conflicts, social differences, and nationality jealousies, often more important than theological and religious concerns. The latter, however, were not insignificant in St. Louis, as United Hebrew's strict adherence to Orthodoxy seems to have disenchanted many of the newly arriving liberal German Jews. "Divine services were held according to the old *Polish* rite," a contemporary recalled; "reforms were not thought of, and thus the numerous young Jewish immigration, intent on its early struggles for existence, felt rather repulsed than attracted." Aversion to other conditions and practices in the "older" Jewish congregation alienated new arrivals. "The Polish congregation is disliked," Isidor Bush wrote to Rabbi Isaac Leeser in 1852, "partly for individuals who are . . . ill-reputed as to moral character, . . . partly for its bad management."

---

12. Minute Book of Board of Trustees of United Hebrew Congregation, AJA; Morris U. Schappes, ed., *A Documentary History of the Jews in the United States, 1864–1875*, 718; Makovsky, "History of United Hebrew Congregation," 276–80.

"The body of Jews here are of Polish origin and habits," wrote another observer, "and have generally followed the clothing trade, which is little calculated to gain the esteem of our fellow-citizens; but even many Jews were unwilling to join them, on account of their intolerance and exactions at every opportunity." The "intolerance" seems to have been United Hebrew's inflexibility in Orthodoxy; the most disturbing of the "exactions" apparently were exorbitant burial charges for nonmembers. Clearly more than theological differences led to the formation of new congregations.[13]

The first of these congregations was Emanu El ("God Is With Us") Congregation, organized in 1847. Unfortunately details of its founding went up in flames during the Great Fire of 1849. We do know, though, that it was also known popularly as the "Bavarian" and the "German" congregation, in contrast with the "Polish" United Hebrew. Its original membership included Max Stettheimer, president; Levy Nathan, secretary; Alexander Suess, treasurer; and Mingo H. Goldschmidt (or Goldsmith), Samuel Prager, Fred Wolff, Joseph Rothan, S. Strauss, Isaac L. Rothan, Jacob L. Long, Joseph Lehman, Simon Louis, Hyman Cohen, Moses Hirschfield, Frederick Schloss, Nathan Markstein, Louis Bauman, Julius Ruthenberg, Aaron Schoen, Simon Obermeyer, Lewis R. Rinestine, Isaac Isaacs, B. Frank, H. M. Reinhardt, Levy Stern, William L. Walter, Meyer Friede, B. Cohn, David Langsdorf, Samuel Haser, Max Morgenthau, and Isaac Lowman. Other members in the congregation's brief existence included Morris Cohn, Joel Eppstein, Isaac Stern, Louis Weil, and William Seligman, as well as some "German Israelites living in the interior of the State" in Boonville, Brunswick, Newport, Weston, and Jefferson City, and one also in Springfield, Illinois.[14]

Emanu El's membership never increased much beyond its original number; in fact, it experienced a disheartening decline. The cholera epidemic of 1849 took a large number. Some succumbed to "gold fever" and went to California, while others relocated in other cities for business purposes. As its membership decreased, Emanu El gradually discontinued weekly Sabbath services, convening only for holiday worship. By 1852, when the congregation went out of existence, its membership had dwindled to only about a dozen.[15]

---

13. Isidor Bush to Isaac Leeser, Carondelet, Mo., July 27, 1852, in Missouri Box, AJA; article signed "I.B." [Isidor Bush?] in *Occident* 9 (June 1851): 135; *Tribune*, December 7, 1883.

14. B'nai El Congregation Minutes, 1; *Tribune*, December 21, 1883; *Voice*, December 5, 1902, October 20, 1916; Makovsky, "History of United Hebrew Congregation," 332.

15. Isidor Bush to Isaac Leeser, Carondelet, Mo., July 27, 1852, in Missouri Box, AJA. One member of Emanu El who became very successful was William Seligman. He

In its brief five-year history, Emanu El conducted services and other congregational business in rented quarters, at least one of which was a room on Fifth Street between Washington and Green over a livery stable in the rear of Samuel C. Davis and Company, not far from where United Hebrew had by then established its first permanent home. As with United Hebrew at that time, Emanu El had no rabbi, and spiritual functions were exercised by individual members. It would appear that congregational demeanor was essentially Ashkenazic Orthodox, with a bit more liberalism than was found at United Hebrew.

Perhaps of greater significance, though, was the action by Emanu El in establishing the second Jewish cemetery in St. Louis. In May 1848 Mingo H. Goldsmith, Isaac Isaacs, Joseph Rothan, and Max Stettheimer, as trustees for the small congregation, purchased a piece of ground 200 by 211 feet on the southwest corner of Gratiot Street and Pratte Avenue, in the "Camp Spring" area just north of the Missouri Pacific Railroad tracks, for which they paid five hundred dollars. A 50- by 50-foot-square area was fenced off for a graveyard. In 1849 a *metaher* (house in which the deceased is prepared for burial) was constructed. Unfortunately the congregation had need for the cemetery all too soon, as the 1849 cholera epidemic took a frightful toll among members and their families.

By the middle of 1852 Emanu El's finances, along with its membership, had dwindled precariously. Accordingly, on June 7, 1852, the congregation sold part of its land, a little more than a third of an acre, to Missouri Pacific for eight hundred dollars, but continued to own and maintain the small cemetery. Despite that profitable sale, the congregation remained strapped for both funds and membership.[16]

Meanwhile, in 1849 another congregation—the fourth in the city—came into being: B'nai B'rith ("Sons of the Covenant") Congregation. (Although the names happen to be the same, there is no connection with the famous fraternal organization founded in 1843 in New York.) Known popularly as the "Bohemian shul," this congregation was founded by German Jews

---

went to California during the gold rush, and with his brother Jesse made a fortune there in the clothing business. Shortly thereafter he moved to New York, where he joined forces with another former member of Emanu El and established the prominent mercantile house of Seligman and Stettheimer. Meanwhile, during the Civil War the Seligman brothers advanced the Union army $1 million worth of uniforms on credit, and through their European banking connections they sold $200 million in bonds in Germany at a time when French and British financial institutions were unfriendly to the Union cause. *Tribune*, December 21, 1883; Steven Birmingham, *Our Crowd: The Great Jewish Families of New York*, 117–21 and passim.

16. B'nai El Congregation Minutes, 1; Makovsky, "History of United Hebrew Congregation," 333–34.

who lived predominantly in the southern part of St. Louis. (St. Louis ran mostly north and south along the Mississippi River, and its western boundary roughly followed Eighteenth Street, though not many people lived then west of Ninth Street.) Like Emanu El, B'nai B'rith came into existence because recently immigrating liberal German Jews considered United Hebrew too "intolerant" in religious matters, too "Polish" in habits and mannerisms, and too "exacting" in financial demands. The original members were Daniel Block, the first *parnass*, referred to as the "father of the B'nai B'rith Congregation"; Solomon Steindler, treasurer; John Fleischman, Moses Epstein, Hyman Epstein, M. Sternbach, Herman Block, Jacob Wachtel, Adolph Wachtel, Joseph Katz, Nathan Aschner, Adolph Aschner, Adolph Klauber, Ludwig [Louis] Schwartzkopf, Julius Augstein, Joseph Levi, Moses Bruml, Ephraim Fischel, M. A. Taussig, Daniel Winkler, Bernard Singer, and Isidor Bush. St. Louis now claimed a "Polish" congregation, a "Bavarian" or "German" congregation, and a "Bohemian" congregation.

As did the other congregations, B'nai B'rith conducted Sabbath and holiday services in temporary rented quarters, not yet possessing its own synagogue. We know of only one location, a second-floor room at the corner of Lafayette and Fulton, a heavily German-populated area in south St. Louis. The room could accommodate seventy people, but we do not know if the congregation ever filled it; in fact, B'nai B'rith's largest membership at any given time was only about thirty families.

Nevertheless, small in numbers and "mostly poor people . . . struggling with the exigencies of their material existence," B'nai B'rith was not without some means. One of its first acts was to purchase about an acre of land for a cemetery, about six miles southwest of the city limits on Gravois Road. The congregation also purchased a lot inside the city upon which it hoped to build a synagogue, but in October 1850, unable to pay the balance due on the land, they returned it to the Benjamin Soulard estate, with partial recompense. Shortly thereafter, when Isidor Bush became president, new efforts resulted in successfully acquiring another plot of land on Jackson Street. But funds for a building still exceeded the small congregation's financial means. Accordingly, in 1852 Bush resorted to a practice common among American congregations at that time, an announcement in Isaac Leeser's *The Occident and American Jewish Advocate*, a periodical published monthly in Philadelphia and circulated widely in Jewish communities all over the country. In an "open letter" addressed "To the friends and Adherents of our Religion," Bush indicated the financial difficulties of his small *kahal* (congregation) and pleaded for support for a "suitable building, but simple." The letter was signed by Bush as president, by M. Taussig, vice president, and by Ludwig Schwartzkopf, secretary.[17]

Thus both new congregations, Emanu El and B'nai B'rith, though dissatisfied with various features of the older and larger United Hebrew, found themselves facing shortages of funds as well as problems of membership. Inevitably the question of merger arose. Ironically, the movement toward merger originated within United Hebrew. Since its inception in 1841, United Hebrew had experienced its share of ups and downs. Its membership had increased, especially after it moved into its newly renovated quarters on Fifth and Green, in spite of the affinity of the new immigrants for religious liberalism. Precise figures are not available, but whereas both Emanu El and B'nai B'rith experienced decreases, United Hebrew's numbers steadily grew larger, to more than a hundred in 1856. Undoubtedly the new synagogue building must have made a difference.[18]

Along with numerical increases, United Hebrew expanded services, both for members and nonmembers. The congregation maintained a *shochet* and a *mohel* for ritual slaughtering and circumcision, and it maintained a *mikvah* in the basement of its building for those who desired such a facility. Its officials performed weddings and funerals, functions taken over later by rabbis when they arrived on the scene. The congregation made available *matzos* (unleavened bread) for Passover. Rudimentary attempts were made toward providing formal religious instruction for children, albeit they amounted to not much more than the *chazzan* teaching youngsters "a little Hebrew . . . at such hours when his other duties give him leisure and opportunity." United Hebrew Cemetery was available for all persons, but nonmembers were charged higher fees. United Hebrew congregants had first options in purchasing seats for the High Holiday services before space was made available to nonmembers. That was important because large numbers of worshipers who rarely attended other services packed the sanctuary for Rosh Hashannah and Yom Kippur services, though most were not members.[19]

---

17. B'nai El File, B'nai El Minute Book, and Isidor Bush to Isaac Leeser, Carondelet, Mo., July 27, 1852, in Missouri Box, AJA; *Occident* 7 (December 1849): 77–81, 9 (June 1851): 136, 10 (September 1852): 294, and 10 (February 1853): 556; *Jewish Free Press* (St. Louis), November 19, 1886; *Modern View,* May 12, 1932; Makovsky, "History of United Hebrew Congregation," 328–37.

18. *Israelite,* March 14, 1856.

19. *Occident* 9 (June 1852): 136. Unfortunately it is not uncommon, even today, that many synagogues fill their seats only on the High Holy Days of Rosh Hashannah and Yom Kippur. Henry Myers, secretary of United Hebrew, wrote in 1849 (after the congregation had moved into the new Fifth Street building) that "during the last

This growth and these accomplishments were not without problems. Disagreements persisted over the virtually unamendable Orthodoxy *(Minhag Poland)* written into the congregation's constitution. Many members desired more liberalism and modernization to reflect the attitudes of incoming liberal German Jewish immigrants as well as the impact of the emerging Reform movement on American Judaism. Meetings of the board of trustees and of the general membership often developed into disputes over finances, especially over fees charged for various services. Disputes persisted over the conduct and decorum at meetings and services. Dissension arose over costs of a Torah scroll and over the honoraria paid to a *ba'al k'riah* (Torah reader) and a cantor. Indeed, its fractured state of finances may have been the main reason why it was the first (in late 1851) to broach the subject of merger, even though on the surface United Hebrew seemed to be the only successful congregation in St. Louis.[20]

An added impetus for merger stemmed from Rabbi Isaac Leeser of Philadelphia. Considered by many as the nearest thing to a "Chief Rabbi of America," Leeser was a leading advocate for unity within American Jewry. A strong traditionalist and opponent of the Reform Judaism championed by Rabbi Isaac Mayer Wise of Cincinnati, Leeser promoted many modernizations in traditional Judaism to make it more meaningful and appealing to American Jews. He was the first, for instance, to incorporate English-language sermons as a regular part of the service. He converted many prayers into English, and eliminated or modified others. He did much to stimulate Jewish education, formally and institutionally as well as informally. He founded and effectively used the widely circulated journal *Occident and American Jewish Advocate* to champion the cause of a modernized Judaism—but withal a traditional Orthodox Judaism as opposed to the rapidly spreading Reform Judaism. Leeser traveled throughout the country on behalf of his advocacy, and one such tour brought him to St. Louis just as the issue of merger arose within its small but growing Jewish community.

On Sunday afternoon, December 14, 1851, more than a hundred people braved "fearfully inclement" winter weather to hear Rabbi Leeser speak at United Hebrew's Fifth Street *shul*. He pointed out the "absurdity" of maintaining three separate congregations, "when the Polish, German, and

---

holy-days the Synagogue was crowded almost to suffocation, not less than from five to six hundred persons being present, whereas, but a few years back, they could count scarcely more than about fifty or sixty." Henry Myers to Isaac Leeser, St. Louis, November 6, 1849, in Missouri Box, AJA; *Occident* 7 (December 1849): 77–81.

20. Isidor Bush to Isaac Leeser, Carondelet, Mo., July 27, 1852, in Missouri Box, AJA; *Voice*, December 5, 1902.

Bohemian customs hardly differ, except in the amount of poetical prayers to be recited on certain days." Those differences were insignificant, he maintained, considering that what he called the "basic forms" remained the same.

Leeser's visit in St. Louis (bitter weather forced him to stay a week longer than he had planned) seemed to bolster sentiment for union. On January 11, 1852, the membership of United Hebrew voted overwhelmingly in favor of merger and designated a committee to make the appropriate overtures and to draw up preliminary guidelines and procedures. For the next two months representatives of the three congregations met and negotiated, but details of their meetings are very sparse. Evidently, however, resistance developed within the two smaller congregations, and over the summer sentiment for merger waned. Apparently United Hebrew negotiators assumed that the two smaller bodies would meld into the larger congregation, with religious practices and procedures remaining *Minhag Poland*; Emanu El and B'nai B'rith disagreed. Since United Hebrew now had its building near the center of the city, its members viewed their synagogue as home for the unified congregation, much to the dissatisfaction of the two smaller groups, who lived preponderantly in the southern part of the city. But perhaps the most important reason why sentiment for merger diminished was articulated by Isidor Bush in his letter to Rabbi Leeser: that personal dislikes as much as religious differences—or perhaps even more—mitigated against merger.

But the merger discussions were by no means a total failure. Feeling that the two smaller congregations "in a divided state . . . would never be able to carry out their intentions for the holding of a worthy public worship," Emanu El and B'nai B'rith decided that at least they would unite. Accordingly, at a general meeting held on October 17, 1852, the membership of the two congregations drew up and ratified a document establishing a "United Israelitish Religious Association" to be known as the "B'nai El Congregation." The new name obviously was a merger of the two older names, though no one knows who was responsible for that suggestion. All the property of the two congregations, "movable and immovable," also was merged. Temporary directors elected to implement the changeover were Alexander Suess, Isidor Bush, Daniel Block, Bernard Singer, and Solomon Steindler. William L. Walter was elected temporary secretary, and Isaac Lowman treasurer. For the time being, however, no one was named president. What proved to be St. Louis's second permanent congregation, B'nai El, had come into existence.[21]

---

21. B'nai El's early history is well documented. The temple itself has conscientiously maintained good records, and copies are in the American Jewish Archives

Five ad hoc committees were appointed for priority tasks. Designated to draw up a constitution were Isidor Bush, Alexander Suess, and William L. Walter. Meyer Friede, L. Block, and John Fleischmann began the search for a suitable synagogue site. Ludwig Schwartzkopf, Ephraim Fischel, and E. Freiburg had the critical task of clarifying the *minhagim* (rituals). Meanwhile, Fred Wolff, Daniel Block, F. L. Dattelzweig, L. R. Strauss, Bernard Singer, and Julius Epstein constituted a fund-raising committee to give the new congregation a sound financial structure. Finally, John Fleischmann, Solomon Steindler, Max Gut, Ludwig Schwartzkopf, and Isaac L. Rothan supervised the continuing operations of both cemeteries, the small Emanu El cemetery at Pratte and Gratiot and the larger B'nai B'rith cemetery on Gravois Road.

The transitional committees reported their progress at a meeting on November 7, 1852, at which time also Ludwig Schwartzkopf volunteered temporarily, at least, to assume the post of *chazzan*, without remuneration. Within a few weeks the constitution and bylaws were ready, and they were submitted and approved, in two special meetings on January 9 and 16, 1853. Written in German script and dated also according to the Hebrew calendar (29 *Teveth* and 7 *Shevat*, 5613), the documents were signed by 152 charter members. The next step was the designation of officers, elected on January 30. The unique procedure required the election first of a board of seven directors, who then chose the executive officers from among themselves. B'nai El's first directors were Isidor Bush, William Walter, Alexander Suess, Daniel Block, Bernard Singer, Isaac Lowman, and Ludwig Schwartzkopf. They then named William Walter to be the first president, Bernard Singer vice president, and Isaac Lowman treasurer. Officially founded a few months earlier on October 17, 1852, B'nai El Congregation now was ready for full-scale operation.[22]

---

in Cincinnati. Perhaps equally important is the contribution made by B'nai El's long-time rabbi (1878–1920), Moritz Spitz. During most of his rabbinate Spitz also edited the *Jewish Voice*, an English-language weekly newspaper that played a prominent role in the St. Louis Jewish community. On at least two separate occasions, Spitz reproduced the minutes of B'nai El Congregation, from its founding up to that particular time. They ran in serial form, spread out over a period of several months, once in 1902–1903 and again in 1916–1917. They obviously constitute an important historical record of B'nai El Congregation as well as of the St. Louis Jewish community. *Voice*, December 5, 1902–August 14, 1903, and October 20, 1916–September 14, 1917.

22. B'nai El's first president, William Walter, did not remain long in St. Louis. In May 1855, before the congregation's first synagogue was ready for occupancy, he moved from the city and "the congregation lost in him one of its founders, and one of the most active, respected and popular members." "History of B'nai El, Compiled from the Congregation's Minutes," as printed in *Voice*, December 19, 1902.

As might be expected, the new congregation faced all sorts of problems. One that did not immediately pose a difficulty, however, was numbers; 152 charter members assured sufficient congregants. (That number would fluctuate, but that is a problem every congregation faces constantly.) However, not all the 152 signers actually became members of B'nai El. Many apparently were only temporary sojourners in St. Louis who either moved elsewhere or did not bother to become formal members.[23]

One reason for the large number of charter members, of course, was the sheer increase in Jewish immigrants in the 1850s from Germanic Europe. Another undoubtedly was that B'nai El was more liberal than United Hebrew. Both congregations clearly advocated and maintained traditional Judaism; nevertheless, whereas United Hebrew adhered very strictly to the practices of *Minhag Poland* and *halachic* Orthodoxy (even to the extent of expelling members who did not), B'nai El's policies were less stringent. Although by no means accepting or advocating the tenets of Reform Judaism, B'nai El's constitution and bylaws acknowledged the liberal tendencies of the newly immigrating German Jews and their desire to acculturate. "We are therefore not permitted to condemn any Israelite," stated the preamble to the congregation's constitution, "for his religious or rather irreligious views, opinions, and acts, not to mention to exclude him, so long as he does not violate the commandments of neighborly love, and desires to come to listen to the word of God."[24]

Some might conclude that such "laxity" toward traditional Judaism classifies early B'nai El already as a Reform congregation. Quite the contrary; despite "modernization" leanings, B'nai El retained its Orthodoxy for decades before becoming Reform. Indeed, years later Rabbi Samuel Wolfenstein, one of B'nai El's early spiritual leaders, in reminiscing about his efforts to lead the congregation toward "moderate Reform," described the status of Orthodoxy and traditionalism when he came to the congregation in 1870:

> The old Siddur and Machzor had been in use, Thora reading and Misheberachs, everything in the old style. That first Simchath Thora was observed in the very same fashion as they used to keep it in Schwihau

---

23. A contemporary St. Louis newspaper reported that of about six hundred or seven hundred Jews in St. Louis in December 1853, B'nai El numbered sixty active members and thirty applicants for membership. *St. Louis Intelligencer,* December 17, 1853. Among those who came from B'nai B'rith to found B'nai El was Moses Bruml. His descendants affiliated with B'nai El to the present. Among them is Helen-Rose Bruml Klausner, whose husband, Bertram Klausner, served as rabbi of B'nai El for thirty-six years, from 1953 until he died in 1991. *St. Louis Jewish Light,* September 26, 1979, and April 17, 1991.

24. From Constitution of B'nai El Congregation, AJA.

in Bohemia, whence many of the members of the congregation had come, and wherefore they used to be called "The Boehmische Shool." Everybody was called up to the Thora on the eve of Simchas Thora. . . . Each section was sold by auction. There were processions by the old and the young, and the women threw down from the gallery raisins and nuts to the youngsters.[25]

Wolfenstein's description, of course, typifies any traditional Orthodox congregation.

Another account of early B'nai El comes from the unidentified author of "Reminiscences of a Former St. Louisan," a series of articles that appeared in *The Jewish Voice* in 1914:

I have in my scrap book, which I call my "Sepher ha-Chayim" (Book of Life), the picture of the first Synagogue of the B'nai El Congregation. . . . Everything was strictly orthodox. . . . My memory dates back to the time when Schwartzkopf was "Chasan" (Rabbi there was none), when "Frenchtown" and a goodly section below it was a ghetto without gates, when people spoke to each other by their Hebrew names, and with one another in Bohemian and German and "Loshon Kodesh" ["Holy Language," that is, Hebrew]. Little wonder they did not master English. In those days people went to "Shul" in the early morning on Yom Kippur, emerging only when the proverbial three stars appeared in the heavens. . . . The congregation remained strictly Orthodox until the advent of Doctor S. Wolfenstein . . . [26]

Isaac Fuld was another who identified the early Orthodoxy of B'nai El. Fuld came to St. Louis in 1853. Reminiscing later about several prominent personalities whom he knew well, he noted that "all belong[ed] to the old *Orthodox* B'nai El Shul." On another occasion, Fuld identified both the "Polische Shul" and the "Boemische Shul" as unquestionably Orthodox.[27]

That, then, was B'nai El, a traditional Orthodox congregation during the first few decades of its existence, albeit with conscious leanings toward modernization and acculturation. Early B'nai El was not only Orthodox but also German. Many early references to the congregation alluded to it as either "German" or "Bohemian." This was due, of course, to its member-ship: men and women who came to this country from the central European Germanic states. Indeed, as late as the 1860s, the congregation's rabbi would write: "My congregation is purely German, everything conducted in the German language."[28]

---

25. *Voice*, November 12, 1909.

26. Ibid., October 30, 1914. The continuation of this series of "Reminiscences" is printed in the issues for November 6, 20, and 27, 1914.

27. Ibid., April 16, 1920; *Modern View 25*, 11.

28. Rabbi Henry Kuttner to Rabbi Isaac Leeser, St. Louis, June 6, 1862, in Missouri Box, AJA.

One of the new congregation's prime objectives was to build a synagogue, to serve as both house of worship and religious school. To that end, it will be recalled, a committee had been designated to find an appropriate site. The committee quickly determined that the Jackson Street land owned by the defunct B'nai B'rith Congregation would not suffice, and so it was sold for $465. Added to the $800 which Emanu El had acquired from the sale of its land to the Missouri Pacific Railroad, B'nai El had a small nest egg with which to start a building fund.

Meanwhile the new B'nai El occupied temporary rented quarters. The first site was two small rooms on the corner of Lafayette and Ninth. When some members urged a more northern location, the congregation rented quarters on Fifth Street near Walnut. In August 1853, when that place proved insufficient, another was found on the corner of Seventh and Lafayette, and the following year even larger facilities were rented at Seventh and Park, a building known as "Decker's House." All this time, of course, the site committee searched for a suitable permanent location. Unable to agree on several possible places, the committee at different times suggested doing what United Hebrew had done: lease an existing church building and remodel it to their needs. But the persistence of Daniel Block, who had been one of B'nai B'rith's influential leaders, led to rejection of leasing in favor of purchasing a lot and building a completely new building.[29]

In October 1853, Abraham S. Jacobs, who had just become a member of B'nai El, offered the congregation a parcel of land at its original cost to him and about half its current market value. The terms were unanimously accepted by the committee, the board of directors, and the thirty-two congregational members who attended a special meeting on October 30. Located on the east side of Sixth Street, between Gratiot and Cerre (closer to the latter), with a seventy-foot front and seventy-five feet deep, the price was $34 a front foot, or $2,380: $380 in cash and notes for $2,000 at 6 percent for four years. Louis Block, Isidor Bush, and Meyer Friede, named as trustees, bonded themselves that the property would "never be used for anything else than a Temple building."

Funds for a building proved more difficult to acquire. Subscription lists were circulated, but they left much still to be raised. One encouraging development was financial support from portions of the non-Jewish community. Responding to newspaper and other solicitations, Catholic,

---

29. Unfortunately Daniel Block did not live to see his hopes for the new synagogue materialize; he died on September 3, 1853, before the building was completed. "History of B'nai El, Compiled from the Congregation's Minutes," in *Voice*, December 5, 1902.

Presbyterian, and Baptist groups demonstrated welcome ecumenism by pledging various amounts of money. This may have been the first instance of such interreligious cooperation in St. Louis history involving the Jewish community. All this support helped, of course, but it still did not solve B'nai El's financial predicament. By December 1853 the congregation had only fifteen hundred dollars in its treasury, still far short of a reasonable amount for definitive action.[30]

Suddenly a seemingly dead issue was resurrected—merger. Reaction within United Hebrew to the creation of B'nai El had been mixed. Some actually took advantage of the new congregation by using it as a lever to pry dues concessions from the older body. That may explain why, in what appears to have been a gesture of malicious vindictiveness, United Hebrew revised its constitution and bylaws, prohibiting its members from belonging at the same time to another congregation or even from aiding one monetarily. Yet members of both congregations associated socially and in business, and even served on a joint committee to review candidates for the position of *shochet*. So despite United Hebrew being the more traditional "north side shul" and B'nai El the more liberal "south side shul," the two were not entirely disassociated.

The issue of building a synagogue, however, affected both congregations. United Hebrew's Fifth Street synagogue was a leased building, remodeled, but nevertheless not secure in permanency. In fact, for some time President Adolph J. Latz had been conjecturing openly about United Hebrew buying land and constructing a permanent synagogue. And B'nai El, of course, was right in the middle of that exercise. Then suddenly, early in 1854, B'nai El initiated a formal proposal to United Hebrew that the two merge. No reasons for the proposal appear in existing records of either congregation, only hints. Undoubtedly B'nai El's membership—especially its leadership—felt frustrated over its inability to raise sufficient building funds; perhaps a combined effort would succeed. Indeed, B'nai El officers and board members openly favored merger, even though some had made rather disparaging observations earlier about United Hebrew's philosophy and membership. Whatever B'nai El's reasons, the reaction from United Hebrew was surprisingly positive, considering what had happened in the earlier merger attempt. On February 12, 1854, President Latz read at a congregational meeting a letter he had received from B'nai El proposing merger. With the approval of his membership, Latz appointed an ad hoc committee to draw up "equitable terms" under which the two congregations might unite. Two

---

30. Makovsky, "History of United Hebrew Congregation," 356–60.

weeks later, on February 26, United Hebrew members gathered at a special meeting and unanimously approved those terms. Another committee was thereupon appointed to contact the B'nai El board and proceed with merger arrangements. The union of United Hebrew and B'nai El, rejected once, now seemed imminent.[31]

Once again, though, it was not to be. Unexpected news from New Orleans created a completely different situation. Judah Touro, the foremost American Jewish philanthropist of the time, had died. Touro, a veteran of the War of 1812 and a wealthy New Orleans merchant, used his wealth generously and was a great benefactor for many causes, Jewish and non-Jewish. He donated ten thousand dollars, half the amount needed, for the purchase of Bunker Hill as a national monument in Boston. Upon his death, he left sixty thousand dollars for the poor in Jerusalem as well as bequests to many Jewish organizations across America. Among the recipients was B'nai El Congregation, which was given three thousand dollars. Isidor Bush apparently played an important role in instigating the bequest, but the details remain unknown.[32]

B'nai El's sudden good fortune had an electrifying effect on its membership. With the Touro bequest, the congregation now felt confident they could raise the remainder of the building fund by themselves. Poised to join forces with United Hebrew, many B'nai El members now had a change of heart. Despite continued strong support for merger by President Bernard Singer and former presidents and board members William Walter, Fred Wolff, Meyer Friede, Isidor Bush, and Abraham Jacobs, the B'nai El membership refused to ratify the move. At a meeting on April 16, 1854, repeated efforts by board members failed to push through a favorable vote. The closest was a 22–22 tie. Five absentee ballots raised the "for merger" count to 27–22, but it was still far short of the two-thirds majority required in the bylaws. Several absent members declared later that they would have supported merger had they been at the meeting, but their votes still would not have been enough. Thus ended the last attempt to unite the two congregations. Bush, who earlier had expressed severe reservations about the "Polishe shul" and the character of some of its members but

---

31. B'nai El's congregational minutes are less detailed on this matter than those of United Hebrew, and give the impression that the latter instigated the move for merger: "The officers of the United Hebrew congregation . . . expressed the sincere wish of uniting with the B'nai El." B'nai El Congregational Minutes, 4.

32. Judah Touro's beneficiaries were legion. In 1850 he bought an old estate in New Orleans, converted it into a hospital, and gave it to the city. Touro Infirmary still exists today (as part of the Tulane University medical school) as a monument to his generosity.

who now strongly supported a union, deeply regretted the failure of the merger, "which would have made one of the largest and most powerful Jewish organizations of the land."

The Judah Touro legacy spurred B'nai El into action. Throughout the remainder of 1854 building fund contributions accelerated, as did membership, and various building proposals were considered. By early 1855 the congregation had approved plans by Koenig and Brothers, Architects, at an estimated cost of sixty-six hundred dollars (the final cost came closer to seven thousand dollars).[33]

The cornerstone ceremony, organized by Isidor Bush and Abraham Jacobs, took place on the afternoon of April 16, 1855. Because this was the first synagogue constructed in St. Louis and also west of the Mississippi, the occasion merits more than just passing notice.[34] More than four hundred persons attended, Bush recorded, "about half of whom were Hebrews," and "over fifty ladies." Prominent citizens in attendance included St. Louis Mayor Washington King, Missouri Supreme Court Justice William Scott, Rabbi Bernard Illowy (recently engaged at United Hebrew), and several Protestant ministers. B'nai El President Bernard Singer introduced Bush, who gave a brief historical background detailing how Emanu El and B'nai B'rith had become B'nai El. He praised the many non-Jews who had generously contributed to the building fund, and expressed especially warm thanks for the Touro bequest. Then,

> the corner-stone being elevated, a glass jar, hermetically sealed, was then placed in a cavity in a foundation stone. In it were a copy of the Constitution of the United States; the Constitution, By-laws, officers and members of the congregation [seventy-five at the time]; a history of the organization of the congregation; a list of the chief Executive officers of the United States and city of St. Louis; a copy of the *Israelite* [Rabbi Isaac Mayer Wise's newspaper]; a view of the front elevation of the temple when completed; a variety of U.S. coins and other small articles.[35]

The actual laying and sealing of the cornerstone was performed by John Hogan. A former circuit-riding, fire-breathing Methodist preacher turned

---

33. "History of B'nai El, Compiled from the Congregation's Minutes," in *Voice*, December 12, 1902. For Bush's role in securing the Judah Touro grant, see Samuel Bowman's biographical sketch of Bush in *Modern View*, September 19, 1924.

34. For details of the historic and impressive ceremony, see B'nai El Congregational Minutes and "History of B'nai El, Compiled from the Congregation's Minutes" in *Voice*, December 12, 1902, as well as in a feature article in *Voice*, May 25, 1906. See also *Israelite*, May 4, 1855.

35. When the building was torn down years later, B'nai El officials sought to retrieve the glass jar and its contents from the cornerstone, but they were unsuccessful. What happened to those contents remains unknown. *Voice*, November 17, 1916.

politician and very successful businessman, Hogan was a distinguished member of the St. Louis financial and political power structure at the time. One St. Louis historian categorized him as "the city's chief drum-beater." Architect Koenig presented Hogan with a ceremonial trowel "of fine workmanship, the blade being made of silver, and the handle of pearl." On the blade was inscribed:

In consideration of
laying the corner-stone of
Temple of the Benai El Congregation,
April 16th.   Nissan 30.   5615.
1855.

Accepting the trowel, Hogan delivered a stirring main address. "I have been placed in a variety of circumstances," he began, "and have addressed various assemblies, but the scene before me begets emotions with which I have never before arisen to make a speech." That set the tone for a presentation highlighted by a characteristic American encomium on religious freedom:

> But there is a land, where they are recognized as men; a land where the arm of the oppressor cannot be raised against them, or any other human being, because of his religious opinion; a land whose broad and beautiful banner is gloriously bespangled with stars and stripes, and as its folds are developed by heaven's free breeze, proclaims to all men, "Here you may worship God under your own vine and fig-tree, according to the dictates of your own conscience, and none dare molest or make you afraid."

One observer wrote: "The address of Mr. Hogan was listened to with marked attention, and impressed every heart by its sincerity and genuine eloquence."

Hogan's address was followed by brief comments in German by Rabbi Illowy, who stressed that a synagogue was not only a house of prayer, but also a house of learning, a center for "divine instruction."

At the conclusion of Illowy's brief remarks, the cornerstone was lowered and fixed into place. Hogan sealed the stone permanently with mortar. Then, with no fanfare, a brief Masonic ceremony ensued, described simply as "those great emblems of the mechanic arts, viz: the *plumb*, the *square*, and the *level*, were applied by Mr. Koenig, who pronounced the work finished."

The cornerstone in place, President Singer called on Isidor Bush to thank the assembly and invite them to the dedication ceremony when the building was completed. Everyone expected a lengthy address, but Bush briefly introduced Mayor King, who also kept his comments short and to the point. On that happy note of brevity, a final benediction concluded the ceremony.[36]

Construction proceeded throughout the summer of 1855, but not without problems. Members lodged all sorts of complaints with the building committee—about the layout of the building, the costs, the quality of the construction, and the painting. Most of the dissatisfaction, however, was viewed as a carryover from the differences engendered earlier in the merger debates. By September the building was ready for occupancy.

Impressive dedication services occurred on a hot Friday afternoon, September 7, 1855. By two o'clock the temple was packed with members and distinguished guests of many denominations. At three o'clock sharp President Singer ceremonially opened the front doors. "The Temple was beautifully decorated with flowers, palms and other plants," recorded an eyewitness, "and amid solemn music and song the scrolls were borne to the new Holy Ark." Seven times they were paraded around the synagogue by the congregation's elders, in time-old tradition. Psalms, prayers, readings, and musical selections, in Hebrew, English, and German, were interspersed throughout the program. Musical selections and choral accompaniments were played on "an old, very bad, and borrowed organ." (Rented for the occasion, the organ later was replaced by a much finer instrument.) Isidor Bush delivered an address in English, and Rabbi Illowy preached a sermon in German. "The solemn service closed with [the liturgical poem] 'Yigdal,' sung by a quartet," B'nai El records indicate, "and nothing had marred the joyous occasion save the oppressive heat." And so the first synagogue built in St. Louis was ready for use.[37]

Only one known photograph of B'nai El's Sixth and Cerre synagogue exists, an exterior shot taken in 1858. It shows an octagonal-shaped building, fifty feet across, topped by a domed cupola and squared crenelated battlements. The domed top appeared to some like a "conventional Turkish Mosque." Others would refer to the temple's "fortress" appearance, and still others affectionately called it the "Coffee Mill" or the "Pepper Pot" because of its apparent resemblance to those common kitchen utensils.[38] In the vestibule was installed a marble slab in memory of Judah Touro

---

36. The trowel is in the possession of the Missouri Historical Society in St. Louis, on loan from Hogan's descendants. B'nai El Congregation has sought for years to get it for its own historical museum, but unsuccessfully.

37. The basement was completed later. *Israelite*, September 28, 1855.

38. *Modern View 25*, 8.

as the benefactor of the congregation. Tall, arched double doors at the front of the building, flanked by even taller, narrow and arched windows, opened onto a sanctuary containing benches seating about three hundred persons. In addition to natural light from the sky-lighted dome, two chandeliers and six urns on pedestals served as gaslight fixtures. The basement, finished after the temple was already in use, housed a *mikvah* and classrooms for religious school use. A gallery surrounding the main sanctuary provided separate seating for women, as customary in traditional Jewish synagogues. On the east wall of the sanctuary stood the altar and the Ark, which held the Torah scrolls. In front of the Ark stood two sizable *menorahs* (candelabras), a gift to the congregation from the Zion Ladies' Aid Society. In the tradition of Orthodox synagogues, a *bimah* (reading platform) stood in the center of the sanctuary, facing the Ark, from which the Torah was read. Alongside the pulpit a small reading lectern accommodated the *chazzan*. Next to it stood an organ.[39]

That organ represented a significant leaning within B'nai El toward liberalism and, later, Reform. The use of musical instruments (particularly the organ) and of non-Jews in congregational choirs had become major issues between Orthodoxy and emerging American Reform Judaism, as had, of course, the more divisive and important issues of theology and prayer. Though in most other respects an Orthodox *shul*, B'nai El's lay leadership (it had no rabbi yet) already had demonstrated its leanings toward liberalism, and not surprisingly would become a Reform congregation within a few decades.

One more congregation appeared in pre–Civil War St. Louis, but it lasted only briefly. Adas Jeshurun, like Gates of Mercy Congregation earlier, and like so many small, transient eastern European Orthodox congregations that sprang up later, seems to have been a "tsu-lochis-nick shul," a congregation organized primarily because of personality and/or operational conflicts rather than important theological or policy

---

39. When the congregation later moved to new buildings, the marble Judah Touro commemorative plaque and the two Zion Ladies' Aid Society menorahs were installed in the new buildings. *Voice*, December 12 and 19, 1902, and October 30, 1914. In 1875, when B'nai El moved to a new location at Eleventh and Chouteau where it had purchased and remodeled the Chouteau Avenue Presbyterian Church, the Sixth and Cerre building was sold to the Good Samaritan Episcopal (Colored) Congregation, which occupied it for a number of years before selling it to business interests that converted the building to a warehouse. In September 1905 the historic edifice was leveled and the site since then has been occupied by a series of commercial structures and parking lots. Nothing of the original building remains on the site, not even remnants of its foundation. *Voice*, September 22, 1905; Compton, ed., *Pictorial Saint Louis*, 111.

differences.[40] In 1854, some of United Hebrew's members broke away and organized a separate congregation. The reasons are not clear; we can only speculate, based on other occurrences within United Hebrew at the time. Perhaps it resulted from resentment against cemetery management; perhaps it came out of dissatisfaction with the Orthodoxy of Rabbi Illowy's ministry; perhaps it represented disapproval of discriminatory policies toward nonmembers. At any rate, on December 10, 1854, a group that eventually grew to twenty-five members seceded from United Hebrew and formed a new congregation, Adas Jeshurun. Officers elected included Abraham Newmark, president; A. S. Meyers, treasurer; H. Myers, secretary pro tem; and L. Waldstein, B. Lithauer, L. M. Prince, I. Turk, and B. S. Rosenthal, trustees. Presumably Adas Jeshurun conducted services in rented or donated quarters, but no evidence exists to indicate where. The congregation's only known achievement was the purchase of ground for a cemetery in St. Louis County on Olive Street Road. (Later, in 1868, the land became the site of United Hebrew's Mount Olive Cemetery.) Within a few months, however, the congregation's differences with United Hebrew were patched up, and in August 1855 the seceders harmoniously reunited with the parent congregation. Some even became officers and board members. Nothing more ever was heard of Adas Jeshurun Congregation.[41]

The resolution of the Adas Jeshurun episode cleared the way for United Hebrew Congregation to tackle the nagging issue of a permanent site. By 1855 the lease on the Fifth Street building was running out. Furthermore, B'nai El's new edifice made that synagogue more appealing to potential new members, especially among newly arriving immigrants. Some in United Hebrew felt that the future of the congregation inevitably depended upon a new building. That decision was accordingly made,

---

40. The author is indebted for this Yiddish tongue-in-cheek sobriquet to a friend, Lazar Sorkin, of St. Louis. Sorkin recalled for the author how so many small congregations, often not much larger than a bare *minyan*, rented an upstairs room over his father's kosher butcher meat market in what was then St. Louis's near-north-side eastern European Orthodox Jewish "ghetto." These groups were invariably temporary and transient, and usually came into being because of seemingly ridiculous and trivial reasons—such as a certain individual not receiving a particular "honor," or a *yahrzeit* being overlooked, or some similarly innocuous or insignificant oversight. The Yiddish term *auf tsu-lochis* refers to something done for spite or to get even; hence the sobriquet *tsu-lochis-nick* for a congregation or a synagogue *(shul)* begun only for spiteful or personality reasons. Indeed, one might even refer to early Emanu El and B'nai B'rith as *tsu-lochis-nick* congregations, considering the reasons why those members preferred not to belong to the already established United Hebrew—the "Polish" congregation.

41. *Occident* 12 (January 1855): 527; Makovsky, "History of United Hebrew Congregation," 362–70.

albeit haltingly and painstakingly. First it became expedient to extend the existing lease on a year-to-year basis. After several grave and introspective deliberations, on August 10, 1855, Mr. and Mrs. Simon (Amalia) Abeles and Mr. and Mrs. Moses (Rachel) Morris, as authorized intermediaries for the congregation, purchased from Judge George W. Beirne for $6,240 a lot on the east side of Sixth Street, between St. Charles and Locust, just to the north of the Benton School. Because a small building stood on that lot, some question apparently existed over possible encumbrances to the title. With that question finally resolved, on March 20, 1856, Abeles and Morris and their wives formally transferred ownership of the lot to United Hebrew Congregation.

United Hebrew now faced the difficult task of funding the building. Selling the small structure on the lot brought in $126, a mere pittance compared with the full amount needed, estimated at about $20,000. That was considerably more than the cost of B'nai El, because United Hebrew planned a much larger building, with more elaborate interior furnishings. Minutes of United Hebrew board meetings are replete with plans to raise funds: across-the-board building assessments for members; gift solicitations from patrons and benefactors; subscriptions from the community at large through newspaper advertising; and other appeals to Jews and non-Jews in the city and elsewhere. The women in the congregation pitched in with money-raising affairs. Not until April 1858, however, did United Hebrew feel secure enough to contract with Joseph Hodgeman for the building.

By June 1859 United Hebrew's new building was complete (there was no elaborate cornerstone-laying ceremony as at B'nai El). It was an impressive two-story Romanesque brick structure, fronting forty-two feet on the east side of Sixth Street and extending more than eighty feet in depth. Unfortunately no known photograph of the building exists, either interior or exterior. The building held about nine hundred people in a main sanctuary on the first floor and a women's second-floor balcony. Stained-glass windows on all sides enhanced the atmosphere and the beauty of the structure. In Orthodox fashion, a *bimah* stood near the front of the main sanctuary, facing the pulpit and the Holy Ark on the east wall, which housed the Torah scrolls. During services officers sat on the pulpit, while the cantor conducted services from the *bimah*; the Torah also was read from the *bimah*. Gas chandeliers illumined the building during the evening, aided in the daytime by a stained-glass skylight containing a large Mogen David design. Occupied mostly by the main sanctuary, the first floor also contained several smaller rooms for classroom or meeting purposes, as well as a well-tailored vestibule. In the basement were more classrooms, furnace and kitchen facilities, and toilet conveniences for men and women, as well as living quarters for a synagogue caretaker. Another important feature in the basement was a *mikvah* with necessary accoutrements. The total cost of the building was about twenty-one thousand dollars.[42]

The formal consecration and dedication of United Hebrew's new Sixth Street synagogue was held on June 17, 1859. Since the departure of Rabbi Illowy four years earlier, United Hebrew had remained without a spiritual leader. Unable for various reasons to replace him in time for the dedication of its new home, United Hebrew did, at least, acquire a cantor. On April 3, 1859, the congregation employed Reverend Isaac Ritterman, a native of Krakow, Poland, who had studied music in Vienna. Ritterman immigrated to the United States in about 1855 and served for several years as cantor at the prestigious B'nai Jeshurun Congregation in New York City before moving to St. Louis in 1859. In addition to his cantorial duties (which included organizing a congregational choir), Ritterman also officiated at weddings and superintended United Hebrew's small religious school.

The main speaker at the new synagogue's dedication, however, was Dr. Morris J. Raphall of New York's B'nai Jeshurun Synagogue. A native of Stockholm, Sweden, Raphall was educated in Hebraic and secular studies, earning both rabbinic ordination and a doctorate in philosophy at the hands of some of Europe's outstanding educators. His scholarly productivity in England and the United States for three decades from the 1820s to the 1850s made him one of the preeminent rabbis of the time and a highly sought-after lecturer. Raphall was a staunch supporter of Orthodoxy, but favored a modernized version more appealing to the times. Though a warm personal friend of Isaac Mayer Wise, he unwaveringly opposed Wise and his new American Reform; this may have been an important reason why United Hebrew chose Raphall as its dedicatory speaker.[43]

---

42. When Donald I. Makovsky wrote his master's thesis on the early history of United Hebrew Congregation in 1958, the original walls of the building still stood. The interior, several times gutted and remodeled by various commercial occupants, then housed the Freund Jewelry Company. The entire block was torn down in the 1980s to become an office building and warehouse complex. Meanwhile, from his own observations of the walls standing in 1958, from contemporary descriptions by eyewitnesses, and from reminiscences of some elderly residents of St. Louis, Makovsky reconstructed in his thesis a very good description of the synagogue, especially its interior. Makovsky, "History of United Hebrew Congregation," 419–27. That thesis remains the most detailed account of the early history of United Hebrew Congregation.

43. One of Raphall's most noteworthy achievements was being the first rabbi to preside as chaplain in the United States House of Representatives, on February 1, 1860. The House chamber was "crowded with spectators, who manifested the most intense interest in the proceedings." *Washington Globe*, February 2, 1860, as reprinted in *Occident* 18 (March 1860): 275.

The consecration ceremony was in many ways similar to that conducted earlier at B'nai El. Prominent St. Louis civic and religious personalities of various denominations attended. Elders of the congregation carried the scrolls of the Torah seven times around the synagogue before depositing them in the Ark on the east wall. Traditional Hebrew prayers and hymns were interspersed throughout the program. Rabbi Raphall then climaxed the evening with a stirring and scholarly dedicatory address delivered in English.[44]

In two important respects, however, the United Hebrew dedication differed from the earlier B'nai El event. Unlike at B'nai El, no organ or non-Jewish choir members were present at United Hebrew's ceremony, nor were there any post-service social activities, since it was the Sabbath. These differences indicated how United Hebrew still was adhering to Orthodoxy while B'nai El was moving in the direction of liberalism and eventually Reform.[45]

Thus, in the two decades preceding the Civil War, the St. Louis Jewish community had organized five known congregations, of which two survived (and still exist today), each in its own permanent synagogue building. Both had started as Orthodox, but both already showed tendencies toward liberalization and acculturation, with B'nai El taking the lead.

---

44. Minute Book of the Board of Trustees of United Hebrew Congregation, St. Louis, 163–71; Makovsky, "History of United Hebrew Congregation," 428–50.

45. The "festive ball" of the B'nai El dedication was just that—a "ball" with food, entertainment, dancing, and accompanying festivities. *Israelite,* May 4, 1855. That is quite different from an *oneg Shabbat* following a Friday evening service, normally a rather reserved and modest reception. Even a very lavish *oneg Shabbat* would fall far short of the "festive ball" celebrated by B'nai El.

——— 6 ———

PRE–CIVIL WAR GROWTH
Culture

The growth of the Jewish community in pre–Civil War St. Louis was reflected in more than new congregations, synagogues, and cemeteries. New benevolent associations also reflected that growth. The pioneer in this field, the Hebrew Benevolent Society, had been established in 1842. For a few years thereafter, the Jewish population increased so slowly that one benevolent association proved sufficient. Besides, other relief agencies existed, both public and private, although not specifically to service a Jewish clientele. They included, among others, some long-standing and some organized only recently, such as the Erin Benevolent Society, St. Andrew's Society of St. Louis, the French Benevolent Society, and the German Emigrant Society. Non-Jewish women's eleemosynary associations included the Female Charitable Society and the St. Louis Samaritan Society. Church organizations also provided help for the needy, especially of their own denominations. This included, of course, the Jewish congregations.[1]

Beginning in 1849, however, more charitable associations came into existence. One reason was the sudden upsurge of immigration from revolution-torn Europe. The 1849 cholera epidemic, along with that year's Great Fire, was perhaps an even more important catalyst. On April 15, 1849, "in consideration of the increased number of suffering and destitute members of the Israelite faith who within a short space of time have called upon individuals for assistance," a group of United Hebrew women organized the "Ladies Hebrew Benevolent Association of the United Hebrew Congregation." Their first meeting gathered at the home of Mrs. Joseph Rothan, on Main Street between Chestnut and Pine, where Dr. F. M. Jacobson addressed them about the problems of cholera. One week later Mrs. H. Harris and Mrs. H. Lichtenstein cochaired a second meeting that drew up a constitution and bylaws. Two days later, on April 24, 1849, the

---

1. See especially Ross, "History of St. Louis," and Scharf, *Saint Louis City and County,* vol. 2, 1752–58.

first officers and directors were elected: Mrs. H. Harris, president; Jeanette Samuel, vice president; Mrs. F. M. Jacobson, secretary; Mrs. S. Jacks, treasurer; and Mesdames H. Lichtenstein, S. DeHaan, R. Frank, I. Flateau, and I. Segar, board members. The first known Jewish women's organization in St. Louis, it turned its attention immediately to helping cholera victims. The price proved fearful. Within a few months three of its officers (including Jeanette Samuel, whose husband was president of the congregation, and her mother, Rachel Levy) themselves became victims of the dread disease. Even as they were replaced, though, the women of United Hebrew Congregation continued their doleful work and served valorously throughout the entire medical crisis.[2]

By the mid-1850s, the acceleration of immigration created a need for more relief agencies. In 1855 more Jewish women, "after devoting their energies individually for several years to the relief of the sick and distressed," decided that their efforts might be more effective if they organized formally. Accordingly, on a hot Sunday afternoon, August 5, 1855, about seventy-five women met and organized the "Hebrew Relief Society of St. Louis." Mrs. S. J. Levi was elected president; Mrs. P. Freiburg, vice president; Mrs. M. Abraham, secretary; Mrs. R. Rosenthal, treasurer; and Mesdames S. L. Moses, S. Dunker, P. Hart, A. Haas, and M. Kuhns, trustees. Unlike the earlier United Hebrew women's organization, membership was open to all women. Like the United Hebrew group, the Hebrew Relief Society sponsored a number of projects, including an occasional ball, to raise funds. One project, a "fun" fair, was "the first time Israelitish ladies call[ed] on their Christian sisters to assist them."[3]

Another early women's benevolent group was the "Zion Ladies Association," organized at least by 1858 to benefit the poor and the sick. Among its many fund-raising activities was a Chanukah ball that became for many years a traditional and well-attended social event within the Jewish community. This organization did not limit its help to individuals; in 1858 it loaned B'nai El Congregation two hundred dollars to meet some of its obligations.[4]

---

2. Van Ravenswaay, *Saint Louis*, 390. In 1880 the Ladies Hebrew Benevolent Association merged with the newly formed Ladies' Aid Society organized by Rabbi and Mrs. Henry J. Messing of United Hebrew Temple. It is known today more commonly as the United Hebrew "Sisterhood."

3. *Israelite*, September 21, 1855.

4. *Voice*, December 25, 1902. The Zion Ladies Society no longer exists, nor do any of its records. We know of it only because of occasional mention in the newspapers. The last known reference was dated February 17, 1888, in the *Voice*, when the organization reportedly numbered some 240 members. This group may have been predominantly,

Joining the women's groups and the earlier Hebrew Benevolent Society was the Judah Touro Society. Organized in January 1858 by Rabbi Henry Kuttner (then at B'nai El) to commemorate the *yahrzeit* (anniversary) of the great philanthropist's death, the Judah Touro Society soon became one of the most widely acclaimed and active organizations in the Jewish community. Within a few months its membership had grown to 150 men. Contemporary correspondence suggests strongly that membership of the Hebrew Benevolent Society was primarily United Hebrew congregants and friends, while the roster of the Judah Touro Society consisted overwhelmingly of B'nai El members and their friends. This may be another indication (like the circumstances surrounding the origins of the synagogues) of the fragmentation within the small early Jewish community along national-origin lines.[5]

The various benevolent societies performed many necessary charitable functions, of course, but they also constituted socializing agencies for their members. Fund-raising projects, such as picnics, dances, and dinners, brought Jews together. Members visited the sick and attended funerals, and they arranged for small loans for those who needed ready cash.

Perhaps no organization fulfilled those services more diligently than B'nai B'rith. Started by twelve German Jewish immigrants on October 13, 1843, in the Sinsheimer Cafe in New York City's lower east side, the Bundes-Brueder (League of Brothers, a name soon changed to The Independent Order of B'nai B'rith) grew rapidly. New lodges appeared in cities all over the country. In St. Louis, a group of men met in about 1853 as the "Society of Love and Friendship," expressly to secure funds with which to organize a B'nai B'rith chapter. That effort culminated in 1855 with the chartering of Missouri Lodge No. 22, the oldest existing B'nai B'rith chapter west of the Mississippi River. Because some early records are missing, full details of Missouri Lodge's origins are somewhat unclear. Nevertheless, sometime in 1855 an application for a charter, accompanied by the required fee, was submitted to District Grand Lodge No. 2.[6] On

---

if not totally, made up of B'nai El women. An article in the *Israelite*, June 10, 1859, identified the officers as all members of B'nai El: Babette Friede, president; Regina Maas, vice president; Eva Dattelzweig, secretary; and C. Pfeiffer, treasurer. Curiously, a similar article appearing at the same time in the *Occident* (June 5, 1859) listed those same women as officers of "the new Mount Vernon Association formed by Jewish ladies of St. Louis." There is no other known record of a "Mount Vernon Association" within St. Louis Jewry.

5. Rabbi Henry Kuttner to Rabbi Isaac Leeser, St. Louis, February 8, 1860, in Missouri Box, AJA.

6. The signatures on the application were Louis Schwartzkopf, Zacharias Maas, Emanuel Wahler, Adolph Amson, Herman Block, Isaac Frank, Solomon Sternbach,

August 12, 1855, Missouri Lodge was formally installed in impressive and colorful ceremonies. Its first officers were Louis [Ludwig] Schwartzkopf (who was also *chazzan* at B'nai El Temple), president; Zacharias Maas, vice president; Adolph Amson, secretary; and Emanuel Wahler, treasurer. Other original lodge officers included Simon Harris, Isaac Frank, Herman Block, Joseph Lustig, Solomon Sternbach, Wilhelm Sicher, Levy Stein, and Jacob Block. Zacharias Maas, Simon Harris, and Joseph Katz were the first trustees.

Missouri Lodge's first meeting place was at the home of the St. Louis chapter of the International Order of Odd Fellows, on Chestnut between Third and Fourth Streets (later the site of the Merchants' Exchange). One of their first activities was to establish a "Covenant Fund" for philanthropic use, to which each member contributed fifteen cents every three months. The fund was donated later to B'nai B'rith's Jewish Orphans' Home in Cleveland when that institution was opened in 1868 to care for children victimized by the Civil War. Missouri Lodge conducted its meetings in German in those early years, as did many other Jewish groups. Lodge life centered around social and philanthropic activities, including disaster relief on the occasion of a fire, an epidemic, or a flood, whether in St. Louis or some other location—this was before the American Red Cross came into existence. Missouri Lodge also provided for visitations to the sick and the bereaved. Some of its reactions to antisemitism in St. Louis presaged the later B'nai B'rith Anti-Defamation League.[7]

Although by the Civil War St. Louis Jewry numbered no more than five thousand people, two very telling characteristics of the Jewish community already had emerged: the absence of unity, and the gradual distancing of

---

Henry Block, Solomon Steindler, Joseph Katz, Jacob Wachtel, Levy Stein, Frederic Wolf, Robert Blum, Elias Schnurmacher, Joseph Loebner, Simon Harris, Wilhelm Sicher, Jacob Block, Solomon Marx, Louis Freiburg, Joseph Lustig, Moritz Hoffman, M. A. Taussig, Solomon Stein, Moses Freund, and Solomon Schnurmacher.

7. The early records of Missouri Lodge No. 22 no longer exist. (Extant records go back to November 19, 1893. The author thanks David Blumenthal, a longtime active member of that lodge, for making them available.) Fortunately, though, in 1880, on the occasion of Missouri Lodge's twenty-fifth anniversary, Brother Abraham Kramer published a pamphlet detailing the organization's history. The pamphlet was printed in German: *Kurzgefasste Geschichte der Missouri Lodge No. 22, I.O.B.B., Zu Ehren ihres 25ten Stiftungs-Festes, gefeiert am 12ten August, 1880, Zusammengestellt Von Bruder Abraham Kramer*. The pamphlet was translated later into English by Rabbi Spitz of B'nai El, himself a member of Missouri Lodge and also editor of the St. Louis *Jewish Voice*, and reproduced in that paper in a series of articles that ran for several weeks. *Voice*, August 10, 17, and 24, September 7, 14, 21, and 28, October 5, 12, and 19, and November 2, 9, and 23, 1907, and January 11, 1908. See also *Israelite*, January 1, 1864; *Tribune*, August 13, 1880; *Modern View*, November 14, 1930; *Modern View 25*, 11; and *This Is B'nai B'rith* (pamphlet), 3–8.

many from traditional Judaism. Despite their small numbers and the fact that they lived in close proximity to each other (on the near south side), St. Louis Jews had no cohesive community spirit. It is true that many spoke the same language and had similar backgrounds. But aside from their business and social activities, any group environment that existed was limited to the synagogues, the cemetery associations, and the fraternal and benevolent orders. To be sure, those institutions carried out their functions well, but individually and separately. No central agency, such as a modern-day representative board or federation, existed to coordinate organizational activities or to create an attitude of Jewish *community* performance. That community spirit was several decades in the future. The only common bond within the pre–Civil War Jewish population seemed to be simply that they were Jews. In fact, their German culture and background may have been a stronger bond than their Judaism.

One of the great ironies of American Jewish history, as analyzed by Jewish historian Henry J. Feingold, was that religious freedom in this country may have undermined the very forces and institutions that for centuries had held Jews together and preserved Judaism despite all sorts of adversities. The Jew in America had no fear of an Inquisition, of a state religion that could oppress Jews, or of a government-sponsored pogrom. Of course, antisemitic prejudices existed, but they never carried the imprimatur of government policy. Religious freedom in America removed those outside threats to Judaism that heretofore had required strong internal religious discipline merely to survive and perpetuate the next generation of Jews. "The Jewish worshipper became aware," posited Feingold, "that the security derived from the religious community was not really necessary in the new environment which did not threaten Jews or Judaism. He no longer had to belong, and when that disappeared the raison d'étre for maintaining Jewish communities also vanished. Jewish community life became voluntaristic."[8]

The drive among those German Jewish immigrants to acculturate to their new American environment cannot be overemphasized. At the same time, that process should not be misunderstood. True, to some it meant distancing themselves completely from their Judaic past by abandoning their ancient faith completely: by intermarrying, assimilating, and becoming in fact Christians. Examples included members of the Taussig family (Isidor Bush's in-laws) and others who became prominent in St. Louis circles: the Carrs, the Edgertons, the Von Puhls, the Taylors, the Meisenbergs,

---

8. Henry L. Feingold, *Zion in America*, 106–7. Other Jewish historians who have posited similar observations include Howard M. Sachar, *A History of the Jews in America*, 61–66, and Hasia E. Diner, *A Time for Gathering*, 141, 232–35.

and the Pulitzers.[9] It must be pointed out, though, that those German Jewish immigrants were not alone in that practice. Jews of many lands and environments have abandoned their faith for untold generations, some voluntarily, some by violent forced conversion, lost forever as the Children of Israel.

Furthermore, not all movement was away from Judaism. In 1855 Rabbi Bernard Illowy presided over a conversion in United Hebrew Synagogue in which a woman with seven children embraced Judaism. The ceremony was described as "very solemn and impressive." On another occasion a "German gentleman of education, residing in the county, came to St. Louis to be received in the congregation of Israel." After performing a circumcision on himself, he was examined by a "committee of judges" composed of St. Louis Jews knowledgeable on such matters, who proclaimed him now to be a Jew. The transition was highlighted by the gentleman being "called to the Torah on Sabbath B'Chukosai." On another occasion Rabbi Isaac Mayer Wise was invited to be part of a *Beth Din* (rabbinic court) when "four proselytes were formally accepted in the Synagogue Bene El. . . . The converts formerly belonged to different Christian denominations."[10]

Most German Jews achieved Americanization not by abandoning Judaism, but by maintaining their faith through one of two more acceptable means. One entailed distancing from Judaism, but in varying degrees. In some instances it meant abandoning or modifying certain traditional practices to make it possible for the individual to live more practically in the non-Jewish environment. For instance, for their economic survival, businessmen and laborers found it necessary to work on the Sabbath or on Jewish holidays rather than to observe them as days of rest or festival observation. Maintaining dietary laws became for some impractical or unnecessary when surrounded by Christian neighbors and associates whose lifestyles were different. Many Jews thus distanced themselves from traditional practice, some more than others. They still maintained their Jewish identification, but in varying degrees and as and how it suited them. Many therefore did not belong to congregations, nor did they consider Jewish education important for their children. Bluntly put, they associated very little with anything Jewish. Yet some purchased seats and made rare visits to a synagogue on a Rosh Hashannah or a Yom Kippur, or attended services to recite the *Kaddish* on the anniversary of the death of a loved one. They had their sons circumcised and their children married by a rabbi; they buried their dead in a Jewish cemetery. Except for such minimal

---

9. *Tribune*, November 23, 1883; *Voice*, October 13, 1914.
10. *Occident* 17 (June 1859): 66; *Israelite*, June 22, 1855, April 15, 1859.

life-cycle concessions to Jewish tradition, however, they lived secular lives, creating doubts among many as to whether they were indeed Jews. Yet as far as they were concerned, they unhesitatingly counted themselves as Jewish. Their number is impossible to ascertain, yet occasional estimates indicate that perhaps more than half the total St. Louis Jewish population fell into this category.

Historians who have analyzed the American Jewish immigrant experience have concluded that this separation and disaffiliation resulted from several forces. One was the liberal political attitudes of many German Jews and their concomitant revolt against any religious autocracy or orthodoxy, in many instances a process started or achieved even before those people left their European environs for America. The determination to "Americanize" undoubtedly was another important factor—to throw off their old ways and become like their new American neighbors. Isidor Bush, an astute observer of that experience—and a part of it—warned against going too far in that distancing direction. In spite of the fact that German Jewish immigrants were well-educated persons of reason and intellect, he observed, many experienced difficulties in reconciling their past with their new present and future. What he described as "ultraism"— one extreme or the other—"drives most of our men and principally our leaders to become either hyper-Orthodox or Deists, if not half atheists, and leaves but few in the happy medium." Moving to those extremes, he feared, was "injurious to our progress, to unity and peace in Israel."[11]

A great many St. Louis German Jews took yet a different approach toward Americanization: they embraced Reform Judaism. Unfortunately, Orthodox Jews have viewed Reform as watered-down Judaism, impelled more by social forces than by *halacha* and theology, an expediency for nonobservers to acculturate by emulating Protestant practices but to still somehow claim to practice Judaism. On the other hand, liberal-minded nineteenth-century German Jewish immigrants recognized in Reform a very positive and meaningful form of Judaism that actually fortified them in their Mosaic faith even as it allowed enough latitude to live in an American environment with a clear religious conscience.

The devoutness of those German Reform Jews cannot be overly emphasized. One has only to look at their support for their temples, their dedication to fundamental Reform Jewish principles, their regular attendance at services, and their social consciousness and consideration for their fellow man, Jew and non-Jew, in the form of *tzedakah* and *tikkun olom*. They may not have observed certain practices that Orthodoxy considered

---

11. Isidor Bush to Editor, in *Israelite*, April 11, 1856.

essential; but Reform, after all, viewed those rituals and observances differently. Indeed, one of Reform's greatest appeals to American Jewry was the distinction between Judaism as a religion and "Jewishness" as a sociological phenomenon, a contrast of major importance to nineteenth- and twentieth-century Reform Jews.

Reform within Judaism in America occurred in various ways and stages. Practically every deviation from Orthodoxy aroused considerable dissension, among both rabbis and the laity. In retrospect, though, many of the early differences seem today relatively bland. In fact, the Cleveland Conference of 1855 actually assembled to focus more on unity and cooperation within the practicing American rabbinate, most of whom were still Orthodox traditionalists, than on disruptive theologic topics; it proved, however, to be a springboard to the much more revolutionary Pittsburgh Conference and Platform of 1885, from which emanated those extremely radical principles most often associated with American Reform.[12]

Even though United Hebrew and B'nai El instituted controversial changes as early as the 1850s, those congregations were still considered traditional Orthodox *shuls*. Changes instituted there sought not to establish Reform, but rather to make traditional Orthodoxy more viable to St. Louis Jewry. Thus the organ was introduced into services; but the *mikvah* remained a vital institution in everyday life. Mixed choirs came into existence; yet congregational members considered *kashrus* and the role of the *shochet* among their uppermost concerns. A new prayer book was introduced and many prayers revised and translated into German and English; but women continued to sit in segregated balconies, and men continued to wear head coverings and prayer shawls. Modifications attracted new worshipers; yet nowhere do the minutes of those congregations (until the 1870s) indicate that the changes were deliberate moves toward Reform. They were, instead, modifications toward Americanization, toward a position somewhere between the extremes of inflexible traditional Orthodoxy on the one hand and assimilation or abandonment of Judaism on the other, a position in which members of the particular congregation could feel themselves to be good Americans in a uniquely American environment and also to be good Jews.[13]

---

12. Many excellent works have been written about the development of American Reform Judaism, including a very readable text by Sylvan Schwartzman, *Reform Judaism Then and Now*. Others include Schwartzman's *Reform Judaism in the Making;* David Philipson, *The Reform Movement in Judaism;* and W. Gunther Plaut, *The Growth of Reform Judaism*.

13. Periodic favorable comments about those modifications by Rabbi Isaac Mayer Wise, and unfavorable observations by Rabbi Isaac Leeser, can be found in the *Israelite*,

Many have concluded that Reform replaced Orthodoxy in the German Jewish synagogues and that almost total secularization came to characterize St. Louis German Jewish lifestyle. That did not occur prior to the Civil War; the changes were gradual and moderate, albeit controversial as any changes are wont to be. It was only after the Civil War years that the German Jewish population evolved overwhelmingly into either Reform or unaffiliated, in both instances quite secular. At the same time, Orthodoxy never disappeared from within St. Louis's German Jewry, and at least two new clearly German Orthodox *shuls* were established during the Civil War era.

Describing pre–Civil War Jewry in St. Louis, then, presents somewhat of an enigma. Although identified among the top fifteen Jewish communities in the country by the outbreak of the war, that distinction had to be based on numbers only. Little or no communitywide consciousness existed. Jewish organizations served their individual beneficent purposes, each active within its own milieu. Individuals were caught up in joint drives for economic survival and Americanization. Indeed, studies by historians of American immigration prior to the Civil War indicate that the Jewish experience was in those respects very similar to that of other European ethnic groups.[14] Yet occasionally circumstances stirred some Jews, regardless of observance or affiliation, into what might be perceived as a Jewish consciousness. Maybe St. Louis Jewry was not yet prepared to organize and cooperate communitywide; nevertheless, in the decade prior to the Civil War it took some important steps in that direction.

At least one phenomenon that Jews shared with other immigrant groups was exposure to hatreds and prejudices reminiscent of what they had fled in Europe. Large numbers of Irish and German newcomers, especially in the rapidly growing urban centers, led to overcrowding and related sociological difficulties associated with expanding city populations. As a result, long-standing and deep-seated nationalist, cultural, and religious prejudices overflowed from the Old Country and spread like a malignant cancer into American life: English versus Irish, German versus Slav, Catholic versus Protestant, privilege and class versus egalitarianism. Passions were enflamed by economic fears, some real and some imagined, as newcomers from Europe eagerly sought land and

---

December 10, 1858, July 23 and 26, 1859, August 14 and November 20, 1863, and in the *Occident* 17 (July 1859): 96, and 21 (June 1863): 139–40.

14. See, for instance, Leonard Dinnerstein, Roger L. Nichols, and David M. Reimers, *Natives and Strangers;* William V. Shannon, *The Irish in America;* and John Higham, *Send These to Me.*

jobs in order to establish roots in the New World, but were perceived by those already here as a threat to their own tenuous security in American society.[15]

For Jewish immigrants, the bigotry came from two directions: if they weren't the "dirty Dutch," they were the "dirty Jews." One individual who grew up in St. Louis in the 1850s later reminisced how as a child he had attended a mission Sunday School in the Soulard market house, "from whence I brought home tracts and other missionary propaganda. Even at that time, 1855, the baiting for Jewish souls was rampant, and, strange to say, devout Jewish families, like my own, were trapped, chiefly because of ignorance of English. Of course this ceased as soon as my parents grasped the situation; only, however, to be succeeded by environments entirely removed from Jewish congregational influence."[16]

This dissentient xenophobia peaked during the 1840s and 1850s with the emergence of the American or "Know-Nothing" Party. Though other minorities also were denounced, in truth Catholics seemed to be the main target of Know-Nothing abuse. New York, Ohio, Massachusetts, and Connecticut passed laws placing restrictions on Catholic Church properties. Violence and riots engulfed Baltimore for a time in the mid-1850s. The Know-Nothing presidential candidate, even though he came in third in the balloting, received about 870,000 votes in the 1856 election. Candidates at local levels won several governorships and numerous important positions in municipal and county administrations. In St. Louis, voters elected Luther M. Kennett as mayor in 1850, and Washington King to the same post in 1855.[17]

Viewed for some time anyway as a rough-and-tumble frontier community, St. Louis witnessed a number of bloody brawls and riots in the 1840s and 1850s, some attributable to the sheer lawlessness of the frontier, some to the bitter feelings generated by the antiforeignism prevalent at the time. Although no episodes of outright violence were associated specifically with anti-Jewish feelings, a number of nonviolent incidents clearly demonstrated at least an insensibility to the feelings of Jews, if not latent or overt antisemitism. In 1854, for instance, a small but zealous Jesuit group published a circular called *Gottesfreund* ("Friend of the Lord"),

---

15. This discordant phenomenon has always been a part of the American scene, an unfortunate by-product of a free society. Evidence of it can be found even in early American history during the colonial period.

16. "Reminiscences of a Former St. Louisan," in *Voice*, November 6, 1914.

17. Luther Kennett's election as mayor of St. Louis in 1850 resulted from more than Know-Nothing sentiment in his favor. For more on Know-Nothingism and antisemitism, see Nathan C. Belth, *A Promise to Keep*, 17–22.

urging Jews to convert. "They not only are ashamed of their religion," the paper stated, "but also scoff at it and blaspheme their God, and totally denying their nationality, are given to atheism and rationalism." It was an obvious reference, of course, to those Jews whose American acculturation had led them to very secular views of Judaism.[18]

Shortly thereafter, in 1855, a controversy developed over a "Sabbath Law" that made it a misdemeanor to engage in certain commercial enterprises "on the first day of the week, commonly called Sunday." Exemptions from that restriction included "any person who is a member of a religious society by whom any other than the first day of the week is observed as a Sabbath." This seemed to recognize those Jews who wished to observe their Sabbath on Saturdays. Nevertheless, most St. Louis Jews conformed with the ordinance and closed their businesses on Sundays. However, a small number of observant Jews closed their establishments on Saturdays and remained open on Sundays, maintaining, of course, that the exemptions of the law applied to them. Making use of a convoluted legal opinion drawn up by the city attorney, Know-Nothing Mayor Washington King persuaded those Jewish merchants to close on Sundays rather than face criminal charges. There is no record, either in newspapers or in court records, of any immediate response from individual St. Louis Jews, let alone a community response. As a matter of fact, pressures to Americanize and to not antagonize the non-Jewish population seemed to have carried the day—temporarily, at least. But visiting St. Louis in 1856, Rabbi Isaac Mayer Wise was outraged by the "unjust, despotical and unreasonable Sunday Laws which disgrace this state and this city." He urged a Jewish initiative to bring the matter before the Supreme Court of the United States, where, he felt, "justice will be done." But nothing happened for a few years because, as Wise observed later, "wealthy" Jewish merchants "do not care about it, and the middle class are unable to carry their point before the tribunals of justice."[19]

---

18. *Israelite*, September 15, 1854. For more on the unsettling events in St. Louis during that period, see Primm, *Lion of the Valley*, 173–86; Scharf, *Saint Louis City and County*, vol. 2, 1835–55; and Charles Van Ravenswaay, "Years of Turmoil, Years of Growth: St. Louis in the 1850s," 303–24.

19. *St. Louis Republican*, May 9, 1855; *Israelite*, May 18, 1855, July 25, 1856, January 8, 1858, and April 15, 1859. A similar issue arose in Cincinnati. The Jewish newspaper there actually cautioned Jewish merchants against any actions that might backfire against them. Even though the Ohio law exempted "those whose religious belief compels them to keep their Sabbath on Saturday," the newspaper urged Cincinnati Jews not to open on Sundays; and for those who did, not "to become offensive in the eyes of other citizens" because "it may possibly do harm to the [Jewish] community." *Israelite*, May 18, 1855.

Some might stigmatize Jews who remained open on Saturdays and closed on Sundays as being more concerned with their public image than with their religious rights. In fairness to them, though, one must consider the harsh realities of making a living in an overwhelmingly Christian society. Nevertheless, one chronicler of St. Louis history has written that the city "never followed a pattern of solemn Sabbaths" anyway. Rather than create an atmosphere of Christianity on Sundays, its residents saw it as a day for relaxation and amusement. "Grog shops, beer houses, fruit stores, cigar stores, saloons, ten-pin and bowling alleys, livery stables . . . the whole town was wide open. Steamboatmen, planters, slave-traders, cotton merchants and sugar dealers, in town to do business, found plenty of ways to while away their leisure hours. Like the restless young bloods of the city, they patronized the glittering bawdy houses and gambling dens, and won or lost vast sums at the race tracks near the town. . . . The old French and Southern families looked on in complacense, secure in their solid social structure; blue-nosed New Englanders found it impossible to suppress the vices with which they were unwilling to temporize. St. Louis was becoming a big city, and the vulgar lived cheek and jowl with the proper."[20]

In 1859 three members of B'nai El Congregation, led by their president Meyer Friede, remained open on Sundays instead of Saturdays in a clear attempt to challenge the discriminatory statute. One of them, Joel Mannheimer, was arrested and fined ten dollars and costs in a municipal court. Friede thereupon called a general meeting of the B'nai El membership, which then passed a series of resolutions protesting the court action and calling for its overturn. Unfortunately, incomplete court records leave unclear just what legal steps then ensued. But when a similar case came up in the St. Louis municipal court later, the judge held that anyone who observed Saturday as the Sabbath could not be required to do the same on Sunday. The Sunday closing law clearly violated some citizens' constitutional rights, in this case the rights of observant Jews. Apparently the action taken by Meyer Friede and B'nai El had been successful.[21]

Nevertheless, most Jewish merchants continued to keep their businesses open on Saturdays. Visitors to St. Louis as well as local rabbis often noted the lack of Sabbath observance, by not only those in business but also those who faced no such economic pressures. Writing in the *Occident* in 1860, one observer decried that "keeping the Sabbath is not as general as it should be." Businessmen in St. Louis, as elsewhere, he wrote, simply

---

20. Van Ravenswaay, "Years of Turmoil, Years of Growth," 310–11.
21. *Israelite*, August 26, 1859.

could not afford to close on Saturdays, and accordingly "have relapsed into their former indifference."[22]

Finally, though, in the summer of 1862, Rabbi Henry Kuttner of B'nai El Congregation reported almost exultantly that "the beginning has been made. The firm of Marx and Schoen observe the Sabbath and their business is completely closed. Also two baker members of my community now observe the Sabbath." That such recognition was accorded to Sabbath observance indicates how unusual it must have been in St. Louis at the time.[23]

While many Jews distanced themselves from traditionalism, some did actively defend their rights as Jews. Perhaps this new activism came as a reaction to the bigoted nativism of the period; perhaps it was an offshoot of the humanitarianism of the antislavery movement; perhaps it resulted from the increase in the Jewish population and a resultant feeling of confidence due to that growth. At any rate, by the late 1850s a number of St. Louis Jews had begun to speak up for their religious rights and freedoms. It was still not communitywide Jewish action, but at least it was a step in that direction.

Probably the beginning of that community feeling occurred in 1857, two years before Friede fought the Sunday closing law. It was manifested in the form of a protest to a treaty between the United States and the Swiss Confederation. That treaty had been negotiated under the administration of President Franklin Pierce and ratified by the Senate in 1855. Although the treaty provided for reciprocal equal protection of citizens of the two countries, it also exempted from that right anyone whose particular situation conflicted with local laws. It so happened that the municipal law in several Swiss cantons overtly discriminated against Jews by excluding them from certain specified industries. Throughout the United States—in New York, Baltimore, Cleveland, Nashville, and Chicago—Jews protested that the treaty negated rights of American Jewish citizens even as it protected the rights of non-Jews. On October 25, 1857, members of United Hebrew Congregation held a protest meeting, appealing to President James Buchanan to nullify the treaty because it violated the constitutional

---

22. *Occident* 18 (June 1860): 87.

23. Henry Kuttner to Isaac Leeser, St. Louis, June 6, 1862, in Missouri Box, AJA. In 1887 B'nai El's Rabbi Spitz, decrying the lack of Sabbath observance, cited specifically Section 1.579 of the "Sunday Closing Law" as clearly exempting Jews from that statute. Nevertheless, economic rather than religious considerations continued to influence Jewish merchants to conduct their businesses on Saturday. M. Spitz to Editor, St. Louis, June 8, 1887, in *Jewish Free Press*, June 17, 1887. For more on the Sunday Closing Law issue, see Morton Borden, *Jews, Turks, and Infidels*, 103–27.

rights of Jewish American citizens. Although the federal government did nothing immediately, at least some St. Louis Jews had demonstrated community concern and had taken collective action—perhaps the first such group action within the St. Louis Jewish community.[24]

Shortly thereafter a local incident provided another occasion for Jews to speak out. A sixty-five-year-old, very ill Bohemian-born Jew, Paul Dietrich, was taken to the Sisters of Charity Hospital by his landlord, a Mr. Barclay. There Dietrich extracted a promise from another Jewish patient, Moritz Gutmann, that if he (Dietrich) died in the hospital, he should receive a Jewish burial. One evening, as Dietrich's health faded and he lay in a partial coma, a priest baptized him, despite Dietrich's feeble signs of refusal and Gutmann's protests. A few days later, when Gutmann was released from the hospital, he brought the news of what had transpired to the presidents of the two synagogues, Adolph J. Latz of United Hebrew and Meyer Friede of B'nai El. The two went immediately to the hospital, only to learn that Dietrich had recently expired. When they sought to provide Dietrich with a Jewish burial, the prioress refused to give them his body, alleging that he had died a Catholic. Latz and Friede immediately protested to Mayor Oliver D. Filley, who in turn contacted Bishop Peter Kenrick, head of the Catholic hierarchy in St. Louis. Sympathetic but unwilling overtly to turn Dietrich over to Jews, Kenrick found a way out of his dilemma by having the prioress give up the body not to Latz and Friede, but to the landlord, Barclay. That done, Latz and Friede had no difficulty in acceding to Dietrich's wish for a Jewish burial. The ensuing funeral occurred, according to a newspaper account, "amidst one of the largest concourses ever seen in St. Louis." Once again portions of the Jewish population had acted collectively and demonstrated a growing community consciousness.[25]

Perhaps a landmark incident leading to energizing Jewish community action was the infamous Mortara Affair. In 1858 Edgardo Mortara, the ailing six-year-old son of a prominent Jewish family in Bologna, Italy, was surreptitiously baptized by a Catholic household servant. The youngster was then abducted and placed in the House of Catechumens in Rome, an institution maintained by the Catholic Church to house potential converts. The case resulted in a universal outcry, including protests from Emperor Napoleon III of France, against blatant infringement of religious freedom and parental rights. In 1859 Sir Moses Montefiore, president of the London

---

24. *Occident* 15 (December 1857): 430–31. See also Borden, *Jews, Turks, and Infidels,* 82–94.

25. *Occident* 16 (January 1859): 503, and 16 (February 1859): 554; *Voice,* January 25, 1889.

Board of Jewish Deputies (the institutional representative body of British Jewry), went to Rome in person to seek the child's release, but the Pope rejected all petitions. A scandal of international proportions, the Mortara incident led to the founding in 1859 of the Board of Delegates of American Israelites (the first nationwide representative body of American Jews) and in 1860 of the Alliance Israelite Universelle (the first modern international Jewish association). Their primary function was to strive for civil rights and religious freedom for Jews all over the world. The creation of those organizations proved to be milestones in modern Jewish history. Among other outcomes, they aroused a new awareness of "peopleship" among those Jews who had been distancing themselves from traditional Judaism, for even as they rejected ritual practices, many Jews found humanitarian and familial substitutes (*tikkun olom*) verifying them as a viable part of the Jewish people.

In St. Louis, the Mortara incident brought an outcry from not only the synagogues but also other elements of the Jewish community. Special meetings of United Hebrew and B'nai El members resulted in resolutions of protest from those congregations to President Buchanan, urging him and Secretary of State Lewis Cass to instruct U.S. diplomatic representatives throughout Europe to use their influence on the Papacy. The Missouri Lodge of B'nai B'rith passed a similar resolution. All three backed their words with financial support to a New Orleans–based agency of Mortara aid. Equally significant in St. Louis history, copies of the protest resolutions, in German and in English, were reprinted in St. Louis newspapers, as well as in the nationally circulated Jewish newspaper *Occident*. A separate protest was penned by Rabbi Kuttner of B'nai El, the only rabbi then serving in St. Louis. Unfortunately, all efforts to save young Mortara proved futile, partially because at the time world Jewry lacked a strong enough unified voice. In St. Louis, too, no one institution spoke for the Jewish community, but the action by some St. Louis organizations was a forerunner of broader communitywide cooperative action.[26]

---

26. Henry Kuttner to Isaac Leeser, St. Louis, December 5, 1858, in Missouri Box, AJA; *Occident* 16 (February 1859): 542; *St. Louis Evening News*, December 5, 1858. For more on the Mortara Affair, see the article in the *Encyclopedia Judaica*, vol. 12, 354–55, and accompanying bibliography, especially Bertram W. Korn, *The American Reaction to the Mortara Case, 1858–1859*, and Borden, *Jews, Turks, and Infidels*, 54–58. An earlier Jewish cause célèbre of the mid–nineteenth century was the infamous "Damascus Blood Libel" incident of 1840, which aroused serious concern in Jewish communities in the United States. But there were so few Jews in St. Louis at the time—enough only for a periodic *minyan*—that it is no surprise the Jewish community had no reaction. Nor is there evidence of any reaction by any individual St. Louis Jew.

The reactions to the Swiss treaty and the Mortara Affair reflect a very significant development within St. Louis Jewry. Up to the late 1850s, actions by Jews in St. Louis centered on their own domestic problems and needs. Concerns were internal, associated with events transpiring locally and involving only local groups, and none seemed to demand community-wide action outside that particular group. Perhaps that reflected a Jewish community so small that its problems still could be dealt with by component groups or even individuals. Perhaps, on the other hand, it reflected a small community already divided by discordant forces.[27] Those who initiated cemeteries and benevolent societies intended them primarily for their own membership, although services were made available to outsiders, for a price. Indeed, despite numerous pressures that should have brought Jews together, history records many instances of disagreement and division among that "stiff-necked people," even when the cost proved detrimental to all. For St. Louis Jewry to coalesce over the Swiss treaty and the Mortara incident, then, marked an important step toward unified action and the emergence of meaningful self-representation. Perhaps, too, it demonstrated that an external issue aroused a broader response than did a matter of purely local or internal concern.[28]

The absence of a communitywide mind-set prior to the Civil War suggests that Jewish life in St. Louis centered on the home and on individual institutions. Unfortunately, little evidence exists to characterize home life. One can only assume that any description would range from homes steeped in traditional Judaism to those in which religion counted little or not at all. Families associated with United Hebrew and B'nai El were exposed at the very least to the holy days and festivals. Congregational records reflect celebrations of Passover, Succos, and Shavuos, for instance, and observance of such "minor" days as Tisha B'Av and Chamisha Osor B'Shvat. Purim and Chanukah were celebrated, as were, of course, Rosh Hashannah and Yom Kippur and the Sabbath. The congregations arranged for merchants to have *matzos* for Passover; they saw to it that a *shochet* was available to provide kosher slaughtering facilities, and that

27. Henry Kuttner to Isaac Leeser, St. Louis, March 13, 1865, in Missouri Box, AJA; "Reminiscences of a Former St. Louisan," in *Voice*, October 13, 1914.

28. Early in 1860 word reached St. Louis of many Moroccan Jewish refugees of the war between Spain and Morocco seeking asylum in Gibraltar. An international movement led by Sir Moses Montefiore sought relief. At a meeting held at United Hebrew Synagogue, St. Louis Jews raised funds for that cause. Participants in the effort included Rabbi Henry Kuttner, Meyer Friede, Israel E. Woolf, Isidor Turk, Henry Myers, W. C. Myers, and G. L. Ensel. Contemporary records associate them with both United Hebrew and B'nai El Congregations. *Occident* 17 (March 1860): 300.

a *mohel* could circumcise newborn sons. But there is no data to indicate how widely those services were used in Jewish homes, or how many households participated in those practices.

Indeed, any evidence pertaining to Jewish life seems to be subjective. The reason, of course, lies in the age-old conundrum of what one means by Judaism. One stressing traditional *halachic* and cultural Judaism could readily conclude that Judaism exercised very little hold on the lives of an overwhelming number of St. Louis Jews. If, on the other hand, one accepted the liberalization of *halacha* and viewed favorably the widespread acculturation and "Americanization"-oriented practices of so many German Jews, then the number of those considered to have lived religious lives would be increased considerably. Thus one Jewish resident of pre–Civil War St. Louis later wrote:

> People, as a rule, performed their religious obligations, and due to the class and intimate social relationship which prevailed, any infringement on religious customs was made conspicuous, and the transgressor was taken to task. . . . "Frenchtown" and a goodly section below it was a ghetto without gates, and people spoke of each other by their Hebrew names, and with one another in Bohemian and German and "Loshon Kodesh" [the "holy language" Hebrew]. Little wonder that they did not master the English. In those days people went to Shul in the early morning, on Yom Kippur, emerging only when the proverbial three stars appeared in the heavens. . . . [The] scene is engraved in my memory; these men, wearing their hats, the "tallis" over their shoulders, the humming of the worshippers intent upon their devotions, . . . facsimiles of that pure and virile Jewish race who helped Solomon build the Temple.[29]

In contrast, certain facts suggest a lesser influence of religiosity among St. Louis Jews. No "Jewish" bookstore existed where one could purchase prayer books, prayer shawls, menorahs, or other accoutrements singularly associated with Jewish practice. The city's lone rabbi had to order them from a dealer in Philadelphia as late as 1865. Boardinghouses or restaurants that provided kosher food existed in other midwestern communities (such as Cincinnati and Louisville), but none could be found in St. Louis. One might expect that with a Jewish population approaching five thousand by 1860, in a city emerging as one of the major metropolitan centers in the country, St. Louis Jewry would have provided those facilities for its own residents or for transients, especially the increasing number of traveling businessmen.[30]

---

29. "Reminiscences of a Former St. Louisan," in *Voice*, October 13, 1914.

30. Henry Kuttner to Isaac Leeser, St. Louis, June 16, 1858, February 8, 1860, and March 13, 1865, in Missouri Box, AJA. Conclusions pertaining to "Jewish" bookstores,

Several rabbis observed the St. Louis scene somewhat disenchantedly. Rabbi Isaac Leeser, in his visit to the city over the 1851–1852 winter, saw a St. Louis Jewish community divided along lines of national origin— Polish, German, and Bohemian. "It is extremely difficult," he opined, "to bring about a good understanding and a concert of action between persons who have come together, without any previous knowledge of each other, from all parts of the world, and who have, many of them, only lately settled in a distant city removed from any influence from abroad." Still, he anticipated optimistically, "the sense of the people is after all right, and it could easily be led into a proper channel, with a little forbearance and some patience." Nevertheless, he noted, except for the creation of congregations, little had been done to educate future generations, "except teaching a little Hebrew." An advocate of traditional Judaism, Leeser decried "affairs in their condition" in St. Louis, referring not only to ethnic divisions but also to tendencies toward liberalism. He hoped the situation would improve. "There are in St. Louis," he mused, "elements of greatness, provided only they cultivate among themselves union and mutual forbearance."[31]

Five years later Rabbi Isidor Kalish noted little change within St. Louis Jewry except increased numbers. Rabbi of Ahavas Achim Congregation in Cincinnati, Kalish toured midwestern Jewish communities as correspondent for the *Israelite,* the journal edited by Reform champion Isaac Mayer Wise. Visiting St. Louis in March 1856, Kalish described Judaism there in markedly less enthusiastic terms than his description of Jews elsewhere in the Midwest. "Judaism is represented here," he wrote, "by emptiness and death; namely by empty synagogues and burial grounds." Sabbath morning services were "very thinly attended." He felt that more concern existed among St. Louis Jews about building larger and newer synagogues than for filling those that existed. Yet, Kalish observed, one should not conclude that "egotism and materialism" ranked above "public spirit," or that an "over-powering inclination for the pursuits of gain" transcended "subjects which could ennoble the heart." Encouragingly, Kalish observed, "I found in this city also a great many, who are glowing with a true love for Judaism, and long for a place where the mind and heart are edified."[32]

When Rabbi Wise visited the city in 1859, he observed: "Religion is still at a low ebb in St. Louis." An outspoken advocate of religious toleration,

---

boardinghouses, and restaurants are based on a perusal of advertisements in the *Israelite,* the *Occident,* and St. Louis newspapers of the 1840s and 1850s.

31. *Occident* 10 (April 1852), reprinted in Marcus, *Memoirs of American Jews,* vol. 2, 76–78.

32. *Israelite,* March 14, 1856.

he attributed one reason for the lack of Sabbath observance to the Know-Nothing Sunday closing law. "None observe the biblical Sabbath," he charged, because that discriminatory legislation "excludes Israelites from the benefit of keeping their Sabbath without losing two days a week." Reform champion Wise was disturbed by the distancing of so many St. Louis Jews from Judaism—a process, he observed, that had begun in many families in Germany and Austria. He accused them of lacking the "moral courage" to stand up for their faith. "They are ashamed of their origin," he charged, and "they are ashamed of themselves." But Wise aimed his sharpest condemnation at the hypocrisy of many lay leaders who purported to be traditional Jews: "men who keep no Sabbath, eat what they please, and do what they should not; still they are set mad when a piece of an old prayer is omitted or an outworn custom is abrogated . . . and would rather see the last spark of Judaism extinct before they think of improvements and reforms." All these forces, Wise observed in 1859, caused that "low ebb" of Judaism in St. Louis.[33]

Often a low ebb can be blamed on the lack of leadership. That was not the case in pre–Civil War St. Louis, at least as far as lay leadership was concerned. Lay leaders of the various institutions included the likes of Isidor Bush and Meyer Friede, as well as Adolph J. Latz, Joel Mannheimer, Nathan Abeles, Louis Schwartzkopf, Frederick Dattelzweig, and Abraham Weigel, all highly regarded as citizens and as Jews. Visitors to St. Louis repeatedly mentioned them as in the forefront of whatever advances St. Louis Jewry achieved. Considering the lack of leadership within St. Louis Jewry for the three crucial decades after Joseph Philipson settled in the city, the lay leaders who appeared during the following three decades must be considered most favorably. Nevertheless, despite that emerging leadership, observers still overwhelmingly considered the Jewish community—the "followership"—to be at a low ebb, undoubtedly due to the strong push toward secularized "Americanism" to replace the "old ways" of the "Old Country."[34]

If any shortcomings in leadership existed, they were in rabbinic leadership—not because the rabbis lacked those important qualities, but rather

---

33. Ibid., April 15, 1859.

34. See dispatches of correspondents and memoirs in *Israelite,* May 4 and September 28, 1855, July 25, 1856, April 30, 1858, July 23, 1859, August 8, 1862, and July 24, 1863, and *Jewish Free Press,* November 19, 1886. That lay leadership was purely local. Historian Bertram Korn observed that in those days, "if American Jewry lacked a single essential element, it was national leadership by laymen possessed of vision and ability." Bertram W. Korn, *American Jewry and the Civil War,* 5. That kind of lay leadership did not appear on the national level until the turn of the century.

because the rabbis in St. Louis were so few and served for such short times. In the entire pre–Civil War era, only two rabbis ministered to St. Louis Jewry. Together they served for no more than a few years, hardly time enough to establish any sort of rabbinic direction, let alone leadership. One should not overlook that despite its burgeoning population, St. Louis was still a western city, far from the larger eastern Jewish enclaves, and therefore not the most enticing post for many rabbis. Furthermore, since at that time all rabbis still were trained in Europe, few were prepared for the American-oriented, "no-longer-fully-Orthodox-but-not-yet-Reform" Judaism demanded by so many of the German Jewish immigrants and especially by those who had settled in St. Louis. One has only to recall the difficulties encountered at United Hebrew by one of the era's most eminent rabbis, Bernard Illowy, who stayed for only one year. Prior to Illowy's arrival in 1854, lay members of the congregation discharged religious functions normally performed by a rabbi, with paraprofessionals employed occasionally for specific duties. The board of trustees designated laymen as *ba'alei t'filah* (readers and leaders of services); it also sanctioned certain lay individuals to perform weddings and to act as *shochet* and *mohel*. In 1844 one S. Samuels was hired as *shochet* and Torah reader. Board minutes of 1845 mention a Mr. Hirschfeld being employed as *chazzan* and *shochet*, but apparently he remained for only a brief time. In 1849 the congregation acquired the services of Nathan Davidson, also as *chazzan* and *shochet*, but he too stayed only briefly.

In 1850 Edward Meier came to United Hebrew, having served previously as *chazzan* at Rodeph Sholom Congregation in Philadelphia and at B'nai Jeshurun in New York. Meier remained until 1853, a comparatively lengthy tenure, during which time he served United Hebrew as *chazzan*, *shochet*, and *mohel*; he also performed weddings. Meier established a rudimentary system of religious education, which consisted mainly of teaching a few boys some elementary Hebrew in preparation for their *Bar Mitzvah*. When financial stresses forced the board of trustees to reduce Meier's salary, he resigned and was replaced by Herman Kohn, who stayed in the position for one year. Then in 1854, with finances in better shape, United Hebrew finally employed a full-time ordained rabbi, Illowy.[35]

With Illowy's departure, United Hebrew remained for two years without a rabbi until March 1, 1857, when it hired Henry Kuttner. Kuttner

---

35. Minutes of the Board of Trustees of the United Hebrew Congregation, 86–112; United Hebrew Board Minutes, 1842–1855 (microfilm), AJA; *Occident* 6 (March 1849): 113.

came to United Hebrew from Honesdale, Pennsylvania, where he had ministered since 1852. For reasons not clear from the otherwise copious United Hebrew records, trustees of the congregation employed Kuttner as *chazzan* and *shochet* rather than as a "rabbi." Of course that was true of others hired earlier, except for Illowy. We know, though, that Illowy was indeed ordained; the others apparently were not. In Kuttner's case, even though he was called "Rabbi" and had served as such in Pennsylvania prior to coming to St. Louis, there is no evidence that he was ordained. But that was not unique to Kuttner. Many scholarly and learned Jews who came to America lacked ordination, yet they assumed the rabbinic title and became spiritual heads of American congregations. Whether that created any difficulties for Kuttner cannot be determined, as he remained at United Hebrew for only a few months. During his brief stay he focused more on sorely deficient religious education than on typically ministerial rabbinic duties. It was during that time, too, that United Hebrew committed itself to a new building, and perhaps that contributed to his disenchantment. For whatever the reasons, Kuttner remained at United Hebrew for only a few months and then resigned. He was immediately employed by B'nai El as its rabbi.[36]

After Kuttner's departure, United Hebrew remained without rabbinic leadership for seven years, until 1864, when the congregation employed Rabbi Henry Vidaver. In the meantime, lay members continued to perform various religious functions. In 1859, however, with the imminent completion of its new building on Sixth and St. Charles, United Hebrew sought to unveil its new edifice with an impressive dedicatory service. After auditioning and interviewing several cantors, the board hired Isaac Rittermann to be its new *chazzan*. Born in Krakow, Poland, and trained in music in Vienna, Rittermann had served for more than two years as *chazzan* of B'nai Jeshurun Synagogue in New York, where he excelled as both cantor and choir director. As in Kuttner's case, United Hebrew records leave unclear Rittermann's exact status. He had responded to a United Hebrew advertisement in the *Occident* seeking a *chazzan* and a *ba'al ko'rei* (Torah reader) who could also superintend an elementary Hebrew school. The program for the consecration of the Sixth Street *shul* identified him as "The Rev. Isaac Rittermann, Minister to the Congregation," suggesting that he might also have performed quasi-rabbinic duties. Clearly, though, he was not an ordained rabbi. Indeed, the only rabbi associated with pre–Civil

36. *Israelite*, April 30, 1858; *Jewish Free Press*, September 9, 1885. Born in 1820 in Schroda, Posen, Henry Kuttner came to America in 1852 and became rabbi of the congregation in Honesdale, Pennsylvania, before coming to United Hebrew in 1857. See Henry Kuttler File, AJA.

War United Hebrew other than Illowy (and perhaps Kuttner) was Morris J. Raphall, the eminent New York Orthodox rabbi who delivered the guest dedicatory sermon at the 1859 consecration service.[37]

B'nai El, meanwhile, had experienced its own birth and growth problems, and like United Hebrew went through its early years without rabbinic leadership, relying also upon lay members for those religious services. Thus, when B'nai El organized in 1852, Louis Schwartzkopf volunteered his services as *chazzan*, a function he continued to perform for five years. Rabbi Illowy occasionally ministered for B'nai El during his brief tenure at United Hebrew; he also delivered the 1855 dedicatory sermon at the consecration of the Sixth and Cerre synagogue. Shortly thereafter Illowy terminated his association with United Hebrew, but before leaving the city he conducted High Holiday services at B'nai El.

Following that very brief association with a rabbi, B'nai El reverted to lay leadership, with Schwartzkopf continuing in his capacity as *chazzan* until 1857. Then once again B'nai El benefited from disaffection within United Hebrew. On August 2, 1857, the B'nai El board of trustees appointed Kuttner, just resigned from United Hebrew, as "Hazan and religious teacher." Again, as at United Hebrew, the terminology in board minutes about his employment raises unanswered questions about Kuttner's exact professional status. Nevertheless, later congregational records indicate quite clearly that Henry Kuttner served B'nai El in the capacity of rabbi, with that title, until 1870, and that he then returned to United Hebrew from 1870 to 1875, also with that title.[38]

By the outbreak of the Civil War in 1861, then, only two rabbis, Illowy and Kuttner, had ministered to the St. Louis Jewish community, neither of them for long enough to have much of an impact, although Kuttner would make his mark in time. In his thirteen years at B'nai El, Kuttner advocated and endorsed enough modernization (such as revised prayers, mixed choirs, the organ) to harmonize rather than clash with the "Americanizing" tendencies of most St. Louis Jews, even though he aspersed many of those "acculturizing influences" as a lack of religiosity rather than as liberalism. Still, he avoided the confrontations Illowy had experienced. Kuttner worked for gradual modernization, championing within his congregation those reforms that he could live with, but at the same time resisting radical religious change. There is no doubt that during

---

37. Minutes of Board of Directors of United Hebrew, 1858–1860; Henry Kuttner to Isaac Leeser, St. Louis, February 2, 1860, in Missouri Box, AJA; *Occident* 15 (October 1857): 357, and 17 (March 1859): 1.

38. See history of B'nai El series in *Voice* (December 5, 1902–August 14, 1903, and October 20, 1916–September 14, 1917).

Kuttner's ministry, innovations adopted at B'nai El paved the way for that congregation to become a Reform institution in the 1870s.[39]

A significant development within the St. Louis Jewish community in pre–Civil War years was the beginning of Jewish religious education. No organized Jewish education existed prior to the creation of United Hebrew in 1841. Even then, nothing in that body's records indicates any educational activities for almost a decade, until after the congregation had moved into its first permanent building, the renovated North Baptist Church on Fifth and Green. Meanwhile, parents taught their children in the home or hired a private *melamed* (tutor). United Hebrew employed several paraprofessionals in the 1840s as *chazzan* or *shochet*, but none are identified as teachers (although some might have been employed privately as a *melamed* by individual families). The first evidence of any congregational education was a rather disparaging observation by Isaac Leeser in 1852, bemoaning the "little having as yet been done for religious instruction, except teaching a little Hebrew by the Rev. Edward Miers [sic] . . . at such hours when his other duties give him leisure and opportunity."[40]

That changed with the arrival of Rabbi Illowy in 1854. What he did with Jewish education in St. Louis can be perceived better in the broader context of Jewish education in America. Observing the biblical precept that "thou shalt teach them diligently unto thy children," Jews historically have made religious education a high priority. Especially after the dissolution of ancient Israel, generations of Jewish diaspora parents taught their offspring, either tutorially or by some other method. Early Sephardic Jews in America, for many years too few in number to maintain schools, sought out private tutors. As congregations came into existence, their synagogues became the centers of both informal and formal religious education, either by a professional *melamed* or in classes instructed by volunteers. Before public schools came into being, these institutions taught religious subjects and secular subjects, just as did church schools in other faiths. Secular and religious education was loosely organized, however, and developed very irregularly and almost haphazardly. Congregations imported scholars from Europe and the West Indies, but these scholars were often viewed more as rabbis and cantors than as educators. Some wealthier Jews established private academies, as did wealthy members

---

39. Writing in his newspaper about the early history of B'nai El, Rabbi Spitz observed that "to all intents and purposes" the congregation was a "Reform House of Worship" by 1862, even though women still sat segregated in the balcony. Nevertheless, B'nai El did not become Reform officially until the 1870s. *Voice*, March 30, 1917.

40. *Occident* 10 (April 1852): 55–56.

of other faiths, but often only their own small circle of children benefited. Most Jewish children attended very poorly structured and equally poorly taught congregational schools, or they received individual instruction from a parent or a hired *melamed.*

German immigrants of the early nineteenth century brought with them two additional concepts of Jewish education that had developed over the past three centuries in central and eastern Europe: the *cheder* and the *talmud torah.* The *cheder* was basically a private elementary school, usually conducted in the home of a *melamed.* Very poorly organized or supervised, many became no more than teacher-centered coteries of a private *melamed* and his followers. The *talmud torah,* on the other hand, was better structured and supervised because it was more of a community school. (Many European Jewish communities enjoyed considerable autonomy and authority in internal affairs within their ghetto walls, and this applied especially to Jewish religious education.) *Chevrai talmud torah* (Talmud Torah societies) supervised local schools, established curricula, hired and paid teachers, and even tested pupils. Funds came from tuition, educational taxes levied by the Jewish community, or both. Of course these institutions were not all the same; differences and modifications resulted from circumstances of time and place. Historically, though, no one system proved more effective than the others.

By the time a rudimentary Jewish community had emerged in the 1840s in St. Louis, then, European and American Jews had used several approaches to educating the young. The American environment, however, offered a completely different milieu. In contrast with Europe, where state churches and state-supported religious schools predominated, so many faiths proliferated in colonial America that no one faith achieved state support. Whether secular or religious, education remained in private hands, often organized and administered by a given church hierarchy or organization. By the early nineteenth century, however, that private and parochial education began to give way to public tax-supported institutions where all children, regardless of religion, could attend (racial segregation continued, of course, well into the twentieth century). That transition occurred very slowly, however—the first public elementary school opened in St. Louis in 1838—and church-centered education remained for a long time, with Christian principles an integral part of the curriculum. In fact, despite the American notion of separation of church and state, secular public education curricula continued for a long time to show a distinctly Protestant flavor.

In the 1840s and 1850s, many German Jews, eager to acculturate, became keenly interested in conducting their religious education in parochial day schools like those of their Protestant neighbors. Secular as well as religious subjects made up the curriculum in Jewish day schools. Schools followed the pattern of the *talmud torah,* but with costs defrayed by the sponsoring congregations and the families attending. A prototype Jewish day school was established in 1842 in New York City by B'nai Jeshurun Congregation, offering a secular elementary education accompanied by instruction also in Hebrew and in topics of Jewish orientation. Within the next few years, similar parochial day schools appeared in several eastern Jewish communities. But as rapidly as that concept spread, so did it also fade away, due primarily to the rise of the free, tax-supported, religiously neutral public schools. By the mid-1850s some Jewish day schools already had closed their doors; by 1870 almost all had disappeared. Most religious education in German Jewish communities was conducted thereafter in "Sunday schools," the first of which was founded by Rebecca Gratz in Philadelphia in 1838. Sunday schools met not only on Sunday mornings but also on Sabbath (Saturday) afternoons. The Sunday school movement gained considerable momentum in the 1860s and 1870s, due mainly to the lessened role by then of Hebrew in Reform Judaism and to the success of Protestant Sunday schools all across the country.[41]

When Rabbi Illowy came to United Hebrew in 1854, then, the parochial day school concept had just become the newest innovation in American Jewish education. Within a few months Illowy established such a school, the St. Louis Hebrew School. It did not last long, but it stands as the beginning of formal Jewish education in St. Louis.

Incomplete and conflicting records leave a very unclear history of that first religious school. Illowy was the superintendent, and also taught Hebrew and (in German) Bible history and ethics. He received no pay because funds were limited. A second teacher, identified only as a "Mr. D.," handled secular subjects; his pay amounted to twenty-five dollars per month. There is no record of the students who attended or where classes were held (since Illowy ran the school, perhaps it was housed in United Hebrew's synagogue at Fifth and Green). The curriculum included subjects in "the Hebrew and German branches of study" and in "the English branches." Only two members of the board of Hebrew School directors are identified, Isidor Bush and Samuel L. Moses.

The St. Louis Hebrew School lasted only three months, from November 1854 to February 1855. Directors conducted the first quarterly examination of students on Sunday afternoon, February 6, 1855. Only a sparse crowd

---

41. A concise yet detailed survey of the unfolding of Jewish education through the centuries can be found in the *Encyclopedia Judaica,* vol. 6, 414–42. An interesting sidelight is the resurgence in the last half of the twentieth century of the Jewish day school concept.

attended, suggesting a rather small student enrollment. The students showed "considerable progress" in the courses associated with Hebrew and German; they did "all that could possibly be expected" in the secular "English branches."

Nevertheless, immediately following the examination, the board opted to change the day school to a Sunday school format. In an address before the group, Bush explained why. One reason was finances, an ever-present problem. A satisfactory school necessitated more teachers and material than the Hebrew School could offer, and there simply was not enough funding to meet the need. More important, though, were the pedagogic and philosophic issues of private parochial education versus public secular education. By 1855 at least three public elementary schools already existed in St. Louis, each employing from six to ten teachers. With the city growing so rapidly, more and better teachers and more and better schools seemed inevitable. A poorly staffed and meagerly financed parochial school could not educate its students nearly as well in secular education. Furthermore, Bush maintained, a parochial school that taught secular subjects actually undermined the primary objective of parochial education, which was to provide Hebrew and religious instruction. By expending efforts and money on secular education, the school diminished the time and energy it could devote to religious education. A staunch supporter of public education, Bush convinced his fellow Hebrew School board members that Jewish youth would be better served by dropping the concept of a parochial day school and replacing it with "good Sabbath, Sunday, and evening schools for religious and Hebrew instruction only."[42]

Sunday schools at both United Hebrew and B'nai El replaced the St. Louis Hebrew School. Little is recorded about the program at United Hebrew, except that one did exist. Since the congregation no longer had a rabbi, one can presume that whoever served as *chazzan* or *shammas* (sexton) also provided religious education. Apparently all did not go well; board minutes contain repeated references to dissatisfaction with what was transpiring. Confirming those difficulties, Isaac Mayer Wise, writing in 1859 about a visit to St. Louis, noted that religious education conducted by Henry Kuttner at B'nai El "is all there is done in the way of instruction in the whole city of St. Louis."[43]

---

42. *Occident* 13 (May 1855): 79–89; *Israelite*, July 25, 1856. For more on the history of education in St. Louis, see Selwyn K. Troen, *The Public and the Schools: Shaping the St. Louis System, 1838–1920.*

43. *Israelite*, April 15, 1859. Additional observations on educational problems at United Hebrew can be found in the United Hebrew File, AJA.

Indeed, Kuttner's educational leadership brought excellent results. When he started at B'nai El in 1857, he described conditions for youth education as "pitiful." One of his first endeavors was to establish a religious school, for which he ordered Hebrew grammar and spelling books, prayer books, and sundry supplies from Philadelphia. Kuttner conducted classes at the Sixth and Cerre synagogue four times a week, at first in German, and then, after a year-long struggle with his board of directors, in English. After the examinations in the spring of 1858, one overseer observed that "the seed of God is zealously planted in the pure, young hearts," and that "a better time is coming, a time when our children here also will know and love the religion of their fathers." Within two years Kuttner's school had grown to at least fifty children who, in the examination at that time, "read the Hebrew grammatically, translated prayers into English, and so, too, the Bible and knew Biblical history and whatever else a Jew ought to know." Such exuberance may have been somewhat inflated; nevertheless Kuttner earned many kudos from inside and outside his congregation for his educational achievements.[44]

One achievement was the introduction of the Confirmation service in St. Louis. Jews today equate Confirmation with a graduation exercise on the holiday of Shavuos (Feast of Weeks) representing the successful completion of a Sunday school or religious school curriculum. Confirmands range from ages fourteen to seventeen, depending upon the particular school program. That is different from Confirmation as originally conceived. Confirmation appeared in the German Reform movement in 1810 as a supplement to the traditional *Bar Mitzvah*, the ceremony in which a thirteen-year-old boy assumed the status of adult for religious purposes within the Jewish community—that is, he could count as a member of a *minyan*. The focal point of that ceremony entailed the boy reading a designated passage from the weekly Torah portion and then rendering a commentary about it. Early Reform leaders felt such a limited ceremony did not demonstrate adequate intellectual growth from childhood to maturity, and so they mandated more before a supervising rabbi could "confirm" the boy into adulthood. Because of their belief in the religious equality of the sexes, early European Reform rabbis soon included girls as eligible for both the instruction and the ceremony, a move that of course incurred additional opposition from traditionalists. At any rate, early

---

44. Henry Kuttner to Isaac Leeser, St. Louis, February 8, 1860, in Missouri Box, AJA. Additional correspondence between Kuttner and Leeser relating to Jewish education in St. Louis can be found in *Israelite*, April 15, 1857, April 30, 1858, July 23 and August 2, 1859, August 12, 1862, and July 24, 1863; and in *Occident* 16 (May 1858): 168, and 17 (March 1859): 1, 96.

Reform rabbis perceived Confirmation and *Bar Mitzvah* as concurrent ceremonies for an individual at age thirteen. By the time Rabbi Max Lilienthal officiated at the first Confirmation in America—in 1846 in New York—the ceremony had become a group exercise, appropriately on Shavuos, the holiday commemorating Moses receiving the Law on Mount Sinai. In time, some Reform congregations abandoned the *Bar Mitzvah* ceremony completely and replaced it with Confirmation; others kept both, but with more emphasis on Confirmation.

Thus, in 1859 the oldest son of Moses Friedman of B'nai El Congregation, "having passed his thirteenth year, was publicly confirmed in the synagogue. . . . The candidate was examined in our religion, and replied in full to every question asked, so accurately and firmly that it astonished the whole congregation." This is the first known record of a *Bar Mitzvah* in St. Louis. That same year, 1859, on the holiday of Shavuos, Rabbi Kuttner conducted the first Confirmation at B'nai El, a service that included both boys and girls. Four years later, on Shavuos in the year 1863, United Hebrew Congregation conducted its first Confirmation, a class of twenty-five boys and girls instructed by a Reverend Loewenthal. By that time, obviously, both B'nai El and United Hebrew had moved from their original Orthodoxy well on their way toward Reform.[45]

---

45. *Israelite*, July 23, 1859, August 8, 1862, and June 5, 1863.

7

Pre–Civil War Growth
Economic and Civic Roles

Although one observer would reminisce that prior to the Civil War, "no one heard of St. Louis Jewry," it would be a mistake to assume that Jews confined their activities to their own narrow circle and to affairs strictly Jewish. In truth, although Jews did not comprise large numbers, they engaged in a variety of activities in St. Louis. Perhaps one of the most important was their growing role in the city's expanding business life. True, no Jews were included among the city's "movers and shakers" in those days. The power structure in the half century prior to the Civil War included bankers, businessmen, and politicians who were usually French, German, Irish, or descendants of earlier pioneers from Kentucky and Virginia. Joseph Philipson may have exercised a little influence during his early prosperous years when St. Louis was still not more than a burgeoning village, but certainly none after his financial demise in the early 1820s. Indeed, as late as the 1880s, only two Jews, Isidor Bush and Meyer Friede, wielded any appreciable influence outside the small Jewish community.

Most Jews were relatively unnoticed ordinary citizens who unobtrusively went about their everyday business along with their equally unnoticed ordinary non-Jewish neighbors. Some, of course, were in and out of the city as itinerant peddlers. Some were skilled craftsmen; a few were professionals, such as lawyers or doctors. Most engaged in small retail and wholesale merchandising and lived satisfying and fulfilling lives in that small-business milieu. Some, though, attained greater business success, and with it, prominence in social and civic ventures within not only Jewish circles but also the broader St. Louis community. The early Philipson enterprises typified the ventures of many later St. Louis Jews. Abraham Myers, for example, opened a retail general merchandising store on Main Street. Louis Krafter and Jacob Emmanuel operated a grocery store on Prune Street on the near south side. Abraham Weigel and Solomon J. Levi were partners in a clothing store; so too were Nathan Abeles and Joseph

Kohn. Hyam C. Cohen sold groceries in his store on North First. Adolph J. Latz and his brother Simon had their clothing business in a store on Front Street. Adolph Abeles and Charles Taussig established a very popular general store at Park and Carondelet that became known widely as "The Jew Store," or more commonly among the Germans in the neighborhood as "Der Juden Store"; its regular clientele spread as far as Jefferson County.

Others deserve at least brief mention as pre–Civil War pioneers who constituted the foundation for later St. Louis Jewry. Some achieved very little, and left not much more than their names on early cemetery records or tombstones. Others achieved more, and have a living heritage of descendants scattered today throughout the country as well as in St. Louis.

Samuel Jacks, for instance, came to St. Louis in 1834 from Wreschen, near Posen, Prussia. One of the twelve founders of United Hebrew Congregation, he became a successful clothing merchant in St. Louis before moving to Wichita, Kansas, where he continued in the same trade. When he died on August 31, 1888, his body was returned to St. Louis, where he was buried in Mount Olive Cemetery, which he had helped to found.[1]

His cousin Morris Jacks, born in Graetz, near Posen, in 1831, came to St. Louis in the early 1840s, where he too engaged in the mercantile business for a few years. In 1849, succumbing to the lure of gold, he trekked overland to California. Unable to make a go there, he returned to St. Louis and opened a profitable clothing establishment on the levee, where he remained until 1874. During that time he also belonged to one of St. Louis's early volunteer fire companies, Missouri No. 11. In 1866 Jacks married Traphenia Levi, daughter of Solomon J. and Matilda S. Levi, both pioneer St. Louis Jews. After he retired from the mercantile business, Jacks became a mortuary clerk in City Hall until 1893, when he was promoted to chief clerk of that office. In 1895 Jacks was appointed to the Sanitary Department of the Board of Health, where he served until poor health forced him to retire in 1901. He died at his home at 5176 Fairmount on Yom Kippur Day of 1904, at the age of seventy-four, and was buried in Mount Sinai Cemetery.[2]

In 1840 Adolph Klauber, a native of Bohemia, established an iron and metal business in St. Louis. He and his wife Betty raised their family in St. Louis, where Klauber was one of the founders of B'nai El Congregation. Their son Daniel, born in 1858, later joined in the metal business, and both father and son became well-known members of the Jewish community.[3]

---

1. *Voice,* September 7, 1888.
2. Ibid., September 23, 1904.
3. *Modern View,* January 31, 1935.

Adolph Isaacs, born in Posen, Prussia, in 1823, came to St. Louis in 1842 and lived a full and productive life until 1904. For many years he operated the "Oak Hill" clothing store, where he employed many immigrants and taught them the trade. An early member of United Hebrew Congregation, he also became active in B'nai B'rith, the Masons, and the Hebrew Benevolent Society. He died at his residence at 4105 Maryland just before his eighty-first birthday, leaving a widow and thirteen children (seven sons and six daughters), four of whom continued to live in St. Louis. Isaacs was buried in Mount Olive Cemetery.[4]

Another pioneer St. Louis Jewish merchant was Isaac Baer (he was not related to the Baers who later made the family name synonymous with department-store merchandising in St. Louis). Born in Alsace-Lorraine on July 10, 1818, Baer served four years in the French army before he came to St. Louis in 1848 by way of New Orleans. The sea voyage alone took nine very trying weeks, typical of the tribulations encountered by so many immigrants of that time. Baer settled in southern St. Louis County on the Carondelet Road and opened a clothing store at 1914 South Broadway, where he remained in business until he retired in 1880. At the outbreak of the Civil War in 1861, Baer was forty-three years old; nevertheless, he joined the Home Guard and was with that unit at Camp Jackson when it severely blunted Confederate aspirations to control St. Louis and the vital Mississippi River supply line. Baer retired from business in 1880, but he remained active in Jewish affairs, especially in B'nai El Temple and in Missouri Lodge B'nai B'rith. In his later years he reputedly walked fifteen to twenty blocks and drank three or four whiskey toddies daily. For whatever reason, longevity seemed to bless his family; his father (who remained in Europe) lived to be ninety-two, and his four sons (Bernhard, Charles, Henry, and Joseph) each lived into their eighties. Isaac Baer died on March 28, 1915, at age ninety-six, and was buried in Mount Sinai Cemetery. At the time of his death, he was reportedly the oldest person living in St. Louis.[5]

The 1850s brought an increase in St. Louis Jewry and a corresponding rise in the number of Jews in the city's business community. Adolph Meyer established the Phoenix Livery Stable at 1334 South Seventh Street, near Park Avenue, where he boarded horses. That inevitably led Meyer into conducting funerals, and for at least three decades he became the unofficial "Jewish undertaker" for most of the community. In 1853 Michael Eisenstadt founded a jewelry manufacturing and jobbing company that

---

4. *Voice*, October 21, 1904.
5. Ibid., July 16, 1909, and April 2, 1915; *Modern View*, May 2, 1915.

bore his name, a firm carried on by his son Samuel. Leon Helman, born in Germany in 1819, came to St. Louis in 1857 after living in Memphis for ten years and established a profitable cotton business. By the turn of the century he too became an active and prominent member of the St. Louis Jewish community. Emil Seidel learned the cabinet maker's trade in his native Saxony. He came to St. Louis in the 1850s and prospered in the manufacture of office and bank equipment and house interiors.[6]

Morris Rosenheim came to this country in 1849 at age twenty-two from a small village near Stuttgart, Germany. Like many others, he sought refuge from the political and social upheavals convulsing Germanic Europe. Two years later, though, he returned to his hometown to marry his childhood sweetheart, Matilda Ottenheimer, and brought her back to America with him. They lived briefly in Philadelphia, where Rosenheim engaged in the mercantile business with his brother. In 1853 Rosenheim and his wife moved to St. Louis. There the enterprising young man established a small millinery firm, Rosenheim and Cook. That firm was succeeded soon by a new partnership with Leo Levis, which in turn expanded to become the Rosenheim, Levis and [W. A.] Zukoski Mercantile Company. That partnership lasted successfully until 1893, when Rosenheim retired from the business, at which time it was incorporated as Levis-Zukoski Mercantile Company, by then a world-renowned millinery establishment. Rosenheim had started the business in a small shop on Main Street, from which it moved to a store on Fourth between Locust and St. Charles. Later the firm moved into larger quarters at the corner of Ninth and Washington, and finally to four adjoining seven-story structures at 1113-15-17-19 Washington Avenue, facilities suitable for an enterprise reputed to be the largest millinery establishment in the United States. Rosenheim gave much to community charitable work, at large as well as within the Jewish community. Above all, though, he was a devoted family man. When Morris and Matilda Rosenheim celebrated their fiftieth wedding anniversary in 1901 at their home at 3806 Westminster Place, they were blessed with the presence of their ten children and numerous grand-children and great-grandchildren.[7]

Jonas Meyerberg, born in Westphalia, Prussia, came to St. Louis in the early 1850s at the age of twenty-three and joined his brother in a small millinery concern. A few years later Meyerberg bought out his brother and organized a new firm, Meyerberg and Rothschild. This too became

---

6. *Tribune*, June 2, 1881, and November 10, 1882; *Voice*, May 25, 1905; *Modern View*, April 25, 1919; Gill, *St. Louis Story*, vol. 1, 236.

7. *Voice*, July 26, 1901; *Modern View 25*, 135; Ernest D. Kargau, *Mercantile, Industrial and Professional Saint Louis*, 587–88.

a well-known and well-reputed St. Louis mercantile institution. When Meyerberg died in 1905, the press eulogized him as "one of the moving spirits of the St. Louis Jewish community."[8]

Robert and William Goldstein, both born in Prussia, came to America in their teens, to Natchez, Mississippi. They survived the devastating yellow fever epidemic of 1853 (many of their relatives died), and two years later came to St. Louis. At first they worked for others in the clothing business. In 1858, though, they went on their own, establishing R. and W. Goldstein, a wholesale clothing business. It grew to be one of the most successful firms in that field. Both brothers became active in Jewish community affairs, but self-educated William Goldstein was especially prominent. He was one of the organizers and then president of Shaare Emeth Temple. He helped found and was an inspiring leader of the Hebrew Free and Industrial School; he was also a guiding spirit behind the Alliance night schools. The latter two organizations were vital acculturating and educational institutions established to help the great wave of eastern European Jewish immigrants who flocked to St. Louis in the late 1800s and early 1900s.[9]

Some early Jews found a niche in the financial sector of the St. Louis economy, although realistically none could be referred to as either financiers or bankers. Jacob Rosenbaum, for instance, was among the incorporators of the St. Louis Mutual Fire Insurance Company in 1851. Isaac Rosenfeld was among nine incorporators of the State Savings Association organized in 1856 under an act of the Missouri state legislature. He was the institution's first cashier.[10]

Among those Jews who were part of the St. Louis business scene before the Civil War, one who later became very highly regarded was Isaac Fuld. Born on April 13, 1834, in Frankfort-on-Main in Hesse, Germany, Fuld came to St. Louis in 1853. Like many others, he started a small clothing business; it eventually grew to be the very successful Fuld-Goodwin Mercantile Company. Fuld's major attainments, however, were in areas other than business. Raised an Orthodox Jew in Germany, his first religious affiliation in St. Louis was with B'nai El at its Sixth and Cerre site. In the 1860s, however, he joined a group that considered B'nai El too conservative and helped organize the first Reform congregation in St. Louis, Shaare Emeth Temple.

Though never prominent in political circles, Fuld was a devoted Republican and a staunch supporter of Abraham Lincoln. He attended

---

8. *Voice*, June 2, 1905.
9. Ibid., February 17 and November 10, 1905.
10. Scharf, *Saint Louis City and County*, vol. 2, 1340, 1397, 1417.

the Republican convention at the "Wigwam" in Chicago in 1860 where Lincoln was nominated, and for the rest of his life Fuld devotedly carried a campaign button of Lincoln the presidential candidate, without the beard he grew later.[11] A week after that convention, Fuld met the future president in person in Springfield, Illinois, where both happened to be staying overnight at the St. Nicholas Hotel, and they chatted amiably until the wee hours of the morning. In February 1861, Fuld visited several eastern cities to purchase goods for his business. By then Lincoln had been elected, several Southern states had seceded, the country was on the brink of civil war, and rumors were rampant that attempts would be made to assassinate the president-elect when and if he dared to go to Washington for an inauguration. On March 3, the day before Inauguration Day, Fuld was in Baltimore, and planned to go to Washington for the great event, but a business friend convinced him not to go because of anticipated violence. Fuld always regretted that he allowed himself to be persuaded to stay away from that historic inauguration.

Fuld's Civil War recollections also included Ulysses S. Grant. He recalled seeing Grant as a poor tradesman before the war, trying to sell a wagon-load of wood near the Old Courthouse in St. Louis; then as General-of-the-Army Grant; and even later, at the end of the war, with General William T. Sherman at the dedication of the Thomas Hart Benton statue in Lafayette Park.

Fuld and his wife, the former Babette Pfeiffer, whom he married in 1863, worked for many Jewish organizations in St. Louis. Their religious activities centered around Shaare Emeth and its affiliate groups. Fuld also gave much of his time and energy to Missouri Lodge B'nai B'rith. In 1925, shortly before Fuld died at his home at 3618 Lafayette, a St. Louis newspaper opined that he was at that time not only the oldest living Jew in St. Louis but also the oldest member of B'nai B'rith in the world.

Like many other St. Louis Jews, Isaac Fuld was a longtime patron of the St. Louis Symphony Orchestra. In fact, he attended his last concert only a week before he died. On Sunday afternoon, November 22, 1925, at the same time that Fuld's funeral was taking place, the Symphony was performing a regularly scheduled concert. Conductor Rudolph Ganz interrupted the program and announced to the audience that at that very moment one of the Symphony's most supportive patrons was being laid to

---

11. Fuld left that campaign button to his son William, who later presented it to the Missouri Historical Society in St. Louis, where it was prominently displayed for many years alongside the Charles A. Lindbergh artifacts. For a long time, too, the Society also displayed a large framed picture of Isaac Fuld. *Voice*, April 16, 1920; *Modern View*, August 1, 1930.

rest in Mount Sinai Cemetery. In his honor, Ganz and the orchestra inserted into the program Handel's "Largo," one of Fuld's favorite compositions. It was a singular tribute, the only time such an honor has been accorded by the St. Louis Symphony Orchestra. "A sudden hush came over the audience," reported a St. Louis newspaper, "and the occasion was indeed a solemn one."[12]

Of the numerous business firms established by Jews in St. Louis prior to the Civil War, one stands out as perhaps the most familiar and prominent in the city for more than a century to follow. Its name became associated with—indeed, synonymous with—the bakery business of St. Louis: Freund.

Moritz and Jetta Freund came to St. Louis from Bohemia during the post-1848 German Jewish immigration wave, seeking refuge from Europe's political and social upheavals. With them came their two young sons Leopold and Simon; three more children were born in this country. Sailing first to New Orleans, the Freunds came up the Mississippi River to St. Louis, where they settled in the "Bohemian Hill" area on the near south side, popularly known today as the Soulard area. It was a neighborhood then heavily populated with Bohemian immigrants, and so the Freunds found themselves in friendly environs. For a while they lived in the home of Isaac Rindskopf, whose son later would be known widely in the livery business and then in the funeral business. Although a baker in Bohemia, Moritz Freund first earned his living in St. Louis as a peddler of dry goods and associated notions and accessories. He was concerned enough about his religion to become an early member of B'nai El Congregation; indeed, he was among those who signed the original charter in January 1853. (He and his family and their descendants remained active in B'nai El Temple for many years; as late as 1986, in fact, the congregation named a new wing the Walter Freund and Eleanor Freund Activity Center.)

In about 1855 or 1856, the Freund family took up residence at 913 Soulard. There, in a wood-fired stove in the cellar of their home, Jetta Freund baked bread for her family, a daily chore common for many housewives since time immemorial. But there was something special about her Bohemian-style rye loaves, and soon friends and neighbors asked her to bake for them. As the requests increased, Moritz and Jetta concluded that a return to baking promised greater rewards than peddling. Thus was born the Freund Baking Company. Thus, too, was introduced Freund's "Old Tyme Rye," a bread that soon became one of the most popular

12. *Voice*, April 16, 1909, April 15, 1910, and April 16, 1920; *Modern View*, November 20 and 27, 1925, and October 1, 1930; *Modern View 25*, 11.

staples sold in grocery stores in St. Louis and eventually all across the country.

The Freunds converted the front room of their home into a store, and sons Leopold and Simon, then only eleven and nine years old respectively, delivered baskets of bread to customers. Soon baskets were replaced by Freund wagons that delivered larger orders to an ever-widening market. Family tradition has it that an early supplier of wood for the baking ovens was none other than Ulysses S. Grant, then a struggling young farmer and tradesman who lived in the nearby south-county Affton area. From the outset the bakery was a family enterprise. Jetta and Moritz did the baking; Moritz and the boys did the selling. Of course, as the volume of business increased, additional bakers and other employees were hired.[13]

The bakery remained at the Soulard location for more than six decades, with several physical additions (prosperity enabled the family to move to more affluent personal living quarters). In 1896 a devastating tornado struck the Soulard area, killing more than three hundred people. The bakery was in the center of a widespread area of destruction, but somehow the building remained mostly intact, withstanding extensive outside damage. Despite harrowing experiences, those inside the building survived. Within a short time the bakery was back in operation, even amid wrecked factories and homes, and it continued to produce its tasty products. As business expanded, in 1921 the Freund family purchased a larger facility at Taylor and Chouteau, near the center of the city. There the bakery blanketed the neighborhood with an almost perpetual and distinctive flavor of fresh-baked bread. Travelers through that part of St. Louis long remembered that mouth-watering aroma and a huge billboard advertising popular Freund products.

The bakery remained in the family for four generations, run by a succession of sons and in-laws. By the 1970s, as family members followed other interests and went into other businesses, the bakery finally lost its family identity, and in 1972 it was taken over by an outside corporate baking organization. After more than a century of being St. Louis's most widely known baking institution, the enterprise faded into St. Louis history. But it had left an indelible mark.[14]

---

13. Freund Bakery newspaper advertisements often appeared in German as well as in English: "Lebkuchen und Pfeffernuess" for sale at the "Freund's Baekerei." *Voice*, December 12, 1900.

14. B'nai El File, AJA; *Tribune*, December 29, 1882; *Voice*, November 28, 1901, January 15, 1909, and June 23, 1916; *Modern View*, September 5, 1924, and April 10 and November 17, 1931; Irving Gersten, "The Freund Story," 182–91; Patricia L. Jones, "What Ever Happened to Bohemian Hill?" 22–31.

Another pre–Civil War business that became widely known and respected was the Louis Bauman Jewelry Company. Louis Bauman was born on March 27, 1812, in the village of Hessdorf, Bavaria, where his grandfather and father had been successful merchants. Young Louis, however, became a watchmaker, and he quickly gained local renown as an exceptionally skillful craftsman. In 1838 he immigrated to the United States, settling first in New York, where he engaged in the jewelry business. There, too, he married Marianna Friede; the marriage eventually produced eight children. The young couple moved to Mobile, Alabama, where Bauman followed his trade as a jeweler. In 1844 a yellow fever epidemic forced the family to move again, this time to St. Louis. With his wife's brother Meyer Friede, Bauman opened a small jewelry shop in a frame building at Fourth and Pine. Before long he expanded to larger quarters on Market Street between Main and Second, where he established an enterprise believed to be the first wholesale jewelry house west of the Mississippi. Then tragedy struck with the Great Fire of 1849. His business was destroyed; a large iron safe survived the fire, but when it was opened, all its contents had been ruined by the heat. Like many others, though, Bauman rebounded, and before long Louis Bauman and Company prospered again, first at the Market Street location, and then on Fifth Street (Broadway), where for many years it continued to be a widely known wholesale and retail jewelry landmark. "A narrow door and a small window constituted the front of this place," wrote a St. Louis business historian, "and it can be said that from this modest retail business emanated the largest wholesale and jobbing house in the watch and jewelry line ever established in this city."[15]

Through all those years Bauman remained an active and contributing member of B'nai El Temple, as well as of the Masonic order and other charitable organizations. He retired from the business in 1872 and turned its operations over to his sons Solomon and Meyer. Two sons-in-law, Meyer A. Rosenblatt and August Kurtzeborn, and a third son, Samuel H. Bauman, later came into the business (Rosenblatt left it shortly to become Collector of the City of St. Louis). For almost ten years after retiring, Bauman actively continued his charitable and temple associations. Then in 1881, at the age of seventy, he died at his home on the corner of Second Carondelet and Utah. In 1882 the family-owned business was incorporated by Bauman's heirs as the L. Bauman Jewelry Company, and it continued as one of the country's oldest and most famous wholesale jewelry houses. Eventually, though, non–family members acquired the company's stock, and control passed out of the hands of the family.

---

15. Kargau, *Mercantile, Industrial and Professional Saint Louis,* 578.

Although no members of the Bauman family are directly associated with it today, the present Bauman-Massa Jewelry Company in St. Louis can be traced to the small firm established in 1844 by Louis Bauman.[16]

In the late nineteenth and early twentieth centuries, when St. Louis became a center of the jeans trade, Marx and Haas Clothing Company was acknowledged as a leading house in that branch of the mercantile business. Solomon Marx came to St. Louis in 1853, and in 1855 opened a small clothing shop on North Third Street. His company did well, necessitating moves to larger quarters, first to Main Street, then to Fifth and Washington, to 616 Seventh Street, to Tenth and Lucas, and eventually to a large custom-designed, multistoried building at the southwest corner of Thirteenth and Washington, described as "one of the most desirable localities on this principal thoroughfare of the city." In 1893 the firm was reorganized and incorporated as "Marx and Haas Clothing Company," but with family members maintaining controlling interest. Employing more than two thousand workers and distributing more than a million garments per year throughout the country, Marx and Haas had an important impact upon the St. Louis business scene by the turn of the century.[17]

These are but some of the businessmen and establishments illustrative of a significant contribution by many Jews to the economic growth of St. Louis. Many others, of course, would come along later. Thanks to the general growth and prosperity of St. Louis business during the 1840s and 1850s (especially because of the city's favorable strategic position in westward expansion), many businesses profited and prospered. Some might attribute their success to merely being in the right place at the right time: America's expanding economy, one might posit, proved uniquely suitable and profitable for those engaged especially in the wholesale and retail distribution of consumer goods. Yet for every one who succeeded, others failed, Jew and non-Jew. None can deny, though, that the ethic of hard work and perseverance aptly suited those resolute Jewish immigrants who established their businesses in pre–Civil War St. Louis and who eventually played a significant role in the city's economic growth.

Some years later, Samuel Bowman, a longtime St. Louis resident, listed an "honor roll" of what he called the "best known" Jewish merchants in St. Louis by the Civil War. His roster of wholesale merchants included:

---

16. Author's interview with Hayden Fisbeck of Bauman-Massa Jewelry Company, St. Louis, September 8, 1987; Louis Bauman File in Director's File, Missouri Historical Society, St. Louis; Hyde and Conard, eds., *Encyclopedia of the History of St. Louis*, vol. 1, 119–20; Kargau, *Mercantile, Industrial and Professional Saint Louis*, 577–79.

17. *Voice*, July 2, 1909; Kargau, *Mercantile, Industrial and Professional Saint Louis*, 598–600.

Suss, Obermeyer & Wise	*Dry Goods*
Joseph Weil & Brother	*Dry Goods*
Joseph Baum & Company	*Shoes*
Henry Shulman & Company	*Shoes*
Kramer & Loth Gents'	*Furnishings*
Judell & Platt Gents'	*Furnishings*
Frankenthal Bros. Gents'	*Furnishings*
Marx & Haas	*Clothing*
R. & W. Goldstein	*Clothing*
Kaufman, Baer & Co.	*Clothing*
M. A. Rosenblatt	*Jewelry*
Louis Bauman & Co.	*Jewelry*
J. Meyerberg & Co.	*Hats & Caps*
L. E. Green & Co.	*Millinery*
Rosenheim, Levis & Co.	*Millinery*
Mandelbaum, Furth & Co.	*Grocers*
Bush & Taussig	*Grocers*
Freund & Loebner	*Bakers*
Strauss & Lowenstein	*Millinery*
Wertheimer-Swarts & Co.	*Shoes*
Jacob Strauss Saddlery Co.	*Harness*
Reilly & Wolfert	*Horses and Mules*
Jonas Isaacs	*Horses and Mules*
Greensfelder Bros.	*Druggists' Sundries*
T. and M. Schiele	*Millinery*

Prominent Jewish retail merchants and firms listed by Bowman included:

Fraley & Pollack
Henry Rosenfield
Kohn & Horwitz
Joseph Emmanuel
Joel Swope & Bros.
M. J. Steinberg
Albert Fischer
A. Gershon
Wm. Sicher
Isaac Baer

Perhaps no one had heard of St. Louis Jewry before the Civil War, as Bowman observed, but some of the Jews he named would become quite prominent in later years. In all instances, their seeds were planted and their roots began to grow in the St. Louis business milieu prior to the Civil War.[18]

Pre–Civil War St. Louis Jewry was not limited to religious and commercial enterprises. One other association was with the field of medicine.

---

18. *Modern View* 25, 8.

Though no extant records indicate just how many Jewish doctors were practicing in St. Louis, at least two physicians stand out as leaders of their profession. In 1842 Dr. Simon Gratz Moses, St. Louis's first known Jewish doctor, established with several other doctors the first dispensary for gratuitous treatment of the poor in St. Louis. Moses served as health commissioner of the city, and as early as 1842 became connected with the Medical Department of Kemper College as lecturer on women's diseases and obstetrics. Later he was elected to the chair of obstetrics in Missouri Medical College, a professorship that he retained until 1853. A Southern sympathizer during the Civil War, he spent most of the war years in Georgia, treating sick and wounded Confederate soldiers in various Savannah hospitals. After the war he returned to St. Louis and resumed his practice; despite his seeming "disloyalty" to the Union, he continued to be held in high esteem among the city's physicians. Indeed, until he died in 1897, St. Louis citizenry considered Moses one of the city's most prominent and successful medical practitioners.[19]

Among those associated with the free medical clinic established by Dr. Moses was Dr. Simon Pollack. He was born in Tauss, near Prague, capital of Bohemia, on April 14, 1814, the son of Austrian Jews Jacob and Sarah (Froehlich) Pollack. His father being a successful and respected wool merchant, young Simon Pollack enjoyed the best of educational advantages. After mastering a classical course of studies at the University of Vienna, he went on to earn a medical degree in 1835 at the University of Prague and advanced degrees in surgery and obstetrics back at the University of Vienna. For thirteen months he honed his medical skills at Vienna's famous Maternal Hospital, the largest and most prestigious institution of its kind in the world, after which he traveled for eighteen months throughout Europe, visiting most of the principal hospitals on the continent. During the 1830s, with cholera spreading devastatingly throughout Europe, the Austrian government sent a special commission of physicians to Russia to study the dread sickness, and Pollack, though then still a student, accompanied the commission and became exceedingly knowledgeable about the disease.

In the late 1830s Pollack decided to go to America, where he arrived in New York on July 4, 1838. He encountered difficulties immediately. He had brought with him a draft for $383 on a mercantile house in New York; three days before Pollack arrived, the company went broke, and the twenty-four-year-old immigrant found himself penniless as well as a

---

19. Hyde and Conard, eds., *Encyclopedia of the History of St. Louis,* vol. 3, 1572–75; Scharf, *Saint Louis City and County,* vol. 2, 1531, 1549–50.

stranger in a strange land. That made it virtually impossible for him to establish himself in medical practice in New York, notwithstanding his talent and education. Learning of the yellow fever epidemic then raging in New Orleans, Pollack thought to go there to tender his services and also to start a medical practice; but his worthless $383 draft stranded him in New York. Then a chance meeting with a New York lawyer resulted in Pollack exchanging his books (actually as a loan security) for the necessary fare, and thus he managed to secure passage on a coastal vessel bound for New Orleans, where he arrived in late 1838.

For the next few years Dr. Pollack seemed unable to establish roots anywhere, even though he practiced medicine uninterruptedly. Shortly after arriving in New Orleans he met Thomas Shearon, who owned a large plantation near Sycamore, Tennessee, on the Cumberland River below Nashville. Emulating a practice common in Europe—that is, serving as a family retainer—Pollack became the physician for the Shearon family. Accordingly, he moved to Tennessee, where, thanks to Shearon connections, he established himself in practice, first in Sycamore and later in Nashville. Among his patients in Nashville was the aging but still high-spirited "Old Hickory," former president of the United States Andrew Jackson. Though his medical practice in Tennessee proved highly lucrative, Pollack invested his money in several ill-fated ventures, and he soon lost the small fortune he had accumulated through his medical talents. In 1844, therefore, he went back to Louisiana, to Point Coupee, where, in addition to practicing medicine, he persisted in speculating in unwise outside ventures, this time a small cotton plantation that soon drained him of his finances.

Once more he moved to New Orleans, to reestablish a medical practice there, but again he did not stay long. Either he experienced further financial problems, or perhaps he concluded that better opportunities beckoned in the rapidly growing river city farther north; after all, many other German immigrants from his native Bohemia were headed in that direction through New Orleans. At any rate, on March 14, 1845, Pollack arrived in St. Louis, with only about one hundred dollars in his pocket with which to establish a new life and career. At that time fewer than a hundred fellow Jews lived in St. Louis, and the only other known Jewish doctor was Simon Gratz Moses.

Dr. Pollack opened his first office in St. Louis on the northeast corner of Third and Olive, in quarters rented for five dollars a month. His sparse equipment, costing only about ten dollars, consisted of a bed, a table, and a few chairs, plus medical instruments he had brought with him. His first patients were fellow Jewish immigrants, like himself quite poor, so his practice at first brought him little financial return. Nevertheless, he rendered professional services to all who called upon him, especially the poor. That was how he soon became associated with the free dispensary. Each doctor there handled patients from a particular city ward; Pollack's patients came from the First Ward, heavily populated with German immigrants. Gradually his practice flourished and he became well established. For sixteen years he made his home in the venerable Planters' House at Fourth and Chestnut, with his office nearby, just around the corner at Third and Olive.

Pollack's European training served him well when the disastrous cholera epidemic struck in 1849. In a city whose population in 1850 numbered 77,860, almost 5,200 (about 6.6 percent) died of the cholera in the two-year span from January 1849 to December 1850. In one week alone (in July 1849), probably the peak of the epidemic, 639 of the 867 burials recorded in all St. Louis cemeteries, a frightening 73.7 percent, were the result of cholera. Of course all medical personnel and facilities were used to the fullest, and Pollack's experience in treating cholera victims made him especially valuable. Then on July 5, 1849, Pollack himself was felled by the disease, but he survived through the care he received at the St. Louis Hospital of the Sisters of Charity.

Following his recovery, Pollack became interested in caring for the blind. He went to Europe to study blindness, and upon his return to St. Louis in 1850 he established, with several other doctors, the Missouri Institute for the Education of the Blind. Originally a private enterprise, the institution later was taken over by the state; today, known as the Missouri School for the Blind, it is a world-renowned agency. For the rest of his life Pollack remained a trustee as well as attending physician at the school. In the late 1850s he went back to Europe, this time for almost two years, to qualify as an oculist and aurist. He then returned to this country, and early in 1861 established an eye and ear infirmary in New York City. From there he came back to St. Louis to open an eye and ear dispensary in the Mullanphy Hospital, believed to be the first clinic of its kind west of the Mississippi.

Dr. Pollack was in St. Louis when the Civil War began. An ardent Unionist, he was one of several medical practitioners who helped organize the Western Sanitary Commission, which operated hospitals, trained male and female nurses, and worked to improve health and sanitary conditions in military camps. (The government still lacked organized medical support institutions, and the Red Cross had not yet come into existence.) By the end of the war the commission was supporting fifteen hospitals in the St. Louis area, including a twenty-five-hundred-bed complex at Jefferson Barracks, as well as facilities in at least half a dozen states, plus mobile units on riverboats and hospital railroad cars. In addition to rendering direct medical treatment to sick and wounded soldiers, Pollack served several years as hospital inspector. He patriotically returned his entire salary to the government, rendering his talents free of charge.

Although Pollack was Jewish and known universally by others as a Jew, he had become very much secularized; in fact, there is no evidence that he ever identified with any synagogue or any other uniquely Jewish institution. In 1873, at age fifty-nine, he married a non-Jew, Sallie Perry of Cincinnati, daughter of a wealthy steamboat owner. Their two sons were not raised as Jews, and they were not known to have affiliated with any Jewish association. Like many other German Jewish immigrants of the mid–nineteenth century, Dr. Simon Pollack and his progeny assimilated and apparently gave little if any thought to the faith of their ancestors. Pollack died in St. Louis in 1903.[20]

In sharp contrast with Doctors Moses and Pollack, others active in broader city life, such as many of the prosperous businessmen, unhesitatingly and openly maintained their Jewish identity, albeit many, scrupulously desiring to become "Americanized," tended toward forms of Judaism more liberal than Orthodox traditionalism. Two merit special mention: Isidor Bush and Meyer Friede.

Isidor Bush was born in the ghetto of Prague, Bohemia, on January 15, 1822, the great-grandson of Israel Hönig Edler von Hönigsberg, who was the first Jew raised to nobility in Austria. As a child, Isidor was pampered by his father, Jacob (his mother Fredericka died when he was three years old), and he enjoyed a very pleasant childhood. Educated by private tutors, he had opportunities to meet outstanding Austrian Jewish intellectuals of the time. In 1837 Jacob Busch moved to Vienna, where he became a partner in "Schmid's Oriental Printing Establishment."[21] Though only fifteen, young Isidor became engrossed in his father's publishing business and turned zealously to the study of Hebrew. Soon he spoke four languages fluently, and could read and write in Greek, Latin, and Hebrew as well as in his native German. Within a short time the firm of Schmid and Busch, in which Isidor was eventually part owner, became one of Vienna's largest publishers of Hebrew books, including Bibles, prayer books, and various editions of the Talmud, Rambam, and

---

20. For Simon Pollack, see the following: "S. Pollack, M.D., The Autobiography and Reminiscences of S. Pollack, M.D.," in Simon Pollack File, AJA; *Israelite,* October 22, 1858; Scharf, *History of Saint Louis City and County,* vol. 2, 1531–32, 1543–50, 1573–86; Hyde and Conard, eds., *Encyclopedia of the History of St. Louis,* vol. 3, 1773–74; Primm, *Lion of the Valley,* 266–70; David A. Gee, *216 S.K.: A History of the Jewish Hospital of St. Louis,* 8; Ross, "History of St. Louis," 98.

21. The name is spelled both "Bush" and "Busch." The "Busch" spelling was used in Europe, the "Bush" spelling in America.

other commentaries. Young Isidor also edited and published the *Kalendar und Jahrbuch fur Israeliten,* the first popular annual of Jewish scholarly articles printed in the German language in Austria. Even before coming to America, then, Bush had established himself as a pioneer in journalism.

Like many other liberal intellectuals in the aftermath of the unsuccessful revolutions of 1848, Bush fled to America, arriving with his wife (he had married Theresa Taussig in 1844) and their son Raphael in January 1849 in New York City. There he opened a small store for stationery and books. Shortly thereafter, on March 30, 1849, the pioneering Bush published the first number of *Israels Herold,* a weekly journal patterned after the one he had produced in Vienna. It began a new and distinguished phase of American journalism, the American Jewish press printed in German. Unfortunately, though, the effort failed financially, and Bush was forced to suspend operations after only three months. Strapped for funds, in July 1849 he moved to St. Louis where his wife's family, the Taussigs, had settled earlier.

The small St. Louis Jewish population in the 1840s foreshadowed disaster should he attempt another enterprise in journalism, so Bush undertook instead a career in business. It proved to be a wise choice, although for the rest of his life he continued to write numerous essays and articles for various local and national journals. He opened a general store in Carondelet with his brother-in-law Charles Taussig, who was already in the grocery business with Adolph Abeles. By 1853 Bush and Taussig bought out Abeles, and they continued profitably in the south St. Louis location for many years.

More important to Bush financially, in 1851 he purchased one hundred acres of land in Jefferson County south of St. Louis, at a place later called Bushberg, where he successfully raised grapes. Before long Bush earned a reputation as a leading authority in viniculture; in 1868, in fact, he published *The Bushberg Catalogue,* a manual for raising grapes for wines, which was translated into many languages and enjoyed international circulation. In 1870 he organized the firm of Isidor Bush and Company, and it grew into one of the most successful wine and liquor enterprises in St. Louis.

Bush's business ventures went beyond wine and liquor. During the 1850s the expanding St. Louis and Iron Mountain Railroad Company named him its General Passenger Agent and Auditor; he later became a director of the railroad, serving until 1865 when the line was taken over by New York financier Jay Gould. Bush dabbled in real estate, and he was also active in banking and finance. In 1857 he helped incorporate the Peoples' Savings Bank in St. Louis, serving for a while as its president. In the late 1860s he was president also of the Mechanics Savings Bank, and later he served as actuary for the German Mutual Life Insurance Company. Despite these many successes, Bush never became extremely wealthy; he suffered his share of financial setbacks, but managed to endure them placidly. Nevertheless, he prospered sufficiently to participate in many endeavors, within both the Jewish community and the larger body politic.

One of his associations was with B'nai B'rith. Shortly after he arrived in the United States in 1849, Bush joined New York's Zion Lodge No. 2; after he moved to St. Louis he became a member of Missouri Lodge No. 22 when it was organized in 1855. In 1863 he and several others organized a new St. Louis chapter, Ebn Ezra Lodge No. 47, with which Bush affiliated for the remainder of his life and which he represented honorably for many years in various capacities in District Grand Lodge No. 2.

One of Bush's greatest accomplishments was the B'nai B'rith Cleveland Orphans Asylum. Bush was one of its organizers and a longtime board member. Intended originally to care for children of immigrants and Civil War casualties, the nationally recognized home opened in 1868 and provided its services well into the twentieth century.[22] Bush also framed several national insurance and endowment programs for B'nai B'rith, which many members adopted. Indeed, B'nai B'rith held Bush in such high esteem that it tendered him a testimonial dinner in Philadelphia in 1890 that was graced by dignitaries from all over the country.

In St. Louis, Bush was one of the original members of the small but short-lived B'nai B'rith Congregation when it was founded in 1849. When it joined with Emanu El in 1852 to form B'nai El Congregation, Bush was prominent in the merger. One of B'nai El's original members, Bush served that congregation faithfully for the rest of his life, occasionally as an officer. His devotion to Judaism and his loyalty to his adopted country both were well illustrated in an incident mentioned by his longtime friend and biographer, Samuel Bowman: "I recall in 1863, when things looked darkest for the Union forces, attending a service at Temple B'nai El and listening to a patriotic sermon delivered by Isidor Bush from its pulpit, exhorting the members to stand loyally by and give their full support to the Government of Lincoln."[23]

Isidor Bush's influence and impact extended considerably beyond just the St. Louis Jewish and business communities. He ardently opposed

---

22. The existence of the B'nai B'rith Orphans Home in Cleveland was one reason why for many years St. Louis Jewry did not build its own orphanage; children were sent instead to the Cleveland facility.

23. Samuel Bowman, "Isidor Bush," in *Modern View*, September 19, 1924; James A. Wax, "Isidor Bush, American Patriot and Abolitionist," *Historica Judaica* 5 (October 1943): 187.

slavery and championed the Union cause. Available records leave unclear how he served during the Civil War. Physical disabilities suffered in a fire as a child precluded military service. But he unquestionably served in a civilian capacity, in one instance, at least, as secretary to flamboyant General John C. Fremont, who for a time early in the war commanded Union forces in Missouri.[24] Bush served also on the St. Louis City Council and the Board of Education. The latter was especially meaningful to Bush, who always held education—and especially public education—as a very high priority.

Probably Bush's greatest mark on St. Louis and Missouri history resulted from his participation in several state conventions during the Civil War period. The first, in February and March of 1861, culminated in a critical political victory of Missouri Unionists over Secessionists. Succeeding conventions—actually a provisional government that replaced a Secessionist legislature—kept Missouri in the Union.[25] Bush stood out in those state conventions as a strong advocate for the immediate and complete freedom for all slaves throughout Missouri. Despite strong abolitionist sentiment, however, emancipation remained a minority view in the state convention until the so-called Radical Republicans came into control toward the end of the Civil War. In 1865 the new Missouri "Drake Constitution" came into being (named after Charles D. Drake, leader of the Radical Republicans), which finally emancipated slaves throughout the state.

Bush lived until August 5, 1898, and was regarded with respect and admiration as one of St. Louis's finest citizens and probably Missouri's most prominent Jew of the nineteenth century. He was, among other things, a vice president of the Missouri Historical Society in 1882; later his oil portrait graced that organization's stately building in St. Louis's Forest Park. He was in constant demand as a speaker at civic functions, and his earlier journalist leanings led him to write numerous articles and essays in many publications.

Throughout a life filled with civic accomplishments and distinguished public service, Isidor Bush retained a strong and open attachment to

---

24. At a B'nai El board meeting on September 8, 1861, Bush announced that he could no longer serve as secretary of the board "since he had received an appointment of U.S. officer on the staff of General Fremont." From history of B'nai El as printed in *Voice*, January 9, 1903. One chronicler of Jews in the Civil War identifies Bush as "Captain" Isidor Bush, aide-de-camp to General Fremont. Simon Wolf, *The American Jew as Patriot, Soldier and Citizen*, 112. Robert J. Rombauer, *The Union Cause in St. Louis in 1861*, xii, 145, 168, does not clear up the matter.

25. Although some question the legality of the pro-Union conventions, during the Civil War many actions throughout the country to preserve the Union often superseded narrower concerns for the "niceties" of strict legality.

Judaism. Indeed, wrote one of his biographers, "the dominant note of his life was his fidelity and loyalty to the Faith of his Fathers." Ironically, one of the greatest sorrows of Bush's life was

> his inability to secure the sympathetic interest of his wife and only son in the noble work he was engaged in for the welfare of his co-religionists. . . . The Taussig family of St. Louis, of which his wife was a member, were not at all interested in Jewish affairs, and soon after their arrival in America became members of the Christian Church. . . . It is a source of regret that their great intellectual talents were not devoted to the cause of their Fathers, just as were those of Isidor Bush. In view of the strong influence of his wife's family, it was a source of wonder, as well as gratification to his friends, that Mr. Bush preserved his affection and interest in the people of his faith.[26]

Another St. Louis Jew whose roots predated the Civil War and who gained prominence outside the small Jewish community was Meyer Friede. Born on September 6, 1821, near Kassel, Germany, Friede came to America in 1838, first to Mobile, Alabama, and then in 1844 to St. Louis. His sister Marianna had married Louis Bauman, and Friede went into the L. Bauman Jewelry Company with his brother-in-law, a business association that lasted for many years. In 1883 Friede joined with Morris Eisenstadt and Benjamin Altheimer to establish the Eisenstadt Jewelry Company, which remained prominent in St. Louis for about a hundred years.

Friede also led a distinguished life in community and public service; his commitment apparently emanated from his strong religious beliefs and his devoted congregational activities. In 1847 he helped found the Emanu El Congregation that later merged with B'nai B'rith to become B'nai El. Friede served on the board of trustees of the new congregation and later became its president. Samuel Bowman, a contemporary and personal friend, later wrote a colorful and poignant description of both Friede and B'nai El:

> In those days it was customary for the President of the Congregation and Vice-President to occupy seats on the pulpit, and I well recall the Hon. Meyer Friede, who was President of the Temple . . . and was a man of fine personal appearance, who sat on the pulpit, with a silk hat covering

---

26. Samuel Bowman, "Isidor Bush," in *Modern View,* September 19, 1924. Other sources for the Bush biographical sketch include Wax, "Isidor Bush," 183–203; Rombauer, *Union Cause in St. Louis,* xii, 145, 168; Jacob Furth, "Sketch of Isidor Bush," in *Voice,* January 1, 1915; Isidor Bush, "The Task of the Jews in the United States," in *Occident* 9 (December 1851): 467–83; Benjamin F. Peixetto, "Isidor Bush," *The Menorah* 9 (September 1890): 123–26 and 9 (October 1890): 190–202; Jacob Furth, "Sketch of Isidor Bush," 303–8; Guido Kisch, *"ISRAELS HERALD:* The First Jewish Weekly in New York," 63–84; and Bertram W. Korn, "Isidor Bush," *Encyclopedia Judaica,* vol. 4, 1535.

his head, and with a Taleth over his shoulders; in those days the men occupied the main auditorium on the first floor, and the wives had the pleasure of sitting in the gallery and looking down on their "lords and masters."[27]

Friede's dedication to civic service resulted in his becoming a commissioner of the Municipal Charitable and Penal Institutions in the 1870s and 1880s. For eight years he remained conscientiously involved in the city's insane asylum, poorhouse, and female hospital.

It was in his service in the Missouri state legislature, however, where Meyer Friede left an indelible imprint that must rank among the magnificent moments of human dignity in the history of not only St. Louis Jewry but also the United States. In 1860 Friede was elected to the lower house of the Missouri General Assembly, where he was the only Jew in the state legislature.[28] Typical of so many German immigrants, he was an ardent Unionist, and opposed slavery. His maiden speech on the House floor in January 1861 endorsed efforts in Washington seeking to settle the slavery question without resort to war. Apologizing for speaking with such a decided foreign accent, he pointed to the strong antislavery and pro-Union loyalties of many German-born Republicans, often derogated by proslavery nativists as the "Black Republican Dutch." "When we left the Fatherland," Friede asserted, "we were guided by the bright light of liberty burning through this land. . . . The hearts of all German citizens beat with gratitude, love and devotion to the Union. They are ever ready to lay down their lives in its defense."[29]

Late in January of 1861 the Missouri House was debating a proposed banking bill. A representative from Jackson County in western Missouri

---

27. "Reminiscences of Samuel Bowman," in *Modern View 25*, 8.

28. Meyer Friede was the first Jew to serve in the Missouri state legislature, but he was not the first elected. In 1855 Adolph Abeles achieved that distinction. However, on November 1, 1855, before he could begin his term, Abeles was killed in a train wreck. Abeles was the brother of Nathan Abeles, who had attended the first *minyan* in St. Louis and who was a founder of United Hebrew Congregation. Though raised in a devout family—his parents had hoped he would be a rabbi—Adolph Abeles, unlike Nathan, rarely observed Jewish ceremonies and practices, kept none of the holidays, and "even withheld his children from the covenant." He became a thoroughly secularized and assimilated Jew. Yet when he ran for the state legislature and his opponent made the point that Abeles was Jewish—an obvious antisemitic attempt to "smear" him— Abeles responded that he was proud to be a Jew rather than the bigot his "intolerant German assailant" had shown himself to be. Isidor Bush to Editor, in *Israelite*, April 11, 1856. See also Scharf, *Saint Louis City and County*, vol. 2, 1152 ff.

29. *Tribune*, January 28, 1881. Friede was correct. German immigrants to America overwhelmingly supported the Union cause during the Civil War, both at the ballot box and on the battlefield.

objected to some benefits proposed in that bill "towards those savings institutions, which are governed in nineteen out of twenty cases, by the descendants of those men who sacrificed Christ." "I do not want any discrimination," he blatantly continued, "in favor of those Christ Killers."

Friede responded. His remarks constitute one of the most stirring orations recorded in the annals of the state legislature:

> Mr. Speaker, I think it incumbent upon me, the sole representative of the Jewish persuasion upon this floor, to reply briefly to the remarks made by the gentleman from Jackson in regard to that "ancient people of God." And, Sir, I thank my God that the United States of America, whose Constitution I swore to support and protect, affords me and my people the rights and privileges of free men. Here we have found an asylum from the oppression of European Monarchies, and in return we give our industry, our labor, our capital, and above all, in these troublesome times, our devotion to the flag which blesses us on our adopted soil and protects us abroad. The great Lord Petersborough observed that he was for a "Parliamentary King and a Parliamentary Constitution," but not a Parliamentary God and a Parliamentary Religion. In the name of my brethren, I thank the fathers of this Republic for the Constitution which they ordained and established and I pray we may never have a "Constitutional God nor a Constitutional Religion."

Friede continued with some broad assertions about banking, conceding that for centuries Jews had engaged in banking and finance, often because it was the only economic avenue open to them due to discriminatory regulations forbidding them from engaging in other occupations reserved for Christians. He reminded his fellow legislators that some of the safest and most celebrated banks of Europe owed their existence and success to Jewish skill and capital. He cited specifically also the St. Louis Savings Bank, in which a few Jews were stockholders and directors, and noted that no businessman in St. Louis had ever complained of its management. Defending the exemplary record of America's Jewish citizenry, Friede continued:

> But, Sir, the State of Missouri has one institution which is not patronized by my people—I mean the penitentiary in sight of this capitol—and I am quite sure if any of my fellow members on this floor ever go there, they will not find a Jew with the brand of disgrace upon him. And, Sir, there is another institution where you will find no Jewish inmates. I mean the poor houses. Their good behavior and moral character, and their custom of minding their own business, keep them out of your prisons, and their names from the criminal records of the country. Their industry, good management and economy keep them out of your almshouses, and no Jew is here supported by the State or by the public authorities.

Friede then concluded:

> Sir, when England was as savage as New Guinea, and Paris but a swamp, and this mighty country known only to our God; when letters were

unknown to Athens; when not a hut stood upon either of the seven hills of Rome, my people had fenced cities and cedar palaces, their schools of sacred learning, their fleets of merchant ships, their great statesmen and soldiers, their natural philosophers, their historians and their poets. Yes, Sir, and they had their exchange and banking system, from which our modern Solons may gather wisdom. Why, Sir, it is a fact vouched for by Mr. [James] Madison, that a patriotic Jew named [Haym] Solomon, who, by his skill and industry, had accumulated a large portion of these worldly goods, actually paid the expenses of many members of Congress during the struggle for independence, and after its achievement. And Mr. Madison expressly says he did not see how the Congress could have kept together without the money and credit of the little Jew Solomon. He helped the cause of liberty here and abroad, and deserves to stand side by side with Robert Morris as the financier of the Revolution, and whose name should be enshrined in the affections of all American freemen. There was no interest or usury in his transactions. No, Sir, he gave his money to the cause without reward, except that which every patriot feels in sustaining a patriot's cause. Then the Treasury of this infant Republic was without a dollar, but a Jew mainly assisted in keeping the wheels of Government moving, and in the present condition of the Treasury of this State, I know of nothing better that can be done than to call to your aid the skill and capital of the brethren of Joseph, who filled the King's treasury with money and his storehouses with corn. There is genius among the countrymen of Isaiah, and heroism among the descendants of the Maccabees.

The record shows that "Mr. Friede was loudly and frequently applauded during the delivery of his remarks."

Meyer Friede retired from the state legislature in 1862, after only one term, but the magnificent Churchillian defense of his faith and his people remains one of the memorable perorations in American history.[30]

---

30. "Speech Delivered by Hon. Meyer Friede in the Missouri Legislature . . . in the Year 1861," in Missouri Box, AJA. The full text also appears in the *Israelite*, February 15, 1861. Friede was by no means the only Jew to stand up to antisemitism in legislative circles. An earlier incident involved Judah P. Benjamin, the first professing Jew to be elected to the United States Senate. Taunted by a fellow senator for being Jewish, Benjamin proudly responded: "The Senator will please remember that when his half-civilized ancestors were hunting wild boar in the forests of Silesia, mine were the princes of the earth." *Modern View*, August 22, 1935. For more on Meyer Friede see *Occident* 18 (February 1861): 286; *Tribune*, December 12, 1880, and January 14 and 28, 1881; *Voice*, December 21, 1888; "Reminiscences of Samuel Bowman," in *Modern View* 25, 8; and Burton A. Boxerman, "Meyer Friede Chartered New Paths as St. Louis Jewish Leader," in *St. Louis Jewish Light*, April 9, 1986.

8

THE CIVIL WAR DECADE

The election of Abraham Lincoln in November 1860 precipitated a series of events that culminated five months later, in April 1861, in the outbreak of the American Civil War. Four years of bloody strife followed, a crucible in which the very survival of this country was tested. At the onset of the war, approximately 150,000 Jews lived in the United States; almost two-thirds (about 100,000) had arrived only during the 1850s. The "old line" Sephardic families, descendants of the early Jewish settlers of the colonial period, had long since been outnumbered by western European Ashkenazic Jews from Britain, the Low Countries, and especially the German states. New York City's Jewish community of 30,000 already had become the largest in the country, home for almost 20 percent of all Jews in the United States; two-thirds of all American Jews were concentrated in fifteen cities, one of which was St. Louis. Historians long have echoed Bertram W. Korn's observation that the "urban tendency of American Jews had already become fixed as a norm: European despots had prohibited them from owning land through too many centuries for many to think of tilling the soil; as a religio-cultural minority they were naturally inclined to dwell together in order to preserve their religious practices and worship."[1]

Because of that inclination toward urbanization, more Jews lived in the American North than in the South. Furthermore, the liberal proclivities that so many brought with them from Europe led many to oppose human servitude. Nevertheless, few Jews took an active role in the contentious debates over the slavery issue, mainly because they were so preoccupied in becoming established in their new environments. At the same time, it should be kept in mind, no single group spoke for America's Jews, who were divided by national origin, by differences between traditional and reforming elements, and by geographic residence. True, the Board

---

1. Korn, *American Jewry and the Civil War*, 1–2.

of Delegates of American Israelites existed and was ostensibly representative of American Jewry, but that body was as split as its constituents.
Furthermore, it had come into being in 1859, later than the proverbial
eleventh hour as far as the longtime slavery controversy was concerned.

In reality, Jews, like others, were influenced by geography, and thus
could be found on both sides of the slavery issue. Whereas some Northern
rabbis stood squarely on the side of abolitionism, Southern colleagues
supported the slave system. But not all rabbis followed the lead of their
particular region. Outspoken opponents of "the peculiar institution" included Rabbi David Einhorn of Baltimore (considered a "southern" city),
who boldly championed abolitionism in spite of his congregation's strong
proslavery attitudes. Even threats to his life did not deter his antislavery
preachings, although in 1861 he had to flee to New York to escape a
vengeful mob. Rabbi Morris J. Raphall of New York defended slavery.
But Rabbi George Jacobs of Richmond, Virginia, owned slaves; and Rabbi
Maximilian J. Michelbacher, also of Richmond, though not an actual slave-
owner, voiced strong support for that institution. Rabbi Isaac Mayer Wise
reflected yet another view, that of the compromiser whose greatest fear
was for the survival of a country that offered sanctuary to freedom-loving
people everywhere. Wise remained silent about not only slavery but also
other divisive Civil War issues, though certainly not because of lack of
concern. Having fled from a Europe rife with tyranny and despotism,
Wise counseled America's Jews to appreciate what they had in America
and to work peacefully to keep the Union together. "We are servants of
peace," he wrote, and so he opted to remain silent on the discordant issues
"until a spirit of reconciliation shall move the hearts of the millions to a
better understanding of the blessings of peace, freedom and union."[2]

Jewish laymen also tended to reflect the views prevailing where they
lived. J. F. Moses of Georgia bought and sold slaves. Judah P. Benjamin
and David [Levy] Yulee, Jewish senators from Alabama and Florida respectively, strongly espoused slavery. After the South seceded, Benjamin
served the Confederacy as brilliantly in his way as did Robert E. Lee in
his; Benjamin held the important posts of secretary of war and secretary
of state under President Jefferson Davis, and was commonly referred to as
"the brains of the Confederacy." Prominent Jewish laymen who engaged
actively in the political struggle to abolish slavery included Philip J.
Joachimsen of New York and Isidor Bush of St. Louis. Thus, American Jews
were "as thoroughly divided as the American population itself," historian

---

2. Ibid., 14–31; *Israelite*, December 14, 1860, and April 19, 1861; Myron Berman,
Richmond's Jewry, 178.

Korn observed, although, he noted, "there were fewer Jews than other Americans, proportionately, at the extreme wings of the controversy, and more in the middle ground, because, as immigrants, the great majority of them would naturally have taken less interest in theoretical and sectional political questions than in the more personal problems of economic and social adjustment."[3]

Of an estimated five thousand Jews living in St. Louis during the Civil War, only one is known to have owned slaves. On the other hand, an outspoken opponent of slavery who earned singular notoriety for his activism was August M. Bondi. Refugees from the unsuccessful liberal uprisings in Vienna, the Bondi family came to St. Louis in late 1848, joining friends who had settled there earlier. Fifteen-year-old August worked in the store that his father opened on Carondelet Avenue, but restlessness and driving idealism eventually led him to Kansas, where he joined up with abolitionist John Brown. Although Bondi played no part in the notorious massacre of proslave settlers at Pottawatomie Creek, historians always include him among the "freedom fighters"—some labeled them instead rascally guerrillas or unscrupulous freebooters—who "rode with John Brown." That group included two other Jews whom Bondi recruited, Jacob Benjamin and Theodore Weiner. None of the three joined Brown in his unsuccessful insurrection at Harper's Ferry—they thought Brown's scenario too far-fetched and incredulous—but they continued their antislavery activities in other ways and fought in the Union army during the war. Bondi eventually settled in Salina, Kansas, but his parents and other family members remained in St. Louis, stalwart members of B'nai El Congregation. August visited them often, and was a familiar sight in St. Louis.[4]

Once Civil War hostilities began, Jews fought on both sides. Some ten thousand Jews served in the armed forces, about seven thousand on the Union side and some three thousand in the Confederate armies. More than five hundred lost their lives. Seven were awarded the Congressional

---

3. Korn, *American Jewry and the Civil War*, 16.

4. August Bondi died in St. Louis on September 30, 1907, while strolling near the corner of Fourth and Walnut. He was buried alongside his wife, Henrietta, in Gypsum Hill Cemetery in Salina, Kansas. Many years later, Governor John Carlin of Kansas proclaimed September 12, 1981, as "August M. Bondi Day" to honor the Jewish "freedom fighter who rode with John Brown" for "his commitment to democratic ideals and human rights." August M. Bondi File, AJA; Marcus, *Memoirs of American Jews*, vol. 2, 165–213; Bernard Postal and Lionel Koppman, *A Jewish Tourist's Guide to the United States*, 179–80; Martin Litvin, *The Journey: The American-Jewish Freedom Fighter Who Rode with John Brown in Kansas*; "August M. Bondi," in *Encyclopedia Judaica*, vol. 4, 1202–3.

Medal of Honor, the highest award bestowed for bravery on the battlefield, and countless others received commendations for other military achievements. Jews did their share on the home front as well, in both the North and the South. They raised relief funds for soldiers and their families; they collected hospital supplies, food, and clothing; they opened their homes to soldiers for Passover *seders* and other religious occasions; and they even recruited Jewish men for military service.[5]

The Civil War involved many complex and interrelated matters of national import. A fundamental issue pertained to the constitutional relationship between national and state sovereignties. Slavery, of course, had divided the nation for decades. So, too, had matters of economic and social differences. Agrarianism and ruralism conflicted with expanding industrialism and urbanism, as did creditor economics and debtor economics. Northern and Southern "ways of life" contrasted with each other, with gaping differences in background and culture. Historians have few difficulties in looking upon the Civil War as two different societies facing each other in mortal conflict. Even religious institutions were affected; some actually divided into Northern and Southern wings of the same denomination. There being no "national" Jewish religious affiliation, American Judaism did not split that drastically; but individual rabbis and congregations, North and South, differed in their biblical interpretations toward slavery, as well as in their views toward other Civil War issues.

At least two significant controversies directly involving Jews arose during the Civil War. One entailed the question of Jewish chaplains in the armed forces. The controversy erupted over an act of Congress, approved July 22, 1861, which provided that a military chaplain must be a "regularly ordained minister of some Christian denomination." Both Jews and non-Jews immediately protested this blatant religious discrimination, especially in view of the large number of Jews already in the service. Considerable debate followed, in religious and secular newspapers and journals, in the pulpit, and in letter correspondence. Among those in the forefront stood Arnold Fischel, Dutch-born rabbi of Shearith Israel

---

5. For Jews in the Civil War, see especially Korn, *American Jewry and the Civil War*. See also Wolf, *American Jew as Patriot, Soldier and Citizen*, 1–8, 106–8, and Melvin A. Young, *Where They Lie*. In a memorial service at a Jewish cemetery in Richmond, Virginia, in 1905, honoring Confederate dead, the main speaker declared that "the proportion of Jewish soldiers in the Confederate army was larger than that of any other faith." He may have exaggerated. Nevertheless, he very accurately referred to Jewish staff officers in both the Confederate army and navy, and specifically to General David DeLeon, the Jewish doctor who was the first surgeon general of the Confederate army. *Voice*, June 23, 1905.

Congregation in New York. Numerous petitions were forwarded to members of both branches of the Congress as well as to President Lincoln. After a year-long struggle of words, a new law signed by the president on July 17, 1862, finally enabled Jews to become military chaplains. The first was Rabbi Jacob Frankel of Rodeph Shalom Congregation in Philadelphia, whose commission was dated September 18, 1862. Others soon followed.[6]

Another significant Civil War issue that directly embraced the American Jewish population centered on the infamous "General Order No. 11." As in other internecine conflicts pitting one part of a nation against another, military encounters were not the only confrontations. Issues involving trade and commerce and personal loyalties were equally critical. That was pointedly true early in the war in the lower Mississippi valley, source of considerable consumer goods, medical supplies, and war materiel (especially cotton) vital to both sides. The fluidity of battle lines, especially in western Tennessee and northern Mississippi, exacerbated a widespread instability existing anyway because of tenuous and divided loyalties. Under the circumstances, military confrontations there often were accompanied by economic perfidiousness and corruption, conducted by unscrupulous individuals who took advantage of both North and South to fatten their own private coffers. Greedy and unprincipled merchants, speculators, and traders swooped into the area like vultures, to buy and sell and often smuggle all sorts of vital goods at outlandish prices. Memphis became notorious as the center of a nefarious traffic that ran into millions of dollars. Unconscionable profiteering became an everyday occurrence, with civilians and military alike sharing in the widespread corruption, from high-ranking officers to lowly privates, and from seemingly respectable business magnates to raunchy peddlers. "A greater pack of knaves never went unhung!" deplored Rear Admiral David D. Porter, commanding Union naval forces on the Mississippi.[7] Suddenly, and with no intimation even that it was coming, on December 17, 1862, the following

---

6. *Israelite*, December 6, 13, 20, and 27, 1861, and January 3, 1862. The Confederacy avoided the Union's problem by requiring only that chaplains be "clergymen," with no denominational stipulations. Nevertheless, no Jewish chaplains are known to have served in the Southern forces, because, as Bertram Korn pointed out, Jews probably were so scattered throughout those armies that "there was probably not a sufficient number . . . in any one Confederate regiment to warrant the appointment of a Jewish chaplain." Jewish Confederate soldiers were served throughout the South by civilian rabbis, Jewish laymen, and fellow Jewish soldiers. For an account of the chaplaincy issue, see Korn, *American Jewry and the Civil War*, 56–97. Feingold, *Zion in America*, 91–95, also deals with it, but in less detail.

7. Korn, *American Jewry and the Civil War*, 122.

order was issued from the headquarters of Ulysses S. Grant, commanding general of the Department of the Tennessee:

> The Jews, as a class violating every regulation of trade established by the Treasury Department and also department orders, are hereby expelled from the department within twenty-four hours from the receipt of this order.
>
> Post commanders will see that all of this class of people will be furnished passes and required to leave, and any one returning after such notification will be arrested and held in confinement until an opportunity occurs of sending them out as prisoners, unless furnished with permit from headquarters.
>
> No passes will be given these people to visit headquarters for the purpose of making personal application for trade permits.[8]

General Order No. 11 was immediately enforced. Jews were forcibly removed from a theater of operations that included most of northern Mississippi and western Tennessee and Kentucky. Whole families were summarily expelled, from Holly Springs and Oxford, Mississippi, and from Paducah, Kentucky. Those forcibly displaced included Jews who had never engaged in trade in the area and some who had even served in the Union army.

Since the expulsion order also precluded appeal to Grant, the only recourse seemed to be to the president of the United States. Accordingly, a small group of Jews from the affected area sought to reach Lincoln, first by letter and then with a personal visit. The leadership centered in Cesar J. Kaskel, a Paducah businessman. En route to Washington, Kaskel wrote to Jewish community leaders and journalists all over the country, and within days a storm of protests bombarded the president, the War Department, and members of Congress. Included were at least two communications from St. Louis Jewry. One was a letter by Rabbi Henry Kuttner, written to President Lincoln; another was a resolution adopted by Missouri Lodge B'nai B'rith in St. Louis and forwarded by Isidor Bush to Lincoln's attorney general, Missourian Edward Bates. Many of the protests pointed to the incongruity of General Order No. 11 at the same time that the Emancipation Proclamation purported to free slaves.[9]

---

8. From *War of the Rebellion . . . Official Records of the Union and Confederate Armies,* as quoted in Korn, *American Jewry and the Civil War,* 122–23.

9. United Hebrew Congregation File, AJA; Henry J. Kuttner to Abraham Lincoln, St. Louis, January 5, 1863, in B'nai B'rith, Missouri Lodge, Papers, American Jewish Historical Society, Waltham, Massachusetts; *Israelite,* January 9, 16, 23, and 30, 1863; Korn, *American Jewry and the Civil War,* 126.

Kaskel's meeting with President Lincoln was brief but dramatically fruitful. In Kaskel's presence, Lincoln angrily penned a terse memorandum to General-in-Chief Henry W. Halleck, directing that he telegraph instructions immediately to cancel the odious and discriminatory directive. In short order, on January 17, 1863, only three weeks after he had issued it, Grant rescinded General Order No. 11.[10]

General Order No. 11 was perhaps the most sweeping anti-Jewish regulation in all American history. Unquestionably the list of unscrupulous profiteers included some Jews—attested to by official trial records of those arrested and found guilty—but Jews constituted a minutely small minority of the culprits. Nevertheless, the order banished *all* Jews from the district, and *only* Jews, whether they were engaged in illicit trade or not. Later investigations revealed that Grant may not have been alone to blame, even though the directive was given over his signature; other officers also exhibited antisemitic tendencies. The causes and pressures, according to one historian, "go deep into the nature of conditions in the Department of the Tennessee. . . . Jews were a scapegoat already, prepared and identified . . . a natural scapegoat, even in the United States, because they had already been the scapegoat for almost two millenia."[11]

Rather than an isolated anti-Jewish episode during the Civil War, General Order No. 11 was alarming evidence of a growing antisemitism throughout the United States. Know-Nothingism, though past its political peak, still thrived, along with its vile WASP-ish cohorts, prejudice and intolerance. Jews were probably fortunate that Mormons and Catholics (especially Irish Catholics) had been the main objects of earlier Know-Nothing vituperation—not that German immigrants were denied their share of that gall! But because of their small numbers, Jews *as Jews* had not been significantly singled out as a serious threat. By the time of the

---

10. This General Order No. 11 should not be confused with another "Order No. 11," an equally odious and controversial directive promulgated in retaliation for the infamous Quantrill sacking of Lawrence, Kansas, which resulted in untoward hardship and suffering among large numbers of civilians, especially women and children. Violette, *History of Missouri*, 382–85.

11. Korn, *American Jewry and the Civil War*, 155; Wolf, *American Jew as Patriot, Soldier and Citizen*, 6–7. Korn, who deals in detail with the General Order No. 11 issue, points out (pp. 121–55) that later, when Grant was president, he appointed Jews to important posts in his administration. In fact, Rabbi B. M. Browne of New York served as a pallbearer at Grant's funeral. *Modern View*, September 13, 1940. See also Joseph Lebowich, "General Ulysses S. Grant and the Jews," 71; Lee M. Friedman, "Something Additional on General Grant's Order No. 11," 184; and I. S. Meyer, "The American Jewish Community during the Civil War," 277.

Civil War, however, increased population and visibility made them a convenient target. Jewish peddlers, traders, and merchants often were deemed "money grabbers" and accused of everything from price gouging to smuggling—just because they were Jewish. Christian "Rhett Butler"–type blockade runners and smugglers of the Civil War have been romanticized as heroes; Jews who traded honestly and legally were subject to vilification. Both in the North and the South, despite patriotic sacrifices for their respective sides, motives and loyalties of Jews were suspect. Northerners and Southerners alike maligned the great Judah P. Benjamin, citing specifically that he was a Jew. The press carried numerous condemnatory stories that pointedly discredited Jews. A Harrisburg, Pennsylvania, Republican paper, for instance, condemned an opposition party parade not because the marchers were Democrats, but because one of its organizers belonged to those "who murdered the Savior and who shed the blood of early Christians." Other newspapers printed comparable vitriol. August Belmont married into a non-Jewish family and reared his children as Christians; that did not prevent his detractors from branding him a "Jew banker" and a "Jew broker." Prominent figures in both public and private sectors of American life expressed similar disquieting sentiments.[12] The *relative* freedom from antisemitism that Jews had enjoyed before the Civil War now became a casualty of that war. True, except for the short-lived General Order No. 11, no federal or state legislation restricted civil or political rights of Jews or in any way diminished their legal status as citizens—as the Dred Scott decision had done to blacks. At the same time, though, no legislation or court action curtailed the shameful discrimination and intolerance of the spreading social and economic bigotry that one historian labeled "American Judaeophobia."[13]

---

12. They included Generals Benjamin F. Butler, William T. Sherman, and Philip Sheridan; Union Senators Andrew Johnson (who became president after Lincoln's assassination), Henry Wilson, and Benjamin Wade; Confederate Congressmen Henry S. Foote and William P. Miles; Parson W. G. Brownlow, Colonel LaFayette C. Baker (chief of the Detective Bureau of the War Department, the equivalent then of the Secret Service); and others, including newspaper editors too numerous to mention.

13. Korn, *American Jewry and the Civil War,* 156. Korn documents many incidents in both the North and the South. He blames the war, though, for precipitating this "American Judaeophobia": it was "the key . . . which unleashed heretofore dormant prejudices. . . . Society had to have scapegoats. . . . There were other scapegoats during the war as well: Yankees who were caught in the South at the outbreak of hostilities; German settlers in Texas; sincerely loyal Democrats in the North; but, apparently, the Jews were a more popular scapegoat in all areas than any of these" (187). See also Wolf, *American Jew as Patriot, Soldier and Citizen,* 1–10 and 425–41; Belth, *A Promise to Keep,* 19–23; Leonard Dinnerstein, Roger L. Nichols, and David M. Reimers, *Natives*

The most decisive events of the Civil War in St. Louis occurred early in the conflict, events important because they determined which way the city—and Missouri—would go. In a border city that held strong social and economic ties with both sides, it is not surprising that the people divided their loyalties. For a while, indeed, it was touch and go whether St. Louis—and for that matter, the slave state of Missouri—would be with the North or the South. Two state legislatures existed, one flying the Confederate colors, the other loyal to the Union. A Missouri representation even sat in the Confederate Congress, and considerable sympathy existed in St. Louis and throughout the state for the South. Realistically, however, St. Louis proved to be the key, because of its strategic location at the confluence of the Missouri and Mississippi Rivers. Early in the war, on May 10, 1861 (even before the First Battle of Bull Run in Virginia), a Union force comprised overwhelmingly of Germans—there is no way to know how many Jews were included among the "Germans"—forced the surrender of nearly one thousand pro-Confederate troops encamped in Lindell Grove, near the western boundary of the city just east of Grand Avenue and south of Olive Street (today part of the St. Louis University campus). This "Camp Jackson Affair" was at first a bloodless victory for the Union forces. But tragedy soon followed. As the Union captors marched their prisoners down Olive Street for temporary incarceration in the federal arsenal and downtown prisons, hecklers assembled along the way, shouting anti-German and pro-Southern epithets such as "Hurrah for Jeff Davis," "Damn the Dutch," and "Dutch Blackguards." The unruly crowd soon became uglier, and words changed to sticks and stones. Someone fired a shot—no one knows who or from where—and before the smoke had settled, twenty-eight people, including children, lay dead, and many more were wounded. St. Louis was saved for the Union, but at a price that unquestionably added to tensions already high in a city divided by political and cultural differences. Those tensions included a virulent antiforeignism, as St. Louisans seemed willing to absolve "Americans" for the bloodshed, and to place the blame instead on the "Dutch"—and most Jews were included among the "Dutch."

This was the atmosphere that pervaded St. Louis at least during the first few years of the Civil War, until its outcome became fairly certain. The milieu was that of a border city divided in its political sympathies,

and Strangers, 85–118; Higham, Send These to Me, 123–27; Mark E. Neely Jr., The Fate of Liberty: Abraham Lincoln and Civil Liberties, 107–9; Sachar, History of the Jews in America, 72–85; and Gary L. Bunker and John Appel, " 'Shoddy,' Anti-Semitism and the Civil War," 43–71.

heavily populated by an immigrant element viewed by many natives as outsiders. Indeed, years later one who recalled that era noted that the prisons in St. Louis not only "entertained" military personnel captured in battle but also "offered free board and lodging" to hundreds of prominent St. Louisans who sympathized with the South and who committed overt acts against the Union.[14]

Developments in St. Louis involving the Jewish community are difficult to pinpoint, because a unified Jewish community did not yet exist and most Jews were considered part of the larger German population. Nevertheless, resolutions by individual congregations and other organizations indicate that St. Louis Jews, at least those affiliated with Jewish organizations, strongly backed the North. Mrs. Rose Harsch Fraley, who grew up in St. Louis, later recalled that her coreligionists overwhelmingly were Republicans who opposed slavery and supported the Union.[15]

Some served in the military as members of the Home Guard. Commanded by ardent Unionist Frank P. Blair, the Home Guard consisted predominantly of St. Louis Germans deeply committed to preserving the Union. This unit participated importantly in the Camp Jackson episode. Because members of the Home Guard were not categorized by religion, we have no way of knowing how many of those "Germans" were Jews. From other records, however, some Jews who later attained prominence can be identified. Michael B. Jonas, for instance, became a noted lawyer and for many years served as secretary of Temple Israel. Meyer Fuld was among the founders of Temple Israel and was also a very active member of B'nai B'rith. Henry C. Schwabe, later cited for numerous activities within the Jewish community, rose to the rank of colonel in the Home Guard. Perhaps the most widely known Jewish member of the Home Guard was Isaac Baer. Baer remained an active and widely respected member of the Jewish community until he died in 1915.[16]

St. Louisans served in other military groups in various ways. Some enlisted in Missouri units, as did Louis Rosen in D Company, 41st Missouri

---

14. "Reminiscences of Samuel Bowman," in *Modern View 25*, 7. See Primm, *Lion of the Valley*, 248–51, for Camp Jackson and 251–78 for St. Louis during the Civil War. See also Violette, *History of Missouri*, 335–48, and Rombauer, *Union Cause in St. Louis*.

15. There were five men to every girl, Mrs. Fraley reminisced, so that no shortage of socializing existed for the women. Those instances included musical gatherings and parties, toffee pulls, and similar social events, many held to support the war effort. Most Jewish young men not in the service clerked in insurance offices or were engaged in wholesale or retail clothing, milling, jewelry, or merchandising enterprises. "Conversation with Rose Harsch Fraley," n.d., in Missouri Box, AJA.

16. *Voice*, October 2, 1903, April 2, 1915, and December 21, 1917; "Reminiscences of Samuel Bowman," in *Modern View 25*, 7; Primm, *Lion of the Valley*, 244–50.

Volunteer Infantry, and Isaac Russack, who earned corporal stripes in K Company, 5th Missouri Volunteers. Russack later became a prominent wholesale clothier and for many years the popular president of United Hebrew Congregation. Andrew Franklin had recently arrived in St. Louis from New Orleans when the war began, and he helped organize the "Simpson Battery," a unit that served throughout the war on a Mississippi River gunboat.[17]

Many who fought in the Union army later established themselves as solid citizens and merchants in St. Louis, and became active members of various Jewish organizations as well. Simon Freund (who had soldiered earlier in Austria prior to enlisting in the Union army) later prospered in the cigar business and actively supported B'nai El Temple and B'nai B'rith. Ignatz Hartmann, who fought with the First Infantry, became very active in the G.A.R. (the major postwar organization of Union army veterans), in B'nai B'rith, and in another popular fraternal organization, the Independent Order of the Free Sons of Israel. (Hartmann's son Moses became a highly respected attorney and was elected several times to be judge of the St. Louis Circuit Court.) Louis Gutman, Civil War veteran and for more than thirty years a successful merchant in south St. Louis, was eulogized at his death as one who "lived and died an observing Jew." Moritz Mayer established an iron and metal business at Ninth and Chouteau and was also a dedicated member of Temple Israel. Isaac Rindskopf, the livery stable owner, fought in the First Cavalry, suffered wounds in action, and returned to St. Louis. These are but a few of many who left St. Louis to fight for the Union cause and who reestablished themselves afterward back on the banks the Mississippi River.[18]

Others enlisted while living elsewhere, but settled in St. Louis after the fighting was over. Solomon Boehm, who had come to the United States with his parents in 1854, enlisted in the Second Iowa Infantry when the war began. He served with distinction throughout the war, rising to the rank of captain. Following the war he settled in St. Louis and founded a retail pharmacy. He became prominent in many activities: as commander of the Frank P. Blair Post of the G.A.R., as treasurer of the St. Louis College of Pharmacy, as a justice of the peace, and for many years as president of the New Mount Sinai Cemetery Association. Simon J. Arnold, known to

---

17. *Voice*, June 22, 1906, April 15, 1910, and June 11, 1915; Temple Israel (St. Louis) *Bulletin*, October 3, 1944.

18. Gutman Family file, AJA; *Voice*, October 2 and December 28, 1902, June 23, 1905, March 15 and September 13, 1907, April 24, 1908, and February 21, 1913; *Modern View*, May 26, 1922, and June 1, 1923; Postal and Koppman, *Jewish Tourist's Guide*, 182; Wolf, *American Jew as Patriot, Soldier and Citizen*, 221, 223.

many friends as "Sam," served as sergeant-major in the 76th Pennsylvania Infantry and was wounded in the savage fighting at Gettysburg. After the war he settled in St. Louis, where he worked in the office of Collector of Revenue Meyer Rosenblatt, one of the few nineteenth-century Jews to hold an elective office in the city administration. Herman W. Kastor, who was living in New York in 1861, was among the first to answer Lincoln's call for seventy-five thousand volunteers; he enlisted in a New York regiment and served throughout the war. He later settled in St. Louis and founded the H. W. Kastor and Sons Advertising Company. Leopold Stahl came to this country in 1858, enlisted in a New York infantry regiment when hostilities began, and fought in many engagements. He settled afterward in St. Louis, prospered moderately in retail merchandising, and became active in United Hebrew Congregation, B'nai B'rith, and the Independent Order of the Sons of Benjamin. These represent but a few of the many Jews associated with St. Louis who served patriotically and diligently in the service of their country during the Civil War.[19]

Very few St. Louis Jews, it seems, joined the Confederate armed forces at the outbreak of the Civil War. One who did, though, was Philip Wohl, who had emigrated to the United States in 1848 from Karlsbad, Bohemia, and came to St. Louis in the early 1850s by way of New Orleans and Leavenworth, Kansas. Wohl, a member of Missouri Lodge B'nai B'rith who worked with his brother Jacob in a store on Walnut Street, enlisted with the Confederacy when the hostilities started, and fought throughout the war. Afterward, he went back to Karlsbad to marry his childhood sweetheart, Lena Samish. Wohl then brought his new bride back to St. Louis, where they settled and raised a family. Their son, David Philip Wohl, became a giant in the shoe industry as well as one of the most honored and esteemed philanthropists in St. Louis history.[20]

Like many non-Jews, a number who made St. Louis their home after the war were former Confederate soldiers. Adolph Proskauer lived in Mobile, Alabama, when hostilities began. He enlisted as a private in the 12th Alabama Infantry Regiment and rose through the ranks in battle after battle, eventually receiving a battlefield promotion to major for bravery in action. After the war, Proskauer moved to St. Louis and became a prosperous merchant and highly respected citizen. Among other achievements, he became president of the important St. Louis Merchants Exchange. A board member of Temple Israel, he backed the establishment of a Jewish hospital

19. *Voice*, January 15, 1900, February 1, 1907, April 1, 1910, December 6, 1912, July 17, 1914, April 9, 1915, and September 25, 1919; *Modern View*, August 12, 1921; Wolf, *American Jew as Patriot, Soldier and Citizen*, 187, 346.

20. Burton A. Boxerman, "David P. Wohl—Shoe Merchant," 233.

for the St. Louis community. Joseph Strauss commanded a troop in the Louisiana Cavalry and was wounded at Vicksburg. He later settled in St. Louis and associated with the Jacob D. Strauss Saddlery Company. Philip Sartorius of New Orleans fought in B Company, 15th Louisiana Cavalry. Wounded in a skirmish at Delhi, Louisiana, in 1863, he was captured and paroled to St. Louis to live with relatives. Aaron Hirsch, who owned several small country grocery stores in Arkansas, volunteered for the Confederate cavalry. Union troopers who captured Hirsch referred to him opprobriously as a "Judische Secess"—as if being just a secessionist was not derogating enough. One former Confederate soldier who achieved considerable success and prestige later in St. Louis was Jacob D. Goldman. Goldman fought in the 54th Georgia Infantry in bloody engagements at Murfreesboro and Chickamauga. He eventually settled in St. Louis, and became one of the most successful cotton traders in the Midwest and an outstanding community leader.[21]

Former Confederates who later moved to St. Louis also included women noncombatants. Hanna Mesritz, widow of a Confederate army officer, had been active in many war-related endeavors in New Orleans social circles. She moved to St. Louis after hostilities ceased. Fannie Tobias lived in Mobile, Alabama, wife of a prosperous merchant there. When the war ended, they fled with their six children to St. Louis. Tobias often told how she hid Confederate bonds in the hems of her skirts. When asked what happened to them after she got to St. Louis, she replied: "I made a big fire with them, as they were worthless."[22]

Although St. Louis Jews fought and died on both sides in the Civil War, no monument or memorial exists to honor their service and sacrifice. Twenty-three years passed after the war had ended before the idea was even broached. At a meeting of the Mt. Sinai Cemetery Association in May 1888, Solomon Boehm, a Union army veteran himself, proposed the erection of such a monument. The proposal was "warmly received," but nothing resulted from it. Apparently a cemetery lot was available, but it was deemed "too small for a fitting memorial." Time and again the subject was brought up, but with no results. As late as 1916 that same Solomon Boehm, by then the "elder statesman" of the cemetery association, tried once again, but to no avail, even though many Jewish G.A.R. veterans lived in St. Louis at the time. Monuments have been erected in St. Louis and

---

21. Vernon W. v.d. Heydt to author, St. Louis, June 15, 1922, correspondence in possession of author; Merchants Exchange of St. Louis and J. D. Goldman files, AJA; *Voice,* January 4, 1907, and October 13, 1911; Marcus, *Memoirs of American Jews,* vol. 2, 38–46; Wolf, *American Jew as Patriot, Soldier and Citizen,* 121, 197.

22. *Voice,* November 28, 1912; *Modern View,* June 15, 1923.

elsewhere to memorialize other Civil War soldiers, but none specifically for the Jewish veterans of St. Louis.[23]

Contrary to popular mythology, the Civil War was almost an economic disaster for St. Louis. Historian James Neal Primm has pointed out that when the Confederacy cut off the lower Mississippi in 1861, St. Louis lost both its northern trade as well as its vital river passage to eastern and foreign markets. Federal restrictions and discriminatory measures aimed ostensibly at weeding out "disloyal" merchants (such as Grant's General Order No. 11) hampered the city's upper Mississippi valley trade. Much of the economic activity that heretofore had nurtured St. Louis shifted to Chicago, and with the onset of a new era in railroading, the Windy City rocketed past St. Louis as the predominant commercial center of the Midwest. St. Louis recovered part of that loss, however, thanks to wartime government spending. Clothing, transportation, and commissary needs for the military accounted for many millions of dollars in new business for St. Louis merchants. By the end of the war, as the South's hold on the Mississippi was broken, the city's trade recovered its prewar volume. That dropped quickly when the war ended and military spending decreased. The city's economy recovered soon thereafter, however, as St. Louis businesses expanded through the "commercial traveler" or "drummer" system, better known as the "traveling salesman." By the 1870s St. Louis was once again healthy and prosperous.[24]

Where did Jewish businessmen fit into that picture? Histories of St. Louis—as well as of other cities—focus on developments that had "major" impacts on the city's economy and financial structure. In mid-nineteenth-century St. Louis, that included mostly ventures entailing banks, steamboats, railroads, fur, and cotton. Leaders in those fields generally were the "movers" of the business and political community. St. Louis histories include only one Jew—Isidor Bush—among this elite, and he is included primarily because of his tenacious political role in the state legislature, and not because of any impact he or his wine business had on the economy.[25]

Yet local tradition has it that many Jewish merchants prospered during the Civil War, some becoming quite wealthy. Certainly by the 1870s a nouveau riche had emerged within the St. Louis Jewish community (and among non-Jews as well), comprised of immigrant businessmen and merchants whose prosperity had come during the Civil War years.

23. *Voice,* June 1 and October 25, 1888, June 12, 1891, May 1, 1914; *Modern View,* June 16, 1916; Young, *Where They Lie.*

24. Primm, *Lion of the Valley,* 270–71, 291–92.

25. Ibid., 291; Scharf, *Saint Louis City and County,* vol. 2, 1217–21, 1340 ff.

Undoubtedly part of their success resulted from diligent business acumen. But certainly it was due also to their being in the right place at the right time. Many dealt in clothing, dry goods, and a variety of mercantile products, in cotton and wool, in food and commissary-type merchandise (including medicines and drugs), and in transport supplies ranging from horses and mules to harnesses and wagons and feed. Many business ventures toward which poor immigrants had gravitated in the 1850s provided the very goods and services that the wartime economy needed in the 1860s. They also provided the types of goods and services that the postwar westward-expanding nation required. By the end of the Civil War era, many small establishments begun before the war had grown into prosperous institutions, and their German Jewish owners had become well-to-do entrepreneurs. Many now lived in some of the finest neighborhoods of large and spacious homes, such as Lafayette Park and westward, in the near south side along the Mill Creek Valley to Compton Heights. They established their own social clubs, and their new economic and social status contributed to the creation of new synagogues and other institutions. Though not yet accepted into the circle of city "brahmins," this new elite became highly influential within the Jewish population and provided an energetic leadership that stimulated St. Louis Jewry into a vigorous and active phase of community life.[26]

This development was reflected in the establishment of several new and important cultural and social institutions. Among them was a new B'nai B'rith lodge, Ebn Ezra. District Grand Lodge No. 2, of which Missouri Lodge was an organizational affiliate, had scheduled a regional meeting in St. Louis for July 12, 1863. That meeting never occurred, however, because Confederate General John H. Morgan's surprise "Ohio Raid" cut railroad communication to St. Louis from the east. What then ensued in St. Louis was succinctly described by Isidor Bush in an address delivered at the twenty-fifth anniversary of Ebn Ezra Lodge:

> . . . Under these circumstances the Grand Lodge meeting could not convene in St. Louis, much to the disappointment and regret of [the Grand Lodge and the host Missouri Lodge]. But as the latter had already

---

26. Dun and Bradstreet records provide no data on the prosperity of those entrepreneurs, but information from other sources attests to their growth. R. G. Dun and Company Collection, Baker Library, Harvard University; "Conversation with Mrs. Rose Harsch Fraley," n.d., in Missouri Box, AJA; "Reminiscences of a Former St. Louisan," in *Voice*, December 11, 1914; "Reminiscences of Samuel Bowman," in *Modern View 25*, 7–8; *Voice*, May 3, 1901, March 14, 1902, February 22, 1907, April 24, 1908, and December 22, 1911; *Modern View*, September 3, 1915, and March 25, 1927; Postal and Koppman, *Landmarks*, vol. 2, 56.

made arrangements for a summer-night's festival [on July 13] . . . at
Union Park, they invited the few delegates present [and many friends].

. . . It was a beautiful night. Union Park, at that time a charming
spot in the Southern part of the city, scarcely a trace of which is now
[in 1888] to be found, was handsomely decorated. The festive glee, the
spirit of exhilaration was further enhanced by the good news that had
just been received of the fall of Vicksburg. The banquet was set under
an arbor's leafy canopy; . . . [St. Louis Congressman] Henry T. Blow and
Rev. Dr. I. M. Wise of Cincinnati being the orators of the evening . . .
and others also delivered felicitous speeches; the ladies and young men
danced in the hall . . .

At the same time and place a petition to the Grand Lodge was signed by
the following members of Missouri Lodge: A. Frankenthal, A. Kramer,
A. Loth, M. Jacoby, M. L. Cohn, L. Maas, A. Isaacs, L. Schwartzkopf,
M. Meyerstein and Isidor Bush. These men were by no means dissatisfied
with their own Lodge, but they felt that the establishment of a new one,
working in the vernacular of this country—for the petition stated that
the proceedings were to be conducted in the English language—would
widen and strengthen the circle of our brotherhood and further its cause,
without weakening or otherwise affecting the prosperity of Missouri
Lodge. This had already over one hundred members, transacting its
business in German, and was perfectly willing to have a new lodge
working in the English language, established in St. Louis.[27]

Thus Ebn Ezra Lodge came about because members of Missouri Lodge
preferred an English-speaking group to one that conducted its affairs in
German. Their petition was formally approved by District Grand Lodge
No. 2 in Cleveland on July 25, 1863. Later that year the first officers of
Ebn Ezra Lodge No. 47 were installed: A. Frankenthal, president; Isidor
Bush, vice president; A. Isaacs, secretary; M. Meyerstein, treasurer; L.
Schwartzkopf, monitor; and M. L. Cohn, warden. Ebn Ezra remains today
an active and productive B'nai B'rith lodge in St. Louis.[28]

In 1869 St. Louis Jews founded Cornerstone Lodge No. 323 of the Order
of Ancient Free and Accepted Masons. Masonic chapters had existed in

---

27. *Voice*, October 26, 1888.

28. Ibid. Ebn Ezra's twenty-fifth anniversary banquet, held in October 1888 at
Covenant Hall, Ninth and Market, showed the strong ties St. Louis German Jews still
maintained with their former homeland. Most speakers addressed the assemblage in
German. A newspaper reporter described the enthusiastic audience response to Rabbi
Adolph Rosentreter's mere mention that it was the birthday of "the sainted" Emperor
Frederick III: "The applause lasted several minutes," he wrote. Several more B'nai
B'rith lodges came into being in St. Louis, but apparently none achieved the staying
power of Missouri and Ebn Ezra. References exist to Judah Touro Lodge, Moritz Spitz
Lodge, Isidor Bush Lodge, Achim Lodge, Menorah Lodge, and Julius Furst Lodge, all
in St. Louis at one time or another. Records and Ledgers, B'nai B'rith Lodge No. 557,
AJA; *Voice*, January 1, 1891; *Modern View 25*, 11; Scharf, *Saint Louis City and County*,
vol. 2, 1810.

St. Louis as early as the 1840s, but for the first time a predominantly Jewish group came into being. Charter members included Moses Fraley, Jacob Furth, Joel Swope, Abraham Kramer, David Levy, and Leopold Schoen, men already or shortly to become prosperous Jewish personalities in St. Louis. Other early members of Cornerstone Lodge were Albert S. Aloe, August Frank, Aaron Haas, Leon Helman, Nathan Stampfer, Jacob Straus, Louis Renard, Leopold Freund, and Aaron Rosenthal; they, too, were or would become prominent members of the St. Louis German Jewish community. Originating shortly after the Civil War, Cornerstone Lodge continued for more than a century before it merged with Benjamin Franklin Lodge No. 642 in the 1980s. During that lengthy period, it attracted many Jewish members and recorded innumerable benevolent and philanthropic achievements.[29]

For years prior to the 1860s, the major outlet for Jewish culture (other than the synagogues) emanated from local subscriptions to the *Israelite* and the *Occident*, journals published in Cincinnati and Philadelphia that contained not only Jewish news but also literary works of prose and poetry.[30] As late as 1858 Rabbi Henry Kuttner observed ruefully that "culture here is rather backward," and he feared that it would be "a long time before it will take an upward swing." Yet on several occasions guest rabbis lectured at the two synagogues, and their orations, some in English and some in German, were well attended and warmly received. Especially popular was a musical program by Cantor Marx Moses and his choir from Anshei Emeth Synagogue in Peoria; they performed before a packed United Hebrew sanctuary. A number of German associations existed in St. Louis, such as the "Polyhymnia" and the "Philharmonic Society," to promote vocal and instrumental music, but there is no indication of how "Jewish" they were.[31]

On several occasions St. Louis Jews sought unsuccessfully to organize cultural groups that transcended congregational affiliation. On August 23,

---

29. Author interview with Ralph Koslow of St. Louis Lodge No. 20, AF & AM, St. Louis, July 3, 1990; *Modern View*, August 18, 1925. St. Louis Lodge No. 20 was another masonic chapter whose members were overwhelmingly Jewish; in fact, it was known popularly as "The Jewish Lodge." *Voice*, December 20, 1907.

30. Ludwig [Louis] Schwartzkopf, already associated with various Jewish organizations, acted also as the local agent through whom St. Louisans subscribed to these publications. *Israelite*, April 14, 1857; *Occident* 1 (July 1843): 170, 1 (January 1844): 527, and 2 (March 1845): 510.

31. Henry Kuttner to Isaac Leeser, St. Louis, June 16, 1858, in Missouri Box, AJA. Visiting lecturers included Rabbi Isidor Kalish of Indianapolis and Rabbi Simon Tuska of Memphis. *Israelite*, July 17 and 31, 1863, and May 19, 1864. For German cultural organizations, see ibid., January 17, 1859, and Scharf, *Saint Louis City and County*, vol. 1, 973 and vol. 2, 1629.

1863, these efforts finally met with success when nine young men banded together as the "Hebrew Young Men's Literary Association." One month later they elected their first group of officers: Albert S. Aloe, president; J. R. Jacobs, vice president; I. H. Lazarus, corresponding and recording secretary; S. Fraley, treasurer; and M. Silverstone, financial secretary. Membership grew to forty-five within only three months, as programs provided debates, recitations, essays, and orations for the culture-starved Jewish community. Secretary Lazarus, describing some of the group's activities, observed that participants did themselves great credit, especially "taking into consideration that many of them have never before undertaken to perform anything of the kind, and I can here safely say, without doubt or hesitation, that there is not a single member who has not derived some benefit in the way of literature." Rabbi Isaac Leeser of Philadelphia, editor of the *Occident*, on becoming an honorary member remarked that the new group promised to be "an ornament to this city and our people," and that such an association presaged a vast increase in Jewish literary efforts in St. Louis. The years ahead proved him quite correct.[32]

In contrast with the Hebrew Young Men's Literary Association, another group that originated for cultural purposes soon became primarily a social organization. On November 13, 1859, "a few gentlemen" met informally at Bremer Schlissel, a popular German café on the southwest corner of Third and Olive, and organized the "Harmonie Club" for "the cultivation of literary attainment and the promotion of social intercourse among its members." "Literary attainment" may have been part of their ongoing program; when the Harmonie Club was formally incorporated on May 31, 1869, the articles indeed identified the group as a "literary society." Realistically, though, the "promotion of social intercourse" apparently became the principal raison d'être. From early on, high dues and limited membership virtually assured that only the more affluent would qualify for club membership. One member described the club's roster as consisting of only "the best Jewish element," meaning no doubt the new wealthy among St. Louis's German Jewish population. At first all proceedings were only in German, but in 1868 they changed to English. Early members included Leon M. Helman (the first president), Augustus Binswanger, Albert S. Aloe, Joseph Greenbaum, Morris Rosenheim, George Levis, Barney Hysinger, Saul Schneider, Louis Renard, Meyer Rosenblatt, and Jacob Furth.

---

32. *Israelite*, January 1, 1864; *Occident* 21 (November 1863): 383 and 22 (April 1864): 46. The "Hebrew Young Men's Literary Association" should not be confused with the later "Young Men's Hebrew Association"—the YMHA—although the latter probably evolved from the former.

The Harmonie Club at first rented modest quarters above Specht's Restaurant on Market between Fourth and Broadway; by 1872 they could afford more elaborate rooms on the third floor of a new white marble-front building on Fourth between Spruce and Elm. Club quarters there were reached by a graceful wide staircase, and included a fine ballroom, a large and well-equipped dining room, an elegant ladies' parlor, and several comfortable card rooms. As more and more Jews attained economic afflu-ence, the Harmonie Club became the place for "fashionable" Jewish social events of all sorts. Samuel Bowman later recalled a delightful custom at Club balls: the midnight supper. "The orchestra would strike up the well known march from the opera 'Norma,' known as the 'Supper March'— and then the President leading, would be followed in formal procession by the members of the Club in a march parade to the dining room." Applauding caterer Ralph Lowenstein's savory preparations, Bowman reminisced that "in those days that great and delectable dish known as 'Stopf Leber,' or stuffed goose livers, was frequently served," to the culinary delight of party-goers and diners. This lavishness typified the highly secularist and garish social lifestyle of the emerging German Jewish nouveau riche of St. Louis, a lifestyle that characterized the extravagance and opulence which American historians have associated with the Gilded Age. The Harmonie Club remained for several decades the center of social life among affluent German Jews, and the place where one would find the movers and shakers of the gradually coalescing St. Louis Jewish community.[33]

One should not assume, though, that the ever-growing number of well-to-do German Jews was imperiously materialistic. Just as Bowman recalled elegant and lavish social occasions, he also pointed out that "literary attainment" and culture were by no means abandoned. The Harmonie Club hosted numerous delightful amateur theatrics, concerts, and orations, and members often were presented with opportunities to broaden their cultural horizons. Furthermore, mention has been made of the increasing number of benevolent associations, both men's and women's, which attended to the needs of the poor, especially among the continuous flow of fellow religionists seeking refuge from oppressive conditions in Europe. The Jewish traditions of *tzedakah* and *tikkun olom*— sustenance and support for any who suffer deprivation—had been alive

---

33. Some sources date the Harmonie Club's "Bremer Schlissel" informal beginning in 1856 and 1857. Since the club was formally organized in 1869, its records go back only to that date. See *Tribune*, July 6 and November 23, 1883; *Modern View 25*, 5, 9–10; *Modern View*, August 28, 1925, and April 19, 1929; Scharf, *Saint Louis City and County*, vol. 2, 1817–18.

and healthy in the St. Louis Jewish community for some time. Noting that prior to 1870 Jewish community affairs in St. Louis still were in a "primitive state," one observer nevertheless singled out the Ladies Zion Society for its philanthropic and altruistic efforts. Those women, led for many years by Leonora Wolfort, raised thousands of dollars by sponsoring annual charity balls "attended by rich and poor, there being no 'money class' distinction among our people in those early days." Dances were held at the Masonic Hall on Seventh and Market, the Germania Club at Eighth and Gratiot, the ever-popular Liederkranz Club at Thirteenth and Chouteau, and, of course, at the Harmonie Club. Years later, old-timers still recalled the midnight suppers—"many of us still smack our lips"— served by the "generous Jewish matrons" of the Ladies Zion Society. They also remembered that the ladies' culinary delights were surpassed by generosity toward many unfortunates in need of assistance.[34]

Even as the Civil War decade of the 1860s witnessed a blossoming of St. Louis Jewry in business, benevolent, and cultural endeavors, religious institutions were not neglected. True, rabbis repeatedly deplored the state of religion, but one would hardly expect them to do otherwise. Besides, such complaints, then as now, often reflect holiday or ritual observance, attendance at services, or congregational affiliation, criteria that can be quite misleading in measuring the allegiance of any people toward their religion. True, many German Jewish immigrants distanced themselves from traditional Judaism, and many separated themselves from Judaism completely; nevertheless, as immigration continued during the Civil War years and after, existing Jewish religious institutions in St. Louis continued to grow, and new ones came into being.[35]

Both United Hebrew and B'nai El Congregations experienced a variety of growth problems. Both now had excellent physical facilities, B'nai El at its original site on Sixth and Cerre where the congregation had been housed since 1855, and United Hebrew in its newer synagogue on Sixth Street constructed in 1859. Though packed on the High Holy Days of Rosh Hashannah and Yom Kippur, both buildings were more than adequate for the far lesser numbers that assembled during the rest of the year. Congregational records indicate growth in membership, but finances continued to plague both institutions. United Hebrew seemed to be especially so smitten, apparently from overextending itself in its new building. Only herculean efforts by presidents Adolph J. Latz and Raphael Keiler "saved [the] congregation from being sacrificed."[36]

---

34. "Reminiscences of Samuel Bowman," in *Modern View* 25, 7.

35. *Israelite,* August 8, 1862.

36. Unidentified writer to Editor, ibid., January 16, 1863. See also ibid., August 12, 1859, November 2, 1860, June 5 and July 6, 1863, and *Occident* 20 (December 1862): 430.

United Hebrew faced one problem that B'nai El had solved: it had no rabbi. Except for the very brief tenures of Rabbis Illowy (1854–1855) and Kuttner (1857), for more than two decades United Hebrew relied upon its own lay members and part-time professionals to perform necessary religious functions. It also benefited occasionally by "borrowing" Rabbi Kuttner from B'nai El. By 1863, however, with its finances apparently under control, United Hebrew instituted a search for a full-time permanent spiritual leader. After seeing several impressive candidates, in 1864 the congregation hired Rabbi Henry Vidaver. A native of Hungary and educated in Germany, Vidaver came to the United States in 1859 to Philadelphia, where he served first at the Julianna Street Synagogue (popularly known as the "Old German Synagogue"), followed by a brief tenure at the famous Rodeph Shalom Synagogue. He then returned for several years to Berlin, and in 1864 answered the call to United Hebrew. Vidaver brought with him a reputation as not only a great preacher in both English and German but also "one of the most elegant Hebrew writers of the day."[37]

Possibly the highlight of Vidaver's ministry at United Hebrew was the occasion of President Abraham Lincoln's assassination. Vidaver delivered a stirring and moving eulogy in the packed black-draped United Hebrew sanctuary. Copies of his address were reproduced throughout the country as part of the outpouring of tributes to the martyred president. Vidaver's words touched the soul of a grieving America, and his literary excellence produced an encomium that has stood the test of American history:

> He [Lincoln] lives in all that can eternalize the memory of man on earth; he lives in those glorious actions he executed in order to rescue his country from peril, shame, and disgrace; he lives and will live forever in those grand and startling principles which he displayed and maintained with an unparalled moral force—principles which not only helped to uphold the power of our Union, but which likewise wiped out the blackest spot which stigmatized our star-spangled banner. Yes, Abraham Lincoln still lives, and will live forever, and "a double portion of his spirit" will rest upon us, the people of the United States, who will strive to follow his examples, and live in his spirit of liberty, justice, and love, and thus he will live in his people eternally. . . . Wheresoever the sway of despotism and slavery will be crushed, and freedom will carry the day, there the great names of our Republic's fathers will be honored and praised; there one more name will be added to the number, and that name will be Abraham Lincoln.[38]

37. *Israelite*, May 13, 1864, and related board minutes of United Hebrew and B'nai El Congregations. Also see *Voice*, December 23, 1902, January 16 and 30, 1903, and January 19, February 2, 9, and 23, March 8 and 30, April 20, and June 1, 1917.

38. The full text of Vidaver's famous eulogy can be found in *Occident* 23 (June 1865): 122–28.

Perhaps the most vexing problem facing United Hebrew and B'nai El was the pull between traditional Orthodoxy and the new Reform Judaism. The issue was not confined to St. Louis alone; it existed in Jewish communities all over the country. Many German Jewish immigrants viewed traditional religious practices as ties to a European life and lifestyle they had finally been able to leave. Interestingly, many actively patronized and even encouraged nonreligious *secular* ties with their former homeland; thus, musical, literary, athletic, and other *vereins* that extolled the *Vaterland*'s language and culture flourished in virtually all German immigrant communities. But the attitude toward their Jewish religious environment was quite different. The French Revolution, the advent of Reform Judaism, and prospects of a new life outside the ghetto led European Jews to question many religious practices that tied them to a vanished social past. This proved especially true among Jews who emigrated to America throughout the nineteenth century. To become Americanized meant to cut those Jewish *religious* ties even as those same immigrants fostered and promoted German *cultural* ties. Thus many abandoned their Judaism for either agnosticism or atheism, or else they assimilated into the Christian community through conversion or intermarriage. But many more took a less drastic approach: they maintained their ancestral faith, but modified traditional Orthodoxy for a more "modern" or "liberal" or "Americanized" form of Judaism. For, in fact, they rebelled not against Judaism, but against *Orthodox* Judaism.

Many writers, for various reasons, have made much of those who abandoned the faith of their ancestors. But the overwhelming majority of German Jewish immigrants *remained Jewish.* Their Judaism ranged from traditional Orthodox theology and ritual as practiced in their European homelands to a new and exceedingly liberal brand of Reform Judaism. But withal, they remained Jewish. Opinions differed as to what constituted "proper" Judaism; they probably will continue to differ as long as Judaism exists. There is no doubt that most German Jewish immigrants, including those in St. Louis, sought to fit their Judaism into the surrounding secular environment by changing some of their religious practices—but with absolutely no intention of giving up their faith. Many had begun that process even before leaving Europe. It meant facing accusations of being no longer "religious Jews"; it meant being referred to as "Jews in name only" or as "High Holy Day Jews" or as "secular Jews." That modifying or dropping certain customs seemed only to emulate practices of Christian neighbors, or to be merely changes of convenience, only added to the controversy. This was a major issue that convulsed the entire Jewish population in the United States, from the long-established Sephardic communities located mostly in coastal communities to the newly arriving immigrant populations spreading throughout the country. It was also a major issue in United Hebrew and B'nai El in St. Louis: where in that broad spectrum between traditionalism and modernism could a comfortable position be found that would enable members to be both "good Jews" and "good Americans." (It should be noted, by the way, that the same problem existed among the Slavic/eastern European/Orthodox Jewish immigrants who flocked to this country in the latter part of the nineteenth and early part of the twentieth centuries. Many of them also intermarried and assimilated, and abandoned their ancestral faith. Many also became nonobservant Jews, practicing the rituals of their faith primarily on the occasion of a life-cycle event such as a *bris* or a *Bar Mitzvah* or a funeral, rarely participating in religious services—yet they still considered themselves Orthodox Jews. Many also became Reform Jews. It is unfair and incorrect, then, to assign those "distancing" actions only to the German Jewish immigrants of the nineteenth century.)

It made no difference, by the way, whether or not one affiliated with a congregation. Undoubtedly most mid-nineteenth-century St. Louis Jews remained unaffiliated; congregational records indicate a relatively small portion of them were members. Yet nonmembers thronged to the synagogues for Rosh Hashannah and Yom Kippur, purchased temporary seating for the holy day services, and packed the few synagogues well beyond their capacities.[39] Congregational records also show, as do cemetery records and press articles (although there was no St. Louis "Jewish press" until later) that even those not affiliated with congregations constantly evinced concern about many Jewish practices, especially life-cycle events such as circumcisions, weddings, and burials.[40]

---

39. As recently as 1982, when the St. Louis Jewish community had changed considerably as a result of the earlier influx of eastern European Jews and refugees from Hitlerian Europe, a demographic study of the city's Jews showed that at least one-third still did not affiliate with a temple or synagogue. And there were many more congregations for them to join in 1982 than there had been in the Civil War era. Gary A. Tobin, "The Jewish Federation of St. Louis Demographic Study, December, 1982: Executive Summary," copy in possession of author. Tobin conducted a follow-up study in 1994, but its results were not available at the time this book went into publication.

40. In addition to B'nai El and United Hebrew records, other evidence points to lack of affiliation by many St. Louis Jews. See, for instance, the article by Henry Myers, secretary of United Hebrew Congregation, in *Occident* 7 (December 1849): 77–81; Isidor Bush to Isaac Leeser, Carondelet, Mo., July 27, 1852, and Henry Kuttner to Isaac Leeser, St. Louis, December 5, 1858, June 6, 1862, and March 13, 1865, in Missouri Box, AJA. B'nai El and United Hebrew Congregations circumspectfully provided a *mohel* for their members; solicitations and advertisements by other *mohels* undoubtedly were aimed at noncongregational Jews. See, for example, advertisements addressed "To

The search in St. Louis for how to be both "good Jews" and "good Americans" actually had begun when the first Jews arrived, and certainly when the first congregations had been formed. By the end of the Civil War decade, United Hebrew and B'nai El had instituted changes that showed them moving unmistakably in a liberal direction. Even before the 1860s, both had introduced choirs and organs; yet both continued to seat men and women separately in services. Both still held traditional *Bar Mitzvah* ceremonies; yet as early as 1862 both had introduced Confirmation of boys and girls at the Shavuos service. By 1863 both had adopted the *Minhag America* form of service to replace the *Minhag Poland*, using the new prayer book developed by Reform Rabbi Isaac Mayer Wise. When United Hebrew advertised in 1863 for a rabbi and preacher "of moderate reform tendency," Isaac Leeser, champion of American Orthodoxy, hoped that "moderate reform" would not lead the congregation in a "downward path" that might "loosen ties in our faith." Whereas Leeser deplored the liberalizing tendencies in the St. Louis synagogues, Isaac Mayer Wise viewed that movement as positive and commendable. Both congregations conducted services in Hebrew and the vernacular, with the biggest debate being whether "vernacular" should be English or German (at first most favored German, but gradually the use of English increased). One of the most divisive internal disputes in United Hebrew centered on whether to hire non-Jews for the choir; the decision, after considerable dispute, was in the affirmative. B'nai El also revised or abolished a number of long-held practices. In 1865, amendments to the congregations' constitution discontinued the wearing of the *talis* (prayer shawl); ended the practice of the *aliyah* (calling men up to the Torah when it was read during services); and provided that the Haftorah be read in German rather than Hebrew. Leadership for these changes came from the congregational rabbis (Kuttner and Vidaver) as well as from the lay boards of trustees. Clearly, then, United Hebrew and B'nai El seemed to be moving inexorably toward Reform. Yet neither was so identified; in fact, the term "Orthodox" continued to be applied to both, both locally and by outside observers.[41]

---

the Israelites of St. Louis, Mo. and Vicinity" in the *Israelite*, January 1, 1864. Rabbi Moritz Spitz of B'nai El served also as editor first of the *Jewish Tribune* and then of the *Jewish Voice* from 1879 to 1920; throughout that entire period he constantly decried editorially the lack of affiliation by so many St. Louis Jews.

41. In addition to board minutes of United Hebrew and B'nai El Congregations for the 1860s available at those institutions, see also United Hebrew File, AJA; Henry Kuttner to Isaac Leeser, St. Louis, June 6, 1862, and March 13, 1865, in Missouri Box, AJA; *Israelite*, July 26 and August 12, 1859, August 8, 1862, March 28, June 5 and 17, July 24, August 14, and November 20, 1863; *Occident* 17 (July 1859): 97, 18 (June 1860):

Therein lay the main reason for the organization of a new congregation, Shaare Emeth, which opened its doors officially in 1869 as the first clearly identified Reform congregation in St. Louis. Shaare Emeth's roots came from B'nai El. In April 1863 Isaac Hoffheimer, a member of B'nai El, approached Isaac Fuld about starting a new Reform group. Recently married, the twenty-nine-year-old Fuld was the youngest full-fledged member of B'nai El. Raised Orthodox, Fuld had attended a Reform service in Frankfort-am-Main about ten years earlier and had been deeply impressed. Over the next few months between ninety and a hundred men joined with Fuld and Hoffheimer, some from B'nai El and others from United Hebrew or unaffiliated, and in 1865 they organized "The Temple Association." Its purpose was candidly to pave the way for a new Reform congregation. Shortly thereafter another group came into being, "The Temple Building Association," whose object was to raise funds for a temple for this new Reform congregation.[42]

The Temple Building Association proved to be phenomenally successful. Within only one year, in 1866, they had acquired sufficient funds to purchase a lot on the northeast corner of Seventeenth and Pine and to hire an architect to draw up plans for their building. Officers of this successful association, all members of B'nai El, by the way, included Alexander Suss, president; Isaac Hoffheimer, vice president; I. Rosenfield (also cashier of the State Savings Bank), secretary-treasurer; Joseph Weil, corresponding secretary; and Bernard Singer, S. Schiele, T. L. Bothahn, Isaac Hellman, Morris Landsdorff, L. R. Strauss, Leopold Steinberger, M. L. Winter, P. Seligmann, S. Marx, and Levi Stern, directors. Their success in raising money undoubtedly reflected the financial success of at least a portion of the St. Louis German Jewish population. On June 24, 1867, in an impressive service joined by the Freemasons of Missouri and addressed by Rabbi Isaac Mayer Wise, the cornerstone was laid for the new Reform temple.[43]

87, 21 (June 1863): 139–40; and *Voice,* January 30 and February 6, 1903, and May 30 and August 31, 1917.

42. Shaare Emeth and B'nai El records are confusing about the Temple Building Association. B'nai El files suggest that the "T.B.A." was an ad hoc B'nai El committee whose original purpose was to look into a new building for B'nai El, but that committee members soon joined seceders and devoted their efforts to funding a building for the new Reform congregation instead. Shaare Emeth records, on the other hand, indicate that the T.B.A.'s objective from the very beginning was to raise funds for a new Reform temple. See B'nai El and Shaare Emeth board minutes in library of Shaare Emeth Temple, St. Louis, and in AJA. See also "Reminiscences of Isaac Fuld," in *Modern View* 25, 11.

43. A detailed description of the cornerstone ceremony is found in the *Missouri Republican* (St. Louis), June 25, 1867, and in *Israelite,* June 28, 1867. In the cornerstone

Meanwhile, sometime in late 1866 or early 1867, the original Temple Association reorganized itself into a congregation now known as Shaare Emeth ("Gates of Truth") Congregation. The membership was guided by the desire to "escape dogmatic discussions and dissensions," and to "bring the Israelitish form of worship into harmony with the views and principles of modern society." The congregation's first officers were Barney Hysinger, president; Isaac Hoffheimer, vice president; and Meyer Linz, sexton. (Actually Levi Stern was elected to be the first president, but he declined, and Hysinger was chosen in his place.) A building committee to overlook the completion of the temple included Morris Landsdorff, Bernard Singer, Abraham Kramer, and Meyer Friede (who had formerly been president of B'nai El as well as a member of the state legislature). Pending completion of the temple, in 1868 the new congregation employed Neuman Tuholske as temporary reader. Tuholske was an excellent scholar "who had earned for himself many years before coming to this country the reputation of being one of the most conscientious, profound and clear-headed teachers in the kingdom of Prussia." Existing records give no indication where Shaare Emeth's "home" was while their temple was under construction.[44]

Dedication services in August 1869 formally opened Shaare Emeth to public worship. Rabbi James K. Gutheim, renowned scholar and preacher who only recently had moved from a New Orleans congregation to the prestigious pulpit of Temple Emanu-El in New York, gave a stimulating dedicatory address. Another New York rabbi, Solomon H. Sonneschein, then delivered a very moving prayer and benediction. So impressed was the congregation with the "unheralded" Sonneschein, described as a "radical reformer, though not an extremist," that the very next day, in a

---

was a box containing copies of three St. Louis newspapers, the *Missouri Republican,* the *Daily Missouri Democrat,* and the German-language *Anzeiger des Westens;* also a sheet of paper on which was written: "The corner stone of this Shaare Emeth Temple was laid on the 24th day of June, 1867, under the auspices of the Freemasons of Missouri. Orator, Rev. Dr. I. M. Wise." Also in the box were several two-cent pieces. In 1880, when Shaare Emeth moved into its next building on Lindell and Vandeventer, that old cornerstone was removed from the Seventeenth and Pine structure and reset in the new one. *Tribune,* July 2, 1880.

44. Tuholske's characterization is by Rabbi Samuel Sale in Hyde and Conard, eds., *Encyclopedia of the History of St. Louis,* vol. 2, 1129. See also *Tribune,* March 19, 1880, and Scharf, *Saint Louis City and County,* vol. 2, 1739. Others associated with the beginnings of Shaare Emeth include Meyer Friede, H. S. Winter, S. Sanfelder, L. Stern, A. Kramer, B. Hysinger, L. Steinberger, and L. M. Hellman. *The Jewish Sentinel* (St. Louis), August 21, 1868.

specially called meeting, Shaare Emeth offered him the position of rabbi. Reform Judaism had come to St. Louis.[45]

The establishment of Shaare Emeth Temple led directly to the organization of one of St. Louis's major Jewish cemeteries, Mount Sinai. As with any congregation, Shaare Emeth placed a high priority on providing burial facilities for its membership. Since the new congregation had evolved mostly from B'nai El, it was logical that its members might continue to use B'nai El's Gravois Road cemetery. That request was duly made. A committee from each congregation was thereupon appointed to consider the question: Messrs. Hirsch, Heller, and J. Frank from B'nai El, and Abraham Kramer, Barney Hysinger, and Morris Landsdorff from Shaare Emeth. On April 27, 1869, they agreed to the formation of the Mount Sinai Cemetery Association, to be incorporated under Missouri law, to provide burial facilities for the two congregations. Shaare Emeth agreed to pay in one thousand dollars. Anticipating that two growing congregations now would need a larger facility, the committee authorized William Sicher and Louis M. Hellman to purchase seven arpents (about six and a half acres) adjoining the original grounds, at a cost of twenty-five hundred dollars. The two congregations quickly ratified that purchase, and then appointed a new committee to draw up a constitution and bylaws for the newly created cemetery association. J. L. Singer, William Sicher, and M. Freund represented B'nai El; Abraham Kramer, D. Cole, and Louis M. Hellman spoke for Shaare Emeth. Among the regulations was a provision that only persons "as are at the time of their death known to be Israelites" could be buried there. Management of the new association was vested in a committee of twelve, six from each congregation.

In 1884 the cemetery association purchased an additional adjoining twenty acres for the bargain price of three thousand dollars, making the size of Mount Sinai Cemetery about twenty-eight acres. That remained the situation until 1886, when another Reform congregation, Temple Israel, came into existence and sought admission into the cemetery association.[46]

---

45. Apparently Shaare Emeth's first choice for spiritual leader was a Rabbi Mayer of Cleveland. He was invited as guest preacher during the summer of 1869, before the temple was formally dedicated, and Shaare Emeth reportedly offered him the position. He declined, however, preferring to remain in Cleveland. *Israelite*, August 16 and September 3, 1869, and January 7, 1870. See also Temple Shaare Emeth File, AJA; *Tribune*, July 2, 1880; *Voice*, April 5, 1910, and April 16, 1920; and Compton, ed., *Pictorial Saint Louis*, 111.

46. *Jewish Free Press*, November 19, 1886; *Voice*, June 8, 1888, July 27 and August 3, 1906, and November 24, 1911. The *Voice* of July 27, 1906, prints the text of the April 27,

Although Reform Judaism emerged during and after the Civil War era, Orthodoxy did not disappear within the German Jewish population. Despite the absence of reliable records, particularly among the many small Orthodox *shuls* that are often not much more than a *minyan*, some information does exist about at least two groups of German Jews in St. Louis who not only retained their Orthodoxy but also became stepping-stones to later congregations that continued traditionalism right up to the present.

Very little evidence can be found on the first of those groups, known simply as the "Chevrah Kadisha" (Holy Society). In fact, only one known reference exists. In 1925 the publishers of the *Modern View*, a St. Louis English-language Jewish newspaper, printed an illustrated magazine-type twenty-fifth anniversary edition in which appeared an article entitled "The Orthodox Community of St. Louis," written by Rabbi Adolph Rosentreter. German born and educated, Rosentreter had come to St. Louis in 1884 and the following year became the spiritual leader of the newly formed Orthodox B'nai Amoona Congregation, where he ministered for more than two decades (although not always on a full-time basis) before going into private business. In that *Modern View* article Rabbi Rosentreter wrote:

> In 1882 there were two distinct Orthodox congregations, the "Chevrah Kadisha" and "Sheerith Israel." These two had "Minyan" in rented rooms and held services on the Sabbath and holidays only. The Members were poor and they had to keep expenses within the limits. *The "Chevrah Kadisha" was in existence since 1862.* [Author's emphasis] Their charter was granted August 28, 1873. This charter was taken over by the congregation "Shirei Thillim" in 1893, and that name adopted in 1904.

Except for Rosentreter's statement, no extant data corroborates a Chevrah Kadisha Congregation as early as 1862. References to a congregation by that name do exist in the 1880s and later, but none can be associated with

---

1869, agreement between representatives of B'nai El and Shaare Emeth. The August 3, 1906, edition lists the contents of the bylaws and constitution. Both were reprinted, according to *Voice* editor Rabbi Spitz, from a pamphlet published in 1869 for members of both B'nai El and Shaare Emeth, in both English and German. See also "History of the New Mt. Sinai Cemetery," (n.d.), in records of New Mt. Sinai Cemetery Association, St. Louis, copy in possession of author; also I. Schlesinger, "The New Mt. Sinai Cemetery Association," in *Modern View 25,* 213. In addition to the cemetery arrangement by the two temples, they soon instituted another very successful cooperative program, the annual joint Thanksgiving morning service. The first was held on Thursday morning, November 27, 1879, at B'nai El's temple on Eleventh and Chouteau. *Tribune,* November 21 and 28, 1879; *Voice,* April 29, 1904. The annual joint Thanksgiving service still continues today, expanded to include additional congregations.

Rabbi Rosentreter's 1862 congregation.[47] A "Shirei Thillim" also came into existence later and indeed still exists today, in the small, merged Mishkan Israel–Shirei Thillim Congregation in suburban University City. Unfortunately that body has no written records of either the earlier Mishkan Israel or Shirei Thillim organizations. Surviving members of Shirei Thillim prior to its merger with Mishkan Israel recall some of its history as far back as the World War I era,[48] when both synagogues were prominent institutions within the Orthodox community in midtown St. Louis. But neither oral nor written evidence supports the alleged merger of a Chevrah Kadisha with a Shirei Thillim in 1893. Nevertheless, despite the lack of corroborative documentation, there seems to be little reason to doubt Rosentreter's account—except, perhaps, the accuracy of his dates. Too many small and short-lived Orthodox congregations have existed in St. Louis that simply left no records. Although Rosentreter said nothing about the members of Chevrah Kadisha, one must assume that originally, at least, they were German Jews dissatisfied with the liberal inclinations of both United Hebrew and B'nai El and who preferred a more traditional religious setting. Like the founders of United Hebrew, they may have descended from Polish Jews who had been annexed to Germanic states, but who were withal "German" Jews. Besides, those whom we identify as "eastern European Jews" did not come to St. Louis in appreciable numbers until the 1870s and the 1880s, and any congregation initiated earlier must have been established by those we call German Jews. This would certainly include the Chevrah Kadisha to which Rabbi Rosentreter referred.[49]

---

47. *Voice*, April 26 and May 24, 1901, and December 5, 1902; *Modern View* 25, 28; Scharf, *Saint Louis City and County*, vol. 2, 1740; John Devoy, *A History of the City of St. Louis and Vicinity, from the Earliest Times to the Present*, 181–88. Unfortunately, the name "Chevrah Kadisha" ("Holy Society") engenders confusion, for virtually any *minyan* or religiously oriented group can bear that title, and many have. Several synagogues and at least one cemetery did indeed later call themselves "Chevrah Kadisha," and many often used that term indiscriminately in referring to any Orthdox congregation, regardless of its size.

48. It was popularly known for many years as the "DeBaliviere Shul," after the street adjacent to Forest Park on which the synagogue was located. Prior to being at that location, Shirei Thillim had been at Thirteenth and Carr.

49. *Voice*, April 26 and May 24, 1901, and December 5, 1902; *Modern View* 25, 28; author interviews with Alan Sabol (former president) and Alan Green (rabbi) of Mishkan Israel–Shirei Thillim Congregation, St. Louis, August 25, 1988. A Chevrah Kadisha Cemetery association came into existence in 1920, but it had no connection with the Shirei Thillim Congregation. See also *Jubilee Book Commemorating the 50th Anniversary of the Chesed Shel Emeth Society of St. Louis*, 16, as well as manuscript records of the Chesed Shel Emeth and Chevrah Kadisha Cemetery Associations in St. Louis.

Just as the early history of Chevrah Kadisha remains obscure, so too are the origins of the other German Jewish Orthodox *shul,* Sheerith Israel, even though it evolved into one of St. Louis's major congregations. Sheerith Israel came into existence after the Civil War, through the efforts mainly of one Abraham Tuchler. A native of Cracow,[50] Tuchler was one of many German Jewish immigrants who fought on the Union side during the Civil War. He then came to St. Louis, where sometime in 1868 or 1869 he helped found the Orthodox congregation "Sheerith Israel" (Remnants of Israel). The congregation was known popularly as the "Krakower Shul," since many members, like Tuchler, had immigrated from the Cracow area of Poland.[51] In addition to Tuchler, others in leadership roles included Joseph Sessel, M. Harris, A. Abrams, H. Abrams, and H. Miller. Even though the congregation continued to rent temporary synagogue quarters, by October 1871 it had established its own cemetery, the Sheerith Israel Cemetery, on a small parcel of land at what is now Blackberry Avenue and North and South Road in suburban University City.[52]

In the early 1880s Sheerith Israel became the largest Orthodox congregation in St. Louis (by then at least one or more Orthodox congregations had arisen among newly arriving Eastern European immigrants). The congregation created a Sabbath School in 1882; students met in the synagogue on Saturday afternoons from 2 to 4 P.M. (regular Sabbath services were held, of course, on Friday evenings and Saturday mornings) and on Sunday mornings from 10 A.M. to noon. Reverend L. Rosenblatt, a scholarly layman, acted in lieu of a rabbi; Reverend R. Grodzky served as *chazzan* and teacher. So popular were Sabbath services that a choir was introduced to accompany the *chazzan.* In the summer of 1883 Sheerith Israel invited Rabbi Aaron Levy of Monroe, Louisiana, to be guest speaker. He delivered such excellent Friday evening and Saturday morning sermons, in both German and English, that on September 15, 1883, the congregation hired him as its permanent rabbi.[53]

---

50. Historically the province of Cracow, adjacent to German Silesia, had long been Polish, and its capital city, also called Cracow, was a center of Jewish culture and learning. In 1818 the province was incorporated into the post-Napoleonic German Confederation, and in 1846 into the Austrian Empire.

51. A characteristic of many congregations founded by Jewish immigrants was the common geographic origins of its members. Thus the earlier "Polish Shul" (United Hebrew), the "Bavarian Shul" (Emanu El), the "Bohemian Shul" (B'nai B'rith), and the "German Shul" (B'nai El). Later groups included, among others, the "Hungarische Shul" (B'rith Sholom).

52. *Tribune,* November 12, 1880, and March 9, 1883; Compton, ed., *Pictorial Saint Louis,* 110.

53. *Tribune,* October 6 and December 22, 1882, and August 31 and September 28, 1883.

Sometime in 1884 a serious schism developed among the members of Sheerith Israel, the result of either personality or doctrinal differences, or perhaps a combination of both. Some evidence suggests that Rabbi Levy might have led the secession of those dissatisfied with the too-conservative Orthodoxy of Sheerith Israel. After they organized their own congregation, however, this group soon became disenchanted with Levy, whom they now viewed as leaning too much toward Reform, and in 1885 they replaced him with Rabbi Adolph Rosentreter, who remained with the congregation on and off for about twenty-five years. At any rate, in 1884, led by Morris Schuchat, David Frey, Mailach Saffier, Pincus Agatstein, David Priwer, Israel Meyerson, and Jacob Goldwasser, a group seceded from Sheerith Israel and organized a new congregation, "B'nai Amoona" (Children of the Faith). The two groups continued their separate ways for a while, but by 1900 the older Sheerith Israel had disbanded completely, with most of its members and its cemetery taken over by B'nai Amoona. B'nai Amoona continued to flourish and prosper, and is today one of the major Conservative congregations in St. Louis and the Midwest.

According to the historian of B'nai Amoona Congregation, "what all these people [the founders and first generation of Sheerith Israel and B'nai Amoona] had in common was their adherence to Orthodox Judaism and the German language." A guest rabbi delivered his sermon in German, the language, according to a contemporary newspaper, "best fitting to his audience." Willie Emmer's *Bar Mitzvah* address was in German, as was Rabbi Rosentreter's eulogy for B'nai Amoona's first president, L. M. Plaut. Rosentreter normally delivered his sermons in German, using English only occasionally. In fact, the historian of B'nai Amoona emphasizes "the common German heritage that B'nai Amoona congregants shared with their more well-placed compatriots" (members of United Hebrew, B'nai El, and Shaare Emeth) as an important factor that "gain[ed] them entry into organizations founded by the reform community."[54]

That B'nai Amoona was a congregation of *German* Jews undoubtedly explains its long-standing cordial relations with the Reform congregations of St. Louis, who demonstrated considerably different attitudes toward institutions created by eastern European Slavic immigrants. In fact, a "committee on congregational cooperation," consisting of members and rabbis of United Hebrew, B'nai El, Shaare Emeth, and Temple Israel—all Reform—and of Orthodox B'nai Amoona, even met periodically to deal

---

54. *Jewish Free Press*, November 6 and December 4, 1885, and August 31, 1888. For the early history of B'nai Amoona, see Rosalind M. Bronsen, *B'nai Amoona for All Generations*, 1–32.

with matters of mutual concern. No other Orthodox congregations were included.[55]

The existence of Chevrah Kadisha, Sheerith Israel, and B'nai Amoona make it manifestly clear that although most German Jewish immigrants who came to St. Louis liberalized their views toward Judaism, an appreciable number—enough to organize at least three congregations—retained their traditional Orthodoxy. Thus, when the great influx of eastern European Orthodox Jews began in the 1870s and 1880s, both Reform and Orthodox German Jews had already established themselves and their appropriate religious institutions in St. Louis.

---

55. *Voice*, May 6, 1904.

Rosa Sonneschein.

Rosa Sonneschein's credentials to First Zionist Congress.

Aurelia Stix Rice.

Rachel Stix Michael.

Fourth Street, 1880.

The Jewish Tribune.

רבר אל בני ישראל ־ רוסיע.

ST. LOUIS, AUGUST 29, 1879.

Vol. I.   No. 1.

Poetry.

'Tis the First Jewish Paper.

DAISY.

'Tis the first Jewish paper
St. Louis has had,
And 'twill make all our people
Feel happy and glad
No edition of this kind
Has e'er been in print,
To tell of engagements
Or weddings give hint.

We greet thee, Oh Tribune,
For many a year
Art our Jewish paper
We wanted here
Of all the large cities,
St. Louis alone
Is the only one thus far
That's been without one.

But now one is started,
And long may it live!
And to us in future
The latest news give,
And when we shall find it
Grown welcome and strong,
Oh, may we all know, that
We've helped it along.

St. Louis, August, 1879.

The River of Life.

The most distant and broad appear
For the life we to-day hazes —
A day to childhood seems a year,
And year like far-ago ages.

The gladness comes and with it,
Keeps our feet beside it,
Steals lingering like a cost smooth
Along it carries for her

But as the current rocks goes wan,
And no ones half the thicker
Ye older, that does not the to-man,
The minute's run is one quicker

When ages hang in full in bloom andgirth,
And lids of self is slip
With all we knew the life of death
Forever in love never rapid

It may be stormy, but no hand change,
Time's course be as a sporting
When we do to our out front have gone
And left for some forling

Heaves us in our years of living strength
Into nothing deep distance
And those of youth, evening length,
Proportioned to their own too

Morris, Magdine

My Coal Black Beard.

BY PERCY FITZGERALD.

CHAPTER I.

I do not recall a greater surprise than when one evening, on the grand stair of the Grand Hotel at Pumping-ton-on-Sea, where even the guests feel grand, I encountered that little figure. A snatch of her laughter, spontaneous as a bird's chirrup, had startled me, even before I had seen the figure, like some tune long unheard, and which we have often vainly striven to recover. The next moment the delicate transparency of the cheeks was glowing with a shell-like pink, simply from the unexpectedness of the meeting. Never was seen so petite and graceful and perfectly shaped a little creature. On both sides there was confusion as well as surprise, and certainly pleasure. Contrast there certainly was, as one of the meeters was tall, broad, and decorated with a coal-black magnificent beard, which the owner flattered himself was the admiration of all who saw it. A truly remarkable adornment; which, were there competitors for such things, would certainly take, or would have taken, the large gold meal. For alas, it is no longer in being! Cutting down a beard is like cutting down a tree.

I must confess that it was the charming Dorinda that first put me in conceit with this adornment, and I noticed her soft eyes often settled on it with an expression half of wonder, and half of admiration. My 'beautiful coal-black beard' she called it; with a pardonable anticipation of possession. I had never been compli-mented on the adornment before, and indeed noticed that it rather attracted hostile glances from those of my own sex. Was it surprising, then, that something of PRIDE began to take possession of me, in connection with this adornment, akin to the feeling with which the Chinaman or Tartar regards his tail?

Now, between this sweet little being and the owner of the locks there had been, some five years before, quite a romance. There had been a country house, where we had been on a visit for more than a month, and where at the end of the period things had, as it were, come to a crisis, and we found that we were made for each other. In short, we were ready to put out to sea in what was no more than a little punt, with-out provisions of even a stock of clothes, and with nothing but love on board. All this was settled, as far as we were concerned, as the punt ready, when the next unexpected step in the transaction was a letter from a guardian whom we had both forgotten, written in the most insult-ing terms, and dated from foreign parts, whither he had once carried his ward. From her too came a little letter of a rueful kind, accepting the situation under pressure of force majeure. The guardian according to report, was a Quilp-like personage, of a raging temper, and the little lady might as well resist an ogre. So there it all ended — 'for ever!' that is for five years, until, as I have said, the Grand Pumpington hotel brought us together.

Need I say what followed. She was there with a mature female. Kindly but stupid, she would have been a nuisance to others under other conditions, but I found myself regarding her tenderly, much as a lad from school regards the fairy queen in spangles on the stage. As a matter of course, the amiable little boy god brought his bellows to work on the mouldering embers, and, in the three blissful weeks that followed, blew them up into a roaring flame. She was indeed a tempting and irresisti-ble little personage, full of what in other would be called romance, but which with her was reality; a steady purpose and firmness surprising in one so young, but overlaid with color and gilding, and looking every bit as well as romance. There was in her too a little air of old fashion or rather quaint-ness, to which corresponded her name which was Dorinda—Dorinda Rob-inson; and here she was now at the hotel whither she had been sent, with her maid, for the sea-bathing. It was perhaps scarcely fair, under these unprotected circumstances, to renew the old state of things; but for the young there is no logic, and the little gentleman with the bellows was blow-ing hard all the time; so very soon matters were restored to the status quo ante, as the diplomatists call it, of five years before, and this without the slightest apprehension of difficul-ties being in the way. That was taking the worst side, but the charm-ing Dorinda had great confidence in me would get the ferocious good-humor, and then of a consent. But it matter. It was his way, that if he took ...ence, or was in any way 'put out' by a particular person, nothing would ever bring him round; so we must take care. Of course there are many people who are affec-ted in the same way, and do not for-give being 'put out' but he was in-variable in his conduct, and never was known to forgive the party who 'put him out.'

Thus we lived on in our Fool's Paradise, when it came to pass that on a little festival, the bewitching Dorinda's birthday, I had set off by the railway to the big town, about ten miles away, to purchase a bouquet of magnificent dimensions, and at a cost as magnificent. With me was a facetious friend whom I should have introduced before, Mr. Bibb—'Jem-my,' as he was invariably called, ac-cording to the law which christens with this disrespectful familiarity any-one of distinctly comic gifts, and whose very name suggested pranks and practical joking. It was an un-fortunate moment for me when I consented to take this companion, for to him I nearly owed the loss of my —but that I must leave to be un-folded in the narrative.

The bouquet was bought and we were returning home in the evening full of spirits, having dined at anoth-er grand hotel, and toasted the sweet Dorinda in foaming beakers; which, as 'Jemmy' remarked with some point but too often lead to beaks. Jemmy was, in short, ripe for mischief, and I was in a sort of amiably compla-cent mood, that was ready to abet, though not to take a leading share. In this frame of mind we entered a carriage, and to Bibb's annoyance, why I know not, found it—that is, on seat—occupied by an old gentle-man with a nose like that of the Duke of Wellington; his face sunk in his great coat, from which he peered forth at us, like an owl from a favor-ite bush. Bibb grew at once very noisy and aggressive, and on the pringiple, he said, of smoking out a badger, proceeded to light his cigar. This at once roused the old gentle-man, who, in an angry croak, said, 'This is not a smoking carriage.' 'Indeed!' said Bibb politely, 'how interesting to know that!' And he got up to look curiously into various parts of the carriage, as though to examine something that had been pointed out to him. This exaspera-ted the old gentleman, who said, 'I'll call the guard at the next station.' 'You are quite full of information to-day, sir,' I replied, taking the cue from Bibb. 'Very well, sir,' said he. And as we presently stopped, he actually did summon the official, who required us peremptorily to abate the nuisance or retire. Naturally, this mortification inflamed our animosity and when presently the enemy, com-placent on his triumph, fell off into a slumber, his face assuming a hideous expression, the mischievous Bibb, on the train stopping suddenly, gave a start of alarm, and abruptly called out 'A smash!' on which the old gentle-man started up frantically and made for the door. He was in so mad a state of alarm, tumbling over us in his selfish eagerness, and roaring for the guard 'to let him out,' that we almost shrieked with laughter. We 'descended' ourselves before he had time to recover himself, and when the real state of things just dawned on him, and as he hurried on, we saw him shaking his fist at us from the window, and foaming with rage. Strange to say, he appeared to set me down as the agent of his annoy-ance, though I was comparatively innocent, and he called out as we hurried away, 'Never mind I you shall smart for it, you fellow with the black beard. I'll know you. I'll hunt you.' And he was so much in earnest, that we thought it best to escape as fast as we could, and leave him gesticu-lating vainly. There were more ri-diculous old fools in the world than one imagined. At the same time, I must fairly admit that our proceeding was undignified and unbecoming, and as the reader may think, unimport-ant and scarcely worthy of being gravely narrated. But all turns upon it, that is, upon my magnificent coal-black beard.

We arrived at the hotel about seven o'clock. That evening there was to be one of the usual Grand Hotel grand dances in the grand ball-room for the grand guests to the music of a grand orchestra—a performance to which I always looked forward with delight. For such occasion furnished a kind of theatrical back-ground for all that was...

Jewish Tribune, volume one, number one, August 29, 1879.

HUMOROUS.

—American flats—Pancakes.

—A dark horse—The nightmare.

—Woman's sphere—A ball of yarn.

—Strictly plain—The Western prairies.

—The only fall opening that ladies avoid is the coal hole in the sidewalk.—[N. Y. Journal.

—A Michigan man who lost both legs in a saw mill, now sits around and tells about the terrible battles of the late war. That's the sawed off man he is.—[Boston Post.

MOTHER SWANN'S WORM SYRUP. Infallible, tasteless, harmless, cathartic; for feverishness, restlessness, worms, constipation. 25c.

—There is a father in Pittsburgh mean enough to call his daughter Misery, because she loves company. The *Telegraph* man is authority for this.—[Oil City Blizzard.

—The man who carries his umbrella on his shoulder in a crowd would throw a banana peel on the pavement if he could borrow money to buy the banana.—[Merchant Traveler.

—There are no authentic pictures of Shakespeare, but the intelligent artist represented him as bald-headed because he knew a great deal, and was very fond of theaters.—[N. O. Picayune.

—Said the druggist: "I didn't see why Mr. Byrnesmonkey kicked because by mistake I gave him strychnine instead of calomel. Strychnine costs twice as much as calomel."—[Boston Post.

"BUCHU-PAIBA." Quick, complete cure, all annoying Kidney, Bladder and Urinary Diseases. $1. Druggists.

—The "Star" system of theatrical management, once so popular, is now so played out that managers who attempted it in London would find it probably tended to something very like "star"-vation.—[London Figaro.

—We read in an exchange of a young lady having been made crazy by a sudden kiss. This should teach young ladies to be constantly expecting something of that kind, and to be prepared for it when it comes.—[Lowell Citizen.

—A Minnesota editor calls a rival journalist "a sizzle-souled, insinuating whiffet." A cyclone of culture has evidently swept through that section of the country; or perhaps it is only a tornado of thought.—[N. Y. Journal.

"Mamma, if Adam had not been so bold,
And Eve not quite so 'fly,'
Would we be having picnics all the while,
And a-living awful high?"
"My child, it's hard to tell what would've been
If there had been no fall.
But though the chances are ten to one,
We would not be here at all!"

—"Mercy!" exclaimed Mrs. F., as she caught sight of the cameleopard, "just look at that beast! What a long neck!" "Yes," replied Fogg, "the most remarkable case of sour throat I ever saw."—[Boston Transcript.

—"Where is the girl of long ago?" sings Joaquin Miller. We saw her the other day, Joaq. But she isn't a girl anymore. She had gray hair and a wart on her nose, and no teeth and wore spectacles.—[Salem Sunbeam.

—A plant has been found that cures bashfulness. It should be promptly tried on the man who leaves the hotel by the back window because he is too diffident to say good-bye to the cashier and clerk.—[Chicago Tribune.

"ROUGH ON CORNS." Ask for Wells' "Rough on Corns," 15c. Quick, complete, permanent cure. Corns, warts, bunions.

—A Vassar college girl has written a novel called "The Foolish Virgin." It is probably about a girl who went off to college without supplying herself with enough gum to last her until vacation.—[Philadelphia News.

—Little Johnny says that all men do not belong to the animal kingdom. For instance, there is the circus proprietor. He doesn't belong to the animal kingdom, but the animal kingdom belongs to him.—[Boston Transcript.

—A garden "waul"—A cat on the fence.—[New York Journal.

—Three years constant study in Italy will make an American girl know too much to sing in church, and too little to be useful in opera.—[Picayune.

—A merchant may make a reduction in the price of his material without making any material reduction in his price.

—Ruskin says no couple should marry until they have courted seven years. This would lead one to think that Ruskin runs a soda mountain.—[Boston Post.

—P. W. Goebel, druggist, of Loulsburg, Kansas, says: "I have sold 'PRICKLY ASH BITTERS' for five years, and I have never handled a medicine which gave more universal satisfaction. It is fast becoming the family medicine of this section. I have warranted dozens of bottles and never had one returned.

—The average young lady wants at least four feet of a seat in a street car for a ride of six blocks, but she will ride half a day Sunday squeezed into a buggy seat beside her young man and not find the least fault.—[Detroit Free Press.

—The speaker who alluded to his candidate as "the war-horse that snuffed the battle from afar," climbed up to the composition-room with a club after reading it in the paper as "the ward boss that snatched a bottle from a bar.—[Boston Bulletin.

—A lady said her husband will sit on a barbed wire fence all the afternoon to see a baseball match, and never move a muscle, but when he goes to church he can't sit in a cushioned pew for fifteen minutes without wiggling all over the seat, and changing his position forty times.—[Peck's Sun.

—One of the letters of introduction Miss Kate Field brought with her to Denver was from Sir Charles Dilke to Judge McCurdy. She sent a note to the Windsor hotel office, asking where the judge could be found. The answer came back: "Don't know; he's been dead eight years."—[Denver Tribune.

POZZONI.

No name is better and more pleasantly and widely known than that of Mr. J. A. Pozzoni. For years he has made himself famous by the elegant perfumes and complexion powder that bears his name, the latter having found its way to the belles of Paris, Germany and London. Everybody admires beauty in ladies. Nothing will do more to produce or enhance it than a use of Mr. Pozzoni's preparations.

TAKING TIME BY THE FORELOCK.

"I want to put a death notice in this paper, but I want to leave the date of the death blank, can I do that?" asked a man of the advertising clerk, the other day.

"Don't you know the date?" inquired the clerk, a little startled by the request.

"No, not yet," replied the man. "The fact is, it's my wife, and she isn't dead, but the doctor says she's got to peg out some time to-night, and I have ordered the funeral for to-morrow morning, so I can leave town in the afternoon. Can't you fix the notice?"

"Have you seen the undertaker?" asked the clerk, interested by the man's quiet, business-like air.

"Yes, and he has made all the arrangements. He measured her for the coffin with his eye, and I don't think she has the remotest notion what his game was. I hang notified all the friends, and my mourning suit is around at the tailor's, waiting for me to try on. The only thing is about this notice. If I can arrange that I'm all right. Stick it in. She won't see the paper, and if she does, I'll tell her it is another woman of the same name."

"All right," replied the clerk, "I'll fix it."

"Much obliged," sighed the bereaved by brevet. "I'll do as much for you some time. Now, I've got to go and look after the flowers. Come and have a drink? I've got a few moments to spare."

But the clerk declined with thanks, and the mourner went away in quest of a florist who would contract to furnish flowers with the understanding that "if anything slipped up he would take 'em back and refund half the money."

A typical page from the *Jewish Tribune*, November 2, 1883.

The Jewish Voice.

A WEEKLY NEWSPAPER DEVOTED TO THE CAUSE OF JUDAISM AND OF THE JEWISH PEOPLE.

Vol. VI. No. 15. St. Louis, Mo., Friday, April 12, 1889. **No. 67.**

Written expressly for the JEWISH VOICE.

THE THREE BROTHERS.

[ADAPTED FROM THE GERMAN]
By Miss Bella Bunsel.

SCHRALGE.
II.

"It was a weary road that over it me here," said Abraham, "I could not land like you did, at Almeria or at Malaga; I had to come by land through France, over the Pyrenees, and all the way through Spain. It was a journey full of fatigue, danger and pain partly because I dared not utter any of the large cities, for there the myriadoms of the inquisition watched and shadowed every new arrival, and only at the hamlets could I seek such refreshments as our law allows; yes, even there none and position, race and religion had to be carefully concealed, and travelling mostly by night, seeking concealed places by day—and yet, how often was I near discovery and arrest! And again, how my heart bled at sight of the few traces of the formerly flourishing Israel, now so terribly despoiled through the short—sightedness of man; their magnificent schools transformed into monasteries, their synagogues into chapels or storehouses for straw and corn, their burial grounds into pleasure gardens and vineyards; how it pained me to see our much beloved Spain, robbed of the industry of the Jews and Moors, already desolate; long stretches of land bereft of population, and even now sending her strong men to the newly discovered India (America), what will be the end of all this!

Such was my way to the meeting place we had agreed upon—and such also was my life during the ten years we were separated. Fatigue, danger and pain succeeded each other by turns. In concealment I had to seek safety, travelling by night that I might not fall into the hands of the persecutors of our race. And still I did not despair, and as I found you, dearest brothers, here in concealment, so I made my way to success.

As little as I wish to dwell on the details of my journey through Spain, so little do I wish to speak of my life during the past ten years; but you know, the Fates often entangle the web of life; if once straightened out it continues smoothly to the end. Such have been the incidents of my life which I will relate to you. You know the occupation of my earlier years—the study of the law. I studied and taught, thus passed my life until the terrible expulsion and flight took place, and let me say even at this date, that many, though not of our faith, helped upon my departure with sorrow whom I had instructed in the sciences. But when I had left Spain I found everything changed, I journeyed through France and everywhere found our co-religionists sunk in ignorance. No traces of former refinement or education were to be found, but instead much filth, both internal and external. Philosophy and Mathematics, Grammar and History were unknown in their schools; they busied themselves in solving casuistic problems of the law and where there were none, trying to find them in order to whet and sharpen their ingenuity; this was the aim and glory of their life. I met them in great numbers separated from all the world, a deep abyss between them and all mankind; they lived in their spheres morally and socially separated from all others! Oh, how different had it been in our beloved Spain! In southern France I met many of our fugitives, but they still wandered here and there, few having found a permanent resting place. In several places I tried to lecture, but either the Rabbis would not allow it, or the people did not understand me and I had to continue my wanderings. No order was observed at their religious services; their pronunciation of our holy language, the

that it became unendurable.

What wonder then that wherever a sufficient number of Spanish and Portuguese fugitives was assembled, they organized a congregation, with services according to their own forms and laws.

This offended the existing congregation so greatly that a rupture ensued between these two, though children of one faith, wider than between members of different religions. In all instances they shun each other, and there is no thought of union or intermarriage between them. Our people are guilty of too much pride and even arrogance; the others of unfeelingly turning our fugitives from their doors.

The observation of all this made me very unhappy. I looked into the future and saw our people trodden under foot—saw the Jews of other lands overlook and even excel us in civilization. I spoke of this to our people, but they did not see it as I did, and thus I alienated their friendship and sympathy.

[To be continued.]

NOTES OF A JOURNEY TO THE EAST.

BY MR. ELKAN N. ADLER, M.A.

The Cave of Adullam and the Road to Hebron.

[CONTINUED.]

The frowning cliffs, on either side, made the scene unspeakably imposing, and the consciousness that one was in the very scene of David's adventures, during the most romantic episodes of his career, peopled the whole country with the shadows of the past. Accordingly, after carefully turning a sharp corner where the cliff took an abrupt turn to the left and then to the right again, it seemed the most natural thing in the world, to come upon a small camp of Bedouins, clustered round two little springs of water which rose in the angle formed by the double bend of the rocky wall. The Arabs looked just like the pictures in our familiar scripture books, and were doubtless dressed in similar garb to what they have worn for the last four thousand years. I rode up to them, and, despite the incongruity, hastened to give them each a cigarette. After that, I felt reassured about their intentions, because the Arab is not civilized enough to betray a man after eating of his salt or smoking of his weed. I dismounted, and one of them hospitably attempted to make my horse drink, as they were drinking, from the tiny pools. The noble steed must have been very thirsty, its rider was, but yet it resolutely declined the water, and persisted in its refusal, until one kind-hearted son of the desert doffed his turban, filled it with water, and lifted it to the horse's mouth. The novel bucket may have improved the water's flavour, it certainly disguised the colour, and anyhow the horse refused no longer. After this success, I thought I would try the water too, and so I did, but my first mouthful was my last, and from another such a sip may I be delivered! The experience of that awful taste elucidated to me, how real David's longing must have been, when he jeopardised the lives of the three warriors, whom he sent for Bethlehem water, with which to wash the taste out of his mouth. The story is told in II. Samuel xxiii., 13-17:

"And three of the thirty chiefs went down, and came to David in the harvest time unto the Cave of Adullam: and the troop of the Philistines pitched in the Valley of Rephaim. And David was then in a hold and the garrison of the Philistines was then in Bethlehem. And David longed, and said, Oh that one would give me drink of the water of the Well of Bethlehem, which is by the gate! And the three mighty men brake through the host of the Philistines, and drew water

that I should do this is not that I should of men that went to jeopardy their lives? Therefore he would not drink it. These things did these three mighty men."

This and other indications he evinced so that I must be in the immediate neighbourhood of the very spot in which David took refuge during his guerilla warfare. But who shall decide whether there was one wonderful hole in the south slopes of the Adullam hill, and the rude soldier-band then offered to show one other.

Three brawny fellows, strong as the Arabs of the Pyramids, conducted up what seemed the most tedious precipices. But for the tennis shoes I was luckily wearing, I could never have preserved my footing; but at last, after a climb of about ten minutes, we reached the narrow entrance to the cave, which expanded like a funnel. Unfortunately, we were unable to see anything but the darkness around us. My last match had been smoked away and our only light was an occasional spark from the flint and tinder with which the Arabs did defiance to Bryant and May. I did not, however, penetrate very far into the gloomy hollow of the mountain, and was not sorry to return to the light of day.

I remounted, took leave of my new friends, and one of them guided me to Artas, a village in a valley much fertilised by Solomon's Pools. The irrigation furnished by these wonderful reservoirs, with their aqueducts carried along the mountain slopes, is wonderfully successful, and proves how remunerative waterworks would be. Artas provides Jerusalem with all its fruit and vegetables, and the whole village is one large smiling garden, which the traveller is loth to quit. Unfortunately, the shade of the palms had to be left, and I had to ride disconsolately on across the Wady, and mount the hill on the other side, till I reached the old caravan track to Hebron. Here I passed some hundred camels, and pressed on till I came to the carriage road. It was past four in the afternoon, and I had to gallop to make up for lost time. The nearer one got to the city, the more people were to be seen on the road. When about a mile from the gates, I was met by Bezaleel Kaminitz and the beadle of the Hebron community, on horseback, who came cantering along. They had been sent by the Congregation to raise the hue and cry, for I had tarried too long in my coming, and they feared I had fallen into the hands of the Bedouins. I did not stop, and Bezaleel, who is an expert horseman, wheeled round in fine style, but the beadle was less fortunate. His horse threw him, but he soon got on again, and onward he galloped, I galloped, we galloped all three. An estimable and well to do Turkish merchant, dressed in all his satins, was soberly ambling along, on a large white donkey, in a reverse direction to ours. The donkey, uneasy at the pattering of our dozen hoofs, picked up its ears and turned tail. Its respectable rider seemed surprised and fell off. Hebron, though nearly 3,000 feet high, lies in a narrow valley, between the mountains. The descent from the North-West is rather steep, and so, owing to the rapidity of our progress, our horses were sometimes sliding down, almost on their haunches. It was quite impossible to stop, and we had to leave the Turk to pick himself up as best he could. We rode on and reached Hebron upon the stroke of five, the beadle had a final tumble from his steed, and so we arrived at our journey's end.

ADVICE TO MOTHERS.

MRS. WINSLOW'S SOOTHING SYRUP should always be used when children are cutting teeth. It relieves the little sufferer at once. It produces natural, quiet sleep by relieving the child from pain, and the little cherub awakes "as bright as a button."

The Jewish Free Press.

Volume 17.— No. 1.　　　ST. LOUIS, OCTOBER 1, 1886.　　　Whole No. 326.

—THE—
JEWISH FREE PRESS.

216 N. Eighth Street, Cor. Office.

PUBLISHED BY

The Jewish Free Press Co.

M. C. REEFER - - Manager,

AND LOCAL EDITOR.

HENRY GERSONI, - Editor.

SUBSCRIPTION PRICE, - TWO DOLLARS.
SINGLE COPIES, 10 CENTS.

RATES OF ADVERTISING.

Complimentary Resolutions and Obituaries...$5.00
Betrothals, Marriages, Births, Deaths, each under $1.00
Rates for display advertisements made known on application.

Complimentary and memorial resolutions of any nature whatever are published in this paper only as advertisements, at a uniform charge of $5 each.

Entered at the Post-Office, in St. Louis as second-class matter.

ST. LOUIS
Business Directory

HAPPY NEW YEAR.

OUR BEST greetings and wishes for the ensuing New Year to our readers and friends.

May happiness and contentment be with all who strive to act well and to be useful to themselves and their fellow-men.

May the grace and forgiveness of Heaven rest upon those who have erred in the past and, having found out their errors, endeavor to mend their ways in the future.

May divine blessings rest upon our public institutions and their managers, inasmuch as they further the commonwealth and are free from selfish motives.

May our Cincinnati contemporaries and other Jewish organs that speak for the people and to the people be imbued with a sense of the responsibilities resting upon them, and work for the furtherance and promotion of truth and justice.

May our ministers be endowed with a sense of dignity, and their respective congregations with the knowledge that their ministers are there to teach more than to please; to impart knowledge more than to flatter the taste and sentiments of a few leaders.

May the mothers in Israel embrace the conviction that their destination is to be, and not merely to appear, what the proud title implies; that the best and noblest qualities of their children are to be cultivated by them; that the peace and comfort of their homes depend on them.

May the fathers in Israel think that their duties are not merely to provide for the physical requirements of their houses and children, but that they are to minister to and conduct the spiritual prompting of those whom God has entrusted to their protection and care.

May our young men and women learn to regard the past with veneration, and to train themselves for a future of usefulness in their respective spheres.

May the idle be quickened with hope and gather strength to mend in the last days.

May we all learn to value earthly possessions not for themselves, but as a means to promote what is good and noble in spirit and in truth.

And the blessing of Heaven will be with us all for the ensuing New Year and for many years to come.

THE NEW CONGREGATION.

As WILL be seen from the report in another column, the movement for a new congregation has taken shape, and it has been organized. The man who for 17 years has officiated in the Temple Shaare Emeth is its rabbi no more, but has accepted a call to serve the new congregation. The struggle is now happily ended, and the man who has been a stumbling-block to most of those who have organized the Shaare Emeth Temple, and have maintained it both financially and morally, has been removed. In the congregation peace and harmony will take the place of contention and bitterness.

WHEN a man has maintained a position for seventeen years, and his associates and adherents, we might say friends, turn their backs upon him, and enter into a relentless struggle for his expulsion, antagonizing friends and relations in the maintenance of their principle, there must be grave causes underlying the current causes which may perhaps not be seen by the naked eye of the careless observer. Had not justice and truth been on the side of the antagonists of the former incumbent of the Shaare Emeth Temple, victory today would not be perched on their banners. Personal enmity alone arrayed against a man of talent; an orator of the highest parts; a scholar of no mean attainments; a man whose name was heralded throughout the land far and wide; a man whose voice was listened to and whose advice taken in the first councils of our Jewish bodies—we say, personal animosity alone would have fallen to the ground as harmlessly as dust of accumulated ages is harmless to the intrinsic value of the most precious metals.

IT IS for the reason that this man is placed at the head of the organization that its development will be watched, not with tenderness, but with jealousy and suspicion. Born under most unfortunate auspices, its virtue will not be extolled, nor its faults belittled, by those who have good reason to have small faith in the man for whom the Congregation was started, or in the profession of faith he might now deem fit to make. It therefore behooves the leaders of the new congregation to be most careful in all their movements, lest through the blindness of enthusiasm incident to every new profession, its existence might be as short-lived as was JONAH's Kikajon. Dangerous is the ocean upon which the frail craft has been launched, and the man whom they chose to stand at the helm has proven himself anything but a trustworthy captain in dangerous waters or in times of peril. Let them above all beware of bestowing praise where blame is deserved. Cauterize the wound before it becomes infectious to the body.

BUT not alone the opponents of the rabbi of the congregation and his friends will be careful observers of its development. No congregation can be maintained by partisanship. Its friends might contribute once and twice and three times; but if merit is lacking, it will die of itself without any outward agency. The element which constitutes a congregation, which makes up its moral support, is the great crowd which is now an interesting onlooker. If the congregation has been started and organized for SONNESCHEIN, if the principles of the new organization are to be fitted to his taste—then we predict an early death for it. Its enemies can afford to put their hands in their pockets and merely watch the time (and it will not be a long one either) before their ominous predictions will be fulfilled. It will die of inanition. But if the principles announced are indeed the foundation of the new congregation; if it has been organized for the purpose of perpetuating true Jewish principles, with "charity to all and malice to none"—if SONNESCHEIN will subject his former erratic actions to the principles of truth, of peace, of justice, of religious morality—then will the vast body of disinterested observers fall into line, and a religious fervor and enthusiasm will take the place of the apathy and lethargy which now so alarmingly pervade the Jewish community of St. Louis.

THIS is the momentous question. One foremost in the movement as well as one of the most intelligent men within the body of the new congregation, assured us that SONNESCHEIN had only been engaged on probation. If his teachings and his bearing does not run in a parallel line with the principles of true Judaism, his days within the Congregation are numbered. The congregation had been erected not for SONNESCHEIN, but SONNESCHEIN had been elected for the purpose of teaching the principles of the body whose rabbi he now will be. If this be the policy they will pursue, then may GOD prosper them in their ways. May they succeed in bringing back within the true fold the man who in his youth had promised to become a shining light, a teacher, a guide, a ruler, a giant in Israel; but who by frivolous action threw his god-given diadem into the mire. May they succeed in helping him retrieve his lost position.

THIS is a time when we prostrate ourselves before our Heavenly Father, and implore him to forgive us our sins, as we are willing to forgive those who have sinned against us. The fight has been a bitter one, but it is past. Let the victors be magnanimous. Lend the drowning man your hand and help him up once more, unworthy though he may have proven himself thereof by his conduct in the past—no matter how grievous the wrongs he perpetrated against you and against the laws of true religion. Let your heart be softened. Give the man a show to redeem himself.

A NEW year is beginning. A bright page in a new book is opened—a page as clear as sunlight, and unsoiled by even the slightest blot. This is the page whereon Dr. SONNESCHEIN begins to write his new record. The eyes not alone of St. Louis, but of the world, are upon him. It is within his power to redeem himself, if he so chooses, or to become a shame and an abomination to his friends for all future times. Another duty is now imposed upon him by circumstance—besides the duties which he owes to himself as a man, to his family as a husband and father, and to the congregation which has entrusted to him the guidance of their spiritual affairs—it is a duty as sacred as all these—the duty of proving his gratitude to his friends who have so nobly stood by him in this terrible struggle—who have bravely battled for him to the last, even though certain defeat stared them in the face.

A beneficent Providence has endowed him with brilliancy, genius, with rare qualities enjoyed by few mortal men. Let him arise and gird his loins; let him prove to the world that he is worthy of the friendship of the men who have championed his cause. He will thereby not only maintain their friendship, but will once more regain the esteem, the respect, aye, the love of the men who have so bitterly opposed him in the past—men whose integrity, whose sterling worth and whose earnestness in the cause of our holy faith has never been questioned. And the grace of God will be with him, and strengthen him in his undertaking.

As TO the attitude of the JEWISH FREE PRESS, it will at all times support and advocate every movement calculated to promote true Jewish principles. And as it is claimed that the new congregation has been established with the same object in view, the FREE PRESS will, with all the power at its command, seek to further the interests thereof.

Marcus Bernheimer.

Isaac Fuld.

J. D. Goldman.

Barney Hysinger.

Major Adolph Proskauer,
Twelfth Alabama Infantry,
Confederate States of America.
(Courtesy Alabama
Department of Archives and
History, Montgomery.)

William Goldstein.

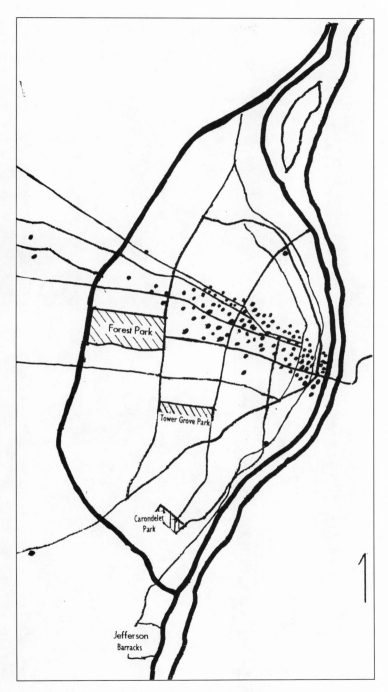

Forest Park

Tower Grove Park

Carondelet
Park

Jefferson
Barracks

1

Jewish institutions and neighborhoods, 1807–1907:
the "Central Corridor."

Alliance Building, Ninth and Carr.

YMHA, 3645 Delmar.

Original Jewish Hospital, 1902–1926, 5415 Delmar.

Columbian Club, Lindell and Vandeventer.

Home for the Aged and Infirm Israelites, 3652 South Jefferson.

Orthodox Old Folks Home, North Grand and Blair. Original building.

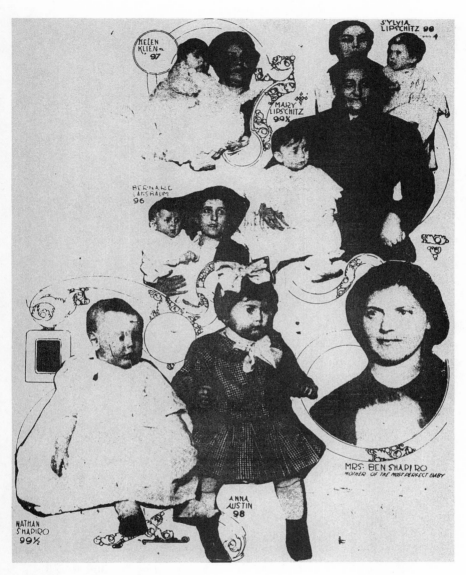

Better Babies Contest, Jewish Alliance.

St. Louis, October 16th, 1871.

A few days since, a number of young Israelites, anticipating the urgent necessity of prompt action on the part of the Israelites of St. Louis to render assistance to our distressed brethren of fire-stricken Chicago, who would soon be in our midst, formed themselves into a " Temporary Relief Committee." Temporary relief, in a number of instances, has been extended.

Now, in view of the fact that many Israelitish families are already, and many more will soon be, here, who will require and are entitled to substantial assistance, we do respectfully urge upon you the pressing necessity of organizing a permanent UNITED HEBREW RELIEF ASSOCIATION, and to that end invite your hearty co-operation.

The Israelites of St. Louis will assemble in Mass Meeting, on next Tuesday evening, Oct. 17th, at 7.30 o'clock, at the Synagogue, on Sixth Street, near St. Charles Street, for the herein mentioned purpose.

His Honor, Mayor BROWN, and the General Relief Committee of the City of St. Louis, assure us material assistance.

ABZ. KRAMER,
Prest. Congregation Shaare Emeth.

ADOLPH ISAACS,
Prest. Congregation U. Hebr.

L. R. STRAUS,
Prest. Congregation Bnai El.

A. BINSWANGER,
Chairman Temporary Relief Committee.

LEWIS HUTZLER,
NATHL. MYERS,
SIMON POPPER, and others,
Of Temporary Relief Committee

Call for United Hebrew Relief Association, 1871. (Courtesy St. Louis Jewish Community Archives.)

Rice-Stix Dry Goods Company, Tenth and Washington.

Stix, Baer and Fuller Dry Goods Company: The "Grand Leader," Sixth and Washington.

Famous-Barr Company, Seventh and Olive.

Freund Baking Company delivery wagon. (Courtesy Missouri Historical Society, St. Louis.)

Levis-Zukowski Mercantile Company, 1113 Washington Avenue.

Isidor Bush and Company, 213 South Second Street.

9

INTO THE BROADER COMMUNITY

The post–Civil War era proved to be a watershed in St. Louis Jewish history. "The real growth of St. Louis [Jewry] came after the conclusion of the Civil War," recalled one who lived through that period. "Our Jewish population grew rapidly, both in numbers, character and in material resources beginning with 1870." Indeed, not only did an identifiably viable Jewish community develop in the 1870s, but so too did a number of individual Jews emerge as recognizable community leaders. By 1879, for instance, two Jews had been elected to the thirteen-man St. Louis city council. And by 1880, according to a scholarly appraisal of the St. Louis community, "the German Jewish community and its descendants were firmly entrenched in the life of the city. They were in the main substantial and prosperous citizens, who, though they attended separate churches, nevertheless formed an integral part of every civic endeavor."[1]

Limited by the paucity of rabbis, religious life in St. Louis had seemed evident only in the synagogues and their relatively small memberships. As in other cities, most Jews in St. Louis did not belong to congregations but exercised their Judaism more in ancillary organizations such as cemetery associations, charitable groups, and fraternal orders. St. Louis Jewry continued to be characterized by what historian Howard Morley Sachar labeled "the Americanization of German Jewry." St. Louis's Jews continued to emphasize two main objectives: gaining security within the explosively expanding American economy, and distancing themselves from what they viewed as an archaic European lifestyle.[2]

At the same time, an environment was evolving in St. Louis in which rabbinic leadership began to assume a new importance that extended

---

1. "Reminiscences of Samuel Bowman," in *Modern View 25,* 7; Merle Fainsod, "The Influence of Racial and National Groups in St. Louis Politics, 1908–1928," 276. See also William A. Kelsoe, ed., *Saint Louis Reference Record,* 183–85.
2. Sachar, *History of the Jews in America,* 61–71.

beyond the synagogue. More trained rabbis began to appear on the St. Louis scene. They included such outstanding figures as Samuel Wolfenstein, Solomon Sonneschein, Henry J. Messing, and Moritz Spitz. In addition, during the 1870s United Hebrew and B'nai El continued to liberalize their religious practices, leading them soon to join Shaare Emeth as Reform congregations, a transformation brought on by not only the new Reform-oriented rabbinic influence but also emerging lay leadership demanding more "Americanization." The growing role of laymen was abetted no doubt by the appearance of German Jews among the nouveau riche of St. Louis. They were no longer poor immigrants; by now they had become successful and wealthy—and increasingly influential— entrepreneurs. True, the broader St. Louis community was slow to accept them among the movers and shakers of the city; but within narrower Jewish circles their business and professional successes propelled them into new leadership roles. That affected both synagogue and secular Jewish activities. But the new rabbinic leaders cannot be overlooked. Along with the emerging lay leadership, the rabbis played a significant role in creating a cohesive community spirit among the Jews of St. Louis.

Perhaps the most significant change affecting the synagogues was the final transformation of United Hebrew and B'nai El from their original Orthodox traditionalism to Reform. By the 1870s both seemed on the verge of finalizing such a move.

B'nai El's transition occurred first. By 1868 its board, after considerable debate, ended the traditional practice of "calling up" worshipers during the weekly reading of the Torah on the Sabbath. The Haftorah (additional reading from the Prophets) would henceforth be read in the vernacular— which meant German—instead of in Hebrew. Wearing the *talis* was also discontinued. Those changes still did not satisfy the many members who left B'nai El for the more liberal Shaare Emeth. Accordingly, a special meeting of B'nai El's membership discontinued segregating women in the balcony during services; women now sat with men in the main sanctuary.[3]

Nevertheless, other traditional practices remained, and they may have been factors in a change of spiritual leadership. In 1870, for reasons not at all clear in B'nai El's records, Henry Kuttner resigned and returned to his former position at United Hebrew. B'nai El chose Rabbi Samuel Wolfenstein as his successor. "I accepted the position," Wolfenstein wrote later, "with the understanding that I should have hands free in introducing such changes in the ritual as I should consider necessary to build up the congregation and to make it a moderate Reform Temple."[4]

---

3. From B'nai El board minutes, as reproduced in *Voice*, January 30 and February 6, 1903.

4. "Dr. Wolfenstein's Reminiscences," in *Voice*, November 12, 1909.

Born in Moravia, Austria, on December 10, 1841, Wolfenstein was educated at the Universities of Vienna, Prague, and Breslau. He received his ordination from Rabbi Zvi Mecklenburg of Koenigsberg in 1865, and duly served as a congregational rabbi in Intersburg, Prussia, for five years. In 1870 he was elected to be director of the Höheren Töchterschule (advanced girls' academy) in Intersburg, but without explanation the Prussian government arbitrarily refused to confirm his election. One can only surmise that it was blatant antisemitism. So Wolfenstein and his wife, the former Bertha Brieger, emigrated to the United States, where he shortly thereafter applied for and was accepted to the post as rabbi of B'nai El Congregation.[5]

Among the first practices Wolfenstein ended, with full support from the lay leadership, was the tradition of auctioning off Torah portions. That change was precipitated by what happened on Simchas Torah of 1870, shortly after he assumed his post. In accordance with long-standing practice for that festive holiday, virtually every worshiper at the *Hakofos* service participated in the ceremonial parading of the Torah scrolls around the sanctuary. Who carried what Torah and in what order was determined by auction. The next morning the *shammas* (sexton), William Sicher, approached Wolfenstein with a broad smile on his face. "Doctor," he saluted the rabbi, *"es hat sich bezahlt"* ("it really has paid off"). From a handkerchief he poured onto a table a pile of coins and bills, nearly two hundred dollars. Elatedly Sicher declared that *"nach nicht ist da gewesen!"* ("That has never happened here before!") "And why did you bring this to me?" the rabbi asked. *"Doctor-leben,"* Sicher replied, "that belongs to the *Rebbe.*" From now on, Wolfenstein asserted, that practice stops. Wrap up this money, he told the unbelieving *shammas,* and turn it over to the *parnass* (the president of the congregation), L. R. Strauss. Thus ended at B'nai El the practice of auctioning off "Torah honors."[6]

Another important ritual change placed the weekly reading of the Torah on the Reform-advocated triennial cycle; that is, the weekly Sabbath reading of the Torah would be completed in three years rather than the traditional one year. Also important was the adoption of the new Szold-Jastrow ritual and prayer book. Appreciably modified from the traditional service, the Szold-Jastrow approach was viewed as moderate Reform, not nearly as liberal as the practices introduced at Shaare Emeth by the very progressive Rabbi Solomon Sonneschein.[7]

---

5. Cyrus Adler, ed., *American Jewish Yearbook, 5666*, 117.

6. "Dr. Wolfenstein's Reminiscences," in *Voice*, November 12, 1909.

7. Ibid. On Simchas Torah of 1873, when the first three-year cycle was completed, B'nai El celebrated with a lavish banquet free to all its members. See summary of B'nai El board minutes, reproduced in *Voice*, February 13, 1903.

Then came the critical event. At the invitation of Rabbi Isaac Mayer Wise, the recognized leader of American Reform, representatives of five congregations met in Cincinnati to lay the groundwork for an organization of America's Reform temples. Wolfenstein represented B'nai El at that meeting. Though he differed with Wise on several issues, Wolfenstein's overall glowing report to the B'nai El board resulted in that body unanimously endorsing the proposed national organization. Two years later, on July 8, 1873, delegates from thirty-four congregations, representing twenty-eight cities in thirteen states—including B'nai El—officially created the Union of American Hebrew Congregations (UAHC), which is still the umbrella organization of America's Reform temples. In 1876 B'nai El found itself in such dire financial straits that it was unable to pay its dues, and it reluctantly withdrew from the UAHC. Later that same year, however, members agreed to a special assessment to cover the cost of those dues. B'nai El thereupon immediately reaffiliated with the UAHC, and it has been a constituent member ever since.[8]

Wolfenstein instituted several more significant Reform modifications. In 1875 the congregation ended the traditional observance of the "additional day" for certain holidays—Rosh Hashannah, Succos, Passover, and Shavuos. The following year, when asked if members could pray in the temple with uncovered heads, Wolfenstein responded in the affirmative, but allowed that it was up to the individual worshiper. As for himself, he said, he would continue to cover his head "with the customary velvet cap and wear ministerial garb."[9]

In 1878 Wolfenstein resigned from B'nai El to become superintendent of the highly regarded orphans home established in Cleveland by B'nai B'rith. There he earned a national reputation as a capable and conscientious social service administrator. In the eight years he served at B'nai El, his most important legacy was leading that congregation through the final stages from Orthodox to Reform.

Wolfenstein was succeeded in 1878 by Rabbi Moritz Spitz. Although Kuttner's and Wolfenstein's service had by no means been unstable, their tenures were marked by constant concern with the incessant issue of Orthodox versus Reform. By the time Spitz arrived, that determination had been made; now all internal religious issues would be handled within the Reform framework. As a result, thanks to the good health and physical

---

8. From summary of B'nai El board minutes as reproduced in *Voice*, February 13 and 20, 1903. For a brief and very readable survey of early American Reform Judaism, see, among others, Sylvan D. Schwartzman, *Reform Judaism, Then and Now*, 188 ff.

9. From summary of B'nai El board minutes in *Voice*, February 20, 1903; "Dr. Wolfenstein's Reminiscences," in *Voice*, November 12, 1909.

well-being of its spiritual leaders, only three rabbis would serve B'nai El for the next century: Spitz, Julian A. Miller, and Bertram Klausner.[10]

Moritz Spitz was born in Csaba, Hungary, on October 4, 1848. The oldest of seven children of Rabbi Jacob Spitz, Moritz was educated at the University of Prague and received his rabbinic *smicha* (ordination) from Rabbi Judah Tebeles of that city. Following the untimely death of Spitz's mother, his father emigrated to Louisville, Kentucky, where he taught Hebrew and sent for his children one by one. Moritz came last, in 1870, as he had to complete his rabbinic studies. He served congregations in Chicago and Milwaukee before coming to St. Louis. In 1872 he married Esther Block, of Cleveland, whom he had met earlier under unusually dramatic as well as romantic circumstances during the great Chicago fire of 1871. A frequent visitor in Milwaukee was Solomon Sonneschein, rabbi of Temple Shaare Emeth in St. Louis. The two had been close friends for many years since their school days in Prague. In 1878 Sonneschein suggested to Spitz that he apply for the position at B'nai El that Wolfenstein was vacating. Spitz was elected unanimously, and served the congregation with distinction and honor until he died in 1920. He proved to be a remarkable asset to not only B'nai El but also the larger St. Louis Jewish population and the broader non-Jewish secular community. He was "beloved by both Jew and Gentile," wrote the *St. Louis Times* at the time of his death. Spitz and his wife were both venerated by their congregation, where they instilled a new and vibrant spirit of Temple life. Spitz became an important and influential force also behind such community institutions within St. Louis Jewry as the Jewish press, the Home for the Aged and Infirm Israelites, and the YMHA.[11]

The transformation to Reform at United Hebrew occurred at a much slower pace and with greater resistance within the congregation. United Hebrew records indicate that in the 1860s and 1870s the congregation was plagued with not only nagging financial problems but also lack of permanency in spiritual and lay leadership. Those records indicate also a recurring desire to continue Americanizing ritual practices, but at the same time not to "stray" too far from popular traditional practices.

---

10. Spitz served from 1878 until 1919, when he became rabbi emeritus, the position he held until he died in 1920.

11. A biography of Spitz would be a welcome addition to the annals of St. Louis Jewry. The archives of B'nai El Temple contain a veritable treasure of untapped primary sources. See also the Moritz Spitz File, AJA, as well as the files of the *Jewish Tribune* (1879–1884), the *Jewish Free Press* (1885–1887), and the *Jewish Voice* (1888–1920), all St. Louis newspapers that Spitz edited. See also Cyrus Adler, ed., *American Jewish Yearbook, 5664*, 101–2.

This overall picture of uncertainty began in 1866 with the departure of the popular Rabbi Henry Vidaver to a post in San Francisco. Because of financial constraints, the congregation replaced him with several temporary appointments, including a Mr. Franzig and the Rev. Isaac Ritterman. Neither was an ordained rabbi; they were referred to as *chazzan*. In 1870 Henry Kuttner left B'nai El, and United Hebrew immediately employed him.

Kuttner's second tenure with United Hebrew started on a positive note. The board offered him a three-year contract, considerably longer than tendered to earlier leaders. At the same time, the board also approved an organ and choir, suggesting further Americanization under Kuttner. Lay leadership soon expressed itself positively in nonspiritual matters. In 1872 the national charitable Kesher Shel Barzel Society requested cooperation from United Hebrew for relief of Rumanian emigrants. Even though the recipients of this aid were eastern European Jews who were overwhelmingly Orthodox, German American United Hebrew congregants Joseph Davis, Aaron Gershon, Abraham Newmark, A. S. Jacobs, and Isaac Russack constituted an active and diligent committee for that worthy cause. It reflected significant secular Jewish community efforts already taking place.

Nevertheless, internal problems continued to plague United Hebrew. Congregational records do not give a clear picture, but they reveal some issues. Financial instability undoubtedly was a major concern, but that was neither new nor unique to any congregation. A nagging controversy over sanctuary seating refused to go away. In fact, it may have caused another serious problem, the resignations of many officers and board members. Such a revolving-door scenario in leadership certainly affected morale within the congregation. Apparently, too, some dissatisfaction with Kuttner began to emerge. When he applied in 1873 for a renewal of his three-year contract, the board approved only a two-year extension; and when that expired, Kuttner was not reemployed. Instead, with congregation records giving absolutely no clue as to why, in 1875 Kuttner left United Hebrew for another rabbinic position in Cincinnati.[12]

For almost three years United Hebrew remained again without permanent spiritual leadership. In 1875 the board elected Rev. M. Treichenberg as

---

12. "Minutes, Board of Trustees of the United Hebrew Congregation, 1859–1868," "Records of U.H.C., 1868–1946," and "Board of Trustees Meetings, 1868–1881," all in archives of United Hebrew Congregation, St. Louis. After leaving United Hebrew, Kuttner served as rabbi in Cincinnati until 1883, and in Louisville from 1883 to 1892. He then retired to St. Louis, where he died on July 11, 1897. See Henry Kuttner File, AJA; *St. Louis Globe-Democrat*, August 26, 1880; *Voice,* May 21, 1909; and Priwer, *United Hebrew Congregation,* 21.

chazzan for one year. Within a few months, however, members registered "great dissatisfaction" over some of his actions (although congregational records do not indicate what those actions were), and he was released. In 1876 several trustees sought to get Rabbi Vidaver back from San Francisco, but in vain. United Hebrew records for 1876 and 1877 are replete with concern over finances as well as efforts to find a spiritual leader. Finally, in September 1877 the congregation advertised nationally for a "Reader, Preacher, and Teacher." From a list of many applicants pared down to three, on December 30, 1877, the board of trustees elected Rabbi Henry J. Messing. He was tendered a two-year contract to become effective on March 1, 1878.

Henry Joseph Messing came from a highly respected eastern European family that claimed nine generations of distinguished rabbis. The youngest of three brothers who all became rabbis, Messing was born in Gostyn, in Posen, Germany. He was educated at the Gymnasium in Glogau and at the University and the Rabbinic Seminary in Breslau. He studied also under the renowned Talmudic scholar Grand Rabbi Elias Guttmacher of Graetz. The Messing family emigrated to London during the 1860s, where the parents remained; in 1867 the three sons sailed to the United States, where all became congregational rabbis. Henry Messing served congregations in Dubuque, Iowa, Williamsport, Pennsylvania, and Peoria, Illinois, before answering the call to United Hebrew in 1877.[13]

Messing's arrival marked a milestone in United Hebrew's development as well as in St. Louis Jewish community history, just as Spitz's arrival at virtually the same time was also so significant to B'nai El and to the larger community. With the advent of the Messing era—his contract was renewed again and again by a very satisfied congregation—rabbinic stability and long-overdue congregational esteem finally came to United Hebrew. Indeed, for the next century, just as at B'nai El, three men would predominate as chief rabbis at United Hebrew: Messing, Samuel Thurman, and Jerome W. Grollman.[14]

---

13. Messing's father, Rabbi Joseph Messing, was a noted scholar and author of at least twelve authoritative Talmudic tracts. He died in London in 1880. In 1872 Henry J. Messing married Jenny May, who became a popular, active, and beloved "rebbitzin" at United Hebrew Temple during all the years she and her husband were there. Author's interviews with Ben Roman and Wilma Messing, St. Louis, June 19, 1992; *Dedicatory Book, United Hebrew Congregation,* 10, 25; Priwer, *United Hebrew Congregation,* 21–22; Adler, ed., *American Jewish Yearbook, 5664,* 81–82.

14. Henry J. Messing was rabbi at United Hebrew from 1878 to 1911, and rabbi emeritus from 1911 until he died in 1913. Rabbi Mendel Silber served with Messing as associate rabbi from 1905 to 1910. *Modern View 25,* 22; *St. Louis Jewish Light,* June 10, 1987; Priwer, *United Hebrew Congregation,* 20–25.

At the same board meeting in which Messing was chosen to be United Hebrew's new rabbi, lay leaders paved the way for the congregation to move toward Reform. President Bernard Cohen, secretary Aaron Gershon, and trustees Charles Bienenstock, Benno Diamant, Louis Halle, Henry Lyon, Samuel Marx, and Isaac Russack spearheaded a resolution that the congregation replace its *Minhag Poland* with the Reform *Minhag America* developed in the 1850s by Isaac Mayer Wise. The exact form of the prayer book would be determined after Messing took over. There seems no doubt that both Messing and the United Hebrew board agreed that St. Louis's oldest congregation would become Reform. The question was, to what extent? Indeed, only two months after Messing arrived, he addressed the board on the new UAHC. "The Rev. Dr. spoke at length upon the subject," United Hebrew board minutes state, "fully explaining the advantages to be derived, after which a motion was made by Joseph Davis, Esq., seconded by I. Gogel, Esq., that this congregation join the American Union of Congregations [*sic*] , which motion was unanimously adopted." Thus in the summer of 1879, by becoming a part of the UAHC, United Hebrew officially became a Reform congregation.[15]

Despite its affiliation with the UAHC and its strong support for Isaac Mayer Wise's new Hebrew Union College to ordain American-trained Reform rabbis, United Hebrew under Messing's spiritual leadership pursued a very cautious Reform regimen. The moderate Szold-Jastrow prayer book and ritual replaced the Orthodox *Minhag Poland*. In 1881, when United Hebrew moved westward into a new temple on Twenty-First and Olive, traditional segregation of women in the balcony was replaced by family pews. The number of persons called up to the Torah on a Sabbath morning was reduced from the traditional seven to only three: the president, the vice president, and the rabbi. (Exceptions could be made for a *Bar Mitzvah* or at the request of members on the occasion of a special celebration such as the naming of a child or an "aufruf" preceding a wedding.)[16]

At the same time, though, many United Hebrew members reacted negatively to the changes. In 1881, traditionalists introduced into a board meeting a resolution to appoint a special committee of four, "two Orthodox and two Reform," who would elect a fifth member as chairman, "to recommend changes in Sabbath and holiday worship that best satisfied both sides." A lengthy and heated discussion in committee of the whole resulted in the resolution being tabled. (A similar controversy erupted

---

15. "Records of U.H.C., 1868–1946," in archives of United Hebrew Congregation, St. Louis.

16. Ibid.

as late as 1910, when some board members complained that United Hebrew's religious practices "to the elderly are too much reformed, to the young people not enough reformed." Again no resolution of the problem was forthcoming.) Traditionalists prevailed in some issues, at least temporarily, when the congregation voted by a narrow margin to retain the "additional days" in Rosh Hashannah, Succos, Passover, and Shavuos (the additional day was later dropped). Lengthy and discordant disputes over the wearing of hats were not resolved until 1913 when the congregation voted that the rabbi could read from the Torah bareheaded. Clearly, then, United Hebrew moved toward Reform, but cautiously and slowly, and with considerable resistance. With good reason has United Hebrew been categorized as a "moderate" Reform congregation from the earliest days of its Reform association.[17]

Much of the direction for both change and the moderation of the change came from Rabbi Messing. As with Spitz at B'nai El, Messing exerted strong influence in his congregation and in the community at large. As will be seen, he had much to do with creating communitywide Jewish education and with developing, among other institutions, a home for Jewish senior citizens.

Meanwhile, another prominent St. Louis rabbinic figure was the young spiritual leader at the newly organized Reform Shaare Emeth Temple. Solomon Hirsch Sonneschein was born on June 24, 1839, at St. Martin Turocz in Hungary, the son of Moses Sonneschein and Charlotte Jassniger. Educated in Moravia and Hamburg, he received his rabbinic diploma in 1863 from the Chief Rabbi of Moravia, and a doctorate from the University of Jena in 1864. Shortly thereafter he became rabbi of a congregation in Warasdin, Hungary. There he met and married seventeen-year-old Rosa Fassel, who was visiting her sister there. Rosa was the youngest of nine children of Dr. Hirsh Baer Fassel, a prominent Hungarian rabbi and scientist. Virtually forced by her father to marry Sonneschein (Rosa considered him the least desirable of three prospective husbands her father proffered), the newlyweds were about as incompatible as two young people could be. The marriage proved to be discordant and tempestuous from the very beginning. Although the Sonnescheins raised four children before they

---

17. Ibid.; *Tribune*, June 10, 1881; Priwer, *United Hebrew Congregation*, 11–12, 21–23. United Hebrew Temple records are frustratingly sparse relating to the transition to Reform. There is no doubt that United Hebrew joined the Union of American Hebrew Congregations early in Messing's tenure, which began in 1878. In 1885, however, the congregation withdrew. Unfortunately United Hebrew records do not provide details. But clearly the congregation reestablished its association later. *Jewish Free Press*, December 4, 1885.

eventually were divorced, their lives took distinctly different directions: he was a hard-drinking, crude, firebrand, radical Reform theologian whose peers would accuse him of being more a Unitarian than a Jew; she was a beautiful, cultivated, avant garde, cigar-smoking feminist, writer, and publisher, much happier in a cosmopolitan salon than in a synagogue, who became an ardent and enthusiastic Zionist supporter of Theodor Herzl and Max Nordau. To say the least, the Sonnescheins were an engaging addition to the St. Louis Jewish scene.[18]

Thus the 1870s ushered in a new era of rabbinic leadership for St. Louis. That leadership was not confined, however, to those clergymen's individual congregations, important though that was. For during this period, St. Louis Jewry embraced a new phase of its Jewish identity. Hitherto St. Louis Jews were identified primarily with congregations, fraternal organizations, benevolent societies, or cemetery associations. Affiliated or unaffiliated, they did little to be identified collectively as a *St. Louis* Jewish community. They were Jews living in St. Louis; they were Jews who belonged to Jewish associations in St. Louis; some individual Jews had even gained some degree of prominence by being active in the overall St. Louis community—but there was not yet a unified St. Louis Jewry. That changed in the 1870s, not only because of the activities of these new rabbis but also through the emergence of newly visible and influential lay leaders. Unfortunately, it took a tragedy three hundred miles away to activate the change.

At about 9:20 P.M. on Sunday night, October 8, 1871, fire broke out in a crowded tenement district in the near west side of Chicago. Long-standing legend has it that the fire began when Mary O'Leary's cow accidentally kicked over an oil lamp in the barn alongside her home. The flames quickly

---

18. In the Rosa Sonneschein file in the American Jewish Archives (Cincinnati) is a fascinating memoir written by David Loth, Rosa's grandson. It details a sense of the impact his grandmother had on the St. Louis scene when she and Rabbi Sonneschein came there. "The St. Louis Jewish community of the 1870s lacked the style and sophistication of those in New York, Cincinnati, New Orleans or even Chicago. Wives and daughters of leading businessmen had no such Paris or Vienna costumes as the new rabbi's young wife wore so gracefully. They were shocked to observe that she powdered her face, and were scandalized when she attended the theater in the company of the congregation's most eligible bachelor on a Friday night . . . Rosa maintained her supply of the latest fashions and her contact with the cosmopolitan society of her girlhood by annual trips to Europe." Rosa Sonneschein File, AJA. See also Solomon Sonneschein and Rosa Sonneschein files, Shaare Emeth Temple, St. Louis; *Voice*, October 9, 1908; Adler, ed., *American Jewish Yearbook, 5664*, 101; Jack Nusan Porter, "Rosa Sonneschein and *The American Jewess:* The First Independent English Language Jewish Women's Journal in the United States," 57–63, and Porter, "Rosa Sonneschein and *The American Jewess* Revisited," 125–31.

spread out of control, and throughout the night and all during the next day an inferno raged through the city. Only herculean efforts finally brought the conflagration under control. Some eighteen thousand buildings were destroyed; upwards of ninety thousand people were homeless; at least three hundred lost their lives. Thousands fled from Chicago, seeking refuge in communities elsewhere.

One of those communities was St. Louis. Before the flames were even extinguished, St. Louis newspapers carried telegraphic dispatches detailing vivid stories of widespread destruction and suffering. Incoming trains brought hundreds upon hundreds of refugees. As did so many other communities throughout the country, St. Louis unhesitatingly and unselfishly responded to the emergency; after all, many St. Louisans vividly recalled the horrors of their own devastating riverfront fire only two decades earlier. Emergency committees sprang into being in practically every segment of St. Louis life. The Merchants Exchange established an ad hoc "Chicago Aid Society" that coordinated the city's efforts. Companies and employees contributed money and clothing. Religious institutions of all denominations gathered relief supplies. School children contributed their pennies, and also collected food, blankets, sheets, and clothing. In fact, the first trainload of relief supplies into stricken Chicago came from St. Louis. Mayor Joseph Brown dispatched fire engines and policemen to assist. St. Louis orphans homes took in destitute youngsters whose parents had been lost in the disaster. Even the St. Louis Empire Baseball Club pitched in with a benefit baseball "match," the proceeds going to Chicago relief.[19]

For St. Louis Jewry, this relief effort proved to be a milestone in community action, because it saw the creation of the United Hebrew Relief Association (UHRA). Established to provide aid for the hundreds of Chicago Jews who sought refuge in St. Louis, the United Hebrew Relief Association soon became the coordinator of charitable and philanthropic activities for the broader St. Louis Jewish community. It was the first time St. Louis Jewry acted consciously as a citywide Jewish community. The United Hebrew Relief Association proved to be the predecessor of what eventually became, after several institutional reorganizations, the Jewish Federation of St. Louis.

Perhaps the one individual most responsible for creating the United Hebrew Relief Association was Augustus Binswanger. Born in Cantonsville, Maryland, in 1844, Binswanger grew up working in his father's vinegar factory. Disliking the hard manual labor, young Binswanger left home

---

19. *St. Louis Democrat*, October 9–17, 1871.

to seek his fortune as a clothing store clerk in Darlington, North Carolina. When the Civil War began, the seventeen-year-old youth found himself in the Confederate army, but he was soon discharged, abetted by a personal letter from General Stonewall Jackson. Binswanger somehow got to Washington, D.C., where he opened a clothing store. Drafted into the Union army, he hired a substitute to serve for him, a common practice throughout the country under the provisions of the draft law. Despite an earlier meager education, Binswanger managed to enroll in Yale University Law School. Admitted to the bar in 1867, he moved west to St. Joseph, Missouri, and shortly thereafter to St. Louis, where he opened a law office. Successful in his law practice, Binswanger also developed a very lucrative commercial association with the Silver Cave Mining and Milling Company. Though never traditionally observant, Binswanger was nevertheless enough concerned about his religion to become an active member of the newly organized Reform Shaare Emeth Temple. He lived in St. Louis for only two decades, until 1888, when he moved to Chicago, but in that brief time he emerged as an important leader within the city's Jewish community.[20]

St. Louis's mobilization to aid Chicago refugees evinced no overt discrimination. Nevertheless, Binswanger sensed that various ethnic and religious relief groups were concentrating on "their" people, whereas no one seemed to do the same for Jews. Binswanger's knowledge of history made him aware that in catastrophic times Jews unfortunately often had to fend for themselves. He knew also that existing Jewish benevolence organizations in St. Louis were too small, too congregationally oriented, and too lacking in organization and resources to take on such a monumental task. This emergency required a broader community undertaking. Accordingly, as Chicagoans poured into the city, on October 11 Binswanger invited to his office a number of fellow St. Louisans to ensure relief for Jewish refugees. That group included Lewis Hutzler, Joseph B. Friend, Nathaniel Myers, Julius Rothschild, B. Summers, Lewis Glazer, Moses Cohn, Simon Popper, Gus Frank, L. Kayser, and Albert Frankenthal,

---

20. As a member of Shaare Emeth, Binswanger advocated celebrating the Jewish Sabbath on Sunday, "in conformity with nine-tenths of the civilized people on Earth." He shocked his fellow Shaare Emeth coreligionists by going to a German theater on Kol Nidre eve in 1868, complaining that because so much of the services were in Hebrew, he derived "so little pleasure or benefit" from them. The following year, 1869, he attended the High Holiday services and was very complimentary, although he still complained that "altogether too much Hebrew [was] used in prayers." Diaries of August Binswanger, Missouri Box, AJA. See also *Tribune*, January 26, 1883; *Jewish Free Press*, January 28, 1887; *Voice*, September 28, 1888, and May 20, 1904.

all established Jewish businessmen. They resolved themselves into "The Temporary Relief Committee," or the "TRC," and designated Binswanger as chairman. The very next day the Merchants' Exchange's Chicago Aid Society designated Binswanger chairman of the "Committee to Provide for Destitute Families," one of several groups organized to implement the city's relief efforts. Binswanger was assured full cooperation especially in assisting Jewish refugees.[21]

The next few days witnessed a frenzy of activity, as TRC members canvassed fellow Jews for funds and relief materials. Binswanger and Popper alone collected five hundred dollars from merchants along Main Street. Funds were raised every evening at the Harmonie Club. TRC volunteers made round-the-clock visits to "The Rink," a recreation center in north St. Louis to which Chicago refugees were conducted from the railroad station; there they saw to the immediate needs of arriving Jewish refugees, both individuals and family groups.[22]

Even as those emergency measures were undertaken, on October 16 Binswanger and others moved to broaden and better institutionalize Jewish benevolence by calling, in a circular letter, for a permanent communitywide organization:

> Now, in view of the fact that many Israelitish families are already, and many more will soon be, here, who will require and are entitled to substantial assistance, we do respectfully urge upon you the pressing necessity of organizing a permanent UNITED HEBREW RELIEF ASSO-CIATION.

That letter was signed by Binswanger, by the presidents of the three major congregations—Abraham Kramer of Shaare Emeth, Adolph Isaacs of United Hebrew, and L. R. Straus of B'nai El—and by Lewis Hutzler, Nathaniel Myers, and Simon Popper of the TRC. Accordingly, on the very next day, October 17, 1871, a crowded mass meeting took place at United Hebrew's sanctuary on Sixth and St. Charles, attended by persons of all facets of St. Louis Jewry. There they organized the United Hebrew Relief Association. The association immediately took over from the Temporary Relief Committee the task of assisting Jewish refugees from fire-stricken Chicago. Officers elected included Bernard Singer, president; A. Jacobs, vice president; William Goldstein, treasurer; Augustus Binswanger, secretary; Nathaniel Myers, corresponding secretary; and William Keiler, Isaac

---

21. Augustus Binswanger Papers, St. Louis Jewish Community Archives, St. Louis; Augustus Binswanger to Samuel Bowman, n.d., in *Modern View*, August 28, 1925; *St. Louis Democrat*, October 14, 1871.

22. Binswanger to Bowman, Chicago, n.d., in *Modern View*, August 28, 1925; *St. Louis Democrat*, October 14 and 15, 1871; Scharf, *Saint Louis City and County*, vol. 2, 1769.

Baer, Moses Fraley, Lewis Hutzler, Simon Popper, and Joseph Baum, directors. The first communitywide institution representing St. Louis Jewry had come into existence. Little could anyone realize that helping the Chicago refugees would be only the beginning of a very active and productive agenda that would continue to the present.[23]

United Hebrew Relief Association members "pushed forward with great energy" the task of aiding Chicago refugees. They collected money, food, clothing, and other personal necessities for direct distribution, and arranged also for housing. Needed resources were raised within the Jewish community by means ranging from direct solicitation to charity balls, the latter often coinciding with such Jewish festivals as Chanukah and Purim. Some of the refugees eventually returned to Chicago; some remained in St. Louis, where the UHRA helped them settle permanently.[24]

Two important points must be clarified about the United Hebrew Relief Association. First, although it came into being to alleviate the needs of Jewish refugees from Chicago, its efforts were not confined to just those people and for just that period of time. Once the Chicago refugee emergency passed, "its province [became]," in the words of one contemporary St. Louis Jew, "to care for indigent Hebrews, whether transient or resident." That soon included refugees from yellow fever disasters in the South and many new eastern European immigrants who began to flock into the city.[25]

Second, one of the most difficult tasks for those concerned with St. Louis Jewish philanthropy has been how it has been organized. In modern times we view the St. Louis Jewish Federation as the umbrella organization that coordinates the efforts of many individual philanthropic institutions. That is accurate only depending upon how one defines the words "umbrella" and "coordinates." Many Jewish eleemosynary institutions exist in St. Louis, with their own functions, officers and boards of directors, budgets, programs for raising needed revenue, and agendas. Each operates independently of the others; yet each tries to work as cooperatively as possible with the others. The Jewish Federation attempts to facilitate that work. The product of decades of federation experiences in Jewish communities across the country, the St. Louis Jewish Federation has its own membership, officers and directors, budget, programs for raising revenue, and agenda. Part of that agenda and budget is to subsidize some

---

23. United Hebrew Relief Association file, St. Louis Jewish Community Archives, St. Louis; Scharf, *Saint Louis City and County,* vol. 2, 1769; Samuel L. Rosen, "The Historical Development of the Jewish Federation of Saint Louis," 58–59.

24. Scharf, *Saint Louis City and County,* vol. 2, 1769.

25. Ibid.; *Modern View 25,* 90.

of the operations of those other institutions. Some of its own structural organization consists of representatives of those other associations who sit on various boards or committees of the Federation. Understanding just who represents whom, who has what function, and how lines of communication and authority are drawn, can be as confusing as trying to trace similar lines within a giant multifaceted corporate conglomerate.

So, too, with the United Hebrew Relief Association. It came into being because existing philanthropic institutions could not handle the load of Chicago relief. It did not replace those organizations; it was a new association that worked alongside them. It had its own membership, its own dues structure, its own organization, and its own agenda. At the same time, because of the caliber of its business leaders and their emerging prominence in the overall St. Louis economic picture, as well as its broad appeal across the entire spectrum of St. Louis Jewish society, the UHRA was soon viewed as the most influential and the leader in Jewish benevolent work. It tried to coordinate the work of all the Jewish philanthropic institutions, and to a small degree it succeeded, at least during the Chicago refugee period. But once that emergency had passed, the other associations insisted upon "doing their own thing." Still, the UHRA did emerge as the leader within St. Louis Jewish philanthropy.[26]

When yellow fever epidemics struck several cities in the lower Mississippi valley in 1878 and 1879, the United Hebrew Relief Association was thus already positioned to take the lead in assisting Jews from those areas who looked for succor in St. Louis. Among them were Jews who had already built some of the leading business firms in Memphis and who, when they relocated farther north, became commercial giants in St. Louis. They included men such as Jonathan Rice, William Stix, and Benjamin Eiseman (Rice-Stix and Company), Isaac Schwab (Isaac Schwab and Company), and Jacob Friedman (Jacob Friedman and Brother.)[27]

Unfortunately, extant records give us very few details of UHRA activities in the 1870s. Some available data, however, reveals at least part of their important work. We know, for instance, that from September 1873 to September 1874, the association provided some thirty-five hundred dollars to help 256 families and 202 single men. The first detailed breakdown of UHRA operations—the earliest available record—is for 1875. One hundred and sixty-five members, who met seventy-three times

---

26. A directory of St. Louis benevolent societies published in 1880 listed the following: United Hebrew Relief Association, Ladies' Hebrew Relief Society, Ladies' Widows and Orphans Society, Ladies' Sewing Society, Mercy and Truth, Hebrew Benevolent Society, and Hebrew Mutual Benefit Society. *Tribune,* May 7, 1880.

27. Ibid., October 10, 1879, and November 26, 1880; *Modern View* 25, 9.

during that one year alone, were led by the following officers: Louis Hutzler, president; Rabbi Samuel Wolfenstein, vice president; Augustus Binswanger, secretary; William Goldstein, treasurer; and Rabbi Solomon Sonneschein, Jacob Furth, Moses Strauss, Moses Fraley, Bernard Singer, Joseph M. Pollack, Albert Fisher, S. Zork, Abraham Kramer, E. Fishel, Leopold Sternberger, and Joseph Baum, board of directors. The UHRA financial statement for 1875 indicated:

Receipts

From Dues	$2,220.00
From Concert	324.17
From Ball	2,503.02
Advances returned	152.00
Donations	237.00
Interest	40.86
Total Receipts	$5,477.05

Expenditures

Cash to 308 families	$2,210.40
Cash to 87 single persons	284.75
Groceries to 112 families	275.85
Coal to 16 families	43.05
Board & Lodging, 272 persons	300.65
Transportation, 167 persons	729.17
Shoes & Clothing	92.35
Funeral expense	45.00
Maintenance expense	259.92
Total Expenditures	4,241.14
BALANCE ON HAND	$1,235.91[28]

In the first ten years of its existence, from 1871 to 1881, the United Hebrew Relief Association distributed more than thirty-eight thousand dollars to alleviate the privations of needy St. Louis Jews. That may not seem like much when compared with dollar amounts in the late twentieth century, but it was a considerable figure for that time—especially when one recognizes that the UHRA drew from limited resources in a St. Louis Jewish community that at that time numbered fewer than 10,000 of a total city population of about 350,000.[29]

---

28. *Modern View 25,* 32.

29. *Israelite,* October 30, 1874; *Tribune,* April 15, 1881; *Voice,* July 6, 1888; Scharf, *Saint Louis City and County,* vol. 2, 1769; Rosen, "Historical Development of the Jewish

In addition to providing direct and immediate relief to fellow Jews, the United Hebrew Relief Association also performed a number of other very important functions. It established and maintained an employment bureau, whose importance to the Jews of St. Louis cannot be overly emphasized—especially to the new arrivals into the city. It undertook what proved to be a long and arduous campaign for a Jewish hospital. It laid the foundations for the Home for the Aged and Infirm Israelites—the first home for St. Louis Jewish senior citizens—and also for the establishment of a kindergarten for the very young. It made possible the creation of the Hebrew Free and Industrial School. And when Russian immigrants began to come to St. Louis, the United Hebrew Relief Association led the movement to help them become a viable part of the St. Louis Jewish community.[30]

Assessing the overall impact of the United Hebrew Relief Association is difficult because of the lack of data. It clearly merits credit, though, as the first organization to achieve communitywide cooperation within St. Louis Jewry. Up to the 1870s, group efforts—"community" efforts, if you will— had focused on limited "communities": synagogues and congregations for a somewhat circumscribed membership; cemetery associations primarily for congregational members; educational programs primarily also for congregational members; even cultural and benevolent societies associated primarily with congregational membership. True, nonaffiliated Jews had access to and benefited from any and all of those activities; but none were really viewed as organizations for the entire St. Louis Jewish community. That is why the United Hebrew Relief Association holds a singular place in the history of the Jews of St. Louis.

One reason for the emergence of the UHRA, of course, was the dramatic nature of its needs: relief for disaster victims. Undoubtedly another was the rise of a new breed of Jewish leader in St. Louis. Three generalizations

---

Federation of Saint Louis," 60. The United Hebrew Relief Association's early records seem no longer to exist. For many years they had been kept in the Jewish Federation office in St. Louis. Based on his bibliography, Samuel Rosen used them in the 1930s for his master's thesis. However, according to administrative personnel in the Federation office, in the course of several office moves since then, "excess" and "extraneous" files were disposed of to reduce the bulk and cost of storage. That seems to have been the fate of those early UHRA records. Persistent efforts by the author and by personnel of the recently organized St. Louis Jewish Community Archives have failed to locate them.

30. *Tribune,* November 21, 1879, and October 13, 1882; Scharf, *Saint Louis City and County,* vol. 2, 1769–70; Hyde and Conard, eds., *Encyclopedia of the History of St. Louis,* vol. 2, 1125–26; Rosen, "Historical Development of the Jewish Federation of Saint Louis," 59–63.

characterized the new leaders: First, they were German Jews, mostly first-generation (but some second-generation) Americans. Second, most were affiliated with Reform congregations. And third, they were prosperous merchants and businessmen who could be counted among the foremost achievers in the St. Louis economy. To identify all would be virtually impossible. Some who started their business careers prior to the Civil War have already been noted. A few more deserve mention here because of their outstanding efforts and achievements from time to time as officers and members of the United Hebrew Relief Association: Barney Hysinger, Leon Helman, Albert Arnstein, Marcus Bernheimer, Bernard Singer, Louis Wolfner, M. J. Epstein, Moritz Block, William Goldstein, William Stix, Moses Fraley, Solomon Boehm, Louis Brey, Samuel Bowman, Jonathan Rice, Moses Summerfield, August Frank, Louis Godlove, J. P. Weil, Adolph Robi, and William Deutsch. This is by no means a complete list, but these men, along with the rabbis, were significant in developing a truly citywide Jewish community spirit.[31]

In addition to their growing role in the city's business and cultural picture, Jews played an increasingly important role in St. Louis public education. Except for Rabbi Illowy's short-lived day school in the 1850s, Jewish education was conducted either by private tutors or in conjunction with synagogues, and, more important, it was always supplementary to public education. Isidor Bush's ardent championship of public over parochial education was well received by a German Jewish population that placed high priority on acculturating to American life.

From the very beginning of the St. Louis public school system in the 1830s, Bible instruction had been included in the curriculum—not necessarily to teach religion per se, but as a vehicle for teaching reading and morality. Nevertheless, bitterly debated confrontations developed between Catholic and Protestant clergy and laymen over which Bible should be used—the Protestant King James Bible or the Catholic Douay Bible. Because of their small number, and even though some public school teachers were Jewish, Jews took no overt part in these debates. Although pro-Protestant forces prevailed, Catholic leaders continued to push their conviction that proper education could not be separated from religion.[32]

---

31. *St. Louis Democrat*, October 15, 1871; *Israelite*, October 30, 1874; *Tribune*, October 10 and November 21, 1879, November 12 and 26, 1880, April 15, 1881, and October 13 and November 17, 1882; Scharf, *Saint Louis City and County*, vol. 2, 1769–70; Hyde and Conard, eds., *Encyclopedia of the History of St. Louis*, vol. 2, 1125–26.

32. Troen, *The Public and the Schools*, 34. One Jewish teacher was Louis Cohen. See Louis Cohen File, AJA. Jews on the Board of Education included Adolph Levi, in the 1850s. *Occident* 18 (May 1855): 85.

A serious dispute arose in 1849 when the Missouri state legislature authorized local school districts to levy general real estate taxes to raise additional school funds. Catholic leaders argued forcefully that if Catholics paid these taxes, then Catholic schools should receive an appropriate share. (At that time Catholic school enrollment constituted almost half the total school population of St. Louis.) The city's school board, whose president was Unitarian minister William Greenleaf Eliot, countered that schools should foster social amalgamation rather than sectarianism, and that this was especially true when applied to public funds. Although the Catholic forces lost again, they remained undaunted in their efforts to retain a tie between religion and public education.

The issue became further politicized in the 1870s, this time with an attempt to push through the state legislature a voucher plan that would allow a child to receive ten dollars from the education tax that could be applied to a school of choice. That bill was defeated in Missouri, as were similar proposals in other states. The defeat of those measures was, of course, important to public education.

Far more significant, however, was the impact the whole issue had on new views expounded on public education, in St. Louis and elsewhere. Nineteenth-century secularized education experienced a radical and revolutionary departure from the millenia-old concept of church-sponsored moral education. Ever since colonial days, American "public" education had stressed moral instruction along with the Three R's, with the Bible as a major curricular vehicle. But the rapidly changing and democratizing American society of the nineteenth century generated new views toward the mission of public schools. The emerging breed of public educators—for whom St. Louis school superintendent William T. Harris stood out as a highly reputed spokesman—argued that American public education should be the crucible in which heterogeneous peoples and cultures could "ascend into a new homogeneous nationality." (Israel Zangwill would later popularize the "melting pot" concept.) This would be done by promoting in the schools "Anglo-American" culture and especially the English language. Ethnoculturalism was encouraged within any group's internal milieu; but the public stance should reflect Anglo-Americanism and the universal use of the English language. Harris was an ardent participant in the "St. Louis Movement," whose philosophical advocacy earned international attention. Proponents of Hegelian thesis-antithesis-synthesis dialectics, these philosophers believed that public education should prepare future generations to become productive and cooperative citizens in the emerging urban-industrial America. To achieve this, though, it was essential that children be in the public schools.

In St. Louis, Harris's greatest challenge was the multiculturalism and sectarianism that prevailed in the large Catholic population and the many immigrant ethnic groups. Since Germans (regardless of their religion) constituted the largest foreign group—and used the German language in so much of their everyday lives—they were potentially the greatest obstacle. To overcome that, Harris incorporated the German language as part of the school curriculum. This would attract German children into the public schools where they could be readily assimilated, but still would retain many opportunities for them to preserve their German identity. (Other ethnic and nationality groups in St. Louis were far less numerous. Besides, coming mostly from the eastern United States or from western Europe, most already spoke English anyway.) Statistical studies during the 1870s showed that the "German curriculum" was proving successful. Even the St. Louis *Missouri Republican,* a newspaper that was hostile to German instruction, admitted in 1871 that the public schools were the greatest force for the amalgamation of the city's population.[33]

Nevertheless, Harris's policy was challenged every step of the way, for a variety of reasons—political, cultural, and economic. The ongoing conflict reached a new peak in 1878, when the "German question" arose in the April municipal elections. St. Louis politics was never a field known for being quiescent, and many discordant issues repeatedly plagued the community. Its multiethnic and multicultural population had been terribly divided during numerous Civil War–era crises, often with heart-wrenching consequences even within close-knit families. Many of those conflicts continued during Reconstruction and after, with political squabbles exacerbated by cultural, religious, and ethnic differences. Since Germans were more closely identified with the Republican Party and the Irish with the Democrats, the question of German instruction in the schools inevitably became a partisan issue.

In 1878 the Irish/Democratic/Catholic/nativist/traditionalist elements of St. Louis, spearheaded by school board member Michael Glynn, attempted to undermine the "German curriculum" by proposing that Gaelic, and even French and Hebrew, be added to the curriculum— expounding the same justifications that Harris earlier had advocated when he introduced German. Fully anticipating that the request would be turned down because of the expense entailed, the Glynn forces insisted that if all legitimate languages could not be treated equally, then simple justice required that no one language—in this case German—merited privileged status.

---

33. Troen, *The Public and the Schools,* 34–65. See also Lawrence A. Cremin, *American Education: The National Experience, 1783–1876,* 520–21.

The reaction of the German community was "immediate and force-ful." The widely circulated German newspaper *Westliche Post* not only defended German language usage in the schools, but editor Emil Pree-torius urged his readers to unite politically to ensure continuation of the program. Of special significance to the Jews of St. Louis, however, was a mass meeting at the Tivoli Hall, where the assemblage unanimously and enthusiastically elected "community activist" Rabbi Solomon H. Son-neschein, "widely known for his support of workingmen's rights and pub-lic education," as their spokesman to argue before the board of education in favor of retaining German in the curriculum.

Sonneschein's advocacy before the school board proved successful. Efforts to undermine the Harris program by including costly additional foreign language options failed; on the other hand, the board by a con-vincing 20–7 vote elected to retain German. In the ensuing few weeks the St. Louis press printed quite a few letters from the public, on both sides of the issue, but even those who disagreed with Sonneschein praised his forceful and lucid advocacy and presentation.

The assault on German proved to be only the opening gambit for disputes over many other issues, not only in the broader municipal envi-ronment, but especially in the schools. The issues included such diverse educational matters as music, art, the new concept of the kindergarten, high schools, and other phases of the structure and curriculum of the public schools. And inexorably, with Sonneschein as a leading spokesman, the German community emerged, according to St. Louis school historian Selwyn Troen, as "the most stalwart defenders of a broadening definition of what legitimately constituted public education"—that is, a broad-based curriculum (in contrast with a narrower parochial school curriculum) that stressed not only a basic excellence in academics but also an expansion of those academics and the creation of good citizenship in an "American" civilization.[34]

Throughout this struggle, Sonneschein was one of the most outspo-ken and strongest advocates of public education. His name appeared repeatedly in the public press. It should be understood, though, that Sonneschein spoke for the German community; did he speak also for the Jewish community?[35]

How did Jews view public education and its new approach? Unfor-tunately, extant records of contemporary Jewish organizations offer no

---

34. Troen, *The Public and the Schools*, 65–67.

35. Sonneschein's strong ties with the German community are manifested by his many addresses to German groups totally unrelated to his rabbinic duties. See, for example, *St. Louis Republic*, August 31, 1879; and *Tribune*, September 5, 1879, and January 14, 1881.

answers. Furthermore, no Jewish newspaper existed in St. Louis at the time to give editorial views. Nevertheless, a few observations might suggest some clues. If Sonneschein spoke for the German community, most of the Jews of St. Louis were, after all, part of that larger German population. Furthermore, a number of Jewish laymen, among whom Isidor Bush can be singled out, were longtime champions of public secular education. In addition, later records of graduates of the public schools included many Jewish students; Jewish newspapers (when they finally came into being) listed those names with pride. Given traditional Jewish attitudes toward education, and considering the high priority German Jewish immigrants placed upon successfully Americanizing in their newly adopted homeland, it seems inconceivable that St. Louis Jewry was not full-square behind one of its own rabbis in this matter. That a Jew was selected so enthusiastically to be a spokesman, and that a Jew stood so prominently in the advocacy of public education, has to reflect positively on the Jewish community. Equally interesting is that although the opposition expressed openly xenophobic views, there is no overt evidence that any who disagreed with Sonneschein focused on his being a Jew; they viewed him as a German who just happened to be Jewish (for example, simple references to him as "the Reverend Dr. Sonneschein" or "Rabbi Sonneschein" or "the good rabbi"). It would seem, then, that this portion of St. Louis history reflects quite positively on the role of local Jewry in the progress of public education in St. Louis.[36]

36. The issue of German in the public schools remained for several decades. Its importance to St. Louis Jewry was underscored by Rabbi Moritz Spitz when he pointed out that fully nine-tenths of the Jews of St. Louis still spoke the language. *Jewish Free Press*, November 11, 1887. For a fuller exposition of the St. Louis public school and ancillary public education issues, and especially the philosophic background of "The St. Louis Movement," see *St. Louis Daily Globe-Democrat*, March 10 through April 15, 1878; Troen, *The Public and the Schools*, 32–78; and Primm, *Lion of the Valley*, 335–44.

10

BEGINNINGS OF THE
ST. LOUIS JEWISH PRESS

For the St. Louis Jewish community, the rise of a public educational system was matched in importance by the emergence of a St. Louis Jewish press. When Isidor Bush came to the city in 1849, he brought the excellent credentials and practical experience that might have initiated a Jewish press in St. Louis, but the small Jewish population made a newspaper an impractical endeavor. It was not until after the Civil War, when many more Jews lived in the city, that a Jewish press finally appeared.

The first Jewish newspaper in St. Louis was the *Jewish Sentinel*. Only fifteen scattered issues (or parts of issues) remain to give us an idea of its contents. The earliest, numbered Volume I, No. 10, is dated Friday, August 14, 1868. That would suggest that the paper first appeared—since it was a weekly—on June 5 or June 12, 1868. The paper had been moved from Louisville to St. Louis in 1868 by publisher and editor Saul Bacharach and associate editor E. B. Getz. Whether Volume I, No. 1 was published in Louisville or in St. Louis is not clear, since no copies of that edition exist. Certainly, though, by August 14, 1868, the paper emanated from St. Louis, with publishing facilities located at 317 Olive Street (in early 1869 operations moved to 309 North Fifth Street).

One might not be sure, though, by examining the contents of the *Sentinel*, that it was truly a *St. Louis* newspaper. Rarely did more than half of one column per issue deal with St. Louis or St. Louis Jewish matters, even though the *Sentinel* was an eight-page folio (two sheets folded into eight pages), each page eighteen inches tall and twelve inches wide, five columns to a page. Only occasionally could one find brief mention of the activities of the Temple Association, then involved in the founding of Shaare Emeth. Several editorial comments decried the need for better Sabbath School education. A singular item of local concern was a brief announcement that Mrs. A. Newmark was opening a Jewish boardinghouse at 11 North Eighth

Street and that her endeavors merited "liberal patronage." Apparently the issues of May 7 and May 14, 1869, upset leaders of B'nai El, for the congregation's board of directors called a special meeting to respond to the *Sentinel*'s charges. (Unfortunately, neither existing copies of the newspaper nor B'nai El's records give any clue to what the dispute was about.) In general, then, not much about St. Louis Jewry appeared in the *Sentinel*. Perhaps that lack of St. Louis orientation was a contributing factor behind the *Sentinel*'s demise after just one year.

Contents of the *Sentinel*, other than advertising, fell primarily into two categories: literary pieces printed in serial form, and reprints from other newspapers about Jewish matters elsewhere in America or abroad. Even the advertisements publicized products or institutions or services in cities other than St. Louis more than those available in the local area. No literary productivity of any St. Louisan, Jew or non-Jew, can be found in the extant copies of the *Sentinel*. Existing copies contain several short stories, none particularly noted in Jewish literary lore. They include *Nina Balatka: The Story of a Maiden of Prague* (author not identified), *The Woman's Kingdom* (author identified only as the author of *John Halifax, Gentleman*), and *Villa Eden: The Country House on the Rhine*, by Berthold Auerbach, not exactly a household name in Jewish literature. The *Sentinel*'s editors apparently had a strong penchant for William Shakespeare, for they reprinted several lengthy exchange articles dealing with the famous Bard of Avon, albeit none of those articles had any particularly Jewish slant.

Nevertheless, one could tell unmistakably that the *Sentinel* was a Jewish newspaper. Across the top of the front page, in large full-cap type, was the masthead "The Jewish Sentinel." Immediately below that masthead, on the dateline, appeared the Talmudic phrase *Tzedek Tzedek Tir'dof*, printed in Hebrew lettering, and its English translation, "Justice, Justice Shalt Thou Pursue." In contrast with later Jewish newspapers, however, no other Hebrew was found on the *Sentinel*'s pages, either in Hebrew lettering or in transliterated English.

One additional item of interest about the *Sentinel* merits mention. A singular characteristic of the Jewish newspapers that followed the *Sentinel* in St. Louis was the avoidance of partisanship in either local or national politics. The St. Louis Jewish press never hesitated to deal with anti-semitism or other aspects of social injustice, but it never made those issues partisan Democratic or partisan Republican or partisan any political party. The same applied to candidates for public office. Paid advertisements appeared aplenty, but the Jewish press rarely, if ever, supported or opposed a candidate—either local or national—purely upon that candidate's religion. The editorial concern was for issues, not religion or partisan politics. In 1868 General Ulysses S. Grant became the Republican candidate for president. Because of Grant's infamous General Order No. 11, many Jews found themselves in a quandary. German immigrants, whose numbers included many Jews, had strongly supported Lincoln and the Republican Party, especially because of their association with the antislavery movement. Now, in 1868, many Jews feared the Republican nominee to be antisemitic. Editorials in the *Sentinel* clearly illustrated that dilemma, and foreshadowed stands that would be taken by later St. Louis Jewish newspapers: concern not for party, but for issues. On August 21, 1868, the *Sentinel* wrote:

> With Grant's politics we have nothing to do. Many Jews, a great many, are Republicans: but they are Jews *first*, and Republicans and Democrats afterwards; and it makes no difference what party the public man belongs to, who does them a wanton and gratuitous wrong; they owe it to themselves, to their faith, and to their nationality to resent it.

The *Sentinel* clearly disapproved of Grant, but not for his political views—only because it viewed him as antisemitic.

Just how long the *Sentinel* remained in existence is not clear. The last issue we know of was dated May 28, 1869; whether any followed is simply unknown. Nothing in the May 28 issue hinted that the paper was going out of existence, but that really is not conclusive. The little we know for sure is that the first Jewish newspaper in St. Louis, the *Jewish Sentinel*, came into being in June of 1868 and lasted for approximately one year; that it was edited by Saul Bacharach and E. B. Getz; that it detailed mostly literary pieces and news of world Jewry; and that very little on its pages dealt with the St. Louis Jewish community.[1]

More than a year passed before the next Jewish publication appeared in St. Louis. It was *Die Warheit: Zeitschrift für Freie Menschen* (The Truth: Periodical for Free People). This publication lasted for only six months, from January to June 1871. *Die Warheit* was a German-language weekly, published and edited by Shaare Emeth's Rabbi Solomon Sonneschein. A sixteen-page folio, *Die Warheit* was more a literary magazine than a newspaper; in fact, the very rare news articles consisted of reprints or exchanges from other sources detailing topics of Jewish interest, as had been the case with the now-defunct *Sentinel*. *Die Warheit* served more as an outlet for

---

1. *Jewish Sentinel*, August 14, 21, and 28, September 11 and 18, and October 2, 1868, January 29, February 5 and 19, March 12 and 19, April 23 and 30, and May 7, 14, and 28, 1869. For more on the *Sentinel* see *Voice*, February 6, 1903, and Scharf, *Saint Louis City and County*, vol. 1, 948, 959. "A Resource Guide: The St. Louis Jewish Press," prepared by the Jewish Genealogy Society of St. Louis, copy in possession of the author, is a useful bibliographical aid for locating available copies of St. Louis Jewish newspapers, especially those on microfilm.

essays, poems, sermons, and an occasional short story. Sonneschein authored some of those writings himself, and when he did, he usually was an advocate for Reform Judaism—a topic that rarely had appeared in the *Sentinel*. Most of the literary contents of *Die Warheit*, however, were reprints or exchanges from European Jewish journals or other American Jewish publications. Sonneschein soon found that without advertising and with no revenues other than subscriptions, the enterprise was too costly to continue. But it was not to be the end of his journalistic endeavors.[2]

Almost four years transpired before the next Jewish journal in St. Louis, the *Jewish Tribune*, came into being. Two papers by that name actually existed; we know very little about the first, much more about the second. The first *Tribune* was published from 1875 to 1878; the second, from 1879 to 1884. No copies of the 1875–1878 series remain; we know of it only from references to it in other sources—and those references are tantalizingly meager. In 1875 three St. Louis Jewish merchants with literary and journalistic proclivities pooled their financial resources and writing abilities as joint publishers and editors: Louis Godlove, Joseph L. Wolfner, and Sam H. Fredman. We know nothing about the contents of the publication. We know only that two and a half years of circulation problems and financial tribulations finally forced them to cease publication in 1878 and to reorganize into what they hoped would be a more effectual operation. That reorganized venture came to fruition on August 29, 1879, with the publication of a new newspaper, also called the *Jewish Tribune*.[3]

Meanwhile, before the new *Tribune* appeared, another Jewish publication emerged on the St. Louis scene, the *Society Record*. No copies of this publication exist either; once more all we know of it comes from other sources. The *Society Record* lasted for just a few months, in 1879. Though referred to as a "Jewish journal"—even mistakenly as the "first" Jewish journal in St. Louis—it really was not a newspaper in the same sense as the *Sentinel* or the *Tribune*. It was instead a literary publication on the order of the earlier *Die Warheit*, except it was printed in English. The *Society Record* was primarily an outlet for the literary abilities of an increasing number of talented St. Louis Jewish young people, some in their teens, who showed proclivities toward literary advancement. In that sense the publication is important, for it was the first known to offer such opportunities to members of the St. Louis Jewish community other than those who ventured into journalism as a profession. Some evidence suggests that the *Society Record* may have been produced by the Young

---

2. In contrast with the *Sentinel*, copies of *Die Warheit* remain plentiful. Complete runs are available in a number of St. Louis public libraries, as well as in other newspaper depositories across the country.

3. *Voice*, December 18, 1914.

Men's Hebrew Literary Association (the organization would later evolve into the much better known YMHA). Although some members of the YMHLA can be identified, only one can be associated directly with the *Society Record:* the journal's editor, seventeen-year-old Henry A. Diamant, who later became a well-known professional actor under the stage name Martin Hayden.[4]

When the reorganized *Jewish Tribune* began publication, it again had the field of St. Louis Jewish journalism to itself. The new paper, although using the old title, began numerically again with Volume I, No. 1. Despite the reorganization, instability and controversy continued to importune the *Tribune* in both ownership and editorship, as an almost ludicrous revolving-door scenario plagued the paper throughout its existence.

Reorganized as the "Tribune Publishing Company," with offices at 105 North Third Street, the journal was headed at first by the same three men, with Fredman as president, Wolfner as secretary, and Godlove as treasurer. Within one month, Joshua Rosenfield Jr. was added as another editor and publisher; the paper now gave the firm of "Rosenfield, Wolfner and Company" as publisher, at a new address, 20 North Fourth Street. In January 1880, Rosenfield bought out his partners and became sole owner, retaining Wolfner as business manager and bringing in B'nai El's Rabbi Spitz as managing editor. In May 1880 Shaare Emeth's Rabbi Sonneschein was added as another editor. Six months later Wolfner left the organization. In February 1881 printer Max C. Reefer bought out the company, becoming the new "Publisher and Proprietor." He retained Spitz as editor, but dropped Sonneschein. Four months later Sonneschein was back as editor and Spitz was out. That remained the picture until August 1883, when Reefer enlisted Chicago liberal Reform rabbis Bernard Felsenthal and Emil G. Hirsch as editors, but that arrangement lasted only four weeks.[5]

In late August 1883 Spitz rejoined the staff as coeditor with Sonneschein. That proved very short-lived, however, when a vitriolic Chanukah-

---

4. *Israelite*, January 1, 1864; *Tribune*, August 29, 1879; *Jewish Free Press*, September 2, 1887; *Modern View*, April 7, 1932; *Modern View 25*, 90. Another literary group contemporaneous with the *Society Record* was one called the "M.F.C." (the "Mythical Folly Club"). Its membership consisted of "some very intelligent boys of from 15 to 18 years," and included as its officers young men who would later emerge as prominent businessmen and leaders within the Jewish community: Louis P. Singer, president; Albert Loth, vice president; and Samuel Fischer, secretary and treasurer. "We trust they will remain a myth only in name," observed the editor of the local Jewish newspaper, "and soon astonish all by coming forth both with credit to themselves and the rising Jewish generation of St. Louis." *Tribune*, August 29, 1879, and June 10, 1881.

5. Bernard Felsenthal and Emil G. Hirsch were leaders in the emerging radical wing of American Reform Judaism, which soon included St. Louisan Sonneschein as a leading spokesman. *Encyclopedia Judaica*, vol. 6, 1222 and vol. 8, 503.

Christmas dispute between the two boiled over from their pulpits into the *Tribune* and even into the St. Louis secular press. Though both were Reform Jews, Spitz championed a more traditional view, emphatically advocating that Jews celebrate Chanukah rather than Christmas; the radical Sonneschein, on the other hand, favored Chanukah being celebrated on Christmas Day, regardless of the Jewish calendar. At the height of the controversy, Spitz departed from the *Tribune* again, replaced by Meyer J. Lowenstein. It appeared on the surface that Sonneschein had emerged the editorial victor. That was not the case. Spitz left for financial reasons; in fact, Sonneschein soon severed his ties with the *Tribune* for the same reason. Both, along with the lay entrepreneurs, had sunk quite a bit—"many thousands," Spitz recalled later—into a "bottomless barrel."[6]

Despite being the only local Jewish newspaper available, and despite editorial and news coverage that seemed to arouse interest and readership, the *Tribune* was doomed to failure. Spitz later observed that two major factors contributed to the newspaper's demise. One was the never-ending conflict among the policy makers, in both editorial and business phases of the operation. The other was the inability to attract adequate advertising; that, after all, determined the all-important financial base upon which the newspaper operated. The paper took a severe financial beating. In March 1884 the Bloch Publishing Company bought out the *Tribune* and moved its operations to its home headquarters in Cincinnati. Publication continued thereafter for only one more month; the edition dated April 18, 1884, proved to be the last issue of the *Tribune*.[7]

Although the *Tribune* survived for only a few years, it retains a prominent position in the history of the St. Louis Jewish press. True, it was not a "first"—although it erroneously claimed to be. But it set a pattern that succeeding Jewish newspapers seemed to emulate. An overview of the *Tribune*'s contents reveals some of those interesting characteristics.

The very first issue printed a "Prospectus" that described accurately what appeared in its columns:

---

6. *Voice*, December 18, 1914.

7. *Tribune*, August 29 and September 26, 1879, January 16, February 6 and 13, April 1, May 7 and 28, June 11 and 18, July 16, August 27, October 22, and November 2, 1880, February 25 and April 1, 1881, October 6, 1882, August 3 and December 21, 1883, January 11, February 1 and 22, March 7 and 21, and April 11 and 18, 1884. An excellent summary of the *Tribune*'s early trials and tribulations can be found in an article on the early St. Louis Jewish press written by Rabbi Spitz for the special twenty-seventh anniversary edition of the *Voice*, December 18, 1914. Another brief summary of the early St. Louis Jewish press can be found in Scharf, *Saint Louis City and County*, vol. 1, 948.

Our chief aim and intention shall be the faithful exposition of all subjects which may affect or enhance the interests of Judaism. Our primary object will be to secure and treat of items of news which directly interest us as Israelites. . . . Literature, the arts, sciences and society will find due notice and appreciation in our columns.[8]

Also in that first issue appeared the following revealing poem:

'TIS THE FIRST JEWISH PAPER

'Tis the first Jewish paper
St. Louis has had,
And 'twill make all our people
Feel happy and glad.
No edition of this kind
Has e'er been in print,
To tell of engagements,
Or weddings give hint.

We greet thee, O TRIBUNE!
For many a year
Not one Jewish paper
Was edited here.
Of all the large cities
St. Louis alone
Is the only one thus far
That's been without one.

But now one is started,
And long may it live
And to us in future
The latest news give.
And when we shall find it
Grown welcome and strong,
Oh, may we all know, that
We've helped it along.[9]

The *Tribune* was a weekly newspaper, published every Friday. Occasionally, if a Jewish holiday conflicted with a Friday publication date, the paper came out on Thursday. True to its prospectus, the *Tribune* contained articles aimed exclusively at Jewish readership. It did not print general news—it left that to the secular press. The *Tribune*'s articles focused on Jewish affairs in St. Louis, in Missouri and neighboring Illinois, in other parts of the United States, and overseas. Articles of Jewish activities in St. Louis came from local sources; news of Jewish affairs elsewhere was excerpted from other journals or from letters to the editor.

---

8. *Tribune,* August 29, 1879.
9. Ibid.

The *Tribune* did not avoid controversial issues, provided they were Jewish in nature. It did not hesitate, for example, to excoriate St. Louis Jewry for its poor Sabbath synagogue attendance; after all, the editors were rabbis, and one would expect them to push for improved attendance at worship services. Openly championing Reform over Orthodox Judaism, the *Tribune* did not hesitate to engage in that debate, but it never degenerated, as it easily could have, into name-calling or character denigration. Even when Spitz and Sonneschein brought the emotional Chanukah-Christmas controversy into the *Tribune*'s columns, their observations remained at a remarkably high intellectual level. One could tell, too, when Spitz was the editor and when Sonneschein headed that department; the tenor of the editorial remarks, though clearly advocating Reform Judaism, reflected either the radical or moderate Reform bent of the editorialist.

One issue that the *Tribune* (and ensuing Jewish papers) championed on an almost annual basis involved the attendance of Jewish children in the St. Louis public schools on the High Holy Days of Rosh Hashannah and Yom Kippur. "We cannot tell schools not to open, nor Jewish children not to attend," wrote the *Tribune*, "but we can call the problem to the attention of the superintendent of the public schools." Invariably school superintendents William Torrey Harris, Edward H. Long, and Frank Louis Soldan viewed the matter with sympathy, and they directed that Jewish children should not be penalized for absences on those days.[10]

Except for the constant harping on the lack of religious observance within St. Louis Jewry, nothing appeared in the *Tribune* that might present a detrimental view of the Jewish community. Certainly disreputable or indiscreet Jews existed in St. Louis, some even occupying cells in the city jail, but one would never read about that in the *Tribune*. No matter who those persons might be, the *Tribune* refrained from sensationalizing those people or affairs. One did not read in the *Tribune* about Jewish gangsters or criminals or prostitutes or lawbreakers of any kind. Certainly they were not glorified, regardless of how the secular press treated them. Instead, the *Tribune* lauded praiseworthy accomplishments of other Jews. One read of Jewish high school graduates—their names were proudly listed for all to see, with special stories about any who achieved particular honors. One read of Jewish musicians and speakers and writers who performed recitals or delivered oratorios or wrote literary items. The picture painted of the Jewish community was of a hard-working people in many economic

---

10. See, for instance, *Tribune*, August 13 and 27, 1880, and St. Louis Jewish newspapers in August and September of virtually every ensuing year, right before the High Holy Days.

and cultural endeavors, generous in charity, and conscientious in service to both its own smaller Jewish community and to the overall larger St. Louis community. It was a pattern that succeeding generations of Jewish newspapers continued to follow.[11]

The *Tribune* energetically encouraged and fostered a strong Judaism for its readers. Printed in English and openly advocating a Reform accommodation with the surrounding secular society, the *Tribune* nevertheless constantly reminded St. Louis Jewry of its biblical and talmudic and cultural heritage, with innumerable essays on those subjects. On the front page, immediately beneath the large masthead in Old English type, appeared in Hebrew letters the phrase *Dah-ber el B'nai Yisroel V'Yis-oo* ("Speak unto the Children of Israel and they shall go forth"). That motto was changed in the May 7, 1880, issue to *Chazak V'Ahmahtz* ("Be Strong and Be Firm"). (The two Hebrew words were printed in the center of the line, with "Be Strong" on one side and "Be Firm" on the other.) Many phrases and expressions regularly appeared throughout the paper in Hebrew print or in English transliteration. Scattered examples include: "This is a *machloko l'shem Shomayim*"; "Our holy *Yom Ha'shviyi*, the Sabbath"; "We hold them up *l'ma'an yishon'u v'yiro-u*, that they may hear of them and be guarded"; and "*Hah-lo ov echod l'chulonu*, is there not one Father for all of us?" This is not to infer that the *Tribune* printed large blocks of Hebrew; it was clearly an English paper. But the widely scattered use of Hebrew was clearly discernible.

Just as Hebrew in the *Tribune* reminded St. Louis Jews of their Jewish heritage, the use of German was indicative of the European origins of many of its readers. Despite increasing acculturation, many St. Louis Jews—like many non-Jews who also had emigrated from Germany—continued to speak German in their homes, businesses, and worship services. It should come as no surprise, then, that Spitz and Sonneschein, who delivered sermons in German in their own synagogues, also used that language in the newspapers for which they wrote. German phrases often appeared, as did advertising and letters to the editors, often reprinted in full in German.

---

11. For example, the *Voice* listed the names of all the Jewish graduates of the Central High School graduating class of 1888. Praises were lavished especially on Bertha Stern, who ranked first in the class and was awarded a four-year scholarship to Washington University, and on Laura Davis, who ranked second in the class. *Voice*, June 8, 1888. Like the annual plea to excuse Jewish youngsters for absences on the High Holy Days, the Jewish press at virtually every graduating time listed the names of Jewish graduates of elementary schools and high schools, with additional laudatory comments about any who received particular honors.

So widespread was the use of German that the *Tribune* even briefly produced a completely German magazine-type supplement, entitled *Sulamith*. (Spitz worked mostly on the *Tribune*, while Sonneschein concentrated on the *Sulamith*. In fact, the editors requested that correspondence for *Sulamith* be addressed to Sonneschein at Shaare Emeth Temple rather than to the *Tribune*'s office.) The supplement appeared on a monthly basis, starting in November 1880, and was free to *Tribune* subscribers. Its contents were entirely articles of wide literary subject matter, written by Sonneschein and by guest rabbis. *Sulamith* lasted for only three issues, however, and then expired. German continued to be used in the *Tribune* proper, but its use decreased. By the turn of the century, its usage had become very rare. In contrast, the use of Hebrew phrases, either in Hebrew type or in transliterated English, continued unabated well into the twentieth century.

True to the goals listed in the first-issue prospectus, the *Tribune* carried news of Jewish affairs throughout the nation and the world. It also stressed literature either by or about Jews. The first issue contained a short story by Percy Fitzgerald entitled "My Coal Black Beard." Shortly thereafter S. M. Gardenheier's "The Jewish Talisman: A Story of Spain in the Fifteenth Century" appeared in serial form in several successive issues, as did "The Gideonite" by Mrs. Marion Hartog. These are typical of the many literary items of Jewish content that appeared in the *Tribune* as well as in its successor newspapers. Undoubtedly they contributed much to the cultural acumen of many St. Louis Jews.

Of equal interest to St. Louis Jews were the many brief accounts of social events transpiring within the community and elsewhere. They ranged from weddings to *Bar Mitzvahs* to birthday parties to organization socials. Some even verged on the gossip side: "Mr. Ben Altheimer has returned from Europe, looking hale and hearty—and still single!"; or "Miss Theresa Glaser is engaged to William Mendel of Versailles, Mo.—we wish them *mazzel tof*." Even bits of humor were scattered throughout. Under the heading "Wit and Humor" appeared: "A young lady shot herself right in the middle of the waist. Of corset didn't kill her!"[12]

The demise of the *Tribune* with the issue of April 18, 1884, left St. Louis once more without a local Jewish newspaper, this time for a full year. In April 1885 another weekly journal appeared, the *Jewish Free Press*. Its publisher was Max C. Reefer, who had been associated earlier with the *Tribune*. Reefer brought in as editor Dr. David Stern, rabbi of a congregation in Wilkes-Barre, Pennsylvania. The arrangement lasted only briefly, though,

---

12. These and similar vignettes are extracted from scattered issues of the *Tribune* from 1879 to 1884.

and Reefer took over the editorship himself. In June 1885 he secured the services of Henry Gersoni.

A product of the Vilna Rabbinical Seminary, Gersoni had already become almost legendary in Jewish letters, as a pioneer in the American Yiddish press, as an editor of the *Chicago Jewish Advance* and the *New York Post*, and as translator of some Ivan Turgenev works into English and of Henry Wadsworth Longfellow's *Excelsior* into Hebrew. At the same time, though, Gersoni had become the center of considerable controversy; Rabbi Spitz later referred to him as "one of the most notorious men in American Jewry of that day . . . too radical . . . and virtually a Christian." Nevertheless, the association of such a well-known personality with the *Jewish Free Press* should have enhanced the newspaper's stature. Unfortunately, though, Gersoni's "other lucrative literary labors" kept him in New York all during this time, and his attempts to edit the *Jewish Free Press* longdistance proved unsatisfactory.

Accordingly, on November 5, 1885, Reefer dropped Gersoni and reassumed the editorship himself. In August 1887 he asked Rabbi Spitz to author a series of articles on current Jewish issues. Their popular reception led to another management change, beginning with the issue of September 30, 1887, when Reefer named Spitz as editor. That lasted only two months—seven issues—for the edition dated November 25, 1887, proved to be the *Jewish Free Press*'s last.

Nevertheless, Spitz's return to journalism—he continued very successfully all those years as rabbi of B'nai El—was of long-range significance to the history of the St. Louis Jewish press. "I cannot exactly state whether [the *Jewish Free Press* died] a natural or unnatural death," Spitz wrote later, "because Reefer had left St. Louis [for Kansas City], and I knew nothing of the financial affairs of the concern. There was an intermission of exactly one month, for on the first Friday of January, the 6th, 1888, appeared the first number of the *Jewish Voice*." Since the appearance of the *Voice* under Spitz, St. Louis has never been without a Jewish newspaper.[13]

The *Voice* flourished under Spitz's editorship until he died in 1920. Without his leadership, the newspaper gradually went downhill, and it finally went out of business in 1923. But during its existence, the *Voice*

---

13. In the lead editorial of the first issue of the *Voice*, Spitz wrote: "Though Jewish Journalism in this city has had a rough and ragged road to travel, yet it has at least done much good: it has prepared the way for a good journal." *Voice*, January 6, 1888. Spitz's recollections of the history of the *Jewish Free Press* can be found in his article "The Jewish Voice and Its Predecessors" in the twenty-seventh anniversary edition of the *Voice*, December 18, 1914. See also Scharf, *Saint Louis City and County*, vol. 1, 948. For more on Henry Gersoni see *Jewish Free Press*, June 26, 1885, and November 12, 1886, and *Encyclopedia Judaica*, vol. 7, 518–19.

played a very prominent role in the St. Louis Jewish community. First and foremost it brought to its readers news of local, national, and international *Jewish* affairs. The *Voice* also acted as an outlet for many budding essayists, poets, and short-story writers. Its pages reflected a variety of cultural and literary achievements by Jewish intellectuals, both famous and unknown. Moreover, its many advertisements (admittedly not all its advertisers were Jewish) indicated the broad spectrum of occupations and businesses in which Jews were engaged. Those advertisements and other items of a demographic nature showed that many Jews lived and worked in a rather narrow corridor from the downtown area due west to the county; but they showed that many Jewish businesses existed also outside that corridor in the northern and southern parts of the city. Editorially, the *Voice* expressed views in a variety of Jewish affairs, whether they were local, national, or international. Editor Spitz always clearly articulated a moderate Reform position. Yet he often showed considerable affinity toward Orthodoxy and Zionism, two issues over which many of his Reform colleagues disagreed. Decrying some of the "medieval" or "archaic" or "oriental" practices and behaviors of some Orthodox Jews, the *Voice* nevertheless sympathized with the problems of the new eastern European immigrants and constantly urged supporting their efforts toward education and accommodation to the American environment. To evaluate the *Voice*'s impact on the Jewish community empirically is perhaps impossible; at the same time, there seems no doubt that for its thirty-four years of existence the *Voice* served the St. Louis Jewish community exceedingly well.

For more than a decade after it came into being, the *Voice* remained the sole St. Louis Jewish community newspaper. But in 1898 journalist/philosopher Abraham Rosenthal and commercial printer Joseph A. Schweich conceived the idea of a weekly illustrated journal to feature "interesting news for all, latest and best illustrations of prominent men and women, noted sights and scenes," as well as "contributions by able writers on vital topics of the day." Concern over finances led Schweich to withdraw from the project, and businessman/writer Benjamin F. Koperlik replaced him. On September 26, 1901, the *Modern View* came into being. Edited very ably by Abraham Rosenthal—he preferred just "A. Rosenthal" to the full name—the *Modern View* became a prominent fixture in the St. Louis Jewish community for the next four decades. Whereas the format and size of the *Voice* was very similar to that of the secular dailies, the *Modern View* was more the size of a magazine supplement. The *Modern View*'s format generally was sixteen pages in size, with larger editions for Rosh Hashannah, Chanukah, and Passover. The newspaper included many photos and pictures; its whole front page, in fact, normally consisted of a full-page photo of a person or a place, with a brief explanatory caption.

Such a format by no means reflected the "yellow journalism" that was prevalent at that time; it was merely a manifestation of the new technology in newspaper journalism. Editorially, Rosenthal's objective was to be the "true" voice of Reform Judaism, since he viewed Spitz and the *Voice* as perhaps not liberal enough in their approach to Judaism. (In time, though, Rosenthal also mellowed, especially toward Orthodox Jewry and political Zionism.) Like the *Voice*, the *Modern View* shunned partisan politics; and like the *Voice*, it dealt exclusively with Jewish affairs—local, national, and international—leaving non-Jewish matters to the secular press.[14]

One cannot accurately evaluate the importance of any newspaper to its readership. Nevertheless, even lacking empirical data, and conceding that several ventures failed before a permanent Jewish press arose with the *Voice*, certain inferences seem valid. By the end of the Civil War era, enough Jews lived in St. Louis to justify a Jewish press. Despite some failures, the Jewish community demonstrated its willingness to support its own publications. The surviving issues of the Jewish press clearly reveal a diverse and heterogeneous Jewish population: in religious observance, in economic activity, in financial and social status. At the same time, this was a press for a clearly viable *Jewish* community. The Jewish press acted as a—perhaps *the*—information conduit within that community, and from that community to outside society. In that sense, then, the emergence of a Jewish press stands as a major watershed in the history of the St. Louis Jewish community.

---

14. Many issues of the *Modern View* remain extant in numerous depositories, and, as with virtually any newspaper, they provide excellent materials about the community in which the journal existed. After Rosenthal died in 1929, his daughter Mignon and a succession of other editors followed until 1943, when the paper closed down because of wartime exigencies. See also Z. Abrams, *The Book of Memories*, pt. 3, 3. Additional twentieth-century Jewish newspapers in St. Louis included the *Jewish Express* (Yiddish, briefly in 1904), *Der Vorsteher* (Yiddish, 1907–1910), the *Jewish Record* (Yiddish and English, 1915–1951), the *Jewish Post and Opinion* (St. Louis edition, English, 1948–present), and the *St. Louis Jewish Light* (English, 1947–present).

11

GROWING PAINS

Several more significant developments during the 1870s and early 1880s further illustrate the growth and character of the St. Louis Jewish community. They include the creation of the United Jewish Charities, the onset of eastern European immigration, the establishment of Beth Hamedrosh Hagodol (the oldest existing Orthodox congregation in St. Louis), and the beginning of a residence demographic pattern that continues to the present.

It will be recalled that the United Hebrew Relief Association had come into being in 1871 to meet the immediate needs of Jewish refugees from the Chicago fire. Once that crisis had passed, the UHRA continued as the city's major Jewish charitable institution, helping the sick and needy in a Jewish population that was still overwhelmingly Germanic in origin. During the 1870s, however, small numbers of eastern European immigrants began to arrive; in the 1880s they became a flood that radically altered the nature of Jewish communities throughout the United States. These new immigrants created the same dilemma for the German Jewish population of St. Louis as they did for Jews living elsewhere in the country. On the one hand, the newcomers were harried and uprooted coreligionists facing formidable social and economic problems, not unlike what two generations of St. Louis Jews had themselves faced and which most had successfully overcome. But on the other hand, these new Jews were cut from a different mold. They were Slavic in background and culture, not Germanic. They spoke a different language—Yiddish. Most were virtually destitute. Most, too, even those who were less observant, associated with Orthodoxy, and steadfastly opposed westernizing and modernizing their religious beliefs and practices. Historians have aptly characterized the dilemma German Jews now felt: *they* had adjusted to their new environment and generally had "made it" in America; these "different" Jews now might undermine all that achievement if they insisted upon maintaining their European ways.

The problem came to the surface in St. Louis in the mid-1870s over what was called the "schnorrer" issue ("shnorrer" is a pejorative term for a "professional beggar" or one who constantly displays groveling or beggarly behavior). It involved a very small but visible number of these new immigrants—"wandering mendicants"—who managed to move from city to city by living off Jewish charity, emulating certain cultural practices common in some eastern European Jewish communities—practices that most of the St. Louis German Jewish community found distasteful and embarrassing. Resenting the refusal of these "schnorrers" to make serious efforts at supporting themselves, UHRA leaders viewed subsidizing them not only as a serious drain on their funds but also as perpetuating and supporting an offensive and opprobrious image of Judaism. One solution sought was cooperation among Jewish relief agencies of different cities in dealing with these itinerants, to force them into trying, at least, to support themselves, and thus "showing that they are worthy of relief. . . . Thus would we get rid of the professional schnorrer and no longer be compelled to support the lazy, the idle, and the profligate."[1]

In 1878 yellow fever struck the lower Mississippi valley, and epidemics ravaged communities from Memphis to New Orleans. As had occurred following the great fire in Chicago, refugees poured into St. Louis, this time from the south. Once more the city responded to the challenge. With the UHRA taking the lead, Jewish social and benevolent associations pitched in to the best of their abilities to repeat their earlier efforts for Jews in need. But "schnorrer" subsidies had depleted their treasuries, and raising necessary funds and materials to help the new wave of refugees required extraordinary efforts.

In 1879, to more effectively carry out their charitable objectives, the city's leading benevolent associations formed the United Jewish Charities. Leading the consolidation were four groups: the UHRA, the Sisterhood of Personal Service, the Ladies' Zion Society, and the Hebrew Ladies' Sewing Society. According to its constitution, the object of the United Jewish Charities was "to relieve the deserving Jewish poor, prevent want and distress, and discourage pauperism by providing a central organization for the distribution of charity in St. Louis."[2]

---

1. Rosen, "Historical Development of the Jewish Federation of Saint Louis," 60–63. See also *Tribune,* August 10, 1883. The "old line" German Jews and the immigrant eastern European Jews soon split into two virtually separate Jewish communities, in St. Louis as in other cities in the United States. It did not take long for German Jews to use the term "schnorrers" when referring to virtually any eastern European Orthodox coreligionist. The latter had their own Yiddish pejorative for "uppity" and "arrogant" German Reform Jews: "Deutschuken."

2. Rosen, "Historical Development of the Jewish Federation of Saint Louis," 63–64.

The United Jewish Charities remained the central agency for Jewish benevolence in St. Louis for two decades, until through a series of reorganizations in the 1890s and early 1900s it eventually became the present Jewish Federation. As when the UHRA had come into being in 1871, the groups that joined the United Jewish Charities retained their independence and separate entities. Lines of authority still were confusing and unclear. The organization remained somewhat haphazard, as each institution within it controlled its own identity, membership, fund-raising programs, and agenda. The UHRA still stood out as the mainstay of Jewish charity in St. Louis, but the other groups also continued their important work. They all served many community functions, trying to coordinate them under the new umbrella United Jewish Charities, and, as will be seen, soon developed additional programs and projects as new needs arose.[3]

The newly arrived eastern European Jews thus found Jewish charitable organizations in place to assist them. The synagogues, however, were a different story: few of the existing congregations were compatible with their religious practices. Most St. Louis German Jews by the 1870s were not Orthodox, although some German Jews preserved their traditional Orthodoxy and established small congregations (for example, Sheerith Israel and B'nai Amoona). The eastern European Orthodox Jews therefore did find a few people in the existing German Jewish community who accorded with their religious practices. But a pervasive characteristic of American Jewry quickly emerged, the same that had manifested itself earlier when German Jews began to come in significant numbers in the 1840s and 1850s: congregations in St. Louis were formed according to nationality, and thus Germanic congregations were "Polish" or "Bavarian" or "Bohemian." In the 1870s the newcomers were not even Germanic; they were Latvians, with a Russian ghetto culture as their background. It should come as no surprise, then, that they did not affiliate with any existing German congregation, even if it was Orthodox. Instead, in 1879 they began their own, the *Beth Hamedrosh Hagodol* ("Great House of Learning") Congregation. It remains today the oldest existing Orthodox congregation in St. Louis (earlier Orthodox congregations either no longer exist or have since changed to Reform).[4]

---

3. Ibid., 64, 72; *St. Louis Jewish Light*, March 31, 1971.

4. The ensuing history of Beth Hamedrosh Hagodol is based upon the following: documents in the Beth Hamedrosh Hagodol Collection, St. Louis Jewish Community Archives; "Beth Hamedrosh Hagodol to Celebrate Its Golden Jubilee," in *Modern View*, August 31, 1933; "Beth Hamedrosh to Mark Centennial," in *St. Louis Jewish Light*, September 26, 1979; Abrams, *Book of Memories*, 51–55; Flaks, "Thirty Years of

The exact date of the first Beth Hamedrosh Hagodol *minyan* cannot be pinpointed due to lack of records. We know, though, that congregants met informally for about two years before they organized, and that for the ensuing eleven years they worshiped in rented quarters. Most of that time those rooms were in the 900 block of North Seventh Street, between Wash (now Cole) Street and Franklin Avenue (now Dr. Martin Luther King Boulevard). By 1890 members finally were able to purchase a building at 1123 North Eleventh, near Biddle Street, from the German Evangelical Protestant Congregation of the Church of the Holy Ghost, for six thousand dollars, and to convert it into their synagogue. Seven years later the congregation remodeled the structure, installing a balcony for women and stained glass windows to lend a more spiritual atmosphere. Beth Hamedrosh Hagodol remained at that location for thirty years, a major landmark in a neighborhood whose population soon became overwhelmingly eastern European Orthodox Jewish.[5]

Meanwhile, the congregation attained legal status. On October 31, 1881, Beth Hamedrosh Hagodol filed a "Constitution and Articles of Agreement" with the Circuit Court of St. Louis. That document contained the signatures of the congregation's first officers: Victor Gerstel, president; Joseph Leskovich, secretary; and Joseph Baum, secretary. The congregation was officially incorporated by the State of Missouri on November 27, 1882. Because it lacked necessary funds—and since Jewish cemeteries already existed in St. Louis—the congregation felt no immediate compulsion in that direction. In 1901, however, a committee consisting of M. Levitt, Joseph Romansky, Selig Fleishman, Abraham Rubinowitz, M. Hollander, and Elias Olschwanger was authorized to look into the matter, and before the end of the year Beth Hamedrosh Hagodol purchased a six-acre plot on Ladue Road, about a mile and a half west of Clayton, to be the congregation's cemetery. It remains today at the same location.[6]

Vaad Hoeir," 25–26; and Averam B. Bender, "History of the Beth Hamedrosh Hagodol Congregation of St. Louis, 1879–1969," 64–89.

5. In 1920, as the Jewish population moved westward, Beth Hamedrosh Hagodol purchased a home on 5877 Bartmer and remodeled it as a new synagogue. As neighborhoods changed further, in 1961 the congregation moved again, to 1227 North and South Road in suburban University City.

6. *Beth Hamedrosh Hagodol Congregation Diamond Jubilee* (pamphlet), 7, in Beth Hamedrosh Hagodol Collection, St. Louis Jewish Community Archives. Others in leadership roles included Mesdames Brochman, Hollander, R. Rabinowitz, R. Levy, I. Stein, J. Singer, and P. Yetter. The original organization included more than forty women. Ibid., 7–12.

Beth Hamedrosh Hagodol, true to its name, was much more than a place of worship. It became a "dynamic center" for all sorts of Jewish activities for the increasing numbers of immigrant eastern European Jews, satisfying intellectual and social needs as well as religious. A *Chevra Mishna G'moro* (society for Talmudic studies) developed into a popular and highly acclaimed Talmudic group whose traditional learning sessions attracted Hebraic students of all ages. As did other congregations, Beth Hamedrosh Hagodol also served the needy and the sick through various men's and women's affiliate groups. One that became very active was the Moses Montefiore Ladies' Charity Society, organized in 1892, led at first by Mrs. Dora Fleishman (president), Mrs. J. Gallant (treasurer), and Mrs. C. Kaplan (secretary). One of the first Zionist societies in St. Louis—if not the first—appeared at Beth Hamedrosh Hagodol.

As early as 1885 members of Beth Hamedrosh Hagodol expressed concern over "the tragic plight of the Jewish children who were growing up without the slightest conception of and respect for Jewish traditions and ideals." That anxiety led to an association with the Moses Montefiore Hebrew Free School, an outstanding and long-lasting institution that for the next four decades provided Hebrew education to countless hundreds, and perhaps thousands, of Jewish boys and girls to supplement their secular public school training. It became, like some of the synagogues that soon came along, a landmark in a neighborhood of predominantly eastern European Orthodox Jews.[7]

Like the earlier United Hebrew and B'nai El Congregations, Beth Hamedrosh Hagodol had no rabbi when it began, and its earliest spiritual leaders had irregular tenures at best. The congregation's first recorded rabbi was Israel Miller, who came in 1886 and remained until 1892, but there is little additional information about him. In 1892 Solomon Elchanan Jaffe became the leader of the *Mishna G'moro* class, and he served as congregational rabbi for the next three years. Though Jaffe was widely respected as a scholar in both Orthodox and Reform circles, Beth Hamedrosh Hagodol experienced considerable internal factional strife during his tenure, and he left in 1895. For the next eleven years the congregation got along without a permanent rabbi, his functions being performed either by knowledgeable congregants or by temporary or visiting rabbis. Included among the latter were Rabbis Aaron Spector and Samuel Freedman. Then in 1906 Bernard Dov Ber Abramowitz became rabbi of Beth Hamedrosh Hagodol and, indeed, the unofficial "chief rabbi" of St. Louis Orthodox Jewry. His scholarship and esteem compared favorably with contemporaneous religious

---

7. *Jewish Free Press*, November 13, 1885, and April 16, 1886.

personalities in St. Louis, not only within the Jewish community but also in the broader Christian community. Rabbi Abramowitz proved to be the forerunner of a series of outstanding Orthodox rabbis in St. Louis that included such twentieth-century greats as Chaim Fishel Epstein and Menachem H. Eichenstein.[8]

Beth Hamedrosh Hagodol was only one of several Orthodox congregations that appeared in St. Louis in the latter decades of the nineteenth century, as more and more eastern European Jews arrived.[9] As so many historians have pointed out, major differences existed between the western European and eastern European Jews. The earlier German Jews, having gone through an emancipation experience in western Europe, placed high priority on distancing themselves from traditional religious practices that they associated with an unhappy medieval European past; the later eastern European arrivals had been very little affected by the French Revolutionary emancipation processes, and instead clung tenaciously to the major force that had enabled them to survive eastern European autocracy and ghettoism—their traditional religious and cultural way of life. In acculturating to the New World milieu, German Jews inclined strongly toward secularism and even complete assimilation, and those who retained their Judaism sought to modernize and Americanize it, viewing with favor the new Reform Judaism as a way to live their religious lives in American surroundings. Eastern European Jews also sought to acculturate to the new environment, but both Orthodox Jewish practice and eastern European ghetto mores had a much stronger hold on them. They viewed with great alarm compromising either. Instead, they chose not to distance themselves from their past, but to transfer their eastern European way of life and religion into their new environment. Rather than accede to the new, they sought to accommodate to the new by preserving the old.

---

8. *Voice,* April 9, 1915, and August 18, 1916; Bender, "History of Beth Hamedrosh Hagodol Congregation," 75–78. Some dates in Bender's history seem to be inaccurate. A directory of Rosh Hashannah services for 1886 listed "Beth Hamedrosh Hagodol—929 N. 7th—A. M. Goldman, Reader." *Jewish Free Press,* September 24, 1886. A St. Louis newspaper identified Rabbi Shlomo Jaffee as "Chief Rabbi" as early as 1887. *Jewish Free Press,* November 18, 1887. That same year an announcement appeared in the press that Rev. Israel Fleishman had been elected rabbi, with the address of the congregation given as 708 Wash Street. *Jewish Free Press,* June 17, 1887.

9. A directory published in the *Voice* in 1901 listed four Reform congregations and six Orthodox. The Reform were United Hebrew, B'nai El, Shaare Emeth, and Temple Israel. Listed as Orthodox congregations were B'nai Amoona, Beth Hamedrosh Hagodol, Chevrah Kadisha, and three new *shuls,* Tipheris Israel, Sheerith Sfard, and B'nai Israel. *Voice,* May 24, 1901.

Thus, just when St. Louis Jewry in the 1870s seemed to be coalescing into a truly united community, along came a second Jewish community, quite different from that which had evolved over a period of two generations. The differences between German Jews and eastern European Jews often bred a mutual ill will that was further stimulated by the concepts of "schnorrer" and "Deutschuken." While all may have been Jews, there were "our kind" of Jews and "the other kind" of Jews. In time, factors such as shared experiences in the St. Louis public schools, more accommodation between Reform and Orthodox leaders and congregations, common tribulations during the Great Depression and World War II, and shared pride in the birth of the State of Israel would break down the barriers between German and eastern European Jews. But for two generations—until about the World War II era and its aftermath—two Jewish communities would exist side by side in St. Louis, with separate institutions and often a duplication of important services.

The arrival of those first eastern European Jews into St. Louis poses an obvious demographic question: where did they live? Did they meld in with the existing German Jewish population? For that matter, where had those earlier German Jews been living? Studies of St. Louis ethnic groups have focused on *nationality* entities, such as the Germans, the Irish, and later the Italians, the Poles, the Greeks, and others. We know, for instance, that the Irish dominated in the northern wards, and the Germans in the southern areas. That would indicate, then, that the earlier German Jews lived mostly on the south side, a supposition that is corroborated by the sparse data available in early institutional records; we find Jews living in such areas as "Frenchtown," Soulard, Carondelet, and Lafayette. But other evidence suggests that some Jews lived elsewhere. When United Hebrew established its early buildings on Fifth near Green and then at Sixth and St. Charles, contemporaries commented on their "central" location to accommodate "all" Jews. Early leaders of B'nai El (and its progenitors Emanu El and B'nai B'rith) several times mentioned servicing mostly the "better" Jews in the "southern part of the city." Yet we know that both B'nai El and United Hebrew counted among their members Jews whose north side addresses did not comport with that strict "nationality" criterion for residency.[10]

---

10. See particularly *Tribune,* December 5, 1879, September 14, 1883, and February 17, 1888; Fainsod, "Influence of Racial and National Groups in St. Louis Politics"; and Troen and Holt, eds., *St. Louis,* 70–74. Other works focusing on St. Louis ethnic groups include Margaret LoPiccolo Sullivan, "St. Louis Ethnic Neighborhoods, 1850–1930," 64–76; Gary R. Mormino, *Immigrants on the Hill: Italian-Americans in St. Louis, 1882–1982;* Nini Harris, *A Grand Heritage;* Mario Pertici, "And Then Came the Italians,"

This suggests that factors other than just nationality or ethnicity characterized neighborhoods where Jews lived. Indeed, with few exceptions, even though one nationality might have dominated, neighborhoods were not entirely monolithic. Considerable housing integration existed. That was because nationality was only one factor that determined where people lived. Affluence was another. In fact, an interesting residential and demographic pattern was set early in St. Louis history even before the Civil War. The core area, where the city had been founded, became the central "downtown" business district. The "south side" became the more affluent residential area. The "north side," with cheaper housing and many tenements, was where less-well-to-do residents lived.[11]

Since so many Germans occupied the south side, we can infer that the Germans as a whole—with exceptions, of course—represented a goodly portion of the affluent populace of St. Louis. St. Louis Jews being predominantly German, we can deduce from where they lived that at least those who resided on the south side could be numbered among the well-to-do. But we know that German Jews lived also in the not-so-affluent north side—indicating that not all German Jews were "rich Jews."

Where they lived tells us something else about early St. Louis Jewry. Just as not all became affluent, so, too, as we have already seen, did not all German Jews modify their Judaism to Reform. Some retained their Orthodoxy; to wit, those who organized the Chevrah Kadisha, Sheerith Israel, and B'nai Amoona Congregations. It would be no historical indiscretion to suggest that most of those who remained Orthodox resided in the north side—simply because that is where those early German Jewish Orthodox congregations were located. Reform Jews had no prohibitions against vehicular travel to attend their services; Orthodox Jews, on the other hand, universally have lived near enough to their synagogues to walk there on the Sabbath and holidays. Where Orthodox congregants lived determined where their synagogues were located. Had Orthodox German Jews been affluent enough to live in the German south side, one would feel reasonably certain that they would have done so, and also would have established their synagogues there. Instead, they lived where their economic status dictated, and they established their houses of worship there too.

When the poor eastern European Latvian Jewish immigrants arrived in the 1870s, they settled in the near north side, in the less affluent part of the

---

59–60; Ed O'Donnell, "Irish Stew," 63–65; George Frangoulis, "The Greek Community," 66–67.

11. Sullivan, "St. Louis Ethnic Neighborhoods"; Fainsod, "Influence of Racial and National Groups in St. Louis Politics"; Mormino, *Immigrants on the Hill*, 20–31.

city, where not-so-affluent German Orthodox Jews already were living. When they established Beth Hamedrosh Hagodol, it was no surprise that the quarters for their *shul*, both temporary and permanent, were also in that neighborhood.

Implications of that demography can be confirmed from additional data that became available with the emergence of the St. Louis Jewish press. Congregational records tell us where only a small number of Jews lived; newspapers provided data about many more. For instance, that Miss So-and-So had a lavish engagement party at the Harmonie Club, or that Baby So-and-So's *bris* was a well-attended *simcha*, seem on the surface to be no more than trendy society news fluff. But many of those stories also included names, and often addresses, of guests. In contrast with other historical records, one can reasonably assume that "Jewish-sounding" names in Jewish newspapers do indeed indicate Jewish people. Checking those names in appropriate city directories furnishes considerable information on where Jews lived in St. Louis. That collective data, covering more than a century of St. Louis Jewish history, provides a clear and significant demographic characteristic of St. Louis Jewry.[12]

Another factor makes it possible to further pinpoint where the Jews of St. Louis lived. St. Louis Jewry is the city's only major ethnic group identifiable demographically by *religious* affiliation. Jews, whether German or eastern European, expanded along a central corridor that ran due west from the downtown area. (After World War I they continued to expand in the same direction, into the central portion of St. Louis County.) That central corridor was bounded very roughly on the north by a line along Cass Avenue to Jefferson Avenue and then westward along Natural Bridge Road; on the south by Arsenal Street to Kingshighway and Forest Park. Protestant and Catholic and other churches proliferate all through the St. Louis area, in German, Irish, Italian, Polish, and even Jewish neighborhoods. Jewish synagogues and temples, on the other hand, as well as other Jewish institutional establishments—community centers, Hebrew schools, social settlement homes, and other eleemosynary institutions—

---

12. In addition to the little available from early Jewish institutions, the author has compiled voluminous residential data beginning with the 1870s, when newspapers provided two major sources of information. One was annual lists of confirmands, which included their addresses. The other was names of St. Louis Jews that appeared in ordinary news items. Those were then checked in St. Louis city directories for addresses. Thus were gathered numerous names and addresses of St. Louis Jews from the 1870s through the 1940s, and from these the author could draw an accurate picture of where Jews lived in St. Louis. See also Gary Tobin, *The Jewish Federation of St. Louis Demographic Study, December 1982: Executive Summary,* and Sullivan, "St. Louis Ethnic Neighborhoods, 1850–1932."

have been located almost exclusively in that central corridor, starting downtown and in the near north and near south sides, and gradually moving westward.[13] The very few exceptions include the Home for the Aged and Infirm Israelites (on South Jefferson near where it runs into Broadway); Mount Sinai Cemetery (on Gravois Road in the southern part of St. Louis County); and the Orthodox Old Folks Home (at North Grand and Blair). Only the cemetery remains in its original location; the two senior citizens homes have merged and exist today as the Jewish Center for the Aged, located on South Outer Forty Road in the central corridor as it has expanded into St. Louis County. In addition, there have been three small isolated enclaves of Jewish residence, consisting mostly of eastern European Jews: in the South Broadway and Cherokee Street neighborhood, and in the Baden and Walnut Park areas in north and northwest St. Louis. None of the three enclaves exists any longer; its Jewish residents have almost all moved into the central corridor.[14]

A further pattern developed within that central corridor almost from the very beginning, with of course some exceptions, and which continued until about the World War II era. Overwhelmingly, Jews of eastern European origin, most of whom professed to being Orthodox, lived in the northern half of that corridor. Most German Jews, many Reform, lived in the southern portion. As the more affluent German Jews began to move west in the 1870s, beyond Jefferson Avenue into the Lafayette and Shaw and Compton Heights areas, some Eastern European Jewish immigrants came into the near south side, in the Soulard area south of downtown and east of Twelfth Street. By the early 1900s, however, as they too could afford to move west, they moved mostly into the northern half of that central corridor, and farther westward there. As that movement westward continued, the "boundary line" between what was to be virtually two Jewish communities was roughly Delmar Boulevard. Shopping areas characterized by kosher butcher shops, bakeries, and delicatessens, as well as all Orthodox *shuls*, were located north of Delmar, readily accessible to Orthodox Jews for whom nearby synagogues and *kashruth* were an everyday necessity. Reform temples, on the other hand, as they moved west, remained south of Delmar. The sole exception was United Hebrew,

---

13. By the 1930s the Jewish population continued to move due westward into the central portion of St. Louis County, gradually vacating the city portion of that central corridor. By the 1980s very few Jews lived within the city proper, nor were more than a handful of Jewish landmarks left there. See Walter Ehrlich, "Jewish Historic Landmarks in St. Louis," 2–15.

14. Abraham Davis to author, St. Louis, February 18, 1985, letter in author's possession; *St. Louis Jewish Light*, April 3 and 10, 1985; Abrams, *Book of Memories*, 97–103.

located from 1903 to 1926 at Kingshighway and Enright—but that was only one short block north of the Delmar "line." Furthermore, as eastern Europeans increasingly joined Reform congregations, more and more addresses of Reform congregants indicated residences north of Delmar.[15]

Along with developing residency patterns, new institutions appeared in the 1870s and 1880s that exemplified the vibrant growth of the Jewish community in St. Louis. Among the first were two that aimed at serving opposite ends of the age spectrum: the Hebrew Free School for the younger generation, and the Home for the Aged and Infirm Israelites for senior citizens.

Following Rabbi Bernard Illowy's unsuccessful attempt in the 1850s to establish a Hebrew day school, religious education remained the province of individual congregations or private tutors. Rabbi Henry J. Messing of United Hebrew was the next to involve the larger Jewish community in creating an educational institution. In August 1879 Messing returned from a Union of American Hebrew Congregations meeting in New York, where he had observed that city's Hebrew Free School in operation. Supported by local Jewish community institutions, the New York school provided not only religious education but also meals, clothing, and other necessities for pupils who could not afford them. Very much impressed with what he had seen, Messing broached the idea to fellow clergymen Spitz and Sonneschein, suggesting a similar community school in St. Louis under the auspices of the UHRA. Spitz and Sonneschein concurred in the need for and import of a school, but they preferred a joint venture by their three temples, concerned that an independent lay organization might undermine and weaken the influence and role of their own institutions in directing Jewish education. Messing went ahead anyway, meeting with lay people and soliciting support for "a free school for instruction in Hebrew and religion, open to all Jewish children of St. Louis."[16]

Controversy erupted immediately. Messing's supporters posited that Jewish children who could not afford to belong to congregations that provided religious education should not be deprived of that instruction just because they lacked financial means. Opponents stressed that those showing greatest interest in attending such a school were mostly from the

---

15. St. Louisan Israel Treiman, the first Jew to be awarded a Rhodes Scholarship, grew up in an Orthodox family in the area east of Twelfth Street and south of the downtown area—the so-called South Broadway neighborhood—and he provided the author with some fascinating reminiscences of that community. Author's interview with Israel Treiman, St. Louis, September 8, 1982, a transcript of which is available in the St. Louis Jewish Community Archives.

16. *Tribune*, October 31, 1879, and March 22, 1880.

"northern" part of the city and often were associated with *chevra* there; in other words, the project seemed to appeal more to the Orthodox-leaning elements of St. Louis Jewry.[17]

There thus came to the surface an issue that plagued and divided St. Louis Jewry for almost a century to come: the nature of and responsibility for Jewish education. One side stood steadfastly for religious education defined, paid for, and independently controlled by the individual congregations. The other side considered Jewish education more the collective responsibility of the Jewish community. Although some viewed this as a Reform versus Orthodox controversy, the issue as it developed was not that simple. It also entailed overtones of social discrimination: affluent Jews versus not-so-affluent Jews; German Jews versus eastern European Jews; "our kind" of people versus "that kind" of people. True, most Reform Jewry favored congregational education, and Orthodox-leaning Jews endorsed the eastern European–style traditional *cheder* or *talmud torah* supported by a *kehillah* or communal structure. Nevertheless, a good many on both sides took quite different stances. Many traditionalists feared that nontraditional elements in a lay-dominated communitywide organization might dilute what Jewish education should be. On the other hand, many liberal-leaning Jews felt a moral obligation to help educate all Jewish children, especially the economically deprived, even if the substance of that instruction might deviate from their own personal religious convictions.[18]

As to Messing's proposal, immediate and substantial support within the community ensured its success. In early January 1880 Messing convened a meeting of prominent Jewish lay leaders. Isidor Bush chaired the meeting, which formally organized the "Hebrew Free School Society." Because of pressing business concerns, Bush declined the presidency of the organization, but he did accept the post of vice president. Joseph B. Greensfelder was chosen president; Jacob Furth, treasurer; and Henry Lyons, Louis Halle, Meyer A. Rosenblatt, H. M. Lowenstein, M. B. Greensfelder, and Bennett Meyer were named directors. Four hundred dollars were pledged, sufficient for the school to get under way. On Sunday, January 18, 1880, the Hebrew Free School opened. About one hundred children attended on that opening day; and with Rabbi Messing acting as superintendent,

---

17. Ibid., October 31, November 21 and 28, and December 12, 19, and 26, 1879.

18. That conflict exists even today, although the programmatic operation of the Central Agency for Jewish Education (CAJE) within the framework of the Jewish Federation has made great strides in overcoming those difficulties. Furthermore, tradition-focused day schools such as the Epstein Hebrew Academy, Solomon Schechter School, and Hebrew Prep School meet the needs of many Orthodox elements.

classes were instructed by three teachers: Messing, L. Weiss, and Isaac Hahn.[19]

Widespread support throughout the community abetted the school's opening. United Hebrew Temple held a fair at Uhrig's Cave, a popular recreation spot, to raise money for the Hebrew Free School. Similar fund-raising functions were sponsored by the Star of the West Lodge, the Independent Order of the Free Sons of Israel, and at least three literary societies. Jacob Furth contributed several boxes of oranges, and Theodore Block several boxes of nuts, as Purim treats for the children. Furth also announced that he would give a ten-dollar gold coin at the end of the school year to the student with the best record in attendance and deportment. All this enthusiasm resulted in increases in enrollment and in faculty. The press reported an enrollment in the next few months of between 140 and 186; and Annie Meyer, S. Rabbinowitz, M. J. Manowitz, and M. W. Holz were added to the faculty. Classes met four times a week, on Saturday and Sunday afternoons, and on Tuesday and Thursday afternoons after regular secular public school.[20]

Closing exercises and final examinations for the first school year occurred on Saturday afternoon, July 3, 1880. The enthusiasm and warmth surrounding the event—it was the first of many annual ceremonies to come—make it worth looking at in some detail. Rabbi Messing offered a brief opening prayer. Winnie Laufferty, "a slight little lady," recited a poem "with considerable vim." Mr. Holz then examined the fourth-grade Hebrew class. That was followed by two more recitations, by students Johanna Giest and Siegmund Abeles. Mr. Rabbinowitz then interrogated the third-grade Hebrew class. Next, "a manly little fellow named Victor Lichtenstein recited 'Belshazzar's Vision,' in good voice," followed by "vivacious" Lena Lichtenstein's recitation of "The Chieftain's Daughter." Mr. Holz examined the second-grade Hebrew class on its lessons,

---

19. *Tribune,* January 2, 9, and 23, and February 13, 1880. At first Spitz and Son-neschein were cool to a community-supported school, endorsing instead congregational schools. Ibid., December 26, 1879. To their credit, however, once the school was established, they became staunch supporters. At the same time, they worked diligently to improve the religious schools of their own temples.

20. *Tribune,* January 2, 9, 23, and 30, February 6, 13, and 20, March 5, and April 30, 1880. That classes were conducted on Saturday afternoons should not be viewed as sacrilegious or impious, even though so many pupils came from the "north side" families "often associated with chevra there." Even among Jews who consider themselves Orthodox, many are not very ritually observant and often do things on the Sabbath (such as work, or ride on private or public conveyances) that more observant Orthodox Jews might not do. Furthermore, even among observant Orthodox Jews, *limud torah* ("studying the Torah") is considered a proper act for the Sabbath.

following which "Nattie Weinstein covered himself with glory in a recitation about Moses." Manowitz followed with an examination of the first-grade Hebrew group, and Rose Harris recited "From the Talmud." Student participation concluded with teacher Annie Meyer examining the entire student body on Bible history. Following a very brief address by Isidor Bush, awards were handed out. Ten-dollar gold pieces went to the outstanding scholars: Rose Weil in the first grade, Victor Lichtenstein in the second, Jennie Harris in the third, and Rachel Franklin in the fourth. Book awards for ranking second in each grade were presented to Rose Harris, David Laufferty, Rebecca Greengard, and Dora Marx. Third-place awards in each grade were granted to Sam Goldman, Johanna Geist, F. Saul, and Willie Gerst. Additional "rewards of merit" went to Hattie Weinstein, Eli Meidner, Esther Golony, and Jacob Heike. A silver medal for "best in attendance and deportment" was awarded to young Victor Lichtenstein. Proud parents k'velled (glowed with pride) at seeing the results of St. Louis Jewry's first successful community educational enterprise. Indeed, for years thereafter, the St. Louis Jewish press regularly publicized activities of the Hebrew Free School, often identifying praiseworthy pupils by name and describing their achievements for all to applaud. It would seem to substantiate a very positive and supportive attitude within the Jewish community toward education.[21]

Like any new and innovative institution, the Hebrew Free School faced a variety of problems that simply took time to solve. One was the instability of the student body. Many came from poor homes and did not live close to where classes were held. Increasing numbers of impoverished eastern European immigrant children began to come in, posing such problems as transportation, clothing, food, educational materials, and language difficulties. Finding adequate teaching personnel was an ongoing challenge. That was in good part resolved when William Deutsch replaced Rabbi Messing as superintendent. A well-qualified and capable educator, Deutsch directed the Hebrew Free School until he died in 1908.[22]

---

21. Ibid., July 2 and 9, 1881.

22. In an environment where "prominence" so often was equated with people successful in politics or business or religion, William Deutsch stood out as a teacher who, in his own unpresuming professional manner, exerted a most positive influence upon untold numbers of Jewish young people growing up in St. Louis. He was born in a rural area of Brandenburg on February 11, 1842. Stifled by the meagerness of small village schools, his parents sent him to Berlin, where he earned degrees in classical languages. Deutsch emigrated to America in 1867 and settled in St. Louis, where he became acquainted with Rabbi Henry Vidaver, then serving at United Hebrew. Together they founded the Western Hebrew College, intended as an institution of advanced learning, especially in the Hebrew language. Lacking adequate support, the

Another concern was where classes would be conducted, since the school lacked a permanent home of its own. Classes were held variously at the temples, but also at a number of rented places; during the first few years of the school's existence, for instance, at least five different sites were used. It was not until 1901, when the cornerstone was laid for the Jewish Educational and Charitable Building (popularly known as the "Alliance Building") on the northwest corner of Ninth and Carr, that the Hebrew Free School finally had a permanent home. By 1905, though, the school had merged with other agencies housed in that center to become The Jewish Educational Alliance.[23]

Another ongoing issue was the curriculum. In the 1880s Reform Judaism liberalized and modernized Reform theology and practice. In St. Louis, some Reform Jews sought at the same time to minimize Hebrew in both religious services and education. Although Sonneschein was in the forefront of the national movement for liberalization, his attitude toward Hebrew in the Free School proved to be just the opposite. When some lay leaders proposed the elimination of Hebrew from the school curriculum, Sonneschein responded vigorously. "That inherited language is sacred," he wrote to the president of the Hebrew Free School Association. "What right have we to abolish it in our school? You just as lief may force down the throat of an old-fashioned pious Hebrew a slice of pork, all because he is hungry and you want to be charitable." Both Sonneschein and Spitz consistently urged more Hebrew, pointing out that "at one time a child of five already could read Hebrew, and even say grace at meals—but no longer," and that efforts were necessary to improve the reading and

---

institution closed within two years. But his scholarship and teaching ability earned Deutsch a position in the St. Louis public schools, where he taught Latin, German, and French at Central High School. For many years he also taught English during the summer months at Bryan and Stratton College, a private business school on the corner of Market and Broadway. Deutsch also headed the Sabbath School at Shaare Emeth. When Rabbi Messing succeeded in getting the Hebrew Free School under way, one of his priorities was to convince Deutsch to associate with the institution, albeit at the same time retaining his responsibilities at Central High School. The arrangement proved highly successful for more than two decades. In addition to his teaching and administrative talents, Deutsch was also a published scholar whose several texts and essays on the teaching of foreign languages were widely used in colleges and universities. *Jewish Free Press*, May 8, 1885, March 5 and June 25, 1886, and June 17, 1887; *Voice*, March 1, 1889, February 15, 1901, January 15, 1904, and February 10, 1909.

23. St. Louis, Missouri File, AJA. See also *Tribune*, January 23, March 5, July 2, and December 12, 1880, January 21 and April 1, 1881, and November 3 and 17, 1882; *Jewish Free Press*, June 17, 1887; *Voice*, March 1, 1889, and February 15, 1901.

knowledge of *loshon ha-kodosh* ("the holy tongue"). Hebrew remained an integral part of the curriculum.[24]

The opening of the Hebrew Free School led to additional important developments in the religious education of St. Louis youth. The first was an immediate upgrading of existing congregational religious schools. (This necessarily refers only to the three Reform temples in existence then, United Hebrew, B'nai El, and Shaare Emeth. Unfortunately the lack of data precludes any description or evaluation of religious education in the Orthodox congregations. That they conducted religious education is undisputed; evidence exists in the form of approximate numbers of pupils. What is not known, though, is who did what, where, and how.) That upgrading entailed curricular modification that included a "new emphasis" on "Hebrew, Catechism, and Biblical History," as well as motivational approaches to attract more pupils. All three temple schools opened their doors to children of families who could not afford congregational membership. An exploration into the possibility of a joint religious school fell through as each temple preferred complete autonomy in its own religious instruction. Those attending the 1880 annual meeting of Shaare Emeth heard that the temple's religious school had enrolled 176 pupils, making it "one of the largest in the country." It had six teachers, and its facilities were so overcrowded that the school had to rent two rooms on Pine Street opposite the temple. In 1882 the United Hebrew Confirmation class numbered eight, Shaare Emeth twelve, and B'nai El sixteen—their largest enrollments up to that time. By 1883 more than seven hundred children were enrolled in the city's Jewish educational programs, Reform, Orthodox, and the Hebrew Free School.[25]

Even as young people's religious education was being upgraded in the temples, the Hebrew Free School expanded its program into a new area that proved remarkably constructive and positive. As early as October 1880, leaders of the school broached the idea of adding vocational courses, starting with sewing classes for girls. The object was not only to provide girls of poor Jewish families with religious education but also to train them for jobs. Spearheaded by the efforts of Jacob Furth, on January 18, 1881, the Industrial Department of the Hebrew Free School opened. About

24. Solomon H. Sonneschein to Jacob Furth, February 22, 1885, in Solomon H. Sonneschein Letterbooks, AJA, letter reprinted in *Jewish Free Press*, April 3, 1885. See also *Tribune*, January 23, March 5, July 2, October 1, and December 12, 1880, January 28, February 19 and 26, March 5 and 19, and April 1, 1881, and November 3 and 17, 1882; *Jewish Free Press*, June 17, 1887; *Voice*, March 1, 1889, and February 15, 1901.

25. *Tribune*, March 26, April 1 and 16, September 10, and October 1, 1880, April 8, 1881, and September 21 and October 5, 1883; *Voice*, June 22, 1888.

fifty girls, ages eight to fourteen, enrolled. Sewing classes were conducted on Tuesday and Thursday afternoons, after regular public school. All pupils also regularly attended the weekend religious classes. Weekend teachers Annie Meyer and Tillie Friedman also taught sewing on Tuesdays and Thursdays, with the aid of volunteers Mesdames Sonneschein, Spitz, Steinberg, Jessel, and Rashky of the Hebrew Ladies Society.[26]

Problems that plagued the Hebrew Free School also affected the subsidiary industrial department: location, curriculum, and personnel. For reasons that are not clear, financial support for the vocational branch lagged behind that of the parent school. Some evidence suggests it might have resulted from attitudes toward the many eastern European immigrant youngsters in the school; a certain amount of unease toward the new immigrants existed among some established German Jews. For whatever reasons, in January 1883 the industrial department was forced to close.

But that proved to be only a temporary setback. Thanks once again to exemplary leadership by Mr. and Mrs. Furth, funding was revitalized, and in December 1883 the industrial department reopened. It remained an integral part of the program for the remainder of the school's existence. Indeed, in 1884 the name of the school itself was modified to reflect that change: henceforth it was officially the St. Louis Hebrew Free and Industrial School.[27]

For the next twenty-five years the school flourished and provided inestimable education for untold numbers of Jewish young people in St. Louis. Pupils included children of German Jewish origin as well as those with eastern European backgrounds; in time the eastern Europeans constituted most of the enrollment. That apparently disenchanted a large number of German Reform Jews, who refused to support the school on the grounds that it "perpetuate[d] Russo-Jewish life and fanaticism [Orthodox Judaism] instead of Americanizing" the students. Nevertheless, adequate financial support continued. Although only Jewish children attended the weekend religious classes, enrollment in the weekday vocational courses was open to all. In 1885, for instance, all 81 pupils (49 girls and 32 boys) who attended the weekend religious sessions were Jewish; 22 of the 54 girls in the weekday vocational courses in cutting, sewing, crocheting, and embroidering were from non-Jewish Italian, Irish, German, and Polish families.[28]

---

26. *Tribune*, October 1 and December 12, 1880, January 28 and December 21, 1881.

27. Ibid., October 27, and November 3 and 17, 1882, January 19, April 6, June 29, September 7, November 9, and December 7, 1883, and February 15, 1884.

28. *Jewish Free Press*, November 6, 1885, May 27, 1887; *Voice*, January 15, 1904. An honor roll of persons associated with the Hebrew Free and Industrial School, both as

Alongside the Hebrew Free and Industrial School and the Reform temple religious schools, another group of schools came into being for similar purposes. These were Talmud Torahs established by the increasing number of Orthodox *shuls* in the growing near-north-side eastern European Jewish neighborhoods. Unfortunately both the *shuls* and the schools were often transient and temporary, and they maintained few if any records; we know of them only through occasional references in the Jewish press. Considering the nature of Jewish education in eastern European communities, one could surmise that almost every *shul* that sprang up also had some sort of *cheder* associated with it. As early as 1885, for instance, a number of such schools existed, referred to in the *Jewish Free Press* as "Talmud Torah Free Schools." Housed in separate congregations, these institutions were created by newly arrived eastern European immigrants and maintained by them through small contributions, often no more than twenty-five to seventy-five cents per month, usually just enough to pay the cost of a *melamed*. The children attended the St. Louis public schools during the day, and then went to the Talmud Torah for Hebrew and religious classes that usually began at about 4 P.M.

In 1885 an attempt was made to combine some of those Talmud Torahs into one school, quartered at the Beth Hamedrosh Hagodol Synagogue in the 900 block of North Seventh. Thus was started the Moses Montefiore Hebrew School, administered and financed by the eastern European Orthodox Jewish population. In 1885 some 135 members contributed enough to cover expenses that amounted to about one hundred dollars per month. The first known president of the organization was a Mr. Lipsky, and its first recorded teachers were a Mr. Yaffe and a Mr. Kaulikoff. By 1886 the school was stable enough to move into its own quarters at 710 Wash Street. It occupied additional sites during the next few decades, and it became one of the most visible and popularly known institutions in the heart of the Orthodox Jewish community.[29]

---

professionals and as volunteers, would be quite lengthy. Teachers included William Deutsch, Emil Mayer, Bertha Sale, and the congregational rabbis, among many others. Mrs. Jacob Furth, Mrs. William Deutsch, and Hannah Stix stand out among the many exemplary lay women who volunteered services. Others who served in a variety of capacities included Jacob Furth, Albert Arnstein, Joseph B. Greensfelder, Isaac Schwab, David Eiseman, Bernard Greensfelder, Julius Glaser, William Goldstein, Elias Michael, David Treichlinger, and many others—a veritable "who's who" in the St. Louis Jewish community. Rare was an edition of the St. Louis Jewish press that did not mention some person or activity associated with the school.

29. *Jewish Free Press,* November 13, 1885, and April 16, 1886. The earliest known board of directors of Moses Montefiore Hebrew School included Abraham Joseph

Even as these developments for Jewish youth unfolded, additional efforts were made to deal with problems of the sick and the elderly. The Home for the Aged and Infirm Israelites had its roots in early efforts to establish a Jewish hospital in St. Louis. In the German Jewish tradition, a "hospital" was described in Hebrew as a *hekdesh* (or "hostel for the poor"), an institution in central European Jewish communities that served the dual purpose of lodging poor or sick travelers as well as providing a place for curing the sick. Because of small and scattered numbers in America, Jews relied on the overall secular community for such services, even if it meant hospitalization in an institution run by a Christian denomination. For those who insisted upon maintaining the traditional kosher dietary laws, often the decision was to risk tragic consequences by staying at home rather than to eat nonkosher food in a non-Jewish medical facility. By the 1860s only three Jewish hospitals existed in the United States: Jews Hospital in New York (name changed in 1869 to Mount Sinai Hospital); Jewish Hospital in Cincinnati; and Judah Touro Infirmary in New Orleans.

As early as 1863 a group headed by Isidor Bush proposed a Jewish hospital for St. Louis. City authorities were very receptive to the proposal; they even offered land near the United States Marine Hospital in south St. Louis, not far from the government arsenal. That offer, however, contained a proviso that the hospital must be erected within two years. Attempts to raise the necessary funds proved unsuccessful, and the property reverted to the city. Apparently the Jewish community was not yet large enough nor prosperous enough.[30]

Spector, Pesach Olchovy, Elijah Olschwanger, Mordechai Levy, Moses Ber Leventhal, Moses Hollander, Selig Fleishman, Abraham Miller, Nathan Cohen, Jonas Razowsky, Joseph Millner, Ruben Horwitz, Mayer Bruchman, Abraham Rubinowitz, Saul Levitt, Abraham Gallant, Yoel Levitt, Isaac Magidson, Ben Zion Goldman, Joseph Romansky, Shabsai Leventhal, Shrage Appelstein, Ephraim Cohen, and Mordechai Seigel. *Beth Hamedrosh Hagodol Congregation Diamond Jubilee* (pamphlet), 7, in Beth Hamedrosh Hagodol Collection, St. Louis Jewish Community Archives.

30. Scharf, *Saint Louis City and County,* vol. 2, 1763; Hyde and Conard, eds., *Encyclopedia of the History of St. Louis,* vol. 2, 1044. An informal history of Jewish Hospital gives 1853 as the date of Bush's attempt, but there is no documentation or supportive data for that date. Gee, *History of the Jewish Hospital of St. Louis,* 8 (several other dates in Gee's account are inaccurate and unsubstantiated). Frances Hurd Stadler, in her popular but undocumented *St. Louis Day by Day,* 204, also gives the date as 1853. Stadler's credentials as a researcher at the Missouri Historical Society are otherwise impeccable, and so this seems to be a simple typographical error, or perhaps she accepted Gee's date at face value. After all, Bush came to St. Louis only in 1849, and although he soon emerged as a leader among his coreligionists, when one considers how difficult it was for him to establish himself economically, it does not seem plausible that in that short time he would carry enough influence with city officials to lead a movement for a

No further overt action on a hospital transpired for almost fifteen years. Then, on October 13, 1878, in his annual presidential report to the UHRA, Bernard Singer included the following:

> There is yet one thing to which I especially desire to call attention, and which I think is within the province of this association, and that is the establishment of a Jewish hospital in this city. Every large city in this country has such an institution, and I believe if that matter was properly taken hold of by a few energetic and enterprising men, we could succeed in establishing such an institution here. In connection with the hospital we could also maintain a home for the aged and infirm. We have paid out to such aged and infirm persons during the last year for rent and necessaries of life nearly $1,000.[31]

Enthusiastic support for Singer's proposal by Rabbi Sonneschein, Augustus Binswanger, Jacob Furth, Joseph M. Pollack, William Goldstein, Meyer Langsdorf, and Leopold Steinberger resulted in immediate pledges of $1,620. Sonneschein, Furth, and Binswanger thereupon drafted an appeal to St. Louis Jewry to organize a "Jewish Hospital Association."

A large gathering duly assembled for that purpose on October 27, 1878, at the Harmonie Club. Initial enthusiasm soon gave way to skepticism. Although widespread support existed for some sort of action, many questioned whether that action should include a hospital. Debate soon centered on the name of the proposed organization, because so many placed a higher priority on a home for the aged than on a hospital. That squabble was settled with a new name, the "Jewish Infirmary and Hospital Association of St. Louis." An additional $870 was pledged toward the project, but with the understanding that it would not be payable unless a total of $5,000 was subscribed. The assemblage then elected temporary officers for the new association: Jacob Furth, president; William Goldstein, treasurer; and Augustus Binswanger, secretary. President Furth then appointed two committees, one to solicit funds and one to draft a constitution and bylaws. Despite some expressed misgivings, the sense of the people there seemed to be that the constitution and bylaws would provide for a hospital as the primary institution and a home for the aged as "an appendage" to the hospital.[32]

---

hospital. Besides, Jews in St. Louis in 1853 numbered only in the hundreds and were without much wealth, and thus were hardly a group that might make a viable attempt to establish a hospital. By 1863, however, that had changed; they now numbered in the thousands and included several quite wealthy merchants.

31. *Voice*, May 31, 1907. Unless otherwise indicated, this early history of the Home for the Aged and Infirm Israelites is derived from Scharf, *Saint Louis City and County*, vol. 2, 1763–64 and from the Home's Minute Book as reproduced in serial form in the *Voice*, March 8–May 31, 1907.

32. *Voice*, May 31, 1907.

Nothing concrete happened for almost a year and a half, primarily because the committee on subscriptions could not raise its goal of $5,000. When the constitution committee completed its document, another public meeting was called, for March 28, 1880. Only thirteen men showed up: the five members of the constitution committee (Jacob Furth, Isidor Bush, Rabbi Sonneschein, William Deutsch, and Augustus Binswanger), plus Rabbis Henry J. Messing and Moritz Spitz, Barney Hysinger, Bernard Singer, Albert Fischer, Theodore Bloch, Dr. H. Newland, and Aaron Gershon. The mood obviously was dampened by the failure to raise the necessary funds. In fact, the evening's discussion focused on whether to even pursue the project. They decided unanimously that action on the constitution and bylaws should be postponed indefinitely and that the documents should be referred instead to the board of directors of the UHRA for further action. For the second time a move for a Jewish hospital had failed.

But not so for a home for the aged. Whereas many questioned the need for a hospital and especially the ability to support it financially, much more enthusiastic and positive feelings existed about a facility for the aged. The UHRA's board of directors devoted several meetings during 1880 and 1881 to that issue. Nevertheless, things seemed to be at an impasse. The editors of the *Tribune* asked repeatedly what had happened to the idea, referring to it as "the all-absorbing topic of the day" among the Jews of St. Louis.[33]

Nevertheless, conversations were taking place between leaders of the UHRA and the Kesher Shel Barzel Society. During the nineteenth century a number of Jewish benevolent fraternal societies came into existence in the United States, modeled frequently on the Freemason pattern, for mutual aid, fellowship, life insurance, relief of distress, and sick and death benefits. Some originated as *landsmanschaften*, some as political groups, some as *chevrah*. The most famous, of course, was B'nai B'rith. Others included Free Sons of Israel, B'rith Abraham, Knights of Joseph, Kesher Shel Barzel, Progressive Order of the West, Sons of Benjamin, and workers' and Zionist groups. (National women's lodges also existed, such as the Fortschrittstoechter Society, Miriam Ladies Society, and Toechter Israels.) Organized in 1860, Kesher Shel Barzel supported Jewish hospitals, orphanages, and similar eleemosynary institutions. In 1880 and 1881, District No. 4 of Kesher Shel Barzel, made up of lodges in the north central states, showed particular interest in establishing homes for aged and infirm Jews. At its annual meeting in Chicago in February 1881,

---

33. Ibid., February 24, 1905; *Tribune,* March 5 and April 1, 1880.

discussion centered on such an institution specifically in St. Louis. But during the next few months negotiations between Kesher Shel Barzel and the St. Louis United Hebrew Relief Association broke down, and Kesher Shel Barzel withdrew a tentative offer. Existing records give no clue as to why this happened.[34]

Into this breach stepped several St. Louis Jewish women's groups, and their action proved decisive. The Ladies' Widows and Orphans Society took the lead. Organized during the Civil War to provide a home for Jewish children orphaned by that conflict, the women solicited funds through bazaars, balls, and similar money-raising projects. But when B'nai B'rith established its large orphanage in Cleveland in 1868, the group dropped the idea of a St. Louis home. It kept its funds intact, however, and donated any interest earned by the corpus to the Cleveland institution. By 1881, when the notion arose for a home for aged and indigent Jews in St. Louis, the women had about ten thousand dollars in their treasury.

Meanwhile, other St. Louis women's groups had been actively promoting a home for the aged. One was the Ladies' Zion Society, headed by Mesdames Joseph Wolfort, Leopold Steinberger, Joseph Cook, and Jonas Isaacs. Another was the Young Ladies' Hospital Aid Society, whose membership included such active young women as Flora Isaacs, Clara Maas, Josie Bush (Isidor's daughter), Sophie Glaser, and Sarah Schiele. They still hoped for a hospital, but now they ardently supported efforts for a senior citizens home. Discussions among these and others led to concrete developments. The UHRA's board of directors pledged seventy-five hundred dollars. The Ladies' Widows and Orphans Society divided its treasury, donated half to the Cleveland orphanage, and pledged the other half (five thousand dollars) to a St. Louis home for the aged. The Ladies' Zion Society pledged fifteen hundred dollars, and the Young Ladies' Hospital Aid Society came up with another fourteen hundred dollars. The Hebrew Ladies' Sewing Society, headed by Kate Skrainka, offered material goods in the form of sheets, pillowcases, napkins, tablecloths, bedspreads, comforts, towels, and nightgowns. The Ladies Pioneer Society, through its president Mrs. Augustus Frank and secretary Carrie Newmark, pledged one thousand dollars. During UHRA meetings in March and April 1882, enthusiastic male and female supporters poured in more pledges. The list of contributors included the names of virtually every Jewish organization, merchant, and community or congregational leader.[35]

---

34. *Tribune,* January 7 and May 6, 1881.

35. As reproduced in *Voice,* March 8 and 15, 1907, in a special feature labeled "Twenty-Five Years Ago." See also *Tribune,* March 23, 1883.

With that solid support, president Barney Hysinger and secretary Augustus Binswanger of the UHRA issued a circular letter on May 4, 1881, calling for a mass meeting to establish "a home for the aged and infirm Israelites of St. Louis, with a hospital as an appendage thereto." That gathering took place on Sunday, May 8, 1881, at Shaare Emeth on Seventeenth and Pine, and a society called "The Home for the Aged and Infirm Israelites" was formed. Barney Hysinger was designated as temporary president and Augustus Binswanger as temporary secretary. During the next few months pledges amounting to more than seventy thousand dollars poured in, ranging from gifts of only a few dollars to some exceeding ten thousand dollars. Not since the great Chicago fire had St. Louis Jewry responded with such enthusiasm.[36]

Before long the society purchased a building at 3652 South Jefferson. The site was deliberately chosen so that inhabitants could live quietly and peacefully in a rural-like setting away from bustling city activities. The large brick building, formerly the "Beauvais Mansion," contained eighteen rooms on two floors, was surrounded by a park and a garden, and was situated about twenty feet above street level on a terraced knoll. Persons sitting on a spacious veranda were treated to a magnificent view almost ten miles in every direction that included bluffs on the Illinois side of the Mississippi River and hills bordering on the Meramec River to the south and west in St. Louis and Jefferson Counties.[37]

The formal opening and dedication of "The Home," as so many popularly and affectionately referred to it, occurred on Sunday, May 28, 1882. Threatening weather failed to keep well-wishers away; a somewhat overexuberant writer for the *Tribune* opined that most of St. Louis's sixty-five hundred Jews were there. The excitement and enthusiasm of the occasion were apparent in his report:

> Though the time set for the dedication was four o'clock, two hours earlier witnessed the arrival of many of our coreligionists to witness the solemn and joyous ceremonies of dedicating the Home. . . . Private carriages lined the wide avenue on both sides for many blocks, and herdic coaches filled to excess began to roll in an hour before the specified time. The extra run of street cars did not suffice to satisfy the wants, and many had to . . . walk the distance. At four o'clock locomotion was a difficult feat either inside of the building or on the grounds.[38]

---

36. Augustus Binswanger Papers, St. Louis Jewish Community Archives, St. Louis.

37. A third floor was added later to provide additional facilities. The Home for the Aged and Infirm Israelites is not to be confused with the more familiar Orthodox Old Folks Home established almost twenty-five years later at North Grand and Blair by eastern European Orthodox Jews.

38. As reprinted in the *Voice*, May 3, 1907.

Those present heard selections by choirs and musical groups, and addresses by Rabbis Messing, Sonneschein, and Spitz, as well as by Augustus Binswanger and Barney Hysinger, all organized by an arrangements committee comprised of Mrs. Joseph Wolfort, Mrs. Augustus Frank, Benjamin Eiseman, Nicholas Scharff, William Goldstein, and Augustus Binswanger. St. Louis Jewry probably had not thrilled to such an exhilarating experience since the laying of the B'nai El cornerstone in 1855.

The Home achieved instant success because of widespread support from the Jewish community. In fact, within four years it was completely occupied, and people began to speak about expansion. Almost every week the Jewish press listed numerous gifts and contributions in cash and in kind made by St. Louis Jewry and by Jews living in scattered Missouri and Illinois communities. The Home was ably operated by a competent professional staff headed for many years by Dr. and Mrs. Samuel Pollitzer, selected from among many applicants as superintendent and matron. Effective lay direction was, of course, indispensable; it ensured the Home's prominent position within the Jewish community for decades to come. Many of St. Louis's most prominent Jewish personalities served as officers and board members. Worthy of note was the very first administration, which set an example of competence and conscientiousness for those who followed: Barney Hysinger, president; Mrs. Albert Fischer, vice president; Augustus Binswanger, secretary; Benjamin Eiseman, treasurer; and Leon M. Helman, Nicholas L. Scharff, William Goldstein, Meyer Lowenstein, Mrs. Joseph Wolfort, Mrs. Moses Fraley, Mrs. Augustus Frank, Mrs. Levy Stern, and Bertha Landsdorf, directors.[39]

The Home for the Aged and Infirm Israelites remained in existence for more than half a century. Extremely popular at first, within a decade the Home became the center of an ongoing controversy over *kashrus* (kosher facilities). The German Jewish leadership persistently resisted demands to convert the Home's food facilities to accommodate the ever-increasing number of eastern European Orthodox Jews. After a protracted and sometimes acrimonious dispute, in 1907 the Orthodox community opened its own facility, the Orthodox Old Folks Home, located at North Grand and Blair. St. Louis thus had two Jewish old folks homes, one supported by the German Reform community and one supported by the eastern European Orthodox community. Over the next few decades, as the eastern European Jewish population outnumbered the German Jews, residency in the South Jefferson institution diminished. Serving fewer and fewer residents, the Home merged with the larger Orthodox institution in 1940, and the facility on South Jefferson was closed.

---

39. *Tribune*, January 12, and May 18 and 25, 1883; *Voice*, January 6 and May 11, 1888.

The creation of the Hebrew Free School and the Home for the Aged and Infirm Israelites could not have come at a more fortuitous time, for those institutions played a vital role when significant numbers of eastern European Jewish immigrants began to arrive in the 1880s. Americanizing and educating their young and caring for their sick and elderly became a matter of immediate concern, and the St. Louis Jewish community fortunately seemed prepared to meet the unexpected crisis. On the other hand, establishing and maintaining those two institutions stretched to the limits the financial capabilities of the UHRA, and the burden of the new immigrants proved extremely taxing.

Although large numbers of Russians began to emigrate to the United States in the 1880s, they were not the first to arrive.[40] Perhaps 50,000 of America's 250,000 Jews in 1880—about 20 percent—had originated in eastern Europe. Some even lived in St. Louis—specifically, the Latvian Jews who had founded Beth Hamedrosh Hagodol in 1879. Although the exact number of St. Louis Russian Jews at this time is not known, from all indications they resided in the near north side east of Tenth Street, between Market and Carr, where the Orthodox *shuls* were known to be located.

Historians of American immigration have written extensively about how some two million Jews poured into the United States from eastern Europe from the 1880s to the 1920s. It was one of the largest refugee movements in history. Only a very brief overview is necessary here as background to the St. Louis story.

Although the migration occurred steadily and continuously during that period, it came in two major waves. The first occurred in the 1880s, triggered by the assassination of reform-minded Tsar Alexander II. His murder brought reactionary forces back to power in Russia, and unleashed widespread latent antisemitism throughout that part of the world. Bloody pogroms and other barbaric acts of inhumanity occurred in 1881 and 1882 in some 167 cities and towns in western Russia and the Ukraine as well as in widespread rural areas. Capping these depredations were the infamous

---

40. For the sake of simplicity, the shorter and more general term "Russian" henceforth will be used to identify the new class of eastern European Jewish immigrants. Accuracy should demand clear identification—Latvian Jews, Estonian Jews, Lithuanian Jews, Galician Jews, Polish Jews, Ukranian Jews, Hungarian Jews, Rumanian Jews, Moldavian Jews, etc.—but the simple generic "Russian" was the term popularly used by contemporaries. When more specificity is required, the more accurate identification will be used. Some would argue that the term "Slavic" is more appropriate than the term "Russian." Be that as it may, contemporaries used the term "Russian," and so will this author.

May Laws of 1882, repressive measures that severely restricted rights of Jews throughout Russia. Thousands fled, often illegally and without passports, most taking a tortuous and precarious route that went through Austrian Galicia. There the city of Brody became an overcrowded refugee center, where unscrupulous profiteers and brigands victimized thousands of desperate, fleeing Jews. The refugees were forced to live under the most abject conditions, crowded into decrepit factories and dirty stables wherever they could find a place, struggling to survive against harsh and miserable impediments created by both man and nature. To help them, Jewish communities throughout western Europe created emergency relief agencies, most importantly in Vienna, Berlin, Paris, and London, to assist the refugees in the resettling process. In May 1881 the New York United Hebrew Charities established a special Russian Relief Committee, anticipating that some of those refugees might emigrate to this country. Four months later the first boatload arrived. What started as a trickle soon became a flood. It simply overwhelmed unprepared American relief agencies. That led to a reorganization and refocusing of the American effort, which now stressed two major objectives: the creation of the Hebrew Emigrant Aid Society (HEAS) to locate Jewish immigrants in cities across the United States (which succeeded), and the attempt to establish refugee agricultural settlements, mostly in the American Midwest (which had some successes, but which overall proved to be a failure).[41]

By 1883 about nineteen thousand Russian Jews had reached the United States (additional thousands resettled in havens throughout western Europe). Just about then the pogroms in Russia abated, the flow of immigrants began to diminish, and the European relief societies gradually liquidated their Brody frontier station operations. By the end of 1883, when it appeared that the worst was over, HEAS phased out its operations in

---

41. The Hebrew Emigrant Aid Society is not to be confused with the later Hebrew Immigrant Aid Society (HIAS) created in 1902. The major impetus for HEAS came from prominent German Jews in America. HIAS was supported by German Jews as well, but perhaps the main reason for its greater success derived from the strong support it received from America's Russian Jews, themselves emigrants whose "making it" in America made them much more sympathetic toward other Russian refugees. An excellent brief analysis of Russian Jewish emigration to America can be found in Sachar, *History of the Jews of America*, 129–36.

At least sixteen Russian Jewish farming ventures were attempted, including Sicily Island Colony in Louisiana, New Odessa in Oregon, Cotopaxi Colony near Denver in Colorado, Cremieux Colony in South Dakota, Beersheba Colony in Kansas, Palestine Colony in Michigan, Alliance and Woodbine Colonies in New Jersey, and Painted Woods Colony in North Dakota. The best account of those agricultural settlements and others is Uri D. Herscher, *Jewish Agricultural Utopias in America, 1880–1910*.

America. Some refugees even returned to Russia, hoping that life there would return to normal. They soon found that they were mistaken; in fact, by the end of the 1880s about 161,000 more Jews fled from Russia for the United States. These people still were aided by various relief agencies, although not on as large a scale as the earlier effort.

By 1885, as a steady flow of immigrants continued to stream into the United States, a group of Russian Jewish émigrés in New York organized the Jewish Emigrant Protective Society. Their purpose was to act as interpreters and agents for naive and uninformed Russian Jews arriving at Castle Garden, where immigrants disembarked in New York harbor (in 1892 Ellis Island replaced Castle Garden as the entry point). The Jewish Emigrant Protective Society was augmented by another Russian Jewish volunteer agency, the Hebrew Sheltering House Society, which supplied kosher food, secondhand clothing, and temporary housing. In 1902 these makeshift groups merged into the Hebrew Immigrant Aid Society (HIAS). It became the major immigration agency for Jews coming into the United States in the twentieth century.

Meanwhile, the second and much longer and larger wave of emigration began in 1891. It was triggered by the notorious Passover-eve decree that expelled Jews from Moscow, and was followed by another wave of harassment and persecution that climaxed in the bloody Kishinev massacre of 1903. For three more years those depredations continued almost unabated, followed by the Russo-Japanese War of 1904–1905 and the revolutionary uprisings that came on the heels of that war. Through all these periods of stress and persecution up to World War I, Jews by the thousands fled Russia in a steady stream, seeking refuge in the United States, the "Goldeneh Medina."[42]

St. Louis Jews, of course, were well aware of these events, which were publicized amply in the secular and the Jewish press. In 1881, following the outbreak of the pogroms that came on the heels of Alexander II's assassination, the UHRA, with Jacob Furth, Marcus Bernheimer, and Augustus Frank taking the lead, appealed to local fraternal lodges and very quickly raised more than seven hundred dollars to help Russian refugees. In February 1882 the New York office of HEAS notified the UHRA in St. Louis that it wanted to send several hundred immigrants to the Midwest. St. Louis was asked to take in some, and to arrange for distributing others to different midwestern and western communities.

---

42. So much excellent scholarship has been published about this great emigration that the author must resist trying to single out those that are the best. Instead, the reader is encouraged to visit libraries and select from the vast availability of fine reading on this subject.

Despite some sympathetic support, the UHRA reacted hesitantly. The Home for the Aged and Infirm Israelites and the Hebrew Free School had just been established, and both needed ongoing support. Aid programs for needy Jews already in St. Louis required continuous funding. The "schnorrer" situation still rankled many as it continued to drain limited resources that many felt should be put to better use. Faced with the new immigrant crisis, the board of the UHRA called for a mass meeting of St. Louis Jewry to decide what course to follow.

It quickly became apparent that large numbers of the community's German Jews were reticent to help the new Russian immigrants. Some pointed out that many Russians did not come under duress as persecuted refugees at all, but were instead seeking to escape military service or to better their own social and economic situation—how ironic the similarity to why so many German Jews themselves had earlier fled to this country!—and were perfidiously taking advantage of free transportation offered by HEAS. Such persons were not "true" victims of persecution, the argument went, and were labeled therefore as of "low moral grade" and unworthy of assistance. It seems quite apparent, though, that behind this attitude lay deep-seated suspicions and latent animosities between German and Russian and between Reform and Orthodox, and especially the fear within a secure and established German Jewish citizenry that a new and different group of Jews might undermine that security. This attitude was openly expressed not only in St. Louis but also in many other German-dominated Jewish communities elsewhere in the country. In its annual report in 1882, published in the local St. Louis Jewish press, the UHRA proclaimed:

> Only disgrace and a lowering of the opinion in which American Israelites are held by this community, can result from the continued residence among us of such an addition to the Jewish population. Every crime against property or person committed by one of these wretches will throw obloquy over our race throughout the land.[43]

In an effort to help the "true" refugees, in March 1882 the Russian Exile Aid Society was formed, the action again spearheaded by Jacob Furth, Marcus Bernheimer, and Augustus Frank. (The group's name was changed in June 1882 to the St. Louis Branch of the Hebrew Emigrant Aid Society.) Many board members of the UHRA refused to serve on the board of this new group. Nevertheless, in the next seven months 514 Russian emigrants were brought to St. Louis. The 257 men among them included 133 mechanics, 18 farmers, and 106 without a trade. Thirty of the boys and

---

43. Rosen, "Historical Development of Jewish Federation of Saint Louis," 66. See also *Tribune*, April 15, 1881, and October 6 and 13, 1882.

28 women were able to work. Total cost of bringing in these immigrants, getting them settled, and finding jobs for them amounted to $9,646.72. It was virtually every cent the St. Louis Emigrant Aid Society had.[44]

Now out of funds, the St. Louis Emigrant Aid Society was forced to disband in September 1882 after existing for only six months. It announced that it expected no new immigrants; any who came must now be cared for by relatives or friends. In effect, the whole immigrant matter was thrown back into the lap of the UHRA. Only two days later Albert Arnstein, secretary of the now-defunct Emigrant Aid Society, notified the UHRA that thirty-one heads of families of recently arrived immigrants (113 people) had requested assistance. The harried UHRA granted that aid, but sent a virtual ultimatum to the New York office of the national Emigrant Aid Society:

> In order to stop this imposition upon our charities, we hereby notify all communities that any person sent here who may become a subject of our charities will be immediately re-transported to the place from which he or they were sent.[45]

That was followed ten months later by a formal UHRA resolution passed unanimously by its board of directors after considerable and lengthy debate:

> Resolved, that hereafter no aid or assistance be granted by this association to any emigrant coming to this city from any point to which such emigrant had been previously sent by any persons or association.

In effect, the UHRA asserted, St. Louis will take care of its own needy Jews or those who came here on their own; St. Louis would not accept, however, any immigrants dumped upon it by any other city or agency.[46]

Only two weeks later, seven Russian families arrived at Union Station from Newport, Arkansas, where they had been part of an immigrant agricultural colony. Stricken with malaria, they had been sent to St. Louis for hospital care. For three days they remained destitute at Union Station while the UHRA refused to grant them succor. Bureaucratic red tape in the city's public charity Mullanphy Board prevented that body from helping. Only after Rev. Isaac Epstein, assistant rabbi of Shaare Emeth, publicized the tragic situation in the St. Louis press was Jacob Furth able to pressure the UHRA and the New York office of HEAS to help the piteous refugees. It was too late, though, for one three-year-old child; she died of malaria.

---

44. *Tribune*, October 13, 1882, and March 16, 1883.

45. Ibid., October 13, 1882; Rosen, "Historical Development of Jewish Federation of Saint Louis," 68.

46. *Tribune*, August 10, 1883.

Ironically, Epstein's own superior at Shaare Emeth, Rabbi Sonneschein, castigated Epstein publicly for airing the depressing matter. "We do not assume the right of criticizing any action of any charitable gentleman," Sonneschein wrote as editor of the *Tribune*. "We don't discourage him in his noble work. But we think such appeals have no other result but that of placing the Hebrew Relief Association in a rather questionable light, while such appeals really do not further the cause for which they were intended." Apparently avoiding humiliation or embarrassment weighed more than helping destitute Russian refugees.[47]

In fact, the attitude of many German Jewish leaders toward the Russian newcomers seemed to reflect a position Sonneschein expressed in a sermon delivered at Shaare Emeth and then printed as an editorial in the *Tribune*. It began as an excoriating denunciation of Russian Jews in general, and an admonition against giving them charity.

> The average Russian Jew, with whom we come in contact, is below par in respect to civilization. . . . I know some of them are worthless, and the sooner they are turned loose to their own starvation the better for them. You have no idea of the pernicious influence of their inveterate, inborn laziness. It is catching, like some infectious disease. The longer we allow them to knock at the door of the [United] Hebrew Relief Association, and send supplies regularly every month into their homes, just so long are we catering to their laziness and helplessness. . . . Don't give them money, for every cent you give them in cash—alms—does more harm than good. If they will not work, let them loose to their starvation, and hunger will teach them to work, if nothing else will, after they have ceased to depend upon begging.[48]

A few weeks later, commenting on the apparent failure of the immigrant agricultural colonies, Sonneschein added to that excoriation by denouncing the waste of thousands of dollars for "a crowd of lazy and dirty good-for-nothings [whose] laziness, impudence and degradation increases . . . in proportion to the amount of money which constantly pours into their tattered pockets." In order to "save the fairness and honor of American Judaism," he urged getting rid of "this Russian Elephant . . . this social pest." Is the United States, he asked rhetorically, the "great and open poor-house for Jewish outcasts of Europe?" Help only those who deserve our sympathies, he urged.[49]

These were stunningly harsh sentiments, especially coming from a man of God. Then, in what seemed to be an incredible reversal, Sonneschein urged St. Louis German Jewry to help the Russians find work, even to

---

47. Ibid., August 31, 1883. See also ibid., September 28, 1883.
48. Ibid., December 22, 1882.
49. Ibid., February 9, 1883.

pay them slightly higher wages if need be to keep them on the job. The children must go to school and become educated. For those too young yet for school, "our noble hearted German ladies" will care for them in a common nursery. As for the adults, though, both men and women, they must work and earn every cent they receive. "You will see that by that very thing you will create in them the spirit of independence and self-assertion, the spirit of industry and thrift."

Sonneschein then rationalized why he felt honest and hard work would transform those Russian Jews from dregs of humanity to industrious and productive members of society. His reasoning would have warmed the hearts of nineteenth- and twentieth-century pan-Germans and racial supremacists:

> Have you forgotten that these Russian Jews, whom you deplore and shrink from today, that they are probably your own great, grand, second, third, or fourth cousins? Do you know where they came from? They are originally *German* Jews—they came from along the borders of the Rhine, from the Isaar and the Danube and all those ancient cities of Germany. They are descended from German ancestry who by reason of persecution at home left everything they had, for the sake of their lives, and fled; being received by the semi-Asiatic princes of Slavic Europe—they dwell in Poland. You see they are not Russian by blood, they are not barbarians; they are by descent German Jews, and by your kindness, by your charity, by your interest in them, show them that you will raise them and their children, so that they shall be as smart, as orderly, as clean, as industrious and as intelligent as your own. . . . In a few years from now [we] will say, "We are glad that these Russian Jews came . . . the brethren and sisters of the Bavarian and Bohemian Jews—they are like them; they also came poor, but they asserted their industriousness, asserted their intelligence, and God has blessed them and by them their country.[50]

Don't give the Russians outright charity! Discipline them to work! With proper direction, they will succeed, just as we German Jews did in America. After all, those Russian Jews are really originally *German* Jews who had the misfortune of coming under the sway of uncivilized and barbaric Slavic Poland and Russia! Just show them the right way, and their true German blood will come to the fore!

That is what it appeared to mean on the surface. But recent scholarship has pointed out that this attitude, expressed widely by other German Jewish leaders in the United States, actually inferred considerable sympathy for Russian Jews, albeit hidden behind overtly manifest Germanic bravado. Very few German Jewish leaders proposed an outright ban on Russian immigration into the United States; they sought rather how best

---

50. Ibid., December 22, 1882.

to Americanize the newcomers, how to make them productive citizens—and yes, how to not at the same time compromise or embarrass German Jewry. Although Sonneschein *seemed* to advocate keeping the least desirable element of the "Russian Elephant" out, he clearly wanted to see the Russians modernized and Americanized like their German precursors, and to have them become part of a sorely needed labor supply in the burgeoning United States industrial economy. That was especially true for the expanding garment industry in St. Louis, in which many German Jews had become established and prosperous. Americanized and disciplined Russian immigrants could—and eventually did—provide much of the labor that German Jewish entrepreneurs needed. Indeed, as some anonymous pundit phrased it, the Russians first worked as low-paid employees in the German-owned factories; then they became the foremen; and soon they became the owners. In a nutshell, so to speak, that describes how many Russians eventually "made it" on a par economically with their German Jewish progenitors.[51]

Perhaps that explains why, with all his seeming personal vagaries, Sonneschein, who so overtly and derisively excoriated Russian Jewry, nevertheless became a popular lecturer and teacher for many when they settled in St. Louis. One might wonder about his rationale and methodology; yet beneath a veneer of Teutonic haughtiness he seemed to possess innate empathy for his Russian coreligionists, and he became one of their staunch supporters. But was it because they were Jews, or because he viewed them as abused Germans?[52]

What is not controvertible, though, is that St. Louis German Jewry *did* provide much needed relief and support for immigrant Russians, in the 1880s and later, which undoubtedly helped the newcomers face and overcome many problems, especially those of sheer survival. One must remember that while Reform Judaism abjured many customs and

---

51. See especially Sachar, *History of the Jews in America,* 133–36, and Gerald Sorin, "Mutual Contempt, Mutual Benefit: The Strained Encounter between German and Eastern European Jews in America, 1880–1920," 34–36.

52. One example might illustrate Sonneschein's active support for Russian immigrants. In 1888, after he had become rabbi of the new and very liberal Temple Israel, Sonneschein appeared, with other St. Louis rabbis, on a program commemorating the twenty-fifth anniversary of Ebn Ezra Lodge B'nai B'rith. At the conclusion of the program, someone suggested an out-of-pocket collection be made to secure funds for the B'nai B'rith orphans home in Cleveland. Sonneschein immediately arose and requested that whatever was raised should be split between the orphans home and "our Russian brethren" of the newly organized Congregation Sheerith Sfard, struggling financially to establish a house of worship. Almost seventy dollars was collected, and half did go to the new Orthodox *shul. Voice,* October 26, 1888.

ritual practices of Orthodoxy, the substitute for those "outmoded" and "no longer meaningful" Mosaic and rabbinic laws was *tzedakah—tikkun olom* and social service. To Reform Judaism and Reform Jews, helping others was a very important manifestation of being a Jew. If those helped happened to be other Jews, so much the better—even if they were Russians!

Thus, under the leadership of its president Barney Hysinger, the UHRA solicited relief funds that helped succor the arriving immigrants. Leon Helman and Albert Arnstein spearheaded the establishment and operation of a UHRA Employment Bureau that found jobs for many Russian Jews. The Hebrew Ladies Sewing Society organized a clothing distribution facility to help immigrants face winter weather hardships. Other women's societies carried out similar projects. The Hebrew Free and Industrial School, with Jacob Furth taking the lead, opened its classes to school-age immigrant children, who received instruction in not only Hebrew and religion but also English to help them in their public school experiences; many also benefited from vocational training there. Night classes were begun for working adults. It did not take long for positive results. Within only two months seven-year-old Russian immigrant Annie Fried starred in an English-speaking Purim celebration at the Harmonie Club. The *Tribune,* by no means a pro-Orthodox journal, reported with felicitousness and pride when Russians began to establish their own businesses—among them Wolff Feinberg as a painter and I. J. Harris as a kosher butcher. By February 1884 enough Russians had achieved sufficient financial means to organize a Mutual Benefit Union, where they and other Russian immigrants might make small business and personal loans. It was the Russian Jewish counterpart of the Hebrew Benevolent Society established by the earlier German Jews back in 1841.[53]

By the mid-1880s, then, hard-pressed Russian Jewish immigrants had become an established part of the St. Louis scene. The clearly Orthodox Beth Hamedrosh Hagodol Congregation already existed, comprised of Latvian Jews. Although Sheerith Israel Cemetery had been founded by German Jews, it at least was indisputably an Orthodox institution, operating under Orthodox *halachic* interpretation. With the founding of the Mutual Benefit Union in 1884, all the rudiments of a Russian Orthodox Jewish community now existed in St. Louis, along with the already established German Reform community.

Of course there were crossovers. Some Germans were Orthodox; some Russians became Reform. Some of each assimilated into Christian society;

53. *Tribune,* October 27, November 3, 9 [*sic*], 17, and 24, 1882, January 26, March 9 and 16, and April 6, 1883, and February 16, 1884.

some of each existed only as "life cycle" Jews who were otherwise quite secular and nonobservant. Nevertheless, German Jews identified most with Reform Judaism, and Russian Jews identified most with Orthodox Judaism. Most Germans by the 1880s had become established economically, and some had become quite affluent; most Russian Jews had not had the opportunity yet to advance beyond the stage of poor immigrants— that would take several decades. Most German Jews lived in the southern half of the "central corridor"; most Russian Jews lived in the northern half. If they came together, it usually was in the workplace, where the German was the boss and the Russian the laborer—at least at first. Despite seemingly cordial relations among leaders and institutions, German Jews continued to look condescendingly upon Russian Orthodox Jews as religious fanatics and "schnorrers," while Russian Jews saw the German Reform Jews as haughty and imperious "goyim." Spiritually and physically, then, German Jews and Russian Jews existed as two almost completely separate Jewish communities in St. Louis.

12

TEMPLE TROUBLES

The 1880s witnessed many important developments for St. Louis Jewry, but none more rancorous and perhaps more traumatic than the events that led to the establishment of Temple Israel. In the middle of this scenario stood the colorful and dynamic—and controversial—Rabbi Solomon H. Sonneschein.

Sonneschein had come to St. Louis in 1869 to become spiritual leader of Shaare Emeth Temple, newly organized, as Sonneschein viewed it, "on the basis of radical reform." He began a tempestuous ministry at Shaare Emeth that lasted for seventeen years. During that time Sonneschein emerged as one of the leading rabbis in the country. His name frequently appeared throughout the nation in newspaper articles that dealt with matters relating to Judaism. He was widely known and very highly regarded in the St. Louis Christian community. In that sense he contributed toward putting himself, Shaare Emeth, and St. Louis Jewry into the public consciousness. From the very beginning of his ministry at Shaare Emeth, Sonneschein encountered what he called "some of the bitterest and sorest of fanaticism." (It should be understood that to him, "fanaticism" described most Jewish traditional practice, including even many of the Americanizing modernizations implemented at other American Reform temples. He viewed Judaism's ethical inheritance as far more important than its "ritual peculiarities.") Nevertheless, he seemed satisfied that he was prevailing over most of those who disagreed with him at Shaare Emeth, and that the congregation was gradually acknowledging, as Sonneschein himself put it, "the saving powers of progress and intelligent independence." But this came at a cost. "Doctor," one of Sonneschein's insightful friends observed, "you are a man of many good qualities, but the best of all is your wonderful talent for making and keeping enemies."[1]

---

1. "Dr. Sonneschein's Statement to the Officers and Members of the Congregation Shaare Emeth," June 29, 1886, in *Jewish Free Press*, July 9, 1886. This letter is found also

Sonneschein was indeed an enigma. He possessed many admirable qualities. A brilliant theologian, he was recognized as one of the finest rabbinic thinkers of the time, albeit many Jews, even fellow liberal Reform Jews, disagreed with the extremism and radicalism of his beliefs. He preached religious universalism as far more preferable to denominational parochialism. He genuinely viewed himself in the forefront of a new Jewish religious movement in this country, and unabashedly dedicated himself to the creation of what he called the "National Jewish Church of America." The principles of his new church entailed "radical changes from all oriental or medieval Judaism," such as the abolition of circumcision "and similar rites," and "the denial of the verbal inspiration of the Bible."[2] Despite his radicalism—or perhaps because of it—Sonneschein was a dynamic and inspiring lecturer and preacher, invited as often by non-Jewish audiences as by Jewish gatherings. His charisma constantly propelled him into the forefront of causes that he supported, for he championed them with vigor. Yet he demonstrated personal flaws that proved to be his undoing. He was overbearingly arrogant, insolent, and often contemptuous, even from the pulpit; one need only recall his shocking excoriations of Russian Jews. Any prominent public figure should be entitled to his or her own personal life; yet many looked with great disfavor upon a man of God womanizing and drinking excessively. Far too often congregants felt they were being addressed from the pulpit by a drunken preacher— yet left convinced they had just heard a brilliant sermon![3] Comparing Sonneschein's intellectual qualities with contemporary St. Louis rabbis Messing and Spitz and Rosentreter is patently unfair and virtually impossible anyway; at the same time, no evidence exists that any of them were ever accused of graceless or reprehensible personal or ministerial misbehavior. In that regard, Sonneschein stood alone.

In the summer of 1881 Sonneschein and his family vacationed in his native Hungary. The congregation sent them off with what Sonneschein described as sentiments "full of tender words of . . . sincere love and respect." When he returned three months later, however, Sonneschein sensed that "chilling and blasting influences" had been at work to undermine his position. Nevertheless, seeking to avoid confrontation—

---

in the Bernard Felsenthal Papers, AJA, and in the Rabbi Solomon H. Sonneschein File, Shaare Emeth Temple Library, St. Louis. Much of what follows about the "Sonneschein Affair" comes from the rabbi's own published statements, from materials in the Felsenthal Papers and the Sonneschein File, and from detailed accounts in the *Jewish Free Press* from March through October 1886.

2. *St. Louis Post-Dispatch*, May 28, 1886; *Jewish Free Press*, June 4, 1886.

3. "Conversations with Mrs. Rose Harsch Fraley," n.d., in Missouri Box, AJA.

something rather unusual for him—he proceeded with his rabbinic agenda, ministering to his congregation's religious and pastoral needs. At the same time, he participated actively and substantially in the secular community. That included his championing of German in the public school curriculum, as well as giving many addresses to Jewish and non-Jewish groups in which he fostered reconciliation and fraternization between Jews and Gentiles. Included was a series of so-called Shylock lectures that earned Sonneschein wide acclaim for attacking long-standing nefarious antisemitic myths about Jews and the merchant world.[4]

At the same time, though, Sonneschein managed to create more than a little consternation within his own congregation as well as in the St. Louis Jewish community at large. One reason was his outspoken religious radicalism, especially as compared with the more moderate Reform of his respected colleagues Messing and Spitz. Perhaps most disturbing, though, was his shocking Chanukah-Christmas declamation in 1883 that the two should be celebrated "by the really naturalized Israelites of this country as the identical national and religious holiday common to both the American and the Jew." It precipitated a rancorous outcry and a heated public conflict that was aired even in the St. Louis secular press, as well as in Jewish newspapers all over the country. The Chanukah-Christmas bombshell led fifty-four members of Shaare Emeth to petition that Sonneschein not be rehired when his contract came up for renewal at the congregation's March 1884 annual meeting. That meeting witnessed an emotionally divisive and bitter debate, with the influential Marcus Bernheimer leading the forces seeking Sonneschein's dismissal, and the equally prominent Moses Fraley championing the rabbi's retention. Shaare Emeth chose to retain Sonneschein. A similar scenario played out at the 1885 annual meeting, although in not nearly as acrimonious an atmosphere, but with the same results. That 1885 meeting was rife, however, with rumors that a new congregation was about to be formed. It seemed apparent that some sort of explosive situation was brewing, not only within Shaare Emeth, but vicariously in the broader Jewish community, considering both Shaare Emeth's and Sonneschein's important status in that larger milieu.[5]

Almost immediately thereafter, Sonneschein and Shaare Emeth became deeply involved in the "Pittsburgh Platform" imbroglio. At issue

---

4. Another example of the esteem in which the non-Jewish community held Sonneschein was reflected in his designation to deliver the baccalaureate address at the University of Missouri graduation exercises in Columbia. *Tribune*, May 28, 1880.

5. "Dr. Sonneschein's Statement," in *Jewish Free Press*, July 9, 1886. See also *Tribune*, December 23, 1883, and January 4 and April 4, 1884; *Jewish Free Press*, April 24 and May 15, 1885, and July 9, 1886.

were basic conflicts within American Reform Jewry that had been festering for several decades, in St. Louis as well as in Jewish communities elsewhere. As Gerald Sorin points out in his insightful study of late-nineteenth-century American Jewish history, the prevailing pattern in Jewish religious structure (as also within most Protestantism) was congregationalism. Individual congregations, especially those that had separated themselves from strict Orthodoxy, established their own parameters in interpreting *halacha*. That had occurred in St. Louis with United Hebrew, B'nai El, and Shaare Emeth. If any other authority existed, it lay in a movement or denomination with which that congregation voluntarily affiliated or associated (such as the Union of American Hebrew Congregations), rather than with a less flexible central rabbinic authority as in Orthodoxy (or in church hierarchy within Catholicism). Thus one Reform congregation or rabbi might foster the *mikvah* or encourage traditional kosher dietary laws; another might view the *mikvah* as outmoded, and consider *kashrus* as meaningless "culinary Judaism." The potential for theologic anarchy was never more traumatically illustrated than by the famous—or infamous—"*trayfa* (non-kosher) banquet" in Cincinnati on July 11, 1883, on the occasion of the tenth anniversary of the Union of American Hebrew Congregations and the first ordination of Hebrew Union College graduates. A dinner that included biblically proscribed shellfish (clams, frog legs, crab, and shrimp) precipitated a disruption by some participating Reform rabbis of a program that many had hoped would bring unity, but which instead resulted in greater dissension. Just at that time, too, the new wave of immigration from eastern Europe was bringing with it a resurgence of Orthodoxy into American Jewish life. And if Reform leaders lacked for sufficient perplexities, another threat to their modernization of Judaism had emerged from the establishment by Felix Adler of the Society for Ethical Culture. A former rabbinic student and son of a prominent New York rabbi, Adler preached a universal moral theology that drew from many religions and that stressed ethics and moral behavior over tradition and ritual. His weekly Sunday morning lectures in New York attracted huge crowds, mostly Jews dissatisfied with the tight strictures of Orthodoxy but still not comfortable with alternatives proffered by Reform.[6]

Faced with challenges from Ethical Culture on the one side and Orthodoxy on the other, Reform leaders in 1885 drew up the so-called Pittsburgh Platform as an expression of Reform principles. "I was in New York a few weeks before," Sonneschein wrote later, "to consult with a colleague

---

6. Gerald Sorin, *A Time for Building: The Third Migration, 1880–1920*, 171–74. Sorin's book is volume 3 of Henry L. Feingold (general editor), *The Jewish People in America*.

about the opportunities and possibilities of a real co-operation with all the rabbis of the land . . . leaning toward progress and reform. We became convinced that a compromise with even the tamest Orthodoxy would simply terminate in a compromise of true and outspoken reform."[7] Compared with earlier pronouncements by Reform leaders, this Pittsburgh Platform articulated principles and beliefs that even many Reform rabbis considered too radical and antitraditional. For some Reform rabbis, the Pittsburgh Platform *was* Reform Judaism; for others, it carried no binding prescriptions. Even though the Pittsburgh Platform was not completely accepted by Reform, its spirit of excessive liberalism, even radicalism, permeated Reform Judaism for decades to come and clearly was a factor in the wide gap between Reform and traditionalism within American Jewry until the middle of the twentieth century.[8]

Sonneschein participated actively in the Pittsburgh conference and returned to St. Louis looking forward to enthusiastic implementation of the new principles in his congregation. Instead he met much more resistance and hostility than he had expected. In spite of his devoting Friday evening sermons to the Pittsburgh Platform, attendance dwindled; Sonneschein couldn't fathom whether it was lack of enthusiasm toward those principles, or a general lack of religiosity within his congregation and thus indifference toward attending any services. On one Friday evening the attendance was so poor—fewer than fifty worshipers in the spacious Shaare Emeth sanctuary—that he angrily canceled his prepared remarks and spoke extemporaneously on an altogether different subject. To boost attendance and to broaden his dissemination of the Pittsburgh Platform, Sonneschein even invited the membership of the recently founded Young Men's Hebrew Association to attend, but much to his publicly expressed chagrin not a single member showed up.[9]

---

7. "Dr. Sonneschein's Statement," in *Jewish Free Press*, July 9, 1886.

8. Sorin, *A Time for Building*, 172–73. The Pittsburgh Platform rejected traditional laws of *kashrus*, practices such as the use of the *mikvah* and the wearing of *tefillin* in daily prayer, many Sabbath and holiday practices, and most of the use of Hebrew in prayer. In recognizing Judaism as a religion rather than a manifestation of historic peoplehood, Reform rejected Palestine as a potential Jewish homeland, thus standing for many years in opposition to political Zionism. Reform Judaism did, however, strongly endorse cultural Zionism. The Columbus Platform promulgated by American Reform in 1937 made major revisions in the Pittsburgh Platform, closing the gap with Orthodoxy (and also the recently formulated Conservative Judaism) on many previously divisive issues. They included, among others, the use of more Hebrew in prayer, the restoration of many rituals and observances, and a vigorous support of political Zionism.

9. *Jewish Free Press*, December 11, 1885. So outraged was Sonneschein toward the YMHA that he publicly discontinued his membership in the organization.

Nevertheless, Sonneschein persisted. One tactic was to change the format of his Friday sermon from a one-way lecture to a quasi-debate, with Sonneschein offering to respond after his presentation to questions from any worshipers. The Friday evening service of December 11, 1885, thus attracted about two hundred people. At the conclusion of the rabbi's sermon, the highly respected Isidor Bush assumed the role of moderator as worshipers questioned Sonneschein. It quickly became apparent that feelings ran very high on both sides, so much so that even the venerable Bush had difficulty maintaining order. The evening concluded with Sonneschein announcing from the pulpit that he would arbitrarily continue a similar format for services in the future.[10]

But the following Sunday, Shaare Emeth's board of trustees, whose membership had become more and more disenchanted with its rabbi, censured Sonneschein for using the pulpit to foster his personal agenda rather than staying within parameters approved by the board. The board also forbade further use of the rabbi's confrontational format during religious services. To get around the "during religious services" limitation, some of Sonneschein's supporters successfully petitioned the board to allow the rabbi to hold his debate in the vestry room *after* services, rather than in the sanctuary *during* services. On succeeding Friday evenings, then, Sonneschein used the approved format to campaign for the Pittsburgh principles within an obviously divided Shaare Emeth.[11]

But now other factors came into play, as the earlier observation about Sonneschein's "wonderful talent for making and keeping enemies" came home to haunt the embattled rabbi. Sonneschein's response to his board's censure—even though the board had retracted somewhat and had permitted debate in the vestry room after services—was to proclaim arrogantly and insultingly from the pulpit the very following Friday evening that "nine-tenths of the congregation" were ignorant of "the meaning of the underlying principles" of their own faith. He denounced those who would not concur with his way of "preserving Judaism in its essential purity," accusing them of favoring instead a return to the "*Schmutzreligion* of former days." Several times he referred to Moses Maimonides, perhaps the most revered of all Jewish philosophers, as a *meshummed*—an apostate traitor to

---

10. Ibid., December 18, 1885.
11. "Dr. Sonneschein's Statement," ibid., July 9, 1886. See also ibid., December 11, 18, and 25, 1885, and January 1, 8, 15, and 22, 1886. The petition to allow Sonneschein to hold his debates was instigated by Frank Block. Others who signed the petition included such well-known Shaare Emeth members as Joseph Wolfort, William Stix, Herman Sonnenfeld, William Goldstein, Joseph Schwab, Isaac Swope, Jonathan Rice, Elias Michael, George Milius, and David Eiseman. Ibid., December 25, 1885. They would later be among the founders of Temple Israel.

his faith—for promulgating much of that *"Schmutzreligion,"* the "rottenest rot of medieval Judaism." Sonneschein even included the editors of the *Jewish Free Press* in his excoriations—because they disagreed with him on the Pittsburgh Platform—and denounced from the pulpit those congregants who allowed that "vile" newspaper to enter their homes. None of these outbursts could have added to Sonneschein's list of friends.[12]

Then matters of a personal nature entered the picture, in the form of vicious and scurrilous rumors and gossip, for which, unfortunately, factual basis existed. There was widespread talk of the rabbi's heavy drinking and uncouth behavior, and of his womanizing. Many were angered and embarrassed at his reportedly "outrageous" (which meant drunken) performance at a wedding ceremony, and shocked at his untoward demeanor before students in a program before the Hebrew Free School. But what may have been the proverbial straw that broke the camel's back devolved from Sonneschein's behavior at the funeral of Eleanor Henriquez on March 1, 1886. Miss Henriquez, only twenty years old, had suffered for a number of years from a ravaging and painful illness. The Henriquez family had only recently moved to St. Louis and, at a friend's suggestion, had requested Sonneschein to conduct the funeral service. Being of Sephardic descent, the Henriquez family adhered to many traditional Jewish practices and rituals, one of which was the custom of covering mirrors in the house of a deceased. Sonneschein arrived late for the funeral, conducted in the Henriquez home; some in attendance later suggested that he seemed to be inebriated. On entering the house and seeing the hall mirror covered with a sheet, Sonneschein loudly and rudely reproached Mr. and Mrs. Henriquez for their "superstition" and contemptuously tore the cloth from over the mirror. One woman friend of the Henriquez family was overheard saying: "Were I but a man, I'd throw the monster out of here." Then, after Sonneschein completed the service, he concluded his benediction with a shocking: "May the God of Truth and Justice in His mercy never visit this house." Only quick and mollifying action by Barney Hysinger, president of Shaare Emeth Congregation, who happened to

---

12. Ibid., December 25, 1885. The *Jewish Free Press* openly and candidly disagreed with Sonneschein on the Pittsburgh Platform. That did not keep the editors from referring to him on other occasions, however, in very complimentary terms as one of the most prominent rabbis in the country. Ibid., December 11, 18, and 25, 1885. In fact, when Shaare Emeth members voted the following year on whether to keep Sonneschein as their rabbi, the *Jewish Free Press* powerfully and in no uncertain terms editorialized that the congregation should retain him. It did so not only in its editorial comments but also in a feature article prominently headlined: "Reasons Why Dr. Sonneschein's Friends Should Be Supported by Your Vote." Ibid., September 10, 1886.

be in attendance, prevented personal violence against Sonneschein. Later suggestions that the rabbi "was not in condition to perform religious rites" neither mitigated criticism of his barbarous behavior nor allayed talk of his heavy drinking. To make matters worse, the whole deplorable episode was widely publicized in the press.[13]

Two weeks later, in a routine and regularly scheduled congregational election, Shaare Emeth members chose a new board of trustees. One of that board's first actions moved the time when the rabbi received his pay from the beginning of the month to the end. Incensed at this change (although it had no effect on his salary), Sonneschein now became convinced that a conspiracy was brewing against him, by those who disagreed with his religious principles and by those who faulted his personal lifestyle. On April 1 he curtly and abruptly resigned. He gave neither reason nor explanation. The resignation would take effect on October 1, with the understanding that if the congregation found a successor in time to officiate for the High Holidays he would step down before then. The board of trustees accepted Sonneschein's resignation unanimously. But a special meeting of the general membership, required to review the board's action, deteriorated into a virulent name-calling session before the board's decision was endorsed by a vote of 82–64. It was a clear majority, but it was equally a clear indication as to how badly the congregation was split. The next day the *St. Louis Post-Dispatch* produced the first inkling of why Sonneschein had resigned: "[S]imply because I am a liberal," he was quoted as saying, "and the present management of my church are Orthodox." Commenting on that allegation, the *Jewish Free Press* pointed out that Shaare Emeth was not and never had been an

---

13. "Conversations with Mrs. Rose Harsch Fraley" and "Diaries of Augustus Binswanger" in Missouri Box, AJA; Augustus Binswanger Papers, St. Louis Jewish Community Archives, St. Louis; *Jewish Free Press*, June 26, 1885, and March 5, 12, and 22, 1886. Among the juicier items involving Sonneschein's womanizing was one that involved his cook. When the Sonnescheins were divorced in 1892, Rosa allowed Solomon to obtain the decree, because if she brought the suit his position as rabbi—he was by then rabbi at Temple Israel—might be jeopardized. "I wished to be rid of him, not ruin him," she later explained to her grandson David Loth. So she offered to let her husband get the divorce, even if it meant she would receive no alimony, provided she could choose the grounds. Sonneschein thought that very generous of her, until he heard the grounds—"refusal to cohabit"—a valid reason under Missouri law. He boasted arrogantly that he would never admit in a court that there could be a woman who refused to sleep with him. But keeping his position as rabbi meant enough that he finally relented and went ahead with the divorce, on Rosa's terms. David Loth, "Notes on the Marital Discord of Solomon and Rosa Sonneschein," in Rosa Sonneschein File, AJA. For some further comments on Rabbi Sonneschein's personal indiscretions, see *Jewish Free Press*, June 26, 1885.

Orthodox congregation, and that whatever theologic differences existed were over Reform principles and had nothing to do with Orthodoxy. More important, though, the *Jewish Free Press* suggested, Sonneschein's own "eccentricities" may have contributed as much if not more to Shaare Emeth's decision to drop him.[14]

But the matter was far from over, as a singular sequence of events unfolded during the summer of 1886. Within two weeks after Sonneschein had resigned, Shaare Emeth began advertising for a new rabbi. Faced with being without a pulpit in the fall, Sonneschein made a brief visit to Boston. What transpired on that trip became a new and overpowering issue in what was becoming a more and more bizarre affair. Sonneschein later told his board that he went to Boston to seek "congenial employment in a literary and intersectarian field."[15] But while there he met with two prominent Unitarian ministers, Reverend J. Minot Savage and Reverend Grindell Reynolds, the latter the secretary of the American Unitarian Association. He saw no rabbis in Boston, nor did he attend any Jewish religious services, but he did deliver a Sunday morning lecture in the Unitarian church of the famed Reverend Edward Everett Hale. Because of Sonneschein's widespread fame in rabbinic circles, what appeared like an extraordinary interest in Unitarianism was reported in unusual detail, not only in the St. Louis press but also in many Jewish newspapers across the country.[16] Also noted was a seeming change in Sonneschein's philosophy

---

14. *St. Louis Post-Dispatch,* April 2, 1886; *Jewish Free Press,* April 9, 16, and 23, May 7, and July 9, 1886. Each week special sections of the *Jewish Free Press* entitled "The Situation" were devoted to developments in the "Sonneschein Affair." They included not only letters taking both sides of the issue but also detailed accounts of meetings that dealt with the matter. See issues of the *Jewish Free Press* for May through September 1886, which also include reprints of articles from newspapers throughout the country.

15. To a reporter of the *St. Louis Post-Dispatch,* however, Sonneschein stated that his trip was to serve three purposes: to deliver an address in Cincinnati, to seek literary work in Boston, and to interview with a New York committee for a position as spiritual leader of a new congregation there. When asked which congregation, Sonneschein replied: "A new church to be established in New York . . . to be called the First Reformed American Jewish Church. It was to be established with the idea of founding a National Jewish Church, just as the Unitarian is a national church. . . . I told this committee I could not accept their call then. To establishing such a National Jewish Church for America my life is devoted. . . . We will have such a Jewish Church, and its principles include radical changes from all oriental or medieval Judaism . . . [among them] the abolition of the rite of circumcision and similar rites, and . . . the denial of the verbal inspiration of the Bible." *St. Louis Post-Dispatch,* May 28, 1886; *Jewish Free Press,* June 4, 1886.

16. M. J. Savage to B. Hysinger, Boston, June 3, 1886, and Grindall Reynolds to B. Hysinger, Boston, June 3, 1886, in Bernard Felsenthal Papers, AJA. See also *Jewish Free Press,* May 21 and 28, 1886, and *Israelite,* May 21, 1886.

away from one of his prior strong rabbinic positions. Before going to Boston he had delivered repeated sermons against intermarriage; shortly after he returned from his Boston trip, he performed a marriage service for a Christian and Jewish couple.[17]

In St. Louis, meanwhile, some Shaare Emeth members, with Moses Fraley playing an important leadership role, took steps to keep Sonneschein as their rabbi. On May 10 a dozen men—they were dubbed "Sonneschein's twelve disciples"—met in Fraley's office and formulated an invitation to Sonneschein to become a candidate for the position he had just vacated. That petition, Sonneschein later averred, eventually was signed by 148 people—more than the total number who had voted *on both sides* at the April 18 general congregational meeting that had approved the rabbi's original resignation. "With feelings of joy and gratefulness," Sonneschein accepted the invitation and applied to replace himself.[18]

Up to this point Sonneschein's foes had focused on only his "moral character as a man and his good name as a rabbi." Now his trip to Boston opened a completely new issue: Sonneschein's predilections toward Unitarianism and whether because of that he might be unfit to occupy a pulpit not only at Shaare Emeth but in any Jewish congregation. What had been dissatisfaction with Sonneschein's personal behavior and with his avowedly theologic radicalism *within Judaism* now had become a much more serious question of whether Shaare Emeth members believed their rabbi to be no longer Jewish. On May 27 Jacob Furth and Nicholas Scharff, two of the congregation's most eminent members, visited Sonneschein "as a self-constituted committee of two." They informed him that they had proof of his alleged apostasy, that they wanted to avoid embarrassment both to the rabbi and to the congregation, and that they would suppress their information if Sonneschein would withdraw his candidacy. The rabbi angrily accused Furth and Scharff of attempting to intimidate him, and he forthwith refused their request. Shortly thereafter the board of trustees appointed a special committee to look into the rabbi's alleged relations with Unitarianism. Sonneschein publicly protested what he considered to be high-handed inquisitorial spying. In deference to the rabbi, and because some members appointed to the special committee preferred not

---

17. Sonneschein asserted that at the request of the couple he had performed only a civil ceremony and not a religious one, "just as any other officer empowered by the State." He pointed out that there was a "decided difference between marrying a couple as a rabbi and as a civil officer." *St. Louis Post-Dispatch*, May 28, 1886.

18. "Dr. Sonneschein's Written Statement," June 23, 1886, in Bernard Felsenthal Papers, AJA; Jacob Furth and Augustus Binswanger to Members of Congregation Shaare Emeth, June 28, 1886, in ibid. and also in Temple Shaare Emeth File, AJA, and in Rabbi Solomon H. Sonneschein File in library of Shaare Emeth Temple, St. Louis.

to serve on so delicate an assignment, the board asked Sonneschein to name ten people of his own choice from whom it (the board) would then select five to form that committee. Sonneschein indignantly refused.[19]

The board nevertheless proceeded with its investigation, through a specially appointed three-man committee. That committee, in turn, secured the services of attorney Samuel M. Lederer to go to Boston to get the facts concerning Sonneschein's contacts there with Unitarianism. Lederer accordingly met with Unitarian ministers Savage and Reynolds, as well as with several liberal Reform rabbis in the Boston area. At Lederer's request, Savage and Reynolds forwarded to the president of Shaare Emeth their assessments of Sonneschein's affinities toward Unitarianism. Neither seemed to feel Sonneschein was ready to abandon Judaism. Yet both worded their statements in such a way that one who wanted to might easily have come to a different conclusion: "[he] was doubtful as to whether he would be able conscientiously to remain in his position as a Jewish Rabbi"; "[he] seemed to be in much the same position which I occupied when I was about to leave [my] former church"; "whether, in event that his views should be too liberal for his own people, he should feel at home among us." In a lengthy notarized affidavit, Lederer summarized his own discussions with those ministers as well as with Boston rabbis Kaufmann Kohler (described as "the guiding force in the creation and adoption of the Pittsburgh Platform") and Solomon Schindler (a very close associate of Reverend Savage). Lederer reported that Sonneschein had complained to Reynolds that "Judaism was becoming too narrow for him," and that he [Sonneschein] "did not think his congregation would follow him in his liberal ideas." Rabbi Schindler, according to Lederer, believed that Sonneschein "belonged to that class of men who were very fond of sensation, and he must have expected that by coming to Boston and making overtures to Unitarianism, he would be received with open arms by them, and that it would be one of the greatest sensations of the day in

19. Jacob Furth and Augustus Binswanger to Members of Congregation Shaare Emeth, June 28, 1886, in Bernard Felsenthal Papers, AJA. Incredibly, throughout this entire "Sonneschein Affair" even the rabbi's opponents seemed to still hold him in high esteem in virtually everything except his personal "eccentricities." "Few men in St. Louis have contributed so much in gaining for us so high a position in the esteem of our Christian fellow-citizens," wrote the editor of the *Jewish Free Press* who passionately opposed Sonneschein on the Pittsburgh Platform. "Dr. Sonneschein stands head and shoulders above all other Israelites in the esteem of the Christian community. . . . Socially and externally Dr. Sonneschein has done more for Judaism in St. Louis than any other single man." *Jewish Free Press,* April 16, 1886. Yet in the adjacent column the *Jewish Free Press* printed a letter accusing Sonneschein of treacherous and deceitful perfidy, and of creating a crisis at Shaare Emeth just to get a higher salary.

the religious world." Lederer concluded that Sonneschein "went to Boston with a view of uniting himself with the Unitarians, provided he found them offering him sufficient inducements to do so, but not having been received as cordially as he had anticipated, he perhaps then abandoned the plan."[20]

The Shaare Emeth board sent copies of the Savage and Reynolds letters to Sonneschein, and asked him to appear at a special meeting on June 23 "to vindicate himself." (The board had not yet received the separate Lederer affidavit.) It was the first time in the history of American Judaism that a rabbi was summoned before his board to answer to such charges. Very careful of his words, Sonneschein read from a prepared statement. He first denied any obligation on his part even to answer to the allegations: "you are by no means a Sanhedrin," he challenged the board. Nevertheless, he agreed to respond in deference to "the large, intelligent element of Liberal Jews here and abroad." He would read his prepared statement in English, but he firmly insisted that he would respond to questions only in German. Asked why, he replied that he could express his indignation more forcefully that way. Told that some could not understand German that well, he arrogantly responded that their ignorance was not his concern. His discussions with the Unitarian ministers, Sonneschein averred, were "to ascertain how far I, as a Hebrew theologian, could conscientiously go to be accepted by the American Unitarian Association as a public lecturer for the advancement of that sacred cause which both the advanced American Jew and advanced American Christian have in common without losing the integrity and identity of my Hebrew affiliations of birth and conviction." Asked to comment about the Savage and Reynolds letters, Sonneschein responded defiantly: "Every word in those two letters is God's truth."[21]

That was about as much as the already hostile board of trustees was willing to take. It now irefully resolved not only to remove Sonneschein from consideration for reappointment but also to dismiss him at once as rabbi of Shaare Emeth rather than wait until October 1. The board's decision, however, as earlier, had to be ratified by the temple membership, and so another general meeting was scheduled for June 30, only one week

---

20. "Telegraphic Instructions to Mr. Lederer," St. Louis, May 31 and June 1, 1886, M. J. Savage to B. Hysinger, Boston, June 3, 1886, Grindall Reynolds to B. Hysinger, Boston, June 3, 1886, Affidavit of Samuel M. Lederer, Esq., St. Louis, June 11, 1886, all in Bernard Felsenthal Papers, AJA.

21. "Dr. Sonneschein's Written Statement," June 23, 1886, and Jacob Furth and Augustus Binswanger to Members of Congregation Shaare Emeth, June 23, 1886, in ibid. For a detailed account of the June 23 meeting, see *Jewish Free Press*, July 2, 1886.

away, for that purpose. During that week several important communications prepared Shaare Emeth membership for their deliberations. One was a lengthy document produced by the board that detailed all that had developed beginning with Sonneschein's sudden and unexplained April 1 resignation. Pointing out that the rabbi's "moral character and good name as a rabbi" might have been the issue before, the board stressed that now it had to be Sonneschein's extreme theologic beliefs and whether he considered himself a Jew or a Unitarian. Appended to the circular letter were copies of the Savage and Reynolds letters, Sonneschein's written statement to the board of June 23, the instructions given to Lederer, and the latter's detailed report on his investigatory interviews. Sonneschein published his own version of those developments, clarifying to Shaare Emeth members his side of all that had transpired. His lengthy statement was printed verbatim in the *Jewish Free Press*.[22]

On Wednesday, June 30, 1886, Shaare Emeth members met to decide on the board's action. By a vote of 112 to 68 they rejected the board's proposal that Sonneschein be dropped at once, and instead approved retaining him until October 1, the date set originally for his resignation. At the same time, the membership postponed for ten weeks, to September 12, the decision whether to consider Sonneschein as a candidate to succeed himself, providing time to get more definitive information on the Unitarian relationship.[23]

That decision was put off for another reason. It gave both sides time to reach an amicable solution, which many felt absolutely necessary considering Shaare Emeth's status by then as probably the most prominent Jewish congregation in St. Louis, and perhaps in the entire Midwest. Furthermore, influential and wealthy leaders and businessmen within the St. Louis Jewish community were arrayed on both sides—the likes of Moses Fraley, Isidor Bush, Nicholas Scharff, Benjamin Eiseman, August Frank, Joseph Schwab, Isaac Swope, William Stix, Jonathan Rice, Elias Michael, Louis Glaser, Adolph Baer, Leo Levis, Marcus Bernheimer, Jacob

---

22. *Jewish Free Press,* July 9, 1886. The circular letter was signed by only two of the three members of the ad hoc committee, Jacob Furth and Augustus Binswanger. The third member, Adolph Baer, did not sign because he did not know Lederer personally. Jacob Furth and Augustus Binswanger to Members of Congregation Shaare Emeth, St. Louis, June 28, 1886, in Bernard Felsenthal Papers, AJA, a copy in Temple Shaare Emeth File, AJA; M. J. Savage to Barney Hysinger, Boston, June 3, 1886, Grindall Reynolds to Barney Hysinger, Boston, June 3, 1886, Dr. Sonneschein's Written Statement, June 23, 1886, Affidavit of Samuel Lederer, Esq., June 11, 1886, and Telegraphic Instructions to Mr. Lederer, St. Louis, May 31 and June 1, 1886, all in Bernard Felsenthal Papers, AJA.

23. *Jewish Free Press,* September 10, 1886.

Furth, and Augustus Binswanger—and many felt that continued good personal and business relationships demanded a harmonious settlement of this erstwhile religious powder keg.

That became very clear at the September 12 general meeting. About two hundred members gathered in the Temple sanctuary in an atmosphere of anticipation. Very quickly and without any bitterness or rancor—indeed, almost anticlimactically, as the product of lots of behind-the-scenes negotiations came to fruition—the members approved a compromise proposed by the spokesmen on both sides, and gave unanimous approval in advance for the board of trustees to carry out the terms of that agreement. The board accordingly met on September 22. Without any expressed objections, the board tendered Sonneschein the post of rabbi for one year, at a salary of five thousand dollars. As prearranged, he promptly declined; and the following week, on October 1, he ceased to be Shaare Emeth's rabbi. Shaare Emeth agreed to pay him the five-thousand-dollar salary anyway; it was obviously a buy-out of his position. Shaare Emeth's search for a new rabbi, begun several months earlier, now would go on in earnest. "But," said the *St. Louis Post-Dispatch*, "there exists hardly a doubt that a church will be organized for him [Sonneschein] before long." That, it seems, was to be the final step in the Sonneschein compromise.[24]

Two days later, on September 24, at the initiative of Moses Fraley, who by the 1880s had emerged as a virtual power broker within the St. Louis Jewish community, a group of Sonneschein backers met at Fraley's sumptuous home at 3650 Lindell and took measures that resulted in the creation of Temple Israel. At that gathering Fraley stressed that no one held any antagonism toward Shaare Emeth; indeed, he hoped the best of friendly relations could be maintained. It was simply that a new congregation had become a necessity after several years of serious differences among intelligent people within Shaare Emeth over basic principles of Judaism. Nor was he concerned that many might view this action as a way "of maintaining a man." This was not a clash over personality or behavior; it focused only on fundamental principles of Judaism, and Sonneschein reflected the views of many who had become dissatisfied with Shaare Emeth's majority's too-conservative views. Accordingly Fraley proposed, and those present unanimously approved, a new congregation based on what he called "true and liberal Judaism," with Sonneschein as its rabbi. "We shall attempt to show," Fraley asserted, "that Judaism is alive in St. Louis, that we are in hearty sympathy with the

---

24. *St. Louis Post-Dispatch*, September 24, 1886. For accounts of what transpired at the meetings of September 12 and 22, see ibid. and *Jewish Free Press*, September 17 and 24, 1886.

progress made by our Christian brethren, and are not willing to remain in status quo." A committee of three—Fraley, Isaac Schwab, and Benjamin Altheimer—was designated to draft an appropriate statement for the public.[25]

Published in the press the next day, that statement focused on the need for a congregation with a "liberal and modern platform, something which . . . was needed in the city and which would have the effect of advancing Judaism in St. Louis." The implication seemed to be that Judaism as practiced elsewhere in St. Louis, and especially at Reform Shaare Emeth, had retrogressed to something not modern or liberal enough, and that was not advancing Judaism. Members of Shaare Emeth reacted immediately to what they considered a slur against them personally and against their congregation. About twenty-five men gathered on September 28 and passed a series of counterresolutions responding to those published by the pro-Sonneschein faction. The leaders of this group were Isidor Bush, Jacob Furth, Marcus Bernheimer, and Augustus Binswanger, as well as

---

25. *Jewish Free Press,* October 1, 8, and 15, 1886. The following account of the establishment of Temple Israel is based primarily upon this newspaper's accounts as well as *The Republican* (St. Louis), October 18, 1886, in Temple Israel File, AJA; *St. Louis Star and Times,* November 14, 1932, in Ferdinand M. Isserman Files, AJA; *Modern View,* October 8, 1936; Joseph O. Losos, *From Leffingwell to Spoede: Highlights in the History of Temple Israel,* 3–5; Samuel Rosenkranz, *A Centennial History of Temple Israel, 1886–1986,* 5–8.

Those who attended the September 24 meeting at Fraley's house—the "founders of Temple Israel"—included Benjamin Altheimer, Charles Bienenstock, Adolph Baer, David Eiseman, Benjamin Eiseman, Moses Fraley, Louis Frank, Meyer Friedman, M. Friedman, August Frank, Morris Glaser, David Herman, L. W. Heyman, M. Holzman, David Joseph, Isaac Koperlik, Abraham Kramer, A. Landauer, Adolph Loth, B. Loth, B. M. Loth, Gus A. Milius, George W. Milius, Leopold Moss, Charles Moss, Simon Mayer, Isaac Mayer, Elias Michael, Jacob Meyer, J. M. Pollack, Samuel Rauh, Jonathan Rice, I. B. Rosenthal, Isaac Schwab, Max Schwab, Leon Schwab, Jacob Schwab, Herman Sonnenfeld, Albert Singer, William Stix, Charles L. Swartz, Isaac Swope, Joel Swope, Meyer Swope, J. J. Wertheimer, Joseph Wolfort, and Raphael Weil. Those who did not attend the September 24 meeting but who shortly thereafter signed the group's statement, and whom Temple Israel accordingly includes among its "founders," are Samuel Bowman, Adolph Glaser, Joseph Glaser, Louis Glaser, Isaac Meyer, and Max Littman.

In addition to his role in the creation of Temple Israel, Moses Fraley was a driving force in such organizations as the YMHA and the United Charities (one of the forerunners of the present Jewish Federation of St. Louis). When he died in 1917, the *St. Louis Post-Dispatch* referred to him as "probably the most widely known Jewish resident of St. Louis." Burton A. Boxerman, "St. Louis Jewish Leaders," 16–25. For more on Fraley, see Moses Fraley File, AJA; *St. Louis Post-Dispatch,* November 4, 1915; and *Voice,* November 19, 1915.

President Barney Hysinger, who throughout the entire disquieting affair had presented an impartial front. This group strongly asserted that the congregation still embraced "liberal and modern" Judaism. The problems at Shaare Emeth, they maintained, did not emanate from differences over principle; indeed, in seventeen years Shaare Emeth had never rejected any *Reform* changes Sonneschein had proposed. But when he "attempted to foist upon them an intersectarian kind of *mixtum compositum* religion," one that appeared more like a form of Christianity than Judaism, that was too much for the congregation to accept. "It was all over a loss of confidence in the man as our Rabbi," this group averred, and Shaare Emeth could no longer abide Sonneschein as spiritual leader. (Sonneschein's investigations into Unitarianism had made it possible to strip completely—publicly, at least—the earlier expressed concerns about his personal behavior.) Although no changes resulted from the two opposing statements, a war of words seemed to have developed, with each side justifying its actions to the broader Jewish community as well as to the Christian community. Each side tried to make it appear that the separation was amicable, but it is questionable whether that was really so.[26]

Sonneschein conducted his last religious services at Shaare Emeth on Rosh Hashannah, Thursday, September 30. For Yom Kippur services on Friday evening, October 8, and Saturday, October 9, the Sonneschein faction rented separate quarters at Memorial Hall (a hall popularly used for art exhibits and lectures), located at Nineteenth and Lucas, where Sonneschein conducted services for the first time for what was to become Temple Israel.[27]

---

26. *Jewish Free Press*, October 1, 1886. Impressions have long persisted that Temple Israel came into existence as much for social reasons as for religious; that is, the "so that we can be with our own kind" syndrome. One can no doubt interpret some statements made by Temple Israel's founders that way, especially since many represented the affluent "elite" of St. Louis German Jewish society. In fairness to them, though, no clear evidence supports that perception. If it was true—and it may have been for some—it was well disguised behind the argument Temple Israel's founders publicized that they wanted a more liberal Reform congregation than what they had at Shaare Emeth, and with it a more liberal rabbi.

27. *Jewish Free Press*, September 24, and October 8, 15, and 22, 1886. Histories of Temple Israel state that their first services with Sonneschein officiating were on Rosh Hashannah of 1886. They are incorrect. Contemporary evidence indicates Sonneschein presided at Shaare Emeth on Rosh Hashannah, September 30. After all, his contract there did not expire until October 1. He officiated on Yom Kippur for an ad hoc gathering that later became Temple Israel. A Reverend H. Posert officiated at Shaare Emeth on Yom Kippur, and Jacob Furth delivered the sermon, "A Layman's Comments on the Judaism of America." Temple Israel was formally organized the day *after* Yom Kippur. *Jewish Free Press*, September 24 and October 11, 1886, *Republican*, October 11,

The day after Yom Kippur, on Sunday morning, October 10, 1886, the events of the past few years reached their climax with the formal organization of the new congregation. About one hundred people met at the Pickwick Theater Hall, on the northwest corner of Washington and Jefferson. Louis Glaser presided as the gathering duly approved a provisional constitution and then elected the first set of officers for the new congregation: Isaac Schwab, president; Charles Moss, vice president; Adolph Baer, treasurer; Adolph Loth, warden; and a board of directors consisting of Moses Fraley, Benjamin Eiseman, August Frank, S. B. Rosenthal, J. J. Wertheimer, Isaac Meyers, Adolph Kramer, Morris Glaser, and Joseph Wolfort. Then, "by a standing vote," the group unanimously elected Rabbi Sonneschein as their spiritual leader. Moses Fraley then led a discussion on topics that included finances, membership, and religious school. Members concurred that activities would be at rented quarters until they could construct a permanent temple site, which now became a project of priority importance. Fraley then proposed a name for the new congregation—"Temple Israel"—to which the membership agreed unanimously. The long-anticipated new liberal Reform congregation had finally come into being.[28]

Temple Israel immediately faced the problems of any new congregation, such as finances, religious school for young people, membership qualifications, and the establishment of a permanent home. Fortunately its founders included a good number of well-to-do families, mostly merchants and business and professional people. The congregation rapidly established a religious school, with Moses Fraley's daughter Sadie in charge. A Ladies' Aid Society was soon organized, as were a choral society and other ancillary groups. A variety of fund-raising projects to finance construction of a temple building reached fruition on August 31, 1888, with the formal dedication of a beautiful stone-faced Romanesque-style edifice located at the corner of Leffingwell and Pine. In the meantime, the congregation rented at least three places for its activities. Religious services were conducted first at Memorial Hall, and then at the First Christian Church on the southeast corner of Seventeenth and Pine. The Pickwick Theater Hall became the temporary home for the religious school, called for a while the Hillel Sabbath School. It was also where Rabbi Sonneschein soon initiated Sunday morning lectures for those who might have missed services on Friday evening or Saturday. The "lectures"

1886, copy in Temple Israel File, AJA. For histories of Temple Israel, see Losos, *From Leffingwell to Spoede* and Rosenkranz, *History of Temple Israel.*

28. *Republican,* October 11, 1886, in Temple Israel File, AJA.

soon became regular Sunday morning services and, as might be expected, became a controversial issue within the Jewish community, even though they did not supplant regular Sabbath services.[29]

One especially vexing problem facing the new Temple Israel centered around burial facilities. As long as the seceders had been members of Shaare Emeth, Mt. Sinai Cemetery had been available, owned and operated jointly since 1869 by Shaare Emeth and B'nai El. But burial there was limited to Jewish families of those two congregations. Now Temple Israel would have to make some arrangement with the existing cemetery association, many of whom as members of Shaare Emeth garnered less than friendly attitudes toward those who had split away. The alternative was to establish a new cemetery, a rather costly venture.

Accordingly, Temple Israel appointed a committee of Abraham Kramer, Isaac Koperlik, and Charles Moss to present the new congregation's application for membership in the Mt. Sinai Cemetery Association. (It probably was not just coincidental that Koperlik was the current secretary of the association and that the other two were active on its board of directors.) In contrast with the very friendly discussions in 1869 when the new Shaare Emeth had entered into its agreement with B'nai El, the negotiations this time were far from amicable. In fact, this cemetery episode may have reflected, perhaps more than any others, the real animosities and hostilities that had been engendered during the Sonneschein controversy. Contributors to various eleemosynary organizations actually canceled their pledges rather than associate even in charitable work with fellow Jews for whom they had come to hold such bitter feelings. "The issues involved are far greater than would appear on the surface," wrote the

---

29. For some of the controversy over Sunday services, see observations and comments in *Jewish Free Press*, October 29, 1886, January 21, August 19, September 16, October 7 and 14, and November 4, 1887, and January 6, 1888. The issue of Sunday services aroused controversies within Jewish communities throughout the United States. The idea was totally rejected by traditional Jewry. Even within Reform congregations many rejected this innovation as a weakening of the traditional Saturday Sabbath and an unwarranted and condescending way to solicit approbation from Christian Americans. Sunday services proved popular for several decades only among the intense advocates of the extremely liberal Pittsburgh Platform. Sunday services were but one of numerous criticisms by St. Louis Reform Jews that Temple Israel had crossed the line from Judaism to something else. When a writer for the *St. Louis Globe-Democrat* expressed surprise at hearing the popular Christian hymn "Abide With Me" sung at a Hebrew temple [Temple Israel], the editor of the *Jewish Free Press*, himself an avowed liberal Reform Jew, responded derisively: "Please, Mr. *Globe-Democrat*, do not mix things up. The hymn 'Abide With Me' was not, and never will be, sung in a *Hebrew* temple. It was no surprise to us [that it was sung at Temple Israel]." *Jewish Free Press*, January 21, 1887.

editor of the *Jewish Free Press*. "We see a heavily-laden cloud threatening disruption to the harmonious feeling which has ever characterized Jewish councils in St. Louis."[30]

Nevertheless, discussion on the cemetery proceeded apace. The main stumbling blocks were finances and personal sentiments. The financial issues proved to be easily overcome, and in short order reasonable men came to reasonable arrangements. A more serious obstacle, however, was the reticence of some members of the existing cemetery association to accept Temple Israel because they felt the new congregation and its rabbi had strayed outside of Judaism. At least two general membership meetings conducted "long and bitter" discussions before the issue finally was resolved, with the association finally admitting Temple Israel by a less than ardent 56–32 vote. On November 7, 1887, a revised corporate charter came into being for what now was called "The New Mt. Sinai Cemetery Association." The association and the cemetery, at its original location at 8430 Gravois Road, remain in existence today.[31]

Despite the new congregation's almost avid eagerness to have him as their rabbi, Sonneschein's tenure at Temple Israel turned out to be short and as tempestuous as his years at Shaare Emeth. Undoubtedly he was held in high regard by the larger St. Louis community, and that undeniably helped the new congregation get a solid start. His many talks, in both German and English, whether as congregational sermons or as community lectures, attracted large and attentive audiences. He was especially popular with new immigrant groups. Nevertheless, his rabbinate at Temple Israel was plagued by "eccentricities" not unlike those that had contributed to his difficulties at Shaare Emeth. Bad feelings soon developed between the rabbi and members of the congregation, and in 1890, after serving for just four years, he was forced to resign. He was only fifty-two years old at the time. His successor, twenty-four-year-old Rabbi Leon Harrison, led Temple Israel, beginning in 1891, for the next thirty-seven years, during which time it emerged as a major institution in the St. Louis Jewish community as well as in the overall St. Louis religious and secular communities.[32]

---

30. *Jewish Free Press*, November 19, 1886. Fortunately those animosities disappeared after several years. Losos, *From Leffingwell to Spoede*, 5.

31. *Jewish Free Press*, November 5 and 19, 1886; *Voice*, November 24 and 30, 1911; *Modern View 25*, 213.

32. After Sonneschein left Temple Israel, he went briefly to Europe, to recuperate from what he said was poor health. Upon his return to St. Louis, his wife Rosa left him, and they were divorced in January 1893. Sonneschein later remarried; Rosa never did. In 1899 Sonneschein accepted the pulpit of Temple B'nai Yeshurun in Des Moines,

Of all the truly outstanding rabbis who have served in St. Louis within all denominations of Judaism, many consider Leon Harrison the most eminent. He was born in 1866 in Liverpool, England, scion of a longtime Sephardic family; he grew up, though, in Brooklyn, New York. He attended public school there and then attended classes at the College of the City of New York before graduating from Columbia University in 1887 with Phi Beta Kappa honors. Shortly thereafter he was ordained at the Emanu-El Theological Seminary in New York and became rabbi of Temple Israel in Brooklyn. The young rabbi earned widespread acclaim when he delivered a notedly impressive oration at the funeral of the renowned Henry Ward Beecher. Then in 1891 Harrison assumed the pulpit of Temple Israel in St. Louis. Fully devoted to his congregation—he never married—Harrison ministered faithfully to its religious and pastoral needs. But it was his exemplary Judaic scholarship and brilliant oratory that elevated him to pinnacles of rabbinic eminence, both in St. Louis and nationally. A consummate champion of liberal Reform Judaism, Harrison emphasized the ethical similarities of all religious faiths and broadened the practice, begun by Sonneschein, of exchanging pulpits with Christian clergymen; at the same time, though, he fervently and passionately stressed the special qualities of Judaism, whether Orthodox or Reform, which he believed made it the most gratifying of all faiths. When he met his tragic and untimely death in 1928, falling from a crowded New York City subway station platform, eulogies proclaimed him "the greatest pulpit orator in St. Louis," an urbane scholar who had enriched the cultural life of the city, and "one of those who helped to make this a thinking community as well as a community of workaday achievement."[33]

Iowa, where he served for six years until 1905. He then retired to St. Louis, where he died on October 3, 1905, at the age of seventy. He was buried in New Mt. Sinai Cemetery. *Voice,* September 10, 1891, October 7, 1908, February 19, 1909, and April 8, 1910; Losos, *From Leffingwell to Spoede,* 7–8. Meanwhile, after her divorce from the rabbi, Rosa Sonneschein went on to a brilliant and colorful career in journalism, publishing the *American Jewess* from 1895 to 1899. It was the first English-language journal in America edited independently by women. In addition, Rosa became ardently active in the Zionist movement, and her journal was one of the first to spread the Zionist message of Theodor Herzl and Max Nordau. She was one of the very few women who participated in the important early Zionist conclaves of the late nineteenth and early twentieth centuries. She died in St. Louis in 1932, at the age of eighty-five, and is buried, like her husband, in New Mt. Sinai Cemetery. Porter, "Rosa Sonneschein and *The American Jewess* Revisited," 125–26.

33. Losos, *From Leffingwell to Spoede,* 8–15; Adler, ed., *American Jewish Yearbook, 5664,* 62. Israel Treiman, prominent attorney and the first Jew ever to achieve a Rhodes Scholarship and whose early career was very much influenced by Rabbi Harrison,

Leon Harrison was one of two new rabbis who appeared on the St. Louis scene at this time. The other, who actually preceded Harrison by a few years, was Samuel Sale of Shaare Emeth. Both served their congregations with dedication and distinction for lengthy tenures, each for more than three decades; and both attained overwhelming respect and prestige not only within the Jewish community but also in the broader St. Louis religious and secular communities.

Internal dissension did not leave Shaare Emeth with Sonneschein. Following his departure, Shaare Emeth first sought to employ David Philipson, then rabbi of a congregation in Baltimore. Even though offered more money, Philipson declined the invitation, preferring to remain in the East, and so lay leaders and guest rabbis continued to lead services at Shaare Emeth. On April 3, 1887, Rabbi Samuel Sale of Chicago's Congregation Anshei Ma'ariv came to St. Louis as guest lecturer for a Sunday evening program conducted at Shaare Emeth and sponsored by the YMHA. So impressed were Shaare Emeth's leaders and members that they shortly thereafter sent a committee (Nicholas Scharff, Louis M. Helman, and Jacob Furth) to Chicago to talk with him, and this resulted in tendering him the offer to be their new rabbi. On Saturday morning, June 18, 1887, more than seven hundred people filled the sanctuary for Sale's inaugural service. His presentation was universally praised, including his attire: he wore a plain business suit rather than the traditional dress coat to which the congregation had been accustomed during the Sonneschein years. Sale's warm reception no doubt was enhanced by the announcement that he planned to alternate his sermons between English and German, a practice many St. Louis German Jews—and non-Jews too—still found quite satisfying.[34]

---

remembered the rabbi fondly: "He was an institution in St. Louis. What a voice! What a personality! . . . Harrison had a facility for speaking with the most beautiful vocabulary I've ever heard anybody use." Author's interview with Israel Treiman, Clayton, Mo., September 8, 1982, text of interview in possession of author and in St. Louis Jewish Community Archives, St. Louis. For more on Rabbi Harrison, see *Voice*, March 21, 1902, June 4 and September 3, 1909, February 25, 1910, June 23, 1916, and October 3, 1919; Adler, ed., *American Jewish Yearbook, 5664*, 62; and John W. Leonard, ed., *The Book of St. Louisans*, 1906 ed., 259.

34. *Jewish Free Press*, October 29, and November 5 and 12, 1886, April 8, May 13, and June 17 and 24, 1887; *Voice*, May 31, 1912. Sale was born on October 29, 1854, in Louisville, Kentucky. He was the first St. Louis rabbi who was a native-born American. He was educated in the Louisville public schools, but received his higher education at the University of Berlin. He was then ordained at the Rabbinical Seminary in Berlin. He then returned to the United States and served as rabbi at Har Sinai Congregation in Baltimore and Anshei Ma'ariv in Chicago before coming to Shaare

Despite the enthusiastic welcome, Sale's first few years at Shaare Emeth proved somewhat tenuous and almost disastrous. In fact, some who knew Sale before he came to St. Louis warned that if Shaare Emeth had had problems with Sonneschein, it could have even more with Sale. "If Sonneschein's peculiar cast of religious sentiments and teachings verged on Christianity," one such observer wrote, "his successor's thoughts and efforts run in the direction of Agnosticism, or rather Atheism sugar-coated with Judaic ardor and Bible quotations."[35]

A major conflict erupted very soon over the convulsive issue of Sunday services. Sale insisted that Sunday services were necessary to attract younger people as well as to "keep progress in America." He claimed this was clearly understood by the committee that had interviewed him in Chicago. The Shaare Emeth board of trustees, on the other hand, preferred more emphasis on Friday evening services; only if that proved unsatisfactory would it consider Sunday morning proceedings. Sale remained adamant and even threatened to resign. The board's response (by a vote of 11 to 1) was that Sunday morning *lectures* would be permissible, but not services, and if that was unacceptable, the board would release the rabbi from his contract. Clearly displeased, Sale impulsively resigned and instituted measures to return to Anshei Ma'ariv in Chicago. But both sides apparently reconsidered and Sale remained after all, agreeing to the board's compromise proposal of Sunday morning lectures rather than services. He continued the practice for a while and then quietly and without fanfare discontinued it when interest and attendance waned.[36]

Sale's early tribulations at Shaare Emeth entailed more than just Sunday services. Neither congregational records nor the press provide the details, but they give clues that something was amiss. Early in 1888 a St. Louis correspondent for the national *American Israelite*, referring to developments in St. Louis and at Shaare Emeth in particular, wrote: "The community is tired of the bickerings, and we ought to have peace for once." Rabbi Moritz Spitz of B'nai El, also editor of the *Jewish Voice* in St. Louis, who disagreed with Sale in the latter's excessive religious liberalism, commented that

---

Emeth in 1887. While serving at Shaare Emeth, Sale also held an adjunct chair in Hebrew at Washington University. Adler, ed., *American Jewish Yearbook, 5664*, 94.

35. Quoted from a Chicago newspaper in *Jewish Free Press*, July 22, 1887. Similar critical comments in Chicago and New York papers about Sale's ultraliberal leanings appeared in ibid., August 19 and 26, 1887.

36. Ibid., August 19, September 16, October 7 and 14, and November 4, 1887; *Voice*, January 6, 1888. Other than briefly at Shaare Emeth, Sunday services existed in St. Louis only at Temple Israel, where they were discontinued by Rabbi Harrison in 1904 due to poor attendance. Losos, *From Leffingwell to Spoede*, 12.

"to retain his services the congregation [Shaare Emeth] has made him concessions and yielded to every one of his wishes, and brought enormous sacrifice for his sake." Rumors abounded that Shaare Emeth and its rabbi were at loggerheads, that another Sonneschein-type falling out was in the making, and that Sale was leaving for a New York pulpit. Regardless of the rumors and speculation, though, Sale and his congregation reconciled their differences. By the end of 1888 reports of internal dissension had disappeared, and Sale settled into what became a widely respected and highly acclaimed rabbinical tenure at Shaare Emeth that lasted until he retired in 1919.[37]

With Sale and Harrison established in their respective congregations, a golden era of Messing-Spitz-Sale-Harrison rabbinic leadership embraced St. Louis Reform Jewry. Remarkably capable and highly respected in both the Jewish and the Christian communities, this "big four" dominated the St. Louis Reform religious scene until the World War I era and beyond.[38]

---

37. *Voice*, January 6, 13, and 27, February 3, and March 2, 16, and 23, 1888.
38. United Hebrew, B'nai El, Shaare Emeth, and Temple Israel remained the only Reform temples in St. Louis until after World War II.

13

HERE COME THE RUSSIANS!

The last two decades of the nineteenth century and the first two of the twentieth, the period roughly covering the Reform "golden era" of Messing, Spitz, Sale, and Harrison, was also a time of rapid growth in the St. Louis Orthodox community. It was an increase that mirrored what happened in cities elsewhere in the United States, as large numbers of immigrant Jews sought refuge from cruel and oppressive measures foisted upon them by tyrannical antisemitic governments and leaders of eastern Europe. About two million Jews came to the United States during that forty-year period; some fifty thousand settled in St. Louis. With them came a concomitant increase in the city's Orthodox Jewish institutions.

In contrast with the earlier German/Reform organizations, especially the congregations, data and records documenting most late-nineteenth-century Orthodox institutions are extremely sparse. That applies especially to the *shuls*. One reason is that most of them no longer exist, and any records they might have had—whether in English, Yiddish, or Hebrew—unfortunately disappeared with them. So many of the new immigrants belonged to small groups that never constituted more than a transient *minyan* anyway. Often they occupied no more than a rented store, or a room over a store, and existed for no longer than weeks or months. So, too, has the passage of time taken away people who might have provided memoirs or reminiscences.

Those groups that achieved a modicum of stability, such as Beth Hamedrosh Hagodol, Sheerith Israel, and B'nai Amoona, eventually found themselves in a position to rent a building—usually a small residence—and to make a few interior changes, and to then become known as *shuls*. The buildings were modest at best. One room (or two) constituted a place for prayer. A makeshift cabinet housed a Sefer Torah that some immigrant had managed lovingly to bring with him on the long voyage from Russia. A few chairs and a table or two, a cabinet in which to store books—and that was it. A back or upstairs room or a basement served as a *cheder* where children were taught to read Hebrew by the *shammos* or some "rabbi" seeking to eke out a meager living. Often the building became a place of respite for poor or itinerant Jews who needed a temporary place to sleep. Many such establishments bore no special name; they were known simply as a Chevrah Kadisha, or the *shul* on Wash Street, or Yonkel Goldberg's *shul* on Seventh Street, or the *shul* across from the livery stable or next door to Sorkin's butcher shop. These congregations—if one can even use the term "congregation"—consisted of immigrants who felt a strong need to perpetuate religious and cultural mores that were generations old, and accordingly who wished to make only the most necessary modifications to accommodate their new environs. Most of these groups flourished only briefly and then simply faded away, as their membership either moved elsewhere, or for a variety of reasons simply changed their views on how to be both American and Jewish. Most maintained neither formal organization nor records; they saw no need for them. Finances were often on a very loose ad hoc basis. In fact, with very few exceptions, frustratingly little data exists about so many of those institutions that nurtured so many Russian immigrants in so many ways.

Fortunately much better documentation is available for Orthodox bodies founded after 1900. What little we know about the pre-1900 Orthodox congregations comes primarily from very brief and terse newspaper notices about religious holiday services and equally brief and terse listings in city directories. What follows, then, is regrettably not much more than a bare "laundry list" of Orthodox institutions rather than a more detailed narrative.

As already noted, by 1880 Sheerith Israel (later B'nai Amoona), Chevrah Kadisha, and Beth Hamedrosh Hagodol had already come into being, although none were well established or affluent enough to have advanced beyond the "rented facilities" stage. On April 13, 1880, Orthodox Jews in the northern part of the city associated with Sheerith Israel established the "Hebrew Family Benevolent Association." Its purpose was to provide financial and medical assistance especially, though not exclusively, for themselves and for other needy immigrant families. (This was in addition to aid already being provided by the German/Reform-dominated and more secular-oriented United Jewish Charities and its various affiliates.) Organized at a meeting held at Sheerith Israel's facilities at 926 North Sixth Street (Sixth and Wash), elected officers of this group included J. J. Isaacs, president, and S. S. Sachs, treasurer. It was a forerunner of numerous similar mutual aid societies, most of which existed for a brief time and then either disbanded or, more often, joined with others to provide better services. Most of them, as with the Hebrew Family Benevolent Association, were natural outgrowths of congregational affiliation—which probably explains their brief tenures and paucity of records. As to this particular association, it seems to have faded into oblivion just as Sheerith Israel itself eventually did.[1]

By September 1883 the *Tribune* estimated that about fifteen hundred Jewish families were in St. Louis. Except for increasing numbers of eastern European immigrants, apparently no major additions had occurred within the Orthodox Jewish community for a few years, unless they were of the small transient *minyan* variety. A very comprehensive 1883 history of St. Louis, which included a detailed section on religious institutions of all faiths, listed in addition to the long-established United Hebrew, B'nai El, and Shaare Emeth only two Orthodox congregations, Sheerith Israel and Chevrah Kadisha. Sheerith Israel, that historian wrote very briefly, "is a religious association of Hebrews who occupy a rented room and worship according to the most ancient forms." Its officers included M. Harris, president; H. Abrahams, vice president; L. Lipman, secretary; J. H. Abrahams, treasurer; and D. Priwer, L. Michael, and P. Wohl, trustees. Rabbi R. Grodsky officiated at services, and J. Lowenstein was the *shammos*. The same historian described Chevrah Kadisha even more tersely, stating only that it "meets for worship on Seventh Street, between Franklin and Wash Street. Rev. M. Liberstin [Max Lieberstein] is rabbi."[2]

In 1884 the schism occurred within Sheerith Israel, the "Krakower Shul," that resulted in B'nai Amoona coming into being. Shortly following that split, the new B'nai Amoona rented quarters at Ninth and Washington and employed Rabbi Adolph Rosentreter as its spiritual leader. What was left of Sheerith Israel moved from Sixth and Wash to a new rented room at Ninth and Franklin, and Reverend L. Rosenblatt led their services. Sheerith Israel eventually lost its separate identity and merged with the more successful B'nai Amoona. While it existed, though, its members conducted their services at several different locations and under different spiritual leaders. In 1885, for instance, Sheerith Israel was still at Ninth and Franklin with Reverend Rosenblatt their spiritual leader. The next year the

---

1. *Tribune*, April 16, 1880. A similar mutual aid group was organized in 1884, the Mutual Benevolent Union. Its officers were H. Berwin, president, and Max Manuel, secretary and treasurer. The organization of this group provided another occasion for the German/Reform–oriented *Tribune* to praise Russian immigrants for their industrious self-help and for becoming Americanized. Like so many other similar groups, the Mutual Benevolent Union eventually faded away. Ibid., February 15, 1884.

2. Scharf, *Saint Louis City and County*, vol. 2, 1740. Based upon the address, this Chevrah Kadisha may have been in actuality Beth Hamedrosh Hagodol. Yet other data identifies Chevrah Kadisha and Beth Hamedrosh Hagodol as separate synagogues and at different locations. See, for instance, *Tribune*, May 11 and 25, and September 14, 1883, and *Jewish Free Press*, September 9, 1887, and August 31, 1888.

dwindling congregation moved to new rented quarters at Eleventh and Franklin, and Reverend M. Feinschreiber replaced Rosenblatt.[3]

By no means does the history of the Jewish community in that period (or since, for that matter) center only on congregations. In fact, when the *Tribune* stated in 1883 that approximately fifteen hundred Jewish families then lived in St. Louis, it also pointed out that fewer than half actually belonged to any congregation.[4] Historians have emphasized the secular and nonobservant nature of so many Jews prior to the arrival of the eastern European Orthodox Jews. The *Tribune* made much of a most unseemly event on Kol Nidre night of 1882, for instance, when four young men emerged from Shaare Emeth after services, lit up cigars, and chattered loudly and most unbecomingly about going to a nearby bar for a drink. "We would rather see a good Christian than a bad Jew," commented editor Rabbi Spitz about this episode. Yet overlooked was that they *had* attended services, even though their behavior afterward was reprehensible. Furthermore, if fewer than half of St. Louis's Jews actually belonged to congregations, many of the *other* half attended services, even if only for holiday worship. For while decrying lack of attendance at many regular Sabbath services, rabbis and congregational officers exulted over packed sanctuaries not only on the High Holy Days but also on the so-called "minor" festivals of Passover, Succoth, and Shavuoth. Every seat was taken, for instance, at B'nai El's Passover services in 1881, with people even standing in the rear; not as many attended on the seventh day, but it was reported at least as still very crowded. "Fun" festivals such as Purim and Chanukah also attracted large numbers, especially for adult dances and balls and for children's programs.[5]

But Jewish community activities extended far beyond just the temple and synagogue. Probably nothing illustrates this better than the different

---

3. *Tribune*, May 11 and 25, and September 14, 1883; *Jewish Free Press*, September 18, 1885, June 4 and September 24, 1886, and September 9, 1887; *Voice*, March 23 and August 31, 1888.

4. *Tribune*, September 14, 1883. This is one of the few available references to the size of the St. Louis Jewish community. One can determine the Jewish population at any given time only by estimates, as census figures then did not identify people by religion. The problem, though, is conflicting estimates, as found in *Tribune*, January 30 and August 6, 1880, February 4, 1881, December 22, 1882, and September 4, 1883. A significant figure, though, was that reported by Elias Michael in 1898 in his annual report as president of the Jewish Alliance. He made a "conservative estimate" of about fifteen thousand Russian Jews alone in St. Louis, asserting that they already outnumbered the "old line" German Jewish population. *Voice*, October 14, 1898.

5. *Tribune*, April 22, 1881, and October 6, 1882. See also ibid., September 26, 1879, April 9, 1880, November 3, 1882, and August 17, September 14, and December 7, 1883.

extracongregational involvements that St. Louis Jewry engaged in *as Jews* (this would exclude business and civic activities that had nothing to do with religious affiliation). For example, some *Jewish-oriented* businesses and occupations catered uniquely and almost entirely (though not exclusively) to Jews simply because of the very nature of the business or occupation. Such was Henry Kohn's Kosher Sausage Factory at 1303 Carondelet. The *Tribune* even commented in a rare editorial endorsement that Jews should patronize this enterprise not only because Kohn's product was not *traif*, but because it even cost less than *traif* sausage. Mr. M. Lederer offered "all kinds of Kosher smoked beef" at his stand in Union Market. Israel Fleischman advertised kosher sausage, smoked tongue, and corned and smoked beef at Fleischman's Kosher Meat Market at 911 North Seventh. Mr. C. Gregor sold kosher sausage and smoked beef at his confectionery at 1521 South Broadway. He also sold matzos, matzo meal, and other appropriate products for Passover, as did L. Lichtenstein at 1415 North Twelfth, and L. Weiss, agent for Korsoski's Chicago Matzos, in his store at 623 Locust. And of course services offered by *mikvahs*—one in the 900 block of North Seventh, another at 910 Biddle, and still another at 211 North Seventh—and *mohels*—Levy Rosenblatt and Simon Gutfreund, for example—represented singularly Jewish enterprises having no congregational affiliation.[6]

Involving many more Jews, however, were the numerous social and eleemosynary associations to which St. Louis Jewry voluntarily gave time, service, money, and energy—activities and associations singularly Jewish in nature. How many of these people also belonged to congregations and participated in congregational-associated organizations (such as ladies' auxiliaries, men's clubs, young people's groups, etc.) cannot be determined; some overlap certainly existed. But an examination of noncongregational Jewish organizations indicates that many Jews who undoubtedly did not belong to temples or synagogues actively participated in the Jewish community in other ways, especially in benevolent and social groups. A directory of Jewish organizations published in 1880 provides an example of the extent of that participation. The directory first listed the existing (in 1880) formally organized congregations: United Hebrew, B'nai El, Shaare Emeth, and Sheerith Israel. Two cemetery associations were included: Mt. Sinai Cemetery Association and Mount Olive Cemetery Association. The directory then listed eight active benevolent societies and their secretaries: United Hebrew Relief Association, Augustus

6. Ibid., February 20, May 7 and 14, and October 29, 1880, January 7 and 28, 1881, October 13, 1882, and February 15, 1884; *Jewish Free Press*, December 18, 1885, and January 1, 1886; *Voice*, April 17, 1891, and May 10, 1912.

Binswanger, secretary; the Ladies' Hebrew Relief Society, Mrs. Henry J. Messing, secretary; the Ladies' Zion Society, Mrs. Joseph Cook, secretary; the Ladies' Widows and Orphans Society, Mrs. M. Linz, secretary; the Ladies' Sewing Society, Mrs. M. J. Steinberg, secretary; Mercy and Truth, Jacob Rawak, secretary; the Hebrew Benevolent Society, Aaron Gershon, secretary; and the Hebrew Mutual Benefit Society, E. Liebreich, secretary. The newspaper indicated that there were more organizations, but they had not submitted their information in time to be included (that would explain the absence of at least Chevrah Kadisha Congregation and Sheerith Israel Cemetery Association). Several, though not all, literary and social societies followed: the YMHA Association, Moses L. Wieder, secretary; the Ladies' Pioneer Society, Carrie Newmark, secretary; and the Harmonie Club, M. Linz, secretary. One community educational institution was listed: the Hebrew Free School Association, Aaron Gershon, secretary.[7]

Perhaps indicative of how broadly St. Louis Jewry was involved in Jewish-oriented activities and affairs was the impressive roster of Jewish fraternal groups, which served all sorts of functions ranging from purely social to educational and mutual aid and charitable, and which had absolutely nothing to do with congregational affiliation. The earliest such association in St. Louis Jewish history probably was Missouri Lodge of B'nai B'rith, established in 1855. By 1880 additional B'nai B'rith lodges in St. Louis included Ebn Ezra No. 47, Achim No. 175, Julius Fuerst No. 106, and Young America No. 309. In addition to B'nai B'rith, at least two more national Jewish organizations—this would exclude groups such as the Freemasons that crossed religious lines—had established lodges in St. Louis. One was the Independent Order of Kesher Shel Barzel; six separate Kesher Shel Barzel lodges existed in St. Louis, five men's and one women's. Four lodges of the Independent Order of the Free Sons of Israel also flourished. In addition, at least six more independent and unaffiliated fraternal organizations were listed in the directory.[8]

A comparable directory of Jewish organizations in 1902 showed a continued active involvement by St. Louis Jewry in Jewish affairs of all sorts. Since so much of the population increase in the 1880s and 1890s resulted from the arrival of eastern European immigrants, one can reasonably infer that these new St. Louis Jews participated just as enthusiastically in all sorts of congregational and noncongregational activities. Thus the 1902 directory listed four Reform and six Orthodox congregations (but none of their affiliated organizations such as men's and women's and young people's auxiliaries); two Reform and two Orthodox cemeteries; fifteen

---

7. *Tribune*, April 9, 1880.
8. Ibid.

charitable organizations, both men's and women's; two lodges of the Independent Order of the Free Sons of Israel; four lodges of B'nai B'rith; two lodges of the Sons of Benjamin; fourteen lodges of the Progressive Order of the West; ten lodges of the Order of B'rith Abraham; nine lodges of the Independent Order of B'rith Abraham (a different fraternal group); two lodges of Kesher Shel Barzel; four of the Independent Order of the Western Star; and four independent women's lodges.[9]

All the above may be a cold and statistical laundry list of organizations, but it says something very important. It indicates that even if fewer than half of St. Louis's Jews affiliated with congregations, nevertheless many more engaged *as Jews* in a variety of other community matters. Furthermore, one cannot overlook the nature of that involvement. True, some was purely social or otherwise internally focused culturally and educationally. But dominating most of those activities were the fundamental Jewish concepts of *tzedakah* and *tikkun olom,* the concepts of helping others, Jew and non-Jew alike. Many of those groups were mutual aid and benefit societies. For if Jews had learned throughout history that they had to rely upon themselves in the face of adversity, they also lived the basic tenet found in *Ethics of the Fathers:* "If I am not for myself, who will be? But if I am *only* for myself, what am I?" That explains why so many Jews participated vibrantly in a variety of community-oriented activities outside the temple and the synagogue, and why that involvement proved so productive and positive for not only the Jewish population but also the larger St. Louis community.

Despite the general paucity of data on pre-1900 Orthodox institutions, two institutions are well recorded. One still exists as a very important part of today's Jewish community: the Chesed Shel Emeth Society, with which are associated a cemetery and a *shul.* The other was the Orthodox congregation Sheerith S'fard, no longer in existence today, but very prominent from the mid-1880s until the World War II era.

The Chesed Shel Emeth Society originated from a need felt by Orthodox Jewish immigrants for more satisfactory burial facilities. As they began to arrive in large numbers in the 1880s, these immigrants, mostly from the Ukraine and western Russia, felt shunned by the German/Reform population, and at ease only among the relatively small number of Orthodox Jews then living in St. Louis. They found only two *shuls* where they were comfortable worshiping, the "Latvian Shul" (Beth Hamedrosh Hagodol) and the "Krakower Shul" (Sheerith Israel). But as their numbers grew, Russian immigrants increasingly sought to be more self-sustaining rather than mere "guests," albeit welcome guests. That applied especially

---

9. *Voice,* December 5, 1902.

to burial facilities. Sheerith Israel had a cemetery, which operated under strict Orthodox *halacha*, but the Russians preferred their own. (The Reform cemeteries, of course, were anathema to them.) Equally important, many of the new arrivals brought with them a strong desire to perpetuate the "mitzvah of honoring the dead," the age-old *halachic* ritual of preparing the deceased for burial.

To those ends, then, during Passover of 1888 a group of immigrants informally organized the Chesed Shel Emeth ("Kindness of Truth") Society. In November of that year they held their first formal meeting and elected officers: Moses Sherman, president; Jacob Laibel, vice president; Mordecai Greenspan, secretary; Isaac Goldman, financial secretary; and Abraham Koplochinsky, *shammos*. They also designated twelve men to be *mis'askim* (those who actually prepare the corpse for burial). Dues of twenty-five cents per member were collected, plus welcome gratuities, and the organization came into being with a modest treasury of $18.60.[10]

Among the Society's first needs was ground for a cemetery. A committee of Chaim Albert, Jacob Laibel, and John Helman eventually found suitable land, costing thirty-one hundred dollars, in what is now suburban University City, at 7500 Olive Street Road where it intersects with Hanley Road. (Meanwhile, the Society rented a small part of Sheerith Israel Cemetery for temporary burials.) Chesed Shel Emeth members diligently raised funds to meet expenses, collecting literally pennies and nickels from poor immigrant Jews. By February 1889 the organization had gathered fifty dollars to make a down payment on a hearse; one of the members, a Mr. Prelutsky, volunteered to drive his own horse without pay. The final payment on the hearse about a year later occasioned a grand celebration at Beth Hemedrosh Hagodol Synagogue, with a festive parade—a *siyum havogen* (a "celebration of the wagon")—through the streets of what was already an overwhelmingly Orthodox Jewish neighborhood, bounded by Sixth and Cass and Eleventh and Franklin. By May 1, 1893, Chesed Shel

---

10. David Epstein, ed., *Jubilee Book Commemorating the 50th Anniversary of the Chesed Shel Emeth Society in Saint Louis, 1888–1938*, 13–18. Those designated as official *mis'askim* were Isaac Jacob Oxenhandler, Hirsch Bortnick, Moses Barash, Solomon Weisman, Zelig Silverman, Menasha Yatkeman, Chaim Lukatcher, Joseph Malinoff, Hirsch Eckert, Hirsch Forman, Faivush Rothman, and Israel Jacob Rovitsky. One of the first persons the Society buried was a woman, a Mrs. Rosenbloom. The wife of the *shammas*, Mrs. Abraham Koplochinsky, performed the ritual services. Female *mis'askot* were soon thereafter selected to prepare deceased women for burial. Ibid., 18. Chesed Shel Emeth's first board of directors consisted of Hyman Elbert, Isaac Jacob Oxenhandler, Nahum Arsht, Hirsch Bortnick, Moses Barash, David Goldberg, Solomon Glassman, Isaac Dubinsky, Echiel Hadas, Solomon Weisman, M. Silverman, Menasha Yatkeman, Joseph Malinoff, Abraham Koplochinsky, and Faivush Rothman.

Emeth made its first payment of six hundred dollars toward the purchase of the burial ground itself, and a few days later an impressive dedication service officially opened the new cemetery. Within a few months a fence and chapel were added. By 1904 the association was able to purchase seventeen acres of adjacent land (for seventeen thousand dollars), considerably increasing the size of the facility that now was being used by not only Society members but also the entire Orthodox Jewish community of St. Louis.

Founders of Chesed Shel Emeth pointed to an early policy decision that they viewed as representing their true raison d'être perhaps more than anything else. At a meeting held on November 2, 1890, the Society forbade public solicitations to pay for burying any specific indigent deceased. Instead, Chesed Shel Emeth would inter such individuals, with full services, at no cost, thereby avoiding any humiliation or embarrassment to the deceased's family. Rich and poor would be treated equally.[11]

As its membership grew and it proved so successful as a burial society, Chesed Shel Emeth became more involved with other activities within the Jewish community. It actively participated in efforts to create a Jewish hospital, an Orthodox Jewish senior citizens' home, and a Jewish orphans' home. All three institutions came into being after the turn of the century. The Chesed Shel Emeth Society assisted actively in organizing and supporting many Hebrew Schools in St. Louis and several educational institutions in Poland and Russia. In 1915 members began to seriously consider building their own *shul*, which they hoped would serve as a center for not only worship services but also cultural and charitable activities. That project reached fruition in 1919, when the Chesed Shel Emeth Synagogue was erected at Page and Euclid. (When the Jewish population moved farther west after World War II, in 1952 Chesed Shel Emeth built a new synagogue at North and South Road and Gannon Avenue in suburban University City.)[12]

Sheerith S'fard Congregation was another institution that became very important in the pre-1900 Orthodox community. Its origins are very murky. We know of its beginnings from a terse "twenty-five-years-ago" newspaper item stating that it was organized by poor Russian immigrants on February 15, 1887. A different account suggests it may have begun informally a year earlier, as a *minyan* in a private home on Wash Street. The name "Sheerith S'fard" first appeared publicly in August 1888 in

11. Ibid., 19.

12. Ibid., 13–35. An interesting overview of the early development of the Chesed Shel Emeth can be found in Abrams, *Book of Memories*, 70–82.

a newspaper directory of High Holy Day services: a simple "Chevra Sheerith S'fard, 715 Carr Street."[13]

We know very little about what transpired at Sheerith S'fard during its formative years. It was served part of the time by Rabbi Shlomo Jaffee, styled by some as "Chief Rabbi" of the St. Louis Orthodox Jewish community, and briefly by Rabbi Abraham Alperstein, a rabbinic scholar who spent an inordinate amount of time between Sheerith S'fard in St. Louis and the "Mariompoler Shul" [sic] in Chicago. More important, though, the congregation flourished well enough to purchase the building at the 715 Carr Street site. It was the first "permanent" home—in contrast with rented facilities—for any eastern European Orthodox congregation in St. Louis. The achievement was quite remarkable in that most of the membership, according to the editor of the *Jewish Voice,* consisted of "poor people living from hand to mouth." The money was raised by the sale of seats in the *shul* and by individual contributions. Neither method was innovative; the singularity lay in the dedication of the membership in working toward its goals. In fact, more than half the four-hundred-dollar price of the building was raised from the sale of seats alone. On Sunday, September 2, 1888—in time for the High Holy Days—the congregation formally moved into its newly acquired building, the interior remodeled into a synagogue. Rabbi Messing of United Hebrew Temple highlighted a dedicatory program attended by more than two hundred guests and congregants. He cautioned them to avoid internal religious conflicts as other St. Louis Jewish institutions had experienced, and he exhorted them to educate their children to grow up as good Jews and good American citizens.[14]

Sheerith S'fard's remodeled building proved to be only a temporary home. Within three years endeavors leading to a new site reached fruition with the purchase of property at 921 North Ninth (Ninth and Wash Streets). This time the congregation built its synagogue from the ground

---

13. "Twenty-Five Years Ago, 1887," in *Voice,* February 12, 1912; Abrams, *Book of Memories,* 67; Flaks, "Thirty Years of Vaad Hoeir," 26. No extant data explains the term "S'fard" in the congregation's name. At no time has any Sephardic congregation been known to exist in St. Louis. On the other hand, many eastern European immigrants in other parts of the United States named their congregations "Anshei Sfard" even though they were Ashkenazic groups. Orthodox congregations listed in addition to Sheerith S'fard included B'nai Amoona (823 Franklin, Rev. Adolph Rosentreter); Sheerith Israel (Eleventh and Franklin, Rev. A. Abrahams); Chevrah Kadisha (930 North Seventh, Rev. Max Lieberstein); and Beth Hamedrosh Hagodol (931 North Seventh, Rev. A. Spector). All these addresses still represented *rented* facilities. *Voice,* August 31, 1888.

14. *Jewish Free Press,* November 18, 1887; *Voice,* January 27, February 17, May 11, August 3 and 31, and September 7, 1888.

up. The cornerstone was laid on Sunday, January 18, 1891. Formal consecration of the *shul* occurred two months later, on Sunday, March 22. Speakers included the congregation's rabbi Shlomo Jaffee, Rabbi Messing of United Hebrew Temple, and Major Adolph Proskauer, a Civil War veteran (of the Confederate army) and a prominent businessman and member of Temple Israel. The congregation flourished as more and more Russian immigrants crowded into the neighborhood. By 1905 the *shul*'s facilities were so taxed that the congregation purchased a larger building about six blocks farther west, at the corner of Fifteenth and Wash Streets. Formerly a church and remodeled to seat about twenty-five hundred worshipers, the new *shul* was dedicated on July 16, 1905. For more than three decades it stood in the heart of a neighborhood widely referred to as "The Ghetto." Sheerith S'fard became a very important center for St. Louis Orthodox Jewry, for cultural and social events as well as for religious services. There St. Louis Jews enjoyed touring cantorial concerts and important personalities speaking on topics that ranged from talmudic issues to American citizenship to Zionism.[15]

Beth Hamedrosh Hagodol, Chevra Kadisha, and Sheerith S'fard were not the only eastern European Orthodox *shuls* that came into being before 1900. An 1887 holiday directory listed a "Chevra Ahavas Achim" at Eleventh and Franklin, with services conducted by Rev. A. M. Goldman. Three years later the Jewish press mentioned another congregation, "Knesseth Israel Anshei Kovno," organized at the Evans Brothers Building, 1107 Franklin, with Leon Berman as president. But that, unfortunately, is about the extent of available information about pre-1900 Orthodox *shuls*. Directories usually listed also the names of individuals in rabbinic roles. They included, in addition to those already mentioned, A. Abrahams, Aaron Spector (or Spiwak) and H. Feinschreiber. Like the *shuls*, available data provides little more than their names. By the turn of the century some of those *shuls* had disappeared, and some new ones had come into being.

---

15. One of Sheerith S'fard's most effective fund-raisers was Abraham Tuchler, who had played an important role in the founding of Sheerith Israel. *Voice*, February 6, 1891. An interesting sidelight on Sheerith Israel's early history is the friendly relations it maintained with the Reform rabbis and community. Rabbi Messing of United Hebrew was the featured speaker at the *shul*'s dedication and consecration services. One of the congregation's first guest speakers after it began regular services was Rabbi Sonneschein, who was enthusiastically received by his Orthodox audience. Evidence exists of many similar episodes, often overlooked, of support to the new immigrant Orthodox Jews from the established German/Reform community. See, for instance, *Voice*, May 11, September 7 and 21, and October 26, 1888, August 16, 1889, February 6, 1891, and April 7, July 14, and December 29, 1905. Sheerith S'fard later metamorphosed into the Jacob R. Probstein Chapel of Jewish Hospital.

Thus a 1901 Passover directory no longer listed Sheerith Israel, Chevra
Ahavas Achim, or Knesseth Israel Ahavas Kovno. Orthodox *shuls* listed
were B'nai Amoona, at Thirteenth and Carr, Rabbi Adolph Rosentreter;
Beth Hamedrosh Hagodol, at 1123 North Eleventh, Rabbi J. Friedman;
Sheerith S'fard, at 921 North Ninth, Rabbi Zechariah Rosenfeld; Chevrah
Kadisha, at 929 North Seventh; and two new congregations, Tipheris Israel
at Ninth and Wash, and B'nai Israel at 1005 North Seventh. Although we
know little about those institutions, their very existence points out how the
religious component of the St. Louis Jewish community had grown from
the nothingness that had existed when Joseph Philipson settled in St. Louis
in 1807. It continued at an accelerated pace into the twentieth century.[16]

Other types of noncongregational activities also helped establish the
eastern European and Orthodox community in the last two decades of
the nineteenth century. They involved both the German Jews and the
immigrant Russians. One of them centered on the Young Men's Hebrew
Association—the YMHA—popularly referred to as the "Y."

Since Jewish settlers in St. Louis during the first three quarters of
the 1800s placed great importance on becoming Americanized and on
attaining economic security, they confined much of their Jewish-oriented
recreational and cultural activity to relatively narrow congregational and
organizational growth; that is, to charitable societies, B'nai B'rith–type
mutual aid and fraternal organizations, and congregational auxiliaries.
Outside those affiliations, literary and debating societies offered additional means of recreation and friendship. Some were men's organizations, some were women's, and some took in both. A random list of the
more popular included the Hebrew Young Men's Literary Association,
the Ladies Pioneer Society, the Disraeli Social and Dramatic Club, the
T.J.B., the Webster Debating Society, the Manette Social Circle, the Olympic
Debating Society, the Longfellow Literary Society, the Wolfner Literary
and Auxiliary Society, the Irving Literary Society, and the Allemania Dramatic Club. All provided Jewish young men and women with a variety of
cultural and social outlets. To that list in the 1880s was added the YMHA.[17]

As with so many institutions, the exact origins of the YMHA are unclear.
It seems to have metamorphosed from the Hebrew Young Men's Literary
Association. On January 25, 1880, the executive committee of the 125-

---

16. *Voice*, September 9, 1887, March 23 and August 3, 1888, January 1 and October
16, 1891, and April 26, 1901.

17. *Israelite*, January 1, 1864; *Tribune*, October 10 and November 7, 1879, January 30
and April 16, 1880, June 10, 1881, and March 16, 1883; *Jewish Free Press*, April 3, 1885;
Voice, February 17 and November 30, 1888, February 1 and April 4, 1889, October 28,
1898, and April 12, 1909. See also "The Pioneers" Minute Book, AJA.

member HYMLA proposed reorganization into a new society, to be known as the Young Men's Hebrew Association. Invitations to join were extended to other Jewish cultural groups. The new association's stated objects were primarily twofold: to improve the moral, social, and physical condition of its members, and to protect and advance Hebrew interests. To that end, the new organization proposed to establish a reading room and library; to sponsor lectures on historical, scientific, literary, and social topics; to provide social, literary, and musical entertainment; to establish a gymnasium; and to organize an employment bureau. Formal reorganization occurred on February 1, 1880. Temporary elected officers included Bernard Singer, president; Isidor Bush, vice president; B. J. Strauss, corresponding secretary; C. B. Sales, recording secretary; and Albert Singer, treasurer. Five committees were appointed to implement the society's programs: an amusement committee, a constitution committee, a charter committee, a lecture committee, and a membership committee. The charter committee wasted little time; on March 6, 1880, the YMHA successfully petitioned the Circuit Court of the City of St. Louis for incorporation under the laws of Missouri. That petition was signed by Bernard Singer, president, Moses L. Wieder, secretary, and Albert Singer, treasurer, on behalf of the "Young Men's Hebrew Association of St. Louis, Missouri." Officially, then, they constituted the YMHA's first officers.[18]

Perhaps the new YMHA's most vocal booster was Rabbi Moritz Spitz, speaking as both rabbi of B'nai El and as editor of the *Voice*, the Jewish community's newspaper at the time. He seemed never to miss an opportunity to stress the cultural and recreational needs of the Jewish community, especially for young people, as he constantly publicized the YMHA's activities and enthusiastically championed support for its programs. Nevertheless, the first few decades of the YMHA proved extremely tenuous, with all sorts of ups and downs, and on more than one occasion concerned Jewish citizenry even feared for its continued existence. Just why that existence was so tenuous is not clear, for the Y's programs and activities appeared to be exciting and appealing. But it was never clear from the very beginning whether the Y was viewed as a Jewish community center or only as an umbrella structure administering a variety of cultural and social programs. If it was meant to be a community center, then there was no "center" location; for many years programs were conducted at scattered sites, until the Y rented rooms to create the appearance, at least, of stability. But rented quarters still lacked the element of permanency.

18. Unless otherwise indicated, the main source for this early history of the YMHA is Ruth Fischlowitz [Marget], *The "Y" Story*, 1–17. See also *Israelite*, January 1, 1864, and *Tribune*, November 14, 1879, January 30 and March 5, 1880, and January 14, 1881.

Furthermore, for a long time the Y's activities seemed to focus only on cultural and social functions primarily for the already established German Jewish population. Meanwhile, as will be seen, the Educational Alliance came into being, providing comparable services—and more—for a completely different clientele, the new eastern European immigrants. Perhaps because the latter's needs were greater and more urgent, especially in the areas of education and Americanization, the Jewish community showed more support for the Alliance than for the YMHA. Unfortunately the evidence is not clear. Only after many eastern European Jews became acclimated to their new environment and began to join in YMHA activities as well as in Alliance programs did the Y's existence take a more positive turn. And it was not until about 1915, when some key Jewish community leaders openly came to its support and the YMHA purchased its own building, that the organization finally turned the corner and achieved the vibrance and wide respect associated with it in the Jewish community.[19]

The YMHA got off to an enthusiastic beginning in October 1880, highlighted by a rousing and widely praised production of the operetta "Chimes of Normandy" performed by a completely local Jewish cast at the popular Olympic Theater. Other activities during that first year included lectures and social gatherings. Nevertheless, interest in the organization soon waned, and membership dropped. A meeting of the board of directors scheduled in November 1880 at the Harmonie Club had to be canceled when not even a quorum showed up. One month later the organization's inactivity prompted a suggestion that it be disbanded and its funds turned over the United Hebrew Relief Association. Some critics pointed to a lack of leadership; others accused the organization

---

19. In her history of the YMHA, Fischlowitz divides the development of the organization into three periods: the "Early Years," 1880–1915; the "Middle Years," 1915–1927; and the "Years of Accomplishment and of Greater Glory," since 1927. One of the fascinating mysteries of this early period is the "Social Settlement on south Eleventh." Scattered references appear in the Jewish press about programs conducted there for Jews living in the "South Side." *Voice,* February 3, 1899, July 4, 1902, and February 3 and August 25, 1905. At the corner of Eleventh and Sidney Streets (2600 South Eleventh) stands a building on which are inscribed, on a third-floor cornice, a Star of David and the date 1885. Examinations by many researchers into city records (directories, tax records, real estate records) proved frustratingly futile in attempts to more clearly identify that building. Legends abound that the site was once a synagogue, and that it was even a community center, but no verifying evidence exists. There is reason to believe only that in the early 1920s South Broadway merchants rented at least one upstairs room where they could conduct a *minyan.* But was this the south-side "Social Settlement"? And even if it was, no extant evidence ties that Social Settlement with the YMHA or any of its activities. *St. Louis Jewish Light,* November 26, 1975; Don Corrigan, "The Neighborhood Tavern," 84; Russell Farber, "A Close Look at History," 18.

of being too social-conscious, of stressing the "Young Men's" instead of the "Hebrew" in the association's programs. Yet the "corpse" managed to survive. In 1882, for instance, the YMHA orchestra merited very high marks for its participation in the dedication of the Home for the Aged and Infirm Israelites. That same year the YMHA's dramatics groups earned similar plaudits for several dramatic and musical presentations.

Still, the 1880s proved to be trying years. Perhaps one reason for a lack of sustained interest derived from the lack of a permanent home. Meetings were held at the Harmonie Club facilities on Fourth Street, and at Temple Israel at Pine and Leffingwell, but the association's popularity and success fluctuated. Picnics and balls at Normandy Grove and Liederkranz Hall proved very popular and successful. Operatic performances entitled "A Trip to Africa," under the direction of Herman and Abraham Epstein, were termed "a crowning glory to the entire Jewish community of St. Louis." Membership in the YMHA rose in the mid-1880s to approximately five hundred, with young men such as Simon B. Sale, Morris Glaser, Albert Arnstein, and Nathan Kaufman taking leadership roles. Apparently renting quarters at 1321 Chouteau tended to raise enthusiasm for the organization, but it proved short-lived.[20]

By the late 1880s widespread concern still existed that the YMHA was a failure. "Have we as yet a YMHA in St. Louis?" the *Voice* bemoaned editorially; if Memphis can do it, with so many fewer Jews, why cannot we? In the presidential address to his congregation in 1888, Temple Israel's Isaac Schwab despaired of "the Young Men's Hebrew Association in this city languishing, not for want of members, not for lack of ability, but from a lack of spirit and encouragement." This seems somewhat surprising when one notes the variety of activities recorded for the YMHA during the 1880s and 1890s: dances, musicals, picnics, boat excursions. Yet the organization floundered.[21]

No one seemed to be able to pinpoint what basic ingredient or ingredients were missing. Social events were successful; but what of the organization's other goals? During the 1890s some new and innovative programs began to stir more interest in the organization. Women began to serve refreshments at meetings and to participate in more group activities; in fact, the YMHA expanded its title to "YMHA-YWHA" to include activities for women as well as for men. A Labor Bureau succeeded in finding jobs for newly arriving Russian immigrants. Some attempts were made to

---

20. *Tribune*, November 3 and 24, and December 22, 1882, February 2 and March 16, 1883, January 11, February 1, and March 21, 1884; *Jewish Free Press*, December 4, 1885.

21. Fischlowitz, *The "Y" Story*, 7–9; *Jewish Free Press*, December 31, 1886, and February 5, 1887; *Voice*, January 5 and February 17, 1888.

conduct educational programs in cooperation with the newly formed Educational Alliance, but those efforts proved less than successful. For some undecipherable reason, the YMHA just did not take hold, and once again its stature and role in the Jewish community diminished. Perhaps the nadir was the brief mention by Rabbi Spitz in the October 4, 1895, *Voice* of a letter he had received addressed to "the late St. Louis Y.M.H.A., *olov hashalom*" ("May peace be with him," a Hebrew term referring to the deceased).

Fortunes took a turn for the better in 1896, when Abraham Rosenthal, Rabbi Samuel Sale and Benjamin F. Koperlik spearheaded a reorganization of the association. Their efforts were abetted significantly by the fledgling St. Louis Chapter of the National Council of Jewish Women. An encouraging boost derived from the renting in 1897 of larger quarters at 2737 Locust. This time it was an entire building, not just a room or two. A variety of facilities became available, including a ladies' salon, a chess and checkers room, and even a gymnasium. Activities ranged from talks on a spectrum of subjects to athletic contests to dramatics to oratorical and musical presentations. For the first time many viewed the YMHA as taking its place in the community; perhaps, many began openly to express, the YMHA's time finally had come. During the 1890s the YMHA was the scene of a number of cultural and social highlights. One of the most popular was the lecture by noted author Israel Zangwill on November 5, 1898. Chess, checkers, and billiard rooms attracted large numbers. Dances in the gymnasium proved popular, as did athletic field days and picnics. A Carnival of Music, Arts, and Industry in 1899 proved successful not only in attracting an enthusiastic attendance but also for raising funds toward a permanent building site.[22]

Yet the turn of the century saw the YMHA's fortunes slip once again, despite a number of events involving highly acclaimed personalities. A move to a new rented building at 3137 Pine in 1902 seemed to revive the association's fortunes somewhat. Still, even though membership numbered in the hundreds—six hundred in 1903—many still questioned whether the YMHA was serving a worthwhile community purpose.

In retrospect, those doubts seem unfounded, especially when one notes some of the personalities who associated with the Y and the many events and activities that it sponsored during the early 1900s. Those prominent in YMHA activities included such important people as Rabbis Harrison, Spitz, Sale, and Messing; speakers Frank Louis Soldan (superintendent of the St. Louis public schools), Charles Nagel (president of the St. Louis city council), and Professor Isidor Loeb (then at the University of Missouri in

22. Fischlowitz, *The "Y" Story*, 8–17; *Voice,* September 10 and December 16, 1898, January 20 and March 9, 1899, and August 4, 1900.

Columbia and later to become dean of the Washington University business school); and Jewish community leaders Moses Summerfield, Abraham Rosenthal, Ben Lowenstein, Elkan W. Glauber, William Sacks, Karl M. Vetsburg, Bernard Greensfelder, Samuel J. Russack, Ben L. Shifrin, and Martin Schweig. One would think that with men of that stature supporting the YMHA—and others equally prominent but too numerous to list—the organization would be on solid ground. Yet doubts continued to be raised. Perhaps it was just one of those instances when naysayers and pessimists seemed to prevail.

Those expressions of doubt continued too in the face of many YMHA activities, which encompassed a variety of themes and people. A very brief list includes such social and cultural events as individual and group athletic competitions, carnivals, dances, lectures and roundtable discussions, musical and dramatic presentations, and art exhibits. The YMHA actively supported the great 1904 World's Fair by arranging housing facilities for visitors to the city.

Still, many doubted the Y's impact and proclivity for survival. Even as the *Voice* became the Y's official organ and reported weekly on all those activities, negatives persisted. Several moves to new quarters seemed to have little impact. In 1902 the YMHA moved from its 2737 Locust site to 3137 Pine. Another move in 1905 located the YMHA at the Beethoven Conservatory Building at Taylor and Olive, and in 1908 a five-year lease was signed for a portion of a building at Euclid and McPherson. And still the *Voice* decried that "the YMHA is still a homeless stepchild in the household of St. Louis Jewry."[23]

Perhaps "homeless" was the key word. In its entire existence since 1880, the YMHA had never had a permanent home; it had always rented quarters for all its activities. Although from time to time some leaders broached the question of owning a permanent site, nothing concrete came from those discussions, even though occasionally a "building fund" seemed to appear. Then in 1912 another reorganization of the YMHA's administrative structure brought into leadership positions the likes of Moses Fraley, J. D. Goldman, Ben L. Shifrin, Walter Freund, Oscar Leonard, Aaron Waldheim, Elias Michael, and Abraham Rosenthal. Rosenthal, editor of the *Modern View*, joined Spitz and the *Voice* in stressing the importance of the YMHA to the whole community. The 1912 reorganization of the YMHA's leadership brought in men who felt very strongly that the time had come when the organization must own its building and its many

23. Fischlowitz, The "Y" Story, 18–28; Voice, June 8 and 29, September 14, October 5, and December 14, 1900, December 27, 1901, February 14, 1902, August 5, 1904, and March 24 and July 28, 1905.

facilities. They created a viable building fund, and complemented it with a variety of fund-raising activities, which included a grand ball and minstrel show, a steamboat excursion on the Mississippi, and an elaborate carnival. The building fund received a tremendous boost from a sizable bequest from the estate of Elias Michael. The outbreak of World War I in Europe in 1914 temporarily slowed money raising; but a final push brought in the required funds. That final push was spearheaded by two of the Jewish community's most prominent figures, Moses Fraley and Walter Freund. In the fall of 1915 the exciting news spread that a newly purchased building at 3645 Delmar was being transformed into a fully appointed home for the YMHA. It opened on December 17, 1915, in an air of exciting anticipation. "From the moment the doors opened," wrote a YMHA chronicler, "the Home on Delmar became the mecca for young St. Louis Jewry. . . . To 3645 came the cream of St. Louis' growing generation—boys and girls in public school, young people in college, in business, and in industry." After thirty-five anxious years, the YMHA had finally arrived.[24]

The tribulations experienced by the YMHA reflected several conflicting forces in the Jewish community in the decades surrounding the turn of the century. One was the aspiration and creativity to develop effective institutions to serve the needs of St. Louis Jewry. German Jews' needs could be met more by social and recreational activities; Russian Jews needed educational and economic programs. Providing both was not an easy task; yet many felt it had to be done. In fact, as already indicated, this may have been one of the difficulties the YMHA encountered: whether the community felt the needs of one group superseded those of the other. At the same time, in implementing those ambitious projects, the Jewish community faced problems not unlike those faced by others in American society: bringing together the necessary combination of leaders and willing followers to fund and achieve those goals.

Nothing more clearly illustrated those frustrations than the efforts to co-ordinate and improve the St. Louis Jewish community's varied charitable and eleemosynary programs. Overtaxed facilities of the United Hebrew Relief Association (resulting from the influx of refugees from yellow fever epidemics in the lower Mississippi valley) led in 1879 to the creation of the United Jewish Charities, a new umbrella organization to coordinate relief and charity endeavors. That reorganization proved most timely, for

---

24. Fischlowitz, *The "Y" Story*, 25–31. The YMHA flourished at 3645 Delmar until the mid-1920s. For more on the early history of the YMHA, see *Voice*, October 28, 1904, March 5, 1909, October 28, 1910, February 24, July 28, and November 17, 1911, May 3 and June 7, 1912, February 21, 1913, April 2 and 9, and December 3, 1915, October 1, 1920; and *St. Louis Jewish Light,* March 31, 1971.

during the 1880s and 1890s the new United Jewish Charities helped thousands of eastern European immigrants who settled in St. Louis. Yet those efforts also entailed some frustrating relations with both national and local immigrant aid societies. Much more satisfactory was cooperation with the Hebrew Free and Industrial School and various labor bureaus that helped immigrants become acclimated to the American environment and to find jobs.[25]

One related development that began under the auspices of the United Jewish Charities which merits special mention entailed the Jewish Alliance. The St. Louis Jewish Alliance was an outgrowth of programs begun in 1889 in New York by "uptown" German Jewish philanthropists. Those programs, at first called the Hebrew Institute, focused on creating community centers in the Lower East Side where all sorts of Jewish cultural activities were conducted for the benefit of newly arriving "downtown" Jewish immigrants. A reorganization in 1893 changed the name of the program from Hebrew Institute to Educational Alliance. This was done partly to deemphasize Jewish sectarianism—by opening the benefits of the program to more than a Jewish clientele—and to promote the "Americanizing, educational, social, and humanizing" scope of the organization. The Alliance movement spread to other cities; in fact, a national Jewish Alliance of America was headquartered in Philadelphia. In 1890 the Alliance program came to St. Louis, where it soon became widespread and very successful. As the YMHA focused on cultural and recreational activities for those Jews already living in St. Louis (primarily the well-established German Jewish population), the new Alliance concentrated its programs to benefit the newly arriving eastern European population. For those people seeking to establish roots in a new environment, essential activities included learning English, finding jobs, getting a basic Hebrew and secular education on which to build a solid citizenship structure, and becoming familiarized with the American way of life.[26]

To those ends, then, after some preliminary discussions, a group of concerned St. Louis Jews, led by Isidor Bush, Jacob Furth, H. Hirschberg, and Jacob Berger, met on July 5, 1891, at United Hebrew Temple on Twenty-First and Olive to formally organize the St. Louis Branch of the Jewish Alliance of America. Rabbis Sonneschein (Reform) and Jaffe (Orthodox) addressed a large and supportive turnout that elected the first officers of

25. *Tribune,* October 10, 1879, and February 17, 1883; *Jewish Free Press,* March 4, 1887; *Voice,* December 14, 1888, and March 1 and June 7, 1889; *Modern View,* November 9, 1933; Rosen, "Historical Development of Jewish Federation of Saint Louis," 63–69.

26. For a brief overview of the Alliance movement, see *Encyclopedia Judaica,* vol. 12, 1093–94.

the St. Louis Alliance: Isidor Bush, president; Moses Fraley, vice president; M. Jacoby, secretary; and Jacob Furth, treasurer. Members agreed to contribute three dollars a year to help meet expenses; additional sources of revenue would be obtained from a variety of fund-raising projects. The St. Louis Board of Education cooperated magnanimously by providing available evening classroom space at no cost. On October 19, 1891, the Alliance Night School opened. Classes met on Monday, Wednesday, and Thursday evenings at the Jefferson School. (When a new Jefferson School building opened in 1899, that new facility on Ninth and Wash Streets was also made available to the Alliance Night School.) Opening enrollment consisted of seventy students, ages ten to thirty-eight, male and female, mostly Russians and Rumanians. Students received books and other supplies free. Three teachers, supervised by William Deutsch, a popular and highly renowned educator in the Jewish community, constituted the original instructional staff.[27]

The Alliance Night School was an immediate success. Within one month enrollment jumped to about 300; in fact, about 150 potential students had to be turned away temporarily for lack of facilities. But with the cooperation of the St. Louis school board and the Hebrew Free and Industrial School, and with very energetic support from the Jewish community, plus financial assistance from the Baron de Hirsch Fund, more space was provided, more teachers were employed, and many more immigrant students were accommodated. Even the deaths of Isidor Bush and William Deutsch, strong Alliance supporters from the very beginning, did not impede progress. Others stepped in and enthusiastically carried on their work. First Bertha Sale and then Emil Mayer became superintendent, and they led a growing corps of very conscientious and competent teachers. Elias Michael was elected president of the Alliance, a position he held for many years, and he was ably augmented by such rising and established lay leaders as Jacob Furth, Louis Bry, Albert Loth, William Goldstein, Louis Glaser, David Treichlinger, Frank Block, Louis Renard, and William Stix.

By the end of the decade, Alliance president Elias Michael reported that enrollment stood at 536 (366 men and 170 women), mostly Jewish immigrants, but with several score of non-Jewish Italians, Germans, French, and Irish. The curriculum included reading, spelling, conversation, composition, geography, history, arithmetic, and basic bookkeeping. Classes expanded to four nights a week, Monday through Thursday. Special guest lectures on Tuesday evenings featured, among others, Dr. Jesse Meyer

---

27. *Voice,* July 3 and 10, September 18, October 23, and November 6, 1891, March 10, 1899, and April 6, 1900; *Modern View 25,* 5; Rosen, "Historical Development of Jewish Federation of Saint Louis," 69.

("The Wonders of the Human Body") and Judge Sheldon P. Spencer ("Our Country: Government, Duties, and Privileges of Its Citizens"). Rabbis Harrison, Sale, Messing, and Spitz were also frequent speakers, as were lay leaders Elias Michael, Isaac Schwab, Benjamin Altheimer, Moses Fraley, and Emil Mayer. Other popular speakers included McKinley High School teacher Philo M. Buck, who spoke on a wide array of topics such as India, Palestine, the Far East, and Latin America. Alexander Langsdorf of Washington University's engineering school lectured on topics dealing with electricity and mechanics. Doctors and nurses led discussions on various health and sanitation issues. Popular classroom teachers included Minnie Kahn, Rose Kahn, Bertha Goldberg, Florence Isaacs, Regina Fischel, Sophie Baron, and Hilda Levy. Discussions on the infamous Dreyfus Case attracted huge audiences. A breakdown of the students in 1900 showed that 97 percent held full-time jobs during the day. Occupations of males included tailors, blacksmiths, carpenters, cigar makers, errand boys, newsboys, clerks, and mechanics; female students worked as tailoresses, seamstresses, clerks, factory hands, and servants—and one photographer. Some students, of course, were unemployed, but never more than 3 percent. (These classes, it should be kept in mind, were separate from those offered primarily for school-age youngsters by the equally popular Hebrew Free and Industrial School. The Alliance served working immigrant adults, providing night-school courses that helped them with basic educational and civic growth.)[28]

By 1898 serious discussions began that led to a closer relationship between the Alliance Night School and the Hebrew Free and Industrial School, as well as to a permanent site. At least the Alliance classes were together in the Jefferson School, although occasionally a special lecture or program had to be held at a different site. But growing enrollment and expanding programs began to stretch the limited facilities of the Jefferson School. The Hebrew Free and Industrial School's classes, on the other hand, were scattered in many places, in temples, synagogues, and a variety of miscellaneous locations that were either donated or rented. The steady popularity and growth of both institutions—one consequence of increasing immigration—led to the need for one large, properly equipped, centrally located, permanent site. Pressures to reorganize the twenty-year-old United Jewish Charities made the idea more plausible. Accordingly,

---

28. The Philip L. Seaman Scrapbook, AJA, contains many contemporary articles from St. Louis secular newspapers that detail Alliance activities. See also *Voice*, November 6, 1891, October 7, 14, 21, and 28, 1898, February 10 and March 10, 1899, February 2 and April 6, 1900, January 4, February 1 and 8, and April 19, 1901, January 4 and 18, 1907, and March 5, 1909; *Modern View*, November 9, 1933.

in 1899 leaders of the Hebrew Free and Industrial School and of the Alliance, with the blessings and cooperation of the United Jewish Charities, organized the United Jewish Educational and Charitable Association. In contrast with other organizations intended to administer various charitable functions, this new association's prime function was to establish and operate one or more buildings for the use of Jewish educational and charitable societies. It was, in effect, a landlord operating specialized building facilities for the Alliance, the Hebrew Free and Industrial School, and any other appropriate eleemosynary institution. In 1900 President William Goldstein of the Hebrew Free and Industrial School reported to his board that some interest had been shown in purchasing a lot at Fourteenth and Biddle, but no concrete action resulted. Meanwhile the two institutions carried on fund-raising efforts for a permanent site.

That reached fruition early in 1901, with the purchase of property at the northwest corner of Ninth and Carr Streets. The cornerstone of the new United Educational and Charitable Association Building was laid in February 1901, and classes began there the following October. Formal dedication ceremonies for what was henceforth referred to as the Alliance Building or the Jewish Educational Building occurred on Sunday, January 5, 1902. Elias Michael, president of the new Association, addressed those assembled, as did St. Louis Mayor Rolla Wells and school superintendent Frank Louis Soldan. The building's first floor contained general offices, a day nursery, and a kindergarten. Six very large rooms, each divisible into smaller sections, occupied the second floor. The third floor consisted of a library and an assembly hall. In the basement were a gymnasium and bathing facilities.[29]

From the time it opened in 1901, the Alliance Building became one of the most important centers of Jewish cultural, social, and educational programming in St. Louis. Standing out, of course, were the educational classroom activities that attracted more and more Jewish immigrants as they settled in the city. Thousands of new arrivals were helped to become solid citizens who placed high priorities on education and participation in everyday political, social, and economic intercourse. Most attended classes from six months to two years, many for even longer. Decades later elderly Jews proudly related to their children and grandchildren how they worked long hours in factories and shops, and then attended night school in Alliance programs, where they acquired the basics for education

29. *Voice,* October 21, 1898, February 10, 1899, February 2, 1900, January 4, 10, and 25, February 8 and 15, and October 25, 1901, January 10 and April 4, 1902, May 15, and October 16 and 30, 1903, April 22 and December 30, 1904, and January 27, 1905; Rosen, "Historical Development of Jewish Federation of Saint Louis," 70–71.

and good citizenship.[30] In the face of poverty and age-old prejudice, and transplanted in a strange and hostile environment, they became through their own efforts productive members of St. Louis society. Undoubtedly the Alliance was a major contributor.

With more facilities available, Alliance activities branched out to include more than the original basic night-school classes. Educational activities during the day expanded to include a variety of programs in the arts, sciences, and business. Guest college professors and scholars led groups on political economy, history, chemistry, painting and sculpting, and especially issues of health and personal hygiene. Lawyers explained the American legal system, and even conducted mock trials. Individuals and groups nurtured and developed musical talents. Rabbi Leon Harrison's brilliant and inspiring lectures always drew full audiences. Aspiring actors and actresses performed in dramatic presentations, and short-story and poetry readings were regular offerings. Readings from Shakespeare were especially well attended and appreciated. Some typical activities, as reported by Rose Lenore Cohn in the *Voice*, included a lecture by Dr. Henry S. Bridges on "Bacteria"; readings by the Short Story Reading Club from "Mrs. Wiggs of the Cabbage Patch"; Charles A. Stix leading the Jefferson Literary Society in debates and orations; the Young Lacledes' tour of Shaw's Garden; Gussie Isaacs leading the Girls' Saturday Evening Club in a discussion of Longfellow's "Tales of the Wayside Inn"; the Shakespeare Class discussion of "Henry V"; discussions of the Hygiene and Physiology Class led by Dr. H. M. Horwitz; concerts arranged by Laura Hellman; and many more.[31]

Even as the Alliance provided these important services to the Jewish community, one of its most singular contributions was in the field of child care. Kindergartens had existed in St. Louis since 1877, when Susan Blow opened hers at the Des Peres School. One of the key features of the Alliance Building was a well-staffed and well-equipped kindergarten to care for children of young working mothers. In addition, the Alliance operated the Selma Michael Day Nursery for prekindergarten-age toddlers. A good half century or more before preschool agencies became widely established, Alliance leaders saw the need for such an important institution. Equally unique and certainly very popular was the Alliance's annual Better Babies Contest. Silver loving cups and spoons, teething rings, medals, and certificates were awarded to those babies selected

---

30. Including the author's parents, grandparents, and many relatives and friends.

31. Evidence of these activities and more can be found in Philip L. Seaman Scrapbook and St. Louis, Missouri File, AJA; *Voice*, February 15, 1901, May 18 and November 9, 1906, January 4, May 3, and November 15, 1907, and March 13, 1908.

as the healthiest. Those prizes, however, masked the real reason for the
"competition": to identify and correct health deficiencies in youngsters
and thereby encourage mothers to aim for a "winner" the following year.
An annual feature in the St. Louis press was a photo collage of bright-
eyed, full-cheeked infants, the type of pictures that in later years graced
labels and advertisements for baby foods. Sponsored by its Mothers' Club,
the Alliance provided important child-rearing consultation and literature
for the community's young mothers, who, because of their immigrant
background, knew little or nothing about proper food or nutrition for
either themselves or their children. Literature was even distributed in
Yiddish to those who could not yet read English. Popular and prominent
Jewish physicians who participated ably and free of charge in these efforts
included Doctors Aaron Levy, G. A. Lippmann, S. T. Lipsitz, M. Meyers, M. A. Goldstein, M. Jacobs, Selig Simon, M. Wiener, and Llewellyn
Sale. Among the women who organized and administered the program
were Mesdames Aaron Waldheim, Charles A. Stix, Elias Michael, Albert
Greensfelder, Nathan Bry, Aaron Rauh, Charles Rice, Sidney Schoenberg,
Albert Arnstein, David Treichlinger, Maurice Weil, Jonathan Rice, and
many others.[32]

From its beginnings in 1891, then, and especially after it operated in
its own Ninth and Carr Educational Building, the Alliance provided inestimable service to the downtown Jewish community and thus indirectly to
the overall St. Louis community. By 1919, when a considerable portion of
the Jewish population had moved beyond Grand Avenue into St. Louis's
west end, the old Alliance Building was closed and the organization's
functions merged with the new and more centrally located Jewish Community Center at 3636 Page Avenue (that Community Center, by the way,
was totally separate from the YMHA). The Alliance's value to those who
participated in its programs was well articulated by Rumanian immigrant
and laborer Fred Horowitz in his graduation address in 1906:

> Mine is only one of the usual cases. Less than two years ago, when I
> came here from Rumania, I did not have the least idea of this language,
> and today, after attending the evening school regularly, I am able to read
> and understand any English book. . . . Those fortunate enough to come
> to St. Louis are soon made aware of the magnificent institution at Ninth
> and Carr Streets. The Jewish Educational Alliance, whose wide doors
> are ever open to receive those who wish to enroll . . . will prove to an
> outsider that the time within these walls is well spent.[33]

32. St. Louis, Missouri File, AJA; *Voice,* August 12, 1904, May 18, 1906, March 27,
1908, January 2, 1914, and December 19, 1919; *Modern View,* November 9, 1933.
33. *Voice,* May 18, 1906.

Nathan Frank.

Benjamin Altheimer.

Moses Fraley.

Jacob Furth.

Elias Michael.

William Stix.

Sigmond Baer.

Julius A. Baer.

Aaron Fuller.

Benjamin Eiseman.

David May.

Moses Shoenberg.

Jonathan Rice.

Dr. Herman Tuholske.

William Deutsch, educator.

J. J. Wertheimer.

Jerusalem Exhibit, 1904 World's Fair.

14

CIVIC AND ECONOMIC STALWARTS

Just as religious, social, educational, and charitable institutions were important to the growth and development of the St. Louis Jewish community, so too were the roles of Jews in the city's civic and economic activities significant for St. Louis Jewry. In truth, Jewish contributions in the field of politics did not rank as extraordinary, at least quantitatively; the Irish and the Germans dominated. Numbers do count in a democratic society, and Jews never constituted more than a small percentage of the city's population (the highest it ever reached was less than 7 percent just before World War I). Nevertheless, Jews individually and collectively did their share and made a worthwhile contribution to St. Louis progress.[1]

The Jewish role in local politics prior to the Civil War can best be described as minimal, but with a few exceptions. After all, so few Jews even resided in St. Louis then. True, some office holders had those beguiling "Jewish-sounding" names. There was Samuel Solomon, who was, among other things, secretary of the board of commissioners in the early 1800s. And there was Thomas Cohen, a popular grocer and avid fisherman, appointed street commissioner in 1829. On three separate occasions voters of the heavily German-populated wards elected Cohen to the city's governing council. Certainly his name and where he lived suggest that Cohen may have been Jewish; yet no extant evidence can verify it. The same applies to five others elected to the city council and the school board between 1833 and 1857: Andrew Krieg, Adolph Levy, A. Renard, Frederick Mosberger, and Morris I. Lippman. Those *last* names appeared later in various Jewish organizational rosters, but with different first names—their

---

1. *Voice*, January 1, 1902, and March 7, 1905; Troen and Holt, eds., *St. Louis*, 212. In 1900 St. Louis had a population of a little more than 575,000. For overviews of St. Louis political and economic development, see such excellent histories of the city as Scharf, *Saint Louis City and County*; Hyde and Conard, eds., *Encyclopedia of the History of St. Louis*; and especially Primm, *Lion of the Valley*.

children perhaps?—yet those five men themselves cannot be identified definitely as Jews.[2] Other prewar political figures, however, were clearly Jewish: Eleazer Block, Solomon J. Levi, Adolph Abeles, Meyer Friede, Isidor Bush.

After the Civil War, as more Jews rose in a variety of economic spheres, so too did Jews gradually become more involved in St. Louis civic and political matters. One of the earliest was Meyer A. Rosenblatt. A native New Yorker, Rosenblatt migrated west at a young age and, apparently smitten by the political bug, was elected when only twenty-three years old to the Nevada territorial legislature. The war over, he moved back east to St. Louis, where he married into the Bauman family, and for several years he worked in his father-in-law's Louis Bauman Jewelry firm. But politics seemed to be in his blood, and he became involved in local Republican circles (this was the post–Civil War era when Radical Republicans dominated politically, and when Isidor Bush was a power in the party and a strong proponent of the "Drake Constitution"). In short order Rosenblatt became chairman of the Missouri State Republican Committee. In 1872 Governor Joseph W. McClurg appointed him to the St. Louis Board of Police Commissioners. The year 1876 saw major changes in Missouri state politics; a new governor reorganized the St. Louis police board, in the process replacing Rosenblatt. But soon thereafter Rosenblatt became Collector of the City of St. Louis, a position he held until 1880, when he resigned to run, unsuccessfully, for the United States House of Representatives. Shortly thereafter, recurring health problems forced Rosenblatt to withdraw from active politics. A diligent and conscientious member of Ebn Ezra Lodge of B'nai B'rith and of Temple Israel, Rosenblatt died in 1889 at age forty-eight, leaving a widow and three daughters.[3]

Several Jews held political office in St. Louis at the turn of the century. By then, of course, the number of Jews in the city had increased—to approximately forty thousand by 1900—but Jews still constituted no more than about 6 percent of the city's population. Yet as German Jewish immigrants and their progeny became more successful economically and more secure in their social environment, they became increasingly involved in citywide civic, philanthropic, and cultural affairs, which led a number

---

2. Eric P. Newman to author, August 15, 1988, relative to Samuel Solomon, correspondence in possession of author; Scharf, *Saint Louis City and County*, vol. 1, 200, 663, 720, 840; Gill, *St. Louis Story*, vol. 1, 112.

3. *Tribune*, July 20 and October 1, 1880; *Voice*, January 4, 1889; Scharf, *Saint Louis City and County*, vol. 1, 705–6. In the latter half of the nineteenth century German Jews related overwhelmingly to the Republican Party, because they associated the party with its antislavery and strong pro-business stances.

into the political arena as well. Web M. Samuel and Moses Fraley, one a Democrat and one a Republican, were elected in 1877 to the St. Louis Board of Aldermen, as were Joseph Stern (in 1881), Albert Arnstein (in 1891), and Julius Lesser (in 1905). (Jews also ran unsuccessfully; one candidate, Solomon Boehm, lost his bid for an aldermanic seat by only three votes.) L. L. Arnold became a member of the school board in 1885. Dr. Jules Baron held the post of city coroner. Jews were elected to judgeships in various municipal courts; they included Jacob Klein, Simon S. Bass, and Moses N. Sale. Still others did not actually hold office but were considered important behind-the-scenes political activists; they included, among others, Louis Wittenberg and J. J. Wertheimer. Others exercised considerable clout and influence because of their prominence in the St. Louis business arena; we shall note some of them shortly. Probably the most important Jewish power brokers, however, were Isidor Bush, Jacob Furth, Jonathan Rice, Nathan Frank, Elias Michael, and Moses Fraley. One or more of them seemed to be associated with virtually every major development within the Jewish community.[4]

Other Jews also exercised influence in the community. The turn-of-the-century Jewish press reveals their names in a variety of fields and activities: Augustus Binswanger, Aaron Waldheim, Barney Hysinger, Herman Bienenstock, Aaron Gershon, Leon Helman, Isaac Fuld, Albert Arnstein, Benjamin Eiseman, Moses Shoenberg, Isaac Schwab, William Goldstein, Marcus Bernheimer, Henry Rice, Nicholas Scharff, William Stix, and David Treichlinger probably stand out as much as any. Several women also received well-deserved wide recognition, for their leadership in not only charitable endeavors but also educational and literary efforts. This group included Aurelia Rice, Anna Freund Weil, and Rachel Stix Michael. Such "women of valor" and the important place they occupied within the Jewish community would increase notably in the twentieth century. It was not just a coincidence that all of these men and women came from the German Jewish community; after all, eastern European Jews had not been in St. Louis long enough to develop viable communitywide leadership, except, that is, for the religious leaders. Nevertheless, some eastern Europeans already had begun to emerge by the turn of the century, especially Benjamin Burenstein, Dr. Michael Golland, Harry (Herschel) Yawitz, and Nathan Harris. They, and others from within the eastern

---

4. *Tribune,* April 15, 1881; *Jewish Free Press,* October 30 and November 13, 1885, and October 15, 1886; *Voice,* March 8, 1889, January 30, March 6, May 1, and June 5, 1891, February 24, 1893, October 28, 1904, March 17 and 24, and April 7, 1905, and November 2, 1906; Kelsoe, ed., *St. Louis Reference Record,* 183–86.

European community, would attain more visible leadership roles as that immigrant group grew in much larger numbers after 1900.[5]

Gradually, then, Jews became, and were recognized, as an integral part of the St. Louis civic scene. Thus a series of articles on men who helped build St. Louis and "contributed to her greatness as a metropolis," published in the *St. Louis Republican* in 1885, included sketches of Jonathan Rice and Jacob Furth. When the cornerstone of the new city hall was laid in 1891, Marcus Bernheimer, then president of the influential Merchants' Exchange, chaired the executive committee that organized the event, and Jonathan Rice was a member of the leadership committee. Jacob Furth, Elias Michael, J. J. Wertheimer, and Simon S. Bass were on other committees for that important city event. When President William McKinley visited St. Louis in 1898, Rabbis Spitz, Messing, Harrison, and Sale were included on the official presidential reception committee, a recognition not only of the stature of those clergymen personally but also of the Jewish community that they represented. Rabbi Harrison delivered one of the prayers at the Democratic National Convention when it met in St. Louis in July 1904; and even though he eschewed Jewish political partisanship, Spitz praised his colleague for that recognition and remarked editorially in the *Voice* that "prayer is the only thing that is non-partisan . . . it is as good at Democratic as at Republican conventions."[6]

References in the press to legal and political issues in the city often identified the community's outstanding lawyers. The names most commonly mentioned included Jewish attorneys Albert Arnstein, Nathan Frank, Augustus Binswanger, Moses Sale, Lee Sale, Joseph Arnold, David

---

5. A history of St. Louis published early in the 1900s listed some "principal citizens" of the city at the time. Included in that group were several Jews: Nathan Frank, "a lawyer and promoter of various newspaper and real estate enterprises"; Moses N. Sale, "a lawyer and . . . a Judge of the St. Louis Circuit Court"; Charles A. Stix, "president, Stix Baer and Fuller, one of our great department stores"; Ben Altheimer, "president of Altheimer and Rawlings Investment Company, stock and bond brokers"; Goodman King, "president of Mermod Jaccard and King Jewelry Company, one of St. Louis's leading jewelry concerns for many years"; Moses Shoenberg, "president of Shoenberg Mercantile Company"; and Jacob Klein, "lawyer and judge of the Circuit Court." Gill, *St. Louis Story*, vol. 1, 130. Some additional names undoubtedly worth mentioning include Aaron Fuller, Bernard Greensfelder, Simon Freund, Leopold Steinberger, Julius Lesser, Solomon Boehm, Samuel Russack, L. R. Strauss, David Eiseman, Isaac Baer, and Nicholas Scharff. See, for instance, *Voice*, November 1, 1901, January 1, 1904, February 17 and November 10, 1905, May 24, 1907, June 18, August 20, and October 7, 1909, and May 5, 1911.

6. *Jewish Free Press*, November 13, 1885; *Voice*, June 5, 1891, October 21, 1898, and July 15, 1904.

Goldsmith, Henry Hart, M. J. Jonas, Montague Lyon, Benjamin Schnur-macher, and Rudolph Wolfner. Similar identification of the city's out-standing physicians included Herman Tuholske, I. M. Epstein, Llewelyn Sale, A. Gratz Moses, Selig Simon, Henry L. Wolfner, A. Goldsmith, E. W. Haase, Harry Jacobson, E. D. Levy, Simon Politzer, H. Marks, and Jacob Friedman.[7]

Meriting special attention as an important Jewish political and civic leader of the period was Nathan Frank. Some consider him the "succes-sor" to Isidor Bush. Frank was born in 1852 in Peoria, Illinois, the son of German immigrants Brannette Weil and Abraham Frank. Following the Civil War the family moved to St. Louis, where Abraham Frank went into what became a very successful clothing business with his Weil brothers-in-law; he was also an early member of Shaare Emeth. Young Nathan graduated from Central High School, ranking first in his class; he attended Washington University and then Harvard Law School, where he received his law degree in 1871. Returning to St. Louis, he built a very successful legal practice, associating professionally with some of the city's leading lawyers and businessmen, and specializing in commercial and bankruptcy law. He soon became active in politics. In 1882 the city Republican Party nominated him for circuit court judge, but he lost in the ensuing election. In 1886 Republicans nominated him as their candidate for the United States House of Representatives, a nomination that stirred considerable dissension within party ranks. Two major newspapers that normally supported Republicans refused to endorse Frank's candidacy, as did some prominent Republican politicians, accusing him of being the handpicked lackey of the city's Republican boss, Chauncy I. Filley. That brought a countercharge that the real opposition to Frank was to his religion. The ensuing election became quite vitriolic, with overtones of religious bigotry expressed both subtly and overtly. Frank lost to his Democratic opponent by only 114 votes out of more than 15,000 cast. Republicans, on the other hand, claimed a victory for their candidate by 185 votes, accusing corrupt election commissioners of counting the ballots improperly. They formally contested the election, but lost. Two years later, in 1888, Frank again ran for Congress. This time, running as the candidate of both the Republican and the Union Labor Parties, he overwhelmed his opponent by about 3,000 votes. On December 2, 1889, Nathan Frank was sworn in as a member of the United States House of Representatives. He was the first Jew ever to represent the state of Missouri in that body. To this day he remains the *only* Jew ever to represent Missouri in Congress,

---

7. As summarized in a "looking back 25 years ago" piece in *Voice*, March 14, 1913.

in either the House of Representatives or the Senate (others have run, but were never elected).

Nathan Frank served only one term in Congress. During that brief period he compiled a very good legislative record, both in measures important at the national level as well as those vital to local constituent interests. He chose voluntarily not to serve more than one term, and returned instead to St. Louis to his lucrative law practice. Still, he had one burning political ambition: the United States Senate. Three times he ran, in 1910, 1916, and 1928, but he could never secure his party's nomination. Nevertheless, he remained very active in St. Louis civic affairs. He served as one of the commissioners for the famed World's Fair of 1904. He helped found the *St. Louis Star*, an important daily newspaper. A prolific real estate investor and developer, he had a hand in the improvement or construction of many landmark downtown and midtown buildings, including the Metropolitan Life Insurance Building, the *Star-Times* Building, and the stately Loew's State movie house.

Throughout his life as a St. Louis civic leader, Nathan Frank remained a leading and conspicuous member of the Jewish community, openly displaying pride in his religious affiliation. He was prominent in many Jewish social circles, especially the Harmonie and Columbian Clubs. He very generously supported the Jewish Hospital, of which his brother August Frank was the first president. Although a devoted member of Reform Shaare Emeth Temple, Frank nevertheless contributed and supported many Orthodox activities and institutions; he was a major benefactor for the Orthodox Old Folks Home when it was constructed on North Grand and Blair. A bachelor all his life, he was a popular figure in all sorts of social and civic activities. Frank was an avid baseball fan; he sat in the president's box at Sportsman's Park when William Howard Taft established the tradition of a president opening the season by throwing out the first ball. He was an excellent speaker and raconteur, and city officials often asked him to chair banquets when visiting dignitaries came to St. Louis. He contributed generously to many minority causes. More than once he provided the Negro Orphans Home with band instruments. A very close friend was Moses Green, prominent in the St. Louis black community; during one of Frank's runs for the United States Senate, Green responded to a request for support with: "Us Niggers and Jews must stick together." When Nathan Frank died in 1931, national, state, and local figures packed the Shaare Emeth sanctuary for the funeral service conducted there by Rabbi Julius Gordon.

Scattered throughout St. Louis are many statues and memorials to a variety of historic figures. One of the most beautiful honors Nathan Frank. It is the stately Nathan Frank Bandstand in the middle of Pagoda Lake opposite the entrance to the huge outdoor St. Louis Municipal Theater (the world-famous "Muny Opera") in Forest Park. Thousands of theater-goers come early each summer evening just to relax in the serenity of the lake and the bandstand, and to feed the myriads of ducks and their quaintly trailing ducklings as they swim gracefully around the memorial to one of St. Louis's most prominent citizens and certainly one of the most important members of the St. Louis Jewish community.[8]

As important as were all those Jewish contributions to St. Louis political and civic history, the role Jews played individually and collectively in the city's developing economy, and thus in its civic development, was perhaps even more significant. This looms especially important since St. Louis at the turn of the century was one of the fastest-growing and most rapidly developing communities in the United States. By 1900 it had become the fourth-largest city in the nation, and its legions of boosters, both local and nationwide, predicted nothing but continued growth and prosperity.

Few if any Jewish businessmen came to St. Louis already wealthy and successful. Whether of German or of eastern European background, they started at the bottom and worked their way up the ladder of economic success. (This was not unique to Jews, of course; it applied to other immigrant groups as well.) By the turn of the century most Jews of eastern European origin had not been in St. Louis long enough and had not had sufficient opportunity to have attained much in the way of business success. Most still experienced the poverty that had burdened them in their native lands. Agencies such as the Hebrew Immigrant Aid Society, the United Hebrew Relief Association, and the United Jewish Charities helped them find employment, often with already established German Jewish entrepreneurs, especially but by no means exclusively in clothing and related needle-goods businesses. In time a good number of those Russian immigrants established their own businesses and emulated successful experiences of many of their German Jewish predecessors. But that played out in twentieth-century St. Louis Jewish history. Most of the

---

8. The biographical sketch of Nathan Frank is based on Burton A. Boxerman, "The Honorable Nathan Frank," 33–51; and from biographical sketches in *Biographical Directory of the American Congress, 1774–1949*, House Doc. 607, 81st Cong., 2d Sess., 1179–80; Walter B. Stevens, *St. Louis, The Fourth City*, vol. 2, 158–60; and Hyde and Conard, eds., *Encyclopedia of the History of St. Louis*, vol. 2, 828–30. See also *Tribune*, October 20, 1882; *Jewish Free Press*, November 12, 1886; *Voice*, September 14, October 13, and November 16, 1888, March 14, 1902, and October 13, 1911; and Kelsoe, ed., *St. Louis Reference Record*, 21, 197. Although known widely as an active member of Shaare Emeth, Frank also belonged to B'nai Amoona. *Modern View 25*, 66.

Jewish successes in nineteenth-century business development were made by German Jews.[9]

As we have seen, some German Jews who had established their roots in the St. Louis economy even before the Civil War grew to prominence after the war. Many more started in St. Louis after the Civil War, and some achieved prestigious and lucrative positions in the St. Louis business environment. Many others, however, remained in that category of small neighborhood businesses, the names of which rarely, if ever, appear in history books. Yet these small businesses are in one sense the backbone and foundation of any city's economy, and St. Louis was no exception. These businesses were owned by individuals of virtually every European nationality, as well as adherents of all religions, and were scattered throughout the city, in contrast with more concentrated residential patterns. Histories of American Jewry stress how many Jews proliferated in the garment industries; no one can dispute that. But Jews could be found in many other fields, and their roles and contributions there should not be minimized. Business advertising in the St. Louis Jewish press in the decades beginning in the 1870s reveals that Jews engaged in a broad spectrum of the city's commercial endeavors.[10]

Several statistical studies verify that widespread involvement. One study covered the early 1880s. The total Jewish population then was estimated at slightly more than ten thousand, which included, of course, women and children, homemakers, and students not in the workforce. The study listed 1,140 jobs and occupations held by Jews, and showed the following widespread distribution:

Occupation	Number	Percentage
Agents, Insurance and Manufacturers'	9	.79%
Agriculture	3	.26
Alcohol, Liquor, Saloon owners	75	6.58
Artists. Painter (Portrait)	2	.17

---

9. Much has been written about the trials and tribulations of German Jewish immigrants and their rise from poverty and peddler status to successful entrepreneurs. Bibliographies in any good American Jewish history give adequate listings of such studies. An especially interesting brief account is Judith Greenfield, "The Role of the Jews in the Development of the Clothing Industry in the United States," 180–204. Alfred Fleishman's "Jewish Community Played Role in Business Growth," *St. Louis Jewish Light,* July 17, 1985, paints a broad overview of Jewish contributions to the St. Louis business environment.

10. Of course Jews were not the only advertisers in the Jewish press, but from those businesses that can be identified as Jewish-owned and/or operated, the "broad participation" generalization certainly stands as valid.

Bands, Musicians, Music Teachers, Dancing Teachers	17	1.49
Bankers, Brokers	7	.61
Barbers, Hairdressers, Wigs	25	2.19
Boarding Houses	9	.79
Bookbinders & Sellers, Stationery, News	10	.88
Boots & Shoes, Manufacturers & Dealers	68	5.96
Butchers, Stockyard dealers	44	3.86
China dealers, Glassware, Cutlery	9	.79
Cigar and Tobacco dealers	42	3.68
Clocks, Watches, Jewelry, Diamonds	27	2.37
Clothing dealers (Second hand included)	153	13.42
Commission Merchants	19	1.67
Cotton buyers and dealers	4	.35
Dentists	3	.26
Druggists	17	1.49
Dry Goods	68	5.96
Fancy Goods and Notions	36	3.16
Furniture dealers	16	1.40
Furs, hats, and cap dealers	19	1.67
Government workers, notaries public	25	2.19
Grocers and Food Dealers	80	7.02
Hardware, gunsmiths, Horse Supply Dealers	27	2.37
Laundry	1	.09
Lawyers	21	1.84
Manufacturers, small goods, machinery, hardware	16	1.40
Midwives	5	.44
Opticians	1	.09
Pawnbrokers, Junk Dealers	9	.81
Photographers	5	.44
Physicians, Surgeons, Chiropodist	18	1.58
Printers	5	.44
Publishers	5	.44
Rag Dealers	3	.26
Real Estate Brokers	7	.61
Restaurants	2	.17
Second hand stores	20	1.75
Skilled Laborers, Architects, Painters, Blacksmiths, Carpenters, Plumbers, etc.	115	10.09
Tailors	47	4.12
Toy dealers	2	.17
Undertakers	2	.17
Wood and Coal dealers	2	.17
TOTAL	1,140	99.97%

(The total percentage is not 100 percent due to rounding off percentages for each occupation.)[11]

---

11. Jan M. Brahms, "An Analytical Study of the Economic Life of the Jews in St. Louis, 1879–1881," in St. Louis, Missouri File, AJA.

A survey of St. Louis Jewish life a decade later, in the early 1890s, identified all these and more as occupations in which Jews were engaged. Records of a St. Louis B'nai B'rith lodge for 1903–1905 showed its members' occupations as merchants, clerks, tailors, peddlers, machinists, traveling salesmen, cabinetmakers, tinners, carriage makers, window decorators, painters, upholsterers, bookkeepers, plumbers, railroad employees, doctors, printers, and druggists.[12]

A critical evaluation of Jews in the St. Louis business economy indicates that they might be divided into four categories. First were those who did not own their own businesses but who worked for others as clerks, skilled and unskilled laborers and craftsmen, sales and office personnel, and the like. Then there were the small, individually owned businesses that provided a decent living for the owners but that never became more than just small neighborhood stores. Grocers, butchers, bakers, delicatessens, dry goods, and clothing stores, as well as diverse businesses such as repair shops, metal processors, and liveries, made up most of this category. By generally accepted sociological standards, both groups would be considered solid middle class, albeit anything but affluent, and they included most of the Jews in the St. Louis economy. Then there were those businesses that started small but became larger and were prosperous enough to pass on to descendants, and engendered enough success that those families became at least somewhat affluent and well-to-do. The final group, very much smaller in number, included those that became business empires and made those families wealthy and influential in both the Jewish community and in the larger citywide community, if not even beyond.

So it was, then, that Manuel Waldman worked as a cutter in a cap factory, and Joseph Seligman as a clerk in the German Savings Bank. Herman Wohl provided musical entertainment at the International Buffet and Restaurant at 917 Franklin. Emanuel Frank was a pharmacist in a drugstore at Grand and Franklin, Sigmund Meier operated a photography studio at 2624 South Jefferson, and Emil Hartman had his grocery store at 1103 North Vandeventer. Adolph Meyer opened a livery stable at 601 Park Avenue, and Henry Roth sold "the finest of wines" in his liquor store at 3334 Olive. Balmer and Weber's Music Store, 311 North Broadway, furnished the latest popular music for all kinds of entertainments, and offered violin lessons as a house specialty. Charles Novack and Joseph H. Kassel owned the West End Piano Repairing Company at 2646 Olive, and Louis Beer of 22

---

12. Harold L. Rubens, "Jewish Life in a Mississippi Valley Metropolis as Reflected in the *Jewish Voice* of St. Louis, 1888–1891, Inclusive," in St. Louis, Missouri File, AJA; "Records and Ledgers, 1903, Isidor Bush Lodge No. 557," in B'nai B'rith File, AJA.

South Third Street manufactured and repaired vaults and safes. Locksmith A. C. Wolfram, 706 Market Street, provided a wide variety of locks and safety devices; he also sharpened and repaired lawn mowers. August Grunewald, 1408 Biddle Street, was available for all kinds of carpentry work, while the Caplan Galvanized Iron Cornice Company had the "best" in guttering and downspouts. Zeller Brothers Catering Company (later to become Dorr and Zeller Caterers) furnished estimates for weddings and other affairs, and advertised the tastiest of lunches for shoppers and businessmen at their 415 North Seventh restaurant. Their new (in 1906) place at 4701 McPherson specialized in ice cream, fruit ices, and other refreshments and delicacies popular at the World's Fair. Jacob Goodman was proprietor of the St. Louis Hebrew Book Store at 828 Carr Street, where one could purchase Judaica items of all sorts, including *taleisim* (prayer shawls) and prayer books with English and German translations.[13]

A few more "success stories" show the wide diversity of Jewish participation in the St. Louis economy. Joel Swope emigrated from Saxony in 1867, and opened a shoe store on Fourth Street opposite the old French Market. Success led to several larger quarters, eventually to Tenth and Olive, with a branch opened later in the "west end" to specialize in women's and children's footwear and hosiery. The Swopes and their children were active in many Jewish affairs. Joel's son Horace became especially active on the St. Louis Art Museum board, and he donated a valuable collection of prints to the museum.[14]

Jacob Lampert prospered with his cigar manufacturing firm at 412 Market Street; Governor Elliott W. Major also honored him by naming him to the Missouri Commission for the Blind. Active in affairs at United Hebrew Temple, B'nai B'rith, and the Jewish Children's Shelter Home, Lampert was also Grand Master of the Masonic Order in Missouri and a highly regarded musician. A bachelor, when he died he divided up the profits of his cigar manufacturing business among his employees, and by his will left the business to them (after also bequeathing some $7 million to various charities).[15]

---

13. Advertisements by Jewish (and non-Jewish) merchants can be found in every issue of the St. Louis Jewish press. Those mentioned here were taken at random from the *Jewish Free Press*, December 25, 1885, and from *Voice*, November 29, 1889, May 5 and November 10, 1893, April 20, 1904, December 29, 1905, January 22 and March 30, 1906, and July 19 and September 13, 1907. See also Cecil M. Baskett, ed., *Men of Affairs in St. Louis*, 55, 81.

14. Swope Papers, Missouri Box, AJA; *Modern View 25*, 120; *St. Louis Globe-Democrat*, October 1, 1940.

15. *Voice*, November 10, 1916; *Modern View 25*, 104.

Elkan W. Glauber, active in B'nai B'rith and Temple Israel, built up a prosperous dry-cleaning business as owner of the Aalco Laundry Company and the Colonial Laundry Company, and he sat on the executive committee of the Laundrymen's National Association of America. Sam Lazarus, a native of Syracuse, New York, worked in various locations in Louisiana and Texas in the mercantile business and in cattle ranching before settling in St. Louis. In St. Louis he established the Acme Cement Plaster Company, which became an important cog in the city's building and construction industry.[16]

In 1896 Henry B. Berger opened the H. B. Berger Livery and Undertaking Company at 925 North Seventh near Carr with "carriages available for all occasions." The firm soon became a major component of the Jewish community, serving both Reform and Orthodox Jews for funeral purposes. In 1914, as the Jewish population expanded westward, Berger's funeral home moved to 4715 McPherson. Throughout the twentieth century it continued to provide its services to the St. Louis Jewish community from that location, its ownership remaining in the family, passing from generation to generation. Even as the mortuary provided professional services to the community, its owners also participated actively in many Jewish activities and organizations, including temple and synagogue affiliation, the Orthodox Old Folks Home, the Jewish Hospital, Hadassah, and numerous philanthropic and service organizations.[17]

These are but a representative few of the many small businesses that Jews built in St. Louis and that were so basic to the Jewish community and to the city's economic growth. "The Jews of St. Louis were interested in many business areas," concluded one historical observer. "They had little businessmen and big businessmen. . . . They had their professional men, their manufacturers, their retailers, their wholesalers, their traveling salesmen."[18]

As is wont in any democratic free enterprise society, some businesses became larger and more influential than others, both within the Jewish community and within the broader St. Louis economic scene. Some of

---

16. *Voice*, July 25, 1919; *Modern View* 25, 71, 120.

17. Author's interview with Richard Stein, president of Berger Mortuary, October 10, 1994, notes in author's possession. See also *Voice*, November 3, 1905, March 30, 1906, March 3 and December 22, 1911, and December 18, 1914. Another early Jewish mortuary was the Isaacs-Rindskopf Undertaking Company, founded by Jonas Isaacs, Walter Isaacs, and Herman Rindskopf. See *Voice*, April 6, 1906, December 13, 1907, May 7, 1909, and December 22, 1911.

18. Rubens, "Jewish Life in a Mississippi River Metropolis," St. Louis, Missouri File, AJA.

these businesses that began before the Civil War and became giants in the decades that followed have been noted: Freund Baking Company; Louis Bauman Jewelry Company; Rosenheim, Levis and Zukowsi Mercantile Company; R. and W. Goldstein Mercantile Company; Marx and Haas Clothing Company; and Fuld-Goodwin Mercantile Company. More giant Jewish-owned businesses came into being after the Civil War.[19]

Because of its strategic location on the Mississippi River, St. Louis has long been a vital link in the cotton trade. Several Jews played important roles in the cotton business; one of the most prominent was Jacob D. Goldman. His career is interesting not only as a success story in itself but also as an illustration of the many difficulties faced by so many immigrants as they built a new life in America.

A native of Essenheim, near Mainz, Germany, Goldman was born on April 26, 1845. He was eight years old when he received the shattering news, while in Hebrew school, that his mother had just died of typhoid fever. Many years later Goldman described how her body was laid out on a bed of straw on the floor at home, as was the Orthodox custom then, and how he dolefully sat on her coffin in the wagon that trundled her body to the cemetery. When Goldman finished public school at age fifteen, his father wanted him to come into his hardware business; instead in 1860 the young man emigrated with friends to America. Later he recalled his excitement when he saw oranges for the first time in his life in the Hamburg port: "I must have eaten a dozen of them in one day," he wrote in his memoirs. Goldman spent fifteen days at sea in third class aboard

---

19. Only a few more might be mentioned here: the Delmar Manufacturing Company, makers of children's and infants' clothing, run by B. M. Silverstein, A. G. Kratz, and Charles H. Block; Simon Bienenstock and Company, wool merchants, who "contributed largely toward making St. Louis the leading wool market of the west"; the Wolff-Wilson Drug Company, for many years at the corner of Seventh and Washington, dispensers of drugs, toiletries, and related items, headed by Edward H. and C. R. Wolff; the New Era Shirt Company, founded in 1886 by T. L. Rubenstein, who built an organization that manufactured more than a million men's shirts a year at its Ninth and Lucas location; Kline's Department Store, opened in 1904 by Isaac Kline as one of a national chain of six department stores, which flourished for decades at its Sixth and Washington location. These firms not only contributed immensely to the St. Louis economy but also their owners were very active in various community affairs, some in leadership roles. Edward H. Wolff, for instance, of the Wolff-Davis Drug Company, served as president of the St. Louis Pharmacal Society. Isaac Kline was on the board of directors of the Associated Retailers' Association of St. Louis, and he served in a similar capacity for both the YMHA and the Jewish Charitable and Educational Union. Among others, see *Voice*, April 24, 1908, and *Modern View 25*, 120, 139, 140. Many more firms came into being after 1907 and contributed much to the economic growth of St. Louis.

the side-wheel steamer *Saxonia,* subsisting mostly on salted herring and black bread. Landing in New York, he worked there briefly in an uncle's wholesale clothing business. Then he went to another uncle, in Hartford, Connecticut, and peddled for him. Distressed because he was robbed so often, young Goldman went to another relative in Griffin, Georgia, where he did general janitorial work and, after he had learned enough English, clerked from behind the counter.

When the Civil War broke out, Goldman joined the 54th Georgia Infantry Regiment. He fought in several bloody battles, including Murfreesboro and Chickamauga. "The South got to be in a pitiful condition," he recalled later. "For food for the Army and its citizens we had to depend upon what the colored people raised for their mistresses and the children while the men were [away] fighting, they being in bondage, and that is why I will always think well of the colored race—on account of the way they acted during the war towards the Southern people."[20]

When the war was over, widespread poverty and unemployment in the South led Goldman eventually to Chicago. There he learned of the need for merchandise clerks in Cairo, Illinois, because so many Union soldiers were traveling through there on their way home and workers were needed to handle the enormous trade in civilian clothing. After a few months in Cairo, Goldman moved across the Ohio River to Paducah, Kentucky, where now, having saved a little money, he opened a clothing business with a friend, Henry Weil. Late in 1865 Goldman went to Jacksonport, Arkansas, as the agent for their Weil and Goldman Company. Two years later, in 1867, the intrepid Goldman formed a new business with Levi Hecht, Hecht and Goldman, in Jacksonport. By 1870 he was on his own, as the Jake Goldman Company. In 1873 he and Benjamin Adler established Adler-Goldman and Company, in Jacksonport, dealers in cotton.

Although Adler-Goldman prospered in Arkansas, in 1875 the company moved to St. Louis, which by then had become a major midwestern center for the cotton industry. The city's importance in that trade was greatly enhanced as a consequence of the widespread yellow fever epidemic of 1878–1879, which led many cotton dealers in the southern Mississippi valley to transfer their operations to a safer location in St. Louis.

Once in St. Louis, Adler-Goldman and Company grew steadily and prospered. In 1889 two more men came into the business, Gus Rosenberg and Julius Lesser, and the reorganized firm was incorporated as the Adler-Goldman Commission Company. By this time Goldman had become a director and vice president of the Fourth National Bank. "Very

---

20. J. D. Goldman File, AJA.

large financial resources, great business experience, and extensive and fair dealing" were characteristics "to which the firm [could] point with well-justified pride," a St. Louis business observer wrote. All who ran the firm were "well known in business and social circles . . . active in public matters and in everything tending to promote the good and welfare of the community." By the turn of the century Adler-Goldman Commission Company ranked as one of the most successful firms in the cotton trade; indeed, Jacob Goldman was chosen several times by his business peers to serve as president of the prestigious St. Louis Cotton Exchange. An active member of Shaare Emeth Temple, Goldman belonged to numerous mercantile, social, and benevolent organizations, and was highly respected for his honesty and integrity in the Jewish community and in the broader secular St. Louis environment.[21]

In 1891 Goldman, Lesser, and Adler organized another company, incorporated as the Lesser-Goldman Commission Company. With Julius Lesser as president and Goldman as vice president, this organization gradually superseded the Adler-Goldman Company. They established twelve branches throughout Arkansas, which then sold cotton to factories in New England, Great Britain, the European continent, and Japan. Like Jacob Goldman, Lesser was also a member of Shaare Emeth and was active in many Jewish community and civic projects. In time the leadership of the company passed on to the next generation, Alvin D. Goldman and Harry Lesser. (In fact, Alvin Goldman married Blanche Lesser, Harry Lesser's sister.) They continued for many years the great success of the business as president and vice president of the increasingly prosperous and influential Lesser-Goldman Commission Company, and were a major factor in St. Louis's prominence in the cotton trade. Equally important was their continuous conscientious participation in the city's civic affairs as well as in matters pertaining to the Jewish community, including Shaare Emeth Temple, the Jewish Hospital, the YMHA, B'nai B'rith, and the Federation of Jewish Charities. In addition, St. Louis voters elected Lesser to the city council in 1905, but he died in 1908, at age fifty-four, before his term of office expired.[22]

Another important Jewish association with the St. Louis cotton trade was A. L. Wolff and Company. Wolff established himself in St. Louis in 1880 as the agent of a British firm, A. Stern and Company of Liverpool, and

---

21. Ibid.
22. Ibid. For more on Goldman and Lesser and the St. Louis cotton trade, see *Modern View,* July 10, 1908, and *Modern View 25,* 97–98; Scharf, *Saint Louis City and County,* vol. 2, 1217–21; Kargau, *Mercantile, Industrial and Professional Saint Louis,* 128–29; and Primm, *Lion of the Valley,* 270–71, 291–94.

he soon emerged as a significant figure in the midwestern cotton market. He extended his operations through branch offices in several cities in Texas, and shipped most of his cotton through Galveston to Liverpool, from where it was distributed to mills throughout England and the European continent. Wolff "enjoy[ed] the highest esteem in the mercantile and social circles of St. Louis," according to a St. Louis business historian, as "one of the best known cotton merchants in the Southern States."[23]

Jews played a role in the St. Louis real estate business as well, including leadership positions from time to time on the important St. Louis Real Estate Exchange. Organized in 1877, the Exchange not only set guidelines for real estate transactions but also advanced the interests of the city itself by recommending and promoting public improvements. Active in the real estate business as well as in the Exchange in those turn-of-the-century years were such well-known Jews as Marcus A. Wolff, William Einstein, Nathan Frank, Meyer Jacoby, Simon Mayer, Samuel Bowman, and J. I. Epstein.[24]

One of the most prominent (along with Nathan Frank) was Samuel Bowman. Born in the small town of Weston, Missouri, in 1851, Bowman came to St. Louis when he was seven years old. His father had prospered as a pioneer merchant in northwestern Missouri, but he died in 1854, leaving his estate to his widow, who moved to St. Louis. Unfortunately her funds soon disappeared, and young Samuel had to quit school at age fourteen to earn a living for the family. He worked at several jobs, first with a real estate firm, and then with the Bluffton Wine Company. Isidor Bush was then treasurer of the wine company, and Bowman became his assistant. When Bush later bought out the business, Bowman became a partner. He was nineteen at the time. A restless young enterpreneur, he soon ventured into the liquor business on his own.

Successful there, in 1887 Bowman branched out into real estate, establishing the firm of Samuel Bowman and Company. Before long he developed into "one of the most active members of that fraternity," according to a St. Louis business historian, and became "identified with some of the most progressive movements for the development of the real estate interest in St. Louis." First-class buildings that he erected included the Railway Exchange Building, the West End Hotel, the Fraternal Building, the Bowman Building, and several blocks of small business establishments on South Jefferson. Bowman played an important role in the erection of the Municipal Free Bridge across the Mississippi and in bringing about

---

23. Kargau, *Mercantile, Industrial and Professional Saint Louis*, 131–32.
24. Ibid., 132–39; Gill, *St. Louis Story*, vol. 1, 225–26.

improvements in the downtown lighting system. Very much a public-spirited citizen, he was a director of the St. Louis Real Estate Board, the Civic League, and the Chamber of Commerce. At the same time, he was very active and highly respected in the Jewish community. A devoted member of Temple Israel, Bowman participated prominently, often in leadership roles, in many Jewish social and charitable affairs, especially those associated with B'nai B'rith.[25]

Several prominent Jews engaged actively in the securities and invest-ment business in St. Louis. They included, among others, Moses Fraley, Benjamin Altheimer, David and William Kohn, Edward Popper, Morris and Joseph Glaser, I. M. Simon, and Richard Singer. All became quite prosperous and influential in their brokerage ventures. Equally important, all participated actively in Jewish community affairs as well as in citywide civic and humanitarian projects.[26] Benjamin Altheimer and Moses Fraley merit special attention.

Born in Darmstadt, Germany, Benjamin Altheimer was educated there and in Frankfort-am-Main, majoring in language and mathematics. In 1868, at age eighteen, he emigrated to America, settling first in Memphis. In 1874 he moved to St. Louis where, with Edward D. Rawlings, he formed the Altheimer-Rawlings Investment Company, which became one of the most prestigious brokerage firms in the city. In 1915 Altheimer moved to New York, for personal as much as for business reasons. Neverthe-less, Altheimer always considered St. Louis his sentimental home, and he returned often for extended stays. When he died in 1938, his body was brought to St. Louis for burial alongside his wife in the Eisenstadt Mausoleum in Mount Sinai Cemetery.

Altheimer's many civic and philanthropic achievements transcended a deep personal tragedy. In 1880 he married beauteous Jennie Eisenstadt of St. Louis; but in 1883, following the birth of their daughter, his wife died. Altheimer never remarried, and he doted lovingly on his daughter for the rest of his life. In fact, when she married Arthur W. Weil of New York and moved there with him, Altheimer transferred many of his business affairs to New York so he could be closer to her.

Altheimer's involvement in Jewish affairs in St. Louis were legion. One of the founders of Temple Israel, he was active in numerous St. Louis

25. *Voice*, September 2, 1898; *Modern View 25*, 7–10, 91; Kargau, *Mercantile, Industrial and Professional Saint Louis*, 137–38. Well into the 1920s, when he finally retired from a lengthy and active career, Samuel Bowman's name was associated with innumerable St. Louis civic projects as well as with many Jewish community activities.

26. Kargau, *Mercantile, Industrial and Professional Saint Louis*, 148–56, 176–80; Gill, *St. Louis Story*, vol. 1, 225–26.

Jewish organizations, including B'nai B'rith, the Jewish Hospital, and the Jewish Charitable and Educational Union, in all of which he held prominent leadership roles. On the national level, he held important positions in the B'nai B'rith Cleveland Orphans Home and in the Union of American Hebrew Congregations. He was a member of the St. Louis Public Library Board and of the Preetorius Library of Washington University. When the St. Louis public schools celebrated the 350th anniversary of William Shakespeare's birth, Ben Altheimer saw to it that every high school in the city received a complete set of Shakespeare's works. So noteworthy was he in interdenominational charitable affairs that Archbishop John J. Glennon, the city's popular Catholic prelate, dubbed him "the Napoleon of charity."

Two nationally important commemorative days resulted directly from Altheimer's humanitarianism and patriotism. One cold night in January 1912, as Altheimer was leaving a banquet given for the opening of the St. Louis Central Library, a shivering, half-starved beggar approached him for a handout. The shocking contrast between that poor wretch and the lavish banquet he had just attended deeply moved Altheimer. First he put the stranger up in a nearby hotel. The next day Altheimer met with some of the city's leading citizens and helped organize a citywide clothing collection to aid the needy. The results were astoundingly successful. Publicized in the press, "Bundle Day" spread rapidly to other cities, and for years thereafter a national Bundle Day Association conducted annual drives to collect clothing for needy people. Throughout the country this humanitarian program was widely accredited to St. Louisan Benjamin Altheimer.

At about the same time, Altheimer spearheaded a similar project, this one more patriotic in nature. In 1913 Altheimer suggested to leaders of the St. Louis Jewish Sabbath schools that they include a special tribute to the American flag in their closing exercises. A "Flag Day" thus became part of the year's activities right before schools adjourned in June for their summer recess. In 1917, with the United States engaged in World War I, Altheimer suggested the same idea to President Woodrow Wilson as a way for the American people to demonstrate support for the war effort. The result was a presidential proclamation declaring June 14 as America's Flag Day. Although a national Bundle Day eventually faded away, June 14 remains to this day our national Flag Day.[27]

With Altheimer, Moses Fraley ranked as another of the most influential Jewish citizens of St. Louis. Born in Frederick, Maryland, in 1843, Fraley

27. *Voice*, June 28, 1904, June 30, 1909, September 9, 1910, May 2 and 16, 1913, March 5 and October 22, 1915, May 12, 1916, and November 14, 1919; *Modern View*, May 16, 1913, June 13, 1930, and May 5, 1938; *St. Louis Globe-Democrat*, May 12, 1913; Kargau, *Mercantile, Industrial and Professional Saint Louis*, 149–50.

began his business career as proprietor of a general store in Parkersburg, West Virginia. In 1863 he and a friend, Joseph Polack, moved west and eventually started a clothing business in St. Louis. Although five years in that undertaking proved quite prosperous, in 1868 Fraley sold out his interest and started the banking and brokerage firm of Donaldson and Fraley. Successful there, Fraley nevertheless changed fields again, and in 1883 he entered the grain commission business. The firm of Fraley and Carter soon amassed a fortune, but just as quickly lost it. When the company went bankrupt, Fraley vowed to pay his creditors all he owed them, a promise he assiduously kept. The restless entrepreneur changed careers once more in 1893, when he entered the insurance business, where he was successful until he died in 1917. His considerable involvement in city affairs included four years of service on the St. Louis city council.

Most of Fraley's nonbusiness activities focused on Jewish affairs, and by the 1880s he had become, along with men such as Isidor Bush, Marcus Bernheimer, and Benjamin Altheimer, a virtual power broker in the St. Louis Jewish community. He played a prominent role, as already noted, in the creation of Temple Israel, and he served that institution faithfully all his life as president and member of its board of directors. He was a driving force in organizing community backing for the YMHA when support for that institution seemed to wane in the early 1900s. Fraley also figured substantially in the creation of the United Jewish Charities (one of the forerunners of the present Jewish Federation of St. Louis). As its president for many years, he organized successful campaigns to raise needed money for the poor and the indigent, and he made certain those funds were dispensed equitably and properly. When Fraley died in 1917, the *St. Louis Post-Dispatch* referred to him as "probably the most widely known Jewish resident of St. Louis."[28]

St. Louis Jews were important participants in the city's lumber industry. Trade in lumber constituted a considerable portion of the area's economy, due in no small part to the city's location as a crossroads of river and railroad lumber traffic. In 1901, for instance, the burgeoning city of St. Louis alone consumed some five hundred million board feet of lumber; yet that was but a small part of the overall lumber trade that passed through to outside consumers. Markets consisted not only in the obvious building and furniture industries but also for other ancillary enterprises such as box and cooper factories, saw and planing mills, wagon and carriage makers,

---

28. Boxerman, "St. Louis Jewish Leaders," 16–25. For more on Fraley, see Moses Fraley File, AJA; *Voice*, January 28, 1881, December 25, 1903, February 7, 1913, and April 9 and November 19, 1915; and *St. Louis Globe-Democrat*, November 4, 1915.

and sash, door, frame, and stair manufacturers. Forest products grown in at least seventeen states were sold by St. Louis firms, and the capital invested in those businesses in St. Louis alone amounted to millions of dollars.[29]

Among the leading dealers in lumber was the firm of Abeles and Taussig, established in 1884. B. J. Taussig withdrew from the company in the early 1890s, and Robert Abeles carried on alone. The firm specialized in timber for railroad cars and ties, and, according to a St. Louis business chronicler, held "an enviable reputation among railroad officials and contractors." That same historian characterized Abeles as "a very active businessman of the strictest integrity, highly esteemed in commercial circles, a member of the St. Louis Merchants Exchange and several mercantile and social organizations." Abeles was a lifelong and active member of United Hebrew Congregation; he served also in several capacities with the YMHA and with several Jewish philanthropic organizations.[30]

Closely associated with lumbering was furniture manufacturing, and part of the city's growth to 1900 resulted from its development as a leading furniture center. By the turn of the century more than fifty furniture manufacturers flourished in St. Louis, employing at least six thousand workers. Furniture sales in 1900 alone exceeded $30 million.[31]

Joseph Smith founded the furniture company bearing his name, at first a modest retail outlet at 816 North Seventh Street. He soon purchased the entire five-story building at that address, which he converted into a manufacturing plant for all kinds of furniture that he then sold through his own retail outlets. Adding to his original store on North Seventh, Smith soon opened three more retail stores, one at 816 Franklin Avenue in the downtown area, one at 2722 Cherokee in the south-side Cherokee Street shopping district, and one at 5955 Easton Avenue in the Wellston shopping area as the St. Louis population after the turn of the century continued to move westward beyond the city limits and into St. Louis County.[32]

In 1891 Morris Goldman founded the Goldman Brothers Furniture Company at 1104 Olive Street. Joined by his brothers Stanley and Gilbert, Goldman expanded his establishment to cover almost half of that block along Olive Street. Goldman Brothers, which manufactured and also sold retail, became one of several firms that ensured the continued stability of the downtown St. Louis business community. All three Goldman brothers were active in Temple Israel affairs, B'nai B'rith, and many Jewish

---

29. Kargau, *Mercantile, Industrial and Professional Saint Louis*, 233.
30. Ibid., 233–34.
31. Ibid., 253–54.
32. *Modern View 25*, 136–37.

philanthropic agencies, as well as in a variety of non-Jewish fraternal and charitable organizations. Morris Goldman's son Jerome was killed in action in the battle of Belleau Wood in World War I; the Jerome L. Goldman Post No. 96 of the American Legion is named in his honor.[33]

Important to any city is the construction of streets and sewers and similar foundations for a variety of building and large engineering projects. This was the trade of the Skrainka Construction Company, started by brothers William, Joseph, and Phillip Skrainka, who had emigrated to St. Louis from Budapest, Hungary, about the time of the Civil War. Skilled in stone and masonry work, they established themselves as contractors for heavy concrete and masonry foundations. By the 1880s all three brothers had died, and their sons took over the business. Under the direction now of cousins Louis, Fred, and Morris Skrainka, the Skrainka Construction Company developed into one of the city's important contractors for this type of heavy industry. They helped construct the city's new waterworks, built several bridge overpasses, and laid the foundation for Union Station. The firm provided almost uninterrupted employment for hundreds of workmen and laborers, and because of its excellent treatment of its workers, according to a St. Louis business historian, it never was troubled by labor problems or strike movements. "All three [partners] are active, energetic businessmen of great ability," this observer wrote, and "they have an excellent standing in the community and take an active interest in all public affairs." Their "active interest" applied also to Jewish community affairs, the cousins and their wives being associated with numerous social, charitable, and humanitarian endeavors.[34]

Despite the city's role as gateway to the raucous western frontier, St. Louis for a long time had included the music profession as part of its cultural and economic environments. One need only recall the role of the early Philipson brothers. The arrival of so many cultured Germans following the European revolutions of 1848 gave a fresh impetus to the city's musical life, especially in the professional activities of talented musicians and music teachers. The Louis Conrath College of Music and the Clement Strassberger's Conservatory of Music were famed throughout the country for the quality of their music education and the performance excellence of their graduates.[35]

Included in this grouping of outstanding St. Louis musicians and music educators was the "powerful team" of brothers Marcus, Abraham,

---

33. Ibid., 87, 95.

34. Ibid., 21; *Voice*, February 7, 1902; *Gould's Blue Book, 1887,* 85–86; Kargau, *Mercantile, Industrial and Professional Saint Louis,* 331–32.

35. Kargau, *Mercantile, Industrial and Professional Saint Louis,* 339–42.

and Herman Epstein. They began their musical studies at an early age, and for more than a quarter of a century gained enviable reputations as concert performers. Marcus Epstein excelled in music composition and instrumentation, and was widely in demand as a conductor for symphony and opera performances. He also directed several musical productions for the YMHA. Abraham Epstein gained eminence as an organist who also earned superlative praises for the difficult role of piano accompanist for touring concert singers and instrumental performers. He played the organ and conducted the choir at Shaare Emeth Temple, and directed musicals for the YMHA. He also conducted various local amateur orchestras, whose popular performances always received excellent receptions. Herman Epstein, the youngest brother, studied for several years in Europe before returning to become a brilliant performer and excellent teacher. The brothers' Beethoven Conservatory of Music at Twenty-Third and Locust Streets produced graduates who, like those from the Strassberger and Conrath schools, vied with the best talent in the country. Consummate professionals, the brothers also spent considerable time at the Educational Alliance Building, where they became popular performers and instructors for many of the immigrants who attended or participated in musical programs there.[36]

Morris Schweig, a young German photographer vacationing in America in 1886, planned to meet a Berlin friend who had emigrated earlier to this country. When he reached New York, Schweig learned that his friend had moved to St. Louis. Thanks to a railroad price war, Schweig was able to get to St. Louis for only one dollar; he then found the city such a pleasant place that he decided to stay. He began working, at eight dollars a week, for J. C. Strauss, at that time a popular photographer for many of the city's wealthy and influential families. Schweig soon sent to Posen, Germany, for his fiancée, Frieda Rosenfeld. She came to St. Louis, the two were married, and they raised six children. Schweig also brought over his wife's mother, brother, and sister. The latter married Samuel Cohl, a photographer friend of Schweig's. In 1892 Schweig went into business on his own, opening a studio at 1717 Franklin. The following year his brother-in-law came into the business, now called Schweig and Cohl Photo Studio. Within a short time "Der Deutsche Photographe" became a favorite photographer for Confirmation classes not only in the Jewish community but also in many German Lutheran and Catholic churches. In 1898 Cohl left to seek a better fortune in the West, and Schweig continued the business on his own.

36. Ibid., 339–58. See also *Voice*, July 22, September 30, and October 14, 1904, August 24, and September 14 and 21, 1906.

Eventually his oldest son Martin came into the firm, which prospered and moved into larger and better-equipped quarters at 4927 Delmar. Four generations of Schweigs continued Morris Schweig's photographic business, which an art editor of the *St. Louis Post-Dispatch* described as "one of the most respected establishments in town."[37]

Precision manufacturing is absolutely vital to the medical and scientific professions, especially for surgical, optical, mathematical, and photographic instruments. A. S. Aloe Company for many years has been one of the country's largest and most respected in that field. Albert S. Aloe came to St. Louis from Edinburgh, Scotland, as a boy, and in 1860 founded the firm that bore his name. First located in a small shop at Third and Olive, the success and growth of the business led to several moves into more spacious quarters. Employing exceedingly skilled artisans, the firm established three major departments for the manufacture and sale of surgical, optical, and photographic instruments. After Aloe died in 1893, his sons, all born in St. Louis, took over the operation of what had already become a vital component of this highly skilled industry. A St. Louis business historian wrote that "cultural gentlemen as they are, [they] enjoy the respect of the business community, the esteem of a large circle of friends, and are public-spirited citizens who never fail to take an active interest in everything tending to promote the general welfare of their native city."[38]

37. *St. Louis Post Dispatch*, December 25, 1983. See also "Morris Schweig, Biography of Morris Schweig," manuscript given to author by Schweig descendant Frieda Kranzberg, St. Louis, April 27, 1986, copy in possession of author. Block Brothers constituted another firm prominent in that business in St. Louis.

38. Kargau, *Mercantile, Industrial and Professional Saint Louis*, 417. One of those brothers, Louis Patrick Aloe, merits special mention. In 1915 St. Louis voters elected him president of the Board of Aldermen. It was the highest elective city office ever held by a St. Louis Jew. After the United States entered World War I in 1917, severe illness incapacitated Mayor Henry Kiel, and Aloe became acting mayor during those critical war years. In 1940 the city unveiled a beautiful and stately memorial to him on Market Street directly across from Union Station: the Louis P. Aloe Plaza. It stands as one of the most well-known monuments in the city. For more on Louis P. Aloe see *Modern View 25*, 68; Kargau, *Mercantile, Industrial and Professional Saint Louis*, 417; and Burton A. Boxerman, "Louis P. Aloe," 41–54.

─── 15 ───

MERCANTILE GIANTS

Of the many economic fields to which St. Louis Jews contributed, the clothing and mercantile industries undoubtedly were among the areas in which they played their largest role. Several organizations founded before the Civil War became renowned locally and nationally: Rosenheim, Levis and Zukowski Mercantile Company, Meyerberg and Rothschild Millinery Company, R. and W. Goldstein Mercantile Company, Marx and Haas Clothing Company, and Fuld-Goodwin Mercantile Company. Several more giants came into being in the post–Civil War era.

Nathan and Jack Friedman started as jobbers for various eastern cloak manufacturers, but in 1878 they established their own factory in St. Louis. The firm of N. and J. Friedman produced cloaks, suits, skirts, and sundry related garments for retail dealers throughout the Midwest and the West. The business was located first at 411 North Eighth Street, but expansion necessitated the erection of an eight-story building at Eighth and Lucas, in which were located manufacturing facilities as well as sales and stock rooms. Employing about five hundred workers, N. and J. Friedman made a significant impact on the city's economy. "The gentlemen composing the firm," wrote a St. Louis business historian, constituted "a most valuable addition to our mercantile and industrial community."[1]

The Singer and Bry families were associated in the manufacture of women's and children's clothing for many years until the mid-1890s, when differences led them to go their separate ways. Nathan and Louis Bry organized the Bry and Bro. Cloak Company, at 1001 Lucas Avenue, where they manufactured women's cloaks, suits, and skirts. Adolph and James Singer, sons of highly respected early community activist Bernard Singer, established the firm of Singer Brothers also to manufacture women's and children's garments. From their eight-story building at Ninth and Lucas,

---

1. Kargau, *Mercantile, Industrial and Professional Saint Louis*, 565–66.

merchandise went out to retail stores throughout the country. "The firm stands in the front rank of its line," a business historian observed, "and enjoys a well-earned reputation here and outside of St. Louis wherever their goods are sold."[2]

Schwab Clothing Company was another significant firm in the St. Louis garment industry. Isaac Schwab was born in Bavaria in 1839 and at age five came to America with his parents, who settled in Pennsylvania. In 1859 the twenty-year-old Schwab moved to Memphis, where he established a clothing business. When yellow fever swept the area in 1879, Schwab moved to St. Louis, as did other Memphis Jewish merchants. Joined by brothers Jacob and Max, the Schwab Clothing Company became a highly prosperous business in St. Louis, occupying a nine-story building at Twelfth and Washington and employing more than five hundred workers. The firm manufactured a complete line of clothing for men and boys, with salesmen selling from coast to coast. Isaac Schwab numbered among those who broke away from Shaare Emeth to organize the new Temple Israel; he served as its first president. For many years he and his brothers stood among the leaders in various charitable organizations of all denominations. Isaac Schwab played an important role in creating the Jewish Hospital, and he served on the boards of several St. Louis banking institutions. He was signally honored by being named to the executive board of the Louisiana Purchase Exposition Company; unfortunately he died in 1902 and never lived to experience the grandeur of the famous 1904 World's Fair. After the first generation of Schwab brothers passed away, the next generation stepped in to keep the Schwab Clothing Company among the finest of the clothing manufacturers and "one of the most important industrial branches" of the St. Louis economic environment.[3]

As noteworthy as these firms were to the Jewish and the St. Louis communities, perhaps most important were the roles St. Louis businessmen played in general merchandising. Three organizations that came into being in the post–Civil War decades stand out. One operated as a major wholesale merchandiser: the Rice-Stix Dry Goods Company. Two were retail establishments, both department stores: the Stix, Baer and Fuller "Grand Leader" and the Famous-Barr Company. The civic responsibility demonstrated by the people who owned these companies was just as important as the firms' economic impact.

In 1861 Henry Rice, William Stix, and Benjamin Eiseman started a retail business, the Rice-Stix Dry Goods Company, in Memphis, Tennessee. They

---

2. Ibid., 566–67; *Modern View* 25, 110.

3. *Voice*, May 16, 1902, and April 28, 1911; Kargau, *Mercantile, Industrial and Professional Saint Louis*, 601; Leonard, ed., *The Book of St. Louisans*, 1906 ed., 515–16.

soon discontinued retailing and focused on jobbing dry goods products of all kinds. In 1865 Henry Rice's brother Jonathan became a member of the firm; in 1873 Benjamin Eiseman's brother David came in; and in 1878 Elias Michael became a partner. Yellow fever epidemics in Memphis so threatened personal health and the firm's commercial operations that in 1879 they all moved to St. Louis.

Rice-Stix's first location in St. Louis was a small store at 410 North Broadway. The company's success led to expansion to larger quarters in an adjacent five-story building at 418–428 North Broadway. Business continued so successfully that by 1889 even larger facilities—half of a newly constructed building at Tenth and Washington—became necessary. By then the Rice-Stix Dry Goods Company was generally recognized as one of the foremost dry goods houses in the country. In 1899 the firm took over another portion of the Tenth and Washington building, and in 1907 it acquired the rest of the structure, so that Rice-Stix now occupied the entire block bounded by Tenth, Washington, Eleventh, and St. Charles. (In future years two annexes were built on adjacent blocks, one at Tenth and St. Charles and another at Eleventh and Locust. The entire plant covered more than 1.5 million square feet. It was the largest space occupied by any one firm in downtown St. Louis.)

In addition to jobbing what others produced, Rice-Stix soon began to manufacture its own products. These included a wide assortment of men's, women's, and children's clothing ranging from underclothing to outerwear, as well as luggage and other accessory items. These were manufactured in the company's facilities in downtown St. Louis, as well as in factories in Lebanon and Bonne Terre in outstate Missouri.

From its start in 1861 with forty employees, Rice-Stix grew until by the early 1900s it employed more than three thousand people, with a capitalization of more than $10 million. One St. Louis paper indicated that dealers from around the world could get virtually anything they wanted in dry goods by merely contacting "The House That Carries the Goods." In 1907 Rice-Stix sales reportedly amounted to the largest of any business house in St. Louis.[4]

In light of such data, to say that Rice-Stix contributed importantly to the St. Louis economy seems redundant. It was to St. Louis in those days what organizations such as Monsanto, Anheuser-Busch, McDonnell-Douglas, and Ralston Purina became in the latter part of the twentieth century. Both directly and indirectly, in terms of people employed, payroll dollars

---

4. As reported in *Voice*, July 19, 1907. See also ibid., February 14, 1902; and *Modern View* 25, 124–25.

that went into the city's economy, and ancillary economic benefits, Rice-Stix held a preeminent position in the St. Louis economy. It is important to note, though, that two generations of its owners—and their wives—became prominently involved not only as leaders in the St. Louis Jewish community but also as important figures in widespread St. Louis civic matters.

Jonathan Rice was born on July 15, 1843, in Bamberg, Bavaria, the son of Seligman and Yetta Rice. Educated and raised in his hometown, Rice worked briefly in a banking house there, but in 1860 he followed his older brother Henry to America. He went directly to St. Joseph, Missouri, where Henry Rice had opened a general mercantile firm with William Stix, who had come to that location from Springfield, Illinois.[5] St. Joseph was then the strategic terminus of railroad transportation to the West, and so their business flourished. When the Civil War broke out in 1861, the firm contracted to sell supplies to the Union army in the West; one regular customer was Ulysses S. Grant. After Union forces gained control of Memphis on the Mississippi River, the firm moved there, where Rice and Stix joined with Benjamin Eiseman to establish the Rice-Stix Dry Goods Company. Jonathan Rice soon became a partner, and the firm continued to prosper in Memphis for more than a decade. After the business was moved to St. Louis, Henry Rice (although still bearing the title of president of the company) moved to New York, and Jonathan Rice, the first vice president, assumed charge of day-to-day operations, a responsibility that he carried out with singular success until he died in 1903. It was under his leadership that Rice-Stix grew into one of the most important mercantile establishments in St. Louis. "Through his genius for business, by his sterling worth as a man," a contemporary St. Louis business historian wrote, "Mr. Rice has made for himself a place among the merchant princes of the city and has gathered about him a host of friends."[6]

Besides his intensive direction of Rice-Stix business interests, Jonathan Rice was a devoted member of Temple Israel and identified prominently

---

5. The Stix and Rice families were closely intertwined in their personal and business relationships, not unlike other German Jewish families who emigrated to America (compare them, for instance, with the New York "uptown" Jewish families described in Stephen Birmingham's *Our Crowd*). The Stix and Rice families both came from Bamberg, Bavaria, where their forebears had lived since at least 1680. Emigrants to the United States from both families settled in the 1830s and 1840s in Cincinnati, where they prospered commercially and became prominent in Jewish community activities there. Members of both families moved to other parts of the Midwest, including St. Louis, and they maintained close family and business relationships wherever they lived.

6. Hyde and Conard, eds., *Encyclopedia of the History of St. Louis*, vol. 3, 1907.

with many Jewish charitable organizations. He became very active also in many secular commercial and civic endeavors, including leadership roles in the Business Men's League, the Commercial Club, and the Mercantile Club. When Kaiser Wilhelm's brother, Prince Henry, visited St. Louis in 1902, Mayor Rolla Wells named Rice to the reception committee that escorted the royal visitor during his stay. Perhaps the apex of his civic recognition came when he was appointed to the executive board of the World's Fair Exposition. He played an active role in preparing for that epic event in St. Louis history, serving most constructively on three planning committees. Unfortunately he died in 1903 and did not live to see the opening of the Exposition in 1904. For his many business and civic achievements, Jonathan Rice unquestionably ranks among the major figures in St. Louis history.[7]

Jonathan Rice's wife, Aurelia Stix Rice, merits attention for her own achievements. The daughter of Henry and Pauline Stix, who had emigrated to America from Bavaria following the failed 1848 revolutions in Europe, Aurelia was born in 1854 in Cincinnati, Ohio, where her father had become an established merchant and a well-known figure in that city's commercial and philanthropic circles, including Jewish community affairs. Educated in Cincinnati schools, in 1874 she married Jonathan Rice, her brother William's business partner. After the move to St. Louis in 1879, Aurelia Rice spent her time raising a family—one son, Charles M. Rice, later attained considerable prominence on his own—and devoting as much time as possible to philanthropic causes, both Jewish and non-Jewish. She was a founder of the Home for Chronic Invalids on Fee Fee Road in St. Louis County, and an active supporter of the Martha Parsons Hospital and the Bethesda Founding Home, nonsectarian institutions that offered refuge and assistance for young women who faced a variety of domestic and familial problems. As a devoted member of Temple Israel and a vice president of the Associated Jewish Charities of St. Louis, she did much for the organization and the implementation of many philanthropic programs to help the poor and needy, especially among newly arriving eastern European immigrants. At the same time Mrs. Rice was known throughout the city as a patron of the arts, especially of music and literature. She also wrote several well-received poems and short stories of her own. Although there is no evidence that she joined with her husband in Rice-Stix business affairs, unquestionably Aurelia Rice ranked with her husband Jonathan as an important participant and leader in numerous

7. Ibid. See also *Voice*, February 28, 1902, November 26, 1903, and June 12, 1914; *St. Louis Globe-Democrat*, March 4, 1902.

civic and philanthropic endeavors. She was indeed, as so many mourners intoned when she died in 1924, a true *ay-shess chai-il,* a woman of valor, in Israel.[8]

William Stix, one of ten children of Mr. and Mrs. Solomon Stix, was six years old when he emigrated with his parents to America in 1844 and settled in Cincinnati. His older brother Louis had already settled there, and his Louis Stix and Company had grown from a back peddler operation to a well-established dry goods firm. Young William Stix was educated in the Cincinnati public schools and at Farmer's College in College Hill, Ohio. Like so many German Jewish immigrants of his generation, William Stix moved from town to town plying his trade and seeking a place to establish roots. In 1854 he opened a small dry goods store in Springfield, Illinois. Two years later he was in St. Joseph, where he joined with family friends and future brothers-in-law Henry and Jonathan Rice in their lucrative business. In 1862 in Memphis he married his partner's sister Dinah Rice. He remained behind in Memphis after the yellow fever epidemic to carry on the business there until 1884, when he rejoined the firm in St. Louis as president of a satellite organization, the Premium Manufacturing Company.

William Stix served as a vice president of the parent Rice-Stix Dry Goods Company until he resigned from active participation in the firm in 1909. His professional and civic associations included some of St. Louis's most prominent and influential figures in the Business Men's League, the Civic League, and the Mercantile Club. He participated actively in Jewish affairs as president of Temple Israel, president of the B'nai B'rith Cleveland Orphans' Home, treasurer of the St. Louis Jewish Hospital, and treasurer of the Jewish Charitable and Educational Union, and he served with other organizations as well. More than eight hundred people attended a reception honoring Stix on his seventieth birthday. "Never before in the history of this community," a St. Louis newspaper commented, "has an individual received such universal tokens of honor and regard . . . as did the much beloved William Stix." That high regard became very tangible when the board of education named a new public school after him. The William Stix Elementary School, opened in 1922, is located at 226 South Euclid Avenue, adjacent to the Jewish Hospital.[9]

---

8. *Voice,* November 26, 1903, and November 17, 1911; *Modern View,* September 19, 1924; Hyde and Conard, eds., *Encyclopedia of the History of St. Louis,* vol. 3, 1907–8.

9. For William Stix see *Voice,* March 1, 1889, July 13, 1900, April 16 and May 1, 1908, and June 19, 1914; *Modern View,* March 28, 1913, and June 19, 1914; Marcus, *Memoirs of American Jews,* vol. 1, 309–10; Leonard, ed., *Book of St. Louisans,* 1912 ed., 576. A son, Ernest W. Stix, attained considerable and well-deserved prominence on his own in

The Eiseman brothers, Benjamin and David, also did much for the city's economy and for the welfare of both the Jewish and the larger secular communities. Benjamin, born in 1833 in Baden, Germany, the son of Joshua and Fannie (Kaufman) Eiseman, was educated in public schools in Baden until age fourteen, then worked for four years in banking and mercantile establishments there. In 1851, at age eighteen, he emigrated to the United States, settling first in Philadelphia. There he worked during the day and studied English in night school. Two years later he went west to Davenport, Iowa, where he clerked in a dry goods store. He then moved to St. Joseph, where he associated with Henry Rice and William Stix. He served as treasurer when Rice, Stix and Company started in Memphis.

Like his associates in Rice-Stix, Benjamin Eiseman also participated prominently in all sorts of Jewish affairs as well as in greater city matters. He was a founder and an active member of Temple Israel. He chaired the congregation's school board for many years. At the celebration of his seventieth birthday during Chanukah of 1903, the children presented him with a testimonial book containing some of his favorite prayers and psalms. He participated actively in many Jewish charitable organizations, and was a founder and for many years treasurer of the Home for the Aged and Infirm Israelites. Eiseman served as a director of several banks as well as of the venerable St. Louis Mercantile Library. His business peers accorded him singular honors, electing him several times to be president of the St. Louis Chamber of Commerce. When a special congressional committee looked into national problems related to business matters, St. Louis merchants chose Eiseman to be their spokesman. His nickname "Old Man Benevolent" probably described best the high esteem in which all held him. No surprise, then, that on one testimonial occasion Benjamin Altheimer conferred upon Eiseman the title of "Ph.D."—not Doctor of Philosophy, Altheimer indicated, but "Doer of Philanthropy."[10]

Eiseman's younger brother David, born in Baden in 1845, received his education in the Baden public schools until age fourteen, and then worked in a retail dry goods store. In 1865 he emigrated to Memphis, where he worked for Rice-Stix. In 1872 he was admitted as a partner and vice president, and with the rest of the firm he moved to St. Louis in 1879.

---

the World War I era and following. At the time of this writing, the St. Louis Board of Education has decided to close the old Stix Elementary School, but a new school, the location still not determined, will continue that name.

10. For Benjamin Eiseman see *Voice*, January 1, 1904, May 24, 1907, February 14, 1908, October 14, 1910, April 28, 1911, and January 3, 1913; Leonard, ed., *Book of St. Louisans*, 1906 ed., 176; Kargau, *Mercantile, Industrial and Professional Saint Louis*, 174; and Devoy, *A History of the City of St. Louis*, 372–75.

In addition to his work with Rice-Stix, David Eiseman became an active member of Temple Israel, president of Jewish Hospital, and a longtime director of the Jewish Charitable and Educational Union. He served also as a director of several banks and a member of several municipal boards. When he died in 1915 at age seventy, the St. Louis Jewish press and the secular press published laudatory editorial eulogies.[11]

Last but certainly not the least of the Rice-Stix group was Elias Michael. He was born in Eschau, Bavaria, in 1854. Shortly thereafter the family emigrated to America and settled in Memphis, where young Elias grew up and received a public school education. At age fifteen he went to work for the Rice-Stix Dry Goods Company as a stock clerk. He worked his way up through several promotions, moved to St. Louis with the company in 1879, and five years later became a full partner. He then held important executive positions within the company, including secretary, several vice presidencies, and finally the presidency. Additional business activities included organizing the Premium Manufacturing Company (a Rice-Stix affiliate) and serving as a director of several St. Louis banks. He served also in leadership roles in various trade organizations, including the St. Louis Business Men's League, the St. Louis Manufacturers' Association, the National Chamber of Commerce (executive committee), and the National Wholesale Dry Goods Association (president). An active member of Temple Israel, Elias Michael identified with many charitable and educational institutions, Jewish and nonsectarian, including the Jewish Hospital, Father Dunne's Newsboys' Home, the United Jewish Charities, and its successor the Jewish Charitable and Educational Union.

Elias Michael's prestige in the larger St. Louis milieu became manifest when he was chosen as a director of the Louisiana Purchase Exposition. He had a special concern for the education of children—his only child, Selma, died in 1894 at age seven. He served for many years on the boards of the Hebrew Free and Industrial School and the Jewish Alliance Night School, and St. Louis voters elected him to the city's board of education. Among the many distinctions accorded him, perhaps the most meaningful was having a school named in his honor: the Elias Michael School for the Orthopedically Handicapped at 4568 Forest Park Boulevard, adjacent to both the Jewish Hospital and the William Stix Elementary School.

Elias Michael suffered a fatal heart attack in 1913 while playing golf with his good friend Louis P. Aloe. His passing was mourned by many. "He was an appreciated member of our community," one newspaper wrote. "His

---

11. For David Eiseman see *Voice,* August 27, 1915; *Modern View,* August 27, 1915; Leonard, ed., *Book of St. Louisans,* 1912 ed., 174; Kargau, *Mercantile, Industrial and Professional Saint Louis,* 160, 183.

personal participation in institutions of charity and education, both Jewish and non-Jewish, was magnificent." Yet his life was almost cut even shorter. In 1886, while honeymooning with his bride, Rachel, at Lake George in New York, Michael's rowboat capsized, and the young couple almost drowned. In all the excitement, they never learned the identity of the "unknown gentleman from the hotel" who jumped into the water and pulled them out.[12]

Rachel Stix Michael merits special consideration because of her own important contributions to St. Louis history. She was born January 1, 1866, in Cincinnati, the daughter of Hanna Reuss (Rice) and Aaron Stix. Her father died when she was only two years old, and she grew up, along with her mother, in the household of uncle William Stix. Rachel attended public school in Cincinnati, graduated from Hughes High School, and then attended the University of Cincinnati. While the rest of the Stix family moved to St. Louis, she remained in school in Cincinnati until 1886, when she married Elias Michael. In addition to the family life expected of her, she took courses at Washington University and the Missouri School of Social Economy that nurtured her strong interest in education. She later wrote:

> In my day, going to College was not regarded as the next logical step to following completion of a high school course but a side step definitely dooming the eccentric student to ways that diverged hopelessly from the path to be followed by all daughters of fond parents, one that should lead to a happy marriage and a secure home. However, experience is proving the need of higher education for both the mother as well as the father of the modern home so that college training is recognized as essential to daughters' and sons' careers alike. . . . Women's sphere and responsibilities in the home have reached a depth and a breadth far surpassing their provision of merely creature comforts to home and family. Their transition has brought, however, not only obligations but interests that in the up-to-date modern home keep parents and children more of one age in life's aims and purposes. Business, politics, education and community service are now joint interests. Every household today aims to be managed scientifically and systematically. Women thus find their sphere for usefulness broadened and some time set free for greater service not only to home but also to community.[13]

---

12. For Elias Michael see *Jewish Free Press*, July 16, 1886; *Voice*, October 14, 1898, June 24, 1904, May 24, 1907, February 2, 1912, and September 19, 1913; *Modern View*, September 19, 1913, and October 25, 1934; *St. Louis Jewish Light*, August 27, 1980; Kargau, *Mercantile, Industrial and Professional Saint Louis*, 568–69; Leonard, ed., *Book of St. Louisans*, 1912 ed., 413. By a singular coincidence, Rabbi Messing of United Hebrew Temple and Elias Michael died the same day, September 15, 1913. Eulogies for both are found in the St. Louis press in the days immediately following.

13. *Modern View* 25, 145.

The tragedy of Selma's death early in her married life undoubtedly nurtured Rachel Michael's dedication to social and community service. She rebounded from the tragedy by turning to kindergarten and child day-care work, pioneering such activities through the United Jewish Charities and the Jewish Alliance. In 1905 she and her husband founded the Selma Michael Kindergarten and Day Nursery, which became an integral part of the Ninth and Carr Alliance Building, and Mrs. Michael remained an active worker there for many years.

Her affiliation with early childhood care proved to be only the beginning of many years of service to the St. Louis community. After her husband died in 1913, Rachel Michael studied for two summers in the Social Service Department of Boston's Massachusetts General Hospital and the Boston Children's Aid Society, followed by additional work at the Missouri School of Social Economy. She became a member of the social service departments of the Washington University Dispensary, the St. Louis Children's Hospital, and the St. Louis Children's Aid Society.

She worked also in the field of occupational therapy. When the United States entered World War I in 1917, Rachel Michael served importantly in at least two areas. She chaired a committee whose responsibilities included planning courses to train women for jobs vacated by men going into the armed forces. She also trained occupational therapists to help rehabilitate the disabled in military and civilian hospitals. From this work she helped create the Missouri Association for Occupational Therapists. She also became a director of the St. Louis Society for Crippled Children.

In addition, Mayor Henry Kiel appointed her to the city library board, and then to the board of education, to which voters later reelected her twice. Throughout all this civic work, Rachel Michael remained active in Jewish community affairs, at the Alliance Building, in the St. Louis Section of the Council of Jewish Women, in the Miriam Society of the Order of True Sisters, and at Temple Israel, where she attended services regularly on Saturday mornings. She died on September 6, 1936, at the age of seventy, mourned by the Jewish and non-Jewish communities as a truly remarkable woman who had made a lasting imprint on the city of St. Louis.[14]

The Rice-Stix organization thus contributed much to St. Louis history. As a giant in the wholesale dry goods business, the firm constituted a very important element in the city's development through the business

---

14. For Rachel Stix Michael see ibid. and *Modern View,* October 25, 1934; also *St. Louis Jewish Light,* August 27, 1980.

it generated, through the people it employed, and through the dollars it pumped into the city's economy. But its impact was more than economic. The Rice-Stix "family" also gave much to the civic, educational, and philanthropic growth of St. Louis. To quantify those contributions in terms of dollars or percentages is probably impossible. But it would by no means be maudlin or overly sentimental to suggest that St. Louis improved as a community thanks to the direct contributions and indirect by-products of the Rice-Stix Dry Goods Company.

The Stix name is associated with another major mercantile organization important to the history of St. Louis, the Stix, Baer and Fuller Department Store, known popularly as the "Grand Leader." The morphology of that establishment was more complex than that of the Rice-Stix organization; it involved three separate firms that finally came together in St. Louis in 1892.

The beginnings emanated from another Jewish family prominent in St. Louis history, the Baers, and especially the brothers Julius and Sigmond Baer. Both were born in Baden, Germany, Julius in 1861 and Sigmond in 1862, and both were educated in schools there. In 1877 Julius emigrated to America and went to work with the Joseph Adler Dry Goods Company in Fort Smith, Arkansas. Fort Smith at that time was a turbulent frontier garrison town and a jumping-off place for Indian and southwestern trade and travel. Sigmond followed Julius in 1879, also to Fort Smith, where he entered the employ of the Samuel, Baer and Joel Dry Goods Company. When that firm went broke in 1880, Julius and Sigmond Baer pooled their meager assets, $350, and opened their own small dry goods establishment, which they called the Boston Store. They did well enough during the next few years to attempt several expansion projects in Fort Smith and elsewhere along the Arkansas–Oklahoma Territory frontier, but they finally abandoned those ventures as too risky and focused on the home store in Fort Smith. It proved to be a very wise decision; as Fort Smith grew from a boisterous frontier post to a settled community, the Boston Store became its leading mercantile establishment.

Meanwhile, in 1873 their fourteen-year-old cousin Aaron Fuller, also born and educated in Baden, emigrated to America. He went first to Chicago, where he lived with a married sister and clerked in a relative's dry goods store. In 1878, at age nineteen, he and a friend, Herman Apple, opened a small general store in Witcherville, Arkansas, under the name Apple and Fuller. Although the store was successful there, Witcherville was a small town, and in 1882 the partners moved to a bigger city, Fort Smith, where their success continued. In 1886, however, Fuller left the company—he had in the meantime married Frieda Baer, Julius's and Sigmond's sister—and joined forces with his two brothers-in-law in the

Boston Store. Together they led their retail enterprise to continued growth and success in Fort Smith.

By 1892, seeking to expand into a larger urban market area, the partners looked into possibilities in St. Louis. With Fuller remaining in Fort Smith to look after the thriving Boston Store, the Baer brothers went to St. Louis. There they teamed up with Charles A. Stix, a cousin of Henry and Jonathan Rice and of William Stix who ran the already successful Rice-Stix Dry Goods Company.

Like many others of the Stix family, Charles Aaron Stix was born and reared in Cincinnati. After graduating in 1880 from Hughes High School, he started as a stock clerk in the family firm in Cincinnati (Stix, Krause and Company) and worked his way up as salesman and buyer until he finally became part owner. In 1886, anticipating going on his own in Wichita, Kansas, Stix ended up instead in St. Louis. There he and a new associate, John Manning, bought out an already popular and established men's clothing store known as The Famous. Five years later, in 1891, Stix bought out Manning and became sole owner. Continued success led to moving The Famous to larger quarters, but no sooner was that accomplished when a fire destroyed the building, putting Stix and The Famous out of business. But only temporarily. In 1892 David May and Moses Shoenberg, of the firm of May and Schoenberg of Leadville, Colorado, purchased The Famous as well as the new building erected on the burned out site, a landmark event in the history of yet another important Jewish-owned St. Louis mercantile establishment, the Famous-Barr Company Department Store. Meanwhile, recognizing the excellent business record Stix had established before the untimely fire, the Baer brothers brought him into their firm. Thus was organized the Stix, Baer and Fuller Dry Goods Company, which went into business in 1892 under the trade name Grand Leader. Shortly thereafter Fuller came up from Fort Smith, and henceforth the four men lived the rest of their very productive lives in St. Louis.

Located first on Broadway between Franklin (now Martin Luther King Avenue) and Morgan (now Delmar Boulevard), the self-styled "Fastest Growing Store in America" moved several times to larger quarters. By 1906 the company erected a new eight-story building at Sixth and Washington on the site of the former popular Lindell Hotel; in 1911 an adjacent eight-story addition went up on the Seventh and Lucas corner. That same year the firm bought the rest of the block at the Seventh and Washington corner and built an eleven-story annex known as the Model Annex. The Grand Leader building thus occupied a full block in downtown St. Louis, between Sixth, Seventh, Washington, and Lucas.

Stix, Baer and Fuller, along with Famous-Barr Company, became one of St. Louis's largest and most important retail department stores. By

1907, according to tax figures reported in the press, it had become the largest retail store in the city. By 1912 it employed more than two thousand St. Louisans; its payroll alone constituted a significant part of the city's economy, and it provided many ancillary benefits. The *Modern View* wrote of Stix, Baer and Fuller and its management: "Firm believers in good organization, it was their ethical standard of being honorable to the people from whom they bought, to whom they sold, and to their associates in the conduct of their business, that has built for them the solid foundation of good will they so happily enjoy."[15]

Like their coreligionists who led Rice-Stix, the men who built the Grand Leader also contributed immensely to the civic, cultural, and philanthropic development of the Jewish community and the larger St. Louis community. What follows is a mere representation of only some of those activities.

Charles A. Stix held prominent leadership positions in the Civic League, in the St. Louis Retail Merchants' Association, and in the Business Men's League. He was also elected to the city council and appointed to the board of directors of the St. Louis World's Fair. A lover of music, he was instrumental in bringing performances of the Metropolitan Opera and the Chicago Opera to St. Louis. In fact, shortly before he died in 1916 at the age of only fifty-five, he was well along in planning for a St. Louis Grand Opera House, but the project collapsed with his death. He was a dedicated member of Temple Israel, and was involved in many activities within the Jewish community. He served for many years as a director of the United Jewish Charities and its successor, the Jewish Charitable and Educational Union. He gave much time and service to B'nai B'rith, especially as director of its Cleveland Orphans Home. His wife, Sadie Fraley Stix, participated in similar activities within the Jewish community. She also served in various capacities in the broader city arena: among other posts, she was a board member of the city library.[16]

Julius and Sigmond Baer participated in a variety of charitable and philanthropic affairs. Julius affiliated actively in the Masonic order, the Elks, the Visiting Nurses' Association, and the Veiled Prophet organization, among others. Within the Jewish community he gave his services generously to many institutions, especially to B'nai B'rith, the Jewish Hospital, and the Jewish Charitable and Educational Union. Brother Sigmond Baer

---

15. *Voice*, July 19, 1907; *Modern View 25*, 128–29; Kargau, *Mercantile, Industrial and Professional Saint Louis*, 561–62.

16. For Charles A. Stix and Sadie Fraley Stix, see *Voice*, September 8, 1916; *Modern View*, September 8, 1916, and April 5, 1918; *Modern View 25*, 105; and Leonard, ed., *Book of St. Louisans*, 1912 ed., 576.

also was involved in numerous secular and Jewish civic affairs. He served the city as president of the Downtown Improvement Association, and was also a director of the National Bank of Commerce and the Federal Trust Company. As treasurer of the Jewish Charitable and Educational Union, he coordinated many of the philanthropic and financial dealings of that organization's numerous charitable affiliates.[17]

Aaron Fuller also left a praiseworthy legacy to the St. Louis community. He served for five years as president of Temple Israel and for the same amount of time as president of the Home for the Aged and Infirm Israelites. He was president also of the Jewish Charitable and Educational Union, and he gave unstinting support to many other philanthropic institutions, especially the Jewish Hospital. He contributed his services to a variety of secular community causes, not the least of which was as a vice president of the St. Louis Community Fund.[18]

A third Jewish-owned retail mercantile establishment that had a major impact upon St. Louis history was the Famous-Barr Company. Like the Rice-Stix and Stix, Baer and Fuller Grand Leader Companies, Famous-Barr came together, in 1892, only after some disjointed and complicated developments.

The saga began in 1849 when Ubsdell, Pierson and Company, a New York dry goods firm, purchased the H. D. Cunningham Dry Goods store in St. Louis at Third and Market and established its own western retail outlet. The home company sent several men out to run the store, among them William Barr, Joseph Franklin, and James Duncan. During the Civil War those three acquired ownership of the store. By 1870, however, Barr emerged as sole owner and the organization became the William Barr Dry Goods Company, popularly known throughout the city simply as "Barr's." The store's success led to several moves to larger quarters, eventually to two buildings on Olive Street extending from Sixth Street to Seventh Street.

Meanwhile, in 1870 two merchants named Motte and Specht opened a modest clothing store on Franklin Avenue between Seventh and Eighth Streets. Originally handling only men's clothing, the store soon added hats, shoes, and other men's furnishings. Catering especially to a farmers' trade, it soon became a popular stop for rural customers coming to shop in

---

17. For Julius Baer see *Modern View 25*, 74, and *Modern View*, December 3, 1931; Leonard, ed., *Book of St. Louisans*, 1912 ed., 31; and Baskett, ed., *Men of Affairs in St. Louis*, 24. For Sigmond Baer see *Modern View 25*, 75; Leonard, ed., *Book of St. Louisans*, 1912 ed., 31; and Baskett, ed., *Men of Affairs in St. Louis*, 17.

18. For Aaron Fuller see *Modern View*, December 22, 1916, and *Modern View 25*, 73; *St. Louis Jewish Light*, September 16, 1987; Leonard, ed., *Book of St. Louisans*, 1912 ed., 213.

St. Louis. The store had no unique name—simply "Motte and Specht"—and the proprietors sought an identifying label that might be catchy and appropriate. One day a customer who had just bought a suit for three dollars commented how so many farmers were talking about the place, and "It's getting to be quite FAMOUS." Suddenly the proprietors found the name they had been looking for, and before long the rapidly growing clothing store became known popularly as The Famous. Shortly thereafter, in 1886, William S. Stix and John Manning acquired The Famous, and within a few years, Stix became the sole owner. Then the firm's success and prosperity came to a traumatic end in the 1891 fire.

Two new merchants now entered the St. Louis business scene, David May and Moses Shoenberg. A native of Kaiserlautern, Germany, May emigrated with his parents to America when he was six years old. The family settled first in New York City but soon moved to Cincinnati, where David received a public school education. After graduating from business college, May worked as a bookkeeper in Cincinnati for the Stix, Krause and Company dry goods firm. After a brief try in South Carolina, he embarked in general merchandising in Hartford City, Indiana, where he did well. Poor health, particularly respiratory problems, prompted him to move to Leadville, Colorado, near Denver, where in 1878 he teamed up with Moses Shoenberg and opened a dry goods store. May's successes in Leadville extended beyond the prosperous business venture. In 1881 voters elected him county treasurer of Lake County (in which Leadville was located) and then reelected him for a second term—as a Republican in an overwhelmingly Democratic county. Later offered the post of state treasurer, May declined because he feared it might interfere with his business activities. Two more important events in Colorado shaped May's future. He married Rosa Shoenberg, his partner's sister (their oldest son Morton was born in Colorado in 1881); and in 1888 he established what became the first May Company department store, in Denver.

Moses Shoenberg was born and raised in Dayton, Ohio. Educated in the public schools there, he began his business career in Dayton in a haberdashery store. In 1878 he moved to Leadville, where he met David May. Shortly thereafter, his sister married May. Nevertheless, the brothers-in-law drifted apart briefly in business when in 1885 Schoenberg left Leadville for Kansas City, where he associated with the mercantile firm of G. Bernheimer Brothers and Company.

Extant data does not indicate precisely what persuaded Shoenberg and May to move to St. Louis. In March 1892 the two brothers-in-law bought the new building under construction on the burned-out Famous site, and then reopened The Famous in September 1892, now under their ownership. By 1907 the firm moved into larger quarters at Sixth and

Washington. Within four years that building became inadequate for their constantly increasing retail trade. Accordingly the firm acquired a fifty-year lease on the entire downtown block bounded by Olive, Locust, Sixth, and Seventh Streets. Barr's highly successful dry goods store already stood in that block. The result was a merger of the two, with the May Department Store Company (David May president, Moses Shoenberg vice president) buying out the William Barr Dry Goods Company, including its name. Thus was born the Famous-Barr Department Store.

A magnificent new building now was erected covering the entire block, an edifice described as an architectural and engineering masterpiece. The fire-proof structure stood twenty-one stories tall, topped by a two-story penthouse, with appropriate basement and sub-basement foundations. Accessible to customers from street-level entrances on all four sides, the "Store Without a Back Door" was at the time the largest building in the world housing a retail store and offices.[19]

Like Rice-Stix and the Stix, Baer and Fuller Grand Leader, Famous-Barr was a mainstay in the St. Louis business environment. The number of people it employed and the payrolls and tax monies it generated for the city's economy reflect only a part of the firm's importance to St. Louis growth and development. Until the post–World War II development of the suburbs and suburban shopping centers, most St. Louisans went downtown by streetcar or bus to shop, and invariably they did much of that retail shopping at "Famous" and "Grand Leader."

Their enterprising efforts toward business did not deter either David May or Moses Shoenberg from significant involvement in widespread philanthropic and charitable matters, in either the Jewish community or in the broader citywide environment. Both were loyal members of Temple Israel; Schoenberg, in fact, served as the congregation's president. May gave both time and funds to many educational and philanthropic institutions. He was for many years a director of the United Jewish Charities and its successor, the Jewish Charitable and Educational Union. Shoenberg also served the latter organization, as a director and as its president. He participated actively in the Jewish Sanatorium and the Jewish Hospital. Of equal significance, other members of the May and Schoenberg families—wives and children—also became active in many community and civic affairs, both Jewish and secular.[20]

---

19. *Modern View 25*, 76–77, 99, 126–27, and *Modern View*, July 29, 1927; Baskett, ed., *Men of Affairs in St. Louis*, 100.

20. For fuller details on the Famous-Barr Company, see *Modern View 25*, 126–27, and Kargau, *Mercantile, Industrial and Professional Saint Louis*, 559–61. For David May see *Modern View 25*, 76–77, and *Modern View*, July 29, 1927. For Moses Shoenberg see

Just as any attempt to quantify the diverse contributions of the Rice-Stix "family" to St. Louis history would be an exercise in futility, so too would be similar efforts focusing on the founders of Stix, Baer and Fuller and Famous-Barr. At a time when St. Louis reveled in being the fourth-largest city in the United States, when people from all over streamed to the confluence of the Missouri and Mississippi Rivers for the World's Fair, Jewish merchants and Jewish-owned businesses did their share to make their visit memorable and to enhance the city's stature.

Voice, November 1, 1901, and June 18, 1909; *Modern View 25*, 99; and Baskett, ed., *Men of Affairs in St. Louis*, 100.

16

INTO THE TWENTIETH CENTURY
The Germans

Several events during the first few years of the twentieth century crowned St. Louis German Jewry's struggle to attain the security for which it and every other immigrant group aspired, not only to feel comfortably "at home" in St. Louis but also to be accepted by the rest of the community. (That is not to say that xenophobic discrimination and antisemitism had disappeared. Unfortunately neither St. Louis nor the rest of American society have ever been able to conquer those cancerous malaises; we have simply learned to live with them.) These landmark events could not have occurred earlier, for they depended so much on the economic successes of German Jewry. By 1900 those successes had been achieved.

First, though, a brief digression to note St. Louis Jewry's participation in the Spanish-American War of 1898. Histories of St. Louis make little or no mention of that generally popular "splendid little war"—and for good reasons: it lasted very briefly (only a few months), it produced relatively few casualties (more from disease than from combat), and it concluded before it made any serious impact on the city. For instance, no great enlistment or bond drives occurred in St. Louis; they were not necessary. Perhaps for that reason no known study has investigated the war's impact on St. Louis. Undoubtedly St. Louis merchants and manufacturers benefited through the sale of food, grain, clothing, and other military supplies, but no scholarly analysis has verified even that.

Furthermore, no study exists describing the specific *Jewish* role in the war or its repercussions in Cuba and the Pacific basin. Fifteen Jews were among the 250 American officers and men who perished when the battleship *Maine* sank in Havana harbor on February 15, 1898. Several Jewish newspapers throughout the country joined the widespread "jingo press" clamoring for war against Spain. They urged young Jewish men to volunteer not only to retaliate against the sinking of the *Maine* but also to avenge the countless depredations inflicted in years gone by against Jews by the invidious Spanish Inquisition. More than four thousand

Jewish young men volunteered. Jewish soldiers and sailors fought in Cuba and in the Philippines, and several were singled out for commendation. Theodore Roosevelt, who led the famous Rough Riders in Cuba, later wrote that "one of the best colonels in the regular regiments, and who fought beside me, was a Jew.... In my own regiment I promoted five men from the ranks for valor and good conduct in battle ... one [was a] Jew."[1]

Participation by the St. Louis Jewish community is as difficult to discern as participation by the overall St. Louis community. While the city's secular press followed the national "jingo" lead in promoting the war spirit and reporting daily events, the lone Jewish newspaper in the city at the time, the weekly *Jewish Voice*, stood as an exception. In fact, one reading the *Voice* would hardly be aware that a war was being fought. This was the result of editor Rabbi Moritz Spitz's clear policy that the paper should deal only with Jewish matters; war news and other happenings remained the province of the secular press. When events of the war involved Jews, however, and especially a St. Louis Jew, the *Voice* printed those stories. Thus we know that St. Louis Jews Harry Landsman and Philip C. Rosenbaum served honorably in Cuba and the Philippines and later became officers in the Spanish-American War Veterans organization. Lieutenant Alfred Aloe, of the prominent Aloe family in St. Louis, earned a promotion to captain for bravery in action in the Philippines. Barnett Bricker, who had come to St. Louis from Vilna, Lithuania, in 1888, saw combat in the Spanish-American War. Probably the most publicized St. Louis serviceman, Jew or non-Jew, was Commander Simon Cook, who as a naval officer engaged in several heated actions in the Philippines, especially a daring raid to rescue a widely publicized "lost detachment" in the jungles of Visayan Island. Certainly these few instances constitute only a very small part of the military and naval developments in Cuba and the Philippine Islands; but at least they clearly represent patriotic participation by St. Louis Jews in those events.[2]

---

1. As quoted in Samuel W. McCall, *Patriotism of the American Jew*, 126. See also Jeanne Abrams, "Remembering the *Maine*: The Jewish Attitude Toward the Spanish-American War as Reflected in *The American Israelite*," 439–55. That Jews enlisted in significant numbers is reflected in a War Department directive granting Jewish servicemen special furloughs for the High Holidays in 1898. George Cohen, *The Jews in the Making of America*, 103.

2. *Voice*, January 5 and March 2, 1900, April 11, 1902, September 13, 1907, and June 21, 1912; Rogal Family File, AJA; the *American Jewish Yearbook* listed the names of several thousand Jews who served in the armed forces during the Spanish-American War; at least forty-four were from St. Louis. Adler, ed., *American Jewish Yearbook, 5661*, 574–75, 578, 622.

For the two virtually separate Jewish communities taking shape in St. Louis, the first few years of the twentieth century proved to be a watershed. For the German community, several developments between 1900 and 1907 seemed to cap their efforts to "make it" in America. At the same time, comparable developments among eastern European Jews between 1900 and 1907 indicated that the newer immigrant group not only possessed a remarkable viability but also seemed to be approaching some sort of parity with the old-line group. Indeed, as eastern European Jewry rapidly increased in numbers in St. Louis and even surpassed the German Jewish population, perhaps the major issues that emerged revolved around the degree to which the differences between the two seemingly antithetical communities could be reconciled. Those issues became apparent as developments unfurled within each community.

Even before eastern European Jews began to arrive in significant numbers, the old-line German Jewish community had been struggling with two major problems: how most effectively to organize and implement Jewish philanthropy in order to meet ongoing needs, and within that framework whether or not to establish a Jewish hospital. These issues were resolved in the first decade of the 1900s.

As immigration from eastern Europe increased during the 1880s and 1890s, more and more philanthropic efforts were directed toward helping those new arrivals. To overcome numerous internal "turf" controversies, the United Jewish Charities employed Adolph Robi as superintendent to oversee the collection and distribution of aid, which took the diversified form of groceries, fuel, tools, medicines, physician and hospital treatment, clothing, and often just plain cash. The United Jewish Charities also established a center to care for children of working mothers, and a library and reading room to assist in the education of new immigrants.[3]

Despite these many achievements, it became apparent that more had to be done, especially because coordinating human and material resources proved to be increasingly difficult. For inexplicable reasons, most charitable institutions refused to come under the umbrella organization of the United Jewish Charities. Active groups such as the Hebrew Benevolent Society, the Judah Touro Society, the Hebrew Ladies Widows and Orphans

---

3. *Modern View* 25, 32–33; Rosen, "Historical Development of Jewish Federation of Saint Louis," 63–69; Hyde and Conard, eds., *Encyclopedia of the History of St. Louis*, vol. 2, 1125–26. Leaders in these efforts included, among others, Moses Fraley, William Stix, William Goldstein, Henry Rice, Albert Arnstein, Solomon Boehm, Lewis Brey, Samuel Bauman, Isaac Schwab, Elias Michael, Moses Summerfield, and Dr. I. M. DeVorkin. Jewish women assumed equally important roles; they included Mrs. Jonathan Rice, Mrs. Louis Glaser, Mrs. Lewis Godlove, Mrs. Morris Sale, and Mrs. Julius P. Weil.

Society, and the Ladies Hebrew Relief Society remained outside and independent, as did virtually all men's fraternal and women's benevolent groups such as B'nai B'rith, the Free Sons of Israel, the Fortschritts Tochters, the Order of B'rith Abraham, and similar societies. Furthermore, as new eleemosynary institutions came into being, albeit with the blessing and even financial support of the United Jewish Charities, those new bodies operated autonomously from the existing umbrella organization. These included the Home for the Aged and Infirm Israelites, the Hebrew Free and Industrial School, and the Jewish Alliance, by no means insignificant institutions. Also remaining outside the United Jewish Charities was the very popular Shoe Fund, an agency initiated by Rabbi Moritz Spitz and the *Jewish Voice* that collected and distributed hundreds of pairs of shoes, especially during the winter, to children of the Jewish poor.

All these institutions maintained their individual identities and followed their own agendas. "Each had its own separate set of officers, each had its separate way of regarding its own work," observed a chronicler of charitable efforts in those days. "The whole scheme was a rather haphazard one . . . Each fended for itself. Each was a distinct entity. As a result, citizens were harassed by hordes of collectors from various organizations." In some instances, money-raising efforts relied principally on large donations from individual board members. Most groups held separate and even competing fund-raisers, from picnics to holiday affairs (Passover, Purim, Chanukah) to dances and balls.[4]

Despite seeming success, many felt the need to better centralize and coordinate the multiplying charitable and educational organizations and projects. This was already happening in other cities, in New York, Philadelphia, Baltimore, Chicago, Louisville, and Milwaukee, where the influx of eastern Europeans created similar problems. But although efforts to reorganize charities made progress in those cities, no such progress occurred in St. Louis. "The local charities," according to a study of the St. Louis Jewish charitable structure, "were not yet ready . . . they were too scattered, too far removed from each other."[5] Exactly what that meant

---

4. *Tribune*, November 26, 1880, and October 13, 1882; *Voice*, July 6 and November 16, 1888, September 9, 23, and 30, and November 4 and 18, 1898, October 27 and November 3, 1899, January 19, August 31, and September 7 and 14, 1900, October 25 and November 15, 1901; Rosen, "Historical Development of Jewish Federation of Saint Louis," 68–72; Hyde and Conard, eds., *Encyclopedia of the History of St. Louis*, vol. 2, 1126; Scharf, *Saint Louis City and County*, vol. 2, 1806.

5. Rosen, "Historical Development of Jewish Federation of Saint Louis," 70–71. Ironically, even though the St. Louis groups resisted local unification efforts, many supported a national "Associated Hebrew Charities of the United States," organized

is not quite clear. All seemed to be involved in the same general effort of helping the needy. Nevertheless the history of social service everywhere is replete with many conflicts that range from seemingly petty "turf" and personality spats to deep and genuine concerns about the specificity and needs of particular social problems.

By the turn of the century, many in St. Louis deplored the serious diffusion and proliferation of philanthropic efforts and began to argue for more centralization. An important step in that direction resulted from the needs created by the organization of the Jewish Alliance in 1898 and the creation in 1899 of the United Jewish Educational and Charitable Association as a landlord to provide facilities for Alliance activities. The subsequent erection (1901) of the Alliance Building on Ninth and Carr as a potential central headquarters and the recent successes in other communities in federating their charities now led to a concerted effort to reorganize the Jewish charitable structure in St. Louis.[6]

With Elias Michael and Moses Fraley in leadership roles, representatives of several organizations met early in 1901 to look into an effective reorganization and consolidation. That small group soon expanded into a "committee of one hundred," with delegates from additional organizations. They met several times that year, usually at the Columbian Club, fine-tuning a proposed organization and eliciting financial pledges. Finally, on December 11, 1901, the group established a new umbrella organization, the "Jewish Charitable and Educational Union." Popularly (but incorrectly) referred to in the Jewish press as the "Federation of Jewish Charities," the name was officially changed in 1915 to "The Jewish Federation of St. Louis." It is still known by that name today.[7]

As provided in its constitution and bylaws, the purpose of the Jewish Charitable and Educational Union was

> to establish and provide an efficient and practical mode of collecting voluntary contributions, and to devote the sums so collected, to the support

---

in 1886 in Chicago largely through the leadership of St. Louisan Marcus Bernheimer. The main thrust of that organization, as it turned out, was an attempt to deal with the problem of migrant "schnorrers" who thrived by drifting from one city to another. Ibid., 71. For the constitution and bylaws of the Associated Hebrew Charities of the United States, see *Jewish Free Press,* July 9, 1886. See also *Tribune,* October 3, 1882, and *Voice,* November 16, 1888.

6. *Voice,* September 9, 23, and 30, and November 4, 1898, October 27 and November 3, 1899, January 19 and September 7 and 14, 1900.

7. Ibid., March 1 and November 15, 1901, February 14, 1902, and June 12 and October 30, 1903; *Modern View* 25, 30–33, 37; *St. Louis Jewish Light,* March 31, 1971; Rosen, "Historical Development of Jewish Federation of Saint Louis," 72–73, 91.

and maintenance of Jewish charitable and educational organizations of St. Louis and to Jewish charitable organizations of other cities now receiving aid from Jewish residents of this city, and to such other charitable purposes as may be provided for . . . to the end that each institution may the more effectively carry on its charitable and educational work by being relieved of the necessity to make separate appeals and collections; to purchase and own or lease one or more buildings and other real estate for the use of the Jewish charitable and educational societies of the city of St. Louis . . . to distribute charities [and supply educational facilities] amongst the deserving Jewish poor of St. Louis.[8]

The original members of the Jewish Charitable and Educational Union in 1901 included the United Jewish Charities of St. Louis (and its constituent organizations, the Sisterhood of Personal Service, the Ladies Zion Society, the Hebrew Ladies Sewing Society, and the Social Settlement League), the Hebrew Free and Industrial School, the Home for the Aged and Infirm Israelites, the Jewish Alliance, the then-organizing Jewish Hospital, the National Jewish Hospital for Consumptives in Denver, and the B'nai B'rith Jewish Orphans Home in Cleveland. The first allocation of funds, amounting to $20,350, was distributed as follows:

United Jewish Charities	$1,250
Hebrew Free and Industrial School	1,100
Jewish Alliance	2,000
Cleveland Orphans Home	6,000
National Jewish Hospital, Denver	2,000
Jewish Hospital, St. Louis	6,000
Home for the Aged and Infirm Israelites	2,000[9]

The Union's first officers consisted of Moses Fraley, president; Marcus Bernheimer and Julius Lesser, vice presidents; Bernard Greensfelder, secretary; and William Stix, treasurer. The first board of directors, sixteen members chosen from the constituent organizations, consisted of Samuel Russack, Emanuel Myers, Morris Glaser, David Treichlinger, Julius Lesser, David Eiseman, Louis Bry, Moses Schoenberg, Louis Glaser, William Goldstein, Isaac Meyer, Benjamin Altheimer, Aaron Waldheim, Isaac Schwab, Solomon A. Rider, and Elias Michael. It was no surprise that those board

---

8. From the Constitution and By-Laws of the Jewish Charitable and Educational Union, 1901, as quoted in Rosen, "Historical Development of Jewish Federation of Saint Louis," 73–74. In the numerous moves of Federation offices, many of the organization's early records unfortunately have been either destroyed or misplaced. Rosen's master's thesis of 1939, for which those records were yet available, is therefore invaluable as a source for the Federation's early history, along with contemporary newspaper materials.

9. *Modern View* 25, 33. Since the Union collected $42,000 in its first year, its allocations of $20,350 proved to be enviably within its budgetary capabilities.

members—and their successors for several decades—were prominent and wealthy businessmen, Reform Jews of German origin. That was, after all, the segment of St. Louis Jewry that contained most of the wealthy and successful businessmen and persons of influence.[10]

According to the constitution of the Jewish Charitable and Educational Union, additional agencies could be admitted "upon such terms and conditions as may be imposed." Within the next few years more did indeed join, including the Jewish Day Nursery, the Jewish Shelter Home, the Jewish Home for Chronic Invalids, and the Miriam Convalescent Home. Each constituent member submitted a budget setting forth its anticipated requirements for the current fiscal year. The central board then apportioned its funds as it deemed necessary and appropriate for each organization. The union had no voice in the day-to-day management of the constituent agencies. Each institution submitted an annual report covering receipts and expenditures; it also reported on a monthly basis on the management and conduct of its affairs. A very important arrangement was that constituent agencies were required to coordinate all their functions—balls, bazaars, picnics, benefits, etc.—through the union so there would be no conflicts. "The whole work of charity collection for the purposes herein named," the union's constitution and bylaws asserted, "shall be assumed by the Union." Although all constituent agencies retained autonomy in function and objectives, the new Jewish Charitable and Educational Union closely monitored their fund-raising activities to avoid as much overlap and competition as possible.[11]

As the St. Louis Jewish community headed into the twentieth century, then, the reorganization of its philanthropic infrastructure under German/Reform leadership boded optimism for the future. As played out in the early 1900s, new programs included, in addition to outright direct

---

10. Ibid. Eastern European Orthodox Jews did not come onto the Federation board until the 1920s. It seemed, in fact, that board members developed a self-perpetuating hierarchy of German Reform Jews. This is not to suggest corruption or lack of principle; it was merely concern that the "right kind" of people ran things. As individual eastern European Orthodox individuals attained economic and social parity with their German Reform counterparts, they were gradually admitted to board membership. But that became part of a broader development in the World War I and postwar eras, 1913–1926, when a separate Orthodox federation came into being and operated for a decade alongside the existing Reform-dominated federation. See *Modern View*, May 23, June 20 and 27, July 14, and December 26, 1913, and January 9, 1914; also Rosen, "Historical Development of Jewish Federation of Saint Louis," 75–76, 98–101.

11. *Modern View*, January 9, 1914. See also *Voice*, January 1, 1904, and January 6, February 10, April 20, July 28, and November 10, 1905; *Modern View* 25, 33–34; and Rosen, "Historical Development of Jewish Federation of Saint Louis," 74–75.

aid, various medical and health-related projects as well as occupational, educational, and housing programs. All those undertakings faced multi-faceted difficulties under any circumstances; the influx of unprecedented numbers of immigrants from eastern Europe as a consequence of the Kishinev massacres and the Russo-Japanese War created a variety of additional problems. Yet relying almost exclusively upon their own human and financial resources, and with excellent leadership coming from the well-to-do German/Reform population, St. Louis Jewry met the new challenges.[12]

Another longtime goal of the German/Reform community finally reached fruition in the early 1900s with the creation of the Jewish Hospital. After the failed efforts of 1863 and 1878, advocacy for a hospital remained alive, even if not in the forefront of Jewish community affairs. Occasionally a supportive letter appeared in the Jewish press, or the matter arose at some social or organizational meeting. Perhaps the most significant impetus, however, was the influx of both German and eastern European Jewish immigrants into St. Louis in the 1880s, and a growing feeling that many could not receive adequate and proper care in existing medical facilities.[13]

In 1890, accordingly, three St. Louis Jewish physicians—Meyer Epstein, Jacob Friedman, and Henry (Harry) Jacobson—publicly urged a renewal of efforts toward establishing a Jewish hospital. They were joined by an influential group of laymen that included Adolph Proskauer, A. M. Hellman, Solomon A. Rider, David Rosentreter, Lewis Godlove, M. A. Summerfield, William Stix, and Rabbi Samuel Sale. Their call resulted in a mass meeting at Addington's Hall (on the corner of Seventeenth

---

12. Institutions involved in those expanded services in the first two decades of the 1900s included the new Jewish Hospital, the Free Dispensary, the Miriam Convalescent Home, the Home for Chronic Invalids (later known as the Jewish Sanatorium), the Jewish Orphans Home, the Jewish Shelter Home, the Dorothy Drey Summers Shelter Home for Children, the Jewish Day Nursery, the Rose Bry Home, the Orthodox Old Folks Home, the Gertrude Boys' Home, and the Ben Akiba Working Girls' Home. The mere volume of those institutions indicates the widespread activity of the Charitable and Educational Union and its successor Jewish Federation. Some of those institutions still exist today; others have been incorporated into reorganized associations.

13. Gee, *History of the Jewish Hospital of St. Louis*, 9–12. Suspicions have long abounded that an important reason to create the hospital was to provide facilities to train Jewish doctors because existing institutions in St. Louis and elsewhere would not take them in for training. That quotas and discrimination existed undoubtedly was true, but they were disguised so as not to be official policy. Jews have faced this problem, after all, in many fields for many years, in colleges and universities and professional schools as well as in labor unions and business and industry. Nevertheless, no evidence exists that this was a specific reason why Jewish Hospital came into being. If it was, it was well concealed.

and Olive) on Sunday afternoon, January 11, 1891. It was reported to be the largest gathering of St. Louis Jews up to that time, attended by persons from both the German Jewish and the eastern European Jewish communities, and also by every Jewish doctor in St. Louis.[14]

From that meeting came the establishment of a temporary Jewish Hospital Association. Permanent organization was deferred to a later meeting, when only those who subscribed at least six dollars would be allowed to vote. Meanwhile, temporary officers were chosen to keep things moving: Adolph Proskauer, chairman; David Rosentreter, treasurer; and Lewis Godlove, secretary. By March 1 more than 150 subscribers had pledged the minimum of six dollars each, and they took steps toward permanent organization. Newly elected officers included Solomon A. Rider, president; David Rosentreter, vice president; William Stix, treasurer; Lewis Godlove, secretary; and a board of managers consisting of those four plus Adolph Proskauer, Dr. M. J. Epstein, Lee Sale, Hannah Stix, Mrs. Joseph Wolfort, Mrs. Nicholas Scharff, Mrs. H. H. Heller, Mrs. Benjamin Eiseman, and Mrs. Adolph Rosentreter. On April 27, 1891, the Jewish Hospital Association of St. Louis received its charter from the State of Missouri, incorporating it "to afford medical and surgical aid, comfort and relief to deserving and needy Israelites and to such other denominations as the Board of Managers can provide for." It is noteworthy that from its very inception the "Jewish" hospital was open to persons of all faiths.[15]

Efforts moved forward rapidly toward establishing the hospital. At an informal meeting of the board of managers at Temple Israel on May 26, one member even offered a site for a building, but certain unspecified "restrictions" led to its refusal. Stories circulated that a site on South Grand was under consideration. Then, at its first annual meeting on May 1, 1892, the hospital association announced that it had purchased a plot of land at the southeast corner of Ridge and Temple Avenues, near Page and Goodfellow in the west end, a site regarded as especially favorable because of its proximity to the Rose Hill and Franklin Avenue cable cars. The association also announced enthusiastic financial support in the amount

---

14. *Voice*, January 9 and 16, 1891; Gee, *History of the Jewish Hospital of St. Louis*, 12–13. Thirteen Jewish doctors are known to have been practicing in St. Louis at the time: Bernhardt Block (who was also a *mohel*), M. J. Epstein, Jacob Friedman, A. Goldsmith, E. W. Haase, Henry (Harry) Jacobson, E. D. Levy, H. Marks, A. Gratz Moses, H. Newland, Simon Politzer, Herman Tuholske, and Henry L. Wolfner. Moses, Wolfner, and Tuholske were identified as the "most famous" of the group. *Voice*, March 16, 1888, and March 14, 1913.

15. *Voice*, January 16, March 13, May 29, and June 5, 1891; also "First Annual Report of the Jewish Hospital Association, 1893," as cited in Gee, *History of the Jewish Hospital of St. Louis*, 13–14.

of $2,482.65, with $1,500 alone coming from one function put on at the Olympic Theater by a group of Jewish young ladies.[16]

Despite these very encouraging beginnings, the hospital association accomplished very little for several years. It became strangely inactive and, in fact, practically defunct. Just why is not clear. Possibly it experienced the frustrations that led to the reorganization of the United Jewish Charities, especially the diffusion of fund-raising efforts with each benevolent group tending to go its own way. Perhaps it relied too much on a few wealthy donors in spite of its seeming appeal to broad-based community support. In 1893 the *Voice* decried editorially the "mode and manner" in which funds were being raised. "We do not blame the officers," editor Spitz wrote, "but what can they do with the extremely scant means at hand? If every Jewish lodge and benevolent organization would pitch in . . . how rapidly could we advance to a final happy pitch in consummation in this direction?" "We need not rely on the wealthier classes in this matter," the *Voice* inveighed two years later. "The masses of the middle and even poorer classes are able and willing to support a Hospital . . . [even] if it takes the nickels of the children and the pennies of the poor."[17]

A brief albeit simplified overview of the 1890s might shed some light on why the movement for a Jewish hospital—and other institutions for that matter—ran into difficulties. American tradition paints a distorted picture of the "Gay Nineties" as a decade of innocence and fun topped off by a popular war against Spain. But the 1890s were a complex decade, politically, economically, and socially, at both the national and local levels. American historians have recorded widening conflicts between powerful business interests and growing labor, between debtor and creditor classes, and between nativist and pluralist forces. The "Gilded Age" was in full flower in the 1890s, characterized by extravagantly flaunted affluence at one extreme—economists referred to it as "conspicuous consumption"—and abject poverty at the other. Furthermore, a stifling and crushing depression blanketed the country between 1893 and 1897, brought on by overexpansion and overspeculation, as well as by widespread labor disorders, and by ever-growing discontent in agriculture. These, in turn, were exacerbated by dissonant problems of urbanization and industrialization as the Industrial Revolution finally overtook the nation in full force from coast to coast. A country that had been rural and agricultural became too rapidly urban and industrial, and few knew how to deal with those new problems. For good reason, then, historians have recorded the

---

16. "First Annual Report of the Jewish Hospital Association, 1893," as cited in Gee, *History of the Jewish Hospital of St. Louis,* 13–14.

17. *Voice,* September 15, 1893, and March 1, 1895.

depression of 1893–1897 as perhaps the most serious economic crisis in the nation up to that time. Ramifications locally in St. Louis were further complicated by a sordid saga of insider influence and conflict in local politics. A destructive tornado in 1896 that laid waste large sections of the city did not help. These may well have been factors that contributed to bringing the fund-raising for a Jewish hospital to a halt.[18]

Momentum for the hospital grew again in 1898, led by Jewish women. In December 1898, after several months of enthusiastic preparation and publicity, the Ben Akiba Frauenverein held a grand ball at the Concordia Club to raise money for a hospital. Women in the forefront included Mesdames G. Mathes, F. Gottschalk, B. Heidingsfelder, R. Archoefer, R. Unger, S. Glick, and S. Haffner. The Ben Akiba women's success spurred additional efforts, particularly by the Jewish Hospital Aid Society, a women's adjunct of the inactive and seemingly defunct Jewish Hospital Association. Led by Rebecca Kahn, Mrs. Julius Weil, and Ida Kohn, the Aid Society organized a mass meeting on June 11, 1899, to which were invited representatives of virtually all Jewish charitable and fraternal organizations. At Mrs. Weil's request, August Frank, prominent businessman and brother of former Congressman Nathan Frank, presided. The well-attended gathering enthusiastically voted to resuscitate the Jewish Hospital Association, adopt its old charter, and provide financial support. They elected August Frank president, and Ida Kohn, Mrs. Weil, and Jacques Levy as vice presidents.[19]

Organizational wheels turned slowly but inexorably. In April 1900 a new charter was adopted, which slightly revised the purposes of the organization: "[To] afford medical and surgical aid and nursing to sick or disabled persons of any creed or nationality. . . . The religious services of the hospital shall be conducted in conformity with the doctrines and forms of the Jewish religion." New permanent officers elected included August Frank, president; Isaac Schwab, vice president; Lee Sale, secretary; William Stix, treasurer; and a board of directors consisting of Julius Lesser, Morris Glaser, David Eiseman, Jacques Levy, Elias Michael, Charles L. Swartz, Abraham M. Hellman, Marcus S. Weider, and Louis Bry.[20]

Establishing adequate funding now became critical. Again Jewish women stepped into the breach. Rebecca Kahn hosted a meeting at her

---

18. For an overview of St. Louis during the 1890s see, among others, Primm, *Lion of the Valley*, 345 ff. It is worth noting that not a single Jewish business or political figure was associated with any of the less-than-honorable developments in St. Louis during that period.

19. *Voice*, October 14 and December 30, 1898, and June 2 and 16, 1899.

20. Gee, *History of the Jewish Hospital of St. Louis*, 15.

home where she and Gertrude Mathes, Mrs. Weil, and Ida Kohn mapped a strategy to raise money. They approached Elias Michael to make a seed pledge of ten thousand dollars. That proved to be a critical turning point, and during the next few months additional pledges came in from more businessmen, including substantial contributions by Isaac Schwab, William Stix, Max and Leon Schwab, Nathan and Louis Bry, David Eiseman, and Nicholas Scharff. By the summer of 1900 sufficient funds had been raised to warrant definitive action. Accordingly, in August 1900, the hospital association purchased a "handsome lot" at 5415 Delmar, adjoining the Masonic Home, and employed architect William Levy to draw up plans for the building. (There is no evidence as to the disposition of the land purchased earlier at Ridge and Temple; presumably the association sold it and applied the money toward the new Delmar Avenue property.)[21]

Hospital construction now moved forward. The cornerstone was laid on Thursday, May 16, 1901, and the building was completed the following year. Dedication services on Sunday, May 4, 1902, were interrupted by a severe rainstorm and put off for two weeks until Sunday, May 18 (the services had to be outdoors because the hospital had no auditorium or room large enough to hold the large crowd). Major speakers included August Frank, Rabbi Leon Harrison, Governor David R. Francis, Mayor Rolla Wells, Dr. Herman Tuholske (chief of the medical staff), and Rabbi Samuel Sale.[22]

Although the architect's plans called for three side-by-side connected buildings, available funds limited original construction to only one building. It measured forty feet across the front and seventy feet in depth, with a columned front porch and a small cupola on top. Its three stories accommodated thirty beds, a kitchen, and necessary administrative and service facilities. An operating room, the furnace, and quarters for student nurses occupied the basement. By 1906, after an intensive fund-raising campaign, adjacent two-story ward buildings were completed, as were additional structures in the rear, one a small isolation ward, one housing kitchen and laundry facilities, and one a new operating-room pavilion.

21. Ibid., 15–17; "Short History of Jewish Hospital of St. Louis," in Herman Schachter Collection, St. Louis Jewish Community Archives, St. Louis; *Voice*, August 31, 1900.

22. *Voice*, May 17, 1901, and May 23, 1902; *St. Louis Globe-Democrat*, May 19, 1902; *St. Louis Post-Dispatch*, May 19, 1902. The cornerstone of the original hospital contained contemporary newspapers, letters, programs, and an American flag. The cornerstone is now located on the first floor of the Jewish Hospital's Shoenberg Pavilion. It was presented to the hospital by the Masonic organization in 1958, when it razed the original hospital building on Delmar Boulevard and replaced it with a new Masonic home on that site. Gee, *History of the Jewish Hospital of St. Louis*, 16–17.

The hospital stood on the north side of Delmar Boulevard, on a grade about ten feet above street level, a few hundred yards west of Union Boulevard. It fronted on Delmar on a lot that extended back to Von Versen Avenue (the name was changed during World War I to Enright Avenue). Completely fireproof, the installation contained the latest in medical and service facilities, and after the two wards were completed could house up to a hundred patient beds. On the day the hospital was dedicated, it already had six patients.[23]

Like any similar institution, Jewish Hospital had rules and regulations for administration, staff, patients, and employees. One could become a member of the Jewish Hospital Association by making a twenty-five-dollar contribution to the Jewish Charitable and Educational Union. Donors were sought for endowed beds or rooms. Private patients in the hospital paid in advance one dollar a day on a weekly basis; wards were free of charge except "where deemed chargeable." The chief engineer was to keep the hospital temperature in winter at no less than 66 degrees nor more than 68 degrees, considered the "extremes" between comfort and economy (nothing in hospital regulations dealt with summer temperatures, so difficult to regulate, this being well before air cooling became a reality). Ward patients (nothing was said about those in private rooms) were forbidden to use profane or indecent language, to talk loudly, to play cards, to smoke, or to use tobacco or liquor. They were enjoined from entering the "dead house" (morgue). Patients were expected to be clean in their habits in lavatories, closets, and bathrooms. They were required to have a bath at least once a week, but nurses were forbidden to permit them to bathe within two hours of a meal. Night nurses were required to wear slippers.[24]

---

23. *St. Louis Globe-Democrat*, May 19, 1902; *Voice*, May 2 and 23, 1902, and June 8, 1906; Gee, *History of the Jewish Hospital of St. Louis*, 19, 23, 117. See also information on St. Louis Jewish Hospital in St. Louis, Missouri File, AJA. Jewish Hospital's first medical staff consisted of the following doctors: Herman Tuholske (surgery), Jacob Friedman (medicine), Robert Luedeking (medicine), Henry Wolfner (ophthalmology), Hanau W. Loeb (ear, nose, and throat), Phillip Hoffman (orthopedic surgery), Sidney J. Schwab (neurology), W. A. Hardaway (dermatology), E. F. Tiedeman (pathology), and Hugo Ehrenfest (obstetrics/gynecology). The associate staff included Doctors John M. Grant (medicine), William M. Robertson (urology), Willard Bartlett (surgery), William S. Deutsch (medicine), Major Seelig (surgery), Jesse Myer (medicine), Louis J. Wolfort (medicine), Gustave Lippman (pediatrics), Aaron Levy (pediatrics), M. A. Frankenthal (general practice), and Meyer Wiener (ophthalmology). Gee, *History of the Jewish Hospital of St. Louis*, 117.

24. "Rules and Regulations, The Jewish Hospital of St. Louis, 1902," in Gee, *History of the Jewish Hospital of St. Louis*, 19–22.

In the same year that the hospital opened, a school of nursing was also started. Called the Jewish Hospital Training School for Nurses, it had a three-year diploma program. Students (no younger than twenty nor older than thirty years of age) received a stipend of three dollars per month for the first year, five dollars per month for the second year, and seven dollars per month for the third year; that money provided for clothing, textbooks, and personal expenses. Room and board were furnished without charge. Student nurses worked a seventy-two-hour week, from 7 A.M. to 7 P.M. five days a week, with a half day off on Sunday and one other day. They wore ankle-length white uniforms (hemlines came up to mid-calf in 1918), a high round cap (in 1905 it became a Dutch wing cap), and a black outer shawl. In addition to their regular duties at the hospital, student nurses spent two months at the Red Cross Public Health Center and two months at the Jewish Dispensary. Hospital rules forbade nurses in training to marry, or, for that matter, even to mingle socially with the staff. "Woe-be-tide the unlucky member of the house staff or nursing staff to be found in each other's company outside of the Hospital," Dr. Paul S. Lowenstein later recalled of his early years at Jewish Hospital.[25]

An important adjunct of the Jewish Hospital was a dispensary located in the Alliance Building at Ninth and Carr Streets, operating there under the auspices of the Jewish Charitable and Educational Union. Extant records do not indicate exactly when the dispensary opened, but certainly it was in operation as early as 1902 when the hospital's regulations required student nurses to spend two months there. The dispensary functioned as an outpatient arm of the Jewish Hospital. More than that, though, its location in the heart of the "Ghetto" (as that downtown neighborhood was referred to by even the St. Louis secular press) meant that the growing number of poor eastern European Jewish immigrants had ready access to necessary medical care. Its importance to those people as part of the overall Alliance programming cannot be overstated. The dispensary remained in its original location at Ninth and Carr even after the building was sold in 1919 to the YMCA. In 1921, however, when fire destroyed the building, the dispensary moved to the Washington University Clinic and ultimately, in 1927, to the new Jewish Hospital located by then on Kingshighway opposite Forest Park.[26]

One additional observation should be noted about the beginnings of Jewish Hospital. It deals with the matter of traditional Jewish dietary laws and *kashruth* (kosher food and facilities), an issue that plagued the

25. As quoted in ibid., 31.
26. Ibid., 26–27.

institution for decades before finally being resolved in the 1920s. Before a "Jewish" hospital existed anywhere in the United States, sick Jews who went into hospitals either ate the duly provided hospital fare or, if the hospital approved, had friends or relatives bring in kosher food at their own expense. Horror stories abounded in St. Louis and elsewhere of observant Jews who chose to stay at home and even risk death rather than enter a hospital that lacked kosher facilities. As the Jewish population increased in the United States in the 1800s, pressures mounted within Jewish communities to correct that problem, as well as others that had developed. Sick Jews faced outright medical discrimination in some communities simply because they were Jews. Furthermore, nativist prejudices against immigrants led in many places to discriminatory hospital admissions restrictions, usually tied to length of residence, so that recent arrivals often found themselves ineligible for hospital care. To counter these forces, as well as to fulfill the age-old *tzedakah* concept, "Jewish" hospitals came into being, the first in Cincinnati in 1850, followed by others in New York, New Orleans, Baltimore, and Chicago. That was the situation when Isidor Bush made his unsuccessful bid for a Jewish hospital in St. Louis in 1863, when the United Hebrew Charities made its failed attempt in 1878, and when the third successful move finally developed in the 1890s.[27]

Missing in the arguments for a Jewish hospital in St. Louis, however, unlike in other cities, was the concern for *kashruth*. When Jacob Furth, Augustus Binswanger, and Rabbi Solomon Sonneschein addressed an open appeal to the Jewish community in 1878, the need for a hospital, as they expressed it, was that "destitute, aged and infirm Israelites must use City Hospital which is filled by the worst elements of a population and are not . . . the proper retreats for worthy Israelites." Certainly those men knew that Jewish hospitals in other cities had installed facilities for their observant Jewish patients. Certainly they were aware too that observant St. Louis Jews wanted comparable accommodations. But the Furth-Binswanger-Sonneschein appeal resulted not in a hospital but in the Home for the Aged and Infirm Israelites; and despite repeated requests by Orthodox Jews in St. Louis that the Home follow the laws of *kashruth*, leaders of the Jewish community repeatedly rejected those appeals, citing cost as the main reason. When the eventually successful push for a hospital came in the 1890s, once again observant Jews pleaded that it be a kosher hospital, but again in vain.[28]

---

27. Ibid., 4–9.

28. Ibid., 9; *Voice*, May 31, 1907; Hyde and Conard, eds., *Encyclopedia of the History of St. Louis*, vol. 2, 1044; Scharf, *Saint Louis City and County*, vol. 2, 1763. See also chapter 11 for earlier attempts to establish a Jewish hospital.

In spite of the cost argument, one can only surmise, as did a study of the early years of the Jewish Federation, that the real reason lay in the religious attitudes of the leadership within the Jewish community. Almost universally they were wealthy and influential businessmen, and they were Reform Jews. Despite continuous and impassioned pleas by Orthodox leaders, the community power structure that established Jewish Hospital rejected demands that it be a totally kosher institution, or, for that matter, even partially kosher, with one separate kosher kitchen. Those who wanted kosher food had to bring it in themselves; the hospital itself remained nonkosher. That dispute continued for several decades, especially as the Orthodox community increased and began to produce its own breed of wealthy businessmen, and it became a key issue leading to the creation of a separate Orthodox Federation and a viable movement to establish a second, fully kosher, hospital. The matter was finally resolved in the 1920s, when the present Jewish Hospital was built at 216 South Kingshighway, made possible by then in part by the willingness of leaders on both sides to reach an amicable and workable compromise.[29]

The consolidation of the Charitable and Educational Union and the creation of Jewish Hospital culminated for the city's German Reform Jews in a series of tangible achievements that reflected their successful transition into a vibrant community that was now comfortably "at home" in St. Louis. If these solidly established institutions are insufficient evidence, three more developments in the early 1900s can be viewed as symbolic icing on the cake. On September 26, 1901, the first issue of the *Modern View* came into being. Planned since 1898 by journalist Abraham Rosenthal, the *Modern View,* together with Rabbi Moritz Spitz's *Voice,* gave the St. Louis Jewish community two newspapers. Openly espousing a more liberal Reform demeanor than did the *Voice,* Rosenthal's paper reflected the editorial viewpoint of much of the emergent power structure within the Jewish population of St. Louis. One should not infer, though, that Rosenthal spoke as the tool of that power structure or of the liberal Reform rabbinate. On the contrary, he was quite independent. Though the *Modern View* advocated liberal Reform, it often spoke out sympathetically for social and economic support for the Orthodox community, in spite of differences over practice and ritual (for instance, the *Modern View* strongly endorsed a kosher Orthodox Old Folks Home, separate from the existing

---

29. For the controversy over *kashrus* in the hospital, see *Voice,* April 26, May 3 and 31, and November 22, 1912, June 27, August 1, October 31, and December 5 and 12, 1919, June 11, 18, and 25, and September 24, 1920; *Modern View,* April 1, 1927; Gee, *History of the Jewish Hospital of St. Louis,* 9–10; Rosen, "Historical Development of Jewish Federation of Saint Louis," 78.

Reform-oriented Home for the Aged and Infirm Israelites). The mere fact that two newspapers now served St. Louis Jewry attested to the comfort and stability of the Jewish community, especially the German Jewish portion.

Equally significant, or perhaps even more so because its impact extended beyond the Jewish community, was the recognition accorded to and the role played by St. Louis Jewry—especially by some German Jews—in the famous 1904 World's Fair. One in particular, Nathan Frank, played a very significant role from the very beginning. As a member of Congress in 1890, he sought (albeit in vain) to have the 1893 World's Fair moved to St. Louis; but planning had progressed too far and the four hundredth anniversary of Columbus's expedition was hosted instead by Chicago. Nevertheless Frank lobbied enthusiastically for a fair in St. Louis in 1903 to commemorate the centennial of the Louisiana Purchase, and this time his (and many others') efforts proved successful. In fact, as early as 1889 a group of civic-minded St. Louisans had already begun planning for the event, and six prominent Jews held important positions on its executive committee: Frank, Marcus Bernheimer, Jacob Furth, Meyer Bauman, Jonathan Rice, and Moses Fraley. In 1898 a delegate convention summoned by Missouri's Governor Lon V. Stephens designated a committee of fifty (later enlarged to two hundred) to undertake more definitive planning; Pierre Chouteau was named chairman of the executive committee and David R. Francis and Nathan Frank were appointed vice chairmen. Soon the Louisiana Purchase Exposition Company came into being to raise funds, and its shareholders elected a ninety-three-man board of directors to bring the fair to its ultimate fruition. Five of the elected directors were St. Louis Jews: Nathan Frank, Isaac Schwab, Jonathan Rice, Jacob J. Wertheimer, and Charles A. Stix. Unfortunately Schwab and Rice died before the fair opened, but shareholders elected Elias Michael to fill one of those vacancies.[30]

Like everyone else in St. Louis, Jews took great pride in the World's Fair. The *New Era Illustrated Magazine*, published in New York, carried an article entitled "The Jews of the World's Fair City." Throughout the summer of 1904 the *Voice* and the *Modern View* (and, of course, the secular press) printed transportation schedules to help people visit the fair; they also publicized special features and events, as well as lodging facilities available for visitors. St. Louis rabbis delivered numerous sermons focusing on the wonders of the fair. Through the efforts of William Stix and Benjamin

---

30. *Voice*, February 17, 1899, and August 14, 1914; "Scholars Assess Jewish Role in 1904 St. Louis World's Fair," in *St. Louis Jewish Light*, June 25, 1986; *Official Guide to the Louisiana Purchase Exposition*, 167–70.

Altheimer, many youngsters in the B'nai B'rith Cleveland Orphans Home were brought to St. Louis and provided with what must have been some very invigorating and exciting experiences.

Two features of the fair proved to be especially interesting to St. Louis Jewry. One was an exhibit by the local Jewish Charitable and Educational Union in the Educational and Social Economy Building, showing some of the charitable and philanthropic work being done by Jews in St. Louis. Much more attractive, however, was the Jerusalem Exhibit, a reproduction of the old walled Holy City as well as portions of the then "new" city (minus certain unspecified "objectionable features"). Occupying more than ten acres right in the heart of the fairgrounds, the exhibit highlighted items of interest to persons of many faiths, including Jews. In fact, a feature article in the *Voice* describing the exhibit was headlined "Judaism at the World's Fair." Though the title exaggerated, it reflected an unmistakable pride many Jews felt in being a part of the fair and of the exhibit. In fact, though, the Jerusalem exhibit was not a "Jewish" exhibit; its purpose was clearly to attract and educate persons of all faiths. True, four St. Louis rabbis (Harrison, Messing, Sale, and Spitz) sat on the exhibit's advisory board—Harrison was actually a vice president—but about seventy ministers and priests representing virtually every Christian denomination in St. Louis also sat on that board and saw to the multidenominational character of the exhibit. Nevertheless, the Jerusalem Exhibit proved to be a very popular attraction for the Jews of St. Louis.[31]

Individual Jews and the Jewish community as a whole, then, participated in the great World's Fair. But of course so did non-Jews. The importance of the Jewish community's involvement lay not in that Jews did anything special, or that they did more than anyone else. Rather, it was simply that Jews were a part of it—and especially part of the leadership team that created and implemented such a magnificently successful civic venture. It should be stressed, however, that Jews on the board of directors were there not because they were Jews; they were there because they were successful and influential activists and businessmen in the overall community. With Jews having already served successfully in various local, state, and national offices, it was only natural that capable Jews, like

31. *Voice*, February 27, 1903, May 13, 20, and 27, and July 22, 1904; "Jerusalem Exhibit, St. Louis World's Fair," in Manuscript File, Klau Library, Hebrew Union College–Jewish Institute of Religion, Cincinnati; "Prospectus of the Jerusalem Exhibit Company," St. Louis File, American Jewish Historical Society, Waltham, Massachusetts. An interesting feature of the fair was the public flying, thought to be for the first time, of the Zionist flag (white with two horizontal blue stripes and a blue Star of David in the center) that later became the official flag of Israel. *St. Louis Jewish Light*, June 25, 1986.

anyone else, would be a part of the World's Fair organization, fitting in where their talents could be best used.[32]

At least one more development in the early 1900s attests to the comfortable status St. Louis German Jewry had achieved: the establishment of Westwood Country Club in 1907. Any depiction of Jewish social life in the turn-of-the-century years necessarily would include a broad assortment of activities: private "at home" social parties; dances, dinners, and similar affairs sponsored by congregations and organizations for a variety of reasons and occasions; and entertainment afforded by amusement parks, picnic grounds, excursion boats, lectures, concerts, and theaters. A *bris*, a wedding, or a *Bar Mitzvah* normally occasioned a special family celebration. Virtually every edition of the Jewish newspapers contained accounts—some only a very brief mention, some in more detail—of all sorts of social gatherings, indicating an active and viable Jewish social environment for all Jews, rich and poor, German and eastern European. Public band and orchestra concerts attracted many; quite a few attended St. Louis Symphony Orchestra performances. Those who could afford it vacationed at the popular Washington Hotel in Okawville, Illinois, to benefit from the baths and "health-giving waters" there. Many of the more affluent vacationed in the German "fatherland" and visited friends and relatives. Theatrical productions performed in German attracted large numbers of German Jews, as they did non-Jewish Germans in St. Louis. As the eastern European Jews arrived, they frequented Yiddish plays presented by popular road companies. The great Boris Thomashefsky played before one packed audience after another at the Imperial Theater; the Lipzin Yiddish Company featured Maurice Moshkowitz and Samuel Tornberg in performances at the Olympic Theater; and the Glickman Players performed before full houses at the Garrick Theater. And certainly not to be overlooked was one of the city's most prestigious social events, the Veiled Prophet Ball, attended by many of the wealthy "elite" of the St. Louis Jewish community.[33]

---

32. There was, however, another side to the relationship between Jews and the World's Fair. For instance, Jewish laborers were denied some jobs at the fair. Observant Jews complained that the fair was open only six days a week, open on the Jewish Sabbath but closed on Sunday. For those who worked long hours throughout the week and had only Sunday off—and that applied to many non-Jews as well—the fair might have been in another city. Nor did the World's Fair contribute toward breaching the gap between the German Reform and the eastern European Orthodox communities; that divisiveness continued to be a major issue for St. Louis Jewry. For some Jewish concerns related to the fair, see *Voice*, May 13, 20, and 27, and July 22, 1904.

33. For some representative examples of Jewish social life during that time period, see *Jewish Free Press*, September 2, 1887; *Voice*, October 5, 1888, October 7, 1898, May 26,

Following the examples of their non-Jewish affluent friends, wealthy St. Louis Jews established their own private social clubs, such as the Harmonie Club. When the Harmonie Club moved its quarters in 1882 to the western part of the city, members living on the south side, unhappy over that new location, seceded and established a new club, the Concordia Club. In 1892 both clubs disbanded and were replaced by the Columbian Club, which quickly became the most prestigious club for affluent St. Louis Jewry. Membership in the Columbian Club included virtually every wealthy and influential person in the Jewish community in business and in the professions. The club's magnificent three-story building on Lindell and Vandeventer became the site of almost every important Jewish gathering. The flavor and tempo of social life at the Harmonie Club was replicated in all its splendor and elegance at the luxurious Columbian Club.[34]

By 1907, however, that was not enough. The Columbian Club contained superb quarters for all sorts of social and cultural gatherings, but it lacked facilities for athletics and the physical development of its members; only the YMHA offered that, and then only in a limited way. During the summer of 1907 some wealthy St. Louis Jews happened to vacation at the same resort in Michigan. There they informally discussed the situation. In addition, they were very much influenced by a growing national phenomenon—especially popular on college campuses—of "a sound mind in a sound body." Accordingly, some of those men and other interested St. Louis Jews met at the Columbian Club in October 1907 and organized the Westwood Country Club. Before the meeting adjourned, seventy men had pledged their support. Official incorporation documents drawn up in 1908 stated the purposes of Westwood: the mental and physical development of its membership through athletics; the enjoyment of "rational" and social amusements; the playing of golf, tennis, and other "lawful" games; the cultivation of aquatic and equestrian opportunities; and as incidental to those, the maintenance of a clubhouse and other appropriate facilities. The club's first officers were David Sommers, president; Dr. Hanau Loeb, vice president; Charles M. Rice, secretary; and Edward Scharff, treasurer. Its board of directors and membership

---

1899, February 27, May 16 and 30, and June 20, 1902, May 22 and July 31, 1903, June 24, August 5, and December 23, 1904, June 2 and 9, 1905, March 16 and November 2, 1906, and March 29 and April 19, 1907.

34. For more on the Columbian Club, see *Jewish Free Press*, October 9 and November 27, 1885, and October 12, 1888; *Voice*, September 20, 1898; *Modern View*, December 22, 1916; *Modern View 25*, 58; Devoy, *A History of the City of St. Louis*, 141; and Gill, *St. Louis Story*, vol. 1, 127.

included, as the *Voice* put it, "the foremost elements of St. Louis Jewish society." Located at the intersection of Manchester Road and the Missouri Pacific Railway on the outskirts of suburban Kirkwood, Westwood's expansive grounds contained tennis courts, golf links, a lake for swimming and canoeing, equestrian facilities, and appropriate capabilities for winter recreation. Its clubhouse provided elegant means for small informal gatherings as well as large and sumptuous gala affairs. In the fullest sense of the word, then, Westwood symbolized the success of St. Louis German Jewry, and especially its "elite," whose business and civic and professional achievements had rendered them finally comfortable and stable in their St. Louis environment. Not only had they emulated other established groups in their philanthropic and fraternal and social organizations; now they also had the most visible and symbolic representation of their success, their own country club.[35]

---

35. *Voice*, May 12, 1911, and January 5, 1912, and especially the article written by Charles M. Rice on the founding of Westwood Country Club in *Modern View 25*, 59. A long-standing suspicion has persisted that the motivation behind the establishment of Westwood lay in two additional factors. One was that many wealthy German Jews seeking recreational and health facilities did not relish associating with the ever-increasing numbers of "lower status" eastern European Jews who frequented the YMHA. The other was that affluent German Jews seeking to join existing country clubs were turned away because of alleged antisemitism. Having the financial means, therefore, they simply established their own country club. Even if only partially true, though, the validity of such contentions is often impossible to document. It is interesting to note, by the way, that comparable assertions were made later when some Jews of eastern European heritage could not become members of Westwood (that situation no longer exists today). In 1928 Westwood Country Club moved from its original location to its present grounds at Conway and Ballas Roads in St. Louis County. Author's interview with Howard F. Baer, June 22, 1981, Frank Wolff, February 17, 1995, and Milton Greenfield Jr., February 20, 1995.

— 17 —

INTO THE TWENTIETH CENTURY
The Russians

Like the city's German Jews, the eastern European Orthodox Jews of St. Louis experienced a time of great transition in the early 1900s. Indeed, just as German Jewry had experienced its "bridge years" during the 1830s and 1840s, so did the eastern European community pass through its own bridge years at the turn of the century.

Although many German Jews viewed the eastern European Jews as a burden, they helped the newer immigrants immeasurably in employment and housing, in charitable and philanthropic efforts, and in educational and recreational endeavors. After all, these were fellow Jews, even if they were very different. The German Jews' efforts brought remarkable results. True, poverty and narrowly prescribed lifestyle conditions continued in the "Ghetto," unquestionably exacerbated by ever-increasing numbers of indigent immigrants. Yet eastern Europeans adapted successfully to their new environment much as their German predecessors had done earlier.[1] In addition to congregations, the new immigrants created their own mutual aid and fraternal societies for small loans and insurance programs. Orthodox-oriented lodges of the Independent Order of B'rith Abraham and the Progressive Order of the West came into being, as did a variety of labor organizations and Zionist groups. Along with the Alliance night schools and the YMHA, those institutions became vital Americanizing and educational agencies for St. Louis eastern European Jewry. Thus in a relatively short time many of the new arrivals evolved

---

1. Not all, of course, adapted that readily. Some insisted upon retaining Old World cultural and social traditions and mores in a way that disturbed even their fellow eastern European Orthodox Jews. At the same time, many who held strongly to their Orthodoxy still adapted culturally to the American scene. For instance, almost all devout Orthodox Jews easily abandoned long-standing European ghetto garb for western clothing styles. Though many found they had to work on the Sabbath for economic reasons, others found alternative incomes so they could remain *shomer shabbos* (observant of the Sabbath).

from a motley community of immigrants for whom so much had to be done into a group that became more and more self-sufficient. And just as successful businessmen and professionals had emerged as leaders within the German Jewish community, so did successful leaders come forward within the eastern European community. True, it took time before any attained the affluence and civic recognition of the German Jewish leaders, but by the early 1900s the process was well under way.

Several significant developments in the early 1900s symbolized that transition, that "crossing of the bridge." They included especially the emergence of a St. Louis Yiddish press, the creation of the Jewish Orthodox Old Folks Home, the formation of Shaare Zedek Congregation, and the spread of the Zionist movement in St. Louis.

An English-language Jewish press had existed in the city for several decades, published by and primarily for St. Louis German Jewry. By its very nature, the new Yiddish press served almost exclusively the eastern European Orthodox population, many of whom continued to speak Yiddish for many years. As with the earlier English-language Jewish newspapers, the origins of the Yiddish press in St. Louis remain murky, because copies of early publications no longer exist. In most instances its history must be re-created from other forms of evidence.[2]

The first Yiddish newspaper in St. Louis seems to have been published in the early to mid-1890s by Ze'ev Shor. Prior to coming to St. Louis, Shor had attained a certain notoriety in eastern Jewish cultural circles by deliberately eschewing Yiddish and writing only in Hebrew. When he came to St. Louis, however, he decided to publish in Yiddish, hoping it would be more financially successful than his earlier Hebrew endeavors. The result was *Der Yiddishe Presse*.[3] Described as "twice as large as a *Shir Ha-Ma'lot* [a small booklet of Psalms of David]," the *Yiddishe Presse* was published half in Yiddish and half in what was described as "German-Yiddish," and contained news articles, editorials, short stories, and "a little bit of everything." Despite its publisher's reputation, the paper survived for only three issues. It could not compete with well-established and very

---

2. The Yiddish press in America originated in New York in the 1870s. Newspapers such as the *Yiddishe Tageblatt*, the *Jewish Daily Forward*, and the *Jewish Morning Journal* became very popular among the highly literate new immigrant population in St. Louis, and they remained popular even after St. Louis began to produce its own Yiddish papers. For more on the American Yiddish press, see *Encyclopedia Judaica*, vol. 12, 1023–56, and its accompanying bibliography. Assimilationists and nativists derided those who persisted in speaking Yiddish as resisting Americanization and Old World ways. Nevertheless, as far as language was concerned, those Jews were no different from other immigrant groups.

3. The title *Der Yiddishe Presse* is a transliteration of the Yiddish lettering.

popular eastern Yiddish newspapers such as the *Jewish Daily Forward* and the *Jewish Morning Journal*.[4]

Shortly thereafter, in March 1895, a second Yiddish paper appeared, *Der St. Louiser Gazette*, put out by a newly created publishing company headed by Moshe Sherman. The paper had four editors during its brief existence, only one of whom can be identified, a Reverend M. Balough. Modestly labeling itself "the best Jewish newspaper in the West," the *Gazette* appeared weekly, on Thursdays. The paper actually was a Philadelphia product, but by arrangement with the publishers Sherman added a few pages with a St. Louis heading and St. Louis news—what the newspaper profession generally labels a "wraparound"—and sold it as *Der St. Louiser Gazette*. The venture lasted a little more than a year before going out of business.[5]

Within a very short time a third Yiddish newspaper appeared in St. Louis, but there is no record of either its title or its dates of publication. We know only that its publisher was a Mr. A. Krishtalka, a man "interested in literary matters" and "not at all lazy with his own pen." Where other St. Louis Jewish newspapers stressed erudite journalism, Krishtalka delved more often into local news verging sometimes on the sensational and even the debasing. An example was a rather vivid and uncomplimentary description of the interior of a small synagogue recently redecorated with red and blue wallpaper. Another story recounted in somewhat fanciful terms the robbery in mid-day of a Jewish butcher in the amount of $3.75. Whether it was the caliber of the journalism or the lack of advertising, Krishtalka's paper lasted only sixteen months before it too expired.[6]

The next Yiddish paper, also short-lived, coincided with the opening of the World's Fair in 1904. It bore the title *Jewish Express*, perhaps because of the train pictured on its front-page masthead. Contents included news of world Jewry, editorials, short stories, and advertising with English subtitles. Although the *Express* lasted for only six issues, its publishers, Yaakov Bernitz and William H. Goldman, would a decade later start what eventually became the most important St. Louis Yiddish newspaper, the *Jewish Record*.[7]

---

4. *Jewish Record* (St. Louis), January 16, 1925.

5. *Die Deborah* (Cincinnati), April 25 and June 27, 1895; *Jewish Record*, January 16, 1925.

6. *Jewish Record*, January 16, 1925; Abrams, *Book of Memories*, 3–4.

7. *Jewish Record*, January 16, 1925; Jewish Genealogy Society of St. Louis, "A Resource Guide: The St. Louis Jewish Press," n.d., 7–8, copy in possession of author. This Yiddish newspaper was published in St. Louis from 1915 until 1951, much of that time under the editorship of Leon Gellman. Its twelfth anniversary edition of January 16, 1925, contained an article by A. D. Weber entitled "The Development of the Yiddish Press."

The first Yiddish newspaper in St. Louis with a modicum of success, *Der Vorsteher (The Representative),* appeared in 1906. Its publishers included M. I. Wolfson, a transplanted Chicago journalist, and Moshe Sherman, former publisher of *Der St. Louiser Gazette.* They started *Der Vorsteher* as a daily paper, but various considerations forced them to convert it into a weekly. *Der Vorsteher* compared favorably in size with most St. Louis secular papers, ranging at different times from four to eight pages, usually seven or eight columns across. Its contents included news—mostly of the broader world Jewish community, but occasionally about important non-Jewish matters—editorials, readers' letters, literary items such as poetry, essays, and serialized short stories, and of course advertising.[8]

Der Vorsteher remained in existence from 1906 until 1910. Its irregular daily/weekly appearance reflected two major problems, both well known in newspaper publishing. One, to no surprise, was finances; the other was instability in ownership and editorship. "Revolving door" associates with *Der Vorsteher* included Sherman and Wolfson, as well as Rudolph Coopersmith, Meyer Shapiro, Barnet Gram, Jacob Shurman, Sidney B. Glass, and John Ellman. Despite the unstable leadership, one consistency in *Der Vorsteher* was its never-ending disagreement with the "Deutsche Yiddin" and the "Reformer Yiddin." That internal conflict was still a long way from being resolved. Furthermore, even the permanence of a Yiddish press was yet to be established. Nevertheless, that Yiddish press had begun in St. Louis—perhaps haltingly, but it was there. At the very least, it reflected a few steps toward crossing the bridge.[9]

While the Yiddish press was developing, another institution emerged to symbolize the growing eastern European Orthodox community. From the day the Home for the Aged and Infirm Israelites had opened its doors in 1882 (and even earlier, during its planning stages), Orthodox Jews in St. Louis had pressed in vain for kosher facilities there. That issue remained a source of often acerbic disagreement during the 1880s and 1890s as the eastern European population increased dramatically. As

---

Copies of the *Jewish Record* are available on microfilm at the Missouri Historical Society in St. Louis and the St. Louis Jewish Community Archives, thanks to the generosity of Eric Newman of St. Louis, who had deteriorating copies of originals microfilmed to preserve their contents.

8. *Voice,* April 12, November 1, and December 20, 1907, February 12, May 28, and August 6, 1909, and September 16, 1910. Copies of *Der Vorsteher* (although not the complete run) are available on microfilm at the Missouri Historical Society in St. Louis and at the St. Louis Jewish Community Archives.

9. *Jewish Record,* January 16, 1925; *Voice,* January 4, April 12, November 1, and December 20, 1907, February 12, May 28, and August 6, 1909, and September 16, 1910.

more and more eastern European Jewish immigrants established roots, and especially as they rose gradually on the economic ladder, pressures developed anew within the Orthodox community to establish a kosher old folks home.[10]

Those efforts reached a climax in the early 1900s. On February 15, 1906, at a banquet given by the Chesed Shel Emeth Society, some of its members proposed "to establish a home for old and infirm Jews and Jewesses where they shall be enabled to spend their remaining days in peace and comfort without being compelled to deny themselves their religious inclinations." With the overwhelming approval of those present, Society President John Ellman appointed a committee of Meyer Shapiro, Hyman Albert, and Selig Feinstein to consider further action. The committee in turn convened a mass meeting chaired by Rabbi Adolph Rosentreter to test reaction from more of the Jewish community. Both turnout and financial pledges at this gathering far surpassed even the most optimistic of expectations. Buoyed by such an enthusiastic show of support, Rosentreter appointed a committee of Dr. M. I. DeVorkin, Samuel Epstein, John Ellman, Michael Novack, and Nathan Harris to look into a possible site. They wasted little time, encouraged no doubt by continuing financial pledges. Within six months the newly organized *Moshab Z'keinim* (Old Folks Home) Society, organized officially on April 14, 1906, purchased an eighteen-room mansion on East Grand and Blair in north St. Louis for eighteen thousand dollars and converted it into the Jewish Orthodox Old Folks Home.[11]

Dedicatory ceremonies on August 25, 1907, attracted more than five thousand visitors onto the Moshab Z'keinim's spacious grounds. Though most represented north-side eastern European Jewry, many south-side German Jews also attended; the *Voice* singled out such prominent German

---

10. Leading advocates for an Orthodox Old Folks Home included Nathan Harris, Dr. M. I. DeVorkin, Rebecca Kahn, Dr. and Mrs. Michael Golland, Sam Sigoloff, and Rabbi Adolph Rosentreter. *Modern View*, July 18, 1930.

11. *Voice*, August 10, 1906, June 28 and August 30, 1907, and May 31, 1912. The building has been referred to variously as the Sturgeon Mansion and as the Forster Mansion. Both are correct. It was built by Beverly Allen for Isaac Sturgeon, a Union activist during the Civil War, and was the site of many pro-Union meetings during that conflict. It later passed into the hands of C. August Forster, a manager of the Hyde Park Brewery. His heirs sold it to the Beth Moshab Z'keinim Society in late 1906, the deed itself being dated January 21, 1907. Famous native St. Louis writer Winston Churchill—not to be confused with the great British statesman—included in his popular novels many episodes that took place in St. Louis. In his best-selling *The Crisis*, for instance, Churchill highlighted a mansion that he called "Bellegarde"; readers easily identified it as the Sturgeon/Forster mansion at North Grand and Blair. See property records for Block 2446 in Assessor's Office, City Hall, St. Louis; *St. Louis Globe-Democrat*, August 14, 1961; Stadler, *St. Louis Day by Day*, 175.

Jewish leaders as Benjamin Altheimer, Marcus Bernheimer, William Stix, Leon Schwab, and Rabbi Moritz Spitz. Newly elected president Dr. M. I. DeVorkin delivered the main address. In addition to commending those whose efforts had brought the Home into being, DeVorkin stressed that the institution "has not been established in opposition to, or out of dissatisfaction with, the Home for the Aged and Infirm Israelites on South Jefferson." He also heaped praise on the German-dominated Charitable and Educational Union as "one of the finest of its kind in the country . . . run by some of the foremost Jewish citizens of this city." DeVorkin's public attempt at reconciliation proved at least partially successful, for in spite of the ongoing rift between the eastern European Orthodox and German Reform Jews of St. Louis, the Old Folks Home was one Orthodox institution that garnered considerable support from both sides.[12]

Many of those involved in the establishment of the Orthodox Old Folks Home had already become or were to be important figures within the eastern European Orthodox community. In addition to President DeVorkin, the Home's first set of officers included Charles Werner and Nathan Harris, vice presidents; Gustave Cytron, recording secretary; Sam Schwartzberg, financial secretary; and John Ellman, treasurer. Mr. and Mrs. Benjamin Wolfsohn served as superintendent and matron for many years. Samuel Epstein (also district deputy grand master of the Independent Order of B'rith Abraham) worked diligently to secure his lodge's support for the Home. Others cited for conscientious efforts in the institution's formative years included Samuel Epstein, Michael Novack, Frank Dubinsky, Dr. Michael Golland, Isadore Mathes, Heiman Elbert, Benjamin Burenstein, Samuel Schwartz, and Sol Kurlander. These names and others would appear more and more in the local Jewish press during the next few decades as emerging leaders of a fast-growing St. Louis eastern European Jewry.[13]

A seemingly minor incident involving the new Orthodox Old Folks Home presaged the emerging self-sufficiency and growing influence of the newer Jewish population. Despite DeVorkin's conciliatory statements

---

12. *Voice,* August 30, 1907. According to documents in the organization's archives, the institution opened for residents on August 20, 1906. When the Orthodox Old Folks Home later undertook a costly expansion program, German Jews rendered substantial financial support. On the other hand, the German-dominated Federation did not include the Orthodox Old Folks Home under its umbrella until 1926. Rosen, "Jewish Federation of Saint Louis," 83–84.

13. *Voice,* August 10, 1906, June 28, August 30, September 6, and October 4, 1907, August 14 and 21, 1908, and May 31, 1912; *Modern View,* May 31, 1912, July 18, 1930, October 11, 1934, and April 14, 1938.

at the Moshab Z'keinim's dedicatory exercises, *kashruth* continued as a sticking point between German Reform and eastern European Orthodox community leaders. Apparently, too, the new North Grand facility seemed to be siphoning financial support from the older establishment on South Jefferson. The seriousness of the situation prompted Moses Fraley, prominent and influential supporter of the south-side Home, to propose a compromise: that the Home for the Aged and the Infirm Israelites on South Jefferson become a strictly kosher installation, and the new North Grand facility become a hospital for chronic invalids. Leaders of the Orthodox Old Folks Home rejected the proposal. Obviously they felt secure enough to do so—symbolic of the growing status of the eastern European Orthodox community and its own resources.[14]

Yet another institution came into being in the early 1900s to signify the growing virility of St. Louis's eastern European Jewry: Shaare Zedek Congregation. Prior to the turn of the century, the newer immigrant population crowded into the "Ghetto"—that area north of Delmar Boulevard and westward to Grand Avenue. In addition to many Jews, the area was home also for large numbers of Polish, Italian, and Irish immigrants—legendary "Kerry Patch" proliferated there—as well as much of the black population of St. Louis. In the Ghetto also stood the Orthodox synagogues, large and small, permanent and transitory: B'nai Amoona, Beth Hamedrosh Hagodol, Tipheris Israel, Sheerith S'fard, and others. In the early 1900s the Ghetto's population grew rapidly. As conditions became more crowded, the more "affluent" residents of the area began to move westward, toward Kingshighway and beyond. With them came their synagogues. Leading the way was a new congregation, Shaare Zedek.

In August 1904 a group of Jews who had moved into the west end rented quarters on the southwest corner of Vandeventer and Finney to conduct High Holy Day services. They hoped also to stimulate opening a Talmud Torah in the neighborhood—in fact, that might have been their primary objective since so many families with children were moving into the new area. Immediately following the High Holy Day services, then, initial steps were taken to organize the school. Reverend L. Rosenblatt, the popular *mohel*, presided over a well-attended meeting convened at the West End Hotel on Sunday evening, September 11, where a committee was designated to head fund-raising endeavors. That committee achieved

---

14. *Voice*, October 4, 1907. The Orthodox Old Folks Home succeeded to such a degree that the physical plant had to be considerably expanded. That expansion included facilities for many events that made the Old Folks Home virtually a social center for St. Louis Jewry.

its goal within nine months. On June 9, 1905, the new school opened at 3935 Finney, with Reverend J. Korn in charge.[15]

The success of the Talmud Torah led to the creation of a congregation. Responding to a call by Reverend Korn and Mr. Robert Horwitz, on August 12, 1905, a number of worshipers assembled in a regular *minyan* at 4126 Finney Avenue for a Sabbath morning service. The turnout for that routine service far exceeded what Korn and Horwitz had anticipated; the spirited response to Korn's service and sermon surpassed their expectations as well. Enthused by the camaraderie and good fellowship that prevailed, the worshipers assembled again on the following morning, Sunday, August 13, 1905, and organized a permanent congregation. They named it *Shaare Zedek* ("Gates of Righteousness"). Robert Horwitz was unanimously elected temporary chairman, and Dr. Alex Horwitz became secretary. The first Orthodox congregation in the west end had come into being.[16]

From its inception Shaare Zedek was more than just an institution for worship. One of its first actions was to take over the operation of the Talmud Torah. Within only a few weeks, thirty young members organized the Shaare Zedek Young People's Aid Society to provide social and philanthropic outlets for its membership. By October this enterprising group, under the leadership of President Dr. Alex Horwitz and Vice President Clara Siegfried, sponsored a well-attended dance that raised funds for a variety of charitable purposes. Their success and élan augured a very active Orthodox congregation.[17]

Shaare Zedek bolstered that expectation by wasting very little time in securing a permanent home. In December 1905 the congregation purchased

---

15. *Voice*, September 9 and 15, 1904, and June 9, 1905. Those who took the lead in that undertaking included Dr. S. S. Kohn, I. Evans, H. Simpkin, Louis Fadem, Louis Stockman, and a Mr. Marx. Ibid., August 12 and 19, 1904. The "west end" at that time was roughly between Grand Avenue on the east, Easton Avenue (now Dr. Martin Luther King Drive) on the north, Kingshighway on the west, and Chouteau Avenue on the south.

16. Ibid., August 18, 1905. Before long additional congregations began to move into the west end. In 1907 a group organized Beth David Congregation, at first renting facilities at Easton and Semple. The following year Beth David members purchased a small church at Belt and Theodosia and converted it into a synagogue. Ibid., August 28, 1908. Shaare Zedek was the first *Orthodox* synagogue in the west end. Three Reform congregations actually preceded it west of Grand Avenue. In 1897 Shaare Emeth relocated from Seventeenth and Locust to Lindell and Vandeventer; in 1903 United Hebrew moved from Twenty-First and Olive to Kingshighway and Von Versen; and in 1905 B'nai El moved from Eleventh and Chouteau to Spring and Flad. Temple Israel did not move from Pine and Leffingwell to Washington and Kingshighway until 1908.

17. Ibid., October 20, 1905.

a building at 4557 Cook Avenue (today it is 4559 Newberry Terrace) just west of Taylor Avenue, and converted it into a synagogue. That it could do this so soon after it had been organized testified that the members of this new Orthodox congregation fit the characteristic picture of upward mobility. In fact, the *Voice* actually referred to Shaare Zedek as one of the two "wealthiest" Orthodox synagogues in the city, the other being B'nai Amoona.[18]

As the first west end Orthodox synagogue, Shaare Zedek attracted increasing numbers of worshipers. As is wont with attendance at services, many more came for holiday services than for the weekly Sabbath worship. In fact, several times Shaare Zedek had to rent a nearby large hall for its High Holy Day services. Membership increased to such a degree that within a few years the congregation outgrew its Cook Avenue building. In due course, then, Shaare Zedek purchased nearby land on the corner of Page Boulevard and West End Avenue and constructed a new and magnificent dome-topped synagogue. Several thousand people attended the cornerstone ceremonies on August 16, 1914, including Mayor Henry W. Kiel, several Orthodox and Reform rabbis, and numerous Jewish and non-Jewish community leaders. Although the building was not yet completed, Shaare Zedek Congregation conducted High Holy Day services there in the fall of 1914.[19]

One might view the founding of Shaare Zedek as just another of many Orthodox congregations established by eastern European immigrants. Indeed, it was not the first and certainly not the last, nor was it the largest or the wealthiest. Its import lay in something else. Its founders were not a wealthy elite comparable with the originators of Temple Israel, but rather Jews just emerging from the abject poverty of the downtown Ghetto who were becoming professionals and small entrepreneurs, a solid

18. Ibid., December 29, 1905, and December 15, 1913. Calling either Shaare Zedek or B'nai Amoona "wealthy" was an exaggeration, unless one compared them with the much poorer synagogues in the Ghetto. Compared with the Reform congregations, they were anything but wealthy.

19. Ibid., September 7, 1906, October 18, 1907, September 16, 1910, March 24, 1911, December 5, 1913, and July 17, July 24, and August 14, 1914; *Modern View*, July 25 and October 24, 1913, July 10, 17 and 24, August 14 and 21, September 18, and October 16, 1914; *St. Louis Jewish Light*, January 16, 1980. In 1913, when Shaare Zedek decided to build its new synagogue, a merger with B'nai Amoona came under consideration. Representatives of both organizations met several times, but the union never materialized. Shaare Zedek built its new edifice at Page and West End in 1914, and in 1916 B'nai Amoona erected a new synagogue at Academy and Vernon Avenues. *Voice*, December 5, 1913; *Modern View*, December 5, 1913; Bronsen, *B'nai Amoona for All Generations*, 78–79, 97–99.

and steady middle class by any standards. They became the leading wave of many more Orthodox Jews who followed as their economic status permitted such a move. The creation of Shaare Zedek represented that upward mobility, symbolically and in reality. Put another way, the new Shaare Zedek—as did the Yiddish press and the new Orthodox Old Folks Home—typified an emerging self-asserting and self-reliant St. Louis eastern European Orthodox Jewish community.

One criterion of a community's importance derives from the recognition accorded it by outsiders. The turn of the century saw the rise of modern political Zionism as a movement for the creation of an independent Jewish homeland in Palestine. Many American Reform Jews reacted apathetically toward that movement, even branding Zionists as unpatriotic to their adopted lands and dangerous to the best interests of all Jewry. At the same time, Orthodox extremists also denounced the movement as antimessianic, irreligious, and incompatible with fundamental tenets of Judaism. Most American Orthodox Jews, on the other hand—including the large number who were not very observant but who nevertheless tended toward Orthodoxy when they had occasion to exercise any ritual observance—viewed political Zionism much more favorably. Zionist leaders therefore courted the larger and more important eastern European Orthodox communities in America as lucrative wellsprings of financial and moral support. One of those communities proved to be in St. Louis. Being so identified was another manifestation of St. Louis Orthodox Jewry crossing an important developmental threshold. That status was exemplified by the early growth of Zionism in St. Louis, and especially by the landmark visit in 1906 of noted Zionist Shmarya Levin.[20]

Even before Theodor Herzl wrote his famous *Der Judenstaat* in 1896, Jewish pioneers known as *Hoveveh Zion* ("Lovers of Zion") had made sporadic efforts to colonize Palestine, supported mostly by British Jewish philanthropist Baron Edmund de Rothschild. Some of those pioneers—

---

20. A most fascinating St. Louis connection with Theodor Herzl and early Zionism lay in the career of Rosa Sonneschein, the multitalented former wife of Rabbi Solomon Sonneschein. One of her articles published in 1896, entitled "Israel's Dream of Nationality," passionately embraced the age-old Jewish supplication *L'Shana Ha'bo B'Yerusholayim*—"Next Year in Jerusalem." This was a year before the landmark First Zionist Congress that met in Basle in 1897. Being in Europe at the time, she attended the conference as the only American woman observer. She duly became a close friend, associate, and ardent supporter of leading Zionists Herzl and Max Nordau. Rosa Sonneschein, "Zionism in the Making," in *Modern View 25*, 145–50. See also Porter, "Rosa Sonneschein and *The American Jewess*," 57–63, and "Rosa Sonneschein and *The American Jewess* Revisited," 125–31.

unfortunately unidentified—came from St. Louis. But after Herzl published his landmark book, and especially following the First Zionist Congress in Basle, Switzerland, in 1897, Zionist organizations sprang into being wherever Jews lived. Whereas political Zionists agreed on the central theme of a Jewish homeland, they disagreed on the nature of that proposed state as well as on the means of attaining it. Accordingly, many organizations advocated differing and even conflicting Zionist philosophies. In St. Louis several groups came into existence, the earliest being B'nai Zion, Dorchai Zion, Daughters of Zion, Poalei Zion, Ahavath Zion, and Ha-Achooza. Affiliating with a variety of national and international Zionist organizations, these groups at first seemed more often to compete with each other than to cooperate. Then in 1905 Simon Goldman founded the St. Louis Zionist Council to better coordinate local Zionist activities. Goldman's achievements also included attracting many young people, especially young women, into the Zionist movement through the organization of more than fifteen Junior Zionist societies and a Young Judaea Council. Clearly, then, Zionism found receptive adherents in the St. Louis Jewish community.[21]

So it was, then, that when prominent national and international Zionists scheduled appearances to solicit support for their cause, they included St. Louis as one of their targets. On January 7, 1906, the Knights of Zion held its eighth annual regional convention in St. Louis. About 160 delegates from several midwestern states, including forty from St. Louis alone, met in a hall at Seventh and Franklin where, after a friendly welcome by Mayor Rolla Wells, they discussed ways to promote Zionism. That afternoon they paraded to Pabst Hall for a luncheon and entertainment. Twenty-five children of the Junior Knights of Zion of St. Louis marched in the parade, as did a fifteen-piece Junior Knights of Zion Band from

---

21. Moses J. Slonim, "Zionism in St. Louis," in *Modern View 25*, 147–48. Leaders in the Young Zionists of St. Louis included Jacob Dubinsky, president; Kate Shipper, vice president; Joseph Yawitz, secretary; C. Dubinsky, financial secretary; S. C. Bierman, treasurer; and committee chairpersons R. Goldberg, B. Weissman, and Kate Levitt. *Voice*, July 31, 1903. For other Zionist group activities, see ibid., June 10 and July 24, 1904, March 3, 17, 24, and 31, April 4, 20, and 28, and May 5, 1905, January 12, February 23, and April 20, 1906; and Bernard I. Sandler, "Hoachoozo—Zionism in America and the Colonization of Palestine," 137–48. The *Voice* estimated in 1903 that active Zionists in St. Louis numbered several hundred. Both the *Voice* and the newly published *Modern View* strongly opposed a political Zionist state, arguing that Jews should be citizens of the country in which they lived. Instead, they endorsed *cultural* Zionism, favoring Palestine as a non-Jewish haven where Jews, along with Christians and Moslems, could practice their ancestral faiths without molestation. *Voice*, February 26, 1906, May 8, 1908, and March 26, 1909.

Chicago. Following lunch, the delegates were regaled by songs, poems, and recitations in English, Yiddish, and Hebrew. Comparable Zionist meetings attracted visitors to St. Louis later that year.[22]

The most significant gathering occurred in December 1906, the main attraction being Shmarya Levin. One of the most dynamic and charismatic spokespersons for the Zionist cause, the former member of the Russian Duma was an internationally renowned Judaic writer and lecturer who attracted huge crowds wherever he spoke. So acclaimed was his appearance in St. Louis that he expanded his schedule to two lectures, which were sold out well in advance. He spoke first in Yiddish to an overflow crowd of more than fifteen hundred people at Sheerith S'fard Synagogue in the downtown Ghetto. His second talk, this time in German, attracted more than two thousand people, another overflow gathering, at Shaare Emeth Temple on Lindell and Vandeventer in the west end. Benjamin Altheimer and Elias Michael chaired the latter meeting, where Altheimer and Rabbis Harrison and Sale also made brief and stirring presentations. Levin's address at Sheerith S'fard dealt entirely with Zionism; his Shaare Emeth talk, entitled "The Position of the Jews in Russia," ended up being another passionate and persuasive argument for a Jewish homeland. In fact, perhaps the dramatic highlight of the evening occurred after Levin finished and chairman Altheimer brought the enthusiastic audience cheering to its feet when he declared emotionally in Hebrew: *"Kol Yisroel Achim"* ("all Israel are brothers").[23]

Shmarya Levin's visit marked more than a cultural highlight for the Jews of St. Louis. The mere fact that he included St. Louis in his itinerary indicated the high regard in which he and other Zionist leaders held the city's Jewish population—particularly the overwhelmingly Orthodox pro-Zionist element. At the very least, his appearance was one more indication of the city's Orthodox Jewish population's growing stature.

---

22. Speakers at these Zionist functions included, among others, Rabbi Leon Harrison, Dr. M. I. DeVorkin, Dr. Alexander S. Wolff, and Dr. S. Bialock. *Voice,* January 12 and April 20, 1906.

23. Ibid., December 28, 1906, and January 11, 1907. Irving Howe, *World of Our Fathers,* 208, 238, 240, and 504, provides interesting observations about Shmarya Levin. One writer later suggested that Zionist leaders in St. Louis deliberately scheduled Levin's Shaare Emeth appearance to make inroads into the Reform "opposition." "In order to introduce Zionism to the Reform element," this observer noted, "the [reception] committee [Dr. Michael Golland, Simon Goldman, I. M. Wolfson, and Louis Goodman] exploited Dr. Levin's visit for that purpose and arranged the mass meeting in the Shaare Emeth Temple (the mecca of the 'other side.') The *Daily Forshteer* [sic] then announced in large captions: 'Zionism in the Temple.' " Abrams, *Book of Memories,* 17.

EPILOGUE
One Hundred Years

By 1907, St. Louis and its Jewish citizenry had made significant advances. When Joseph Philipson settled in the city in 1807, it was a bustling and roisterous frontier town of fewer than fifteen hundred people, most of whom were French Creoles or emigrants from Virginia and Kentucky. One hundred years later, St. Louis ranked as the fourth-largest city in the United States, with a population exceeding six hundred thousand. People with German, Irish, Italian, African, or Jewish ancestry made up most of the population. Jews alone numbered more than forty thousand, approximately 6 percent of the total. St. Louis had developed into one of the country's major industrial and commercial centers, and Jewish merchants and businessmen had become an integral part of that scene. Jews also had held important political and civic positions.

Major changes had taken place also within the Jewish community. If 1907 marked the one hundredth anniversary of the first permanent Jewish resident in the city, few if any realized it at the time. Far from being concerned about their local roots, St. Louis Jewry at the turn of the century was occupied by more pressing contemporary problems: how to attain and solidify economic and social stability in its non-Jewish American surroundings, how to assist eastern European immigrants in acclimating to their new environment, and how to achieve Jewish continuity—despite internal differences over what constituted Judaism—so that future generations would be able to nourish and perpetuate their faith.

Nevertheless, St. Louis Jewry had crossed important thresholds. There were more Jews in St. Louis by the turn of the century than in any midwestern city other than Chicago. In a reflection of immigration patterns elsewhere in the country, those Jews who came to St. Louis for most of the time period prior to 1907 were predominantly German Jews from central and western Europe. They brought with them the skills of the craftsman and the merchant, and they prospered in those areas. They were an important part of the small neighborhood merchant class so necessary to the

409

growth of a city; some of their businesses grew into the giants exemplified by Rice-Stix, Famous-Barr, and Stix, Baer and Fuller. Jewish manufacturers proliferated among the Washington Avenue manufacturers of clothing apparel, and their products reached diverse markets all over the world.

In addition to economic growth, much had transpired within the Jewish community itself. The original *minyan,* congregation, burial association, and benevolent society—those institutions that almost universally have marked the existence of a Jewish community—had expanded percepti-bly and dramatically. One congregation had grown to many. From the standpoint of religion, St. Louis Jewry reflected what other German Jews had done in America. To break away from what they viewed as repres-sive characteristics of European life, many sought to distance themselves from religious practices that they felt contributed toward that denigra-tion. Because of this objective and the pervasive urge to "Americanize," St. Louis German Jews followed several different paths. Some assimilated and abandoned their Judaism completely, like countless numbers of Jews had done for centuries before. Most, however, retained their Judaism, but led lives that placed very little emphasis on religion. Except for life-cycle events such as a *bris* or a wedding or a burial, their existence was very secular. For them, being part of the Jewish community meant taking part in cultural or fraternal or philanthropic activities, participating in a B'nai B'rith or a YMHA or a Jewish charitable institution. Finally, those who overtly maintained their Jewish religious beliefs fell into two groups. The smaller group retained traditional Orthodoxy and founded several *shuls,* only one of which, B'nai Amoona, survived. A larger number, however, found the new Reform Judaism more to their liking. United Hebrew and B'nai El, originally Orthodox, became Reform, and Shaare Emeth and Temple Israel came along later. By 1907, these congregations, along with B'nai Amoona, ranked as the leading religious institutions in the Jewish community.

Just as significant as the economic and religious institutions were the many philanthropic and cultural organizations that enhanced Jewish community cohesiveness. Leading the way, perhaps, was the evolution of cooperative philanthropy, which ultimately led to the Charitable and Educational Union and the Jewish Federation. Institutions such as the Home for the Aged and Infirm Israelites, the Hebrew Free and Industrial School, the YMHA, the Alliance, and the Jewish Hospital, though plagued by developmental and growth pains, stood as monuments of prideful Jewish community achievement. So too did the many men's and women's charitable, philanthropic, and mutual aid organizations that reached out to help all needy Jews and, indeed, many non-Jews as well. Young people found stimulating cultural and social outlets in a variety of literary and musical societies. The Jewish press, exemplified by the *Voice* and the more recent *Modern View,* acted as another bonding agency by communicating Jewish awareness to all St. Louis Jewry.

By the beginning of the twentieth century, then, German Jewry had, in a sense, attained its goal. It had been able to maintain its own Jewish identity, and at the same time had become part of the overall St. Louis community. Jews contributed to and participated in virtually every phase of St. Louis life, and, despite rare instances of antisemitism, felt very comfortable in their midwestern environment. Although many still associated with German *vereins* and similar German cultural organizations, they considered themselves to be fully American, albeit with German ancestry and German affinities. But their most comforting sensibility was the confidence that as Jews they had found a secure home in America.

Yet a pervasive and gnawing concern remained: the refugees from oppressive life in eastern Europe. Slavic rather than Germanic in tradition, Orthodox rather than Reform in religious outlook, culturally and linguistically more attuned to the eastern European *shtetl* and ghetto than to the more liberalized lifestyle of western Europe, the new immigrants were personified by an unmistakably different kind of Jew. More than that, though, the new immigrants represented the very type of religious and cultural lifestyle from which the German Jews had distanced themselves. Indeed, many now comfortably established in their new American environment viewed the newcomers as a distinct threat, fearful that their "backward" ways might actually undermine the status German Jews had finally achieved. Many actually questioned helping the Russian "schnorrers." Yet the strong Judaic concepts of *tzedakah* and *tikkun olom* prevailed. Philanthropic efforts by German Jewry unquestionably helped many eastern Europeans escape from terrorist antisemitic depredations. Comparable efforts helped those refugees when they came to St. Louis, through support and assistance in such basic needs as clothing, housing, medical care, and employment. Institutions such as the Alliance and the Hebrew Free School—and, of course, the St. Louis public schools—educated many and paved the way for productive employment. The new immigrants responded phenomenally, as they too acclimated to the new American environment.

Despite that successful acclimatization, though, the newer immigrants remained different from the older German element in two significant ways. Overwhelmingly, the German Jews had embraced Reform; eastern European Jews virulently rejected Reform and sought to transplant their Orthodoxy to their new St. Louis environment. Furthermore, where German Jews had readily and willingly acculturated in lifestyle to fit into their non-Jewish environment, the eastern Europeans strove to retain as much as possible of their eastern European culture and way of life. True, they did "Americanize," but usually just when it was absolutely necessary for physical survival. In the process, too, eastern European Jewry conscientiously and diligently established its own community requisites—*minyanim,* synagogues, cemeteries, benevolent institutions—making sure they satisfied Orthodox standards.

The result was that in a very short time two separate Jewish communities resided in St. Louis, the German/Reform community and the eastern European/Orthodox community. Despite cooperation and amity in some areas and ventures, bitter and acrimonious differences emerged in others; none was more divisive than the issue of *kashruth.* As long as the German/Reform element predominated numerically and financially, its philosophies and ways prevailed. But as the newer immigrants grew in numbers and financial abilities, some sort of showdown was inevitable. That conflict pervaded the creation of the Jewish Hospital, in which the German/Reform element had its way. Yet the eastern European/Orthodox side had its way in the establishment of the Orthodox Old Folks Home on North Grand and Blair. Indeed, those and other developments in the first few years of the twentieth century foreshadowed the growing need to resolve the serious divisiveness between the two St. Louis Jewish communities.

The year 1907, then, represents a historical watershed in St. Louis Jewish history. It was the time when one could look back upon a century of considerable progress. It was the time also when one could look ahead to the next century with more than a modicum of anticipation. Would the Jews of St. Louis remain in two separate communities? Could they afford to? Was reconciliation of their deep differences possible? How would existing institutions and forces affect the future? What new forces, either internal or external, would affect St. Louis Jewry? Could the second hundred years be as productive as the first hundred? Only time would tell.

BIBLIOGRAPHY

PRIMARY SOURCES

Archival Collections

AMERICAN JEWISH ARCHIVES (CINCINNATI)
Bernstein, Jeanette, Journal
Binswanger, Augustus, File
Biographies File:
    Baer Family
    Bush Family
    Furth Family
    Lowenstern Family
    Spitz Family
    Waldheim Family
Block Family File
B'nai B'rith File
B'nai El Congregation Minutes, 1847–1860 (photostat)
B'nai El File
Bondi, August M., File
Cohen, Louis, File
Correspondence File:
    Isserman, Ruth
    Shaare Emeth Temple
    Solomon, Samuel D. (St. Louis)
Felsenthal, Bernard, Papers
Fraley, Moses, File
Goldman, J. D., File
Grant, Rosa Mayer, File
Gutman Family File
Isserman, Ferdinand, Papers
Kuttner, Henry, File

Merchants Exchange of St. Louis File

Minute Book, Board of Trustees of the United Hebrew Congregation of Saint Louis, State of Missouri, 1841–1859 (photostat)

Missouri Box

Mount Olive Cemetery, St. Louis, Records, 1849–1880

Philipson Family Papers

Pollack, S., M.D., "The Autobiography and Reminiscences of S. Pollack, M.D., St. Louis, Mo."

Pollack, Simon, File

Rogal Family File

Seaman, Philip Louis, Scrapbooks

Shaare Emeth Congregation File

Sonneschein, Rosa, File

Sonneschein, Solomon H., Letterbooks

Spitz, Moritz, Papers

St. Louis, Missouri File

St. Louis, Missouri. B'nai B'rith, Isidor Bush Lodge No. 557.

St. Louis, Missouri. Congregation B'nai El Minutebook, 1847–1866

St. Louis, Missouri. Hoachoozo Palestine Land and Development Company. Records, 1908–1921

St. Louis, Missouri. Mount Sinai Cemetery. Register of Deaths, 1859–1872 (microfilm)

St. Louis, Missouri. The Pioneer. Minutebook

St. Louis, Missouri. United Hebrew Congregation, Records, 1841–1870 (originals in United Hebrew Congregation in St. Louis)

Swope Papers

Taussig, Anna Abeles, Memoirs, 1830–1886

Temple Israel File

Temple Shaare Emeth File

United Hebrew Temple File

MISSOURI HISTORICAL SOCIETY (ST. LOUIS)

"Autobiography and Reminiscences of S. Pollack, M.D., St. Louis, Mo., The" (reprinted from St. Louis Medical Review, 1904)

Bauman, Louis, File

Cohen, H. H., Pictorial Collection and Biographical Data

Director's File

Early St. Louis Envelope, 1820–1846

Estates of Simon and Joseph Philipson, 1841–1844, Envelope

Index to Marriage Records, St. Louis and St. Louis County, 1808–1836 (originals in Office of Recorder of Deeds, Marriage License Office, St. Louis County)

Index to St. Louis Cathedral and Carondelet Church Baptisms

Index to St. Louis Cathedral and Carondelet Church Burials
Index to St. Louis Cathedral and Carondelet Church Marriages
Index to St. Louis Register: Baptisms, Marriages and Burials 1766–1781
Philipson's File, Director's File, 1843–1855

ST. LOUIS JEWISH COMMUNITY ARCHIVES
Beth Hamedrosh Hagodol Collection
Binswanger, Augustus, Papers
Schachter, Herman, Collection
United Hebrew Relief Association File

OTHER ARCHIVAL COLLECTIONS
B'nai B'rith, Missouri Lodge, Papers. American Jewish Historical Society,
    Waltham, Massachusetts
Dun, R. G. and Company, Collection. Baker Library, Harvard University
    School of Business Administration, Cambridge, Massachusetts
"Jerusalem Exhibit, St. Louis World's Fair." Klau Library, Hebrew Union
    College–Jewish Institute of Religion, Cincinnati
Philipson, Joseph, Account Book, 1807–1809. Mercantile Library, St. Louis
Register of Marriages of the St. Louis Cathedral, 1774–August 13, 1781.
    St. Louis Cathedral, St. Louis
Sonneschein, Solomon H., File. Shaare Emeth Temple Library, St. Louis
St. Louis File. American Jewish Historical Society, Waltham, Massachu-
    setts

Congregational Records. Minute Books, Etc.
B'nai El Temple, St. Louis
Nusach Hari B'nai Zion Synagogue, St. Louis
Shaare Emeth Temple, St. Louis
Shaare Zedek Synagogue, St. Louis
Temple Israel, St. Louis
United Hebrew Temple, St. Louis

Cemetery Records
Bais Hamedrosh Hagodol Cemetery Association, St. Louis
B'nai Amoona Cemetery Association, St. Louis
Chesed Shel Emeth Cemetery Association, St. Louis
Chevrah Kadisha Cemetery Association, St. Louis
New Mount Sinai Cemetery Association, St. Louis
United Hebrew Cemetery Association, St. Louis

St. Louis Municipal Records
Estate of Jacob Philipson, Estate No. 5154, Probate Court, St. Louis
Estate of Joseph Philipson, Estate No. 1907, Probate Court, St. Louis

Estate of Simon Philipson, Estate No. 1666, Probate Court, St. Louis
1438 E. Grand Blvd. (Orthodox Old Folks Home), Office of the Recorder
of Deeds, St. Louis

Personal Interviews and Letters

Baer, Howard F., June 22, 1981
Davis, Abraham, February 18, 1985
Ehrenreich, Bernard, November 20, 1984
Elbaum, Jacob, June 17, 1981
Fisbeck, Hayden, September 8, 1987
Fleishman, Alfred, August 5 and 12, 1981
Green, Alan, August 25, 1988
Greenfield, Milton Jr., February 20, 1995
Koslow, Ralph, July 3, 1990
Kulfinski, Kay B., February 4, 1985
Messing, Wilma, June 19, 1992
Newman, Eric P., August 16, 1988
Pulitzer, Joseph Jr., October 13, 1988
Raskas, Ralph, July 8, 1981
Roman, Benjamin, June 19, 1992
Rosenwaike, Ira, May 23, 1989
Sabol, Alan, August 25, 1988
Schwabe, Mrs. Max, August 13, 1990
Stein, Richard, October 10, 1994
Treiman, Israel, September 8, 1982
v. d. Heydt, Vernon W., June 15, 1992
Wolff, Frank, February 17, 1995

Other Primary Materials

Barnes, C. R., ed. *The Commonwealth of Missouri: A Centennial Record.*
St. Louis: n.p., 1877.
Bennitt, Mark, ed. *History of the Louisiana Purchase Exposition.* St. Louis:
Universal Exposition Publishing Company, 1905.
Biographical Directory of the American Congress, 1774–1949. House Docu-
ment 607, 81st Cong., 2d sess. Washington, D.C., 1950.
Blau, Joseph L., and Salo W. Baron. *The Jews of the United States, 1790–1840:
A Documentary History.* 3 vols. New York: Columbia University Press,
1963.
Bush, Isidor. "The Jews in St. Louis." *Missouri Historical Society Bulletin* 8
(October 1951): 60–70.
———. "The Task of the Jews in the United States, 1851." *American Jewish
Archives* 18 (1966): 155–61.

Compton, Richard J., ed. *Pictorial Saint Louis: The Great Metropolis of the Mississippi Valley.* St. Louis: Compton and Company, 1876.

Coyner, David H. *The Lost Trappers: A Collection of Interesting Scenes and Events in the Rocky Mountains.* New York: n.p., 1847.

Edwards, Richard, and M. Hopewell, eds. *Edwards' Great West and Her Commercial Metropolis.* St. Louis: n.p., 1860.

Epstein, David, ed. *Jubilee Book Commemorating the 50th Anniversary of the Chesed Shel Emeth Society in Saint Louis, 1888–1938.* St. Louis: n.p., 1938.

Goodman, Abram V. "A Jewish Peddler's Diary, 1842–1843." *American Jewish Archives* 3 (1951): 81–85.

Gould's Blue Book. St. Louis: n.p., 1887.

Illoway, Henry. *Sefer Milchamot Elohim: Being the Controversial Letters and the Casuistic Decisions of the Late Rabbi Bernard Illowy, Ph.D., with a Short History of His Life and Activities.* Berlin: n.p., 1914.

Irving, Washington. *The Adventures of Captain Bonneville.* In *The Complete Works of Washington Irving,* edited by Herbert L. Kleinfeld, vol. 15. Boston: Twayne Publishers, 1976.

———. *Astoria: or Anecdotes of an Enterprize beyond the Rocky Mountains.* In *The Complete Works of Washington Irving,* edited by Herbert L. Kleinfeld, vol. 16. Boston: Twayne Publishers, 1976.

Jewish Genealogical Society of St. Louis. "A Resource Guide: The St. Louis Jewish Press." St. Louis: n.p., n.d.

Marcus, Jacob R. *American Jewry: Documents, Eighteenth Century.* Cincinnati: American Jewish Archives, 1959.

———. *Memoirs of American Jews, 1775–1865.* 3 vols. Philadelphia: Jewish Publication Society, 1955.

Official Guide to the Louisiana Purchase Exposition. St. Louis: n.p., 1904.

Pancoast, Charles E. *The Adventures of Charles Edward Pancoast on the American Frontier.* In *A Quaker Forty-Niner,* edited by Anna P. Hannum. Philadelphia: University of Pennsylvania Press, 1930.

Philipson v Mullanphy, 1 Missouri Reports 620–26 (1821).

Schappes, Morris U., ed. *A Documentary History of the Jews in the United States, 1864–1875.* New York: The Citadel Press, 1950.

Schweig, Morris. "Biography of Morris Schweig." Manuscript in possession of author, n.d.

Stewart, William Drummond. *Edward Warren.* London: n.p., 1854.

Taylor, Jacob N. *Sketch Book of Saint Louis.* St. Louis: G. Krapp and Co., 1858.

Tobin, Gary A. "The Jewish Federation of St. Louis Demographic Study, December 1982: Executive Summary." St. Louis: n.p., 1982. Copy in possession of author.

Tyrrell, Frank G., ed. *The Universal Exposition: A Portfolio of Official Photographic Views of the Louisiana Purchase Exposition, St. Louis, 1904.* St. Louis: Portfolio Publishing Company, 1904.

SECONDARY WORKS

Books

Abrams, Z. *The Book of Memories.* St. Louis: Hub Printing, 1932.

Adler, Cyrus, ed. *American Jewish Yearbook, 5662.* Philadelphia: Jewish Publication Society of America, 1901.

————. *American Jewish Yearbook, 5664.* Philadelphia: Jewish Publication Society of America, 1903.

————. *American Jewish Yearbook, 5666.* Philadelphia: Jewish Publication Society of America, 1905.

Baer, Jean. *The Self-Chosen.* New York: Arbor House, 1982.

Baron, Sidney. *Brewed in America: A History of Beer and Ale in the United States.* Boston: Little Brown, 1962.

Baskett, Cecil M., ed. *Men of Affairs in St. Louis.* St. Louis: Press Club of St. Louis, 1915.

Belth, Nathan C. *A Promise to Keep.* New York: Times Books, 1979.

Berman, Meyer. *Richmond's Jewry, 1769–1976.* Charlottesville: University of Virginia Press, 1979.

Billon, Frederic L. *Annals of St. Louis in Its Territorial Days from 1804 to 1821.* 2 vols. St. Louis: G. I. Jones, 1888.

Birmingham, Stephen. *The Grandees: The Story of America's Sephardic Elite.* New York: Dell, 1971.

————. *Our Crowd: The Great Jewish Families of New York.* New York: Harper and Row, 1967.

Blake, Robert. *Disraeli.* New York: St. Martin's, 1967.

Bogen, Boris D. *Jewish Philanthropy.* New York: Macmillan, 1917.

Borden, Morton. *Jews, Turks, and Infidels.* Chapel Hill: University of North Carolina Press, 1984.

Bronsen, Rosalind M. *B'nai Amoona for All Generations.* St. Louis: Congregation B'nai Amoona, 1982.

Cohen, George. *The Jews in the Making of America.* Boston: Stratford, 1924.

Cox, James. *Notable St. Louisans in 1900.* St. Louis: Benesch Art Publishing, 1900.

————. *Old and New St. Louis.* St. Louis: Central Biographical Publishing, 1894.

Cremin, Lawrence A. *American Education: The National Experience, 1783–1876.* New York: Harper and Row, 1980.

Davis, Edward. *The History of Rodeph Shalom Congregation of Philadelphia.* Philadelphia: Jewish Publication Society of America, 1927.

Devoy, John. *A History of the City of St. Louis and Vicinity, from the Earliest Times to the Present.* St. Louis: John Devoy, 1898.

Dimont, Max I. *The Jews in America.* New York: Simon and Schuster, 1978.

Diner, Hasia E. *A Time for Gathering.* Baltimore: Johns Hopkins University Press, 1992.

Dinnerstein, Leonard, Roger L. Nichols, and David M. Reimers. *Natives and Strangers.* New York: Oxford University Press, 1979.

Ehrlich, Walter. *They Have No Rights: Dred Scott's Struggle for Freedom.* Westport, Conn.: Greenwood Press, 1979.

Emmanuel, Isaac S. *Precious Stones of the Jews of the Netherlands Antilles.* Cincinnati: American Jewish Archives, 1970.

Encyclopedia Judaica. 17 vols. Jerusalem: Keter Publishing House, 1972.

Endelman, Judith E. *The Jewish Community of Indianapolis, 1849 to the Present.* Bloomington: Indiana University Press, 1985.

Feingold, Henry L. *Zion in America.* New York: Twayne Publishers, 1974.

Feingold, Henry L., gen. ed. *The Jewish People in America.* 5 vols. Baltimore: Johns Hopkins University Press, 1992.

Fischlowitz, Ruth. *The "Y" Story.* St. Louis: Jewish Community Centers Association, 1964.

Forrestal, Dan J. *Faith, Hope, and $5,000: The Story of Monsanto.* New York: Simon and Schuster, 1977.

Fredman, Joseph G., and Louis A. Falk. *Jews in American Wars.* New York: Jewish War Veterans of the United States, 1943.

Gee, David A. *216 S.K.: A History of the Jewish Hospital of St. Louis.* St. Louis: Jewish Hospital of St. Louis, 1981.

Gill, McCune. *The St. Louis Story: Library of American Lives.* 3 vols. St. Louis: Historical Record Association, 1952.

Glanz, Rudolph. *The German Jews in America.* Cincinnati: Hebrew Union College Press, 1969.

Glazer, Nathan. *American Judaism.* Chicago: University of Chicago Press, 1957.

Hafen, LeRoy, and Carl R. Rister. *Western America.* New York: Prentice-Hall, 1941.

Hagen, Harry H. *This Is Our St. Louis.* St. Louis: Knight Publishing Company, 1970.

Handlin, Oscar. *Adventure in Freedom: Three Hundred Years of Jewish Life in America.* New York: McGraw-Hill, 1954.

Hannum, Anna P., ed. *A Quaker Forty-Niner.* Philadelphia: University of Pennsylvania Press, 1930.

Harris, Nini. *A Grand Heritage.* St. Louis: DeSales Community Housing Corporation, 1984.

Hart, Arthur Daniel, ed. *The Jews in Canada.* Toronto: n.p., 1926.

Herscher, Uri D. *Jewish Agricultural Utopias in America, 1880–1910.* Detroit: Wayne State University Press, 1981.

Higham, John. *Send These to Me: Immigrants in Urban America.* Baltimore: Johns Hopkins University Press, 1984.

Hirschler, Eric E., ed. *Jews from Germany in the United States.* New York: Farrar, Straus, 1945.

Houck, Louis. *A History of Missouri.* 3 vols. Chicago: R. R. Donnelley and Sons, 1908.

———. *The Spanish Regime in Missouri.* 2 vols. Chicago: R. R. Donnelley and Sons, 1909.

Howe, Irving. *World of Our Fathers.* New York: Simon and Schuster, 1976.

Hyde, William, and Howard L. Conard, eds. *Encyclopedia of the History of St. Louis.* 4 vols. New York: Southern History Company, 1899.

Jennings, Marietta. *A Pioneer Merchant of St. Louis, 1810–1820: The Business Career of Christian Wilt.* New York: Columbia University Press, 1939.

Kargau, Ernest D. *Mercantile, Industrial and Professional Saint Louis.* St. Louis: Nixon-Jones, 1902.

Karp, Abraham J. *The Jewish Experience in America.* 5 vols. Waltham, Mass.: American Jewish Historical Society, 1969.

Kelsoe, William A., ed. *St. Louis Reference Record.* St. Louis: Von Hoffman Press, 1928.

Kimbrough, Mary, Justin L. Faherty, and David R. Brown. *Movers and Shakers: Men Who Have Shaped Saint Louis.* St. Louis: Patrice Press, 1992.

Korn, Bertram W. *American Jewry and the Civil War.* Philadelphia: Jewish Publication Society of America, 1951.

———. *The American Reaction to the Mortara Case, 1858–1859.* Cincinnati: Hebrew Union College Press, 1957.

———. *The Early Jews of New Orleans.* Waltham, Mass.: American Jewish Historical Society, 1969.

Lebeson, Anita L. *Jewish Pioneers in America, 1492–1848.* New York: Brentano's, 1931.

Leonard, John W., ed. *The Book of St. Louisans.* St. Louis: *St. Louis Republic,* 1906, 1912.

Litvin, Martin. *The Journey: The American-Jewish Freedom Fighter Who Rode with John Brown in Kansas.* Galesburg, Ill.: Galesburg Historical Society, 1981.

McCall, Samuel W. *Patriotism of the American Jew.* New York: Plymouth Press, 1924.

Marcus, Jacob R. *The Colonial American Jew, 1492–1776.* 3 vols. Detroit: Wayne State University Press, 1970.

———. *Early American Jewry.* 2 vols. Philadelphia: Jewish Publication Society of America, 1951–1955.

———. *United States Jewry, 1776–1985.* 2 vols. Detroit: Wayne State University Press, 1989, 1991.

Monypenny, William F., and George E. Buckle. *The Life of Benjamin Disraeli, Earl of Beaconsfield.* London: John Murray, 1912.

Morais, Henry S. *The Jews of Philadelphia.* Philadelphia: Levytype, 1894.

Mormino, Gary R. *Immigrants on the Hill: Italian-Americans in St. Louis, 1882–1892.* Urbana: University of Illinois Press, 1986.

Neely, Mark E. Jr. *The Fate of Liberty: Abraham Lincoln and Civil War Liberties.* New York: Oxford University Press, 1991.

Paris, Norman, ed. *Brocho L'Mnachem: Essays Contributed in Honor of Rabbi Menachem H. Eichenstein.* St. Louis: Vaad Hoeir of St. Louis, 1955.

Philipson, David. *The Reform Movement in Judaism.* New York: Macmillan, 1907.

Plaut, W. Gunther. *The Growth of Reform Judaism.* New York: World Union for Progressive Judaism, 1965.

Postal, Bernard, and Lionel Koppman. *A Jewish Tourist's Guide to the United States.* New York: Fleet Press, 1954.

Postal, Bernard, and Lionel Koppman, eds. *American Jewish Landmarks.* 4 vols. New York: Fleet Press, 1979–1984.

Primm, James Neal. *Lion of the Valley.* Boulder, Colo.: Pruett, 1981.

Rammelkamp, Julian S. *Pulitzer's Post-Dispatch, 1878–1883.* Princeton: Princeton University Press, 1967.

Rivkin, Ellis. *The Shaping of Jewish History.* New York: Charles Scribner's Sons, 1971.

Rombauer, Robert J. *The Union Cause in St. Louis in 1861.* St. Louis: Nixon-Jones, 1909.

Rosenbloom, Joseph R. *A Biographical Dictionary of Early American Jews: Colonial Times to 1800.* Lexington: University of Kentucky Press, 1960.

Rosenkranz, Samuel. *A Centennial History of Temple Israel, 1886–1986.* Creve Coeur, Mo.: Congregation Temple Israel, 1986.

Sachar, Howard M. *The Course of Modern Jewish History.* New York: Dell, 1958.

———. *A History of the Jews in America.* New York: Alfred A. Knopf, 1992.

Scharf, J. Thomas. *History of Saint Louis City and County from the Earliest Periods to the Present Day, Including Biographical Sketches of Representative Men.* 2 vols. Philadelphia: Everts, 1883.

Schultz, Joseph P. *Mid-America's Promise: A Profile of Kansas City Jewry.* Kansas City, Mo.: The Jewish Community Foundation of Greater Kansas City and the American Jewish Historical Society, 1982.

Schwartzman, Sylvan D. *Reform Judaism in the Making.* New York: Union of American Hebrew Congregations, 1955.

————. *Reform Judaism Then and Now*. New York: Union of American Hebrew Congregations, 1971.

Shannon, William V. *The Irish in America*. New York: Macmillan, 1966.

Sharfman, I. Harold. *Jews on the Frontier*. Chicago: Henry Regnery, 1977.

Snow, Marshall S. *History of the Development of Missouri and Particularly St. Louis*. 2 vols. St. Louis: National Press Bureau, 1908.

Sorin, Gerald. *A Time for Building: The Third Migration, 1880–1920*. Baltimore: Johns Hopkins University Press, 1992.

Stadler, Frances H. *St. Louis Day by Day*. St. Louis: Patrice Press, 1989.

Stevens, Walter B. *Saint Louis: The Fourth City, 1764–1909*. St. Louis: S. J. Clark Publishing Company, 1909.

Stiritz, Mary M. *St. Louis: Historic Churches and Synagogues*. St. Louis: St. Louis Public Library and Landmarks Association of St. Louis, 1995.

Troen, Selwyn K. *The Public and the Schools: Shaping the St. Louis System, 1838–1920*. Columbia: University of Missouri Press, 1975.

Troen, Selwyn K., and Glen E. Holt, eds. *St. Louis*. New York: Franklin Watts, 1977.

Universal Jewish Encyclopedia. 10 vols. New York: Universal Jewish Encyclopedia Company, 1943.

Urofsky, Melvin I. *Louis D. Brandeis and the Progressive Tradition*. Boston: Little, Brown, 1981.

Van Ravenswaay, Charles. *Saint Louis: An Informal History of the City and Its People, 1764–1865*. St. Louis: Missouri Historical Society Press, 1991.

Violette, Eugene M. *A History of Missouri*. Cape Girardeau, Mo.: Ramfre Press, 1957 reprint edition.

Wolf, Simon. *The American Jew as Patriot, Soldier and Citizen*. Philadelphia: Levytype, 1895.

Young, Melvin A. *Where They Lie*. Lanham, Md.: University Press of America, 1991.

Dissertations and Theses

Becherer, Floyd O. "The History of St. Louis, 1817–1826." Master's thesis, Washington University, St. Louis, 1950.

Blum, Virgil C. "German Element in St. Louis, 1859–1861." Ph.D. diss., St. Louis University, 1945.

Fainsod, Merle. "The Influence of Racial and National Groups in St. Louis Politics, 1908–1928." Ph.D. diss., Washington University, St. Louis, 1929.

Kellner, George H. "The German Element on the Urban Frontier: St. Louis, 1830–1860." Ph.D. diss., University of Missouri–Columbia, 1973.

Kirkpatrick, Robert L. "History of St. Louis, 1804–1816." Master's thesis, Washington University, St. Louis, 1947.

Lindhurst, James. "History of the Brewing Industry in St. Louis, 1804–1860." Master's thesis, Washington University, St. Louis, 1939.

McHugh, George. "Political Nativism in St. Louis, 1840–1857." Master's thesis, St. Louis University, 1939.

Makovsky, Donald I. "Origin and Early History of the United Hebrew Congregation of St. Louis, 1841–1859." Master's thesis, Washington University, St. Louis, 1958.

Mayer, Herbert T. "History of St. Louis, 1837–1847." Master's thesis, Washington University, St. Louis, 1949.

Olson, Audrey. "St. Louis Germans, 1850–1920: The Nature of the Immigrant Community." Ph.D. diss., University of Kansas, 1970.

Robinson, James F. "St. Louis in the Gold Rush Era, 1848–1858." Master's thesis, St. Louis University, 1940.

Rosen, Samuel L. "The Historical Development of the Jewish Federation of Saint Louis." Master's thesis, St. Louis University, 1939.

Ross, Oscar M. "The History of St. Louis, 1848–1853." Master's thesis, Washington University, St. Louis, 1949.

Sherman, Moshe D. "Bernard Illowy and Nineteenth Century American Orthodoxy." Ph.D. diss., Yeshiva University, 1991.

Spitz, Lewis W. "The Germans in Missouri: A Preliminary Study." Master's thesis, Washington University, St. Louis, 1930.

Stygar, Mary M. "St. Louis Immigrants from 1820–1860." Master's thesis, St. Louis University, 1937.

Williams, Helen D. "Factors in the Growth of Saint Louis from 1840 to 1860." Master's thesis, Washington University, St. Louis, 1934.

Pamphlets

Beth Hamedrosh Hagodol Congregation Diamond Jubilee, 1879–1954. St. Louis: Beth Hamedrosh Hagodol Congregation, 1954.

Dedicatory Book, United Hebrew Congregation. St. Louis: United Hebrew Congregation, 1927.

Epstein, David, ed. *Jubilee Book Commemorating the 50th Anniversary of the Chesed Shel Emeth Society of St. Louis, 1888–1938.* St. Louis: Chesed Shel Emeth Society, 1938.

Losos, Joseph O. *From Leffingwell to Spoede: Highlights in the History of Temple Israel.* St. Louis: Temple Israel, 1977.

Makovsky, Donald I. *The Philipsons: The First Jewish Settlers in St. Louis, 1807–1858.* St. Louis: St. Louis Rabbinical Association, 1958.

One Hundredth Anniversary, United Hebrew Congregation, 1838–1938. St. Louis: United Hebrew Congregation, 1938.

Priwer, Jane. *The United Hebrew Congregation, 1837–1963.* St. Louis: United Hebrew Congregation, 1963.

Rosenkranz, Samuel. *Golden Jubilee History of Temple Israel*. St. Louis: Temple Israel, 1936.

This Is B'nai B'rith. Washington, D.C.: B'nai B'rith International, 1979.

Journal Articles

Abrams, Jeanne. "Remembering the *Maine:* The Jewish Attitude toward the Spanish-American War as Reflected in *The American Israelite.*" *American Jewish History* 76 (June 1987): 439–55.

"A Woman's Cultural Club." *Missouri Historical Society Bulletin* 6 (1949): 109.

Bender, Averam B. "History of the Beth Hamedrosh Hagodol Congregation of St. Louis, 1879–1969." *Missouri Historical Society Bulletin* 17 (1970): 64–89.

Bernard, Burton C. "Brandeis in St. Louis, 1878–79." *St. Louis Bar Journal* 11 (winter 1964): 17–20.

"Biographical Sketches of Jews Prominent in the Professions in the United States." In Cyrus Adler, ed., *American Jewish Yearbook, 5665* 6 (1904–1905): 52–225.

"Biographical Sketches of Jews Who Have Served in the Congress of the United States." In Cyrus Adler, ed., *American Jewish Yearbook, 5661* 2 (1900–1901): 517–24.

Blum, Virgil C. "The Political and Military Activities of the German Element in St. Louis, 1859–1861." *Missouri Historical Review* 42 (January 1948): 103–29.

Boxerman, Burton A. "David P. Wohl—Shoe Merchant." *Gateway Heritage* 9 (fall 1988): 24–33.

———. "The Honorable Nathan Frank." *American Jewish Historical Quarterly* 61 (1971): 33–51.

———. "Louis Patrick Aloe." *Missouri Historical Society Bulletin* 21 (October 1975): 41–54.

———. "Rise of Anti-Semitism in St. Louis, 1933–1945." *YIVO Annual of Jewish Social Service* 14 (1969): 251–69.

———. "The St. Louis Jewish Coordinating Council: The Formative Years." *Missouri Historical Review* 65 (October 1970): 57–71.

———. "St. Louis Jewish Leaders." *Gateway Heritage* 6 (spring 1986): 16–25.

Bunker, Gary L., and John Appel. " 'Shoddy,' Anti-Semitism and the Civil War." *American Jewish History* 82 (1994): 43–71.

Cohn, Fritz L. "Saint Louis and Poker Flat in the Fifties and Sixties: From the *Jugenderrinnerungen* of Henry Cohn." *California Historical Society Quarterly* 19 (1939): 289–98.

Corrigan, Dan. "The Neighborhood Tavern." *St. Louis Magazine* 12 (September 1980): 84–86.

Czillag, Andras. "Joseph Pulitzer's Roots in Europe: A Genealogical History." *American Jewish Archives* 39 (April 1987): 49–68.

Ehrlich, Walter. "The First Jews of St. Louis." *Missouri Historical Review* 83 (October 1988): 57–76.

———. "Jewish Historical Landmarks in St. Louis." *Gateway Heritage* 6 (spring 1986): 2–15.

———. "Origins of the Jewish Community of St. Louis." *American Jewish History* 77 (June 1988): 507–29.

Ellenson, David. "A Jewish Legal Decision by Rabbi Bernard Illowy of New Orleans and Its Discussion in Nineteenth Century Europe." *American Jewish History* 69 (December 1979): 174–95.

Eliafson, Herman. "The Jews of Chicago." *Publications of the American Jewish Historical Society* 8 (1900): 108–17.

Farber, Russel. "A Close Look at History." *Soulard Restorationist*, August 1, 1985, 18–20.

Forbes, Cleon. "The St. Louis School of Thought." *Missouri Historical Review* 26 (October 1931): 68–77.

Frangoulis, George. "The Greek Community." *The Marketplace—A Forum* 1 (1983): 66–67.

Friedman, Lee. "Something Additional on General Grant's Order No. 11." *Publications of the American Jewish Historical Society* 40 (1950): 184–86.

Furth, Jacob. "Sketch of Isidor Bush." *Missouri Historical Society Collections* 4 (1914): 303–8.

Gersten, Irving. "The Freund Story." *Missouri Historical Society Bulletin* 13 (January 1957): 181–91.

Greenfield, Judith. "The Role of Jews in the Development of the Clothing Industry in the United States." *YIVO Annual* 2 (1947–1948): 180–204.

Higham, John. "Social Discrimination against Jews in America, 1830–1930." *Publications of the American Jewish Historical Society* 47 (September 1957): 1–33.

Holmes, Reuben. "The Five Scalps." *Glimpses of the Past* 5 (1938): 3–54.

Jacobson, Laura D. "The Pioneers." *American Jewess* 1 (1898): 240–43.

"Jews in the Spanish-American War." In Cyrus Adler, ed., *American Jewish Yearbook, 5661* (1900–1901), vol. 2, 529–622.

Jones, Patricia L. "Whatever Happened to Bohemian Hill?" *Gateway Heritage* 5 (winter 1984–1985): 22–31.

Kanter, Harvey A. "The Barth Family: A Case Study of Pioneer Immigrant Merchants." *Missouri Historical Review* 62 (July 1968): 410–30.

Kisch, Guido. "*ISRAELS HEROLD:* The First Jewish Weekly in New York." *Historia Judaica* 2 (October 1940): 63–84.

Kohler, Max J. "Some Jewish Factors in the Settlement of the West." *Publications of the American Jewish Historical Society* 16 (1907): 33–35.

Lebowich, Joseph. "General Ulysses S. Grant and the Jews." *Publications of the American Jewish Historical Society* 17 (1909): 71–79.

Liebman, Charles S. "American Jews: Still a Distinctive Group." *Commentary* 64 (August 1977): 57–63.

Makovsky, Donald I. "Jewish Haven of Freedom." *The Marketplace—A Forum* 1 (1983): 69.

Meyer, I. S. "The American Jewish Community during the Civil War." *Publications of the American Jewish Historical Society* 50 (1961): 277–303.

O'Donnell, Ed. "Irish Stew." *The Marketplace—A Forum* 1 (1983): 63–65.

Osofsky, Gilbert. "The Hebrew Emigrant Aid Society of the United States." *Publications of the American Jewish Historical Society* 49 (1960): 173–87.

Peixotto, Benjamin F. "Isidor Bush." *The Menorah* 9 (October 1890): 190–202.

Pertici, Mario. "And Then Came the Italians." *The Marketplace—A Forum* 1 (1983): 59–60.

Philipson, David. "The Jewish Pioneers of the Ohio Valley." *Publications of the American Jewish Historical Society* 8 (1900): 43–57.

Porter, Jack Nusan. "Rosa Sonneschein and *The American Jewess:* The First Independent English Language Jewish Women's Journal in the United States." *American Jewish History* 68 (September 1978): 57–63.

———. "Rosa Sonneschein and *The American Jewess* Revisited: New Historical Information on an Early American Zionist and Jewish Feminist." *American Jewish Archives* 32 (November 1980): 125–31.

Rosenberg, Elliot. "1843." *B'nai B'rith International Jewish Monthly* 108 (October–November 1933): 12–16.

Rosenwaike, Ira. "Eleazer Block—His Family and Career." *American Jewish Archives* 31 (November 1979): 142–49.

———. "The Mussina Family: Early American Jews?" *American Jewish History* 75 (June 1986): 397–404.

Sachs, Howard F. "Development of the Jewish Community of Kansas City, 1864–1908." *Missouri Historical Review* 60 (April 1966): 350–60.

Sandler, Bernard I. "Hoachoozo—Zionism in America and the Colonization of Palestine." *American Jewish Historical Society Quarterly* 64 (December 1974): 137–48.

Sorin, Gerald. "Mutual Contempt, Mutual Benefit: The Strained Encounter between German and Eastern European Jews in America, 1880–1920." *American Jewish History* 81 (autumn 1993): 34–59.

Sullivan, Margaret LoPiccolo. "St. Louis Ethnic Neighborhoods, 1850–1930." *Missouri Historical Society Bulletin* 33 (January 1977): 64–76.

Swichkow, Louis J. "The Jewish Community of Milwaukee." *Publications of the American Jewish Historical Society* 47 (September 1957): 34–58.

"Trailblazers of the Trans-Mississippi West." *American Jewish Archives* 8 (1956): 59–130.

Van Ravenswaay, Charles. "Years of Turmoil, Years of Growth: St. Louis in the 1850s." *Missouri Historical Society Bulletin* 23 (July 1967): 303–24.

Wax, James A. "Isidor Bush: American Patriot and Abolitionist." *Historica Judaica* 5 (October 1943): 183–203.

Weinryb, Bernard D. "East European Immigration to the United States." *Jewish Quarterly Review* 45 (1954): 497–512.

INDEX